Understanding Architecture

Understanding Architecture

Its Elements, History, and Meaning

Leland M. Roth

IconEditions
An Imprint of HarperCollins*Publishers*

HarperCollins books may be purchased for educational, business, or
sales promotional use. For information, please write: Special Markets
Department, HarperCollins Publishers, Inc., 10 East 53rd Street, New
York, NY 10022.

FIRST EDITION

Designed by Abigail Sturges

Library of Congress Cataloging-in-Publication Data
Roth, Leland M.
    Understanding architecture : its elements, history, and meaning /
Leland Roth. — 1st ed.
        p.   cm.
    Includes bibliographical references and index.
    ISBN 0-06-438493-4 (cloth) / ISBN 0-06-430158-3 (paper)
    1. Architecture.   2. Architecture—History.   I. Title.
NA2500.R68   1992
720'.1—dc20   88-45540

93 94 95 96 97   NP/CW   10 9 8 7 6 5 4 3 2 1
93 94 95 96 97   NP/CW   10 9 8 7 6 5 4 3 2 1 (pbk.)

With thanks to Carol,
who brought this from disk to desk

Contents

List of Maps

Maps by Greg Koester.

List of Illustrations

Introduction

PART ONE: THE ELEMENTS OF ARCHITECTURE

1 "Commoditie": How Does the Building Function?

2 "Firmeness": How Does the Building Stand Up?

3 "Delight": Space in Architecture

4 "Delight": Seeing Architecture

5 "Delight": Architectural Acoustics, Shape, and Sound

6 The Architect: From High Priest to Professional

7 Architecture as Part of the Environment

8 Architecture, Memory, and Economics

PART TWO: THE HISTORY AND MEANING OF ARCHITECTURE

9 The Invention of Architecture: From Caves to Cities

10 Egyptian Architecture

11 Greek Architecture

12 Roman Architecture

13 Early Christian and Byzantine Architecture

14 Early Medieval Architecture

15 Gothic Architecture

16 Renaissance and Mannerist Architecture

17 Baroque and Rococo Architecture

18 Architecture in the Age of Enlightenment, 1720–1800

19 Architecture in the Nineteenth Century

20 Early-Twentieth-Century: The Perfection of Utility

21 Late-Twentieth-Century Architecture: A Question of Meaning

Color Plates (following page 78)

Preface

This book is about learning to perceive and understand our man-made environment. It is about architecture as a physical vessel, a container of human activity. But since architecture is a social activity, building is also a social statement and the creation of a cultural legacy. Every building, therefore, whether a commanding public structure or a private shelter—whether a cathedral or a bicycle shed—is constructed in accordance with the laws of physics in ways that crystallize the cultural values of its builders. This book is an introduction to the artistic urge that compels humans to build as well as to the structural properties that make it possible to make buildings stand up. It is also an introduction to the silent cultural language that every building expresses. This book, then, might be thought of as a primer for visual environmental literacy.

Since the Protestant Reformation, there has been a tendency in the West to stress the written cultural record, whether historical or literary, and to give little serious attention to the meaning of visual imagery. Hence very few students are taught how to "read" or interpret the physical environment in which they certainly will have to live and work. In some schools students are offered classes in the visual arts, music, and dance, even though only a fraction of them will be able to put such knowledge to use when they enter the work world. Yet, concerning the built environment with which they will have to deal, most people are taught next to nothing. What they know is what they gain "in the streets" through

experience by trial and error. This environmental illiteracy has been readily accepted as the normal state of affairs. Most people learn little of the history of their built environment or how to interpret the meaning of the environment they have inherited.

This book seeks to help correct this situation. It is aimed at the inquisitive student or general reader interested in learning about the basic operation of the built environment and the layered historical meaning embodied mute within it. This book is not intended as a historical survey tracing the complex evolution of building forms, but as a basic introduction to how the environment we build works on us physically and psychologically, and what historical and symbolic messages it carries.

The basic structure of this book grew out of an outline I developed in 1977 for Sandee Harden for the architecture section of a telecourse, "Humanities Through the Arts," produced by the Coast Community College, Fountain Valley, California, and the City Colleges of Chicago. As a result, the idea for this book was that architecture be examined as a cultural phenomenon, as well as an artistic and technological achievement. The content of the book then evolved from an introductory course on architecture taught to college freshmen during a period of thirteen years, at Ohio State University, Northwestern University, and now the University of Oregon.

The form and organization assume that the reader knows nothing in either a technical or historical sense of the built environment. Hence the division into two parts, the first of which deals with the basic properties of architecture. Basic design and technical concepts are outlined and a working vocabulary introduced in Part One; then the historical evolution of architecture in the West is treated in Part Two by examining basic cultural themes, with selected buildings as case studies. Such a division makes it possible in the chapter on Roman architecture, for example, to focus on the symbolic image presented by the vast dome of the Pantheon since the structural properties of domes have already been dealt with in Part One.

Part One begins with a definition of what architecture is, and continues with chapters that explore function, structural principles, and elements of design. There are individual chapters dealing with how architecture affects—and is affected by—climatic elements, what the role of the architect has been over time, and what has been considered "good" or "economical" architecture. The discussion in Part One is illustrated by building examples drawn from all parts of the world, past and present.

Part Two is a historical survey of architectural development in the West, from prehistoric times to the present. In these chapters the focus is on architecture as a cultural artifact, as a systematized statement of values. This leads to the concluding argument that what we build today, whether privately or on a grand public scale, is an embodiment of our own values.

In writing this book, I have been influenced by numerous historical studies, including detailed general works, specialized monographs, and recent theoretical studies. Perhaps the most formative was Niels Luning Prak, *The Language of Architecture* (The Hague, The Netherlands, 1968), which is also divided into two parts, but whose historical coverage begins with the Early Christian mausoleum/church of Santa Constanza and ends with Philip Johnson's Glass House and Le Corbusier's chapel at Ronchamp. Since the construction of those buildings, in the early 1950s, much has happened. Similar to Prak's book is Christian Norberg-Schulz, *Meaning in Western Architecture* (New York, 1975).

For the formal analysis of architecture, I am indebted to Steen Eiler Rasmussen, *Experiencing Architecture* (Cambridge, Mass., 1959, second ed., 1962), and the similar treatment in Sinclair Gauldie, *Architecture* (London, 1969). Especially enlightening has been Stanley Abercrombie's *Architecture as Art: An Aesthetic Analysis* (New York, 1984). I also found especially interesting the book prepared by the architects Caudill, Peìa, and Kennon, *Architecture and You* (New York, 1978), aimed at prospective clients. In the passages dealing with values in architecture, I drew from Peter F. Smith, *Architecture and the Human Dimension* (Westfield, N. J., 1979), and Melvin Rader and Bertram Jessup, *Art and Human Values* (Englewood Cliffs, N. J., 1976).

A survey such as found in Part Two cannot help but be influenced by Nikolaus Pevsner, *An Outline of European Architecture* (Harmondsworth, England, 1943; seventh ed., 1963), still one of the most important books of its kind, and by Robert Furneaux Jordan, *Concise History of Western Architecture* (New York, 1970). These compact surveys have now been superseded by three massive studies: Spiro Kostof, *A History of Architecture* (New York, 1985), Marvin Trachtenberg and Isabelle Hyman, *Architecture: From Prehistory to Post-Modernism* (Englewood Cliffs, N.J., 1986), and David Watkin, *A History of Western Architecture* (London and New York, 1986). Unlike these encyclopedic works, however, this brief introduction treats architecture as a cultural expression and focuses on selected examples as types rather than trying to treat in detail the intricacies of the development of style.

Like Kostof, I believe that all of the built environment rewards study, for it is all built in response to human need. In a book of this compact scope, however, it is not possible to provide a survey of vernacular architecture, even though that forms a significant part of our living environment. Nor has it been possible to elaborate on how Islamic, Indian, or Oriental buildings embody deeply rooted cultural values differing from those of the West.[1] I am sensitive that this may be viewed as a shortcoming in this book, and that some reviewers also may find fault with the Western emphasis as well. Inasmuch as most of the students I encounter will be working in a Western culture, and considering the modest scope of this book, the full range of vernacular building and the plurality of modern worldwide contacts could not be examined here. I acknowledge the importance of these studies and hope for suitable treatment in future volumes.

Whatever I may have absorbed from all these studies was modified and enlarged in the classroom in accordance with what worked best. And I must acknowledge, too, the contributions made by my students over the years in their questions, expressed both verbally and in furrowed brows. It is impossible to thank adequately my colleagues who have read the manuscript, but my special gratitude is extended to G. Z. Brown, Jeffrey

Hurwit, John Reynolds, and Richard Sundt.

A word, too, should be said about the plans illustrated throughout the book, for here too students contributed significantly. Aside from those that I prepared, many were drawn to uniform conventions by architecture students in several special media courses that I taught during 1985-86. They are individually identified in the List of Illustrations.

As with my previous books, this too would not have been realized without the encouragement and enthusiasm of Cass Canfield, Jr., my editor at HarperCollins, who nurtured this through a long period of gestation. The most special thanks are due Carol, who read this with a critical eye and among whose inestimable services were spotting the errant commas and preparing the final hard print copy.

pro domo humano

NOTES

1. For Indian architecture see: Susan L. and John C. Huntington, *The Art of Ancient India: Buddhist, Hindu, Jain* (New York, 1985); R. Nath, *Islamic Architecture and Culture in India* (Delhi, 1982); and Benjamin Rowland, *The Art and Architecture of India,* third ed. (Baltimore, 1977). For Chinese architecture see: Nelson I. Wu, *Chinese and Indian Architecture* (New York, 1963); Laurence Sickman and Alexander Soper, *The Art and Architecture of China,* third ed. (Baltimore, 1971). For Japanese architecture, see: William Alex, *Japanese Architecture* (New York, 1963); and Robert Treat Paine and Alexander Soper, *The* *Art and Architecture of Japan,* third ed. (Baltimore, 1981). One study of Japanese architecture as a cultural phenomenon is Kiyoyuki Nishihara, *Japanese Houses: Patterns for Living* (Toyko, 1967). Detailed studies of Islamic architecture have recently begun to appear in English; see: Richard Ettinghausen and Oleg Grabar, *The Art and Architecture of Islam, 650–1250* (Harmondsworth, England, and New York, 1987); John D. Hoag, *Islamic Architecture* (New York, 1977); and George Michell, ed., *Architecture of the Islamic World: Its History and Social Meaning* (New York, 1978).

Understanding Architecture

1. Nest of the South American rufous-breasted castle builder, an example of deliberate construction in the animal kingdom.

Architecture, the Unavoidable Art

Architecture is the unavoidable art. Every moment, awake or asleep, we are in buildings, around buildings, in spaces defined by buildings, or in landscapes shaped by human artifice. It is possible to take deliberate steps to avoid looking at painting, sculpture, drawings, or any of the other visual arts, but architecture constantly touches us, shapes our behavior, and conditions our psychological mood. The blind and deaf may not see paintings or hear music, but like all other humans they must deal with architecture. More than being merely shelter or a protective umbrella, architecture is also the physical record of human activity and aspiration. It is the cultural legacy left us.

The architect Louis Kahn wrote that "architecture is what nature cannot make."[1] Humans are among several animals that build, and indeed some structures built by birds, bees, termites, to name but a few, are like human engineering in their economy of structure. The rufous-breasted castle builder of South America weaves two chambers connected by a cantilevered tube between the two, creating a double-chambered nest in the form of a dumbbell [1]. Certain blind termites build soaring arches of mud, starting at two distinct springing points, pushing their sections upward until they meet in the air. Mollusks, such as the chambered nautilus, build their houses around them, creating a hard shell of calcium carbonate.

The shell of the chambered nautilus can serve as a useful metaphor for the human built environment. As the nautilus grows, it adds a new and larger chamber to its curved shell, the vacated chamber then being filled with nitrogen gas to add buoyancy to the enlarged mass; the older parts of the shell, however, remain as a record of the history of the animal [2]. Architecture is the chambered nautilus shell of the human species; it is the environment we build for ourselves, and which, as we grow in experience and knowledge, we change and adapt to our expanded condition. If we wish to retain our identity, we must take care not to eliminate the "shell" of our past, for it is the physical record of our aspirations and achievements.

It was once customary to think of architecture as consisting only of those buildings

2. Section through the shell of a chambered nautilus. The shell is constructed by means of an unconscious biological process.

3. *Lane Transit District Bicycle Shed, Eugene, Oregon, 1984. The bicycle shed is part of a cluster of buildings, including an area bus terminal, designed to encourage use of public transportation.*

that we deemed "important," the great buildings for church and state that necessitated substantial expenditure of energy and funds. Perhaps this was because, in past centuries, histories of architecture were written largely by architects, princely patrons, or court historians who wished to sharpen the distinction between what they had achieved in contrast to the surrounding mass of vernacular buildings. In his compact *Outline of European Architecture,* first published in 1943, Nikolaus Pevsner began by making the distinction that "a bicycle shed is a building; Lincoln Cathedral is a piece of architecture" [3, 4].[2] Conventional wisdom often makes the same distinction, as demonstrated in the story, now a part of folklore, of the metal building manufacturer who made barn structures and offered the buyer a wide choice of historical ornamental clip-on door frames—Colonial, Mediterranean, Classical, among many others. After a windstorm had damaged a number in one area,

the factory representative telephoned customers to find out how the structures had fared. One customer, whose Colonial door frame had been stripped off while the barn itself survived, replied, "The building's fine but the architecture blew away."[3]

If, in fact, we were to study the "architecture" of Lincoln Cathedral, or of Notre-Dame in Amiens, France, or of any cathedral for that matter, without taking into account the "buildings"—that is, all the humble houses that made up the city around them—we would arrive at an erroneous concept of the position occupied by the church in the social and cultural context of the Middle Ages. We must examine *both* the cathedral *and* the ordinary houses surrounding it, for all of the buildings as a group constitute the architecture of the Middle Ages. So, too, if we wish to understand the totality of the architecture of the contemporary city, we need to consider all its component elements. For example, to understand Eugene, Oregon, we would need to examine the bicycle sheds and the bus transfer shelters that are an integrated part of the transportation system [3]; there bicyclists can lock their bikes under a roof and transfer to motorized public transit. The bicycle sheds are part of a municipal ecological response, an effort to enhance the physical living-environment by encouraging modes of transportation other than private automobiles.

Pevsner's emphatic distinction between architecture and building is understandable, considering the limits of his compact book, for it made the material he needed to cover much more manageable. Pevsner's view grew out of the extended influence of the nineteenth-century critic John Ruskin, who made the same distinction in the second sentence of his book *The Seven Lamps of Architecture* (London, 1849). He began this by observing, "It is very necessary, in the outset of all inquiry, to distinguish carefully between Architecture and Building." Ruskin wanted to concentrate his attention on religious and public buildings, but he also recognized that architecture was a richly informative cultural artifact. In another of his many writings, the preface to *St. Mark's Rest* (London, 1877), he cautioned that "great nations write their autobiographies in three manuscripts—the book of their deeds, the book of their words, and the book of their art. Not one of these books can be understood unless we read the other two; but of the three, the only quite trustworthy one is the last."[4] As Ruskin correctly recognized, to understand the architecture of the past, of any period or culture not our own, we must absorb the history and literature of that period, the record of its acts and thoughts, before we can understand fully what message the architecture conveys. Architecture, then, is like written history and literature—a record of the people who produced it—and it can be "read" in much the same way. Architecture is a nonverbal form of communication, a mute record of the culture that produced it.

These ideas—the totality of the built environment as architecture, and the environment as a form of dialogue with the past and future—underlie this book. Architecture is

understood to be the whole of the environment built by humans, including buildings, urban spaces, and landscapes. And while it is not possible in a book of this size to examine in detail all types of buildings in all ages, the reader needs to keep in mind the idea that the broad spectrum of building of any period, and not just a few special buildings, constitutes its architecture.

Unlike other creatures that build, humans think as they build, so that human building is a conscious act, a reflective act, an act that embodies countless decisions and choices. This is what distinguishes human building from birds' nests and bees' combs, for they build as the result of genetic programming. Humans build to satisfy a need, but even as they do so, they give expression to feelings and values; they are expressing in wood, stone, metal, plaster, and plastics what they believe vital and important, whether it is a

4. *Lincoln Cathedral, Lincoln, England, 1192–1280. This building was constructed as a public demonstration of both church power and civic pride.*

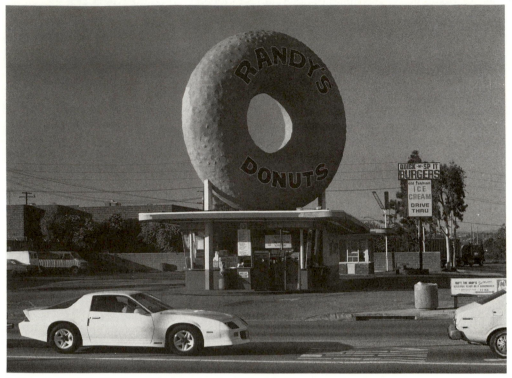

5. *Henry J. Goodwin, Big Donut Shop, Los Angeles, 1954. A building created in response to an automobile culture and a public desire for instant alimentary satisfaction.*

bicycle shed or a cathedral. It may be a message clearly understood and deliberately incorporated by both client and architect, or it may be an unconscious or subconscious statement, decipherable by a later observer. Hence, the United States Capitol in Washington, D.C., has as much to tell us about the symbolism of republican government in the nineteenth century as the Empire State Building in New York City has to tell us about capitalism and urban land values in the twentieth century. Equally important as cultural artifact and as architecture is the Big Donut Shop in Los Angeles, built in 1954 by Henry J. Goodwin [5], for it reflects Americans' love of the automobile and their desire for instant alimentary gratification.

Architecture is the unavoidable art. We deal with it every waking moment when not in the wilderness; it is the art form we inhabit. Perhaps this familiarity causes us to think of architecture as only a utilitarian agent, as simply the largest of our technical contrivances, requiring of us no more thought than any other appliance we use throughout the day. And yet, unlike the other arts, architecture has the power to affect and condition human behavior; the color of walls in a room, for example, can help to determine our mood. Architecture acts upon us, creating a sense of awe such as one might feel walking among the huge stone columns of the hypostyle hall of the Egyptian temple at Karnak; or being pulled, as if by gravity, to the center of the vast space covered by the dome of the Pantheon in Rome; or sensing the flow of space and the rootedness in the earth of Frank Lloyd Wright's Fallingwater.

Part of our experience of architecture may be based largely on our enjoyment of these physiological responses—which the skillful architect knows how to manipulate to maximum effect—but the fullest experience of architecture comes from expanding our knowledge of a building, its structure, its history, and its meaning, while reducing our prejudices and ignorance.

We need to remember, too, that architecture, besides providing shelter, is a symbolic representation. As Sir Herbert Read wrote, art is "a mode of symbolic discourse, and where there is no symbol and therefore no discourse, there is no art."[5] This symbolic content is most easily perceived in religious and public buildings where the principal intent is to make a broad and emphatic proclamation of communal values and beliefs. If a building seems strange to us it is likely because the symbol being presented is not in our current vocabulary. To Americans who have no Gothic architectural heritage, the construction of the Houses of Parliament in London in the mid-nineteenth century in the medieval Gothic style might seem at first anachronistic. Yet it becomes more understandable when we remember that actual Gothic buildings were to be incorporated into the new complex and that, to nineteenth-century Englishmen, Gothic architecture was viewed as being inherently English and thus had a long connection with parliamentary government. The argument could be made that for them Gothic was the *only* appropriate style.

Architecture is the science *and* the art of building. To understand more clearly the art of architecture and its symbolic discourse, it is best to gain first an understanding of the science of architectural construction. So, in the following chapters of Part One, the pragmatic concerns of function, structure, and design are explored. Then, in Part Two, the symbolism of architecture as a nonverbal means of discourse is taken up.

NOTES

1. Louis I. Kahn, "Remarks," *Perspecta*, the Yale Architectural Journal 9–10 (1965): 305.
2. Nikolaus Pevsner, *An Outline of European Architecture* (London, 1943). This has remained a standard work and continues to be reprinted in its seventh edition.
3. Walter McQuade tells a similar story in "Where's the Architecture?" *Connoisseur* 215 (November 1985): 82.
4. Ruskin's *Seven Lamps of Architecture* is still in print. Because of the many editions of Ruskin's writings, the best source is the multivolume standard edition edited by E. T. Cook and A. Wedderburn, *The Works of John Ruskin* (London, 1903–12); for *St. Mark's Rest* see vol. 24.
5. Sir Herbert Read, "The Disintegration of Form in Modern Art," in *The Origins of Form in Art* (New York, 1965), p. 182.

6. *Stonehenge III, Salisbury Plain, Wiltshire, England, c. 2000–1500* B.C. *Detail of a central trilithon.*

PART ONE

The Elements of Architecture

1.2. *Adler and Sullivan, Guaranty Building, Buffalo, 1895. Louis H. Sullivan gave clear expression on the exterior of three major functional zones of the modern office skyscraper.*

CHAPTER 1

"Commoditie":
How Does the Building Function?

Haec autem ita fieri debent, ut habeatur ratio firmitatis, utilitatis, venustatis. (Now these should be so carried out that account is taken of strength, utility, grace.)

Marcus Vitruvius, *De architectura,* c. 25 B.C., 1.iii.ii

In architecture as in all other operative arts, the end must direct the operation. The end is to build well. Well-building hath three conditions: Commoditie, Firmeness, and Delight.

Sir Henry Wotten, *The Elements of Architecture,* 1624

Perhaps the most basic definition of architecture was written by the ancient Roman architect Marcus Vitruvius, about 25 B.C. As we learn from his treatise, architecture was the subject of critical writing long before his time. Several Greek architects compiled books on their profession during the centuries before the birth of Christ, and their works led to that written by Vitruvius. He lists sixty-three Greek and Roman books on architecture he consulted, some of them dating back to the fourth century B.C.[1]

The basic elements of architecture described by Vitruvius have remained essentially unchanged since antiquity. Architecture, he wrote, must provide utility, firmness, and beauty, or, as Sir Henry Wotten later paraphrased it in the seventeenth century, commodity, firmness, and delight. By utility, Vitruvius meant the arrangement of rooms and spaces so that there is no hindrance to use and so that a building is perfectly adjusted to its site. Firmness meant that foundations were solid and that the materials of the building were wisely selected. Beauty meant that "the appearance of the work is pleasing and in good

taste, and [that] its members are in due proportion according to correct principles of symmetry."[2] No matter how this notion of beauty, or *venustas,* may have been construed in the intervening centuries, the Vitruvian triad still remains a valid summary of the elements of good architecture. The ultimate tests of architecture are these: First, does a building work by supporting and reinforcing its use; does it enhance its setting? Second, is it built well enough to stand up; will its materials weather well? But third and equally important, does the building appeal to the senses, does it provide a full measure of satisfaction *and* enjoyment—does it provide delight?

The Vitruvian three-part definition of architecture will be the basis of the discussion in the following seven chapters, beginning with the element that, on the surface, would appear most straightforward, but that, in the mid-twentieth century, has proved extremely troublesome. That element, the first one cited by Vitruvius, is *function.* Function, or the pragmatic utility of an object—its being fitted to a particular use—was a criterion analyzed by such Greek philosophers as Plato, Aristotle, and Xenophon.[3] Part of the difficulty we have faced in the last three-quarters of a century is that there is only one word in English for function, just as in English and most European languages we have but one word for snow, whereas the Inuit (Eskimos) have numerous words to describe its many properties under different weather conditions. Similarly, we need variations to describe different kinds of function. Our alternative is to make compound words such as "circulatory function" and "acoustical function."

Making the problem worse, about 1920 the definition of function became restricted to a purely mechanical sense with the rise of what became called International Modern architecture, the "International Style," as it was christened in 1932 by Henry-Russell Hitchcock and Philip Johnson. The model of this type of building was provided by the AEG Turbine Factory, Berlin, 1908–9, by Peter Behrens and by the Fagus factory, Alfeld, Germany, 1911, by Walter Gropius [20.7, 20.8]. In both of these, the form of the building was almost totally determined by internal industrial processes. In 1926 Gropius designed the new building for the Bauhaus school in Dessau, Germany, the workshop wing of which exemplified the same industrial determinism. At nearly the same time, Gropius wrote of the new architecture: "A thing is determined by its nature and if it is to be fashioned so as to work properly, its essence must be investigated and fully grasped. A thing must answer its purpose in every way, that is fulfill its function in a practical sense, and must thus be serviceable, reliable, and cheap."[4] The Swiss-French architect Charles-Édouard Jeanneret (who wrote under the pen name "Le Corbusier") described the functional inadequacy of the contemporary house, saying that, for the new age and the new architecture demanded by it, "the house is a machine for living in."[5] The architect Bruno Taut summarized the intent of International Modern architecture in 1929: "The aim of architecture is the creation of the perfect, and therefore most beautiful, efficiency."[6] In short, beauty would result *automatically* from the leanest, strictest utility.

The problem that became increasingly manifest as the twentieth century unfolded, however, was that few buildings (other than factories or other industrial structures) have the kind of internal process that can determine form in such a direct and utilitarian way. Most human activities cannot be so quantified or reduced to a kind of mechanical formula. The American architect Louis I. Kahn believed that "when you make a building, you make a life. It comes out of

life, and you really make a life. It talks to you. When you have *only* the comprehension of the function of a building, it would not become an environment of a life."[7]

Another problem we have had to face in the last two centuries is that few buildings have continued to accommodate the function for which they were originally designed. This has necessitated enlargements, modifications, or the construction of wholly new buildings, with the original building being converted to a new use. The temptation is to say that the old building was never functional because it cannot accommodate the new use we want to put in it. It may, in fact, have accommodated its original use very well.

An alternative is to design a building in such a way that any possible future activity can be accommodated. This approach was taken in the mid-twentieth century by Ludwig Mies van der Rohe, who devised what he called the *Vielzweckraum,* the "all-purpose space" or "universal space." Indeed Mies is reported saying that he and his associates did not fit form to function: "We reverse this, and make a practical and satisfying shape, and then fit the functions into it. Today this is the only practical way to build, because the functions of most buildings are continually changing, but economically the building cannot change."[8] This is demonstrated in the huge single room of Crown Hall, the school of architecture of the Illinois Institute of Technology, Chicago, 1952–56 [1.1]. While such a vast single room can indeed hold any of a variety of future activities, it does not function at all well acoustically, for a sound generated in any part of the room ripples and reverberates through the entire space. Mies van der Rohe simply put into built form what a number of International Modernist architects had believed since the 1920s: that there was a universality of human needs and function. Le Corbusier even claimed it was possible to design "one single building for all nations and climates."[9] Unfortunately this notion, so appealing because of its apparent scientific simplicity, ignores the truths that function is socially and culturally influenced, and that a building's form is also

1.1. Ludwig Mies van der Rohe, Crown Hall, Illinois Institute of Technology, Chicago, 1952–56. The interior consists of one vast room designed to house a variety of differing utilitarian functions.

a response to its physical setting and climate.

Function, therefore, has many components, the most basic of which is ***pragmatic utility,*** or the accommodation of a specific use or activity in a specific room or space. A room might be used to contain a single bed for sleeping, it might be an office cell containing a desk, or it might be a large assembly chamber or some other public space.

Most buildings, of course, are composed of numerous rooms with interrelated functions. People therefore need to move from one room to another, so that nearly as important as the utilitarian function is the ***circulatory function,*** the making of appropriate spaces to accommodate, direct, and enhance movement from area to area. When Charles Garnier designed the Paris Opéra, 1861–75, he analyzed just what the "function" of the opera was. Certainly Parisians went to hear the latest opera, but as Garnier correctly realized there was per-

haps an even more important social reason for going to the opera—people went there to see and be seen. Therefore the circulatory areas were every bit as important as the stage house and the auditorium, and, as the plan clearly reveals, the grand stair, the foyer, and the vestibules make up a significant portion of the total area [19.14, 19.15].

Like Garnier, when Louis Sullivan set out to design some of the first metal-framed commercial skyscrapers toward the end of the nineteenth century, he first examined just what this new type of building enclosed.[10] He discovered there were four distinct zones, the bottom-most of which was the basement, containing machinery, storage, and other strictly utilitarian uses. Above that were three distinctly different visible functional zones: the ground floor (containing the entrances, the elevator lobby, and shops at the perimeter facing the street), the central section (floor upon floor of office cells arranged around the elevator),

1.3. Mies van der Rohe, Boiler House, Illinois Institute of Technology, Chicago, 1940. With its towerlike chimney and high clerestory windows, this building has the physical attributes of early churches.

and the terminating, upper floor (with elevator machinery, water tanks, storage, and other miscellaneous uses). Since the new, tall office block was decidedly vertical in form, Sullivan argued that it was the architect's responsibility to emphasize that verticality and to express clearly the three functional zones, as he did in the Guaranty Building, Buffalo, New York, 1895 [1.2].

Another architect who exploited the potential for expressive form by celebrating different functional activities was the Finnish architect Alvar Aalto. Among his best examples is one of the two buildings he designed in the United States, the library for the Benedictine Monastery at Mount Angel, Oregon, 1967–71 [21.36]. The principal pragmatic function is to contain books, which are arranged in bookcases that fan out northward from the central reading and circulation core. But the other support activities require different spaces; on the south side are closely fitted rectilinear office and work rooms for the staff and a wedge-shaped auditorium. Each of the spaces is placed where it needs to be and is shaped in the best way to accommodate its use, joined by the architect with the other spaces to form a harmonious whole.

A building also has a *symbolic function* and makes a visable statement about its use. We usually expect some correspondence between what the building appears to *suggest* its use is and what its use *actually is.* Among the Egyptians, Greeks, and Romans, and for the Renaissance and the Baroque architect from 1400 to 1750, there were general guidelines as to the form and appearance of buildings for certain uses, but nowadays there is much greater latitude. Since roughly 1920, therefore, architects have had to do two things simultaneously— invent original forms using new building technologies and devise appropriate new symbolic representations for the functions they are housing. Often the exploitation of new technologies has taken precedence over symbolic representation, and many twentieth-century buildings tell us almost nothing about what goes on inside them. As an example, compare two buildings designed by Mies van der Rohe for the cam-

pus of the Illinois Institute of Technology during 1949–52 [1.3, 1.4]. One is the boiler house, perhaps the most utilitarian building of the ensemble; the other is the chapel. Yet there is nothing in either the form or the material of the chapel that tells us how its function differs from that of the boiler house. It may be that Mies van der Rohe was viewing the chapel as an all-purpose space and wished not to create a fixed image so that a new use could be accommodated in it later. One might contrast the I.I.T. chapel with the interior of the Zion Lutheran Church, Portland, Oregon, 1950, by Pietro Belluschi [1.5], which to most observers embodies the functional character of a religious building without attempting to recreate Gothic vaults, crockets, or finials.

In the United States the national Capitol building in Washington has established an

1.4. Mies van der Rohe, Chapel, Illinois Institute of Technology, Chicago, 1949–52. Although a chapel, it has none of the conventional clues as to its function.

1.5. Pietro Belluschi, Zion Lutheran Church, Portland, Oregon, 1950. Through the simple use of colored glass and laminated arches in wood, the traditional image of a church is suggested.

image of government, and since 1830 that image has been recalled many times. One notable example is the Minnesota State Capitol, Saint Paul, 1895–1905, by Cass Gilbert [1.6]. Like the national Capitol, this has two chambers, on either side of a central circulation chamber capped by a tall dome. In this case the dome is specifically patterned after that of the basilica of Saint Peter's in Rome, but the image conveyed is of a building in which the legislature does its business; the bright dome of white marble proclaims that function across the landscape of Saint Paul as it rises over the surrounding buildings. In another example, when Eero Saarinen was engaged in 1956 to design a terminal building for Trans World Airlines at Idlewild (now Kennedy) Airport, New York, he set out to shape a building that, in architectural terms alone, would convey

symbolically the sensation of flight. He and his associates conceived a building with great concrete shells stretching out from the center, like giant wings, and interior surfaces that curve and rise without sharp angles or corners [21.14]. Hence the form alone prepares us for the miracle of flight as we pass through to board a plane.

No building is devoted wholly to one kind of function. Most buildings contain a mixture of purely utilitarian function and symbolic function. Figure 1.7 represents the "universe" of combined utilitarian and symbolic content for any given building; the diagonal lines cutting through the diagram show what relative percentage a garage might contain (90 percent utilitarian and 10 percent symbolic), whereas a memorial structure or a church might be just the opposite (10 percent purely utilitarian func-

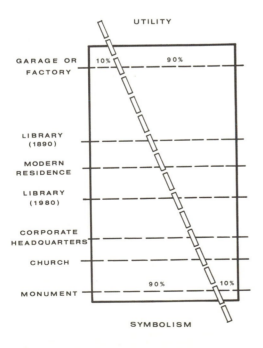

1.6. Cass Gilbert, Minnesota State Capitol, Saint Paul, 1895–1905. Based on the Capitol in Washington, D.C., this building clearly evokes the image of an American government building.

1.7. Diagram of the relative components of function in different building types. A garage or factory is largely utilitarian, whereas a shrine or monument is largely symbolic.

1.8. Louis I. Kahn, Jonas Salk Institute for Biological Studies, La Jolla, California, 1959–65. View of the interior court. The working areas are housed in large multifunctional spaces, whereas small, individual private studies are clustered in the central courtyard.

tion and 90 percent symbolic). A private house might be somewhere in the middle, with equal concern given to accommodating utility and symbolic representation. A public library or city hall today might be in much the same location on this graph, perhaps favoring symbolic or representational function over strictly utilitarian, but in the nineteenth century such buildings favored symbolic function much more. Thus, the diagram in Figure 1.7 shows the mix of utilitarian and symbolic functions at only one point in time. For a different period, past or future, the lines for different building types would cut across the field at different locations.

Good architecture also has physical and physiological functions to fulfill. As an example, a waiting room at a doctor's office or a hospital emergency room is a place where most people experience heightened anxiety. The architect might determine that creating a domestic atmosphere like that of a home living room, with a view out to an enclosed garden, rather than an antiseptic clinical atmosphere, would help to reduce those anxieties.

There is also a ***psychological function,*** which we might define as the optimum satisfaction of all the types of function just described. Perhaps the modern architect who best achieved psychological function was the American architect, Louis I. Kahn, as represented in his Jonas Salk Institute for Biological Studies in La Jolla, California, 1959–65 [1.8]. Just as Garnier did for the Paris Opéra, Kahn penetratingly analyzed what the range of functions was to be in the laboratory, and he saw that satisfying the purely utilitarian function of providing space for conducting experiments was only part of his task. He was fortunate, too, that his client, the scientist Jonas Salk, already perceived the need for something more than the utilitarian. As Kahn said, Salk recognized that "the scientist . . . needed more than anything the presence of the unmeasurable, which is the realm of the artist."[11] So the laboratory spaces were separated into two parts, large spaces for work and small private spaces for reflection. The large universal spaces for setting up the experiments are on the outside of the U-shaped plan, and budding from their inward faces are the private studies. The work spaces are expansive and functionally efficient, whereas the studies are small, intimate, and private, paneled in teak, with windows angled so that the researchers look out westward toward the Pacific Ocean. The work spaces are focused on the empirical research; the studies are designed to encourage a community of minds and private contemplation of the meaning of the research. As Kahn and Salk wished to make clear, science is more than the accumulation of data. Although science grows out of the inextinguishable human desire to know, such knowledge inevitably influences the quality of human life and hence calls for the most penetrating reflection. Science is more than data-accumulating, as Salk knew well. Similarly, architecture is more than functional utility or structural display—it is the vessel that shapes human life.

NOTES

1. Most regrettably, all those ancient manuscripts are now lost, so that Vitruvius's book, originally on ten scrolls, has acquired special historical significance. It provides us our only glimpse into the thinking of the architects of antiquity. The oldest complete copy of the Vitruvius manuscript dates only from the eighth century A.D. and was copied out by monks of the Saxon scriptorium in Northumbria, England. The other surviving sixteen copies of Vitruvius derive from this and date from the tenth through the fifteenth centuries. The most recent translations of Vitruvius in English are: Frank Granger (trans.), Vitruvius, *On Architecture*, 2 vols. (Cambridge, Mass., 1931), which lists the various medieval Vitruvius manuscripts; and Morris Hickey Morgan (trans.), Vitruvius, *Ten Books on Architecture* (Cambridge, Mass., 1914), which puts Vitruvius into easier, idiomatic English. The major translations of Vitruvius into European languages are listed in Granger, xxxiii–xxxiv, including the paraphrase version by Sir Henry Wotten, *The Elements of Architecture*, London, 1624.
2. Vitruvius, *Ten Books*, Morgan trans., 17.
3. For a discussion of utility and adaptation to use in antiquity, see Edward Robert De Zurko, *Origins of Functionalist Theory* (New York, 1957), 15–31.
4. Walter Gropius, "Where Artists and Technicians Meet," *Die Form*, new series, 1 (1925–26): 117–20.
5. Le Corbusier, *Towards a New Architecture*, trans. Frederick Etchells (London, 1927), 10.
6. Bruno Taut, *Modern Architecture* (London, 1929), 9.
7. Louis I. Kahn, interview in John W. Cook and Heinrich Klotz, *Conversations with Architects* (New York, 1973), 204.
8. *Architectural Forum* 97 (November 1952): 94.
9. Le Corbusier, *Précisions sur un état présent de l'architecture et de l'urbanisme* (Paris, 1930), 64.
10. Louis H. Sullivan, "The Tall Building Artistically Considered," *Lippincott's Magazine* 57 (March 1896): 403–9, reprinted in Leland M. Roth, ed., *America Builds* (New York, 1983), 340–46.
11. Louis Kahn quoted in Ann Mohler, ed., "Louis I. Kahn: Talks with Students," *Architecture at Rice* 26 (1969):13.

2.1. Column, Temple of Poseidon, Paestum, Italy, c. 550 B.C. *This stone column, larger than structurally necessary, conveys a clear impression of its strength.*

CHAPTER 2

"Firmeness": How Does the Building Stand Up?

Architecture . . . is the crystallization of its inner structure, the slow unfolding of form. That is the reason why technology and architecture are so closely related.

Mies van der Rohe, speech to Illinois Institute of Technology students, 1950, in U. Conrads, ed., *Programs and Manifestoes on 20th-Century Architecture.*

The most apparent part of a building is its structure, or what makes it stand up. This may be more noticeable nowadays than it once was, since architects and engineers take delight in making structures do more and more work with less and less material, seemingly defying gravity. The tension we may feel when looking at a structure so delicate as to seem in danger of imminent collapse illustrates the difference between the ***physical structure,*** the literal bones of the building that do the work, and the ***perceptual structure,*** or what we see. They are not the same, for a column may be much larger than structurally necessary simply to reassure us that it is indeed big enough for the job. Such is the case with the thick columns of the Temple of Poseidon at Paestum, Italy [2.1].

In a comparison between Lever House, New York, by Skidmore, Owings and Merrill, 1951–52 [2.2], and the neighboring New York Racquet and Tennis Club, by the office of McKim, Mead & White, 1916–19, we see the difference between a wall of glass that hides the structure and a massive masonry wall. The wall of the Racquet and Tennis Club looks stronger than need be, and gives us the assurance of structural excess, whereas the actual physical columns

of Lever House are covered by a suspended skin of green glass, and there is no readily perceptible clue as to what holds the building up. We know from experience that sheets of glass by themselves cannot hold up a building of that size, so we must hunt for the actual structure (the architects force us into a kind of game) until we finally see the columns emerge at the base of the building. This play between what we know to be a heavy building and its suggested weightlessness is part of the appeal of these glass-skinned skyscrapers; modern viewers take delight in the idea that gravity has been cheated (although observers of earlier periods might have considered the structure of the building poorly expressed).

We grow up with a good sense of gravity and how it affects objects around us, for from the first moment we try to move our limbs (once removed from the relatively weightless state of the womb) we experience the pull of gravity. As infants, we must figure out how to raise our bodies erect and maintain a state of stasis while standing and then how to move on two legs. So, long before we can articulate the idea in scientific terms, we have a clear concept that objects not supported will fall straight down, or, to be exact, toward the center of the earth. And that is the essence of architectural structure—making sure that objects will not fall to earth, despite the incessant pull of gravity.

We develop early a way of understanding objects around us through ***empathy,*** of imagining ourselves inside the object and feeling how gravity works on it. So, for

2.2. Skidmore, Owings and Merrill, Lever House, New York, 1951–52. With its glass envelope suspended from the inner skeleton, Lever House visually hides its structure, whereas the adjacent New York Racquet and Tennis Club (by McKim, Mead and White, 1916–19) has a boldly expressed wall structure.

example, when we see the pyramids in Egypt, we sense that they are inherently stable objects, whereas when we see something like the inverted Shapero Hall of Pharmacy at Wayne State University, Detroit [2.3], we feel a sense of instability, and perhaps marvel at the expertise of the architect and the engineer who placed such a building on its head. In the case of Lever House, the architect played with our differing perceptions of solid stone and transparent glass, knowing that we would sense one building as solid and "heavy" and the other

as "light." Some architects, in fact, have taken pains to accentuate the sense of weight, particularly the nineteenth-century American architect from Philadelphia, Frank Furness, as in his Provident Life and Trust Company, Philadelphia, 1876–79 [2.4], regrettably now demolished. The building projected a sense of immense weight, so that the parts of the building seemed to be compressed and telescoped into one another, sliding ever downward.

Part of our perception of architecture has to do with this empathetic analysis of how

2.3. Paulsen and Gardner, Shapero Hall of Pharmacy, Wayne State University, Detroit, 1965. This unusual building, resting on its smallest point, makes the viewer wonder how it is held up.

2.4. Frank Furness, Provident Life and Trust Company, Philadelphia, 1876–79 (demolished c. 1950). The architect deliberately exploited strong contrasts in form, scale, and texture to create an image that was bold and unique.

2.5. *Choir of Saint-Pierre, Beauvais, France, 1225–1569. In this building, devoted to the aspiration to heaven, the vertical line dominates everywhere.*

forces are handled in buildings. Hence, when we see the Parthenon in Athens [11.25], the careful balance of vertical and horizontal elements, in which neither dominate, suggests a delicate equilibrium of forces and thus exemplifies the Greek philosophical ideal. In contrast, Gothic architecture, as represented by the east end of the cathedral of Beauvais, France [2.5], is characterized by soaring, thin vertical supports, and a multiplicity of vertical lines. All of this suggests ascent, lift, weightlessness, aspiration, and a visual denial of the tremendous forces generated 140 feet (42.7 meters) in

the air and insistent on being conducted safely down to the ground.

The Post and Lintel

The beginning of structure is the wall, whether the wall is made of stone, brick, adobe or mud blocks, glass blocks, or any of a variety of materials. But a room enclosed with walls has no light or view, so the wall must be opened up. The blocks or bricks over that opening must be supported against the pull of gravity, and this is done either by means of a beam (of wood, or of

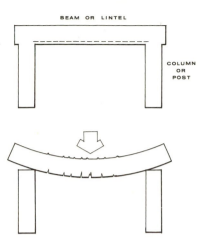

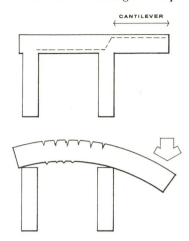

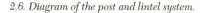

2.6. *Diagram of the post and lintel system.*

2.8. *Diagram of a cantilever.*

metal after 1750) or an arch. Such a beam inserted in a wall to support the wall above is called a **lintel.** The wall could also be cut away, so to speak, and replaced with slender stacks of blocks to form columns, with lintels spanning the spaces between them. The architect Louis Kahn spoke of "the momentous event when the wall parted and the column became."[1] The column and beam, or the post and lintel, system [2.6], is as old as human construction in permanent materials. Archaeological and anthropological evidence suggests that post and lintel systems

of wood or bound papyrus reeds were used long before they were translated into more durable stone, and in fact humans may have been using posts and beams for several hundred thousand years. Such a system is called a **trabeated** system, from the Latin *trabs,* or beam. One of the most straightforward examples of post and lintel construction is the Valley Temple east of the pyramid of Khafre, Giza, Egypt, built between 2570 B.C. and 2500 B.C. [2.7]. Here, finely polished square lintels of red granite rest on square piers of the same material, contrast-

2.7. *Valley Temple, Pyramid of Khafre, Giza, Egypt, c. 2570–2500 B.C. This is one of the purest and most direct expressions of the post and lintel system.*

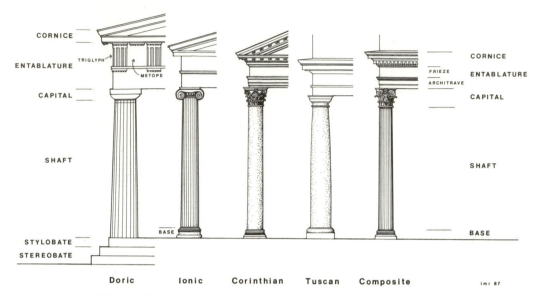

2.9. *Comparison of the five Classical orders. The Greek orders consisted of the Doric, Ionic, and Corinthian. To these the Romans added the Composite (a combination of the Ionic and Corinthian) and the simpler and heavier Tuscan Doric.*

ing with the alabaster floor. Extending the beam over the end of the column, results in a *cantilever* [2.8].

All beams, whether of stone, wood, or any other material, are acted upon by gravity. Since all materials are flexible to varying degrees, beams tend to sag of their own weight, even more as loads are applied. This means that the upper part of a beam between two supports is squeezed together and is compressed along the top surface, while the lower part is stretched and is said to be in tension [2.6]. In a cantilever, the situation is exactly reversed [2.8], for as the extended beam sags due to the pull of gravity, the upper part is stretched (put in tension) and the lower portion experiences compressive stresses. In the cantilever these forces are strongest just over the support. In fact, it is the continuity of the material of the beam over the support that makes the cantilever possible.

Wood, being a fibrous material, resists tensile stresses well, as does wrought iron and modern steel, and beams of these materials can span significant distances. The tensile forces along the bottom of a beam (or along the top of a cantilever) are deter-

mined by the length of the span and the load placed on the beam, so that eventually, given a span and a load sufficiently great, the tensile strength of the material will be exceeded; the beam will crack at the bottom or deform along the top (or both) and will collapse. Stone and solid concrete, being crystalline materials, have less tensile strength than fibrous wood, and a wooden beam over a given span can carry a load that would crack a stone beam carrying the same load. Of course, the stone beam starts out being far heavier by itself. The solution, in beams of concrete, which has great compressive strength, is to place something within the concrete that will take the tensile forces. This was done by the Romans, as well as in modern times, by placing iron (and now steel) rods in the formwork into which the liquid concrete is then poured. The result is reinforced concrete. As the dotted lines in Figures 2.6 and 2.8 indicate, the steel is placed where the tensile forces accumulate—on the bottoms of beams and at the top of cantilevers. The Greeks also faced this problem. The central opening of the gateway to the Akropolis in Athens, the Propylaia, built 437–32 B.C. [11.19], had to accommodate the passage of pairs of sacrificial oxen with their handlers; the result was a span of 18 feet (5.5 meters), far too great for a solid block of marble that also had to carry the roof. The solution adopted by the architect, Mnesikles, was to hollow out the beam to reduce its own weight (it still weighed eleven tons) and to place iron bars along the top of the beam, apparently to carry the weight of the marble blocks above. In this unique instance, the iron bars are at the top of the beam, not the bottom, where they would be expected. Even so, over the centuries cracks developed in this lintel beam.

The columns of the Propylaia are splendid examples of one of the three column types the Greeks evolved for their civic and religious architecture [2.9]. These three columnar types, or orders, were then adapted by the Romans, who added more ornate variations of their own, and became part of the basic architectural vocabulary from the Renaissance in the fifteenth century to our own times. Each order consists of three basic parts—base, shaft, and entablature—and rises from the three-stepped temple base composed of the *stylobate* (from *stulos,* "column," plus *bates,* "base"), with a two-layer *stereobate* below. In all the orders, the height of the column and the relative size of its component parts and of the entablature are all proportional derivatives of the diameter of the column.

Doric columns [2.9], the most massive of the three Greek orders, are four to six and one-half times as tall as the diameter, and the Doric *entablature* (the stylized system of beams and beam ends) carried by the column is about one-fourth the height of the column. The shaft of the Doric order rises directly from the stylobate; it has no base. The shaft itself has twenty broad scalloped indentions, or *flutes.* Atop the shaft, the *capital* consists simply of a banded necking, a gently outward-swelling *echinus,* and a square *abacus* slab. Each order has its distinctive *entablature* formed of three parts. That of the Doric order is made up of (1) the lower *architrave* (from *arch,* "main," and *trabs,* "beam"), (2) the middle range, of alternated *triglyphs* (stylized beam ends)

and *metopes* (infill sculpted panels), and (3) the uppermost *cornice,* formed of several projecting moldings.

The more slender **Ionic order** [2.9] has a base from which the shaft rises. The column itself is roughly nine times as high as its diameter, and the shaft has twenty-four flutes. The capital has distinctive curled **volutes** resting on an egg-and-dart molding. The Ionic entablature is roughly one-fifth the height of the column, and is made up of an architrave of two or three faces, with a middle **frieze** often filled with a continuous narrative band of sculpture. Atop this was the cornice.

Slightly more slender still is the **Corinthian order** [2.9], whose column is ten times the height of its diameter. It rises from a base similar to that of the Ionic order, and similarly has twenty-four flutes. The Corinthian capital is the tallest of the three, with two or three concentric bands of outward-curling *acanthus* leaves. The entablature is similar to that of the Ionic order.[2]

The Greek orders were subsequently adopted by the Romans, who used them largely as decorative elements; the principal changes introduced by the Romans were making the Doric order into the more slender Tuscan Doric, with the addition of a base and often a smooth, unfluted shaft [2.9]. The other major addition was the **Composite order,** formed by placing the volutes of the Ionic atop the curled acanthus

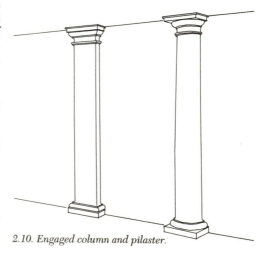

2.10. *Engaged column and pilaster.*

2.11. Steel frame.

2.12. Balloon frame.

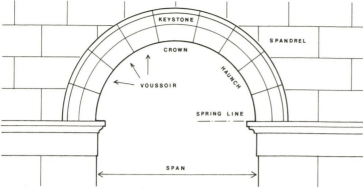

KEYSTONE

SPANDREL

CROWN

HAUNCH

VOUSSOIR

SPRING LINE

SPAN

2.13. Diagram of an arch system.

leaves of the Corinthian. The Romans also introduced a decorative adaptation of columns, merging the column with the wall, so that a half-column seems to emerge from the wall; this is the **engaged column** [2.10]. The Romans also developed a flat, pier-like projection of the wall, complete with base and capital corresponding to those of a column of the same order; this is the **pilaster.** Both these devices allow the rhythm of a colonnade to be continued along an expanse of what would otherwise be a flat wall.

Frames

If the two-dimensional planar structural system of posts and lintels is imagined extended into three dimensions, the result is a frame. This can be a frame like that of the stone columns and beams of the Valley Temple, but today it is more typically made of riveted steel members [2.11] or of nailed wood lumber [2.12], the conventional "balloon frame" used for home construction in North America since the mid-nineteenth century.

The Arch

If we return to the basic masonry wall once again, we find there is an alternative for spanning an opening—the *arch* [2.13]. Like the lintel the arch can be made up of stone, but the arch has two great advantages. First, the masonry arch is made up of many smaller parts, the wedge-shaped **voussoirs,** so the critical necessity of finding a large stone lintel free of cracks or flaws is elimi-

nated, as are the logistics of handling large blocks of stone. Second, because of the physics involved, the arch can span much greater distances than can a stone lintel. The gravitational forces generated by the wall above the arch are distributed over the arch and converted in the voussoirs to diagonal forces roughly perpendicular to the lower face of each voussoir. Each voussoir is subjected to compressive forces. One of the drawbacks of arch construction is that during construction all the voussoirs must be supported by a wooden framework, the **centering,** until the uppermost voussoir, the **keystone,** is put in place. At that instant the arch becomes self-supporting and the centering can be removed to be used to build the next arch.

Traditionally, centering was semicircular in form, as this shape was the easiest to lay out on the job site with pegs and rope. Unfortunately the semicircular arch is not a perfect structural form, for the forces at the base of an arch of this shape are not going straight down. In almost every traditional structural form, there are *lateral* (sideways) forces in additional to *vertical* forces (those generated by gravity and going straight down). This is especially true of the semicircular arch, and the problem increases in direct proportion to the vertical forces the arch carries. These lateral forces would cause the base of the arch to spread unless suitably restrained, as in a large arched bridge in which the feet of the arch push against the bedrock on either side of a gorge. In an arch that has no wall bearing

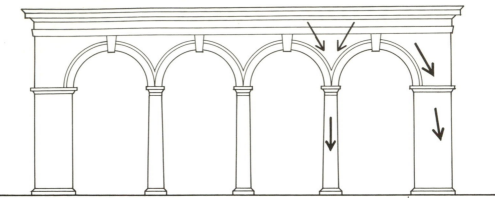

2.14. Diagram of an arcade.

down on it there is another problem—the arch's own weight. A single load focused at the apex, or crown, of the arch will cause the arch to rupture or spread apart on its upper surface at roughly 40° up from the horizontal, but this problem quickly diminishes as an additional uniform load (such as a wall above) is spread over an arch.

If several arches are placed end to end, then the lateral forces of one arch are exactly counteracted by the lateral forces of the adjacent arch [2.14]. When this is done, the arches can be placed on slender piers or individual columns, for the lateral forces are canceled out (except, that is, at the very ends). The Romans used this to excellent advantage in their *arcades*, as for example in the Pont du Gard, a combination bridge and aqueduct over the Gard River near Nîmes, in the south of France, built in the late first century B.C. [Fig. 2.15]. The total length of the bridge is 900 feet (274.3 meters), with arch spans of 64 feet (19.5 meters), except for the center span, which is 80 feet, 4 inches (24.5 meters). In an arcade standing on tall piers or columns, there would still be unresolved lateral forces at the ends, but these can be transmitted to the ground by

2.15. Pont du Gard, Nîmes, France, c. 25 B.C. A combination bridge and aqueduct with superimposed arches.

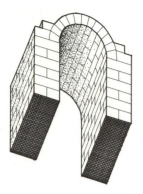

2.16. *Tunnel or barrel vault.*

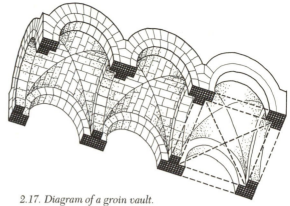

2.17. *Diagram of a groin vault.*

sections of walls or buttresses at the ends of the arcade.

Vaults

An ***arcuated*** structure, one built up of arches, acts structurally on a flat plane, but if the arch is imagined pushed through space, the form that results is a vault. In the case of a semicircular arch, the resulting vault is called a ***tunnel*** or ***barrel*** vault [2.16]. Usually such vaults are placed up on walls, but since the solid barrel vault is heavy, this causes the walls to spread out

at the top. These lateral forces can be resisted by substantial buttresses along the walls or by thickening the wall. An example of a barrel vault raised to great height is the nave of Saint-Sernin, Toulouse, France, begun 1080 [14.22]. But, as Saint-Sernin also shows, solid barrel vaults result in dark interiors. A solution devised earlier by the Romans was to run additional barrel vaults at right angles to the main vault so that they intersected, resulting in a ***groin vault,*** opened up by wide semicircular ***lunettes*** at each end and along the sides [2.17]. With this arrangement, the forces are channeled

2.18. *Basilica of Maxentius, Rome,* A.D. *307–312. This legal hall, now largely destroyed, demonstrated how the Romans could cover vast public spaces with concrete vaults.*

2.19. Giovanni Paolo Panini,
Interior of the Pantheon, c. 1750.
Samuel H. Kress Collection,
National Gallery of Art,
Washington, D.C. This painting
conveys better than any modern
photograph the effect of the space
inside the Pantheon.

down along the groins where the vaults intersect and are concentrated at points at the foot of the vaults. A three-section, or three-bay, groin vault was used by the Romans in many of their large public buildings, such as baths and basilicas. An excellent example is the immense Basilica of Maxentius, Rome, A.D. 307–12 [2.18, 12.10]. Built with a form of concrete developed by the Romans, this had three center bays measuring 88 by 83 feet each, for a total length of 265 feet (80.8 meters). The lateral forces of the groin vaults, lifted nearly 80 feet into the air, were absorbed by walls of adjoining chambers on each side, each chamber measuring 76 by 56 feet (23.2 by 17.1 meters). Three of these side chambers, themselves barrel-vaulted, are the only portions that survive today.

An arch rotated in three dimensions about its center generates a dome; a semicircular arch thus makes a hemispherical dome. The dome, too, was much used by the Romans. The largest, clearest, and most impressive of all was the immense dome of the Pantheon, Rome, A.D. 120–27 [2.19, 12.12]. Here the clear span is 142 feet 6 inches (43.4 meters). The dome is a massive shell of concrete, 4 feet (1.2 meters) thick at the top, where there is the broad, single opening of the eye, or oculus, 30 feet (9.1 meters) across. The thickness of the dome was increased at the point where rupture would tend to occur, and at its base the dome is 21 feet (6.4 meters) thick. The wall of the drum below, also 21 feet (6.4 meters) thick and supporting the five thousand tons of the dome, is hollowed out by niches 14 feet (4.3 meters) deep, so that in fact it functions structurally as sixteen radial buttresses, connected at their tops by radial barrel vaults. Moreover, both the dome and the drum wall are interlaced by arches and stubby barrel vaults set in the concrete to help direct the forces.[3]

The weight of the concrete per cubic foot

in the Pantheon was varied by the Roman architects and engineers by means of the materials used to make up the concrete. Concrete is a thick viscous material mixed of water, an aggregate of broken rock (*caementa* in Latin), and a binding material derived from lime that will cement everything together. In the concrete of the Pantheon, the rock aggregate was varied from the very densest and heaviest basalt in the foundation ring, where the greatest weight had to be carried, to frothy pumice in the part of the dome nearest the oculus, in an effort to reduce the loads from above.

It might be well to pause at this point to clarify the difference between Roman concrete and what is commonly used today. In both instances the basic composition is similar, but the binding agent in Roman concrete was *pozzuolana,* a volcanic ash that underwent a chemical action when ground and mixed with water, forming an artificial stone. In modern concrete, developed in 1824 in England by Joseph Aspdin, the binding cement is made of chalk and clay, carefully burned, with the resulting nodules ground to a fine powder. When mixed with water, sand, and fine gravel, the resulting artificial stone closely resembles the fine-grain natural limestone found in the region of Portland, England, as Aspdin first noted. As a result, this artificially produced cement is still called Portland Cement to this day. For both the Romans and us, the cement itself is too costly to make entire buildings, sidewalks, or other constructions from it alone. Even the mortar used between bricks and stone is stretched by adding sand; and in making concrete, gravel and sand are mixed in as the **aggregate.** In Roman concrete, the brick and tile relieving arches also served as a kind of large aggregate. Like stone, concrete is immensely resistant to compressive or squeezing forces, but relatively weak resisting tensile or stretching forces. Realizing this, the Romans added iron bars to concrete in some instances, but they preferred to use integrated relieving arches of brick and tile. Since the mid-nineteenth century, iron or steel rods have been placed in the formwork for modern concrete wherever tensile forces will occur.

Formwork is one of the cost disadvantages of concrete. As first mixed, concrete is a thick viscous material and must be contained in forms, or molds, until it has cured and dried; the formwork (called shuttering in England) is like the centering used for arch construction. In large structures, both in Roman times and now, this means the construction of substantial and expensive wooden structures, significant in themselves, which are then destroyed once the concrete has cured sufficiently for the forms to be removed.

Domes, particularly of the size of the Pantheon in Rome, are powerfully evocative spaces, but they require circular plans, making it difficult to add adjacent spaces. This problem became acute by the fourth century A.D., but the solution devised by Byzantine architects was to place the dome over a square plan below. What made this possible was the curved triangle-shaped spherical segment called a **pendentive** [2.20]. Imagine a square over which you wish to place a dome. First cover the square with a larger hemisphere, which just touches the corners of the square. Then slice downward along the sides of the square so that looking down on the cut hemisphere you see a square. Then, just at the top of the semicircles

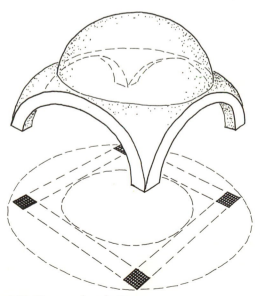

2.20. *Diagram of pendentives.*

2.21. *Hagia Sophia (Church of Divine Wisdom), Istanbul (Constantinople), Turkey, 532–537. Interior view.*

now forming the sides, slice off the top parallel to the square on the bottom. The resulting form has a circular shape at the top while at the bottom it is a square. The four curved segments that remain are the pendentives, making the transition from the square plan below to the circular plan above. An excellent example of the use of pendentives is found in the church of Hagia Sophia (Holy Wisdom), Istanbul, Turkey, 532–37, designed by Isidoros of Miletos and Anthemios of Tralles [2.21, 13.15, 13.16]. As with the Pantheon in Rome, the space enclosed is huge; here the dome is 107 feet (32.6 meters) across, but with the extended half-domes below and the barrel-vaulted spaces beyond, the total clear distance from one end of the church to the other is more than 250 feet (76.2 meters).

The base of the dome of Hagia Sophia is raised up nearly 132 feet (40.2 meters), from the floor, and the considerable weight of the brick dome gradually caused the walls to spread. After two earthquakes, in 553 and

557, the dome collapsed; although rebuilt, it collapsed after another quake in 989. To prevent further spreading, enormous buttresses were then built against the pendentives, but only on the northeast and southwest sides, since along the main axis the dome was already well buttressed by two half-domes, which in turn were buttressed by smaller half-domes and stubby barrel vaults resting on columns and piers. The result was that along the main axis the forces exerted outward and downward by the dome were conducted by this cascade of half-domes and vaults to the broad expanse of the lower part of the church. But on the shorter cross axis, on the other two sides, the original piers proved inadequate to resist the stresses accentuated by earthquakes; it was here that the later external buttress towers were added.

Once the Roman dome was placed on pendentives, it became possible to put the dome over a square or rectangular room, and add additional spaces to the sides, perhaps with their own lesser domes, as in the arrangement of the cross-shaped church of Saint Mark, Venice, with five domes [13.24–13.26].

As serviceable as the Roman groin vault was, its disadvantage was that it worked well only over square bays; when the bays became rectangular or trapezoidal, the lines of the groins (where two vaults intersect) became curved and the vault lost structural strength; besides, such vaults were difficult to cut in stone. The solution to this problem was achieved about 1100 at Durham, England, and at Saint-Denis, France. It consisted of building ribs, or freestanding diagonal arches, along the lines of intersection of the groin vault, as well as along the outer edges of the vaults [2.22]. The webs of the vaults could be filled in afterward. One advantage of the rib vault was the great reduction in the amount of centering needed; in a structure with repeated bays, only one set of centering supports was needed. Once the ribs and webs were up in one bay, the centering could be moved to the next bay. In addition to the rib vault, medieval masons used broken, or pointed, arches, made up of two segments of circles. By shifting the centers of the two arcs making up the arches, masons could create arches on all sides of a trapezoid or any irregular square or rectangle, all of equal height. The result was rib vaulting as used in most French, English, and German Gothic cathedrals, such as Notre-Dame of Amiens, France, begun in 1221 [2.23].

Trusses

The Romans also used another structural type that has proved basic to large constructions in the nineteenth and twentieth centuries—the *truss*. The traditional truss was made up of timbers arranged in triangular shapes or cells [2.24]. The triangle, by virtue of its built-in geometry, cannot be changed in shape without distorting or bending one of its sides. Hence, by adding triangle to triangle, it is possible to construct extended figures that are quite strong despite being relatively light. Wooden trusses were used in a wide variety of forms for roof construc-

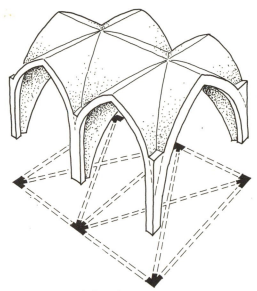

2.22. *Diagram of rib vaulting.*

2.23. *Robert de Luzarches, Notre-Dame de Amiens, Amiens, France, 1221–69. The vaults of Notre-Dame in Amiens are quadripartite, having four curved webs in each bay section of the choir and nave.*

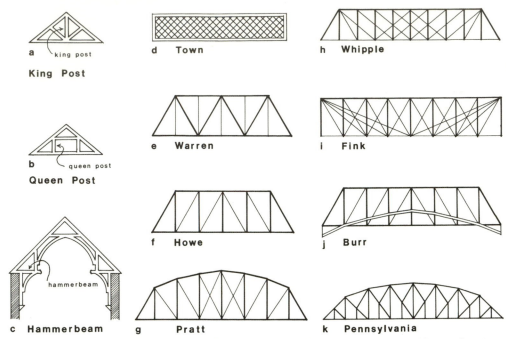

2.24. *Comparison of truss types. The trusses include medieval types (queen post, king post, and hammerbeam) and patented nineteenth-century forms (Howe, Pratt, Whipple, Warren, Fink).*

tion in Roman buildings and continued to be used during the Middle Ages, especially in the roofs of the large tithe barns. One superb example of medieval wooden truss construction is the hammer-beam truss roof of Westminster Hall, London, built in 1394–99 by Henry Yevele and Hugh Herland and spanning 68 feet (20.7 meters); it is the broadest wooden span of medieval times [15.16]. The great Gothic cathedrals such as Amiens were covered by such a wooden roof over the rib vault.

During the nineteenth century, many new forms of trusses were devised, often identified by the name of the engineer who first used them (some of these are shown in Figure 2.24). The truss, particularly when built up of steel members, proved capable of great spans, and hence was used to enclose vast spaces. An example is the Galerie des Machines, the largest of the buildings in the international exhibition held in Paris, 1889 [19.22], in which a series of curved arch trusses spanned 377 feet (114.9 meters). Here, as with any arch, there were considerable lateral forces at the base, but massive buttresses were made unnecessary because the ends of the arched trusses were connected by steel rods just beneath the floor.

Space Frames and Geodesic Domes

As with the post and lintel or the arch, so too the truss can be extended in three dimensions, forming a new type of structure. The truss extended in three dimensions becomes a *space frame*, a relatively new structure in widespread use only since about 1945. Like the planar, or flat, truss, it can span considerable distances. Properly designed, it can be supported at virtually any of the junctures of its members, permitting large cantilevers, as in McCormick Place, Chicago, 1970–71, by C. F. Murphy and Associates [2.25]. An intriguing variation is the R. Kemper Crosby Memorial Arena, Kansas City, Missouri, 1975, also by C. F. Murphy and Associates [2.26]. Substantial three-dimensional trusses, built up of tubes of steel, have a clear span of 342

2.25. C. F. Murphy and Associates, McCormick Place, Chicago, 1970–71. Designed by Gene Summers, this has spans of 150 feet (45.7 meters) in both directions and covers a total area of 19 acres.

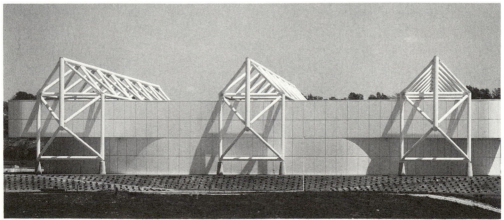

2.26. C. F. Murphy and Associates, R. Kemper Crosby Memorial Arena, Kansas City, Missouri, 1975. Designed by Helmut Jahn, this has three trusses, each 27 feet high and spanning 324 feet (8.2 by 98.8 meters), from which the roof is suspended.

2.27. R. Buckminster
Fuller, United States
Pavilion, 1967 World's
Fair, Montreal, Quebec,
Canada (destroyed by
fire, 1976). In this a
space frame is curved to
enclose a sphere.

2.28. Félix Candela, restaurant, Xochimilco, Mexico, 1958. The building shell is built of concrete applied over a
mesh of steel wire, with a total thickness of about 4 inches.

feet (104.2 meters) and carry the roof slung on their underside.

Just as the arch can be rotated to form a dome, so a truss can be curved in three dimensions to form what R. Buckminster Fuller christened the "geodesic dome." Like the truss, this is built up of small, light, easily handled steel members. Fuller began designing and building these domes after 1945, and in 1967 he was asked to design the United States Pavilion for the international exhibition held in Montreal, Canada [2.27].

Shells

Another structural type employs shells. Typically constructed of concrete, shells can be very thick and heavy or extremely thin and light. The American architect Eero Saarinen was particularly interested in shell forms and used a portion of a sphere cut to a triangular plan in his Kresge Auditorium at Massachusetts Institute of Technology,

Cambridge, in 1954. He then devised sweeping, reinforced concrete cantilevered shells for the Trans World Airline Terminal at Idlewild (Kennedy) Airport, New York, 1956–62 [21.14]. The total covered space is 212 by 291 feet (64.6 by 88.7 meters), with enormous cantilevers at the ends of 82 feet (24.9 meters). Typically the edges of such shells are subject to significant internal stresses and deformation, so large beams run along the edges of such shells to stiffen them. As can be imagined, the feet-shaped piers that support the cantilevered shells are packed with reinforcing rods to take up the enormous tensile stresses generated by the 82-foot overhangs.

It is possible to build shells with much less material, as the Mexican architect Felix Candela demonstrated in a number of buildings in the 1950s and 1960s. A good example is his restaurant at Xochimilco, Mexico, 1958 [2.28]. The concrete, applied by hand over steel wire mesh, is only about

2.29. *Cerny Associates, Minneapolis International Airport Terminal, 1962–63. The roof has the form of a folded plate similar to a simple accordion-fold fan.*

4 inches (10.2 centimeters) thick, but what gives the structure its strength is not the mass of the material itself but the curves of the shell. The rigidity of the structure is, in a truly mathematical sense, a function of its double curvature, for it is curved radially as well as circumferentially.

A shell may also be curved or folded in only one direction. A good instance of this is an accordion-fold shell, as in the Minneapolis International Airport Terminal building, 1962–63, by Cerny Associates [2.29]. A particularly interesting use of a folded shell is in the Assembly Hall at the University of Illinois, Urbana, 1961–62, by Harrison and Abramovitz, with the engineers Ammann and Whitney [2.30]. This dome consists of a folded plate, 394 feet (120 meters) in diameter, which rests on a series of radial supports reaching upward from a footing ring at the base. The enormous lateral forces exerted at the outer edge of the dome are taken up by a belt of almost 622 miles (1,000 kilometers) of steel wire wound under tension around it.

Suspension Structures

Technologically primitive societies have used vines and ropes for suspension bridges since time immemorial. Beginning in the early nineteenth century, suspension bridges began to be built of iron chains, and then bundled steel wire cables. The classic example of the modern suspension bridge is the Brooklyn Bridge, begun by John Augustus Roebling in 1867 and finished by his son, George Washington Roebling (with construction supervised by George's wife, Emily), in 1883 [2.31]. In this bridge steel wire was used in the cables for the first time. It has remained the model for suspension bridges since its construction.

Only since 1955 has the principle of cables in tension been used extensively for buildings other than bridges. A tension structure is especially efficient, since the entire cable is in tension, whereas most other structural forms have mixed stresses (as in a simple beam, which is in compression along the top and in tension along the bottom). A suspended cable assumes a curve described mathematically as a catenary (very close to a parabola) and is an ideal structural form, for it is entirely in tension. In fact, if it were possible to freeze that form and invert it, the result would be a catenary curve or parabolic arch virtually entirely in compression. Such arches, and vault forms derived from them, were used by the Spanish architect Antoni Gaudí at the turn of the last century in Barcelona, Spain [19.39].

Eero Saarinen, so interested in powerfully expressive shell forms, also used sus-

2.30. Harrison and Abramovitz with Ammann and Whitney, engineers, University of Illinois Assembly Hall, Champaign, 1961–62. This folded plate shell dome has corrugations radiating from the center.

2.31. John Augustus Roebling, Brooklyn Bridge, New York, 1867–83. This bridge established the structural basis for all modern suspension bridges; it also employed the first steel used in an American structure.

2.32. Eero Saarinen, Dulles International Airport Terminal, Washington, D.C., 1958–62. The roof is suspended on cables anchored in the beams running along each side of the building.

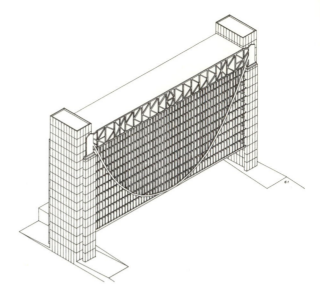

2.33. Gunnar Birkerts, Federal Reserve Bank, Minneapolis, 1971–73. Diagram of the structural parts, showing the principal structural cables and the restraining truss at the top.

pension in a number of buildings. In his Ingalls Hockey Rink, Yale University, New Haven, Connecticut, 1955–56, Saarinen put up a reinforced concrete parabolic arch the length of the rink, suspending cables from that arch down to curved walls on either side of the rink. A wooden roof deck was then laid on the cables. Saarinen enlarged on this idea in his Dulles Airport Terminal, outside Washington, D.C., 1958–62 [2.32]. Here he created two rows of outward-leaning columns, curving over at the top to carry beams running the length of the terminal. Between these two parallel beams, cables were suspended. Concrete slabs were placed on the cables to create the roof deck. This may not seem a lightweight structure, but the dead weight of the roof deck was necessary to keep the roof from fluttering in the wind.

Another building using the same principle is the Federal Reserve Bank in Minneapolis, Minnesota, 1971–73, by Gunnar Birkerts. The written requirements for this building stipulated that there be a large area below the paving at ground level; within this covered area, free of supporting columns, armored vans could deliver and pick up shipments of currency. This meant there could be no supporting columns coming down from any structure above, and Birkerts's solution to this dilemma was to carry the entire building on cables suspended from the tops of two towers, much like a suspension bridge [2.33]. The outer walls are rigid grids attached to the cables and all floor beams are fastened to these cable-supported wall grids; hence all floor and wall loads are carried by the cables back up the to the tops of the towers. With the towers being pulled in and down in this way, the tops inevitably would be drawn together; hence, spanning the top of the building is a truss serving to keep the towers apart. Birkerts also provided for the construction of two arches atop the towers from which additional floors could be hung when it proved necessary to enlarge the building vertically. If that is ever done, the outward lateral forces created by the arch carrying the added floors will counteract some of the inward lateral forces created by the lower floors hanging from the cables.

Buildings can also be suspended by cables from a single mast support, and most buildings are built nowadays using such a suspension device in the cranes that lift materials. These have cables or steel rods from a central mast supporting the end of the boom of the crane. A striking example of this technique as the principal structure of a building is the Westcoast Transmission Building, Vancouver, British Columbia, Canada, 1968–69 [2.34], by Rhone and Iredale, architects, with Bogue and Babicki, engineers. In this building the floors are suspended by cables coming out from the central core that rises above the topmost floor.

Membrane (Tent) and Inflated Structures

Since the early 1960s, a number of new materials have permitted ever more exotic construction techniques. Eventually these may become just as commonplace as metal framing, which was itself a highly novel technique when used for building the Crystal Palace in London in 1851, but which is today one of the most common framing materials. One variant technique is the tent membrane structure, a variation on the oldest of human building types. The German architect and engineer Frei Otto has focused his energies on developing membrane structures in which the tent is supported by masts carrying a net of interwoven

cables stretched to tie-downs anchored in the earth (this prevents the membrane from fluttering in the wind). To this net the membrane itself is attached. A good example was his German Pavilion for the international exhibition in Montreal, Canada, 1967 [2.35].

Another new building type is the inflated structure, made possible by new advances in textile fibers, weaving, and plastic impregnation. One application is for temporary covers over swimming pools and other such seasonal facilities. Often the structure has a single membrane sealed to the ground or floor deck, and the atmosphere within the structure is pressurized by fans, inflating the structure. An alternative is a double wall inflatable (a sort of enlarged version of the inflated tubular child's swimming pool), in which tubes are fastened together so that the inflated tubes have structural integrity and the atmosphere inside the building need not be pressurized. A good example of

2.34. Rhone and Iredale, with Bogue and Babicki, engineers, Westcoast Transmission Building, Vancouver, British Columbia, Canada, 1968–69. The floors are carried on beams and columns attached to exterior cables that angle back to the central structural mast.

2.35. Frei Otto, German Pavilion, 1967 World's Fair, Montreal, Quebec, Canada. In this building the protective enclosure is provided by a membrane held taut by cables stretched from masts to the ground.

this type was the Fuji Pavilion at the international exhibition at Osaka, Japan, 1970, designed by Yutaka Murata [2.36]. The disadvantage of inflated structures is that they require a nearly constant input of energy to power the fans to maintain the pressure, and they are susceptible to holes and rips in the fabric. Gradually, membrane and inflated structures are being used to cover sports areas, but these technologies are so new that we have limited information as to how the materials will stand up over decades of exposure to the elements.

Technology and Risk

It seems part of the expression of human aspiration that, when a new technology is developed, there is a compulsion to put it to use. There is the insatiable human desire to "push the edge of the envelope," as test pilots express it. And, as is often sadly the case, the risks and disadvantages of a new procedure or material are discovered only *after* a structure is in use. Perhaps Greek architects learned by bitter experience just how big a stone lintel could be lifted into

2.36. Yutaka Murata, Fuji Pavilion, 1970 World's Fair, Osaka, Japan. Tubes of inflated fabric provide their own rigid support.

place before cracking occurred, and Gothic architects realized they had reached the limits of their technology when the vaults of the Beauvais cathedral collapsed. The compulsion toward structural leanness and novelty became particularly evident in modern architecture after 1920, when the goal was the visual dematerialization of architecture (as in the transparent glass wall of Lever House). The objective has been to get the maximum structural performance from the minimum amount of material, with joints and connections made as small as possible. The result has been that some designs have proved deadly, as in the case of the "skywalks" of the lobby of the Hyatt Regency Hotel, Kansas City, Missouri. The way the walks were fastened to the slender rods was defective, and the aerial walkways crashed to the floor in July 1981, killing 113 people and maiming 180 more.[4]

Structure as Cultural Expression

Structure is more than just a simple matter of creating a frame or envelope. The materials that are selected and the way they are assembled, suggesting either massiveness or dematerialization, are part of the view that a culture has of itself and its relationship to history. So, as will been seen in Part Two, the massiveness of the pyramids was an expression of the unchanging view of the universe held by the Egyptians, the balance in Greek temples a representation of the ideal of equilibrium in Greek philosophy, the upward reach of the Gothic cathedrals an expression of the hope of heaven, and the slender supports of the Hyatt Regency skywalks were our smug boast of the conquest of gravity through modern technology. *How we build says almost as much as what we build.*

NOTES

1. Louis I. Kahn, from a lecture at the School of Architecture, Pratt Institute, New York, 1973, quoted in John Lobell, *Between Silence and Light* (Boulder, Colo., 1979), 42.
2. Recent investigations by George Hersey indicate that the Greek orders were first developed in imitation of the trunks of trees in sacred groves and that the names of the many parts that make up the orders can be traced to the sacrificial offerings made to the gods. This is discussed further in Chapter 11.
3. For a structural analysis of the Pantheon, see Robert Mark and Paul Hutchinson, "On the Structure of the Roman Pantheon," *Art Bulletin* 68 (March 1986): 124–34. See also the discussions of the structure of the Pantheon in R. Mainstone, *Developments in Structural Form*, and in M. Salvadori, *Why Buildings Stand Up* (cited in the preceding Suggested Reading).
4. See the analysis of the failure of the Hyatt Regency skywalks in Steven S. Ross, *Construction Disasters: Design Failures, Causes, and Prevention* (New York, 1984), 388–406. In January 1986, the state of Missouri revoked the professional licenses of two structural engineers who had designed the walks, after they had been cited for gross professional negligence in November 1985.

SUGGESTED READING

Carl W. Condit, *American Building: Materials and Techniques from the Beginning of the Colonial Settlements to the Present*, second ed. (Chicago and New York, 1982).
———. *American Building Art: The Nineteenth Century* (New York, 1960).
———. *American Building Art: The Twentieth Century* (New York, 1961).
Norman Davey, *A History of Building Materials* (New York, 1971).
James Edward Gordon, *Structures: Or Why Things Don't Fall Down* (New York, 1978).
Rowland J. Mainstone, *Developments in Structural Form* (Cambridge, Mass., 1975).
Steven Ross, *Construction Disasters: Design Failure, Causes, and Prevention* (New York, 1984); includes discussion of the Hancock Tower fiasco, the failure of the Kemper area roof, and the Hyatt Regency sky walk collapse.
Mario Salvadori, *Why Buildings Stand Up* (New York, 1980).
Mario Salvadori and Robert Heller, *Structure in Architecture: The Building of Buildings*, third ed. (Englewood Cliffs, N.J., 1986).
Stephen Timoshenko, *History of the Strength of Materials* (New York, 1983).
Alexander J. Zannos, *Form and Structure in Architecture: The Role of Statical Function* (New York, 1986).

3.10. Salisbury Cathedral, Salisbury, England, 1220–66. Interior, nave. The repeated bays and strong horizontal layering draw the eye strongly along the axis.

CHAPTER 3

"Delight": Space in Architecture

The history of architecture is primarily a history of man shaping space.

Nikolaus Pevsner, *An Outline of European Architecture,* 1943

Architecture is the art into which we walk; it is the art that envelops us. If Nikolaus Pevsner distinguished a questionable division between "architecture" and "building," there is little disagreement with his further observation that architecture is the making of space.[1] As he notes, painters and sculptors affect our senses by creating changes in patterns, and in proportional relationships between shapes, through the manipulation of light and color, but only architects shape the space in which we live and through which we move. Frank Lloyd Wright believed space was the essence of architecture and discovered that the same idea was expressed by Okakura Kakuzo in *The Book of Tea.* The reality of architecture lay not in the solid elements that seem to make it, but rather "the reality of a room was to be found in the space enclosed by the roof and walls, not in the roof and walls themselves."[2]

The architect manipulates space of many kinds. There is first the purely *physical space,* which can be imagined as the volume of air bounded by the walls, floor, and ceiling of a room. This can be easily computed and expressed as so many cubic feet or cubic meters.

But there is also *perceptual space*—the space that can be perceived or seen. Especially in a building with walls of glass, this perceptual space may be extensive indeed and impossible to quantify.

Related to perceptual space is *conceptual space,* which can be defined as the mental map we carry around in our heads, the plan stored in our memory. Buildings that work well are those that users can grasp easily in their mind's eye and in which they can move about easily with a kind of inevitability; such buildings can be said to have good conceptual space.

The architect also decisively shapes *behavioral space,* or the space we can actually move through and use. All these basic types of space can be illustrated by examining the Lloyd Lewis house in Libertyville, Illinois, 1939, by Frank Lloyd Wright [3.1]. From within the living room, looking toward the fireplace, the view is defined by the built-in bookcases, the brick of the fireplace mass, and the floor and ceiling [3.2]; all the surfaces are opaque and suggest a clear sensation of confinement; the physical space is evident. Looking toward the left, the view stretches out through a broad bank of French doors to the meadow and woodland beyond [3.3]; from this vantage point the perceptual space reaches out across the field and to the sky, as far as the eye can see. Moving toward the dining area, we see the built-in dining table, fastened to a brick pier [3.4]. To move from the living room through the dining area and into the kitchen, we must move around that built-in table, since it cannot be moved. In purely physical terms, the table takes up very little volume, a very few cubic feet compared to the many hundreds of cubic feet in the combined living and dining space, but in behavioral terms it determines in a dramatic and deci-

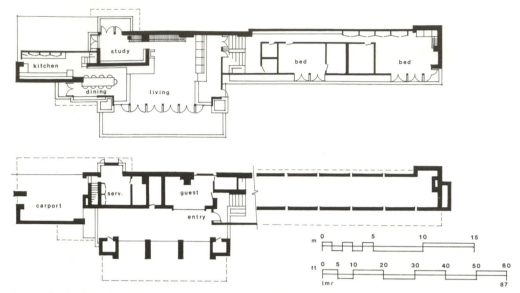

3.1. *Frank Lloyd Wright, Lloyd Lewis House, Libertyville, Illinois, 1939. Plan of the lower level and the upper living level.*

3.2. *Lloyd Lewis House. View of the living room, looking toward the fireplace. From this vantage point, the space is sharply defined and suggests comforting enclosure.*

3.3. Lloyd Lewis House. View of the living room, looking toward the screen of French doors. From this direction, a person's view can pass out into the countryside, into a large perceptual space.

3.4. Lloyd Lewis House. View of the dining area, showing the built-in table. The fixed table clearly determines how a person is directed through this space, thereby determining behavior.

sive way how we can move about in that space.

Architectural space is a powerful shaper of behavior. Winston Churchill understood this well when, in 1943, before the House of Commons, he said, "We shape our buildings, and afterwards our buildings shape us."[3] The chamber in which the Commons had been meeting for nearly a century had been gutted by a German bomb in 1941, and Parliament was beginning to consider alternative ways of reconstructing the chamber. When Parliament had first begun to meet, in the thirteenth century, it had been given the use of rooms in medieval Westminster Palace and had moved into the palace chapel. A typical Gothic chapel, it was narrow and tall, with parallel rows of choir stalls on either side of the aisle down the center. The members of Parliament sat in the stalls, dividing themselves into two groups, one the government in power and the other the loyal opposition. Seldom did members take the brave step of crossing the aisle to change political allegiance. When the Houses of Parliament had to be rebuilt after a fire in 1834, the Gothic form was followed, and Churchill argued that this ought to be done again in 1943. There were those who advocated rebuilding the House with a fan of seats in a broad semicircle, as used in legislative chambers in the United States and France. But Churchill convincingly argued that the form of English parliamentary government had been shaped by the physical environment in which it had first been housed; to change that environment, to give it a different behavioral space, would change the very nature of parliamentary operation. The English had first shaped their architecture, and then that architecture had shaped English government and history. Through Churchill's persuasion, the Houses of Parliament were rebuilt with the

3.5. *Piazza di San Marco (Piazza of Saint Mark's), Venice, Italy, 830–1640. This exterior enclosure contains aspects of physical, perceptual, and behavioral forms of space.*

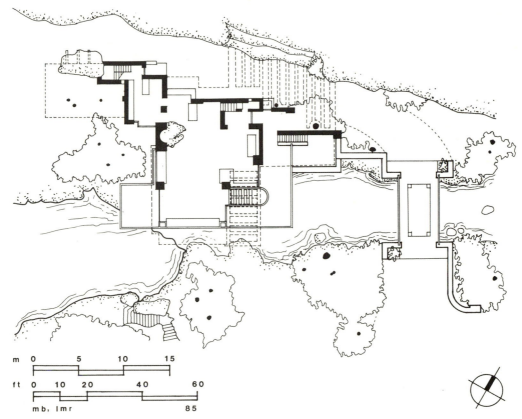

3.6. Frank Lloyd Wright, Edgar Kaufmann residence, Fallingwater, near Mill Run, Pennsylvania, 1936–38. Plan. Here space is molded in a fluid way; it opens out through the banks of glass on the south to the wooded ravine.

medieval arrangement of facing rows of parallel seats looking across a central aisle [19.8].

These concepts of physical, perceptual, and behavioral space have been applied here to spaces within individual buildings. With slight redefining, these terms can be used to describe experiences in large outdoor spaces as well. Consider the huge outdoor living room in Venice—the Piazza di San Marco [3.5]. If we are standing in the piazza and looking west, the space is clearly defined and enclosed by the walls of the buildings on either side and straight ahead; much the same is true if one turns and faces east, toward the church of San Marco, but the light coming from the right in the distance gives a hint of an opening. Moving eastward, near the front of the church, it is necessary to move around the soaring tower of the Cam-

panile which stands *in* the piazza, determining walking behavior. Once one is around the Campanile, one sees the smaller piazzetta, which extends toward the south. Past the pair of free-standing columns that mark the boundary of the piazzetta, one's view crosses the canal, and the enclosed physical space opens up in a much more expansive perceptual space.

The plan of the Lloyd Lewis house also illustrates clearly the possibility of duality of space—***interwoven spaces*** as contrasted with ***static spaces.*** Wright was a master of interweaving connected spaces, creating what has been described as fluid or flowing spaces, beginning in his Prairie Houses of 1900 to 1910 and continuing in Fallingwater, near Mill Run, Pennsylvania, built for the Kaufmanns in 1936–38 [3.6]. In these houses there is no separation of the living

3.7. *Shokin-tei (Pine-Lute Pavilion), Imperial Villa of Katsura, near Kyoto, Japan, 1645–49. View from inside the pavilion out toward the Middle Islands.*

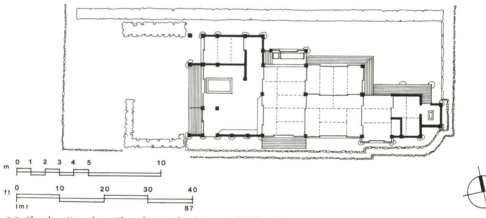

3.8. *Shoi-ken (Laughing Thoughts Pavilion), Imperial Villa of Katsura, 1645–49. Plan.*

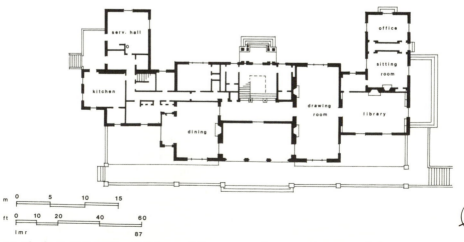

3.9. *Charles A. Platt, William F. Fahnestock House, Katonah, New York, 1909–24 (demolished). Plan. In this building the spaces are clearly compartmentalized for separation of activities and for acoustical privacy.*

and dining rooms or the library alcove; all are loosely defined as component parts of a larger space. Wright developed this conception of space as a result of studying Japanese architecture. In the traditional Japanese house, a wooden structural frame supports rails along which screens slide. These screens define the "rooms" of the Japanese house by being closed, or they permit the house to be opened up by being pushed back [3.7, 3.8]. In the traditional Japanese house there are no rooms in the conventional Western sense. The influence of Wright's earlier decompartmentalized Prairie House plans on European architects is illustrated in Ludwig Mies van der Rohe's German Pavilion for the international exposition held in Barcelona, Spain, in the summer of 1929 [20.13]. There are no rooms in the ordinary sense here either, but rather a series of planes arranged in space, defining a group of interrelated areas.

Conversely, the more traditional European or American house of the turn of the century was clearly subdivided into separate rooms, each with a clearly understood and discrete purpose: for lounging, dining, reading, receiving guests, and so forth. One example is the William F. Fahnestock house at Katonah, N.Y., 1909–24 (now demolished), by Charles A. Platt, with its cluster of individual rooms [3.9]. This was similar in many ways to Platt's Harold F. McCormick house in Lake Forest, Ill., 1908–18. Originally, a far different house had been designed for the McCormicks in 1908 by Frank Lloyd Wright (it would have been his largest up to that time), and in it he devised a number of broad interlocked spaces that opened up and flowed into one another. As it happened, Mrs. McCormick wanted a more formal and compartmentalized lifestyle, and for that, Platt's plan proved far more suitable.

Space can determine or suggest patterns of behavior by its very configuration, regardless of barriers or hindrances. We speak of **directional space,** as distinct from **nondirectional space.** The plan of the German Pavilion at Barcelona illustrates well nondirectional space, for there is no one obvious path through the building, but

rather a variety from which to choose. In contrast, in the Gothic cathedral the emphatic axis directs movement toward the single focus—the altar [3.10]. This gravitational pull seems especially strong in English cathedrals, for, since they are lower than their French counterparts and have emphasized horizontal lines, an optical illusion seems to make the bays leading toward the altar seem to extend even farther.

We can speak, too, of **positive** and **negative space.** A positive space is one that is conceived as a void, then wrapped in a built shell erected to define and contain it. An example would be the plaster shell of Vierzehnheiligen (Fourteen Saints), the pilgrimage church in Franconia, southern Germany, 1742–72, by Johann Balthasar Neumann [17.43]. There is nothing structurally substantial about the shell; it is there solely as an envelope to define a particular space and create a particular architectural and religious experience. In contrast, negative space is created by hollowing out a solid that already exists. Perhaps the earliest habi-

3.10. *Salisbury Cathedral, Salisbury, England, 1220–66. Interior, nave. The repeated bays and strong horizontal layering draw the eye strongly along the axis.*

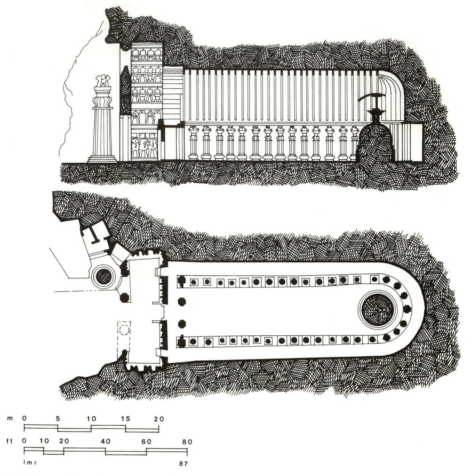

m	0	5	10	15	20
ft	0	10 20	40	60	80
l m r					87

3.11. *Cave, Karli, India, c. A.D. 100. Plan and section. This example of "negative space" was created by hollowing out the rock of the cliff, leaving columns and a vaulted chamber inspired by traditional wooden architecture.*

tations of the human species were naturally hollowed-out caves. That memory lingers in such rock-cut caves as those at Ajunta and Karli, India, carved out from 2000 B.C. through A.D. 650 [3.11], where the space has been created by laboriously cutting away the existing solid to create the desired void.

The concepts of positive and negative space can be applied to urban space as well. In this context, negative space might be defined as open space that is simply left over after the construction of buildings, whereas positive urban space would then be defined as deliberately shaped and defined in accordance with a preconceived plan. These two differing ideas can be seen in the city of Flo-

rence, Italy. The major public space is the Piazza della Signoria, next to the principal municipal building, the medieval Palazzo Vecchio, built from 1298 through 1310, which juts out into the irregularly shaped open space [3.12]. The irregular Piazza della Signoria, defined as buildings were erected over several centuries, could be described as a negative space. However, as the Renaissance developed in Florence during the following century, an entirely new attitude toward space and its definition arose in that city. When Filippo Brunelleschi designed his Ospedale degli Innocenti (Foundling Hospital) about half a mile north of the Piazza della Signoria in 1419, he divided the

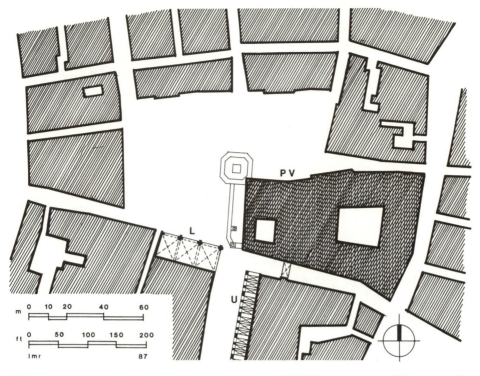

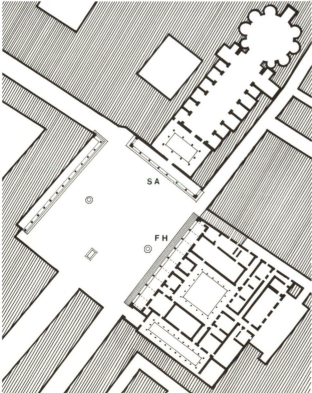

3.12. *Piazza della Signoria, Florence, Italy, 1298–1310. This "negative urban space" developed out of what was left after the construction of the surrounding buildings.*

L = *Loggia della Signoria
    (Loggia dei Lanzi)*
PV = *Palazzo Vecchio*
U = *Uffizi (municipal offices)*

3.13. *Filippo Brunelleschi and others, Piazza Annunziata, Florence, Italy, begun 1419. This "positive urban space" was deliberately planned in conjunction with the modular facade of Brunelleschi's Foundling Hospital.*

FH = *Foundling Hospital (Ospedale
    degli Innocenti)*
SA = *Santa Annunziata*

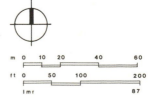

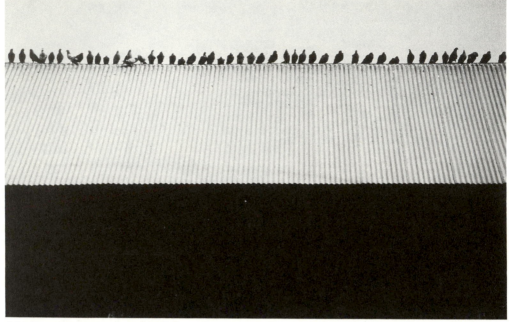

3.14. *Pigeons resting on the ridge of a barn, demonstrating the "personal space" maintained between members of the same species.*

facade into a row of identical arcade modules. The space in front of the hospital was then opened up into an urban square, the Piazza Annunziata, and the architects of all the surrounding buildings based their facades on the Brunelleschian arcade module, so that the square became an orderly rectangle governed by a mathematical grid that seems to determine the placement of every part of its defining walls [3.13]. The Piazza Annunziata could be described as a positive space, defined in accordance with preconceived ideas.

There is still another way of defining space, and although it is not strictly architectural, the architect nevertheless must take it into account. This is **personal space,** the distance that members of the same species put between themselves. This is illustrated by the way birds space themselves along the ridge line of a building or on a telephone wire, or in the way strangers space themselves in sitting on benches waiting for a bus [3.14].[4] For most animals, this zone of comfort is genetically programmed. On rocky coastal outcroppings, seals and

walruses heap themselves up on top of each other in apparent bliss, while swans and hummingbirds take great care to avoid contact or close proximity. Experiments in which animals are forced to exist in crowded conditions, in violation of their genetic code, can produce aberrant behavior.

Humans, however, have proved themselves to be extremely flexible in their determination of personal space; they seem not to have any programmed genetic spatial code. Instead, among humans personal space is culturally determined and is fixed in childhood, so that enforced changes in personal distance later in life may produce anxiety. The Italians and the French prefer much more densely packed arrangements, as in seating arrangements in outdoor cafés, than do the English, northern Europeans, and Americans. Even in the same culture, different sets of rules are adopted by men and women. Two unacquainted men will maintain a greater distance than will two unacquainted women, particularly in the United States. If an architect violates these unstated rules of personal space and places workers in an office arrangement too close together, even if every other architectural variable is optimized, the result may prove to be an environment that is resisted by the users. There is a special risk if an architect is designing for users of a culture or class to which he or she does not belong, as vividly demonstrated in the design of the Pruitt-Igoe public housing of Saint Louis, Missouri, 1952–55. This housing was so designed that its inhabitants could not supervise the public spaces and hallways in their long apartment blocks and muggings steadily increased. Eventually the housing proved so hazardous to live in that the city destroyed large parts of it in 1972.[5]

NOTES

1. Nikolaus Pevsner, *An Outline of European Architecture,* 7th ed., 15.
2. Frank Lloyd Wright, *The Natural House* (New York, 1954), 220; he refers to Okakura Kakuzo, *The Book of Tea* (New York, 1906), 24, who in turn paraphrases Lao-tzu.
3. Winston Churchill, speech before House of Commons, October 28, 1943, in *Onwards to Victory: War Speeches by the Right Hon. Winston S. Churchill* (Boston, 1944), 317.
4. This concept is discussed in Edward T. Hall, *The Hidden Dimension* (Garden City, N. Y., 1966), and in Robert Sommer, *Personal Space* (Englewood Cliffs, N. J., 1969).
5. Territoriality was another important but ignored design issue in the creation of Pruitt-Igoe; see the analysis of Pruitt-Igoe in Oscar Newman, *Defensible Space* (New York, 1972).

SUGGESTED READING

Andrew Baum and Stuart Valins, *Architecture and Social Behavior: Psychological Studies of Social Density* (Hillsdale, N. J., 1977).

Amos Ih Tiao Chang, *The Tao of Architecture* (Princeton, N.J., 1956).

C. M. Deasy, *Design for Human Affairs* (New York, 1974).

Clovis Heimsath, *Behavioral Architecture: Toward an Accountable Design Process* (New York, 1977).

Bill Hillier and Julienne Hanson, *The Social Logic of Space* (Cambridge, England, 1984).

Glenn Robert Lym, *A Psychology of Building: How We Shape and Experience Our Structured Spaces* (Englewood Cliffs, N. J., 1980).

Christian Norberg-Schulz, *Existence, Space and Architecture* (New York, 1971).

Yi-Fu Tuan, *Space and Place: The Perspective of Experience* (Minneapolis, Minn., 1977).

Dom H. Van der Laan, *Architectonic Space* (Leiden and New York, 1983).

Bruno Zevi, *Architecture as Space* (New York, 1957).

4.5. Notre-Dame de Chartres, Chartres, France, 1194–1260. The simpler south tower, built 1134–55 in the early Gothic period, contrasts sharply with the more ornate north tower, begun in 1507 in the late Gothic period.

CHAPTER 4

"Delight": Seeing Architecture

Our eyes are made to see forms in light.

Le Corbusier, *Towards a New Architecture,* 1927

Life is not life at all without delight.

C.V.D. Patmore, *The Victories of Love,* 1863

As Sir Henry Wotten put it, the third element in Vitruvius's description of architecture, following utility and sound structure, is delight. This is the most complex and diverse of all the components of architecture, for it involves how architecture engages all of our senses, how it shapes our perception and enjoyment of (or discomfort with) our built environment. It is perhaps the area with which most people, architects and users alike, have difficulty. This is partly because it involves, at every turn, subjective responses which differ from individual to individual. But perhaps even more important, for more than half a century, from 1910 to 1960, Western architects and others around the world whom they influenced preferred to believe that delight in architecture had no independent existence, that it came about automatically by the maximizing of functional utility and the exposure of structure. Advocates of what came to be called International Modernism argued that the Vitruvian formula had been forever changed, so that commodity plus firmness *equaled* delight; or, as Bruno Taut wrote, architecture was the creation of "the perfect, and therefore most beautiful, efficiency."[1] Since about 1965, however, architects, critics, and historians have begun to reverse this position, arguing once again that there can be delight in architecture and

that good architecture endeavors to produce the greatest pleasure for the price, so long as function and durability are satisfied as well.

Visual Perception

Since what pleasure we derive from architecture is generated by our perception of it, we must start by considering how the human eye and mind receive and interpret the visual data of architectural experience. How does the psychology of vision and sensory stimulation affect our perception of architecture?

Perhaps the most fundamental concept is that the mind, particularly the human mind, is programmed to seek meaning and significance in all sensory information sent to it. This, no doubt, is linked with the instinct for survival, for eons ago the eye, the ear, and the mind learned to interpret a change in color in the grass or the snap of a twig as indications of a predator on the prowl. The result, as far removed from our primeval origins as we believe ourselves to be, is that the mind seeks to place all information fed into it into a meaningful pattern. The mind does not recognize that incoming data mean nothing. Even purely random visual or aural phenomena are given a preliminary interpretation by the mind on the basis of what evaluative information it already has stored away. Hence, what we perceive is based on what we already know.

How the mind interprets forms and patterns presented to it is the subject of Gestalt psychology (from the German *Gestalt,* "form" or "shape").[2] Faced with random or

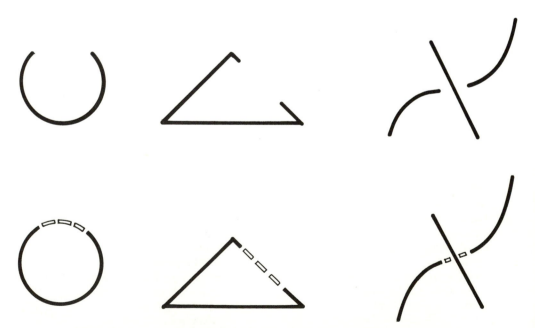

4.1. *Diagram of seven dots illustrating the concept of proximity. They are close enough to be interpreted as a unified figure, commonly called the Big Dipper.*

4.2. *Row of dots with slight inequalities in their spacing, illustrating the concept of repetition.*

4.3. *Diagrams illustrating the concept of continuity and closure. The mind attempts to complete each form on the basis of known forms in the simplest way possible (the principle of simplest and largest form).*

unknown visual information, the mind organizes the data according to certain built-in preferences. These preferences are for proximity, repetition, simplest and largest figure, continuity and closure, and figure/ground relationship.

Proximity: Objects are seen to represent a pattern, and points in space are interpreted as lying on a single plane, even if one is distant and another is far. The ancient interpretation of star constellations as the figures of the Zodiac and as gods and goddesses is a classic illustration [4.1]. Although the seven stars making up the Big Dipper are in fact at various distances from the earth, we cannot see those astronomical differences in distance and so we interpret the stars as being on a single plane, forming the outline of a dipper with a long handle (or a bear with a long tail).

Repetition: Equalities of spacing or distance are seen even where none exist, so that a row of lines or dots will be seen as being equidistant; and two parallel lines, slightly different in length, will be seen as equal in length [4.2]. This is one reason why the corner columns of Greek temples are of interest, for they were purposely made a little thicker than the others and were positioned a little closer to each other, so that what we *want* to see as a series of equal objects arranged in space is, actually, a carefully calculated sequence of inequalities [11.25].

Simplest and largest figure: When presented with elements that suggest an image it can recognize, the mind fills in the missing pieces to form the simplest and largest figure. The related mental operation that makes this possible is the impulse toward *continuity and closure* [4.3]. What appears to be a fragment of a circle will be completed as a circle rather than a crescent or some other shape, and the curved line will be seen as being broken where the short line "crosses" it.

Figure/ground relationship: A shape seen in the context of an enclosing shape will be interpreted as a form against a background, with the mind choosing which is which [4.4]. In the standard illustration of this phenomenon, we can choose to see

4.4. Figure/ground illustration. Depending on what the mind chooses to interpret as the background, one sees a turned white vase or the profiles of two faces.

either a turned white vase against a dark background or two dark faces against a white background. This principle, too, seems to have been employed in the Greek temple colonnade [11.24]. The corner columns were thickened, since they alone of all the columns were seen silhouetted against the sky; these corner columns would have been seen as a dark mass against a light sky, whereas the others would have been seen as light masses against the shaded *naos* wall behind them.

On the surface, the principles of Gestalt psychology would suggest that the mind seeks to find utmost order and regularity, and might even suggest that the preferred state is absolute calm and uniformity. In actuality, the mind craves information, constantly varying information, and when that input is cut off—when sight, hearing, smell, and touch are completely unstimulated, as in a flotation tank—the mind will eventually invent its own stimuli and hallucination will result. When information becomes repetitive, the mind tunes it out and focuses instead on the deviations from the anticipated pattern. This happens automatically, or it can be made to happen as the result of a conscious decision; we choose not to hear

4.6. Mies van der Rohe,
Federal Center, Chicago,
1959–64. In this late design,
Mies van der Rohe pulled the
glass curtain wall outside the
columns, resulting in
absolutely uniform window
bay units.

street traffic at night so we can sleep, but
the slightest cry of an infant rouses parents
from sleep as a distress signal—it is the
information that deviates from the expected
norm. Again the Greek temple illustrates
this point [11.25]. One reason the Athenian
Parthenon has been considered good architecture for so long may be because there is
not a single straight or regular line in it.
What appears at first glance to be repeti-

tively uniform is (as will be shown in Part
Two) a subtle and mathematically precise
arrangement of inequalities and curves. So,
too, many observers prefer the facades of
the Gothic cathedrals of Chartres [4.5, page
56] and Amiens, because their facades are
not bilaterally symmetrical. In fact, the towers of the west end of Chartres were built
four centuries apart (1134 and 1507) and
represent two different stages of architec-

4.7. *Kallmann, McKinnel and Knowles, Boston City Hall, 1961–68. In this building, similar in function to the Federal Center in Chicago, the variety of internal offices and functions is suggested by the variations in external forms.*

tural development in France. Or, to take more contemporary examples, we might contrast the repetitive facades of the Federal Center buildings in Chicago, by Mies van der Rohe, 1959–64 [4.6], which exploit industrial production of building parts, with the variation of window shapes and sizes in Boston City Hall, by Kallmann, McKinnel and Knowles, 1961–68 [4.7].

There is also a kinesthetic body response to forms and lines. Thus the horizontal line is sensed empathetically as being at rest, just as the body is at rest when horizontal. Frank Lloyd Wright exploited this in his Prairie Houses around Chicago [20.4], stressing and emphasizing the horizontal lines and planes of his houses, not only to relate their form to the flat, midwestern prairie but also to convey the image of domestic tranquillity. In contrast, the vertical line is sensed as one of aspiration, reaching, assertiveness [2.5]. There is a sense of dynamic equilibrium as a result of forces at work in the vertical line (just as our bodies are maintained erect by a multitude of muscle actions). But the line that most strongly conveys dynamic action and movement is the diagonal. This phenomenon was exploited in numerous compositions in Baroque and Romantic paintings from 1600 through 1900, but it has also been used for dramatic effect in such architecture as Walter Gropius's *Memorial*

to the March Victims at Weimar, Germany, 1920 [4.8]. It can be seen, too, in the Marine Corps War Memorial in Washington, D.C., 1945–54, by the sculptor Felix W. de Weldon, based on the gripping Pulitzer Prize-winning photograph taken on Iwo Jima on February 23, 1945, by Joe Rosenthal.

The angularity of Gropius's memorial also

4.8. *Walter Gropius,* Memorial to the March Victims, *Weimar, Germany, 1920. A sharp diagonal is used for dramatic effect in this memorial to victims shot in a street uprising. The pointed angularity can also be described as being "hard."*

enhances its effect. Such faceted objects can be described as hard, in contrast to the rounded Einstein observatory tower in Potsdam, Germany, 1919–21, by Erich Mendelsohn, which, in contrast, could be said to be soft [21.1]. In literal fact both are hard, for the Einstein observatory is built of brick covered with stucco.

Proportion

The mind also seeks out mathematical and geometrical relationships—or proportions—in patterns. The ancients believed that all nature was governed by abstract universal laws. The Greek philosopher Pythagoras demonstrated that two taut strings, having a ratio in their lengths of 2 to 3, would produce what is called a fifth when plucked together. And a string twice as long as another (having a ratio of 2 to 1) would produce the same tone an octave lower. Moreover, since the ancients also believed that human form was based on that of the gods, universal and divine geometric and proportional relationships could be observed in the proportions of the human body. Vitruvius describes how, by taking the navel as the center, the extremities of the human body lie on the edges of both a square and a circle, the most basic and ideal of geometric figures [16.3].

Vitruvius also described how to generate geometric figures with irrational numbers (that is, numbers that cannot be expressed as the ratio of two whole numbers). His demonstrations all start with a square. The particular advantage of this system, and the basis of many Greek proportional systems before Vitruvius, was that such geometric figures could be laid out on the flat earth of the construction site with only wooden pegs and lengths of rope. Whole building plans, therefore, could be scratched out on the ground with utmost regularity of part to part. By measuring off the diagonal of a square, and then rotating it down along one side of the square, one creates what is described as a $\sqrt{2}$ rectangle [4.9] in which the sides have the proportional relationship of 1 to 1.414 (or 1:$\sqrt{2}$). Or one might lay out two squares, end to end, measure off the diagonal of this rectangle, and then rotate it down to the long side to form a $\sqrt{5}$ rectangle [4.10] in which the sides have the proportional relationship of 1 to 2.2361 (or 1:$\sqrt{5}$). Many medieval churches show these proportional systems in the arrangement of their plans. Another proportional system followed by the Greeks was the relationship of x to $2x + 1$, so that Greek temples normally had six columns across the ends and thirteen along the sides (6 to $2 \times 6 + 1$) or, less often, eight columns by seventeen (8 to $2 \times 8 + 1$).

Perhaps the proportional system most associated with Greek architecture and design, and with Classical architecture as a whole, is what is called the Golden Section or Golden Mean. Just as gold is the most incorruptible and perfect of metals, so too this proportional relationship was believed to be perfect. It can be described as the relationship of two unequal parts so that the smaller part is to the larger as the larger is to

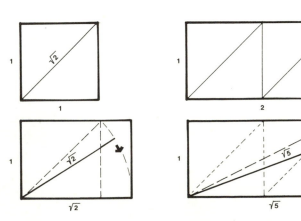

4.9. *Square root of 2 rectangle.*

4.10. *Square root of 5 rectangle.*

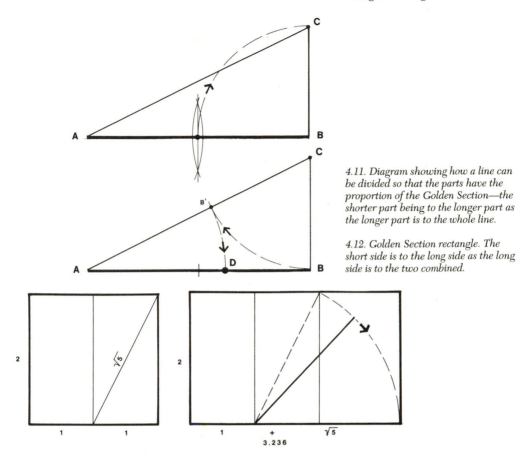

4.11. *Diagram showing how a line can be divided so that the parts have the proportion of the Golden Section—the shorter part being to the longer part as the longer part is to the whole line.*

4.12. *Golden Section rectangle. The short side is to the long side as the long side is to the two combined.*

both combined. Today we can write this algebraically, with *a* being the smaller unit and *b* the larger:

$$\frac{a}{b} = \frac{b}{a+b}$$

This can be rewritten as an equation: $b^2 = a^2 + ab$. If *a* is assigned a value of 1 and the equation solved for *b*, the result is that *b* equals 1.61804. Or, if *b* is given the value of 1, the result is that *a* is 0.61804; the proportional relationship between 1 and 1.618 and between 0.618 and 1 is exactly the same.

The Greeks worked this theory geometrically in one of two ways, with ropes and pegs in the field or with drafting instruments on a sheet of vellum (or paper). The problem is to divide a line A-B into two parts so that the short part is to the long part as the long part is to the entire original line [4.11]. First, the line A-B is bisected; then half of

the line is swung up to the perpendicular to form the triangle A-B-C. Using *C* as the center, the line *B-C* is swung up to strike the hypotenuse A-C to locate the point B'. Then, using A as the center, the line A-B' is swung back down to the original line, A-B, to fix the desired point of division, *D*. The result is exactly the same; D-B is to A-D as A-D is to A-B.

Even more simply, a Golden Section rectangle may be generated from a given square. First the square is divided in half, so that each half measures one unit by two units [4.12]. Then the diagonal of one of these rectangles is rotated down along the side of the original square. From the end of the rotated diagonal the desired Golden Section rectangle is constructed. The proportions of the finished rectangle are 2 to $(1 + \sqrt{5})$, which is 2 to 3.236, or 1 to 1.618. There is a further derivative from the

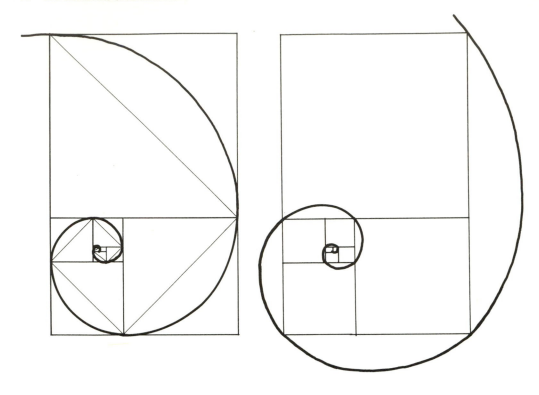

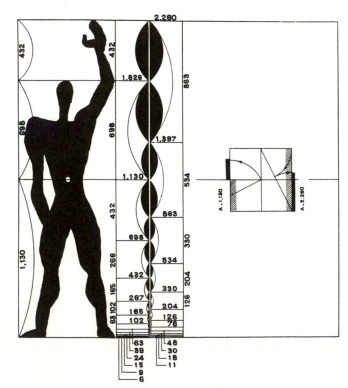

4.13. Logarithmic spirals based on the Golden Section.

4.14. Le Corbusier, diagram of the Modulor man, 1947.

Golden Section rectangle which results in a most interesting curve [4.13]. In a Golden Section rectangle, mark off the square at one end; a smaller square is drawn in the end of the remaining rectangle, and another square is then drawn in the leftover rectangle, and so on until no more squares can be drawn. If the corners of these nested rectangles are then connected by a curved line, the result is a logarithmic spiral or volute very much like that found in the patterns of seeds in a sunflower or in the section of a chambered nautilus. It was such a curve that the Greeks used in the volute of the capital of the Ionic order.

There is yet another intriguing correspondence to a proportional system based on a numerical series, first described by the medieval mathematician Leonardo Fibonacci (c. 1170–c. 1240). The numerical sequence is generated by starting with one, adding that to itself, and then generating the next in the series by adding the preceding two numbers together, thus: 1, 2, 3, 5, 8, 13, 21, 34. . . . The larger these numbers become, the closer the last two approach the Golden Section; for example, 21:34 =

1:1.61905, and 34:55 = 1.61765. On the basis of the Fibonacci series, the architect Le Corbusier developed a proportional system in the late 1930s that he called the Modulor [4.14]. He used this as the basis of design for a large apartment block, the Unité d'Habitation in Marseilles, France, 1946–52, casting the image of the Modulor man with upraised arm in the concrete of its elevator tower. In fact, among twentieth-century architects, Le Corbusier was the most frequent user of proportional systems, both in arranging the placement of walls and structural supports and in the sizing and placement of windows and doors in exterior walls [4.15].

Scale

Architecture (including landscape architecture) is the largest and most encompassing of the visual arts. One of the challenges faced by the user is to determine just how big a building is, and the yardstick against which we measure the size of a building is our own size. How big a building is, relative to the size of the average human being, is

4.15. *Le Corbusier, Unité d'Habitation, Marseilles, France, 1946–52. The entire building, in all its parts, was proportioned using the Modulor and its numerical relationships based on the Fibonacci series (1:2:3:5:8, etc.).*

4.16. Michelangelo, Basilica of Saint Peter, Rome, 1549–64. East end. In an effort to give visual unity to this huge building, Michelangelo deliberately used overscaled elements to reduce the number of parts, but the result also makes it difficult to judge the true scale of this building relative to human size.

said to be its *scale*.[3] In the case of the Unité d'Habitation, Le Corbusier conveniently cast into its side a clear ruler by which we can see just how big the building is. Frank Lloyd Wright designed his houses for what he considered the ideal height, 5 feet 8½ inches (which just happened to be his own height). Had he stood 6 feet 2 inches tall his architecture might have been significantly different.

For the most part, there are many clues in a building as to its size—windows, doors, steps—but even they may be enlarged so that our sense of scale is distorted. Such is the case with the exterior of Saint Peter's in Rome, built under the direction of Michelangelo, for the windows and pilasters are two and three times larger than what we would expect [4.16].

One of the problems inherent in the austere and industrially inspired architecture of the International Modernism of the mid-twentieth century was that it lacked such clues. Architects were quite proud of the way they stripped away details that for centuries had provided visual clues. The dilemma is well illustrated in the Beinecke Rare Book Library at Yale University, New Haven, Connecticut, 1960–63, by Skidmore, Owings and Merrill [4.17], especially when viewed in the context of the surrounding buildings dating from the 1920s. The older buildings provide many clues as to their size relative to human beings, but the library provides few. Only when the students and bicycles in the foreground are viewed in relation to the library does its size begin to be revealed. Although in some situations the game of trying to guess the scale can be amusing—and this is the basis of the whimsy in the sculpture of Claes Oldenburg—ordinarily the task of trying to determine scale, when it occurs again and again in the modern urban cityscape, becomes unsettling.

Rhythm

There are a number of ways by which ordered variety can be given buildings. One is the use of rhythm, or the alternation between incident and interval, between solids and voids. Rhythm in architecture is the pattern created in windows spaced in a wall, or columns in a colonnade, or piers in an arcade. This architectural rhythm is read by scanning the surface, much as one might scan a musical score, reading the patterns the notes make in time. This is one way that architecture is like music, for both must be experienced in time. So, too, one can experience the rhythm of a colonnade or arcade by walking along it, sensing the passage of the piers. We can also speak of the continuous, unvarying rhythm of Mies van der Rohe's federal buildings in Chicago, for the pattern of the windows does not change at all, whether one reads from top to bottom or from left to right. We can see a similar, even rhythm in the arcade that runs across the facade of the Foundling Hospital in Florence, 1419–36, by Brunelleschi [16.6]. There are slight differences in the end bays, added later, where the Corinthian columns of the arcade are framed by taller Corinthian pilasters. If we take the center line of the columns or piers as marking the edge of each bay, and we scan the facade

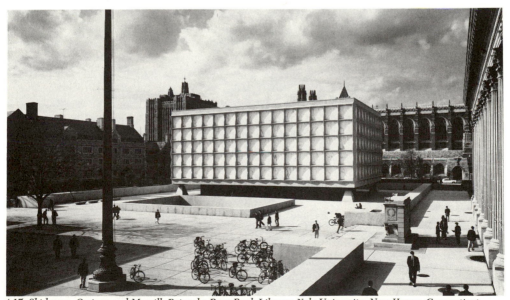

4.17. Skidmore, Owings and Merrill, Beinecke Rare Book Library, Yale University, New Haven, Connecticut, 1960–63. The large-scale forms of the library contrast sharply to the much finer and more easily interpreted scale elements of the Yale Law School, in the distance.

4.18. Giulio Romano, Palazzo del Te, Mantua, Italy, 1527–34. Garden facade. What appears at first glance to be a simple repetition of arcade units turns out, after closer examination, to be a complex series of variations on a theme.

left to right, we find that the first bay differs from the next to the right, and that it in turn differs slightly from the next; after that the bays are identical until we approach the other end. So, we can assign symbols to this reading, saying that the facade has this rhythm: a-b-c-c-c-c-c-c-c-b-a.

Such order and clarity of form are characteristic of the Renaissance in Italy, which began with the Foundling Hospital. But we might compare that arcade to the garden facade of the Palazzo del Te in Mantua, Italy, 1527–34, by Giulio Romano [4.18]. At first glance, there appears to be an equally even rhythm in the arcade, except, of course, that the center element is slightly larger. But closer observation reveals that no two adjacent bays are the same. Reading the rhythm left to right, we find that the end bay is butted up against the wall of the garden enclosure and framed with doubled pilasters on the other side. The next bay is framed with doubled pilasters and a wall with a niche on the left and doubled pilasters and an opening to the right. The next bay is framed with a single column and a pilaster; the next one is a flip-flop inversion, but with its pilaster lying behind the large pilaster of the larger central unit. The next bay is the outer bay of the enlarged central pavilion and is framed with a pilaster and a column on the left and a pair of columns on the right. Finally, the centermost bay is framed with doubled columns (actually it is a cluster of four, two in front of the others). Assigning symbols to this reading, we get a-b-c-d-E-F-E-d-c-b-a. It is a bilaterally symmetrical composition, with every element to the left of the center mirrored by what is on the right, but each part

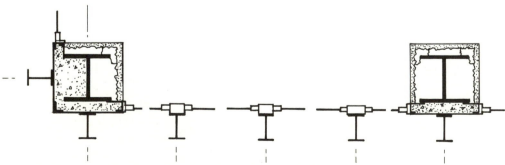

4.19. Lake Shore Drive Apartments. Plan of windows and structural columns.

4.20. *Le Corbusier, Secretariat Building, Chandigarh, India, 1951–58. In this elongated building, Le Corbusier varied the rhythm of the shape and sizes of the sun screens, breaking up the long facade.*

of that rhythm varies from the part next to it—an excellent example of ordered variety.

As in music, we can find two rhythms played against each other simultaneously. This occurs in many of the arcades and colonnades of the Renaissance and Baroque periods, as well as in more recent times. Consider the facades of Mies van der Rohe's apartment towers at 860–880 Lake Shore Drive, Chicago, 1948–51 [4.19, 20.14]. Mies devised a structural frame of square bays, so that each tower measures three by five bays. The structural steel columns, in accordance with Chicago building codes, had to be encased in protective concrete fireproofing. Mies then divided the interval from the center lines of the structural columns into four equal parts, using these secondary dividing lines for the centers of the mullions supporting four windows. The windows were made flush with the edge of the structural column, so that the thickly insulated structural column used up some of the width of the adjoining window, making the outer windows in each structural bay narrower than those in the middle. The result is two overlaid rhythms. The larger structural rhythm is absolutely even, A-A-A, but the window rhythm within the structural bay is a-b-b-a. As will be shown in Part II, the rhythms in Italian Renaissance buildings were normally governed by deliberate mathematical Vitruvian relationships, but

the rhythms in Mies's Lake Shore Drive apartments were the result of the application of mass production techniques to window frames. In his later buildings, such as the Seagram Building, New York, 1954–58 [7.10], and the federal buildings in Chicago [4.6], Mies pulled the plane of glass in front of the structural columns, causing the structural rhythm to disappear behind an absolutely even window rhythm.

In architecture, rhythm can also be created by the alternation of solid and void. In his later architecture, Le Corbusier excelled in this. One particularly interesting example is the elongated Secretariat Building he designed for the new capital of Punjab State in India, Chandigarh, 1951–58 [4.20]. This office building required a number of identical office cells, expressed externally by the repetitive rhythm, whereas at the center the rhythm changes dramatically in favor of larger, asymmetrical patterns corresponding to larger chambers and differing internal functions.

It is also possible to speak of rhythm in architecture in reference to undulating or curving walls. Buildings with frame construction, whether of wood or steel, tend to have rectilinear forms; hence their facades tend to be flat planes. Curved forms, however, have more dramatic impact. During the Baroque period, curved walls were exploited extensively, for they suggested not only that they bound space but that space pushed back on them. A good example is the facade by Francesco Borromini of the church of San Carlo alle Quattro Fontane in Rome, 1655 [17.14]. The facade is a series of curves and countercurves that establishes a play of rhythms. Such curved buildings have been rare in the twentieth century, particularly before 1960, but a notable exception is Baker House at the Massachusetts Institute of Technology, Cambridge, 1946–48, by the Finnish architect Alvar Aalto [4.21, 21.7]. Here the undulating form was not only a way of fitting what needed to be a long building into a restricted site but also a response to the oblique views across the Charles River that Aalto discovered the students preferred.

Texture

Another of the many devices used to add variety to architecture is texture, a term that has various meanings. The **optical texture** of a building refers to its visual pattern at the large scale, whereas its **tactile texture** refers to what can be physically felt with the human hand. So, for example, the Secre-

tariat at Chandigarh, seen from a distance [4.20], has a rich optical texture in the variation between the uniform office cells and the more irregular "texture" of the larger meeting rooms. Another of Le Corbusier's buildings, the Unité d'Habitation apartment block in Marseilles [4.15], has a similar bold texture pattern when viewed from a distance. But we can also speak of the tactile texture, the roughness of surface that can be felt. When one gets close to the Unité apartments, it can be seen that the concrete was poured in forms made of rough lumber so that when the forms were removed a bold pattern was left imprinted in the concrete. Moreover, Le Corbusier had the workmen turn alternate panels of the formwork, creating a basketwork checkerboard pattern in the concrete that adds to the textural richness at both the optical and tactile levels. In addition to the visual rhythm of Baker House, Aalto also had the wall laid up with rough clinker brick—those that had become twisted and overburnt during firing and normally would have been rejected. These were placed randomly to add a visual and tactile texture to the walls [4.21]. At certain times of the day, when the sun rakes along

4.21. *Alvar Aalto, Baker House, Massachusetts Institute of Technology, Cambridge, 1946–48. Viewed at close range, the randomly placed rough bricks create a visual and tactile texture in the wall.*

4.22. Paul Rudolph, Art and Architecture Building, Yale University, New Haven, Connecticut, 1958–64. Detail, showing the rough texture of the broken concrete ridges in the cast-concrete walls.

the surfaces, the protruding misshapen bricks cast shadows along the wall.

Concrete lends itself to the creation of texture, for it must be poured into a form of some kind. It is virtually impossible to make the joint invisible between successive pours of concrete, for even slight variations in the composition of the cement will cause color variations. An architect can take care to design the details where the panels of the formwork come together, accentuating that line, and in this way create a texture in the finished concrete that is a record of the act of construction. Louis I. Kahn did this with great care, especially in the concrete for the Salk Institute at La Jolla. Another attempt to create a special texture in concrete led to an even rougher texture than planned. When erecting the Art and Architecture Building for Yale University, 1958–64 [4.22], the

architect Paul Rudolph used forms made of plywood panels to which champhered strips of wood had been screwed [4.23]. The forms were oiled in the hope that the concrete would not stick, enabling the forms to be removed easily for reuse. Nonetheless, the concrete bonded to the formwork. When the forms were pried off, either the wooden battens pulled away from the plywood, sticking fast in the concrete, or the corners of the concrete stuck fast to the wood and chipped off the building. Rudolph then had all the edges of the concrete ridges hammered off, exposing the sharp crushed-rock aggregate and creating minute variations in color as well as a brutally abrasive surface.

Architects may also make strong contrasts between strikingly different textures, as Michelozzo di Bartolommeo did in the

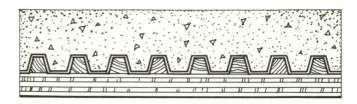

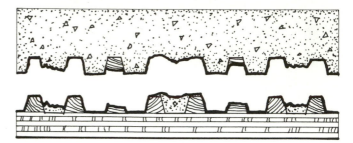

4.23. Art and Architecture Building, Yale University. Diagram of the wooden forms for the concrete; the concrete adhered to the forms, creating a rough, uneven texture.

Palazzo de' Medici in Florence, 1444–60 [16.25]. He began with aggressively rough stone masonry (called **quarry-faced ashlar masonry**) at the lower level, changing to **rusticated masonry** in the middle level (the individual blocks have their edges cut back to emphasize the joints), and then completely smooth ashlar masonry in the upper-most level where the joints between the stone blocks are almost impossible to see from the street. Frank Lloyd Wright created an equally dramatic contrast in Fallingwater, near Mill Run, Pennsylvania, 1936–38. The house was built in a ravine about 51 miles (82 km) from Pittsburgh where the client, Edgar Kaufmann, Sr., liked to get away from the city [4.24]. Wright learned from Kaufmann that he most enjoyed sitting on a large rock ledge over the stream. Wright then built the house at that spot, leveling part of the rock outcropping for the floor of the house. Stone from the site was used to build up the major structural piers of the house, laid in a rough and random pattern emulating the texture of the rock outcroppings themselves. But the concrete used for the cantilevered balconies was made especially smooth, so that the greatest possible contrast was created between the rough, dark verticals and the smooth, light-colored horizontals.

Variation of texture is a large part of landscape architecture and garden design, in which plants with different foliage patterns, colors, and heights are played against one another. To this can be added the textures of gravel, rock, and water. In the sprawling gardens of Versailles, first laid out in the seventeenth century, nearly all these variations can be found, from the geometrically laid-out and close-clipped parterres near the château itself, with their hedge-framed flower beds, gravel walks, splashing fountains, and quiet reflecting basins, to the large masses of trees and rustic woodlands farther out [4.25].

Modern architects have, in a sense, had to rediscover tactile texture, for it was suppressed by International Modernism from 1920 to 1960. Since early time, roughness of surface was equated with unskilled craftsmanship, and smoothness of surface was achieved by careful handwork. But with the rise of industrialization, smoothness became easier to achieve in factory-made products. Smoothness then became equated with cheap mass production. The great irony was that much International Modern architecture was made to appear machine-made, but its smooth, textureless surfaces were often achieved by the most painstaking of handwork. By 1930, avant-garde architecture had no tactile texture. Rudolph's Art

4.24. *Frank Lloyd Wright, Edgar Kaufmann residence, Fallingwater, near Mill Run, Pennsylvania, 1936–38. Strong contrasts are created between the rough vertical masonry piers (with stone slabs laid to imitate natural rock strata) and the smooth horizontal concrete floor slabs.*

4.25. *André Le Nôtre, Château de Versailles, Versailles, France, 1661–c. 1750. The gardens, designed by Le Nôtre, exhibit a variety of textures in plant materials, paving, architectural embellishments, and the use of water.*

4.26. *Imperial Villa of Katsura, near Kyoto, Japan, 1620–58. The central gate, combining a wide variety of textures in architectural and landscape materials.*

and Architecture Building at Yale is important, therefore, as one of the first to exploit texture once again.

Perhaps the most sensitive interplay of textures is to be found in the traditional Japanese house and its surrounding garden. In this fusion of building and landscape, plant materials, rocks, gravel, water, and architecture employ a full range of textures from rough to smooth. This exploitation of texture is summarized in the most elegant and understated way in the pavilions and gardens of the imperial villa of Katsura, about three and a half miles (6 km) southwest of central Kyoto.[4] This was built in three stages, on a site of about 16½ acres (66,000 square meters), from 1620 to 1658; included were a main house and five tea

pavilions around a series of ponds fed by the Katsura River. As one approaches, a hedge, or screen, of living bamboo trees is seen first, leading to a fence of cut bamboo; this in turn leads to a hedge that frames the Imperial Gate protected by a gable roof of thick thatch. One then proceeds along a broad path paved with carefully fitted flat pebbles. The entrance to the main house is through the Central Gate [4.26]. The view through that gate is a study in the play of textures—gravel and pebble walkways, a fieldstone threshold, and a bamboo fence and gate with a thatch roof contrast and complement the house beyond, which has smooth plaster surfaces and dark-stained wood frame members.

Within the villa buildings, one finds varied textures—thick, grass-covered tatami mats on the floor contrasted with the grain of the wood in the verandas at the house's edge. The walls are defined by paper- and silk-brocade-covered sliding screens. The ceilings in the main house are a carefully finished wooden lattice, whereas in the garden teahouses one looks up to the bamboo rafters and bamboo mat beneath the thatch. As viewed from the various openings in the house and tea pavilions [3.7], every square inch in the gardens is a study of the interplay of plants, rock, and water, an interplay that changes through the cycle of the seasons.

Light and Color

Perhaps the most powerful element in our perception of architecture is light. Louis I. Kahn insisted that there was no true architecture without natural light. Our principal receptors for sensing the environment are our eyes, and the light illuminating that environment is critical for the information we receive. The perception of textures is dependent upon the quality of light falling on the building. Moreover, light creates strong psychological responses and has a definite physiological effect.

In doing close, exacting work—such as sewing or reading—the eyes become strained if there is too strong a degree of contrast between high light levels in the immediate work area and darkness in the surrounding area. Consequently, for normal office work a relatively high level of evenly diffused light, creating the minimum of harsh shadows, is standard. This can be achieved by banks of fluorescent tubes with diffusing grates below them, by careful handling of reflected sunlight, or by a combination of the two. The goal is to avoid strong pools of light that will direct and focus attention.

For other activities the opposite effect is desired, since a strongly focused pool of light against a background of general darkness is a highly effective device for focusing attention. Baroque architects were especially sensitive to this phenomenon, and in their churches they created hidden sources of light, focusing the light on specific areas to direct attention. Painters of the Baroque period, such as Rubens and Rembrandt, did much the same, similarly creating areas of strong illumination to direct our attention. Film directors also use strongly focused light to direct the attention of their audiences, a technique they borrowed, in turn, from the theater.

In 1647, in designing the chapel for Cardinal Federico Cornaro for the left transept arm of the church of Santa Maria della Vittoria in Rome, the sculptor and architect Gian Lorenzo Bernini designed a miniature theater, with portrait figures of the cardinal and members of his family in "boxes" to the sides observing the *Ecstasy of Saint Teresa* depicted on a "stage" at the center [17.5]. The action is lit by a window hidden behind the architectural frame of the stage, and the image of the flood of heavenly light down on the miraculous event is intensified by the golden rays that radiate down from that hidden light. Everything else in the chapel is dimly lit, so that one's eye is automatically drawn to that brightest spot in the entire composition.

Light is a most effective element in creating a sense of mystery and awe, and the manipulation of light is a principal agent in the creation of shrines and religious buildings. In his later architecture, Le Corbusier proved himself extremely sensitive to the atmospheric role of light, beginning with the chapel Notre-Dame-du-Haut at Ronchamp, France, 1950–55 [21.10, 21.13]. A pilgrimage church on a promontory in the Jura foothills, near the alps of the French-Swiss border, it was reconstructed after being severely damaged during World War Two. Le Corbusier covered the church in white stucco, so that from afar its gleaming whiteness, seen over the surrounding green landscape, acts as a beacon. As one approaches the hill, only the swelling gray concrete roof of the chapel is visible, but as one ascends the hill the white southern wall comes increasingly into view. When the pilgrim reaches the top of the hill, especially at midday, the full brunt of the sunlight is reflected his or her face. Proceeding through the southern door into the chapel, the visitor is suddenly plunged into darkness, as if going into a cave. Through this device, Le Corbusier suggests the separateness of the world outside and the mystical world created inside, at first shrouded in darkness. Then, as if in revelation, the details of the interior space gradually become clear as one's eyes adjust to the dim light, and the silo-like towers seen from outside are discovered to be giant scoops capturing and filtering light down onto devotional altars below. It is an architecture that, from the inside, is almost entirely shaped and defined by the careful manipulation of light.

The term *light* has been used so far to mean the entire visible solar spectrum, with its mixture of various wavelengths. But sunlight is composed of many colors; and color, too, is a powerful evoker of moods and physiological response.[5] During the nineteenth century, much was written about the effect of color on humans. Johann Wolfgang von Goethe discussed optics and the physiological effects of colors in 1810; in 1877 Niels Finsen began color therapy for patients. As with all stimuli, the human organism adjusts to and compensates for continuous unvarying stimuli, but, even so, it is possible to measure distinct physiological responses to colors in the spectrum. Exposed to red, for example, the body experiences an increase in muscular tension, the release of adrenalin, increase of the heartbeat, and a stepping-up of gastric activity. In other words, the human organism prepares for digestion at the sight of blood.[6] It is for this reason that restaurants often employ red or red-checked table linens; dark, so-called warm colors (oranges and browns, for example), and candles with low light output, rich in the red and orange portion of the spectrum, augmented with directed beams of concentrated low-level light to enhance the physiological effect of red while also creating an intimate psychological environment—all directed to enhancing the dining experience.

On the other hand, exposed to green or blue (so-called cool colors), the body experiences a release of muscular tension, a slowing of the heartbeat, and a slight lowering of the body temperature. This is why summer clothing is often in pale blues and lime greens. This is also why fast-food eateries, at least until recently, tended to make the eating experience less genial by using high light levels, achieved by using fluorescent tubes rich in blue light, and color schemes avoiding reds and oranges, thus encouraging a rapid turnover of customers and thereby increasing the volume of food sold.

A color wheel [Plate 1] shows the principal hues divided into two major segments. The area made up of red, red-orange, orange and yellow-orange is said to consist of **warm colors,** while the area made up of yellow-green, green, blue-green, blue, and blue-violet is said to consist of **cool colors.** The so-called primary colors (when mixing pigments for paint, for example) are red, yellow, and blue, and all other colors can be created by mixing these together; when all three are mixed in proper proportions the result is a deep gray approaching black. When mixing light itself, however, the three primary colors are different (reddish-blue, or magenta, yellow, and bluish-green, or cyan), and a mix of these three produces white light; this is the principle of color television. We say a color, or chroma, is **saturated** when it cannot be made any stronger than it is, that a red or a blue cannot be made any redder or bluer. If gray is added to a color, darkening it, that is said to produce a **shade.** If white is added to a color, that produces a **tint,** commonly called a pastel.

To an extent, warm colors heighten bodily functions, while cool colors slightly depress bodily functions. In addition, various theorists suggest an optical phenomenon in which the mind interprets warm colors as being closer to the eye than physically true, while cool colors are interpreted as being slightly farther away. The same is true for dark shades and light tints, the darker shades being sensed as closer and the lighter tints as slightly farther away. So, in selecting paint for a room, if the room is small, the color of choice to make it seem larger would be a tint of green or blue. If a room is extremely large and barnlike and the desire is to make it seem smaller, a shade in the warm part of the spectrum might be the color of choice. Even in selecting an off-white, the choice of the pigment to be mixed in will have perceivable results, a subtle warm pigment making the room more intimate, and a cool pigment making the room more expansive. Thus, without affecting the physical space at all, the psychological perception of that space can be changed.

Color has been used effectively in architecture since Paleolithic times, as the paintings in caves suggest. Fragments of plaster used to cover the wooden Neolithic houses at Habasesti, Romania, built c. 3500–3000 B.C., are covered with decorative painted patterns. Dwellings built on Crete during the Minoan period in the Mediterranean (c. 2000–1300 B.C.) had brilliant red columns and ceremonial and living chambers vividly painted with murals and decorative bands, as seen in the restored palace at Knossos, built c. 1600 B.C. Later, the Greeks similarly painted their white marble temples, a fact that long went unnoticed, since the exposed ruins had been bleached by centuries of exposure to the sun. Only in the mid-nineteenth century did the French architect Jacques-Ignace Hittorf discover in the protected recesses of the ornament of Greek temples the traces of red, blue, and other colors that had been used to pick out and accentuate parts of the orders. In the Doric order, for example, the flat part of the sculpted metope panel was painted a deep saturated red, to point up the raised relief figures [Plate 3]. Egyptian temples were also brilliantly painted, particularly the engraved hieroglyphic inscriptions, but since these too have been bleached out by thousands of years of exposure, the nearest approximation of the rich colors of the temples is to be seen in Egyptian tomb walls, whose murals were never exposed to the light of the sun.

Early Christian churches, built after the end of the Roman Empire, were exceedingly plain externally, but inside the walls and vaults were covered with mosaics made of tiny bits of stone and glass, forming images of biblical figures and Christian symbols. The dazzling brilliance of such murals, combined with veined marble columns and inlaid floor patterns, is evident in the decoration of the apse of San Apollinare, a church built c. 532–49 in Classe, then a suburb of Ravenna, Italy [13.7], and in the church of San Vitale, built in 532–48 in Ravenna by the Byzantine Emperor Justinian. The two mosaics of the sanctuary area in San Vitale show the emperor and his court presenting the bread and wine used in the Eucharist service.

Gothic churches were also alive with color, although much of their painting (unlike the earlier mosaics) has faded and disappeared. The stained glass windows, however, and the patterns created by the light that passes through those color filters as it strikes the internal walls, have endured. In the mid-nineteenth century, Eugène-Emmanuel Viollet-le-Duc restored the small royal chapel in Paris, the Sainte-Chapelle, 1242–48, repainting the deep-blue vaults with twinkling golden stars [Plate 4].

Perhaps the most colorful buildings of all were those built by Muslims in what is now Iran and in Spain. The practice originated in the ancient Near East in the Tigris-Euphrates valley, where buildings were made of soft brick. Since the structural brick was soft-fired, to save wood used for the firing, it was susceptible to damage by rain. Hence the soft-brick buildings were covered with a protective skin of hard-fired ceramic-glazed tiles, so that the outer surfaces of the buildings were ablaze with brilliant colors. This practice is well illustrated in the mosques of Isfahan, Persia (now Iran), especially the Masjid-i-Shah Mosque, 1611–1638, in which the tile is used to convey passages from the Koran in stylized calligraphy [Plate 2]. This practice of using ceramic tile as covering and embellishment was carried to Spain where, as part of Moorish architecture, it eventually became part of traditional Spanish vernacular architecture; from Spain it was carried to Mexico and the Spanish colonies in the New World.

Renaissance architects were far more interested in clearly delineating the component volumes of a building than in exciting the eye, but they did use dark stone for the pilasters and entablatures of their interiors to draw the mathematical edges of their geometrical designs [16.9, 16.13]. Otherwise the walls of their interiors were of plain white plaster. Andrea Palladio restricted the color schemes of his mid-sixteenth churches even more, creating interiors that are essentially studies of creams and whites. In the Baroque period that followed, however, architects deliberately set out to captivate the eye of the beholder, so that once again color became a major element of design and embellishment. This reached its culmination in the Late Baroque-Rococo architecture of the early eighteenth century, and perhaps nowhere better than in the carved and gilded stuccowork of the artisans Joseph Feichtmayr and Johann Übelhör in the church of Vierzehnheiligen (Pilgrimage Church of the Fourteen Saints) in Franconia, Germany, designed by Johann Balthasar Neumann and built in 1742–72 [Plate 5]. The colors and patterns evident in such south German Rococo interiors, however, were largely the result of highly skillful painting on polished plaster, so that what appears to be marble usually is not.

Color continued to be an important element in nineteenth-century European and American architecture; but, in accordance with the view held then that architecture ought to be real and truthful, building materials were used to exploit their inherent color—the red of brick contrasted with polished marbles, white and cream limestone, and the wide spectrum of slate from gray, green, red, to beige. Color of this kind, employing the rich effects achieved in building materials, was restricted with the rise of International Modernism. The exception was Mies van der Rohe's elegant German Pavilion in Barcelona, 1929, with its polished marble and onyx panels [20.12]. In large measure, the color scheme of International Modernist architecture—as it was crystallized in the 1920s by the designers associated with the Bauhaus in Dessau, Germany—was inspired by the architects of the Dutch De Stijl movement. De Stijl architects proposed an objective and systematic use of saturated primary colors applied as paint to the planes shaping space, with black being reserved for structural members. In their fifth manifesto, 1923, De

Stijl theorists asserted, "We have given color its rightful place in architecture" [Plate 6].

How effective primary colors can be, especially when used in conjunction with carefully controlled lighting, is demonstrated in the chapel design by Le Corbusier for the monastery of La Tourette near Lyons, France, 1956–59. The chapel is a large rectangular box of reinforced concrete with only a few narrow slits for windows. At the bottom of the box and extending to the sides are lateral extensions containing the numerous altars at which the monks must say Mass once a day. The light coming into the chapels is admitted through tubular light monitors, extending up from these side-altar extensions; the light is thus caught and thrown down across the walls behind the side altars, where it rakes the roughcast surfaces painted in deep saturated reds, blues, and yellows. Thus, using concentrated light and pure color to direct the eye, Le Corbusier has focused attention on the most important functional part of the monastic chapel, the altars used by the monks.

In recent years architects have turned with renewed vigor to exploiting a rich complexity of ornament, color, and texture in an effort to entice and stimulate the eye of the observer. One architect who has done so with particular gusto is the American Charles Moore, as is dramatically evident in his design for the Piazza d'Italia in New Orleans, Louisiana, 1975–80 [Plate 7]. In most instances, however, as with Late Baroque and Rococo architecture, the colors arise not from the natural weathering of materials but from applied paint that must periodically be renewed. Nonetheless, such environments have reinstituted a measure of vivacity and energy which was forbidden by the austerity of International Modernism in the mid-twentieth century.

Ugliness

Among the major contributions of philosophy in the late eighteenth century were the notions of the "picturesque" and the "sublime," extolling the virtues of irregular and rough forms, and the delight in the thrill of

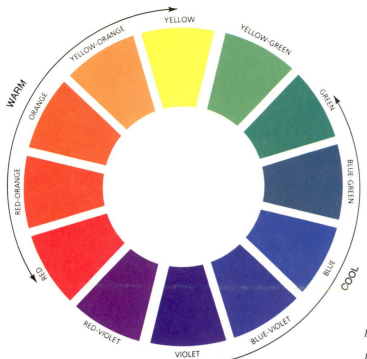

WARM

YELLOW

YELLOW-ORANGE

YELLOW-GREEN

ORANGE

GREEN

RED-ORANGE

BLUE-GREEN

RED

BLUE

COOL

RED-VIOLET

BLUE-VIOLET

VIOLET

Plate 1. Color wheel.

Plate 2. Masjid-i-shah Mosque, Isfahan, 1611–38.

Plate 3. Greek Temple, Doric order, as reconstructed by Jacques-Ignace Hittorff, 1860.

Plate 4. Royal Chapel of Sainte-Chapelle, Paris, 1242–48. Restored by Viollet-le-Duc c. 1850.

Plate 5. Johann Balthasar Neumann, Vierzehnheiligen (Pilgrimage Church of the Fourteen Saints), Franconia, Germany, 1742–72.

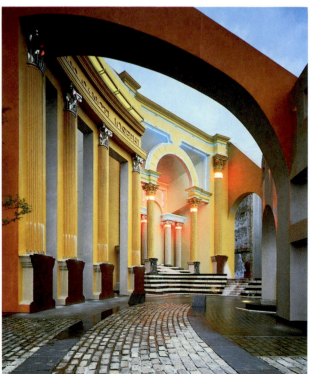

Plate 6. Theo van Doesburg and Cornelius van Estern, Color Construction (Project for a Private House), 1922.

Plate 7. Charles Moore, Piazza d'Italia, New Orleans, 1975–80.

physical danger. Out of the sensibility of the picturesque came an awareness of the aesthetic value of ugliness.[8] Certain nineteenth-century architects, such as William Butterfield in England and Frank Furness in the United States, took pleasure in devising compositions that reveled in awkward juxtapositions of forms and collisions of colors.

Ugliness can be defined in a number of ways: as a quality that is confusing because it is ambiguous or displays an absence of a perceivable pattern of relationships; as a quality that is monstrous because it does not conform to accepted norms; or as artistic willfulness and capriciousness. Frank Furness's Provident Life and Trust Company Building, Philadelphia, 1876–79, now destroyed [2.4], for example, had a facade that displayed a clear bilaterally symmetrical pattern, but it deviated emphatically from accepted norms of its own period (and even more of the mid-twentieth century), suggesting a certain artistic willfulness. This deliberate "ugliness" is even more pronounced in other designs by Furness which were asymmetrical.

The late twentieth century is an age of pluralism, in which various conflicting artistic values and standards, present and past, are mutually acceptable or at least tolerated. But this is a recent development. Most periods have looked down upon the art and architecture of the period immediately preceding. During the Renaissance, for example, the architecture of the Middle Ages was despised, since it seemed formless in comparison to the newly rediscovered Classical humanist architecture; this was said to be the work of barbaric Goths (hence Gothic). Similarly, to the rationalists of the late-eighteenth-century Enlightenment, the exuberantly embellished and curved architecture of the preceding century and a half was said to be misshapen and formless; the critics of the Enlightenment applied to it the term baroque, for to them the curved architecture of the seventeenth century was as much a freak as the twisted and misshapen "baroque" pearl, originally called barroco by the Portuguese. During the 1970s the angular forms of Art Deco of the 1930s, as well as the pseudo-streamlined

forms of the early 1950s, were nostalgically appreciated, but the structurally determined architecture of Mies van der Rohe of the late 1950s and 1960s was ridiculed. And in the 1980s, the precision and clarity of Mies van der Rohe's architecture are just beginning to elicit renewed acclaim.

Each generation thus rejects its fathers and embraces its grandfathers; it tends to think of the work of the previous generation as barbaric, since it does not conform to contemporary standard of values. In the same way, during the 1950s the work of Furness in Philadelphia was considered irredeemably ugly and much of it was wantonly demolished before a new sensitivity to Furness's deliberate "ugliness" arose during the 1960s. In part the prejudice against Furness may have been due as much to the accumulation during three-quarters of a century of atmospheric pollution on the rough surfaces of Furness's buildings as it was to the bold and very personal ornament that Furness invented. As the mid-twentieth-century International Modernist propagandists tried to convince us, ornament was a crime against nature and society. And yet, as Furness's deliberate flouting of the rules of taste of his time show, the value of ugliness is that it forces us to examine our accepted conventions; we may find that our preconceptions do not have much substance.

Ornament

In the past century and a half, the value attached to architectural ornament has swung from one extreme to another. In the mid-nineteenth century, the English critic John Ruskin could readily persuade his readers that "ornament is the chief part of architecture."[9] And yet, in 1908, the Viennese architect Adolf Loos laid the groundwork for International Modernism with his article "Ornament and Crime," asserting that "the evolution of culture is synonymous with the removal of ornament from utilitarian objects."[10] He equated the use of ornament in modern architecture with degeneracy and the smearing of erotic graffiti on lavatory walls. It is a risky proposition to use this equation to evaluate architecture in

4.27. Adolf Loos, Steiner House, Vienna, 1910. Garden facade. A good example of the elimination of ornament that Loos advocated in his article "Ornament as Crime," published in 1908.

the absence of other information. For example, using Loos's criteria literally, what are we to make of a comparison between his Steiner house in Vienna, 1910 [4.27], in which he exemplified his principles, and the Carson house in Eureka, California, 1884–85 [4.28]? The temptation would be to say that the first was the work of a virtuous person and that the second the work of someone deranged. If we look into historical circumstances, however, a very different picture emerges. Loos was working in Vienna in a cultural environment that very much wanted to create a new and scientifically objective architecture suited to the new century. The William M. Carson house, designed by Samuel and Joseph Newsom, was built by the developer of the California redwood lumber industry. The year 1884 was marked by a severe though short-lived business recession. As there was, temporarily, no demand for redwood, Carson had this house built as a kind of public works project to keep his millhands busy and also as a demonstration of what could be done with redwood. Small wonder that so much attention was lavished on this showpiece while

Carson and his employees waited for the economy to recover.

The ornament of the Carson house, then, served specific economic and social purposes, but there are many other purposes that ornament serves as well. There is nothing wrong with saying, at the very outset, that ornament can be used solely for the reason given by Vitruvius and Wotten— pure visual delight. This would be the case for the remarkable interior of the sacristy, the Cartuja, in Granada, Spain, built in 1730 and decorated in 1742–47 [17.4]. There is, underlying all the carved plaster flourishes, a Classical pilaster and entablature system, but the intent here was to add element upon element for the delight of the eye. The same is true of the mirrored interior of the small Amalienburg pavilion in the grounds of the Nymphenburg outside Munich, Germany, 1734–39, designed by François Cuvilliés and decorated by J. B. Zimmermann and Joachim Dietrich [17.40]. Every surface is covered either with glass or with small-scale gilded ornament, and the whole is a treat for the eyes. It is all there solely for visual delight.

Ornament can also have a strictly utilitarian purpose, such as enhancing the longevity of a building. For example, the demonlike gargoyles stretching out from Gothic cathedrals, from a purely functional point of view, are water spouts to throw the water collected from the upper roofs away from the building [4.29]. The same purpose is served by the many projected moldings that serve as horizontal ridges on Gothic buildings, dripping the water away from the wall surface. When these details are reused on later buildings, under similar climatic conditions, the same weathering effect is achieved. Even though the Gothic revival limestone veneer of the Chicago Tribune Tower of 1922–25 was once ridiculed, because this medieval shell was said to be inappropriate for the twentieth century, the Gothic detailing has meant that the building has stood up to weathering much better than adjacent skyscrapers built three decades later.

Ornament can also serve an acoustical function. An excellent case study is Philharmonic Hall, designed by Harrison &

4.28. Samuel and Joseph Newsom, William M. Carson House, Eureka, California, 1884–85. This elaborate house was built of redwood to illustrate the extreme versatility of this durable soft wood and also to keep Carson's lumber mill workers busy during a recession period.

4.29. *Notre-Dame de Amiens, Amiens, France, 1221–69. The gargoyles on the buttresses of the choir serve the very practical purpose of throwing rainwater away from the building.*

Abramovitz in 1960–62 as part of the prestigious Lincoln Center, New York, which became the official home of the New York Philharmonic Orchestra. The unusual plan was quickly christened the "Coke bottle" plan. From the ceiling, elongated hexagons were suspended as "acoustical clouds," to disperse the sound to the audience [4.30]. As quickly became clear, however, the room did not function well. Among several problems, the sound was unevenly dispersed throughout the hall. Eventually, a number of important soloists and orchestras flatly refused to perform there. In 1971, with the donation of funds, it was decided to rebuild the interior of the hall. The revised plan, devised by the architect Philip Johnson and the acoustical consultant Cyril M. Harris, was a more traditional rectangular box room, and among the important changes was the incorporation of large, solid ornamental reflecting panels [4.31]. Today the rebuilt concert house, renamed Avery Fisher Hall, is considered among the fore-

most symphony halls in the world, but the mistakes took $4.5 million to correct!

Articulation (clear expression) of parts of a building is another function of ornament. A good example is Adler & Sullivan's Guaranty Building in Buffalo, New York, 1895 [1.2], in which each of the distinct functional zones, as analyzed by Sullivan, is expressed by a change in the terra cotta blocks enclosing and protecting the steel skeletal frame. The separate functional activities are directly indicated in the skin of the building.

Ornament can serve an expressive utilitarian purpose as well. One example might be to accentuate a functional part of a building. Looking at the west front of the Gothic cathedral of Reims, France, we see the doors announced unmistakably by broad, recessed archways [4.32]. At close range, the carvings of individual figures from the Bible, showing the life of Christ and episodes from the Old Testament, are evident. But from somewhat farther back,

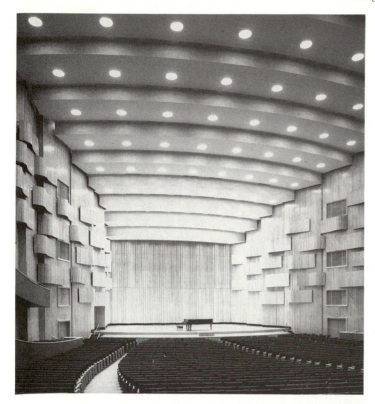

4.30. *Harrison and Abramovitz, Philharmonic Hall, New York, 1960–62. The original interior shows the suspended "acoustical clouds" intended to disperse sound.*

4.31. *Cyril M. Harris with Philip Johnson, Avery Fisher Hall (formerly Philharmonic Hall), New York, 1971–74 (1973, during renovation). Gutted, redesigned, and rebuilt, Avery Fisher Hall bears little resemblance to its original state; the acoustical results, however, are far superior.*

4.32. *Notre-Dame de Reims, Reims, France, begun 1241. The observer immediately recognizes where the entrances are in the west front of the cathedral.*

these merge in a series of concentric arches to form hoods over the doors, showing clearly where to enter.

Gothic ornamental devices were used later in the twentieth century for a different purpose. At the beginning of the twentieth century, when the modern metal-framed skyscraper was developed, some architects employed Gothic details in early skyscrapers to emphasize and accentuate their vertical character. Such is the case with the Gothic detailing of the Chicago Tribune Tower, as well as with the earlier and taller Woolworth Building, New York, 1911–13, by Cass Gilbert, which inspired the Chicago skyscraper [4.33].

Up until the early years of this century, one of the major purposes of figural ornament was to be didactic, to tell a story through images of men and animals related to the building's function. This story-telling is most evident to us, perhaps, in Gothic cathedrals, in the portals where the sculpture (as in the west front of the Reims cathedral) related the life and work of Christ and the Last Judgment. The general disposition of figures and narrative had been established in the portals of Notre-Dame at Chartres, France, carved between 1145 and 1170 (the rest of that church was destroyed by fire but was immediately rebuilt, 1194–1220 [4.34].[11] On the right (south) side, in the tympanum panel over the door itself, are three depictions of Christ's birth. The tympanum panel on the left (north) portal shows Christ's ascension into heaven. The center and largest tympanum depicts Christ in Judgment, framed by symbolic representations of the four Evangelists. By means of such coherently organized story-telling images, arranged across the breadth of the church, the message of the Bible is presented for the illiterate, and the building itself became a bible in stone.

Such a fusion of pictorial imagery and building function was true for Greek temples as well. The correspondence of ornament and function is clearest perhaps in the sculpture carved to fit into the low triangular pediments at the ends of the roof of the Temple of Zeus at Olympia.[12] The site had been sacred since about 3000 B.C., and, as

4.33. Cass Gilbert, Woolworth Building, New York, 1911–13. In order to express the height of this building as dramatically as possible, Gilbert used vertically soaring Gothic details.

4.34. Portal in west front, Notre-Dame de Chartres, Chartres, France, 1194–1220. The sculptural embellishment of the entrance portals is carefully organized to illustrate the life and teaching of Christ, the Last Judgment, and the foretelling of Christ's life in the Old Testament.

with most sites in Greece, various myths gradually evolved relating to the gods and demigods associated with that region. By the eighth century B.C. the site had become sacred to Greeks of all the various interminably quarreling city-states, yet at four-year intervals a general truce was declared so that athletes could come from across Greece to Olympia to participate in the games. Gradually the site was divided into two sections [4.35, 11.15]. To the west was a sacred precinct, with temples, altars, and treasury buildings along the north edge; to the east was a stadium for the games and the chariot races. During 470–456 B.C. a large, new marble Doric temple to Zeus was built after designs by the local architect Libon. Placed inside was a colossal seated figure of Zeus, made of gold and ivory by the Athenian sculptor Pheidias.

The temple to Zeus had six columns across the ends and thirteen along the sides. As was customary in Greek temples, within the encircling outer Doric colonnade was the chamber for the image of the god, the *naos;* this had porches at each end formed of two Doric columns framed between projections of the *naos* walls. In the Doric entablature, there are two sculptural metope panels above each support, and this meant that there were six sculptural panels at each end of the *naos*. At Olympia these panels portrayed the twelve Labors of Herakles; thus, in his fabled endurance and strength Herakles was associated with the games.

Zeus' temple was oriented roughly on an east-west axis, and in the pediment on the west side was a representation of the story of the Lapiths and the Centaurs [4.36]. The Centaurs, half-man and half-beast, were invited by the Lapiths (mythical inhabitants of this land) to a royal wedding. When the centaurs had consumed too much wine, for which they had virtually no resistance, their animal nature took over and they began to carry off the women. A brawl ensued from which the Lapiths emerged victorious. Thus, the fighting portrayed in the pedi-

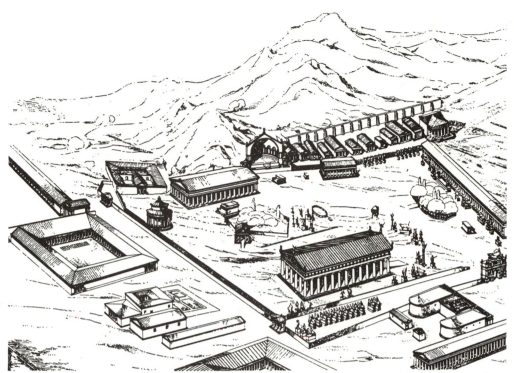

4.35. *Aerial view of the sacred precinct, Olympia, Greece, showing the Temple of Zeus, fifth century* B.C. *To the east of the sacred precinct (temenos) was the stadium where the Olympic Games were played.*

4.36. *Libon (architect), Temple of Zeus, Olympia, Greece, 470–456* B.C. *West end. In the pediment triangle were sculptural figures depicting the story of the battle between the human Lapiths and the part-beast Centaurs.*

4.37. Temple of Zeus, Olympia. East end. In the triangular pediment of the east end of the temple, looking out toward the Olympic stadium, were figures depicting the race between King Oinomaos and Pelops, won by Pelops through deception and murder.

ment was a representation of right over wrong, of human civilization over unthinking barbarism. Everywhere in the figures there is the strongest contrast between the snarling, grimacing faces of the violent beast-men and those of the composed Lapith women, who keep their emotions under control even in the face of physical threat.

In the east pediment, however, was depicted a story that had special meaning to this site and the games [4.37]. It concerned the mythical chariot race between King Oinomaos and Pelops, a young suitor who hoped to gain the right to marry the king's daughter, Hippodameia. Oinomaos loved his beautiful daughter (some authorities say incestuously) and had pledged to give her up only to the suitor who could beat him in a chariot race. But since Oinomaos had been given special horses by the god Ares, all previous suitors had lost, forfeiting their lives. When Pelops arrived, Hippodameia fell in love with him and conspired with her father's charioteer, Myrtilos, to replace the metal linchpin in her father's chariot with

one made of wax. During the race Oinomaos' chariot disintegrated and he was killed. What the east pediment presents is the moment just before that mythical race, as the contestants pledge an oath before Zeus. One lone figure seated to the right, a seer, suddenly reels back in horror, for though he has seen into the future, he is powerless to avert the murder. When the temple was first built, this pediment could be seen from the starting blocks in the stadium. As the athletes gathered for the games, therefore, they could look back over their shoulders to see this image of the mythic chariot race. They would be reminded of the oath they themselves had just taken before a similar statue of Zeus, when, together with their brothers, fathers, and trainers, they vowed to do no wrong to the games. As they put themselves on the mark, they would be reminded by Zeus to reflect on the treachery of Hippodameia and Myrtilos: they must not do likewise in their games; they are commanded not to cheat.

NOTES

1. Bruno Taut, *Modern Architecture* (London, 1929), 9.
2. The importance of the psychology of vision is stressed in Niels Luning Prak, *The Language of Architecture* (The Hague, 1968). See also K. Koffka, *Principles of Gestalt Psychology* (New York, 1935); the many books by Rudolph Arnheim, especially his *Art and Visual Perception* (Berkeley, 1971) and his *Visual Thinking* (Berkeley, 1969); Carolyn M. Bloomer, *Principles of Visual Perception* (New York, 1976), which has a good bibliography; and Gyorgy Kepes, *The Language of Vision* (Chicago, 1944).
3. See Heath Licklider, *Architectural Scale* (New York, 1965); this includes a chapter devoted to proportional systems. See also Frank Orr, *Scale in Architecture* (New York, 1985).
4. For Katsura, see Walter Gropius and Kenzo Tange, *Katsura: Tradition and Creation in Japanese Architecture* (New Haven, Conn., 1960), and Akira Naito, *Katsura: A Princely Retreat* (Tokyo, 1977).
5. For discussion of the effect of color, see the many studies by Faber Birren, especially *Color and Human Response* (New York, 1978); see also Roy Osborne, *Lights and Pigments: Color Principles for Artists* (New York, 1980).
6. This may be a learned cultural response. Published evidence so far has focused on experiments made in the West. Individuals from non-meat-eating cultures may react differently.
7. Written in part by Theo van Doesburg, "De Stijl Manifesto V" is translated in English in Ulrich Conrads, ed., *Programs and Manifestoes on 20th-Century Architecture* (Cambridge, Mass., 1970).
8. See Peter Collins, *Changing Ideals in Modern Architecture* (London, 1965), 243–48.
9. John Ruskin, addenda to Lectures 1 and 2, *Lectures on Architecture and Painting* (London, 1854).
10. Adolf Loos, "Ornament and Crime," 1908,

translated in Conrads, *Programs and Manifestoes,* 19–24.
11. For Chartres, see Robert Branner, ed., *Chartres Cathedral.* (New York, 1969); and Adolf Katzenellenbogen, *The Sculptural Programs of Chartres Cathedral* (Baltimore, 1959; New York, 1964).
12. For Olympia, see J. J. Pollitt, *Art and Experience in Classical Greece* (New York, 1972). See also Jeffrey M. Hurwit, "Narrative Resonance in the East Pediment of the Temple of Zeus at Olympia," *Art Bulletin* 69 (March 1987): 6–15. Although the temple was destroyed long ago, a great deal about its appearance is known from the descriptions of Pausanias, a second-century A.D. physician who devoted twenty years traveling through Greece, making detailed descriptions of everything he saw; see Pausanias, *Guide to Greece,* 2 vols., trans. Peter Levi (New York, 1972).

SUGGESTED READING

Stanley Abercrombie, *Architecture as Art: An Aesthetic Analysis* (New York, 1984).
Rudolf Arnheim, *Art and Visual Perception* (Berkeley, Calif., 1971).
———, *Principles of Visual Perception* (New York, 1976).
Faber Birren, *Color and Human Response* (New York, 1978).
Sinclair Gauldie, *Architecture,* Oxford Appreciation of the Arts Series (New York, 1969).
Heath Liklider, *Architectural Scale* (New York, 1965).
Frank H. Mahnke and Rudolf H. Mahnke, *Color and Light in Man-Made Environments* (New York, 1987).
Frank Orr, *Scale in Architecture* (New York, 1985).
Roy Osborne, *Lights and Pigment: Color and Priciples for Artists* (New York, 1980).
Steen Eiler Rasmussen, *Experiencing Architecture,* second ed. (Cambridge, Mass., 1962).

5.1. *Antonio da Sangallo the Younger, courtyard of the Palazzo Farnese, Rome, begun 1535. The massive piers of the palazzo are large enough to echo the sounds of footsteps, enabling a person to hear the architecture.*

CHAPTER 5

"Delight": Architectural Acoustics, Shape, and Sound

Architecture is frozen music.

Friedrich von Schelling, *Philosophy of Art*, 1805

. . . but music is not melted architecture.

Susanne K. Langer, *Problems of Art*, 1957

In a multitude of ways, architecture shapes human behavior. As Winston Churchill observed, "We shape our buildings, and afterwards our buildings shape us." In a similar way first we shape our buildings and afterward our buildings shape our music, for architecture shapes acoustical space which has its own unique properties.

We can also speak about "hearing" architecture, although for sighted people the aural perception of architecture is nearly completely overpowered by the visual perception of architecture. Yet, if a sighted person loses that sense, then gradually hearing becomes more sensitized, so that it becomes possible to navigate by listening to the echoes bounced off buildings. This is how flying bats locate their prey, by emitting high-pitched sounds that are reflected by objects and insects, and this is how blind people navigate, by listening to the reflected sounds of the tapped cane or the reflections of their own footsteps. It is a good exercise for one who is sighted to walk through an arcade or colonnade having large massive piers, to close one's eyes and to listen as the piers pass; in this way one can hear the architecture [5.1].

Sound is air in motion; it is a succession of pressure waves in the air. The actual movement of the atoms in the air is quite small; for a tone at 256 cycles per second (cps), or middle C on the piano, the atoms in the air are vibrating over a distance of only about one-tenth of a millimeter. But since there are so many atoms, there is kinetic energy in sound. If sound is to be stopped, that energy must be absorbed either by a large mass capable of absorbing the movement without itself moving much, or by a resilient, acoustically spongy material, such as a mat of loose fiberglass.

In acoustical terms, we speak of "live" spaces as those that have highly sound-reflective surfaces, such as dense, polished marble, ceramic tile, mosaic on massive walls, or other hard rigid surfaces. Glazed tile securely attached to massive walls reflects nearly all the sound coming toward it, roughly 98 percent. Eventually, as the sound bounces around it loses its energy to the surfaces it bounces from and gradually the sound will die away. The time required for that to happen is called reverberation time. In large spaces with hard surfaces, the reverberation time may be six seconds or more.

Conversely, "dead" spaces are those that have sound-absorbing surfaces, such as heavy draperies, thick rugs, upholstered furniture, and other soft resilient surfaces. A living room with wall-to-wall carpeting, upholstered furniture, draperies, filled bookcases, and other resilient materials may have almost no reverberation time at all, generally less than half a second.

To study low-level sounds, scientific acoustical measurements are taken in special rooms isolated from the outside environment by being built with multiple massive layered walls, floors, and ceilings. The surfaces of the innermost walls of such **anechoic chambers** are lined with deep pyramidal wedges of foam rubber or fiberglass. The operational floor of such a room is a web of steel cables suspended above more absorbing pyramids. In such chambers, all sound generated is immediately absorbed; reverberation time is absolutely zero. If one stands in such a chamber for a short time, the total absence of sound is almost alarming; soon one can hear the heart beating and the pulse pounding in the head. In such a chamber, the blind could not navigate. This experience suggests that even the sighted may use their hearing in a subliminal way to perceive architectural space.

Except for such special anechoic chambers, all spaces reflect sound to some extent. Out of doors, tree trunks and cliff faces reflect sound. The problem the architect and the acoustical engineer face is designing a space in such a way that sound is reflected in the desired way. To an extent, reflected sound behaves somewhat like reflected light, so that the angle at which a sound approaches a hard surface is equal to the angle at which it bounces off, or the angle of incidence is equal to the angle of reflection [5.2]. But this applies only to the higher tones with frequencies over 1,000 cps.

Moreover, the surface reflecting a sound must be roughly three times larger than the wavelength to be reflected. The length of the wave of a given tone, λ (lambda), is directly proportional to the speed of sound in the transmitting medium, V (in air this is approximately 1,125 ft/sec at 68° F at sea level, or 343 m/sec at 20° C), and inversely proportional to the frequency, f. The wavelength can easily be determined by this formula:

$$\lambda = \frac{V}{f}$$

For middle C, at 256 cps, the wavelength is approximately 4 feet 5 inches (1.3 meters), and the reflecting surface would need to be roughly 13 feet across at the minimum (4.0 meters). For C an octave below, the reflecting surface would need to be 26 feet (7.9 meters) across, and for C at the bottom of the piano keyboard, 32 cps, it would need to be 105 feet (32.0 meters) across. The tone C two octaves above middle C, at 1,024 cps, has a wavelength of nearly 1 foot ¾ inches (0.34 meters), and surfaces to reflect this frequency need only be 3 feet 6 inches across (1.0 meters).

As a consequence, optical models, using light to study how sound is reflected, work only for sounds higher than two octaves above middle C, a very high range occupied only by flutes, violins, and the piccolo. Such models can be constructed with miniature wall segments made of mirrors, with a narrow beam of light simulating the source of sound. To study the reflections of sounds lower than 1,000 cps, radio signals may be bounced off models, or sound may be played electronically in a model at a speed raised in proportion to the size of the model. It is a costly exercise, but making such a model may prove far less expensive in the long run than rebuilding a concert hall, as in the case of Avery Fisher Hall in New York.

Echoes are a form of reflection. The human ear may not be as receptive to

5.2. *Diagram showing reflection of sound waves and how curved surfaces can disperse or focus reflected sound.*

sounds at the high end of the sound spectrum as that of a dog or a bat, but it can still make extremely minute discriminations in the arrival times of different sounds. When a sound is produced, an echo or a distinct reflected image of that sound will be heard if it arrives at the ear only 30 to 45 milliseconds after the original sound, or, in other words, if the reflecting surface is about 35 to 40 feet (10 to 12 meters) away. However, a particular form of echo, a ***flutter echo,*** can occur in a small room having parallel walls with hard surfaces, for conversation bounces back and forth from side to side, causing a buzzing sound. Aside from paneling one wall with absorptive acoustical tile, another solution is to avoid parallel walls. In the small lecture room/auditorium at the Mount Angel Abbey Library, Mount Angel, Oregon [21.36], Alvar Aalto used this solution, with the addition of sound-absorbing material at the back of the room to prevent reflections from returning to the stage.

Since the Italian Renaissance, with the increasing number of enclosed theaters and auditoriums, architects have been fond of designing auditoriums with domed ceilings. Curved shapes are not particularly unsatisfactory *so long as they are high enough from the source of sound,* but all too often the focus of the curve of the dome is near the floor, so that sound is concentrated there in what are called acoustical hot spots. Dome vaults are particularly troublesome since they have a distinct sound focus and do not disperse sound evenly. A similar problem occurs if the rear wall is curved, for sound from the stage is focused back toward the front of the audience. A classic example of a building in which almost everything was done wrong in acoustical terms is the vast Royal Albert Hall, London, 1867–71, designed by Captain Francis Fowke with the architect George Gilbert Scott [5.3, 5.4]. The building, a huge oval in plan, is covered by an ellipsoidal dome, 185 by 219 feet (56.4 by 66.8 meters), so there are curved surfaces both in the plan and in the dome. Because of the combination of curves and size, the result was that in portions of the hall the audience received clear reflected images one fifth of a second late, well over

the limit for echoes. The solution adopted was to hang a heavy velarium drapery overhead to absorb the bulk of the sound formerly reflected from the dome.[1]

In designing an auditorium, an architect must arrive at the optimum realization of a number of requirements. There should be good sight lines to the performance area or stage; good "presence," or strong, even dispersion of initial reflections; good reflection of all frequencies in the sound spectrum; and an even decay of sound during the reverberation time. It is this reverberation time that bears special consideration, for the optimum time depends on the activity in the room. For a lecture hall or a theater in which it is vitally important to hear speech clearly and distinctly, the reflections of previous words need to die away rapidly, so that 1 second is considered the maximum reverberation time. Slightly more reverberation time is desired for the music of small ensembles, such as modern jazz groups or chamber orchestras in which each note produced by each instrument must be clearly heard—perhaps 1½ seconds. For choral church music, symphonic music of the nineteenth century, or Romantic music for the large orchestra, 2 to 2½ seconds is desirable. Opera, therefore, where both music and speech are intertwined, requires a reverberation time somewhere in the area of 1¾ seconds. The problem was that, until 1900, there was no way to determine in advance what the reverberation time of a particular space would be, except to say that small rooms had shorter reverberation times and large rooms had longer reverberation times.

Of course, reverberation time was not a problem until the Renaissance, for theaters in antiquity were open to the sky. The semicircular concentric rings of seats in such theaters, such as that at Epidauros, Greece, built about 340–300 B.C. by Polykleitos the Younger [11.13], did reflect sound directly back to the center of the orchestra circle, but because the seats were so steeply sloped on the hillside, the reflections went upward into the air. In any case, the thirty-four thousand legs wrapped in tunics (the theater seated seventeen thousand) would have provided good sound absorption. The

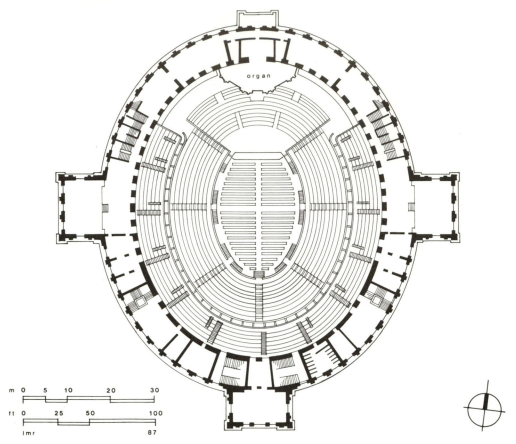

m 0   5   10   20   30

ft 0   25   50   100

l m r   87

5.3. Captain Francis Fowke with George Gilbert Scott, Royal Albert Hall, London, 1867–71. Plan. Because of its size and its curved walls and ceiling, this building was an acoustical disaster.

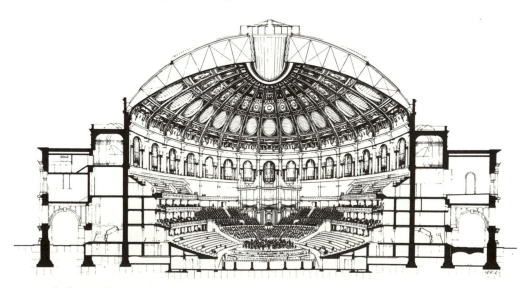

5.4. Royal Albert Hall. Section.

5.5. Andrea Palladio, Teatro Olimpico (Olympic Theater), Vicenza, Italy, 1580–84. Interior. Palladio's theater was built to house revivals of Classical Greek drama and, hence, was patterned after Classical models. It is like a small Roman theater, but covered with a permanent roof.

Romans modified the Greek theater form by using a strict semicircle of seats (the Greek theater was about 200° around) and by constructing large multistory permanent backdrops, or *scenes* (from the Greek *skēnē*) [12.20]. Since hillsides were not always conveniently available, the Romans often ramped the seats on tiers of barrel vaults carried by heavy arcades. The well-preserved example at Aspendos, Turkey, built about A.D. 155 by Zeno of Theodorus, however, is placed on a hillside; it seats seven thousand. A Roman theater—and the larger amphitheater formed by placing two theaters face to face (minus the scene)—was often covered by a *velarium,* a huge awning supported by a web of rope.

With the suppression of theatrical pro-

ductions by the medieval church, the construction of theaters stopped, but with the rise of interest in Classical literature in the Renaissance, the need for this building type emerged once more. Humanists in the area around Venice were especially keen on mounting productions of Greek drama, and they wanted a building shaped for such an undertaking. In Vicenza, near Venice, in 1580, a group of enthusiasts engaged Andrea Palladio to design the Teatro Olimpico as a reproduction of a Classical theater [5.5, 5.6, 5.7]. It was far smaller than a Greek theater, seating only 750, and it was more Roman than Greek, but it provided the right atmosphere. Because of the smaller size, Palladio was able to put a trussed roof on his theater and in that way

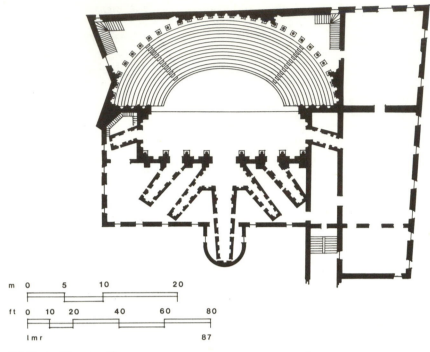

m 0   5   10   20

ft 0 10 20   40   60   80

l m r   87

5.6. *Teatro Olimpico. Plan.*

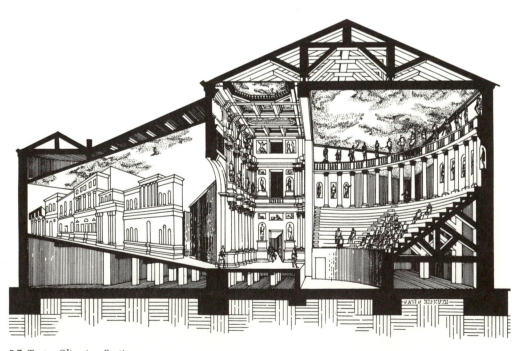

5.7. *Teatro Olimpico. Section.*

make a closed volume. Suddenly, reverberation time became a consideration.

Since the end of the Roman Empire, reverberation time had literally been shaping the development of Western church music. When the early Christians adopted the form of the Roman basilica meeting hall for use as a church, they adjusted themselves to buildings with large volumes, hard stone surfaces, and long reverberation times. It was not possible simply to preach the good news in such halls, for the words resounded up to six and eight seconds after being uttered, and the multiple overlays were unintelligible.

The solution was to chant the liturgy, and by a process of trial and error a basic acoustical principle was discovered. Virtually every enclosed volume has a resonant frequency. In the case of a long, closed tubular organ pipe, the resonant frequency is twice the length of the pipe; hence, in Figure [5.8], for middle C with a wavelength of nearly 4 feet 5 inches (1.3 meters), the length of the pipe is approximately 2 feet 2.4 inches (0.7 meters). Long, narrow basilicas functioned much like organ pipes.[2] So, San

Apollinare in Classe, Ravenna, Italy, built in 530–49, with a length of 185 feet (112.8 meters), has a resonant frequency of about 3.0405 cps. All musical tones consist not only of the basic note but also of a series of ascending harmonics, and the upper harmonic of this extremely low frequency is near F below middle C. The triad up from F is A, meaning that if the priest chanted the liturgy using harmonic intervals around A, the air in the vast volume of such basilicas would soon vibrate on its inherent upper resonant frequencies, and the building itself would carry the message to the worshipers. Thus the plainsong, or Gregorian chant, was born.

A particular musical development of the later Renaissance merits special attention, for it represents a clear case of a building shaping music. The palace church of the doges, or dukes, of Venice, Saint Mark's, was built not in the traditional form of the Latin cross (with a T-shaped plan) but in the form of a Greek cross with four equal arms, each arm and the center bay capped by a dome. Moreover, the interior surfaces were covered with gold-backed glass mosaic, a

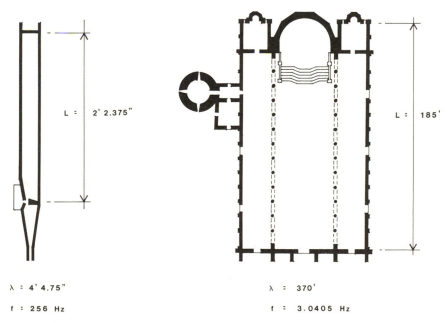

L = 2' 2.375"

λ = 4' 4.75"

f = 256 Hz

L = 185'

λ = 370'

f = 3.0405 Hz

5.8. Diagram comparing the shape of a closed organ pipe and the long basilica church plan of San Apollinare in Classe, outside Ravenna, Italy, built 530–49.

5.9. Thomaskirche (Church of Saint Thomas), Leipzig, Germany. Interior. This engraving by O. Kutschera shows the church as it was when Johann Sebastian Bach was organist and choir director there.

hard reflective surface [13.24]. In each of the arms of the plan there are upper-gallery choir lofts, and during the sixteenth century the choirmasters at Saint Mark's, especially Giovanni Gabrieli, developed a technique of using multiple choirs and multiple instrumental ensembles in the separated lofts performing antiphonally, singing against one another and tossing the melodic line back and forth across the space of the church. As many as four groups would perform simultaneously. This technique was then taken up by German composers as well, including Heinrich Schütz in Munich and Johann Sebastian Bach in Leipzig. The volume of Saint Mark's is considerable, and the reverberation time today is about 6 to 7 seconds,

although tapestries hung in the church probably shortened this somewhat in Gabrieli's time. Still, Gabrieli's music moves slowly, avoiding passages of rapid notes that would pile up acoustically.

At the same time, the princely families of the Italian city-states assembled private chamber groups to perform secular music in their households. Because such secular and dance music was performed in much smaller rooms, or even out-of-doors, it involved faster rhythms and more rapid passages of notes. Such was the background of the court music of Versailles in France, written by Louis XIV's master of music, Jean-Baptiste Lully.

Church music underwent a change in the

north of Europe after 1500, partly as the result of adaptation to smaller churches, partly as the result of changes introduced by Martin Luther when he embarked on reforming the church and thereby touched off the Protestant Reformation, and partly in response to the development of better and more sensitive organs. The result was a body of church and organ music that remains, in many respects, unsurpassed, most notably the music of Bach from the early eighteenth century. Bach, too, adapted his music to the acoustical conditions in the places where he worked. His well-known Toccata and Fugue in D Minor was written about 1708 for the small palace chapel of his employer the Duke of Saxe-Weimar at Weimar. When Bach was employed by the Prince Leopold of Cöthen, he wrote the rapid arpeggios of the Brandenburg Concertos to be played in the small music room there. When Bach then moved to Leipzig and the larger church of Saint Thomas, he began his program of cantatas for the calendar of the church year [5.9].[3] When the choral school there was closed for over a year in 1730–31 for rebuilding, Bach turned his attention to secular instrumental works

for public performance in Zimmermann's coffeehouse.

By the time Bach died, in 1750, there had been established in Leipzig an orchestral ensemble to play public concerts in a large room in the Gewandhaus (Garment Merchants Hall). By the early nineteenth century, under the direction of Felix Mendelssohn, it had become a major symphony orchestra. But in Vienna, where Ludwig van Beethoven was writing his epochal symphonies, there was neither an orchestra to perform them properly nor a hall to perform them in. When large orchestral pieces were performed in Vienna, theaters were pressed into service, as was the large rectangular ballroom, the Redoutensaal, in the Austrian imperial residence. Not until the mid-nineteenth century was the Vienna Philharmonic Orchestra formally organized and finally a special building erected for its use in 1867–70 [5.10, 5.11]. This hall, the Musikvereinsgebaude, was designed by Theophil von Hansen and patterned on the Redoutensaal. The Musikvereinsgebaude worked so well that it served, in turn, as model for the new building for the Gewandhaus orchestra in Leipzig, built in 1882–84

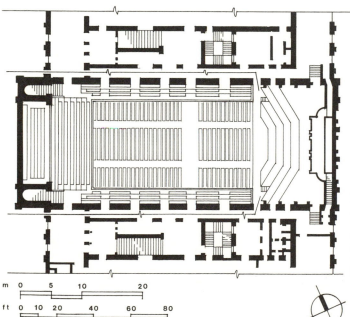

5.10. Theophil von Hansen, Musikvereinsgebaude, Vienna, 1867–70. Plan. Designed especially for use by the Vienna Philharmonic Orchestra, this rectangular orchestral hall set the pattern for many subsequent halls.

m 0   5   10   20

ft 0   10   20   40   60   80

l m r   87

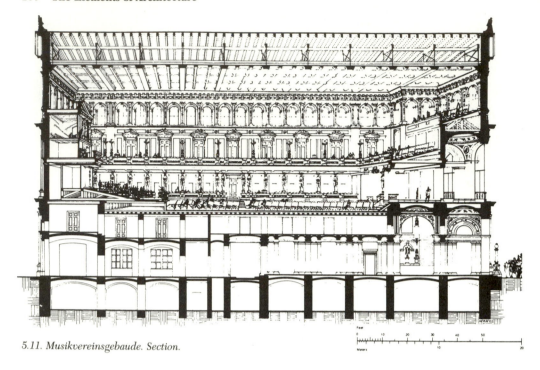

5.11. Musikvereinsgebaude. Section.

by Martin Gropius and Heinrich Schmei-
den.

Meanwhile, opera houses expanded in
size during the nineteenth century, based
on models provided by eighteenth-century
theaters. Often the sight lines were not
good, the acoustics were less than ideal, and
the facilities on the stage were cramped.
During the 1840s, in the course of conducting his early operas in opera houses across
Europe, Richard Wagner discovered that
none of them could provide the facilities he
required for the opera cycle he was then
composing, the four-part *Ring of the
Nibelungen.* His only alternative was to create a new kind of opera house, shaped to
accommodate the music he was writing. He
obtained the patronage of Ludwig II, the
king of Bavaria, who provided him with a
site and the funds to construct his new
opera house, the Festspielhaus (Festival
Hall) at Bayreuth, built in 1872–76 from
designs sketched out by Wagner himself
and designed by the architects Otto Brückwald and Carl Brandt [5.12, 5.13]. The
Bayreuth theater served, then, as the inspiration for the even larger Auditorium in

Chicago, 1887–89, by Adler & Sullivan, in
which excellent acoustics were developed
by the engineer and architect Dankmar
Adler.

Wagner's success, and that of Adler in the
Auditorium, were largely the result of careful observation and informed intuition. The
first building in which the acoustical
performance was mathematically calculated
beforehand was Boston Symphony Hall.
The first steps to build a permanent home
for the Boston Symphony Orchestra, were
taken by Henry Lee Higginson (the principal patron of the orchestra) and the architectural firm McKim, Mead & White in
1892–94, but a business depression then
halted the project. This proved most fortu-
itous, for in 1898 Wallace Sabine, a young
physicist at Harvard, was asked to investi-
gate severe acoustical problems in some of
Harvard's lecture halls. Sabine developed
several mathematical formulas to define
acoustical performance and devised experiments to test the troublesome rooms. The
most difficult to achieve was a formula to
account for reverberation time. Then it
occurred to Sabine that while reverberation

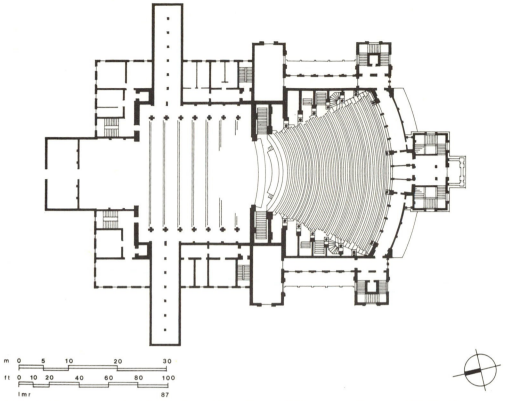

```
m   0     5    10        20          30
ft  0  10  20    40    60    80    100
     1 m r                         87
```

5.12. *Otto Brückwald and Carl Brandt, Festspielhaus (Festival Hall), Bayreuth, Germany, 1872–76. Plan. Designed on the basis of instructions from the composer Richard Wagner, this opera house was to enhance the experience of the opera.*

5.13. *Festspielhaus, Bayreuth. Section.*

5.14. McKim, Mead and White, Boston Symphony Hall, 1892–1900. Exterior. Although patterned after the Musikvereinsgebaude in Vienna and the Gewandhaus in Leipzig, this design was modified in accordance with acoustical calculations made by the engineer Wallace Sabine, making this the first building acoustically planned.

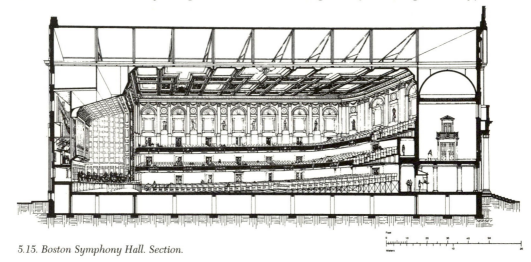

5.15. Boston Symphony Hall. Section.

time was clearly directly proportional to the volume enclosed by a room, it was also inversely proportional to the capacity of the room to absorb the sound. That absorptive capacity was determined by all the materials used in the surfaces of the room, so he set up more experiments to determine just what the absorptive capacities of various materials were. Quite incidentally he had just concluded his investigations when McKim, Mead & White was asked to prepare final designs for Boston Symphony Hall in 1899. Following instructions from Higginson, the architects had used as their model the new Leipzig Gewandhaus, but enlarged nearly 50 percent [5.14, 5.15]. McKim, Mead & White then let Sabine examine the drawings for the building. Sabine concluded that, with certain modifications in the surface treatment, the reverberation time would be 2.51 seconds, only one-hundredth of a second longer than in the orchestra's old hall in Boston. When the first concert was given in 1900, Sabine was proven correct and a new scientific basis had been given to acoustical design.[4]

Yet acoustical engineering, particularly in the design of opera houses and symphony halls, is far from an exact science, as is evident in the costly errors made in the design of Philharmonic Hall in New York, 1960–62, by Harrison & Abramovitz, with the acoustical consulting firm Bolt, Beranek & Newman (this is discussed in Chapter 4 in connection with ornament). Fortunately, given sufficient funds, Philip Johnson and Cyril M. Harris were able to correct those mistakes and create a superior acoustical space. It should be noted that Avery Fisher Hall (as Philharmonic Hall was renamed) is extremely close in volume and form to Boston Symphony Hall.

The most successful orchestra halls of recent years have been those viewed by their architects as the largest of the instruments of the orchestral ensemble. In describing his proposed auditorium for the Fort Wayne Arts Center in Indiana, planned in 1965, Louis I. Kahn said, "Being in the chamber is like living in the violin. The chamber itself is an instrument."[5] This is also how Hans Scharoun conceived of the new hall for the Berlin Philharmonic Orchestra, the Philharmonie, 1956–63 [21.15, 21.16, 21.17, 21.18]. Here the audience surrounds the players; they are part of a body united in a musical experience, for as Scharoun wrote, "Music in the center, that is the simple idea which determined the new concert hall."[6] And as a result, the angled balconies reflect and disperse the sound, as do the convex curves of the ceiling, creating the intimate feeling of participation with the orchestra.

Architecture affects all our senses, not just the eyes. The perception of architecture, then, is an activity in which the whole body is involved—basking in the warmth of a sun-filled court or feeling the cool shadows of its encircling arcade, scanning the rhythm and scale of a facade, listening to the volume of a room, feeling the roughness of stone, the smoothness of tile, smelling the bite of a boxwood hedge along a garden's edge, tasting the cool water of a fountain.

NOTES

1. Acoustical renovation in 1971, by Ronald Ward and Partners, architects, and Kenneth Shearer, acoustical consultant, significantly improved the acoustical performance of Royal Albert Hall.
2. There is some difference of opinion whether such complicated spaces, with side aisles, function so precisely as closed pipes.
3. Hope Bagenal has suggested that in Bach's time the church of Saint Thomas was lined with wooden paneling, greatly reducing its reverberation time, so that Bach's early organ pieces worked equally well in this later environment. Hope Bagenal, "Bach's Music and Church Acoustics," *Journal, Royal Institute of British Architects* 37, no. 5 (January 11, 1930): 154–63. See also his *Planning for Good Acoustics* (London, 1931).
4. See the discussion of Boston Symphony Hall in Leland M. Roth, *McKim, Mead & White, Architects* (New York, 1983), 223–27.
5. Louis I. Kahn, "Remarks," *Perspecta* 9–10 (1965): 318.
6. Hans Scharoun, *Akademie der Kunst* (Berlin, 1967): 95.

SUGGESTED READING

Hope Bagenal and Alexander Wood, *Planning for Good Acoustics* (London, 1931).

Leo L. Beranek, *Acoustics* (New York, 1954).

Leslie L. Doelle, *Environmental Acoustics* (New York, 1972).

M. David Egan, *Architectural Acoustics*, 2nd ed. (New York, 1988).

Michael Forsyth, *Buildings for Music: The Architect, the Musician, and the Listener from the Seventeenth Century to the Present Day* (Cambridge, Mass., 1985).

George C. Izenour, *Theater Design* (New York, 1977).

Peter Lord and Duncan Templeton, *The Architecture of Sound: Designing Places of Assembly* (London, 1986).

Wallace C. Sabine, *Collected Papers on Acoustics* (Cambridge, Mass., 1922; New York, 1964).

6.8. *Tombstone of Hugh Libergier, Notre-Dame de Reims, thirteenth century.
The inscription running around the border reads: "Here lies Master Hugh
Libergier, who began this church in the year 1229 and died in the year 1267."
The architect is surrounded by instruments of his trade; he holds a measuring
rod and a model of a church.*

CHAPTER 6

The Architect:
From High Priest to Professional

The architect . . . must be looked upon as something much more than a designer of buildings—lovely, elegant, charming, and efficient though they may be. His greater role is that of being the delineator, the definer, the engraver of the history of his time. . . .

Eugene Raskin, *Architecture and People,* (1974)

In the discussion of the design of Boston Symphony Hall in the last chapter, it was noted that the patron, Henry Lee Higginson, instructed the architects, McKim, Mead & White, to base their scheme on the successful new Gewandhaus in Leipzig. Unlike painting or poetry, which can be pursued by the artist on his own, architecture results only when a client or a patron calls it into being. Thus the history of architecture is also a history of the relationship between architect and patron.

The first recorded architect is Imhotep, who was active in Egypt under the Pharaoh Zoser from about 2635 B.C. to 2595 B.C. On the base of his portrait statue his titles are listed as "Seal-bearer of the king of Lower Egypt, chamberlain, ruler of the great mansion, hereditary prince, greatest of seers, Imhotep, carpenter, sculptor."[1] Other portions of the inscription indicate he was also a physician. Imhotep's important status is the result of his many accomplishments. He introduced stone construction in Egypt, invented the pyramid, and in many ways laid the basis for all later architecture in the West. His importance was such that he was described as a demigod, and by the Twenty-sixth Dynasty was in fact considered a god. Other Egyptian architects are known as well, particularly Senmut, who was described in contemporary carvings as the

"confidant" of Queen Hatshepsut, who ruled as pharaoh, in 1503–1482 B.C. Inscriptions describe Senmut as "the greatest of the great in the entire land."[2] Portrait figures of Senmut, showing him holding the royal princess in his lap or with coiled, knotted measuring ropes and other tools of his profession, were found in large numbers in the Queen's Mortuary Temple at Deir el-Bahri, which he designed. As inscriptions on portrait statues reveal, these architects held exalted positions in the priesthood, for indeed all education was provided by the priests. Working under these priest-architects were hosts of overseers and craftsmen. Concerning such craftsmen during the Middle Kingdom we have abundant evidence from the tombs they made for themselves near their workmen's village, now called Deir el Medineh, a short distance from the tombs of the pharaohs in the Valley of the Kings.[3]

Loose sketch designs by Egyptian architects have been found on *ostraka,* flat flakes of limestone chipped off larger building blocks, but more formal drawings, showing how a design was to be transferred to the work in progress, were done in various colored inks on papyrus sheets. One of the few surviving drawings, now in Turin, Italy, shows front and side elevations for a shrine chest. A grid, to establish proportions, was drawn in red ink, while the shrine itself was drawn in black [6.1].

In Mesopotamia, the land watered by the Tigris and Euphrates rivers, plans of buildings were inscribed on clay tablets. One small tablet, about 2.3 by 3.5 inches (6 by 9

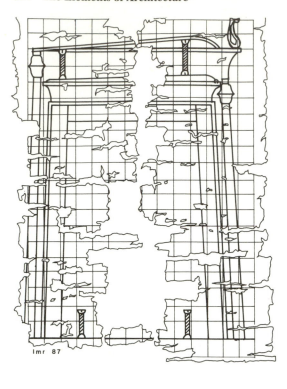

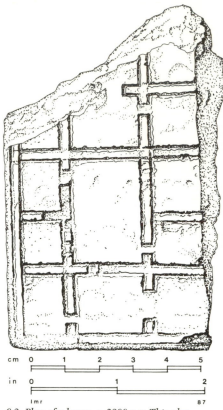

6.1. Reconstruction of an Egyptian papyrus drawing showing the side elevation of a shrine, c. Eighteenth Dynasty (Turin, Italy). The lighter lines (in black ink on the original) are a proportional grid; the heavier lines (red ink) show the profile of the shrine.

6.2. Plan of a house, c. 2300 B.C. This plan, inscribed on a clay tablet, shows the thickness of the house walls. The tablet was found in Tell Asmar, Iraq (the ancient city of Eshnunna).

centimeters), made about 2300 B.C., shows what appears to be a house plan, indicating the thickness of the walls and the placement of doors [6.2]. Two official portrait statues of the Sumerian ruler Gudea of Lagash, about 2200 B.C., show him holding a plaque on his lap engraved with the plan of a building [6.3]. As in Egypt, in Sumerian cities and later in the Babylonian Empire, buildings were devised and built by the rulers and the priests.

The word *architect* is Greek, and its components—*arkhi*, "chief," and *tektōn*, "builder" or "craftsman"—indicate that to the Greeks the architect was far from being a priest or "greatest of the great." As Plato wrote in *Politicus*, architects were not workmen but directors of workmen, and consequently they possessed theoretical knowledge as well as practical skills. None-

theless, they were artisans, not priests. Still, one of the first Greek architects has the mythical quality of Imhotep. Daedalus, who is credited with designing the labyrinth where the Minotaur lived on Crete, was also a sculptor and inventor; he devised the apparatus that enabled Queen Pasiphaë to mate with a bull, resulting in the Minotaur. The word *daedalus* means in Greek "cunning worker" or "skillful one." When he fell into political disfavor, Daedalus fashioned wings so that he and his son, Icarus, might fly to Sicily. In the legend, when Icarus flew too close to the sun the wax holding his feathers melted and he fell into the sea. Daedalus made it to Sicily, where he built an underground steam bath for King Kokkalos.[4]

Real-life Greek architects lived far more prosaic lives, and although we know the names of more than a hundred, we can piece together almost nothing of their lives.[5] Official legal descriptions of buildings survive in detailed inscriptions, but we have none of the Greek theoretical treatises Vitruvius said he consulted, nor do we have any drawings. Some scholars have suggested that Greek architects made no drawings as we think of them, suggesting that they worked in the stone yard in close connection with the masons and had little need for abstract drawings.[6]

The position of the architect rose during the Roman Empire, as architecture became a more important symbolic statement. Cicero classed the architect with the physician and the teacher (*De officiis,* 1.151) and Vitruvius speaks of "so great a profession as this" (*De architectura* 1.1.11). Vitruvius (c. 90–c. 20 B.C.), a practicing architect during the reign of Augustus Caesar, recognized that architecture required both practical and theoretical knowledge, and he listed the disciplines he felt the aspiring architect should master: literature and writing, draftsmanship, mathematics, history, philosophy, music, medicine, law, and astronomy—a curriculum that still has much to recommend it. All of this was necessary, he wrote, because

> architects who have aimed at acquiring manual skill without scholarship have never been able to reach a position of authority to correspond to their plans, while those who relied only upon theories and scholarship were obviously hunting the shadow, not the substance.[7]

The practice of drawing, as described by Vitruvius, also sounds remarkably modern, for he writes of ground plans (*ichnographia*) being laid out with compass and ruler, of elevation drawings (*orthographia*) being "a vertical image of the front," and of perspectives (*scaenographia*) with shaded and

6.3. *Portrait figure of Gudea of Lagash, c. 2200 B.C. Resting on the lap of this ruler of Lagash is an inscribed plan of a building.*

6.4. Cubiculum (bedroom) from Villa Boscoreale, Italy. Buried by the eruption of Mount Vesuvius in A.D. 79, this room has been restored in the Metropolitan Museum of Art, New York; its wall paintings illustrate well the skill of Roman perspective draftsmanship.

retreating sides converging on a vanishing point. Although none of these architectural drawings survive, splendid examples of wall painting from Pompeii attest to the skill of Roman draftsmen [6.4]. In addition, there are a number of building plans engraved in stone, including one particularly interesting engraved plan of what may have been a funerary monument, dating from the middle of the first century A.D.

The building trades in Roman cities became more highly organized as well, and gradually became subject to government control. Each building operation had its *collegium,* or trade organization—blacksmiths and ironworkers, brick makers, carpenters, stone workers, general construction workers, and even demolition experts. Brick making was standardized, and for over a century bricks were stamped with the abbreviated names of the reigning consuls and the brick maker, making it possible to date Roman buildings. The process of construction and the deployment of the building trades were highly organized, particularly important for the building of

scaffolding and centering and for timing the laying and curing of concrete.

One of the last architects in the tradition described by Vitruvius was Anthemios of Tralles, born in western Asia Minor sometime before A.D. 500 and who died about 540; he was the designer of the church of Hagia Sophia in Constantinople, working closely with the architect-engineer Isidoros of Miletos.[8] He came from a distinguished family; his father was a well-known physician, as were two of his brothers, and another brother practiced law in Rome. Anthemios was an architect, an engineer, a geometrician, and a physicist. He wrote on mathematics and may have been the first to describe how to draw an ellipse by using a loop of string around two pins.

In the extolling of the piety of the Middle Ages, many misconceptions have arisen as to the medieval architect; for example, that he was a selfless, uneducated master mason, that he worked from no plans, using strictly traditional knowledge, and that he gloried in his anonymity. There is some basis for these notions, but they are far from the truth.

Admittedly, abbots of monasteries or their historians tended to downplay the contributions of their designing masons when writing of their accomplishments.

State sponsorship of building had dropped rapidly in the western part of the Roman Empire after the fifth century A.D. Only about 800, with the amalgamation of a new empire under Charlemagne, did building begin again on an ambitious scale. One particularly pressing need was the construction of new monastic communities. One of the most important documents of early medieval architecture is a drawing done about 814 on parchment showing how an ideal monastery might be laid out [6.5, 6.6]. Specially prepared by Abbott Haito of the monastery at Reichenau, it was sent to his colleague Abbot Gozbertus at the monastery of Saint Gallen, or Saint Gall, Switzerland, who was planning on building a new monastic complex.[9] The ink drawing is on several sections of parchment sewn together to form a large sheet roughly 44 by 30 inches (112 by 77

centimeters) and is one of the oldest surviving medieval drawings. Such drawings on sheepskin were used during the Middle Ages, but because the parchment was so valuable it was sometimes scraped clean and reused, or turned over and other documents written on the back; several drawings survive for this reason, having been filed away in monastic libraries under the heading of the manuscript written on the back. This is exactly how the Saint Gall plan survived, for in the late twelfth century another monk inscribed on the back side the *Life of Saint Martin* and then folded it several times to book size.

The *collegia* of workmen survived the fall of the Roman Empire, gradually becoming the guilds of the Middle Ages. These were vitally important organizations, not only providing training for youths but also providing a network for the transmission of ideas across Europe; medieval masons traveled extensively from one masons' guild lodge to another, viewing work under way

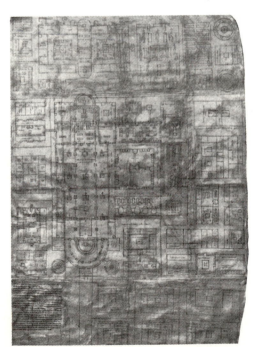

6.5. *Plan at Saint Gall, Switzerland, c. 814. Photograph of the original parchment drawing, c. 112 × 77 centimeters, Library of the Monastery of Saint Gall, Switzerland.*

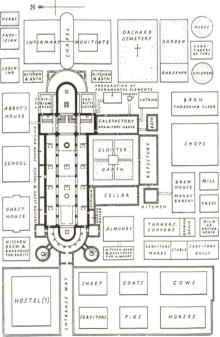

6.6. *Plan at Saint Gall. Layout of the various buildings. Diagram by Kenneth Conant.*

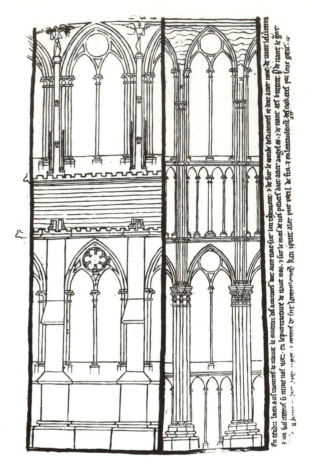

6.7. *Villard de Honnecourt, exterior and interior elevation drawings of Notre-Dame de Reims, Reims, France, c. 1220. This page, from the travel sketchbook of this medieval mason, tells much about the travels of medieval builders, how knowledge was dispersed among brothers in the crafts guilds, and how medieval artists abstracted symbolic images instead of making literal images.*

and jotting down personal observations. Villard de Honnecourt assembled just such a "scrapbook" with eighty-two pages originally, intending to make it available to other guild members.[10] He was born in northern France and trained as a stonemason. About 1190, he became a journeyman while working on the cathedral at Vaucelles, which he drew in his book. He traveled to Reims and Chartres, and about 1220 set out for Hungary to aid in the construction of a monastery there. On his return trip he stopped in Reims, where he assisted in building the cathedral, making a number of drawings of the interior and the exterior of the choir [6.7]. Other drawings showed roof framing, pulpits, ornamental carving, and a perpetual motion machine, with disarming notes such as "This is good masonry" and "I drew it because I like it best."

One reason the role of the medieval archi-

tect became poorly understood may have been due to the many titles used. In addition to *architectus* and *magister* (master, maestro, *Meister*) for master mason, we find *ingeniator* (engineer), *artifex, operarius, mechanicus,* and also words more directly connected with stonework—such as *lapicida, cementarius, lathomus.* The inscription on the gravestone of Pierre de Montreuil, designer of parts of the abbey church of Saint-Denis and of Notre-Dame in Paris, who died in 1254, describes him as *doctor lathomorum,* or professor of freemasons. By the mid-thirteenth century, master masons were accorded a position of privilege and were buried with honors, as is evident in the gravestone of Hugh Libergier, architect of the cathedral in Reims, who died in 1263 [6.8, page 104]. He is shown framed in a trefoil (three-lobed) Gothic arch; in his left hand is a measuring rod, with a mason's square and dividers at his feet, and in his right hand he holds a model of a building. What distinguished the medieval architect-master mason from those of the Renaissance, Baroque, and modern periods that followed was this: as workmen trained in stone-cutting or carpentry, they understood from the inside out how a building was put together. When they undertook contracts to erect buildings, they functioned as both designer and contractor/builder.

The nature of the medieval master craftsman-architect must be understood, as well as the established position of the construction guilds, to appreciate the revolutionary change brought about by the Renaissance. In a list of the most important Renaissance designers, such as Filippo Brunelleschi, Leon Battista Alberti, Donato Bramante, Michelangelo Buonarroti, Giulio Romano, Sebastiano Serlio, there is not one trained architect in the medieval sense of the word. In the fifteenth century, with the rise of Classical humanism and the study of ancient literature, the ideal individual was one who mastered all the liberal arts, and the master craftsman-architect was replaced by the humanist artist. Nearly all of the major architects in Italy after 1400 were trained as painters, sculptors, or goldsmiths; like Leonardo da Vinci or Michelangelo, they worked in all the arts. In the Middle Ages, scholars and teachers were considered to profess a learned discipline, whereas builders, painters, and goldsmiths were viewed as merely practicing a craft. Renaissance architects sought to change that and to elevate their position.

In 1505, Donato Bramante (1444–1514) began construction of the immense new basilica of Saint Peter in Rome, replacing the ancient church built by Constantine in 333.[11] The plan of the church was derived from the new theoretical and geometric ideals of the Renaissance, meant to symbolize God's omniscience and omnipresence as well as to celebrate the intelligence He had given humankind. It was to be a vast Greek cross within a square, centered on four huge piers carrying pendentives and a gigantic dome rivaling that of the Roman Pantheon.

Bramante, then sixty-one years of age, started work on the piers, but died leaving only the arches silhouetted against the sky [16.23]. At the same time, Bramante's patron, Pope Julius II, was having Bramante's nephew, Raphael Santi, paint four mural frescoes in the adjoining Vatican Palace. In one of the semicircular panels, Raphael depicted the gathering together of all the great Greek philosophers, arranged in two groups about the central figures, Plato and Aristotle [6.9]. Those who pursued Platonic abstraction were arranged on the left (stage right), while those who favored observation of natural phenomena were associated with Aristotle on the right (stage left). The figures descend stairs and terraces in an architectural setting of immense proportions, of Classical piers and vaults supporting pendentives and a circular colonnade silhouetted against the sky. This hypothetical building, exemplifying Greek ideals and Greek philosophy, is in fact the incomplete shell of the new Saint Peter's. On the Aristotelian right, bending over to work out a theorem on a slate, is the figure of Euclid, the great geometer—it is a portrait of Donato Bramante (Raphael even included himself, peeking toward the viewer on the far right side). And on the Platonic left side, brooding over a block of stone in the foreground, is the figure of Michelangelo (who at that time was painting the ceiling of the Sistine Chapel). The artist-architect of the new epoch was therefore to be seen as the equivalent of the ancient philosophers—but he was a philosopher in pigment and stone.

The ideal to which many aspired was achieved by Leon Battista Alberti (1404–1472), a humanist scholar and theorist.[12] His designs for churches and palaces set the standard for architecture for the next two hundred years, but he did not construct his own buildings, relying on the mason Matteo de' Pasti to translate his instructions into stone. On the one hand, this meant that ever afterward architects were removed from the constructive process; but on the other, it meant they were freed from working only with established conventions to pursue intellectual exploration and creative artistry—what the Italians called *disegno*.

6.9. Raphael, School of Athens *fresco, Stanza della Segnatura, Vatican Palace, Rome, 1509–11. In this painting praising human intellect, Raphael depicted all the great Greek philosophers grouped around the central figures of Plato and Aristotle. Many of the faces are portraits of living Italian artists and architects, and the setting is the unfinished shell of Bramante's new Basilica of Saint Peter.*

The Renaissance was a period of intense intellectual probing, of the reexamination of Classical literature, art, and architecture. The Renaissance artist-architect shared in this curiosity. Beginning with Brunelleschi, architects made the pilgrimage to ancient Rome, then a sleepy medieval town greatly shrunken from its imperial grandeur, to study and measure Roman ruins. They proposed to equal or surpass the artistic achievement of antiquity, but not to make literal copies of ancient architecture. The great irony is that, although they measured and recorded much, they also destroyed much; the modern notion of historic preservation had no attraction for them.

The Renaissance was able to sweep across Europe by means of the printed page. Printing with movable type spelled the end of medieval orthodoxy and the rule of tradition; architects soon took advantage of this new technology.[13] In the 1440s, Alberti first wrote a manuscript in Latin, *De re aedificatoria,* in ten books patterned after Vitruvius, aimed at improving the taste of classically educated patrons. It was published in Latin in 1485, then in translations of vernacular Italian in 1546 and 1550. Meanwhile numerous editions of Vitruvius had begun to appear in the original Latin, some of them illustrated (Leonardo's drawing of the man in the circle and square, Figure 16.3, was one such illustration). An Italian translation followed in 1521. In rapid succession other original treatises appeared in Spanish, French, and German, along with translations of Vitruvius into various European languages. These were aimed not only at the potential patron, but at the practicing architect and builder. Detailed descriptions on how to proportion each of the Classical orders were provided in the books published by Sebastiano Serlio and Giacomo da Vignola [6.10].

The career and the book of Andrea Palladio (1508–1580) summarize well the goal of the Renaissance architect—the creation of ordered and balanced architecture that might serve as an example for subsequent architects. Palladio, however, is the exception; since he was the son of a miller, he was not classically educated but apprenticed to a stonemason.[14] He worked in Vicenza, not far from Venice, where his abilities attracted the attention of a wealthy and cultivated humanist nobleman, Giangiorgio Trissino, who made Palladio his protégé, tutored him in Vitruvius, and took him to Rome several times to measure Roman buildings. Palladio also later worked closely with Daniele Barbaro in illustrating a translation of Vitruvius. The result of this combination of practical wisdom and theoretical study was that Palladio's architecture was clear in its harmonic mathematical proportions and direct in its form. Palladio published a four-volume work, in Italian, *I quattro libri dell' architettura,* or *The Four Books on Architecture* (Venice, 1570), which presented plans and elevations of his best work around Vicenza, as well as restorations of some of the major Roman ruins [6.11]. Of all architectural books except that of Vitruvius, Palladio's has had the greatest continuing impact; translations and new editions appeared through the eighteenth century, and the English translation of 1738 is still published in paperback.

During the Renaissance there evolved architectural working methods similar to those used in design and construction today. Numerous drawings have survived, on parchment and paper, showing sketches, plan studies, elevations, details, and perspectives. Leonardo da Vinci seems to have invented the technique of drawing small aerial perspectives suggesting both plan and building masses at the same time. Curiously, although Renaissance architects were inventing a new architectural language, one that the traditionally trained workmen did not at first understand, there are few surviving drawings for use in the field showing ornamental details. Models were the preferred method of showing how work was to be done, and a number of these detailed

wooden models survive, including Michelangelo's model for completing the dome of Saint Peter's in Rome.

During the fifteenth century, in Spain and France, this renewed Classical architectural idiom was exploited to create a royal architecture, and in France this necessitated the formation of a corps of architects and builders to carry out the many royal building projects—the Royal Building Administration. By the time of the reign of Louis XIV, in the seventeenth century, this had become a large organization, administered by Jean-Baptiste Colbert, Louis's chief minister. Under Colbert was Louis Le Vau, the king's

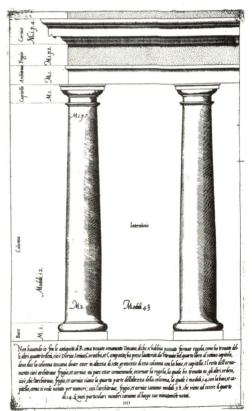

6.10. Giacomo Barozzi da Vignola, the Tuscan Doric order, Plate 4 from *Regola delli cinque ordini d'architettura,* Book IV (Rome, 1562). *This book, along with others by Sebastiano Serlio, Vincenzo Scamozzi, and Claude Perrault, made the proportions of the Classical orders available to builders and gentlemen amateur architects. Vignola's plates were the first to show the relative proportions of each order based on the diameter of the column.*

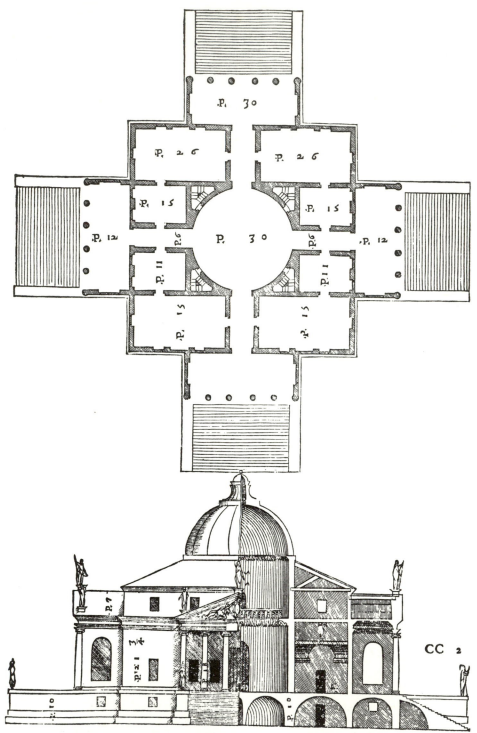

6.11. *Andrea Palladio, Villa Capra (Villa Rotonda), outside Vicenza, Italy, c. 1550. Plate 13 from Book II of Palladio's* Four Books of Architecture. *The English version, edited by Isaac Ware (London, 1738), carried Palladio's influence throughout Great Britain and to the American colonies.*

6.12. *Gianlorenzo Bernini, first design for the east facade of the Louvre, Paris, 1664–65, ink on paper. Bernini's curved and sculpturally molded facade incorporated the latest in Italian plasticity but was rejected by the French.*

chief architect, and under him scores of lesser designers and administrators who worked on Versailles, Marly, and the many other royal building projects. Aside from the continuing expansion of the royal château and village at Versailles, the other major building project was the extension of the royal residence in Paris, the Louvre. Begun in 1547 and continued in 1624 for Louis XIII, it had proceeded in several stages under different royal architects, until the interior court had been completely enclosed by Le Vau. The east front, however, the principal face toward the city of Paris, had not been finished, and in 1665 a competition was held to obtain the best design. Various French and Italian architects submitted entries; the winning design was the work of

the most famous Roman architect of the day, Gian Lorenzo Bernini [6.12]. His artistic reputation was such that, in journeying to Paris, Bernini was honored in cities along the way with festivities that rivaled treatment given kings and princes. He made a triumphal entry into Paris, modified his design at the request of Colbert, and then returned home. Work began on the foundations, but very soon Bernini's scheme was scrapped and a final, eighth design was prepared by a committee composed of the king's architect Le Vau, the king's painter Charles Le Brun, and Claude Perrault, a physician well known for his architectural studies [6.13].

The confusion and mis-starts on the east front of the Louvre suggested that French

6.13. *Claude Perrault, Louis Le Vau, and Charles Le Brun, east wing, the Louvre, Paris, 1667–71. This restrained design, developed by a committee of architects, was considered more appropriate in expressing the French character.*

architects did not have the training to provide the kind of grand symbolic designs the king and his ministers wanted. The result was the establishment of the Royal Academy of Architecture in 1671, which grew during the eighteenth century, was reorganized as the École des Beaux-Arts during the French Revolution, and provided architectural instruction for students around the world during the nineteenth and early twentieth centuries. In France this meant that the path to success in the profession required study at the École, and, ideally, winning the culminating and coveted Grand Prix de Rome, which ensured the recipient thereafter of public building commissions and an appointment to teach students at the École.

The course of architectural education in England (and by extension in the United States) was much different. During the eighteenth century, English buildings were designed either by gentleman amateurs, widely traveled and read in Classical literature and architecture, or by professional architects trained in architects' offices but with little or no theoretical education.[15] An excellent example of the former is Richard Boyle, Third Earl of Burlington (1694–1753), an aristocratic patron who made many trips to Italy, particularly to the region around Venice, where he closely studied the work of Palladio. In England, he built for himself Chiswick House, 1725, closely patterned on Palladio's Villa Rotonda, and championed the cause of Palladian architecture [18.1]. An example of the professional architect would be Henry Holland (1745–1806), an architect and builder educated by his father, also an architect.

6.14. Sir John Soane, breakfast room, Soane House (Soane Museum), Lincoln's Inn Fields, London, 1812–13. In the rooms of his own house, Soane experimented with techniques of day lighting he then used in the Bank of England.

6.15. Benjamin Henry Latrobe, Baltimore Cathedral, 1804–21. Longitudinal section/elevation, 1805. The meticulous colored drawing testifies to Latrobe's professional training in England and to the care with which he specified all the details of the design.

Sir John Soane (1753–1837) represents a fusion of these two types, and his career marks the emergence of the modern architect in England.[16] Soane was the son of a builder; he was trained in the architectural offices of George Dance the Younger and Henry Holland. While working in Holland's office, Soane attended lectures on art at the new Royal Academy of Arts and participated in the design competitions it sponsored. He won a gold medal in such a competition in 1776 and was sent on a tour of Italy. In 1788 he was appointed architect to the Bank of England, a position that kept him occupied for the remainder of his life, although he had a great deal of additional work as well. This combination of practical experience and theoretical education set Soane's work apart, and his ingenious solutions to structural and lighting problems marked a new direction in architecture [6.14]. At the same time, however, he conscientiously supervised the training of young architects in his office, approximately forty in all, for in England (and in the United States) the normal way to become an architect was to spend a period as an apprentice and assistant in an architect's office.

In England's American colonies during the eighteenth century, buildings were designed by gentleman amateurs such as Peter Harrison, merchant turned architect, and Thomas Jefferson, who taught himself Italian so he could read Palladio in the original language. After 1790 several professionally trained architects emigrated from Europe, among them Joseph-Jacques Ramée and Joseph-François Maguin, but the architect who had the most significant impact was Benjamin Henry Latrobe, who arrived from England in 1797.[17] With the arrival of Latrobe, the United States had its first professional architect in the modern sense—an individual who makes a living solely by designing buildings for others to construct; who has received practical and theoretical training (academically, in an office, and on the job site); who supervises construction to make certain it follows the plans agreed on; and who is paid a monetary fee based on the cost of the building being constructed (rather than being paid in goods or services). Working with carpenters' companies and builders rooted in the medieval guild tradition, Latrobe encountered resistance to the rights he claimed as an architect. Once, when he was away from Baltimore on business and unable to supervise work on the Baltimore cathedral, designed in 1804 [6.15], the builder changed aspects of the building. Upon his return Latrobe threatened to resign unless his contract drawings were followed explicitly. Latrobe won this challenge to his authority.

There were no architectural schools in the United States in the early nineteenth century, so aspiring architects trained themselves as best they could, working for other architects. Latrobe trained William Strickland, who in turn trained Thomas U. Walter. American architects faced a problem unknown to their European counterparts—the dispersal of their jobs over a much vaster landscape. Because Ithiel Town traveled extensively, supervising the construction of bridges that employed a truss pattern he patented, in 1829 he took into full partnership Alexander Jackson Davis, thereby creating the first architectural firm. Thereafter, architectural firms with two and three partners became increasingly common in the United States. Although national and municipal architectural agencies were known in Europe, such private architecture firms were rare there until well into the twentieth century.

By the mid-nineteenth century, American architects had begun to attend the École des Beaux-Arts in Paris, beginning with Richard Morris Hunt in 1845 and Henry Hobson Richardson in 1860. At the turn of the century, Americans made up the largest single group of non-French students at the École. These American graduates of the French school combined the sensitivity to plan organization and expression of building character they learned there with their Yankee pragmatism and practicality. Architecture firms that exemplified these attributes were Adler & Sullivan of Chicago (Sullivan attended the École) and McKim, Mead & White of New York (McKim had been at the École). Meanwhile, schools of architecture were established in the United States during the 1870s at the Massachusetts Institute of Technology, Cambridge, and the University of Illinois, Urbana, and French instructors were brought over to apply École teaching methods.

By the end of the nineteenth century, the character of the modern architectural profession had been established, and the question concerning the social responsibility of the architect had begun to emerge. It is a question that has remained unresolved ever since. Should the architect assume the position of an activist and attempt to reform society, to shape environments according to how life *ought* to be lived (in the view of the architect); or should the architect reflect prevailing social values and shape environments according to how life actually *is* lived? Environments carefully designed to realize the architect's philosophical ideal have too frequently turned out, in the long run, to be very poor living environments. The best known example is the Pruitt-Igoe housing complex in Saint Louis, Missouri, built in 1952–55, which provided residents no sense of identity and did not allow them to supervise their immediate environment. It became so dangerous to live in that portions had to be demolished in 1972.[18] Since roughly 1965 architects have begun to take a more enlightened and inclusive approach. For example, some architects have begun to discover that ancient traditional building methods and forms may have distinct practical advantages in the twentieth century, such as the traditional mud brick architecture of Egypt rediscovered and put to new use by the Egyptian architect Hassan Fathy.[19] Mud brick is readily made, cheap, provides thermal protection, and works exceedingly well in dry climates.

The desire to find absolute answers to philosophical questions, to invent a universal and pure architecture, is our idealistic legacy from the Renaissance. Perhaps it would be more appropriate for us to scrutinize each building task as it arises to see what opportunities it provides for creating a dialogue with the past as well as a legacy for the future.

NOTES

1. See Alexander Badawy, "Imhotep," *Macmillan Encyclopedia of Architects* 2:455–64.
2. See Alexander Badawy, "Senmut," *Macmillan Encyclopedia of Architects* 4:33–37.
3. See T.G.H. James, *Pharaoh's People* (Chicago, 1984), and John Romer, *Ancient Lives: Daily Life in Egypt of the Pharaohs* (New York, 1984), for discussions of the lives of the workmen at Deir el-Medina.
4. Daedalus' exploits are described by Apollodorus and Ovid; see the narrative account in Edith Hamilton, *Mythology* (Boston, 1940).
5. See J. J. Coulton, *Ancient Greek Architects at Work: Problems of Structure and Design* (Ithaca, N.Y., 1977).
6. Lothar Haselberger recently suggested that lines engraved on the walls of the Temple of Apollo at Didyma are in fact drawings for proportioning the columns; see *Scientific American* 253 (December 1985): 126–32.
7. Vitruvius, *Ten Books on Architecture,* 1.1.2, trans. Morris Hicky Morgan (Cambridge, Mass., 1914).
8. See William L. MacDonald, "Anthemios," *Macmillan Encyclopedia of Architecture* 1:84–87.
9. Walter Horn and Ernest Born, *The Plan of St. Gall,* 3 vols. (Berkeley, 1979); this exhaustive analysis of the plan is summarized in Lorna Price, *The Plan of St. Gall: In Brief* (Berkeley, 1982). More recent research has indicated that contrary to what Horn writes the plan was not prepared as an outgrowth of a council of abbots in 816–17, it was not a copy of another drawing, and it was not meant as an exemplar of monasteries to be built throughout Charlemagne's empire. See Warren Sanderson, "The Plan of St. Gall Reconsidered," *Speculum* 60 (July 1985): 615–32.
10. See François Bucher, "Villard de Honnecourt." *Macmillan Encyclopedia of Architects* 4:322–24; and Theodore Bowie, ed., *The Sketchbook of Villard de Honnecourt* (Bloomington, Ind., 1959).
11. See Peter Murray, "Donato Bramante," *Macmillan Encyclopedia of Architects* 1:269–82.
12. See Eugene J. Johnson, "Leon Battista Alberti," *Macmillan Encyclopedia of Architects* 1:48–58.
13. For a discussion of architectural treatises, see Dora Wiebenson, *Architectural Theory and Practice from Alberti to Ledoux* (Chicago, 1982).
14. See James Ackerman, *Palladio* (Baltimore, 1966), as well as Douglas Lewis, *The Drawings of Andrea Palladio* (Washington, D.C., 1982).
15. "Amateur" is used here in its original sense (from Latin, *amator,* Latin, "a lover"), meaning a person who pursues an activity as a pastime, for the pleasure it provides, rather than as a profession.
16. See Dorothy Stroud, "John Soane," *Macmillan Encyclopedia of Architects* 4:95–101.
17. See Samuel Wilson, Jr., "Benjamin H. Latrobe," *Macmillan Encyclopedia of Architects* 2:611–17.
18. For the reasons Pruitt-Igoe failed, see Oscar Newman, *Defensible Space* (New York, 1972).
19. See the assessment in J. M. Richards, Ismail Serageldin, and Darl Rastorfer, *Hassan Fathy* (Singapore and London, 1985).

SUGGESTED READING

Martin S. Briggs, *The Architect in History* (Oxford, 1927); somewhat dated but still very useful.

Edmund B. Feldman, *The Artist* (Englewood Cliffs, N.J., 1982), surveys the parallel history of the painter and the sculptor.

Spiro Kostof, ed., *The Architect: Chapters in the History of the Profession* (New York, 1977); now the basic resource, it consists of chapters written by experts in their respective fields.

Leland M. Roth, *America Builds: Source Documents in American Architecture and Planning* (New York, 1983); includes partial transcript of the suit, 1861, brought by R. H. Hunt against E. Parmly for nonpayment of architect's fees.

———, *A Concise History of American Architecture* (New York, 1979).

Andrew Saint, *The Image of the Architect* (New Haven, Conn., 1983); examines the self-image of the architect in the nineteenth and twentieth centuries, including a discussion of the fictional architect Howard Roark in Ayn Rand's novel *The Fountainhead,* 1943.

7.10. *Le Corbusier, High Court Building, Chandigarh, Punjab, India, 1951–56. Detail of facade. The deeply recessed windows and the extra parasol roof keep the intense subtropical sun away from the interior rooms—a simple nontechnical solution to a pressing problem.*

CHAPTER 7

Architecture as Part of the Environment

... an effective relationship of building to earth is fundamental to architecture.

Stanley Abercrombie, *Architecture as Art,* 1984

Another part of our legacy from the Renaissance is the tendency to think of buildings only as objects of social or artistic significance, but not, until recently, as objects with environmental significance. Landscape architects escape this shortsightedness since they deal with living objects, and their success as designers depends on whether they know that the soil and the climate in a particular area will support the plant materials they propose to use. Especially after the development of effective heating, ventilation, and air conditioning equipment about the turn of the century, architects in the industrialized West stopped thinking about such concerns as sun exposure, wind patterns, and prevailing temperature because they felt confident that, given enough equipment, they could overcome any difficulty. There was a price to be paid, of course, but that was borne by the client and the user in the long years after the completion of the building, and architects did not worry much about that.

Once a building is built it becomes as much a part of the environment as a tree or a rock. This fact has double importance. First, it means that the architect needs to consider, at all steps of the design process, how the proposed building will affect its setting, whether an urban context or a natural landscape. Does the proposed building augment and enhance the existing context, or does it stand in distinct and deliberate con-

trast to the context? Second, once completed, the building is subject to the same incessant effects of sun, rain, and time as everything else in the environment. There are those cases in which the patron and the architect wish to make a deliberate statement, as in the case of temporary exhibition buildings, and place their lowest priority on how a building responds to environmental concerns. But for other, seemingly permanent buildings, it would seem to make good sense to consider the impact environmental forces have on a building, as well as the effect the building has on its immediate microenvironment.

Buildings by so-called primitive peoples almost invariably reveal subtle and sophisticated responses to the environment. Consider, for example, the thick adobe construction of the typical house in the American Southwest, a material and construction technique similar to that used north of the Sahara from Morocco to Egypt and in other places with similar climate. The problem is the constant exposure to the sun, which in June radiates 2,750 British thermal units (Btu) of energy per day on one square foot.[1] Translated, that means that a roof in Albuquerque, New Mexico, at 35° latitude, measuring 10 feet to a side (100 square feet or 9.3 square meters), receives enough energy each day to raise the temperature of 4 tons of water (8,000 pounds) from 66° F to 100° F. It is a significant amount of heat.

One way of dramatically cutting down that heat gain is to prevent the sun from touching the roof, as the Anasazi people did nine hundred years ago in building their vil-

121

7.1. *Anasazi village, Mesa Verde, Colorado, c. 1100. These closely clustered houses were pushed just far enough back so that the overhang of the cliff provided shade at midday during the hot summer months.*

lages up in the recesses of caves, as at Mesa Verde, in southwestern Colorado [7.1]. The houses are positioned just far enough back that, in summer, the overhang of the cliff prevents the sun from reaching the roof surfaces. In the winter, however, the low-slanting sun reaches to the back of the cave. But if no cliffs are nearby, an alternative is to put a large mass of material between the dwelling space and the sun so that the mass slows down the absorption of heat, just as the thick mud brick walls and roofs of adobe construction do [7.2]. Even when the afternoon temperature reaches 140° F on the surface of the roof, the internal temperature

of the room is 80° F rising gradually to 85° at 9:00 P.M.; and when the outside temperature plummets to 60° at 2:00 A.M., the internal temperature of the room will be easing down from 80° to a low of 75° at 8:00 A.M. the next morning [7.3].[2] In traditional adobe construction, the windows and doors were kept intentionally small to prevent hot drafts from entering and disturbing the relatively cool temperatures inside. And, of course, if a number of such rooms are piled atop one another, those at the core of the pile will remain quite cool, as is the case in such pueblos as Taos, New Mexico.

As the Inuit (Eskimos) of the Arctic and

the Mandan discovered, building mass works just as well for cold temperatures. The Mandan, who lived along the Missouri River before the arrival of Europeans, built large, round houses with an internal wooden frame on which earth was heaped to a thickness of 1½ feet at the top. This thick insulation prevented the searing heat of late summer from penetrating to the interior and it kept the most frigid winter winds from lowering the internal temperature (the low, round form also presented the least resistance to the wind). In the most severe Arctic climate, there is neither wood nor earth, and so the winter dwelling of the Inuit is built of packed snow cut into blocks and laid in a closing spiral to form a dome— the igloo [7.4]. Entry is through a barrel-vaulted tunnel, made of snow blocks, that comes up from beneath the igloo; the tunnel is blocked with numerous hide curtains to keep out the wind. The thick snow also acts as a thermal barrier, and the whiteness of the snow and the dome shape may help to reflect heat back into the center of the igloo, so that when the outside temperature fluctuates from −10° to −30° F, the internal temperature in the upper half of the igloo

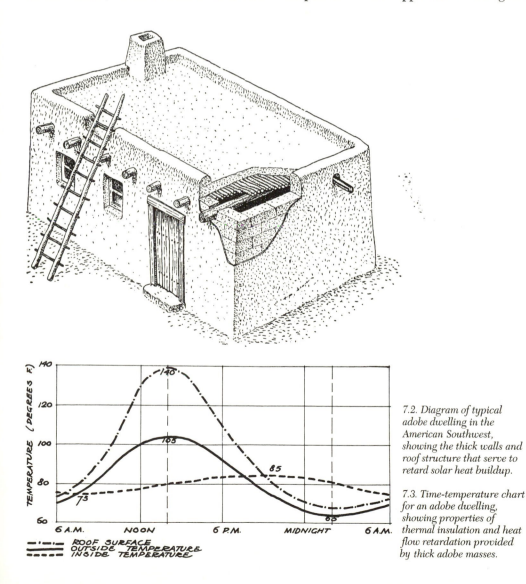

7.2. *Diagram of typical adobe dwelling in the American Southwest, showing the thick walls and roof structure that serve to retard solar heat buildup.*

7.3. *Time-temperature chart for an adobe dwelling, showing properties of thermal insulation and heat flow retardation provided by thick adobe masses.*

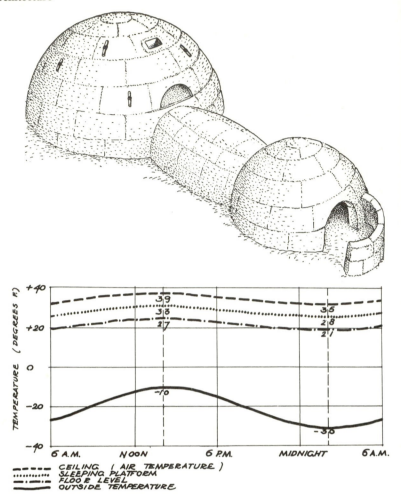

7.4. Diagram of an Inuit (Eskimo) igloo.

7.5. Time-temperature chart for an igloo, showing properties of thermal insulation of packed snow.

will be 35° to 39° F due to the heat generated by a few blubber lamps and the humans themselves [7.5].[3]

The heat generated by the human organism is itself significant. Humans, like all living beings, are in a constant state of slow combustion, but as the human organism can use only about 20 percent of the heat it creates, the rest must be thrown off. Even seated and not moving, the human body dissipates up to 245 Btu's per hour, but moving or working raises this to 580 Btu's per hour.[4] A person doing heavy physical labor, in other words, radiates nearly enough heat in an hour to heat 4 pounds of water from room temperature almost to the boiling point. In the igloo this radiated heat is urgently needed, but in buildings in moder-

ate or hot climates this simply adds to the internal heat load that must be radiated to the outside.

Since 1970, architects and engineers have adapted many of the principles demonstrated in this ancient architecture, devising "new" and yet old ways of heating buildings. For residences it is often possible to use a *passive solar heating system,* in which the solar radiation is allowed to fall on thermal masses, such as brick floors or masonry walls, which soak up the heat and then radiate it back into the building at night. For more precise control, an *active solar heating system* may be installed, using collector panels to absorb solar radiation, a fluid circulating in pipes through the panels to pick up this heat, pumps to move the fluid to another area, a thermal mass (a water reservoir or a mass of rock) to store the moved heat, and an additional secondary system of air ducts or water pipes to carry the heat from the storage mass to the rooms where it is needed. In addition, two electrical sensing systems are needed to turn both the collecting and the secondary systems on and off as required. As the description suggests, it is a complex network of interconnected systems that may fail if any one of its components breaks down.

The solution for keeping a building cool, as the Anasazi pointed out, is to keep the sun off a building, but the development of air-conditioning during 1902–6 by Wallis Haviland Carrier (1876–1950) kept architects from exploiting passive means of preventing solar heat gain until economic pressures and awakening sensibilities caused widespread changes after 1973. It is also possible to keep internal temperatures in a building comfortable by increasing the flow of air through the building, removing heat and encouraging the sensation of being cooled by evaporation of perspiration—in other words, by keeping the light out while letting the air in. This has been done with delicate grace in the Islamic architecture of Iran (ancient Persia) and northern India [7.6]. In these hot locations, windows are covered not with glass but with perforated screens of carved marble, cutting down significantly on the intrusion of light (but creating a dappled pattern within the building) and encouraging the flow of air. Such devices were used throughout the mosques in Isfahan and can be seen clearly in the

7.6. Islamic pierced stone screen. Ustad Abdul Qasim, Masjid-i-Shah Mosque, Isfaham, Persia (Iran), 1611–38.

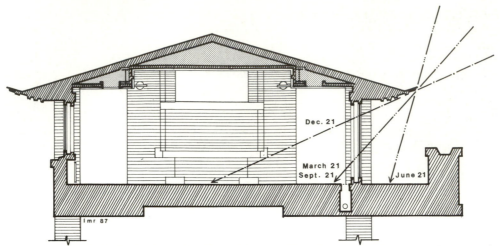

7.7. *Frank Lloyd Wright, Frederick C. Robie House, Chicago, 1908–9. Section of the living room, showing roof overhang and angle of the sun at noon at midsummer, the equinox, and midwinter.*

royal tombs at Agra, India. In designing the United States Embassy in New Delhi, India, 1958, the architect Edward Durell Stone similarly used precast concrete block to prevent direct sunlight from reaching the inner glass envelope; he also used a cantilevered roof to keep much of the sunlight off the wall altogether.

For all the transparency and visual lightness that glass has made possible in architecture, it has also resulted in problems in heat gain. Sunlight, including the invisible infrared portion of the spectrum, easily passes through glass, but once the sunlight strikes a surface in a room, the heat generated can no longer pass back through the glass to the out-of-doors. The result is a gradual heat gain, as was discovered long ago and used to good effect in orangeries and similar glass-enclosed buildings to house tropical plants in the winter—what is commonly called the greenhouse effect. But it occurs in all glass-enclosed buildings, whether intended as greenhouses or not. Again, the solution is to keep the sun off the glass while retaining the view, by using projections outside the wall, either above the window or to the side, depending on the orientation of the window. In addition, these projections need to be proportioned to the latitude of the building. The canvas awning is an example.

Frank Lloyd Wright exploited many of these devices in many of his Prairie houses from 1900 to 1910. In his Robie house of 1907–9, he had no alternative but to orient his building east and west on a narrow Chicago lot; the main facade would face south and was to have a continuous bank of glazed French doors from floor to ceiling [20.4]. He proportioned the roof overhang to the south so that in the summer the sun just misses the edge of the glass [7.7]; and, by greatly extending the roof to the west, he could keep the lower afternoon sun off the west windows as well.[5] George Fred Keck and William Keck, two brother architects of Chicago, pursued this strategy in a series of houses from the mid-1930s through the 1970s, using southerly orientations and carefully calculated roof overhangs to keep sunlight off the window-wall until the cooler months of the year. The Keck brothers were inspired to develop their passively heated buildings as a result of an all-glass house George Fred Keck designed for the Century of Progress exhibition held in Chicago in 1933. During construction in the dead of winter of 1932, the workmen inside had stripped down to shirtsleeves because the glass box acted as a greenhouse.

At almost the same time, the French architect Le Corbusier had a similar experience. He was building a long multistory block with a southern exposure for the Salvation Army in Paris, 1929–33 [7.8]. It was to be fully rational and scientific architecture, its functions analyzed and its form purified; Le Corbusier even spoke of it as an *usine du bien,* or "a factory of goodwill." Its dormitory block was to be a hermetically sealed glass box.[6] Unfortunately, the double glazing and the cooling equipment specified by Le Corbusier were deleted due to cost. The building was opened for use in the winter of 1933, but by the following summer it was a hothouse. The lesson was not lost on Le Corbusier, for in 1936, when he designed the Ministry of Education in Rio de Janeiro, Brazil, in a tropical climate, he added vertical louvers in front of the glass, calling the panels *brise-soleils,* "sun breakers."

If the sun could be kept off the glass, so too could prevailing winds be used to cool a building. When Le Corbusier designed the Unité d'Habitation for Marseilles in 1946,

he used exterior balconies to create horizontal and vertical *brise-soleils,* and by extending the apartment units through the building, he made it possible for residents to open windows at each end and let air flow through [4.15]. And in 1950, when he began work on the new capital buildings for the Punjab in India, again a hot climate, he responded to the nature of the environment. For the High Court at Chandigarh, he used deep *brise-soleils* both vertically and horizontally, and even had a double roof system, with the upper parasol roof carried aloft on spaced piers and cooled by the winds that pass underneath it [7.9; 7.10, page 120].

Perhaps it was because he realized elaborate air-conditioning systems could not always be relied upon that Le Corbusier turned to more integral architectural ways to control the environment in his last buildings. His contemporary, Mies van der Rohe, never felt so compelled, and retained pure

7.8. *Le Corbusier, Cité de Refuge (Salvation Army Hostel), Paris, 1929–33. Like the Robie House, Le Corbusier's Salvation Army Hostel ran east-west, its broad southern glass front exposed to the sun. The heat buildup was to be countered by double glazing and an air-conditioning system, but these were not installed.*

7.9. *Le Corbusier, High Court Building, Chandigarh, Punjab, India, 1951–56. In this semitropical climate, Le Corbusier used the traditional Indian parasol to keep the sun off the roof of the building. The double roof is raised so that breezes can carry away any heat buildup.*

glazed forms and their dependence on extensive mechanical systems. In 1948, when Mies designed the Lake Shore Apartments in Chicago, he was able to have the all-glass wall he had dreamed of since 1919, but the air-conditioning equipment originally specified was deleted to reduce building costs. Limited comfort from the summer heat gain was given by small operable panels in each window bay—but they were placed at the *bottom* instead of the top of the window-wall. In 1954, with the help of an elaborate cooling apparatus atop his Seagram Building [7.11], Mies was able to achieve the sealed box that Le Corbusier had attempted in the Salvation Army building. By the time the Seagram Building was designed, mechanical systems for vertical transportation, lighting, heating, and cooling were consuming more than half the budgets of new buildings. It was as if the building now *was* the mechanical system, wrapped in a membrane. A night view of the Seagram Building shows just how transparent to radiant energy the new architecture was [7.12]. Such buildings proved to be superb sponges of radiant energy in summer afternoons, and excellent radiators of precious heat energy during the long winter nights.

Philip Johnson, Mies's associate architect

in designing the Seagram Building, then shared Mies's purist views. In 1949 he built for himself a glass box weekend house in New Canaan, Connecticut [7.13]. Like Mies, Johnson did not want to compromise the form with the addition of sun screens, but he discovered a "natural" way of having his transparent bubble without roasting in it. He placed the house immediately east and north of a group of mature deciduous oak trees; in the summer their foliage shaded the house, and in the winter, with the leaves dropped, the sun filtered through the bare branches, helping to warm the house. There *was* a way to create an abstract architecture that could still be reconciled to the environment.

Buildings are affected not only by their exposure to the sun but by wind, and they have a reciprocal effect on wind patterns. As moving air encounters an object, it moves over and around it along the path of least resistance. On the windward side a high pressure zone develops, and on the leeward or downwind side a low pressure zone develops. As the wind rises to go over the dome of the Pantheon in Rome, it speeds up and creates a negative pressure that is called the Venturi effect, which draws the air out of the oculus opening at the top. By anticipating prevailing winds, and consider-

7.11. *Ludwig Mies van der Rohe with Philip Johnson, Seagram Building, New York, 1954–58. This building is totally sealed, relying on an extensive heating and cooling system to regulate the temperature.*

7.12. *Seagram Building. This night view reveals how transparent the building is to radiant energy. During the day sunlight passes into the building just as easily as artificial light escapes at night.*

7.13. Philip Johnson, Johnson House, New Canaan, Connecticut, 1945–49. Although the house that Philip Johnson built for himself has walls entirely of glass, it is shaded in the summer by trees to the west and warmed in the winter when sunlight filters through the bare branches.

ing building form and orientation, outside movement of the air can be used effectively to ventilate and cool. In Iraq and Pakistan, traditional houses are built with air scoops on the roofs to catch prevailing winds and provide ventilation.

So long as buildings were relatively low and built with thick walls, the mass of the building was enough to resist lateral forces exerted by the wind. In low masonry buildings, the lateral forces generated by wind pressure are less significant than the vertical forces generated by gravity. This remained generally true until the mid-nineteenth century, when, as building volumes increased and the mass of material diminished, buildings such as the Crystal Palace and the great train sheds began to behave like bubbles in the wind.[7] Suddenly the lateral forces caused by the wind began to sur-

pass the downward forces generated by gravity. The lacy ironwork of Joseph Paxton's Crystal Palace in London, 1851, had to be stiffened by diagonal braces, making the building a vast truss [19.20]. When the skyscraper was first developed in Chicago in the 1880s, architects turned to Paxton's techniques and tied together the steel framing members with diagonals, creating a trussed spine through the center of the building. Then, in the mid-1960s, as a new generation of skyscrapers rose to heights of one hundred stories, or nearly 1,000 feet (304 meters), architects and engineers began to view them as vertical cantilevers whose principal structural task was to resist lateral wind pressure. The resulting buildings were not braced frames but rather rigid tubes.[8] The tapered Hancock Center in Chicago, 1965–70, is an example [7.14].

Large buildings and especially groups of modern skyscrapers also have an effect on wind patterns. As the wind nears a tall building, some of it rises over the building, creating an updraft on the windward side and a downdraft on the leeward side. Some of it goes down and, as it nears the ground, turns around the building. As a result, under the right conditions at sidewalk level, there may be hurricane-force winds that make walking nearly impossible. At times the negative pressure may be great enough to suck windows out of their frames.

Viewed in this way, skyscrapers affect the movement of air just like massive forms in nature, such as mountains. In a way sky-scrapers are man-made mountains, and like mountains they are incessantly worn down by heat, frost, galvanic action, and all the other agents of nature that are forever building up and tearing down. In addition, for more than a century, buildings have been assaulted by chemicals wantonly dumped in the atmosphere. It is the architect's task to select materials and to detail the ways they are joined so the building may endure these attacks for whatever is the desired period. The Egyptians of the Fourth Dynasty thought it right and proper to build the Valley Temple for their Pharaoh Khafre of red granite so as to last him through eternity, and it has stood unyielding to nature

7.14. *Skidmore, Owings and Merrill, John Hancock Center, Chicago, 1965–70. In buildings of great height, the lateral pressure of the wind becomes a more significant structural design factor than vertical gravity-generated forces; hence, as in the Hancock Center, diagonal bracing stiffens each of the external vertical columns.*

7.15. I. M. Pei, John Hancock Tower, Boston, 1966–75. The failure of modern architecture was graphically illustrated by the plywood sheets used to replace the windows of the Hancock Tower sucked out by turbulent winds.

for over four and a half thousand years.

Modern civilization tends to take a shorter view. First, we generally do not want buildings to last very long, or at least clients are not willing to pay for materials that will last much longer than it takes to amortize the building's mortgage. Second, increasingly we are using new materials and methods of assembly whose long-term durability can only be guessed at. A well-known instance concerns the John Hancock Tower in Boston, designed by the office of I. M. Pei in 1966–67. Built during 1966–75 on Boston's Copley Square near the clustered towers of the Prudential Center, it had double-glazed windows with a metallic reflective film on the inner pane of glass. Unfortunately, the windows failed to stay in place, and during 1972 and 1973 the streets and blocks around the soaring tower were periodically and unpredictably rained with shards of glass [7.15]. Some experts said a heat buildup between the panes of glass, due to the reflective film, caused the windows to crack, while others said inadequate frames allowed the glass to be sucked out by the turbulent aerodynamics around the building. As successive legal suits were followed by countersuits, the double glass was replaced with single sheets of one-half-inch-thick mirrored tempered glass. The city of Boston approved the reglazed building for occupancy in 1975, but only in 1981 was the litigation settled out of court (with the terms of the settlement sealed).[9]

This recent and dramatic example of the shortcomings of new materials and technologies is only one instance of an old problem. Even before the birth of Christ, Vitruvius cautioned Roman architects not to use inappropriate materials or unsuitable forms of construction.

NOTES

1. The British thermal unit is the amount of heat required to raise the temperature of one pound of water one degree Fahrenheit. The figure of 2,750 Btu's per square foot on a clear day in June in Albuquerque is derived from G. Z. Brown, *Sun, Wind, and Light* (New York, 1985), 21.
2. These statistics are cited in J. M. Fitch, *American Architecture: The Environmental Forces That Shape It,* second ed. (Boston, 1972), 269.
3. Figures cited in Fitch, *American Architecture,* 266–67.
4. These figures are cited in Brown, *Sun, Wind and Light,* 38.
5. The environmental qualities of the Robie house are analyzed in Reyner Banham, *The Architecture of the Well-Tempered Environment,* second ed. (Chicago, 1984), 115–21. This should be consulted too for the development of air-conditioning by Wallis H. Carrier.
6. For a discussion of the functional parts of the Salvation Army building, the Cité du Refuge, see Stanislas von Moos, *Le Corbusier: Elements of a Synthesis* (Cambridge, Mass., 1979), 154–57; for its environmental shortcomings see Banham, *The Architecture of the Well-Tempered Environment,* 155–58. See also Brian B. Taylor, *Le Corbusier: The City of Refuge, Paris, 1929–33* (Chicago, 1987).
7. Such lateral forces had been encountered before in Gothic cathedrals. The high roofs, lifted 120 or 140 feet in the air, were subject to winds nearly three times higher in velocity than at ground level. The Gothic solution was trussing in the wooden roof and externalized diagonal braces, or flying buttresses. Robert Mark of Princeton University has conducted a number of experiments on models of Gothic cathedrals to measure the effect of wind pressure; see Robert Mark, *Experiments in Gothic Structure* (Cambridge, Mass., 1982).
8. See Carl W. Condit, "The Wind Bracing of Buildings," *Scientific American* 230 (February 1974): 92–105.
9. For a review of this celebrated failure, see Steven S. Ross, *Construction Disasters: Design Failures, Causes, and Prevention* (New York, 1984), 274–87.

SUGGESTED READING

G. Z. Brown, *Sun, Wind, and Light: Architectural Design Strategies* (New York, 1985); a guide book for those learning architectural design, filled with essential data and historical examples, and concluding with a glossary of terms and an extensive bibliography.

Ken Butti and John Perlin, *A Golden Thread: 2500 Years of Solar Architecture and Technology* (New York, 1980).

Hassan Fathy, *Natural Energy and Vernacular Architecture* (Chicago, 1986); a study by one of the leading architects advocating a return to traditional construction methods.

James Marston Fitch, *American Building: The Environmental Forces That Shape It,* second ed. (Boston, 1972).

Benjamin Stein, John S. Reynolds, and William J. McGuinness, *Mechanical and Electrical Equipment for Buildings,* seventh ed. (New York, 1986).

8.1. McKim, Mead and White, Pennsylvania Station, New York, 1902–10, demolished 1963–65. Interior of the Waiting Room, once one of the great public spaces in the United States.

CHAPTER 8

Architecture, Memory, and Economics

Therefore, when we build, let us think that we build for ever. . . . Let it be such work as our descendants will thank us for, and let us think, as we lay stone upon stone, that a time will come when . . . men will say as they look upon the labor and wrought substance of them, "See! this our fathers did for us."

John Ruskin, *The Seven Lamps of Architecture*, 1849

In his most influential book on architecture, *The Seven Lamps of Architecture* (1849), John Ruskin drew a distinction in the opening sentences between architecture and building, making it clear that what he proposed to talk about was *architecture*. The tendency since that time has been to assume that some buildings are more important than others, that some are worth detailed deliberation in their design while others are "Kleenex" buildings, deserving no second thought in design nor any particular care in their use. The result has been that we have a few splendid isolated buildings, but that on the whole we live, work, and play in perfunctory environments, made only as good as it is believed they absolutely need to be. *Perfunctory* is the perfect word to describe much of what has been built since the dawn of the Industrial Revolution. Derived from a Latin root, *perfungi,* it means "to get through with."

Just as we cannot properly understand the past without considering the "buildings" around the "architecture"—the houses around the cathedrals—we need to view all of our built environment as a whole of interrelated parts. Some buildings may have more public significance than others, being the focus of communal or civic life, but all are important. The act of building should

not descend to being perfunctory but should seek to celebrate. This Latin word, derived from *celeber,* originally referred to honoring someone or something by going in great numbers to praise and proclaim, to draw attention to something as being special, to give high value, to enjoy. In 1926, in one of his earliest writings about architecture, the social critic Lewis Mumford observed:

> The great problem of the architect is to mold the essential structural form in such a way as to perform all the purposes for which the building exists. It must fit its site, harmonize with or stand out from its neighbors, fulfill its own function as a shelter, a work-place, or a play-place, and give a special pleasure to every one who passes it or enters it.[1]

Mumford's suggestion that architecture should be a pleasurable experience raises the question of economy. Once again Vitruvius is the source of ancient advice, for he observed that *oikonomia,* the Greek term he used, is essential to good architecture, suggesting that this would result from selection of a good building site, use of good materials, and wise control of expenses. It also involved, he wrote, creating a character in the building appropriate to its use.[2] *Economy,* and all of the modern derivatives drawn from this word, comes from the Greek *oikos,* "house," plus *nemein,* "to manage," referring to good stewardship through wise management of resources. Yet in modern usage, to say something is economical is nearly synonymous with saying it is cheap (a word that comes from Old English and means "to haggle in the marketplace"). True economy, in the sense of good stewardly management, suggests that tearing down an old building may, in the long run, be very bad management on several counts. On a practical level, a considerable investment in human and mechanical energy was required to erect the building, and it may not be desirable to expend additional energy to replace it once it is destroyed (not to mention that it will take more human and mechanical energy simply to remove it). On a deep psychological level, our architecture is our built memory; it is a legacy, both the acclaimed *architecture* and the anonymous *building*. When we remove any part of it, we erase part of that memory, performing an incremental cultural lobotomy.

In every period of human history, what had been built before was replaced by new buildings to accommodate prevailing needs. In the Middle Ages, perhaps, more buildings were adapted to new uses than had been customary before, but that was more a reflection of the generally depressed economic conditions than of a conscious conservationist ethic. One of the ironies of the Renaissance was that, despite the interest in Roman architecture, much ancient architecture was destroyed. With the rise of a more scientific interest in antiquity in the eighteenth century, however, the impulse arose to preserve old buildings as a way of

retaining the knowledge of the past. The difficulty is that not every building can be frozen in time and converted to a museum. Those buildings that have survived are those that could be put to new uses. Historical imagination is required to conceive new uses for old buildings.

New construction need not be halted, nor the past swept away entirely for the new, as some International Modernists proposed in the 1920s. What is needed is a flexible and tolerant affection for the past. In our cities, where space is limited, several questions arise: should old buildings be refitted for a new use, should they be moved, or can they be incorporated into a new design? Good management requires an answer to yet another question: is the proposed building better than the one it will replace? If not, we risk shortchanging not only ourselves but posterity [8.1, 8.2]. To aid in determining answers, many countries have established agencies to inventory and assess their built heritage. In the United States, important buildings and landscapes are listed on the National Register and by state agencies on state registers.

On this last point, Ruskin held very strong views. Writing about the ancient medieval architecture of England, he said: "It is again no question of expediency or feeling whether we shall preserve the buildings of

8.2. *Charles Luckman Associates, Pennsylvania Station, New York, 1966–68. The soaring 150-foot spaces of the old station were replaced by efficient but cramped and unrewarding spaces.*

8.3. *Taj Mahal, Agra, India, 1630–53. Built of white marble by Shah Jahan, this was a tomb for his consort Mumtaz i-Mahal.*

past times or not. *We have no right whatever to touch them.* They are not ours. They belong partly to those who built them, and partly to all the generations of mankind who are to follow us."[3] Blind veneration of the past is counterproductive, but Ruskin's injunction should prompt us to exercise informed appraisal before we turn the bulldozers loose.

True economy is measured in the quality of performance over the long run, not merely in initial cost. In the preface to their survey, *The Architecture of America,* John Burchard and Albert Bush-Brown emphasize that "a design that fails to provide full emotional and physical performance is not economical, however cheap. Indeed cheapness has never been a criterion of great building."[4] So, what is true economy in architecture? John Kenneth Galbraith, one of the most enlightened economists of the mid-twentieth century, served as Ambassador of the United States to India and was familiar with the social impact of both affluence and poverty. He has proposed an intriguing yardstick by which to measure economy, saying that beauty and elegance in public construction are worth having but they are not cheap. He illustrates his point by focusing on the Taj Mahal in India [8.3]:

The return on a public structure is not merely the task that it facilitates. It is the whole pleasure that it provides the community. Accordingly, a building can be very expensive but a rare bargain for the pleasure it provides. A modest structure at modest cost would have provided durable and hygienic protection for the mortal remains of Mumtaz Mahal and Shah Jahan. But by spending more—by some estimates, about $8 million—Shah Jahan got the Taj Mahal. It has rejoiced the whole world ever since. Surely this was sound economy. Our test should be similar. The most economical building is the one that promises to give the greatest total pleasure for the price.[5]

NOTES

1. Lewis Mumford, *Architecture* (Chicago, 1926), 25–26.
2. Vitruvius, *Ten Books on Architecture,* I.2. 8–9.
3. John Ruskin, "The Lamp of Memory," *The Seven Lamps of Architecture* (London, 1849), ch. 6, § 20. The italicized emphasis is Ruskin's.
4. John Burchard and Albert Bush-Brown, *The Architecture of America: A Social and Cultural History* (Boston, 1961), 5; the preface to the hard-cover edition of the book, "The Nature of Architecture," is a perceptive introduction to the study of architecture; regrettably it was deleted from the paperback edition.
5. John Kenneth Galbraith, *Economics, Peace, and Laughter* (Boston, 1971), 158.

CHRONOLOGICAL TABLE

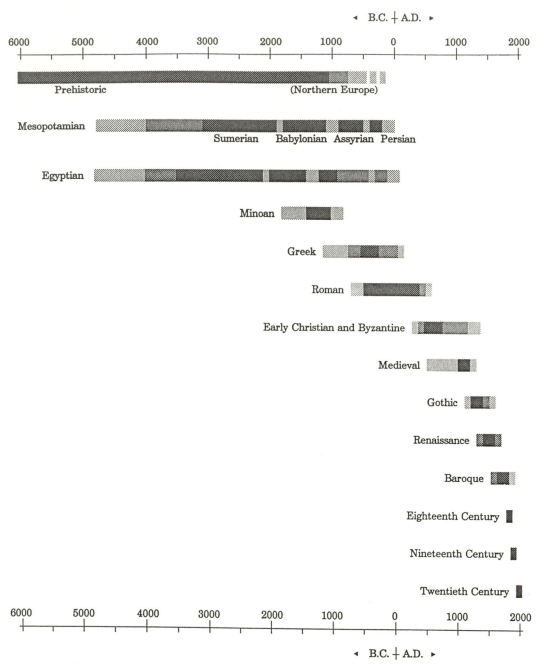

A comparative chart showing the duration of the successive Western cultures and cultural periods discussed in Part Two. The darkest parts of each line show the period or periods of most intense development and activity; the lighter sections represent periods of growth or decline.

PART TWO

The History and Meaning of Architecture

9.16. *Aerial view of the Ishtar Gate and the walls of Babylon, late Assyrian, c. 575 B.C. Restored view. Now restored to its original form in the State Museum, Berlin, the imposing Ishtar Gate, clad in brilliantly colored tiles with heraldic bulls and dragons on a deep blue background, illustrates well the rise of Mesopotamian civilization. Drawing on the same techniques used at Ur, nearly 1,500 years before, it has a hard tile exterior protecting a core of soft brick.*

CHAPTER 9

The Invention of Architecture: From Caves to Cities

Early man's respect for the dead, itself an expression of fascination with his powerful images of daylight fantasy and nightly dream, perhaps had an even greater role than more practical needs in causing him to seek a fixed meeting place and eventually a continuous settlement. Mid the uneasy wanderings of paleolithic man, the dead were the first to have a permanent dwelling: a cavern, a mound marked by a cairn, a collective barrow. . . . Urban life spans the historic space between the earliest burial ground for the dawn man and the final cemetery, the Necropolis, in which one civilization after another has met its end.

Lewis Mumford, *The City in History*, 1961

Architecture is shelter, but it is also symbol and a form of communication; as Sir Herbert Read observed, all art is "a mode of symbolic discourse."[1] Architecture is a physical representation of human thought and aspiration, a record of the beliefs and values of the culture that produces it.

In an introductory study such as this, it is necessary to start at the beginning, but this raises the intriguing question of exactly when it was that humans began to reshape their living environment and to formulate symbols that were given expression in architecture. We need to move well back from the period of recorded history, to the dim ages when the ancestors of the *Homo sapiens* appeared. In doing so we uncover suggestions of the origins of human society and human institutions. We discover, too, that what we build is shaped only in part by the need to provide for a particular functional use; architecture seems to have been built from the very first as a symbol of communal belief. Architecture accommodates psychological as well as physiological needs of the human family, whose basic social institu-

tions are perhaps a million years old. Thus the strictly utilitarian or functional considerations of modern architecture defined during the last century are only the smallest part of the broad social and cultural functions that architecture fulfills.

The first humanoids appeared about five million years ago in central Africa [9.1]. The human ancestor *Australopithecus*, or "southern ape," stood erect and made simple stone tools, and most probably tools of wood as well, although these have disappeared without a trace. These protohumans lived on the warm equatorial savannas and may have had no pressing need for shelter nor, apparently, did they use fire. About two million years ago there appeared a second species of early humanoids, *Homo habilis* or "handy man," who seems to have lived alongside *Australopithecus*. *Homo habilis* moved northward, out of central Africa, capturing fire from natural sources and inventing the hearth. A particularly important scientific discovery, made in a cave at L'Escale, France, is the oldest-known hearth, the remains of a fire that blazed 750,000 years ago. Around such fires, protected and warmed at night in these northern colder climates, early humans gathered and the first social bonds began to form.

Terra Amata (Nice, France)

The next human ancestor, *Homo erectus*, appeared about 1.6 million years ago, at the end of the first ice age, the Danube Glaciation, and endured the rigors of the following ice ages, the Günz Glaciation (one million to

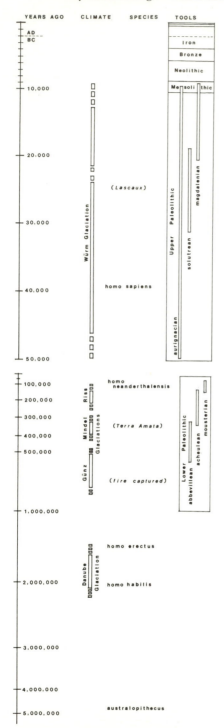

9.1. *Chronological table showing relationship between successive ice ages, human evolution, and prehistoric cultures; the scale expands roughly logarithmically so that more recent events are on a larger scale.*

900,000 years ago) and the Mindel Glaciation (700,000 to 600,000 years ago). As the Günz glaciers retreated, *Homo erectus* spread from central Africa along the north African Mediterranean coast into Europe, and eastward to India and the Indonesian islands. The humans left remarkable stone tools in what is called the Acheulean tool-making tradition, and they used fire, perhaps having learned how to make fire through friction.

As *Homo erectus* groups moved into the less gentle climates of Europe, they had to find or make their own shelter. Because earlier excavations had turned up Paleolithic (Old Stone Age) tools in Nice on France's Mediterranean coast, anthropologist Henry de Lumley watched closely in October 1965 as bulldozers cut through ancient sand banks to prepare a site for new high-rise apartments.[2] When more tools were uncovered, he had the work halted to allow for intensive and painstaking excavations. As a result, de Lumley and his associates discovered what turned out to be a springtime camping ground for a group of *Homo erectus* hunters who visited this spot annually during a period of several decades sometime during 400,000 to 300,000 years ago. At this spot, since called "Terra Amata" (Latin for "beloved land"), de Lumley found the remains of the oldest known fabricated shelter, what might be called the first architecture. There were remains of twenty-one huts, eleven of which were rebuilt on the same spot year after year on the top of an ancient sand dune above the primeval Mediterranean coast. Oval in plan, measuring about 26 to 49 feet in length by 13 to 20 feet in width, they had side walls made of a palisade of branches, 3 inches (7.6 centimeters) in diameter, pushed into the sand [9.2]; against the edges were piled rocks, some of which were 1 foot (0.3 meters) in diameter. Down the center were posts up to one foot (0.3 meters) in diameter, although the roof they supported left no trace (perhaps the side branches leaned against a center ridge beam supported by the posts). In each hut was a central hearth, with a windbreak of stones on the northwest side, the direction from which prevailing winds still blow in Nice. In one hut were indications of a toolmaker, for around a stone stool were chips and flakes of rock, some of which could be reassembled like a jigsaw puzzle to form the original cobble.

That a group of people returned here year after year suggests a regular hunting cycle, but even more important is the hearth. The fire suggests the gathering of the group, of the establishment of a community. Pieces of ocher found within the huts also suggest the inhabitants used these to draw on their skin. In using fire and building artificial shelters, these human ancestors took control of their environment, shaping it to their own convenience. The first steps toward architecture—the deliberate shaping of the living environment—had been taken.

Neanderthal Culture

During the fourth ice age, the Riss Glaciation (350,000 to 225,000 years ago), *Homo erectus* gradually was replaced by an archaic species of *Homo sapiens*. Then, 100,000

years ago, during the warm Riss-Würm interglacial period, another species appeared, *Homo sapiens neanderthalensis* (or Neanderthal man), so called because the first remains were found in 1856 in the Neander valley (*Thal*) in Germany. Although Neanderthals were heavier than modern humans, they were not the brutish, hunched figures once imagined. It happened that one of the first skeletons found was that of a stooped, arthritic old man. The Neanderthals spread throughout upper Africa, Europe, and the Near East. There have been numerous finds, including many stone tools of the Mousterian toolmaking tradition, but only scant finds of remains of built structures. For the most part, the Neanderthals seem to have been cave dwellers.

Through Neanderthal burials, however, much has been learned of their communal existence and something of their perception of life itself. At La Chapelle-aux-Saints, France, in 1908 were discovered the remains of a very elderly man, buried care-

9.2. *Terra Amata,* Homo erectus *dwelling, Nice, France, c. 400,000–300,000 B.C. Reconstructed from holes left by decayed wooden structural members and by the rocks placed around the perimeter, this represents the earliest known human-constructed dwelling.*

PREHISTORIC EUROPE
C. 5000-1000 B.P.

--- Some former shorelines, 15,000-10,000 B.P.

Extent of Glaciation, 3,500-2,500 B.P.

fully with stone tools laid around the body, with a bison leg placed on top of the man's body. A great majority of the other burials have revealed bodies laid out on an east-west axis, suggesting perhaps an alignment with the movement of the sun. Perhaps the most suggestive is the burial in a cave at Shanidar, in the mountains of Iraq.[3] Tests of the soil found around the male skeleton revealed that he had been interred resting on a bed of pine boughs and flowers, and was then covered with blossoms of grape hyacinth, bachelor's buttons, hollyhock, and groundsel. Another man buried in the same cave had a congenitally deformed arm that would have made hunting impossible, and yet he had lived a long life. This, along with the old man buried at La Chapelle-aux-Saints, suggests that a complex Neanderthal social structure had been created in which the old and the infirm were valued, nurtured, and sustained. The flowers of Shanidar suggest the Neanderthals sensed that life continued somehow after death, in a renewed cycle or on a different plane; the flowers indicate that the Neanderthals had come to think in symbolic terms.

Homo sapiens's Houses

The Neanderthals disappeared about 40,000 years ago, about midway through the last ice age, the Würm Glaciation (90,000 to 10,000 years ago). They were replaced by modern humans, Homo sapiens sapiens. Various toolmaking traditions were perfected by the Cro-Magnon people, succeeding each other rapidly—the Perigordian, the Aurignacian, the delicate Solutrean, and the Magdalenian—characterizing what is called the upper Paleolithic period, the Old Stone Age [9.1].

A number of dwelling sites of early Homo sapiens sapiens have been uncovered across Europe. Those of eastern Europe show a type of house that was apparently typical. Round, perhaps domed or conical in shape, with frames of wood covered presumably with hides, they were braced at the bottom with massive mammoth bones and skulls [9.3]. Remains of such houses have been found in several locations in Moravia (Czechoslovakia), at Ostrava-Petřkovice and Dolní-Věstonice, and also in the Ukraine in Russia, near the Dniester River. The

Ukraine site revealed superimposed habitation levels going back to about 44,000 years ago, with the most recent dating from about 12,000 years ago. These dwellings may have accommodated extended family groups, for some houses measured roughly 30 feet (9.1 meters) in diameter. Both Moravian sites were occupied by successive generations from roughly 29,000 to 24,000 years ago. These dwellings were nearly the same as those found in the Ukraine, ringed with massive bones and measuring about 20 feet (6.1 meters) in diameter; one, however, measured about 50 by 20 feet (15.2 by 6.1 meters) and had five hearths. These early *Homo sapiens sapiens* clearly knew how to create fire quickly and at will, for they left flints and iron pyrites used to strike sparks; one piece of pyrite found in a Belgian cave had a groove in it from repeated striking.

The site at Dolní-Věstonice proved to be especially important, for set apart from the five residential huts was a sixth built into the side of a hill, with a larger hearth covered with an earthen dome. Lying about on the floor was ample evidence of what went on there—hundreds of bits of fired clay, some bearing the fingerprints of the primeval potter. Nor was pure clay alone used for the implements, but clay mixed with crushed bone, perhaps the oldest example of what might be called industrial production, in which two dissimilar substances were mixed to create a new and stronger artificial material.

Cro-Magnon humans, our *Homo sapiens sapiens* grandfathers, also buried their dead with elaborate ceremony, to judge by the elaborate ivory and bead jewelry and tools with which they were interred. Perhaps they took leave of the dead with song, playing the bone flutes they left in the graves. But the most compelling evidence of the intellectual capacity of these forefathers is found not in their huts or burials but in the visual evidence they left, the painting and sculpture they created. They seem to have become aware of a cycle of life, of a unity of the cosmos, in which male and female entities participated in the renewal of life. Across Europe have been found carved figures, described now as fertility figures, of women with enlarged breasts and buttocks, most with no discernible faces. Some of these were portable, small figures in stone or ivory, such as the rounded so-called Venus found in Willendorf, Austria, while others were mural art, carved into the rock on the walls of caves. The most imposing and intriguing of these is the Venus of Laussel, France, carved 22,000 to 18,000 years ago. She raises aloft in her right hand a horn marked with thirteen grooves.

Even more impressive than these figures are the paintings discovered in caves in southern France and northern Spain. In

9.3. Cro-Magnon dwelling, Ukraine, c. 44,000–12,000 B.C. These dwellings, some of them 30 feet (9.1 meters) across, had masses of mammoth bones piled around the perimeter and apparently were covered with hides.

9.4. *Middle Stone Age village, Lepenski Vir, Yugoslavia, c. 5000–4600 B.C. Numerous houses were built in terraces consisting of about twenty each. They had trapezoidal plans, measuring from 8 to 11 feet lengthwise, and hard limestone plaster floors with central stone-lined hearths.*

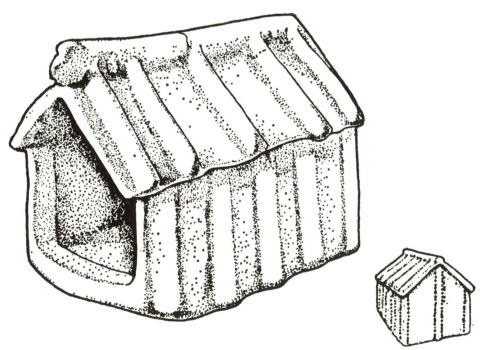

9.5. *Clay model of a house, Střelice, Czechoslovakia, c. 4500 B.C.*

1879, the daughter of a Spanish nobleman, exploring with her father a cave on his estate, looked up and saw the images of twenty-five bison, deer, boars, and other animals. It seemed at first impossible that images of such grace in execution and grace could be of the same date as the remains found on the floor of the caves. As other caves were then discovered, the fact that the images were painted sometime between 34,000 and 12,000 years ago became clear. Then, in 1940, the most famous cave of all was opened, at Lascaux, France, at the edge of the Massif Central above the Vézère River not far from Montignac. By the light of small lamps, which in places left smudges on the walls of the cave, Cro-Magnon humans had painted hundreds of images of aurochs (prehistoric oxen), woolly rhinoceroses, prehistoric horses, deer, elk, and other animals. The colors were achieved using pigments of powdered minerals—iron oxide or ocher ranging from bright red, orange, yellow to warm browns, and manganese oxide (or charcoal) for black—often packed in tubes made of hollowed-out bone. The pigments were mixed with animal fat, egg white, or other liquids, and were brushed on, blown on through tubes, and daubed with the fingers. There is some evidence to suggest that the higher portions of the cave "vault" were painted from a wooden scaffold—architecture in the service of art. The artists and their assistants fashioned images unsurpassed for clarity of outline, grace of form, and sensitivity to perspective until the time of the Greeks and Romans. A good example is the so-called Chinese Horse, in which the outlines of the rear legs fade away as they near the mass of the body to suggest the distance from the legs in the foreground.

The question that has puzzled anthropologists since the discovery of these caves is *why* such striking and realistic images were painted. They were not scribbled in idle moments on the ceilings of inhabited caves. Most are found deep in the innermost recesses of special caves, in secluded chambers reached only by arduous crawling. The lamps, pigments, and scaffold materials had to be carried into the caves with care and deliberation. In some caves there is evidence to suggest the practice of fertility or initiation rites. Are these images of hunting magic, in which the spirit of the animal is captured and killed before the actual hunt, or are these images meant to impregnate the earth with the spirit of the animal after the hunt to ensure its continued survival?[4] If this was hunting magic, why are there no bones of the painted animals in the midden, or refuse, piles adjacent to the settlements? The images of reindeer, whose bones *are* found in human settlements, are comparatively rare. Perhaps these lifelike images are the first human expressions of a sense of something terribly wrong in the ecological balance, a desperate attempt to propagate the animals that were gradually disappearing from the face of the earth. The womb of mother earth was lovingly impregnated with the images of the great disappearing beasts. Perhaps this is why the caves themselves were never altered, the narrow openings never widened, the difficult passages never made easy. Cro-Magnon people seem not to have built sacred buildings, but practiced their religion in the inner sanctuaries of their earth mother.

Neolithic Dwellings

Beginning about 8000 B.C., or 10,000 years ago, the glaciers retreated once again and the harsh climate of Europe was transformed; the tundra and steppes were gradually replaced by lush forests. A new age had begun, the Neolithic or New Stone Age, and humans increasingly settled in one place, building permanent settlements.

In some areas the old hunting and gathering traditions lingered, as indicated by the remains of a settlement at Lepenski Vir on the Danube in the Iron Gates region of north-central Yugoslavia, dating from about 5000 B.C. to 4600 B.C. Facing the river, a series of huts of trapezoidal plan were built in a technique that was not much different from that used by *Homo erectus* at Terra Amata, with a palisade of branches on either side of the house supported by a central ridge pole. Here the floors of the huts were of packed earth plastered hard around a central stone-lined hearth [9.4]. At Střelice, in Czechoslovakia, in the remains of a Neolithic settlement of about 4500 B.C. was found a clay model of a rectangular house [9.5, page 140]. It had straight vertical walls and a double-pitched, or gable, roof; the walls of the model suggest that actual houses had walls made of woven wood mats covered with mud plaster, perhaps with a roof of thatch. Fragments of a similar clay model found at Ariușd, Romania, are inscribed with curved geometric patterns, suggesting that the actual houses were painted.[5] Remains of houses of this type have been found at the Cucuteni-Tripolye settlement at Hăbășești, Romania. At Sittard, in what is now the Netherlands, the wood houses were much longer, up to 260 feet (80 meters) long, and accommodated several families or an extended family.

That these settled communities early developed a complex social structure is suggested by evidence of a division and specialization of labor. Whether these groups were egalitarian or whether ruling families emerged is difficult to tell, but the structures they built clearly reveal a communal purpose and the ability to devote substantial energy to the building process. The community as a whole was no longer involved solely in physical sustenance, so that a growing portion of the community's energies could be directed at expressing, in increasingly durable and symbolic ways, the values of the community. Architecture in stone was invented, so that where previously one or two individuals could put up a wood-framed and hide-covered house in a day or two, now teams of workers could devote their entire energies to quarrying massive stone megaliths (from the Greek mega plus lithos, meaning "great stone") and transporting them to the building site; construction could take weeks, months, or years.

The first of these megalithic constructions were freestanding stone columns called menhirs (a Celtic word meaning "long stone"), cut in large numbers and erected vertically in circular patterns or parallel rows, marking a spot for some ritual purpose whose precise meaning is now lost to us. Such megalithic arrangements, the most

numerous of all ancient stone constructions, appear across northern Europe, but the oldest are those of Brittany in northern France. There, at Carnac, are rows of stones stretching 4 miles (6.4 kilometers), begun as early as 4500 B.C. [9.6]. Nearby, at Kerloas, is the largest megalith still standing, 39 feet high (11.9 meters).

About 4000 B.C., at roughly the same time that the stones at Carnac were being set up in their long rows, a group of temples was begun on the islands of Malta, in the middle of the Mediterranean Sea. By 2700 B.C. the sites were built over with the temple ruins we see at Malta today. These temples are spatially more complex than any of the other buildings of the Neolithic period. One of them, in fact, is carved into the limestone hill at Hal Sallieni. Given the Greek name hypogeum, "cellar," it was a catacomb for housing seven thousand dead. On the Maltese island of Gozo is found the temple complex called Ggantija, Maltese for "gigantic" [9.7]. Similar to many of the thirty other Maltese temples, this complex was built in stages, with connected clusters of rounded rooms defined by parallel walls of large limestone facing-blocks, the space between them filled with stone rubble and earth. The inner walls were partially finished in more carefully cut blocks of a limestone of deep yellow color, some carved with spirals and other curvilinear patterns. What the upper structure of these temples may have been is not clear, but beams and rafters of wood may have formed the roofs.

In northern Europe, roofed structures were also built, the simplest of which are the dolmens (Celtic for "table stones"), consisting of three vertical stone slab supports on top of which rests a massive horizontal slab [9.8]. On the basis of tools, bones, and other remains found inside some of these, it is presumed they were built as tombs and covered with mounds of earth that have eroded away. In some cases, four large roughly rectangular slabs make up the base, forming something like a gigantic stone box, with an immense stone lid. Often these dolmens were extended, with a series of stone slabs forming two parallel walls, capped with numerous roof slabs, all covered with earth.

9.6. Aerial view of aligned stone uprights, Carnac, Brittany, France, c. 4500 B.C.

These long barrows were gallery graves, with a series of bodies placed in the extended chamber. In several locations, the barrows ended in a roughly circular chamber roofed with small stones laid in rings that closed in as they rose, each stone cantilevered over the one below, forming a corbeled vault. Of these passage graves, one that has survived nearly intact structurally is the New Grange tomb near Dublin, Ireland, begun about 3100 B.C., with an entrance passageway, sloping upward and bent in the middle, leading to the domed chamber [9.9]. The tomb is oriented to the southeast in such a way that at sunrise at the winter solstice, around 3000 B.C., the rising sun would penetrate, for a few magic minutes, to the farthest depth of the tomb.

Stonehenge

Of all the prehistoric megalithic constructions, the best known, certainly, is Stonehenge, on the chalk downs of Salisbury Plain not far from Salisbury, England. Strictly speaking, there are three Stonehenges, for the complex was built in three major stages over a period of more than 1,200 years, not by one group of people but by successive generations living in the area. The first stage consisted of marking out the location, sometime between 2950 B.C. and 2750 B.C. With a leather thong or a woven rope 160 feet long affixed to a central stake, a circle was drawn 320 feet in diameter. A circular trench was dug into the white chalk, with the chips piled up largely on the inside, cre-

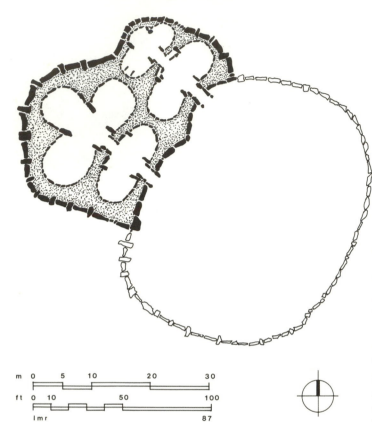

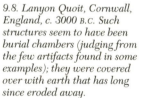

9.7. Temple complex called Ggantija, Malta, c. 4000–2700 B.C. This is only one of many buildings in stone on the Maltese islands, built over several centuries, apparently as religious centers.

9.8. Lanyon Quoit, Cornwall, England, c. 3000 B.C. Such structures seem to have been burial chambers (judging from the few artifacts found in some examples); they were covered over with earth that has long since eroded away.

ating an inner wall originally about 6 feet (1.8 meters) high. An opening was left at the northeast side and a large menhir, the heelstone, erected just outside the entrance.

Then, between 2200 B.C. and 2075 B.C., in the second phase of construction, a crescent of bluestone uprights was erected inside the circle, including a large upright stone aligned with two others outside the entrance near the heelstone. The bluestones are of special significance, since they could have come from only one possible quarry, in the Prescelly Mountains in southwestern Wales, nearly 300 miles (500 kilometers) away. It seems most likely that they were dragged to what is now Milford Haven in Wales and then shipped by sea to the vicinity of Bristol and up the Avon River; from there the stones were hauled to the plain of Salisbury and then along a long curved causeway or avenue to the site.

The third and last phase of Stonehenge, almost as we see it today, was started as early as 2000 B.C. and was finished by 1500 B.C. [9.10]. The bluestones were temporarily removed, and immense sandstone sarsens, or stone uprights, quarried in Marlborough Downs about twenty miles away, were raised

to form a circular colonnade 20 feet (6 meters) high, with curved lintels. Within the enclosure were erected five large trilithons (two uprights carrying a lintel) enclosing a horseshoe opening toward the heelstone to the northeast. It was a prodigious effort, requiring the labor of roughly 1,100 laborers over a period of seven weeks to move each individual stone from quarry to building site, not to mention the stonecutters at work in the quarry and the finishers carrying out final dressing of the monoliths at the site. Each upright had to be tilted, in small increments, perhaps supported by wooden towers of crossed logs, until it slid into the waiting hole and was made properly plumb. The lintels were levered up on similar log towers and moved sideways into place. The stone surfaces may be rough compared to contemporaneous work in Egypt or Greece, but this was not the handiwork of primitive people. It required careful social organization and cooperation of a high order.

Yet the essential question remains: what was it for? The effort of many generations over so many centuries was undertaken for some compelling purpose. As recent investigations suggest, this complex served as an

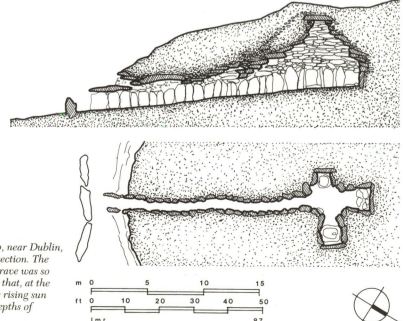

9.9. New Grange tomb, near Dublin, c. 3100 B.C. Plan and section. The entry passage of this grave was so positioned and curved that, at the midwinter solstice, the rising sun would penetrate the depths of the tomb.

astronomical observatory, for the alignment of the heelstone with the stones in the center of the circle is such that at the summer solstice, about 2000 B.C., the sun would have risen directly over the heelstone. Other alignments within the complex suggest that Stonehenge might have been used to mark phases of the moon and other astronomical phenomena. But as the discovery of the remains of an enormous similar round wooden structure two miles away makes clear, the same results could have been achieved with much less work. Stonehenge may indeed have served such an astronomical function, but it was built with such care and expenditure of labor that it also became a tribal expression of identity, a social covenant, a symbol of communal purpose. It was a gathering place where each year the recurring cycle of the sun and of life was celebrated by the assembled tribes.

Skara Brae

It is significant that such prodigious effort in building in stone seems to have been expended only on houses of the dead and on sacred monuments. The houses of workers who built the dolmens, the barrows, and Stonehenge have long since disappeared.

9.10. Stonehenge III, Salisbury Plain, England, c. 2000–1500 B.C. Aerial view. The present Stonehenge is the last of three distinct building phases carried out over almost one and a half thousand years.

But we do have a remarkable record of at least one village, dating from about 2500 B.C. and abandoned about 1500 B.C. Skara Brae, located in the forbiddingly harsh and stony Orkney Islands north of Scotland, was revealed by accident after a lashing storm in 1850 blew off the sand that had covered the village for more than three thousand years (it had most likely been buried by such a storm). Because there is virtually no wood on the islands, the houses were built almost entirely of stone, with stone shelving, tables, and beds. Hence, they were preserved from decay, affording us an intimate glimpse of how life was lived in Neolithic Britain [9.11, 9.12]. There were ten houses in all, with narrow alleys winding between them. The walls were partially collapsed, but judging by the whale bones found in the huts, the roofs may have been of hides or thatch supported by whalebone rafters.

The First Cities

The major change in human settlement, and the resulting creation of architecture as we usually think of it, was the result of adaptation to the dramatic tempering of climate that accompanied the retreat of the glaciers. Humans chose a settled existence, establishing permanent settlements and building houses and other structures. This was made possible by the domestication not only of the human species itself but also of animals and plants, especially a number of grasses whose seeds could be ground into meal and flour. The deliberate growing of grain began in southern Egypt as early as 15,000 B.C. to 10,000 B.C., as is evidenced by the well-used grinding stones found there. By 8000 B.C., agriculture had been firmly established in what is called the Fertile Crescent, along the valley of the Nile, up the coast of the eastern Mediterranean, and through the valleys of the Tigris and Euphrates rivers, as well as in what is now southern Turkey.

Once the Neolithic period, or what the historian V. Gordon Childe called the "Neolithic revolution," had begun, the patterns of human activity were profoundly changed.[6] Large stone tools were replaced by implements with small cutting pieces of

volcanic glass, obsidian, fitted into wood or bone armatures, allowing for easy replacement of broken or dull cutting segments. But the most sweeping changes grew directly out of the development of agriculture. Permanent residence in one spot, near the fields, encouraged more substantial buildings, and as towns and cities grew in size, social organization became more complex, requiring varied building types. Modern civilization has added very few new basic building types to those that arose from the needs created in Neolithic times— houses, governmental and civic buildings, and religious shrines.

Çatal Hüyük

Large, permanently inhabited cities appeared at almost the same geological instant the glaciers retreated, about 8000 B.C. Archaeological excavations down through the mound of the ancient city of Jericho in modern Israel have shown that this was an established city as early as 8000 B.C., but our most detailed understanding of how a Neolithic city functioned comes from the successive layers of the city of Çatal Hüyük in south-central Turkey. Inhabited by 6500 B.C., this city had about ten thousand residents by 5500 B.C. It was not only a farming community but also a vital link in the trade network that transported highly prized obsidian from the volcanic areas to the north to cities throughout the Fertile Crescent of Palestine and Mesopotamia. But besides obsidian and the Neolithic technology it implies, implements of copper and lead were found at Çatal Hüyük, hinting at the beginnings of the Bronze Age.

Çatal Hüyük covered an area of 32 acres (12.9 hectares), of which less than a quarter was excavated during 1961–66, an area that turned out to be a residential quarter. There were no streets as such, but tightly clustered rectangular houses with an occasional courtyard that served as a rubbish dump [9.13]. Entry to the houses was by means of a hole in the roof that also served as the vent for the smoke of the central hearth. The residences were built with timber frames, the panels between the posts and beams filled

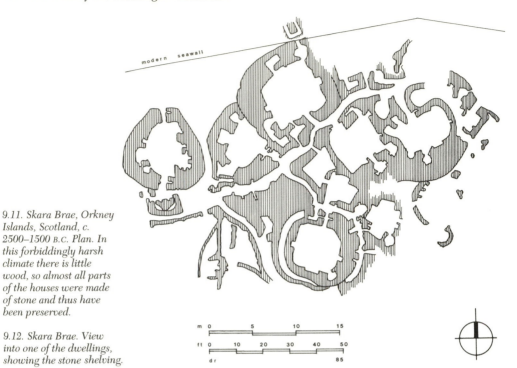

modern   seawall

9.11. Skara Brae, Orkney Islands, Scotland, c. 2500–1500 B.C. Plan. In this forbiddingly harsh climate there is little wood, so almost all parts of the houses were made of stone and thus have been preserved.

9.12. Skara Brae. View into one of the dwellings, showing the stone shelving.

m 0   5   10   15

ft 0   10   20   30   40   50

d r   85

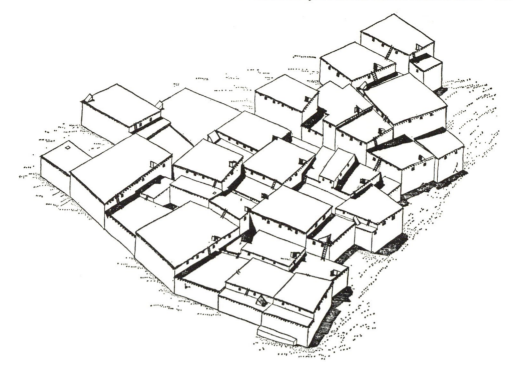

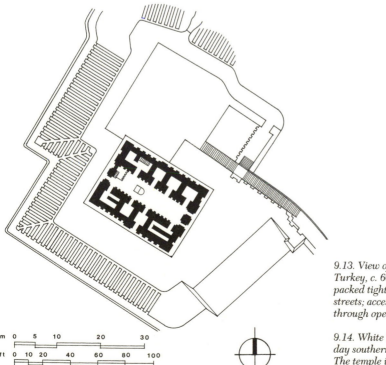

9.13. View of Level VI, Çatal Hüyük, Turkey, c. 6000 B.C. The houses were packed tightly together, with no streets; access to the dwellings was through openings in the roof.

9.14. White Temple, Uruk (in present-day southern Iraq), c. 3500–3100 B.C. The temple itself was built atop a ziggurat mound.

9.15. *Ziggurat of the moon god Nannar, Ur (in present-day southern Iraq), c. 2113–2006* B.C. *Sumerian ziggurats were built with soft brick cores covered with a veneer of hard-fired brick laid in a mortar of thick bitumen.*

with mud brick, plastered, and often painted. In one house a wall was painted with a landscape of the view toward the volcanic mountains in the distance, with a plan of the city in the foreground; in another house were painted figures of dancers. Most remarkable, nearly a quarter of the chambers excavated consisted of shrines devoted to a mother goddess and a bull cult.

Mesopotamian Cities

The growing of grain meant that, after harvest, the surplus of seeds had to be stored, necessitating the development of clay pottery vessels that resisted moisture and attack by insects and rodents. Even more important was the need for some permanent way of recording communal decisions and the tallies of stored grain. In the broad valley watered by the meandering Tigris and Euphrates rivers—what the Greeks called *mesopotamia*, the "land between the rivers"—writing was developed, augmenting (and eventually replacing) ritual, dance, and song as ways of transmitting human memory. By 6000 B.C., primitive villages were scattered across the lower Tigris-Euphrates valley, and by 3500 B.C. larger cities were being built. Within another four or five hundred years, cuneiform was perfected, with a stylus used to impress wedge-shaped marks in soft clay.

The first of the large cities in Meso-

potamia were near the mouths of the two rivers (alluvial deposits have since moved the shore of the Gulf of Arabia 140 miles, 225 kilometers, to the southeast). Wood was scarce here, so the developing urban architecture consisted of mud brick masses covered with a protective layer of fired brick laid in a bitumen mortar. What remains of the protoliterate period are the great pyramidlike mounds, the ziggurats, which served as artificial mountains on which temples were built. The White Temple at Uruk, with its whitewashed brick walls, built between 3500 B.C. and 3100 B.C., is among the first examples of a ziggurat surmounted by a temple [9.14]. The plan of the temple is much like that of the building engraved on the plaque in the lap of the statue of Gudea, governor of the city of Lagash [6.3]. The ziggurat of the moon god Nannar in the city of Ur, built by King Urnammu about 2113 B.C. to 2006 B.C. [9.15], illustrates the development of this form during the Sumerian period. It was built of earth and soft brick, with an outer facing of hard-fired brick laid in bitumen, rising in a series of terraces, ascended by long straight stairs, and surmounted by a temple.

Inventing Architecture and the City

Exactly when human culture dawned is difficult to pinpoint. Early humans gained important and fundamental achievements by beginning to fashion tools and then by using those tools to create an artificial environment around them. Such unassuming huts as those at Terra Amata were the beginning of architecture, for those simple shelters marked the beginning of deliberate place-making.

As the technology of shelter construction improved, the next important step was the enlargement of human settlements that agriculture made possible. Shelters were clustered together to make the first villages, then towns, and finally cities, beginning in the Tigris-Euphrates valley. This pooling of human resources released an inventive energy formerly consumed in eking out individual subsistence livings, and the inevitable result was the development of writing, which made it possible to carry human thought and memory from generation to generation in fixed symbols. In the valley of the Tigris and Euphrates rivers an irrigation system ensured that the supply of food was relatively steady, resulting in a surplus of goods and human energy expendable on the construction of ever larger cities [9.16, page 140]. As with megalithic stone building in Europe, so in Mesopotamia, the first permanent buildings served the most encompassing public need, attempting to bridge the gulf between humans and the gods. Even if the individual buildings were sponsored by individual kings, they were still the embodiment of public purpose. Human civilization and its architectural expression had been invented.

NOTES

1. Sir Herbert Read, "The Disintegration of Form in Modern Art," in *The Origins of Form in Art* (New York, 1965), 182.
2. Henry de Lumley, "A Paleolithic Camp at Nice," *Scientific American* 220 (May 1969): 42–50.
3. Robert S. Soleckei, *Shanidar: The First Flower People* (New York, 1971).
4. A. Leroi-Gourhan, *Préhistoire de l'art occidentale*, third ed. (Paris, 1973), has attempted to organize the cave paintings as a system of symbols rather than naturalistic images.
5. There is always the possibility that these models were children's toys and should not be interpreted literally.

SUGGESTED READING

R.J.C. Atkinson, *Stonehenge* (Baltimore, Md., 1960).

George Bataille, *Lascaux* (Geneva, Switzerland, 1955).

Dale Brown and Edmund White, *The First Men* (New York, 1973).

V. Gordon Childe, *Man Makes Himself* (London, 1936; New York, 1951).

———, *Skara Brae* (London, 1931).

Desmond Collins, *The Human Revolution: From Ape to Artist* (Oxford, England, 1977).

George Constable, *The Neanderthals* (New York, 1973).

Brian Fagan, ed., *Avenues to Antiquity: Readings from Scientific American* (San Francisco, 1975); contains articles by de Lumley on Terra Amata, and on Ukrainian settlements.

Henri Frankfort, *The Art and Architecture of the Ancient Orient*, fourth ed. (New York, 1970).

Sigfried Giedion, *The Eternal Present:* Vol. 1, *The Beginnings of Art*, (New York, 1962).

———, *The Eternal Present:* Vol. 2, *The Beginnings of Architecture*, (New York, 1964).

Dora Jane Hamblin, *The First Cities* (New York, 1973).

Gerald S. Hawkins, *Stonehenge Decoded* (Garden City, N.Y., 1965).

Paul Lampl, *Cities and Planning in the Ancient Near East* (New York, 1968).

A. Leroi-Gourhan, *Préhistoire de l'art occidentale*, third. ed. (Paris, 1973). Trans., *The Art of Prehistoric Man in Western Europe* (London, 1968).

Euan Mackie, *The Megalith Builders* (Oxford, England, 1977).

James Mellaart, *Çatal Hüyük: A Neolithic Town in Anatolia* (New York, 1977).

Tom Prideaux, *Cro-Magnon Man* (New York, 1973).

Ann Sieveking, *The Cave Artists* (London, 1979).

Robert S. Soleckei, *Shanidar: The First Flower People* (New York, 1971).

Robert Wernick, *The Monument Builders* (New York, 1973).

Ruth Whitehouse, *The First Cities* (Oxford, England, 1977).

10.18. Hypostyle Hall, Temple of Amon, Karnak, Thebes, Egypt, c. 1315–1235 B.C. *The huge columns along the central axis are 11.75 feet (3.6 meters) in diameter and rise 69 feet (21 meters); the axis they define is aligned to the rising sun at midwinter, pointing directly to the Valley of the Kings on the west side of the Nile.*

CHAPTER 10

Egyptian Architecture

At the temples' centers stood airless complexes of sunless rooms, chambers that only the ritually pure could enter, surrounding the small central shrines. In these dark sanctuaries elaborate rituals were celebrated through days and nights: rites that spanned years, decades and centuries, communions with eternity, the designs of numberless lives absorbed in deep pieties, built upon the impulses that sustained life in the Nile Valley: the tremendous power of the gods, the daily passage of the sun over the river valley, the river's annual flood and liquefaction of its fields, the germination of the seed, the ripening of the crop. The endless rhythms of the ancient state.

John Romer, *Ancient Lives,* 1984

For most people, to think of ancient Egypt is to evoke the enormous crouching figure of the Sphinx or the great pyramids rising from the edge of the desert on the west bank of the Nile. Egypt is not only an ancient nation but a state of mind, a mystery wrapped like a mummy in a mystique of death. Its greatest architectural remnants are buildings dedicated to funerary practices, its pyramids serving as man-made mountains of burial, its temples lining the Nile with endless repetitions of column after column, of court and chamber leading to yet more courts and chambers. It is an architecture of great mass and monotonous regularity, deliberately adhering to established forms and details over a time span equal in length to everything that has followed it up to the present day. The contribution of Egyptian architecture to the development of the architectural traditions of the West is perhaps less evident than that of Greece, Rome, medieval Europe, or Renaissance Italy; yet, Egypt is where West-

ern architecture begins, rooted in ancient Egyptian religion and science.

Egypt is for most people a great mystery, for it is so remote both in time and in culture. When the ancient Greeks, such as Herodotus, visited Egypt five hundred years before the birth of Christ, or later when the Romans annexed it to their empire just before the Christian era, Egypt was already an ancient land with a culture three thousand years old. Even Herodotus understood Egyptian life imperfectly, and since his time another two and a half thousand years have passed, so that Egypt is for us that much more exotic and remote.

The Landscape of Egypt

As Herodotus wrote in his *Histories,* Egypt "is the gift of the river."[1] Egypt *is* the Nile, and to understand the land, its people, and the architecture they built, we must first understand the river. It is the longest river in the world, 4,130 miles (6,648 kilometers), formed by three tributaries: the Blue Nile and the Atbara, which originate in the mountains of Ethiopia (what the ancient Egyptians called Abyssinia), and the White Nile, which flows from Lakes Albert and Victoria in equatorial Africa.

In what is now the Sudan, the Nile makes a large S-curve, cutting its way through a valley with steep cliff sides, and passing over four cataracts. It passes over another cataract just north of the Aswan High Dam, whose impounded waters now cover a cataract south of the dam. The last and most northerly cataract marked the edge of the ancient land of Egypt. From that point the river flows 750 miles (1,207 kilometers) to the north and into the Mediterranean Sea. This passage is through two distinctly different landscapes. For the greater distance, about 650 miles (1,046 kilometers), it is through a valley cut in limestone, varying in width from 10 to 14 miles (16 to 22.5 kilometers) in width, with steep cliffs rising sometimes to 1,500 feet (457 meters) on either side. Beyond the cliffs, to the east and west, is the desert. Just north of modern Cairo the cliffs end and the river splits into branches, spreading out in a delta that is 100 miles (161 kilometers) long and 155 miles (249 kilometers) wide at the Mediterranean Sea.

In Egypt rainfall is negligible, decreasing from 8 inches a year at Cairo to 1 inch or less in the valley to the south, so that the Nile is the major source of water. In the Abyssinian uplands, however, 60 inches (152 centimeters) of rain fall in a typical summer. The result (until massive dams were put in the path of the Nile in the middle of the twentieth century) was that year after year the Nile was filled with water rich in the eroded soil of the Abyssinian highlands carried down to the valley below. The waters rose in a flood that began late in June, crested in mid-August, and ended by November. The river gave the ancient Egyptians their three seasons, beginning with Inundation from June through October; followed by Emergence of the Fields from the Water from November through February when the fields were planted; and Drought when there was harvest and threshing. The relatively gentle if warm climate also meant that two or three crops could be harvested a year. Some years the crest was higher than normal, sometimes less, but the cycle of inundation and drying repeated itself endlessly year after year, decade after decade, century after century. When the waters receded they left a precious gift, the black soil carried down from Ethiopia. The Egyptians themselves called their river Ar or Aur, one of their words for *black*, because of its burden of soil (Nile is from the Greek, Neilos, from an ancient root meaning "river val-

ley"). The Egyptians called their country Kemet, meaning "the black land"; what lay beyond to the east and west was the desert, "the red land."

Egypt is a great linear oasis in the desert, running north and south, 750 miles long, and (except for the broad delta) only 1 to 12 miles wide. Every year the new soil deposited by the inundation swept away the landmarks that established field boundaries, so very early the Egyptians perfected a system of geometry and mathematics to redefine the boundaries the river had obliterated. The bureaucracy and the science this surveying required would later be put to the service of building the pyramids.

The Nile, then, was one cultural determinant, flowing south to north, from the higher lands that the Egyptians called Upper Egypt to the flat delta, or Lower Egypt, flowing in a rhythm of rise and fall and replenishment that never varied greatly. The other major determinant was the sun, which moved with similar unvarying precision, east to west, perpendicular to the river, in a usually cloudless sky, day after day, pursuing its own endless cycle. The river and the sun, then, established the two perpendicular axes that dominate Egyptian life and architecture. As a study of the Egyptian temple reveals, it is a linear, axial architecture, turned at right angles to the axis of the river. And those two axes of river and sun form the basis of the orthogonal grid of Egyptian fields and cities, exemplified by the city built by the Twelfth Dynasty pharaoh, Sesostris II (also called Senusert II), 1897–1878 B.C., at what is now El Kahun, across the river from his pyramid, on which the workers labored [10.1].

The Egyptian climate varied little, and, with the annual gift of water and fresh soil, life could be pursued with relative ease. There were occasional periods of turmoil, but for centuries on end life went on in peaceful monotony. To the Egyptian, time flowed in cycles that repeated themselves without end; a phrase from early Christian liturgy sums up a view the ancient Egyptian would have easily understood: "As it was in the beginning, is now, and ever shall be, world without end."

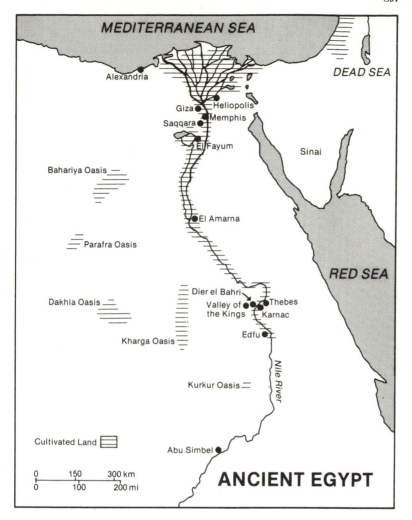

MEDITERRANEAN SEA

DEAD SEA

Alexandria

Giza — Heliopolis
Saqqara — Memphis

El Fayum

Sinai

Bahariya Oasis —

Parafra Oasis

El Amarna

RED SEA

Dier el Bahri
Dakhla Oasis — Valley of — Thebes
the Kings — Karnac
Edfu
Kharga Oasis

Nile River

Kurkur Oasis

Cultivated Land

0   150   300 km
0   100   200 mi

Abu Simbel

ANCIENT EGYPT

The broad valley of Mesopotamia had given easy passage to successive invaders, and the history of that region is one of successive peoples, each modifying the culture absorbed. In contrast, Egypt was protected by desert to the east and west, by mountains and cataracts to the south, and by the Mediterranean to the north; until late in their history the Egyptians kept no standing army. Although trade was actively carried on with the rest of the world, Egypt was geographically isolated; thus protected, the Egyptians very early began to develop a civilization that survived nearly three thousand years.

The Culture of Egypt

Secure in their desert-protected paradise, the ancient Egyptians were content in the endless cycles of life determined by sun and river; they perceived the cosmos not as subject to the whims of the gods but as an unchanging continuum. As a result they developed early a deeply conservative view of life. Unlike the citizens of twentieth-century Western civilization, who believe in progress, in things getting progressively better through the intervention of human ingenuity, the ancient Egyptians had no such concept. To them things were never as good

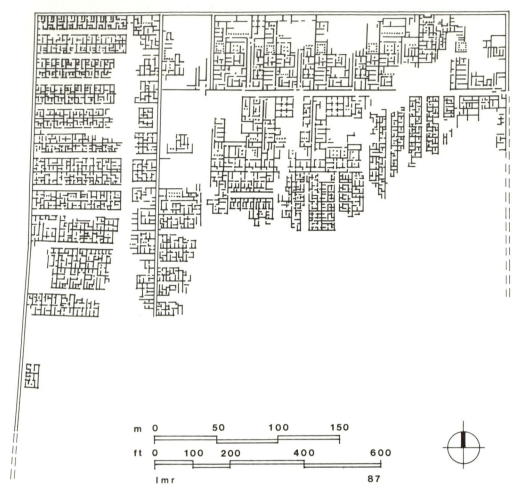

m 0   50   100   150

ft 0   100   200   400   600

I m r   87

10.1. *Village at El Kahun, c. 1897–1878 B.C. This village, built by Sesostris II just east of his pyramid, was to house officials, craftsmen, and laborers working on his burial place.*

as they had been at the time of creation. That had been a golden age, when the gods inhabited the earth. They continually tried to re-create that perfect time. As a consequence, once the forms of Egyptian religion, literature, art, and architecture had been developed, during the predynastic period through the Fourth Dynasty, they changed very little during the following two and a half thousand years.

Almost imperceptibly over the centuries the details of painted or carved images changed, and the proportions of building parts varied, allowing scholars of Egyptian art to identify a statue or building as belong-

ing to the Fourth Dynasty or the Eighteenth Dynasty, but the essential form was fixed. This conservatism was reinforced by Egyptian religion. Most of the many gods represented forces of nature, and their images incorporated aspects and images of humans and animals. Supremely important during the Old Kingdom (Third to Sixth dynasties) was Ra, the sun god, usually shown as a hawk-headed human, with a sun disk resting on his head. Later, during the Middle Kingdom and the Empire, Amon became chief among the gods. More of a pervasive spirit, he was shown as a human figure with a tall headdress shaped like two feathers. Amon was often associated and fused with other gods as well, particularly with the older Ra, resulting in Amon-Ra, who combined aspects of both. The god Osiris, slain by his jealous brother, Seth, and dismembered, was restored to life by his wife, Isis, who carefully gathered the parts of his body. Hence Osiris came to symbolize the land and its cyclical death and rebirth after the flood; he presided over the judgment of the dead. The pharaoh was believed to embody all of these gods. He *was* Ra and Amon, so that the priests in the temples throughout the land, in elevating, feeding, and dressing the images of Amon in their temples, were enacting what Pharaoh, Amon-incarnate, was doing himself at that very moment in his own palace—rising, dressing, and eating. These priestly ceremonies of the state religion were not public ceremonies; the peasants and artisans worshiped any of the scores of local gods associated with their particular province, or nome. But several times during the year the great temple complexes were the sites of public festivals that went on for days.

What served to reinforce the inherent conservatism of Egyptian religion and life was the concept of *ma'at*. It is a term impossible to translate into any European language, for it combines aspects of truth, justice, order, stability, security, a cosmic order of harmony, a created and inherited rightness. It was the goal of the Egyptian farmer, artisan, noble, and priest to live in accordance with *ma'at*, the right order of things created at the beginning of the world. Thus, to advocate radical change, whether material, social, or religious, was to violate *ma'at*. This is no doubt part of the reason why the imposition of a radical new monotheism in religion, and a dramatic realism in art, undertaken by the Pharaoh Akhenaton in the Eighteenth Dynasty, was quickly swept away after his death by the priests of Amon, who reestablished their temples.

Another concept that resists full comprehension in the Western societies of the twentieth century is the fusion of religion and daily life in ancient Egypt; perhaps only orthodox Jews and those who advocate fun-damental Islamic republics so intertwine civil and religious life today. The daily life of the ancient Egyptian was filled with his religion, with the worship of Amon-Ra, of the god-king Pharaoh, and of local deities.

The Egyptian reveled not only in the pleasures of this life but worked to ensure that those pleasures would continue into the next. Perhaps the sense of the continuity of life and the pervasive nature of religion arose in response to what the predynastic peoples observed happened to the bodies of the dead placed in pit graves dug in the desert sands. The bodies were rapidly desiccated; thus dried, they were no longer susceptible to attack by bacteria—they did not rot. Perhaps this survival of the body after death promoted the idea that the human spirit likewise endured, passing to a different realm of existence. The Egyptians conceived of a soul with four distinct attributes. The *Ka* resided with the body in the tomb or nearby, perhaps occupying one of the statues placed in the later, more elaborate tombs. The *Ba* was a more active physical vitality which left the body at death and could move about. The two other aspects of the soul were *Akh* ("effective spirit") and *Sekham,* which seems to have been a twin of the *Ka*. Predynastic burials were made with the bodies surrounded by tools and jars filled with provisions for the next life. Soon the practice developed of artificially drying and wrapping the body, preparing it for the long afterlife. For the most elaborate burials of the pharaohs, several months were required for the many rituals observed by the priests. (Concerning the ancient dried and wrapped bodies, Arabs used the word *mumiyah,* or bitumen, for by the time of the Roman conquest the practice had degenerated to dipping bodies in pitch as a preservative; our word *mummy* comes from this.) Even after death priests provided for daily symbolic feeding of the dead. The present life, in all its security and comforts, was lived to the full, but the next life, stretching out to eternity, was ultimately more important. Hence, while mud brick was sufficient for the houses of peasants, nobles, and pharaohs alike, carefully dressed stone was used for the houses of the gods and of the dead, beginning with the Third Dynasty.

It is all too easy for modern observers to see in mummification, elaborately decorated tombs, and costly funereal stone architecture a morbid fixation with death on the part of the ancient Egyptians. It was in fact quite the reverse; the Egyptians had a fixation with life. The easy and relatively carefree life made possible by the Nile was simply too good to end. Properly provided for, the dead could enjoy the warm kiss of the sun, the pleasure of onions, figs, and beer, the sound of music, and the companionship of loved ones for all eternity.

Egyptian History

Farming villages began to appear along the Nile as early as 5500 B.C., gradually developing into two cultures, one in the harder geography of the southern valley of Upper Egypt, and another in the more moderate climate of the flat, northern delta of Lower Egypt. Forty provinces became defined (called *nomes* by the Greeks, and administered by nomarchs). Towns flourished, agriculture became organized, and writing was developed with pictorial imagery. An architecture was developed of mud bricks reinforced with straw. Coated with a hard plaster, this was sufficiently durable in a climate with little rain, and some of these structures have been in use for four thousand years. About 3100 B.C. the forty nomes of the two separate kingdoms were united by the legendary king Menes, the first of the pharaohs of the thirty following dynasties. Menes established a new capital at Memphis, south of the delta, or Lower Egypt, but north of Upper Egypt and thus at the nation's very center. There followed a five-hundred-year period of peace and prosperity known as the Old Kingdom, c. 2700 B.C. to 2200 B.C.

Control of the Nile's flood water was essential, and this led very early to a centralized government administering the water. The measurement of the river flow, the annual surveying of the land after the crest, and the stockpiling of surplus grain against lean years all encouraged the rapid development of a large bureaucracy and fostered the creation of an absolute monarchy in which the ruler was more than mortal, serving as the representative of the gods. Pharaoh was viewed as a god, the son of Ra the sun god, and upon Pharaoh's death his place as the living god was taken by his son, while the spirit of the dead pharaoh became an even more powerful deity, joining Ra in his boat or barge in the heavens.

Governing such a far-flung nation re-

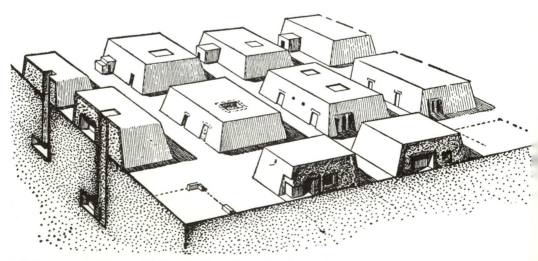

10.2. Cutaway view of a mastaba. The actual burial was below the mastaba.

quired the pharaoh to give gradually more power to the regional nomarchs. By the end of the Sixth Dynasty, 2200 B.C., this had led to a breakdown in the administration of the Old Kingdom and had brought about the decentralization of power known as the First Intermediate Period, c. 2200 B.C. to 2052 B.C. During the Twelfth Dynasty, centralized government was restored and the Middle Kingdom began, lasting from 2052 B.C. to 1786 B.C. The center of power now shifted to a new capital, at Thebes in Upper Egypt. The once unquestioned and absolute authority of the pharaoh of the Old Kingdom was replaced by the increasing power of the priests of Amon, who trained and operated the vast bureaucracy. Another bureaucratic breakdown began in 1786 B.C., resulting in the Second Intermediate Period, which lasted until 1575 B.C.[2]

With the return of strong central government during the Eighteenth Dynasty in 1575 B.C., Egypt began to extend its influence south into Nubia (the Sudan) and north through Palestine to Mesopotamia. This period is called the New Kingdom or the Empire, and it lasted from 1575 B.C. to 1087 B.C. Among its vigorous rulers were Thutmose III and Hatshepsut, the only woman to rule as pharaoh in her own right. Particularly remarkable during this period was the attempt at radical religious, administrative, and artistic reform by Amenhotep IV, who changed his name to Akhenaton and attempted to introduce a monotheistic religion (the first name had meant "Amon-is-Satisfied-with-this-Person," whereas the new name meant "He-Who-is-Serviceable-to-Aton"). However, the dramatic changes in religion and art he initiated did not survive his reign and were suppressed after his death. Akhenaton was succeeded by the young Tutankhamen, whose short reign ended with his unexpected death at age eighteen. Deprived of the opportunity of spending a long reign preparing an elaborate tomb, Tutankhamen was hastily buried in a small tomb cut in the cliffs of the Valley of the Kings. Later the entrance to Tutankhamen's tomb was buried in the debris of a tomb cut above it, and so was hidden from grave robbers until it was found by the archaeologist Howard Carter in 1922. It was a minor tomb of a minor pharaoh, and it was the only one to survive virtually untouched by ancient grave robbers. It took Carter eight years to remove and catalogue the two thousand priceless objects he found there.

Among the most active builders of the Empire was Ramses II, 1304–1237 B.C.; the Egyptian landscape is dotted with temples he erected. So potent did his name become that nine successive Pharaohs after him adopted it. By 1000 B.C. the empire had ended, and Egypt began a slow decline in power until it was conquered by the Persians in 525 B.C., made part of Alexander's empire in 332 B.C., and then annexed by the Romans in 30 B.C. Nonetheless, so great was the power of the culture of Egypt that it took a thousand years for it to subside.

The Step Pyramid of Zoser at Saqqara

The earliest predynastic burials had been made in graves scooped out of the sand, sometimes covered with stone slabs, but jackals made short work of digging up the bodies. The practice developed of building mound structures over the graves, enclosed by sloping mud brick walls. As these grew larger, small rooms were incorporated to contain offerings of food and perhaps a chamber to contain a sculpture of the deceased [10.2]. These tombs were rectangular and resembled the benches found outside Arab houses, and so came to be called *mastabas* ("bench" in Arabic). Clusters of them would be built together for members of a family, so that in death the family group maintained the physical proximity it had enjoyed in life.

If there was one successful and abrupt revolution in Egyptian architecture, it was that created during the Third Dynasty by Pharaoh Zoser (also spelled Djoser) and his architect and chief minister, Imhotep, in the construction of a tomb complex at Saqqara just south of the capital city of Memphis. Construction began about 2750 B.C., twenty years after Zoser came to the throne. Imhotep's innovations were twofold. First,

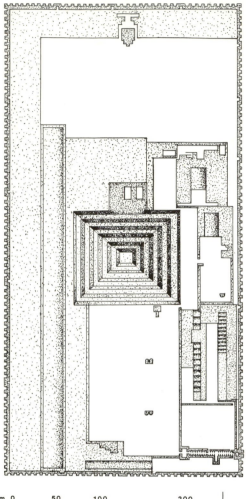

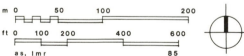

10.3. Imhotep, Pyramid of Zoser, Saqqara, Egypt, c. 2750 B.C. Plan of the pyramid sanctuary complex. Aside from the pyramid itself, nearly everything inside the walls was doubled, representing the two united kingdoms of Upper and Lower Egypt.

measuring 1,788 feet (545 meters) north to south by 909 feet (277 meters) east to west [10.3]. There were several false gates, but only one true entrance, at the southeast corner. This led to a long covered corridor with twenty projecting spur-walls on each side, ending in tapered engaged columns resembling bundles of reeds; at the end was a broader chamber. It is believed that this passage was a symbolic representation of the Nile, with the forty nomes along its banks and the broad delta at the end. Beyond the entry hall was a large open court, perhaps used in the Heb-Sed ceremonies to symbolically rejuvenate the pharaoh (he had to perform all rituals twice, as king of both Upper and Lower Egypt). Immediately to the right of the entrance gate was another long narrow passage, running north to another court; beyond this farther to the north were two identical buildings called House of the South and House of the North, another reference to the pharaoh's dual reign. The engaged columns in these buildings have lotus bud capitals (symbolic of Upper Egypt) and papyrus-plant capitals (typical of Lower Egypt's delta). Just west of the House of the North was another court; at its southwest corner, up against the base of the pyramid was the Serdab chamber. Just west of the Serdab room, and on the axis of the pyramid, is a building seeming to be a replica in stone of the king's palace in Memphis, but with all rooms doubled for the king in his dual role.

The stepped pyramid was started as a broad mastaba with a subterranean tomb cut into the rock plateau; the walls of this tomb chamber were lined with green glazed tile, recalling the reed mats on the walls of the king's palace. To contain burials of other members of Zoser's family, the original mastaba was then extended at its sides, but then the decision was made to transform the traditional horizontal mastaba into a vertical monument by placing four more mastabas over the original mastaba, which then became the base for the pile [10.4]. Another change was made, further enlarging the base and changing the number of superimposed mastabas to five. The final result,

he substituted limestone for the mud brick, bundled reeds, and tree trunks that had been used in royal buildings up to that time (although the stone was cut in small blocks and used like bricks). Second, he literally invented the pyramid.

Zoser's tomb and pyramid complex was enclosed in a wall 34 feet high (10.4 meters), sheathed in fine white limestone, was a stepped pyramid measuring 459 feet (140 meters) east to west, 387 feet (118 meters) north to south, with an original height of 197 feet (60 meters).

Why Zoser should have ordered this unprecedented change, and why Imhotep should have devised it, is impossible to tell. But the form was immediately seized upon by successive rulers, who further modified it by filling in the steps to arrive at the familiar smooth surface.

The Pyramids at Giza

The historians of the ancient world recognized the special character of the pyramids at Giza; they were foremost among the Seven Wonders of the World [10.5, 10.6]. Perhaps no other monument has been sub-

jected to such probing analysis, serious scientific study, and silly conjecture. The Giza trio represents the culmination of pyramid building and was never surpassed by the Egyptians. Each of the great masses is perfectly aligned toward the North Star and the perpendicular axis of the sun. The first pyramid constructed was the northernmost and the largest of the three; it was built for Khufu (called Cheops by Herodotus), the second pharaoh of the Fourth Dynasty, which lasted from c. 2680 B.C. to c. 2560 B.C. Next, to the south was built the pyramid for Khufu's son, Khafre (called Chephren by Herodotus), the third pharaoh of the Fourth Dynasty. Then, south and west of the center pyramid, the last and smallest of the three pyramids was built by Khafre's son, Menkare (called Mycerinus by Herodotus).

The unending fascination with the Giza

10.4. *Pyramid of Zoser. View of the pyramid. Now missing much of the outer casing, the steps of the pyramid once rose to a height of 197 feet (60 meters).*

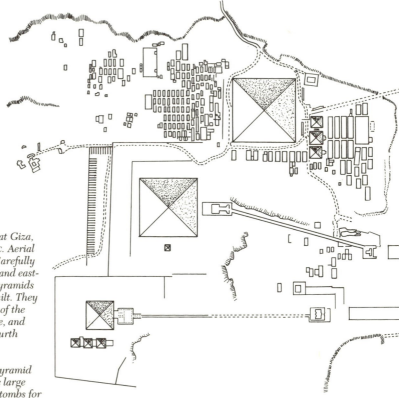

10.5. Pyramid complex at Giza, Egypt, c. 2680–2560 B.C. Aerial view to the northeast. Carefully aligned on north-south and east-west axes, these three pyramids were the largest ever built. They were built as the tombs of the pharaohs Khufu, Khafre, and Menkare during the Fourth Dynasty.

10.6. Plan of the Giza pyramid group. Surrounding the large pyramids were smaller tombs for members of the royal family, mortuary temples where the last stages of mummification were completed, and causeways that reached to the floodwaters of the Nile.

m   0   100   200   300   400   500

ft   0   500   1000   1500   2000

a s   85

pyramids is due no doubt to two factors—their sheer size and the precision with which they were built. The pyramid of Khufu, the largest, originally measured 440 Egyptian cubits on each side (755 feet, 230 meters), and rose to a height of 479 feet (146 meters); today it is shorter, since the outer casing of finely fitted limestone was removed to build portions of Cairo. Its sides have an angle of 51° 50'. At first Khufu's pyramid was to cover a subterranean burial chamber cut deep into the rock of the plateau, but, as the layers of blocks were put in place, this was changed to a slightly elevated burial chamber, and then there was a further change to an even more elevated chamber at almost the exact center of the pyramid's mass [10.7]. The pyramid of Khafre was 707 feet square (215.5 meters), and rose 470 feet (143.5 meters), and is the only one of the three to retain a portion of its original limestone casing at the top; in places this still has something of its original polish. Its sides have a slope of 53° 10'. The smaller pyramid for Menkare measured 356 feet square (108.5 meters) and rose 281 feet (66.5 meters), with slides sloping 50°; it too

is missing its casing, the lower sixteen courses of which were of granite.

The pyramids are virtual mountains, hauled block by block up to the plateau from the Nile. The base of Khufu's pyramid covers just over 13 acres (5.3 hectares); it is big enough to contain the plans of the cathedrals of Florence, and Milan, the basilica of Saint Peter in Rome, as well as Saint Paul's and Westminster Abbey in London, and still have room left over. Including the casing stones, it contained about 2,300,000 blocks, each weighing about 2.5 tons, although some weigh as much as 15 tons. When Napoleon sat at the foot of the pyramids he is said to have calculated that there was enough material in the three to build a wall 3 meters high and 1 meter thick around the whole of France.

The individual pyramids were the most visible part of extensive funereal complexes. Each was approached through a canal cut from the high-water bank of the Nile. At the end of this was a valley temple and auxiliary structures connecting to a causeway sloping up to the foot of the pyramid over which the stones for the pyramid were dragged, a mor-

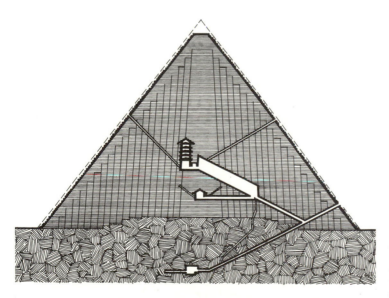

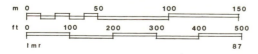

10.7. Pyramid of Khufu, c. 2680–2560 B.C. The cross section reveals the changes in the design, with the first burial chamber deep below the pyramid, the second shifted to a position above the initial layers of stone blocks, and the final burial chamber shifted to a point nearly at the center of the mass.

tuary temple at the foot of the pyramid, and a surrounding necropolis (Greek for "city of the dead") of small pyramids, tombs, and mastabas for members of the royal family. The Valley Temple of Khafre, mentioned before as an example of pure post and lintel construction, has columns and beams cut of red granite placed on a floor of alabaster [2.7]. Inside were twenty-three statues of the king, temporary abodes of the *Ka,* and in the temple it is likely that Khafre's body was ritually washed and the complex process of mummification carried out. Just to the north of the Valley Temple the king's sculptors took advantage of a rock outcropping and carved an enormous figure, the Sphinx, with the body of a crouching lion and the head of the pharaoh, with the forepaws built of stone blocks.

Two questions arise: *How* was this stupendous construction done? More important: *Why* was nearly the whole of the working force of Egypt occupied with such a gargantuan task for years on end? To appreciate the accomplishment it must be remembered that the Egyptians used only tools of wood, stone, and copper and employed no wheeled vehicles (they adopted the war chariot only after 1750 B.C.). The stone blocks were either lashed to sledges and rolled over logs, or possibly crescent-shaped wooden pallets were tied to square stone blocks enabling a few workmen to roll the stones. Most of the journey, from quarry to building site, however, was made easy by shipment along the Nile. One of the most critical steps was leveling the platform of the plateau to receive the base of the pyramid, for a slight misalignment would cause severe problems toward the top of the pyramid. The leveling was achieved by means of trenches filled with water, and so exact was this work that modern surveying instruments have detected a rise of only ½ inch (less than 2 centimeters), at the northwest corner of Khufu's pyramid. Once the huge platform was dressed and made ready the blocks were put in place, layer upon layer, year after year.

How were the stones lifted layer upon layer? A conventional notion is of a single long ramp of earth, but as the pyramid rose this would have necessitated the continual raising and lengthening of the ramp at each level; half the workmen would have been doing nothing but building the ramp. A more logical procedure would have been to have four helical ramps going up each side of the pyramid and wrapping around it— three ramps for teams hauling sledges or rollers up to the working level and one for the empty sledges to come down. Once the capstone was put in place, and as the final casing was polished, the earth ramps could be removed working from the top down.

There are no contemporary accounts of how the pyramids were built nor how many workmen were employed. Herodotus was told two thousand years after the fact that one hundred thousand men were engaged for "periods of three months," and that it took twenty years to erect Khufu's pyramid. Herodotus believed that four crews of one hundred thousand worked year-round, but it now seems likely that most of the workers were employed during the height of the inundation, when farming came to a halt and when the waters rose closest to the quarry sites and to the pyramid plateau. Based on estimates of the weight of the blocks, the distances they had to be moved, and the capacity of teams of eight or ten workmen, it seems likely that one hundred thousand men moved the rough-cut stones from quarry to building site during Inundation. Excavations have revealed what appear to have been lodges for up to four thousand workmen at the base of the pyramid of Khafre. This would be approximately the correct number of skilled masons required year-round to do the finishing work.

The most essential question remains: why was such stupendous effort expended? Conventional wisdom, reinforced in numerous fictional depictions and motion pictures, tells us that the workmen were under the whip, that they were slaves forced to build for the aggrandizement of the pharaoh. The Old Testament informs us that the Israelites performed labor of this kind, but this was at least 850 years later, during a very unsettled time in Egypt. The Fourth Dynasty was a kind of Golden Age in Egypt, a time of peace, security, and plenty. During the Old

Kingdom, the god-king Pharaoh ruled supreme, aided by the priests of Ra, the sun god. At this point the idea of an afterlife was confined largely to the pharaoh and his immediate family (only after the upsets of the First Intermediate Period and the emergence of the Middle Kingdom did there arise the egalitarian notion of an afterlife for everyone). In the Old Kingdom, at death the pharaoh became a god joining Ra in his daily passage through the heavens; the spirit of the dead pharaoh became an intercessor to the gods on behalf of his people, their sole link to the gods. For three months of the year, work in the fields came to a halt. In all but the worst times, the fields yielded more food than was required in a year, so that by attentive study of the river, and through careful management of the surplus of grain, it was possible to have levies of men from each of the forty nomes sent to Giza during Inundation as a kind of public works project during the flood. There were no whips, but willing laborers instead. For the workmen this was an investment in their families' future, since if the pharaoh were properly conveyed to Ra it would benefit them all. One foreman wrote that the men worked "without a single man getting exhausted, without a man thirsting" and that they "came home in good spirits, sated with bread, drunk with beer, as if it were a beautiful festival of a god."[3]

The pyramids may have been viewed as serving a purely practical purpose. In the ancient temple of Ra in the sacred delta city the Greeks called Heliopolis (City of the Sun) was a pointed stone called the *ben-ben,* said to symbolize the primordial mound that first emerged from the water, catching the first light of the sun at creation. The pyramids were considered gigantic *ben-bens:* their capstones were gilded, and from them the spirit of pharaoh greeted Ra on the dawn after his burial. This interpretation is suggested by the Egyptian word for pyramid, *m(e)r* (*pyramid* is a Greek term). In Egyptian hieroglyphs the prefix *m* means "place" or "instrument." The character *'r,* meaning "place to ascend," was written with the symbol resembling back-to-back stairs ⏢ or perhaps a side view of a step pyramid.

This suggests that when the Egyptians spoke of the *m(e)r* of Khufu they meant literally "The-Instrument-by-Which-Khufu-Ascends." And the texts inscribed in the chambers and passageways of later Fourth Dynasty pyramids (the so-called Pyramid Texts) contain passages that reinforce this interpretation. For example, Spell 267 reads: "A staircase to heaven is laid [for Pharaoh] so that he may mount up to heaven thereby." Under certain afternoon conditions, with dust in the air catching the light of the lowering sun as it pierces an opening in clouds, a pyramid of light seems to reach to earth; perhaps this is what Spell 508 means: "I have trodden thy rays as a ramp under my feet whereupon I mount up." And as Spell 523 relates, "Heaven hath strengthened for thee the rays of the sun in order that thou mayest lift thyself to heaven as the eye of Ra."[4] Perhaps, then, the pyramid was the king's launching place, the mountain whose gilded summit would catch the first rays of the sun, from which the soul of pharaoh would rise to greet Ra in his eternal endeavor to ensure *ma'at,* the never-ending rightness of things for his living subjects below.

Egyptian Villages and Houses

The ancient Egyptian metropolises of Memphis and Thebes have disappeared, for they were built of mud brick. Under Pharaoh Akhenaton a new capital city called Akhetaten (The Horizon of Aten) was built, c. 1379–1362 B.C. at a site at the virtual geographic center of ancient Egypt, now called Tel el Amarna. It was to be the headquarters for the religious revolution being attempted by Akhenaton. After Akhenaton's death the city and its new temples were deliberately pulled down by the priests of Amon, and the stones of the temple were reused in later buildings. Yet fragments of Tel el Amarna survive, permitting a reconstruction of a commodious villa in a northern suburb [10.8, 10.9]. From the street one entered through a gate in the surrounding wall; immediately to the left was a small gatekeeper's lodge. Within a walled garden was a small temple to Aton, the new god.

10.8. Suburban villa, Akhetaten (Tel el Amarna), Egypt, c. 1379–1362 B.C. This reconstruction (Oriental Institute, University of Chicago) of a villa outside Akhenaton's new capital city shows the basic elements of a large household, including a small private temple for worship of the newly declared god Aton.

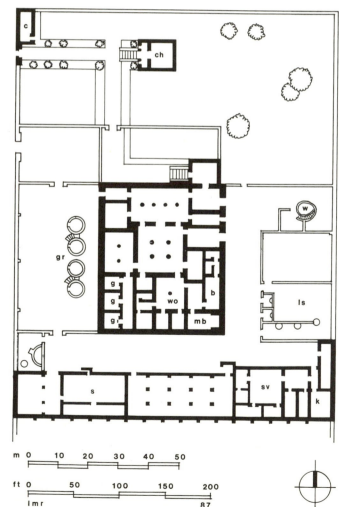

10.9. Plan of villa at Tel el Amarna.

    b   = bathing room
    c   = caretaker's room
    ch   = private chapel
    g   = guest rooms
    gr   = granaries
    k   = kitchen
    ls   = livestock
    mb   = master's bedroom
    s   = store rooms
    sv   = servants' quarters
    w   = well
    wo   = wives' quarters

Past an inner garden court was the house complex, focused on the North Room and the Central Room at the core of the house. Around this core were arranged a West Room for guests, the wives' quarters on the south side, and the master's suite in the southeast corner. Windows in the thick mud brick walls were evidently quite small to reduce heat gain, and the center portions rose to permit light and ventilation through clerestory windows.

Around the principal house were a granary on the west side, stables and a chariot room in the southwest corner of the compound, servants' quarters in the south-central portion, and storerooms and the kitchen in the southeast corner, with a cattle barn and a well along the east side. This was clearly the abode of a favored and successful administrator, perhaps a priest who served in the temple.

Scribes and artisans also lived reasonably well, for their services were crucial to the operation of temple services and the creation of inscriptions and paintings in the temples and tombs. The temple artisans' quarter in Thebes has long since disappeared, but the town built for the artisans working on the tombs in the Valley of the

10.10. Plan of the tomb artisans' village Deir el Medineh, Egypt, begun c. 1530 B.C. This village was inhabited by the scribes, painters, and sculptors who constructed the tombs of the kings and queens of Egypt; it was located on the cliffs overlooking the green Nile valley to the east and the Valley of the Kings to the west.

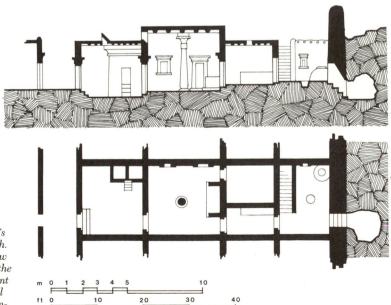

10.11. One of the artisan's houses at Deir el Medineh. The plan and section show the basic components of the Egyptian house, with front reception room, principal room, bedroom, and open-air kitchen.

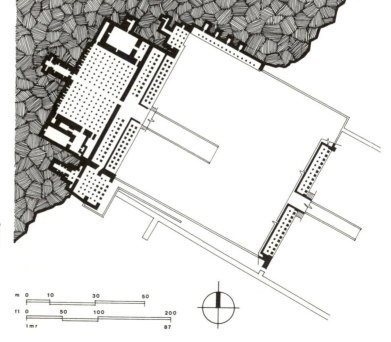

10.12. Senmut, Tomb of Queen Hatshepsut, Deir el Bahari, Egypt, c. 1500 B.C. This remarkable tomb-temple complex is integrated into the base of the cliff west of the Nile, and originally included a grove of myrrh trees brought back by the queen from Punt (Somalia).

10.13. Plan of the Tomb of Queen Hatshepsut.

Kings has survived in part [10.10]. It was founded by Tuthmose I about 1530 B.C. to house an elite corps of artists, craftsmen, and scribes. Now called Deir el Medineh, it was placed in a depression atop the cliffs overlooking the green fields of the Nile valley and Thebes and Karnak to the east, with a path leading down to the desert Valley of the Kings just to the north. The houses, one room wide and several rooms deep [10.11], have the same major parts as the larger, Amarna villa. The dimensions range from 13 to 20 feet wide (4–6 meters) and 65 to 83 feet long (20–25 meters). The front room, with a door to the narrow street, was a reception room with a small shrine to the household god Bes. Beyond that was a taller, larger room, presumed to have had clerestory lighting, with a bedroom behind it. To the rear was a court with stairs to the roof and the kitchen open to the sky for ventilation. Often a small storage cellar was excavated beneath the house.

The Tomb of Hatshepsut at Deir el Bahri

The absolute theocratic power of the pharaohs during the Fourth Dynasty was never equaled, and as a consequence the Giza pyramids were never surpassed. Smaller pyramids were built by subsequent kings, but after the disruption of the First Intermediate Period, tombs and temples replaced pyramids as the major royal building enterprises. Even the gods felt this upheaval, for Ra was displaced as the principal god by Amon, whose priests were centered at Thebes, a city in middle Upper Egypt. Thebes became the capital city, and south of it two large temples to Amon arose, at Karnak and Luxor. Across from the temples, on the west bank of the Nile, beyond which the sun set, tombs were built at the edge of the cultivated valley floor, cut into the face of the cliffs. The model for this type of tomb was provided by the terraced complex built against the base of the western cliff at Deir el Bahri by the Eleventh Dynasty pharaoh Mentuhotep, about 2120 B.C. Its large middle colonnaded terrace, aligned on the axis of the Temple of Amon

at Karnak across the river, perhaps was pierced by a pyramid measuring 70 feet square (21.5 meters) at its base.[5]

That tomb now survives in fragments, but next to it, in much better condition, is the tomb of Queen Hatshepsut, pharaoh of the Eighteenth Dynasty, who ruled 1503–1482 B.C. [10.12, 10.13]. Among her many accomplishments was a commercial expedition to the Land of Punt (modern Somalia), which brought back myrrh trees. Hatshepsut gave her architect and administrator, Senmut, the task of building a terraced mortuary chapel complex next to that of Mentuhotep, to serve also as an earthly paradise for Amon, with a myrrh tree garden recalling those of Punt. Along the axis that runs to the temple of Amon at Karnak across the river, Senmut laid out a Valley Temple opening to a long causeway lined with figures of sphinxes, leading to a broad forecourt lined with trees. Along the west wall runs a colonnade of blunt square piers, behind which are more delicate faceted sixteen-sided columns (they begin to approach the severity of early Greek Doric columns); the colonnade is interrupted at its center by a ramp that rises to an upper terrace. Along the west side of this terrace, too, is a double colonnade, serving as a porch to temples at the far ends dedicated to Hathor, the goddess of love and associated with the arts and music, and Anubis, god of mummification. Deeper inside this porch was an open peristyle court flanked by temples of Amon and Ra cut into the face of the cliff.

The entire temple complex is rooted in the axial and orthogonal traditions of Egyptian geometry and spatial organization. But its unique features are the way Senmut integrated the terraces into the horizontal layers of the cliff, with the vertical lines of the colonnades echoing the vertical weathered grooves of the cliff faces, making temple and cliff seem to be extensions of each other.

The Temple of Amon at Karnak

Temples were more than places of worship, combining centers of learning and administration for the nation. The Egyptian temple,

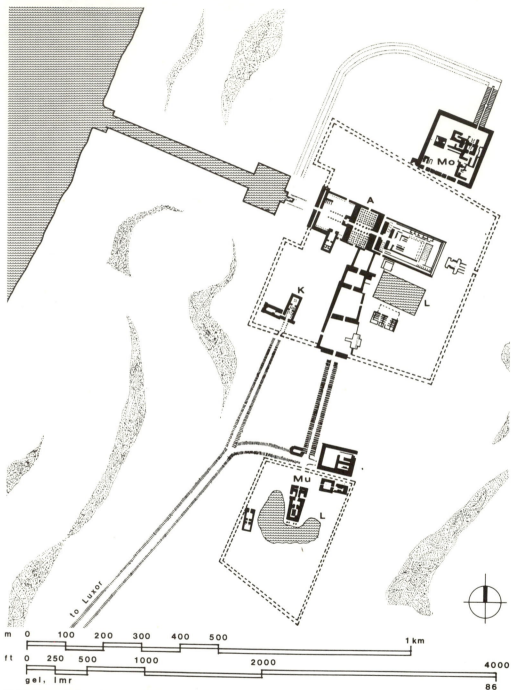

10.14. *General plan of the temple complex at Karnak, Thebes, Egypt, c. 2000–323* B.C. *The core of the ancient Middle Kingdom temple was wrapped with new chambers, courts, and pylons by successive pharaohs for more than 1,700 years. This was the greatest and richest administrative/religious center in ancient Egypt.*

A = Temple of Amon   Mo = Temple of Montu
K = Temple of Khonsu   Mu = Temple of Mut
L = sacred lakes

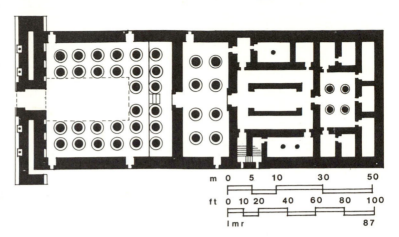

10.15. Temple of Khonsu, Karnak, Thebes, Egypt, c. 1170 b.c. This simple temple illustrates the basic elements of all Egyptian temple design, with an entry forecourt, a public hypostyle hall, and the inner sekos, a chamber reserved for the priests.

the most important public building by the time of the Middle Kingdom, was far more than a church as we understand the concept. It was the residence and training ground of the immense bureaucracy that ran the country. Priests taught writing and painting (to ensure that the images and inscriptions in the tombs were correct). The large temples included schools, universities, libraries, and archives; they were centers for government administration, scientific and medical study, and agricultural administration; and they served as public granaries and workshops. They were also the site of elaborate, prolonged theatrical religious festivals celebrated at the time of the inundation, when work came to a halt in the fields.

At Karnak, south of Thebes, the temple of Amon gradually became the religious and administrative center of the Egyptian Empire. As a temple of Amon it had been a sacred site since the Old Kingdom, but after the Tenth Dynasty it steadily rose in prominence as the major sacred site in Egypt. As Thebes prospered with the influx of spoils of war and the trade of the expanding Egyptian Empire, the temples to Amon at Karnak and Luxor were enlarged by succeeding pharaohs.

There were two principal sacred areas immediately south of Thebes along the east bank of the Nile: a Middle Kingdom temple to Amon at Karnak and another about half a mile to the south at Luxor [10.14]. The tem-

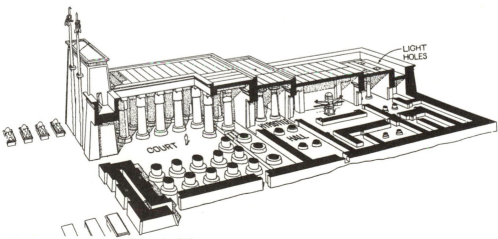

10.16. Cutaway perspective of Temple of Khonsu.

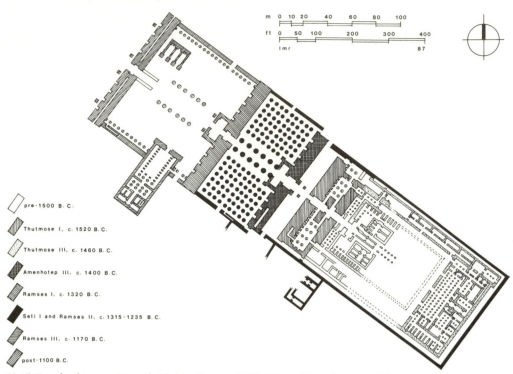

pre-1500 B.C.

Thutmose I, c. 1520 B.C.

Thutmose III, c. 1460 B.C.

Amenhotep III, c. 1400 B.C.

Ramses I, c. 1320 B.C.

Seti I and Ramses II, c. 1315-1235 B.C.

Ramses III, c. 1170 B.C.

post-1100 B.C.

10.17. Temple of Amon at Karnak, Thebes, Egypt, c. 2000–323 B.C. Plan. The parts of the temple still standing include the middle sanctuary built by Thutmose III (c. 1460 B.C.) and the soaring Hypostyle Hall built by Ramses II (c. 1315–1235 B.C.).

ple at Luxor was aligned roughly parallel to the bank of the Nile, but that at Karnak had its axis pointing toward the mid-winter sunrise. Both of these were replaced during the Eighteenth Dynasty, and then successively enlarged. Additional temples were placed around the compound at Karnak, including smaller temples dedicated to Montu, Mut, Ptah, and Khonsu.

Because the larger temple of Amon at Karnak became exceedingly complex as it was enlarged, the smaller temple of Khonsu built by Ramses III about 1170 B.C. illustrates more clearly the basic components of the New Kingdom temple [10.15, 10.16]. The temple was approached along an avenue marked by sphinxes, leading to an entrance *pylon,* or a massive sloped (battered) wall pierced by a narrow door. Slots in the battered wall accommodated flagpoles from which brightly colored banners hung. One passed through the pylon into an open forecourt enclosed by massive colonnades. Proceeding along the axis through this colonnade, one reached the *hypostyle hall,* a chamber filled with columns and lit by clerestory windows. Beyond this lay the *sekos,* the sanctuary reserved for the priests, focusing on a chamber containing the ceremonial boat, or barge, in which the statue of the god was moved during festivals.[6] At the rear of the temple was a chamber in which the image of the god resided, typically a wooden statue covered with gold. At daybreak the statue would be removed from its chamber for ritual washing, dressing, and feeding, before being replaced.

As this description suggests, the main sections of the temple were much like those of a residence (for this was the house of the god), with an entrance garden court, a formal reception hall whose roof was supported by a series of painted columns, and private chambers. Once perfected in the Middle and New kingdoms, the temple form was used for one and a half thousand years into the period of Roman annexation; most temples were built on an axis that ran perpendicular to the river, so that in the ritual washing of the image of Amon-Ra in the morning the priest faced the rising sun.

The huge temple of Amon at Karnak follows this same pattern [10.17]. The core of the sanctuary, already of considerable size, about 265 by 170 feet (81 by 52 meters), apparently survived from the Middle Kingdom. In front of this Thutmose I added two massive entrance pylons about 1520 B.C., enclosing a narrow forecourt. All of this was then encased in a new outer wall, with additional sanctuary chambers added to the rear by Thutmose III about 1460 B.C., bringing the overall dimensions to about 548 by 275 feet (167 by 84 meters). An even larger entrance pylon was built 48 feet (14.5 meters) to the front by Amenhotep III, about 1400 B.C. About 1320 B.C., roughly 161 feet (49 meters) farther to the northwest, Ramses I added yet another, even larger entrance pylon, nearly 41 feet (12.5 meters) thick at its base. During 1315 B.C. to 1235 B.C., Seti I and his son, the prodigious builder Ramses II, connected this pylon to that of Amenhotep III with an enclosing wall and built between them the great hypostyle hall enclosing an area measuring 320 by 160 feet (97.5 by 48.75 meters). In this were placed 134 enormous columns [10.18]. The 122 shorter, lotus-bud columns rise 42 feet and are 9 feet in diameter (12.8 by 2.75 meters), whereas the 12 lotus-blossom or bell columns marking the central axis are 69 feet high and are 11.75 feet (21 by 3.6 meters) in diameter. All were carved and painted with inscriptions; and in this Hall of the Two Crowns the pharaohs' coronations were celebrated. The taller central columns permitted clerestory lighting through stone louvers. Ramses II added yet another enclosing wall around the temple at Karnak. About 1170 B.C., Ramses III built a small temple house for himself south of the entrance axis and adjacent to Ramses I's entrance pylon. Two and a half centuries later, during the Twenty-First Dynasty, the walls enclosing the great entrance forecourt were built, and the enclosure of this vast space, 330 by 275 feet (100.5 by 84 meters)

was made complete by the erection of the entrance pylon just after the conquest by Alexander in 332 B.C. Altogether, construction continued over 1,700 years, and the final dimensions were 1,200 by 320 feet (366 by 98 meters).

Around the temple itself were smaller auxiliary temples, a sacred lake, gardens, granaries, administrative buildings, schools, and other buildings in an enclosed compound more than a quarter of a mile square. The sacred lake and the ceremonial boats housed in the temple for carrying the images of the gods from temple to temple during festivals reaffirmed the connection

10.18. *Hypostyle Hall, Temple of Amon, Karnak, Thebes, Egypt, c. 1315–1235 B.C. The huge columns along the central axis are 11.75 feet (3.6 meters) in diameter and rise 69 feet (21 meters); the axis they define is aligned to the rising sun at midwinter, pointing directly to the Valley of the Kings on the west side of the Nile.*

with the river, which lapped at the eastern boundary of the temple. The entire temple complex, with its lotus- and papyrus-shaped columns connoting marsh vegetation, and its sacred lake and pools, was in fact a formal representation of "the island of creation" when the world first appeared. The orientation of the Karnak temple axis towards the winter solstice sunrise makes clear the connection with the sun. This relationship is confirmed by the descriptions given to the parts of the temple, for as the temple complex was extended to the west its constituent parts were said to represent the hours of the day. For nearly three thousand years Egyptian builders continually reasserted the primeval rhythm of sun and river, guarding against change and preserving *ma'at*.

Late Egyptian Architecture

What so distinguishes Egyptian architecture is the deliberate resistance to change, or rather the acceptance of only the most gradual modification in architectural form over a span of almost 2,700 years. This persistence of form, especially in temple design, is well illustrated by examples built during the Ptolemaic period, when Egypt had been conquered by Alexander. The new temple of Horus, at Edfu, 237–212 B.C., might pass, at first glance, for a temple of a thousand years earlier. Like the temple of Khonsu at Karnak, it is entered through a massive pylon forming the end of the entrance court; beyond this is a shallow hypostyle hall connecting with the inner sanctuary. All parts are aligned on an orthogonal grid, and everything is organized along a dominant axis. Yet one detail suggests its late period and a sense of experimentation among its designers: the columns of the court do not carry the lintels directly on their open palm capitals but instead tall blocks are inserted, lifting the lintel into the air and denying the weight of the mass of the stone lintel block. The sense of mass and unending timelessness that had characterized Egyptian architecture since the Third Dynasty began to

dissipate after the end of the Thirty-first Dynasty. The world was no longer viewed as changeless, following an endlessly recurring cycle, for indeed these temples were built not at the direction of Egyptian pharaohs but by Greek rulers placed on the throne by conquering Alexander. The world was changing, and the fixed rules of Egyptian architecture were being stretched with these changes.

An Architecture of Permanence

Egyptian architecture changed only in subtle ways during thirty-one dynasties, over 2,700 years. The goal of Egyptian culture, and the architecture which housed its institutions, was continuity and order; this unending effort to thwart time, death, and decay bound the architect to the service of tradition. In part this arose due to the need for proper management of the Nile, which required continual social cooperation and strict discipline. As E. B. Smith wrote, the "beneficent tyranny of the Nile" created in Egypt a benign "environmental despotism" rather than a "social tyranny."[7] Ancient Egyptian society was one in which man and nature were bound into a fixed pattern, and the pharaoh became the divine symbol of that absolute and permanent man-nature relationship. In response, Egyptian architecture was one of massive geometric forms, sharp-edged and crystalline. The Egyptians valued bigness, mass, and solidity as the expression of durability, a guarantee of unlimited security and indestructibility. The constant repetition of their sacred chants found a parallel in the repetition of pylon and column in their temples. And yet, out of obelisk, pylon, hypostyle hall, and all the other architectural elements, the Egyptians never fashioned an organic architecture; for all their pragmatic science they never speculated or theorized. The Egyptians never stepped back from the architectural object, studied it reflectively as an abstract thing, because, as E. B. Smith recognized, "they saw not the stone but the symbol."[8]

NOTES

1. Herodotus, *The Histories,* ii. 5.
2. It may have been during this unsettled period that the Hebrews were in servitude in Egypt; another interpretation is that it was during the reign of Ramses II.
3. Quoted in Lionel Casson, *Ancient Egypt* (New York, 1965), 134.
4. These passages are quoted in I.E.S. Edwards, *The Pyramids of Egypt,* revised ed. (Baltimore, 1961), 288–91. See also the translations in J. H. Breasted, *The Development of Religion and Thought in Ancient Egypt* (New York, 1912).
5. The evidence for a small pyramid is scanty; some other structure may have stood at the center.
6. The pyramid of Khufu was surrounded by pits cut into the rock plateau for full-scale wooden boats in which he could travel with Ra; one of these pits was uncovered and the boat recovered intact in 1954.
7. E. B. Smith, *Egyptian Architecture as Cultural Expression,* 246–48.
8. Ibid., 249.

SUGGESTED READING

Alexander Badawy, *Architecture in Ancient Egypt and the Near East* (Cambridge, Mass., 1966).

————, *A History of Egyptian Architecture,* 3 vols. (Berkeley, Calif., 1954–68).

M. L. Bierbrier, *The Tomb-Builders of the Pharaohs* (London, 1982).

Lionel Carsen, *Ancient Egypt* (New York, 1965).

I.E.S. Edwards, *The Pyramids of Egypt,* revised ed. (Baltimore, Md., 1961).

Ahmen Fakhry, *The Pyramids,* second ed. (Chicago, 1969).

James Fitchen, "Building Cheop's Pyramid," *Journal, Society of Architectural Historians* 37 (March 1978): 3–12.

Sigfried Giedion, *The Eternal Present: vol. 1, The Beginnings of Architecture* (New York, 1964).

T.G.H. James, *Introduction to Ancient Egypt* (New York, 1989).

Paul Jordan, *Egypt the Black Land* (New York, 1976).

Kurt Mendelssohn, *The Riddle of the Pyramids* (New York, 1974).

John Romer, *Ancient Lives: Daily Life in Egypt of the Pharaohs* (New York, 1984).

Earl Baldwin Smith, *Egyptian Architecture as Cultural Expression* (New York, 1938; reprint, Watkins Glen, N. Y., 1968).

W. Stevenson Smith, *The Art and Architecture of Ancient Egypt,* second ed. (Baltimore, Md., 1981).

Desmond Stewart, *The Pyramids and the Sphinx: Egypt Under the Pharaohs* (New York, 1977).

Jon Manchip White, *Everyday Life in Ancient Egypt* (New York, 1963).

John A. Wilson, *The Burden of Egypt: An Interpretation of Ancient Egyptian Culture* (Chicago, 1951).

11.18. *Temple of Athena Nike, Athens, c. 435–420* B.C. *This tiny jewel was built to commemorate the Greek victory over the Persians; it stands over an ancient Bronze Age defensive bastion protecting the gate to the Akropolis. It has Ionic columns only at the front and rear.*

CHAPTER 11

Greek Architecture

The Greek architect . . . dealt with forms both natural and constructed. With them he celebrated his three deathless themes: the sanctity of the earth, the tragic stature of mortal life upon the earth, and the whole natures of those recognitions of the facts of existence which are the gods.

Vincent Scully, *The Earth, the Temple, and the Gods,* 1962

The Greeks were proud of their public and sacred architecture, and even in antiquity the white marble Parthenon atop the Akropolis hill in Athens was recognized as a special achievement. One writer of the second century B.C., in describing his visit to Athens, wrote admiringly of the "costly, remarkable, and farseen temple of Athena called the Parthenon" rising on the Akropolis to greet those coming into the city.[1] In the following centuries the Parthenon continued to be praised in literary works even though Greece was seldom visited by Europeans once that country was absorbed into the Ottoman Turkish Empire. Only in the mid-eighteenth century did an English expedition, led by James Stuart and Nicholas Revett, venture to Athens to record in a scientific way the actual appearance of the fabled Parthenon. The reputation that the ancients had attributed to the building was confirmed, and the Parthenon became a symbol of the clarity and precision of ancient Greek architecture. In the nineteenth century this led to a revival of Greek architecture in which the form was understood even if the spirit that created the Parthenon was missing. Since the mid-nineteenth century, as study of Greek history

and literature has ceased to be the measure of a well-educated person, ignorance of Greek culture increased. Hence to understand the intellectual clarity of ancient Greek architecture we must know something of the civilization that gave rise to it.

The ancient Greeks of the period 750 B.C. to 350 B.C. learned much from Egypt, apparently adapting their earliest sculpture and post and lintel stone architecture from Egyptian models. They readily admitted this, for as Plato wrote in *Epinomis,* "Whatever the Greeks acquire from foreigners is finally turned by them into something nobler."[2] Quickly, however, the Greeks shaped an art and architecture distinctly their own, creating a system of values celebrating human capacities that has formed the basis of Western civilization ever since.

The Geography of Greece

As in Egypt, where the river and desert created a particular culture, so too in Greece a specific geography and climate influenced culture, but here it fostered a much different view of mankind's place in the world. In ancient times Greece included more than the broad peninsula extending from the Balkans at the southeast corner of Europe; from the second millennium B.C. onward it also included the scores of islands scattered to the south and east of the peninsula as well as along the coast of Anatolia or Asia Minor in what is now Turkey. The ancient Greeks, in fact, spoke of the Aegean Sea between the Greek peninsula and Asia Minor as "the pond," since their countrymen were scattered about its edges.

Everywhere the Greek landscape is rough, a corrugated mass of limestone and marble mountain ridges extending into the sea like fingers, sheltering innumerable bays and coves. The land is divided into three main parts, centered on the principal peninsula. To the southeast of the main peninsula is Attica and the city of Athens. East of the peninsula lies the large island of Euboea, close to shore. To the south, like a gigantic hand with its fingers outstretched and pointing the way to Crete and Egypt, is the lesser peninsula of the Peloponnesus, attached to the mainland mass by a narrow isthmus at Corinth.

There is little flat soil except in coastal plains and occasional valleys. Farming was always difficult and it became more so as the forests were cut and the thin upland soil was washed into the sea. This erosion was well advanced even in ancient times, for Plato observed in *Critias* that "the fertile soil has fallen away, leaving only the skeleton of the land."[3] Travel from one valley or plain to the next was always treacherous; hence very early the Greeks turned to the sea as their major highway, and this risk-taking on the seas, in turn, bred in the Greeks an adventurousness of spirit, a love of action, and a readiness to put their strength to the test. The tough, resilient fiber of the Greeks was formed in response to a environment that could change dramatically in an instant, for besides violent thundershowers the region is prone to earthquakes, dangers seldom encountered by the Egyptian. The agricultural economy of the Greeks was based on small farms individually owned and operated, and both this economy and the rugged landscape prevented consolidation of the many Greek city-states into a centralized nation. Nonetheless the Greeks shared a

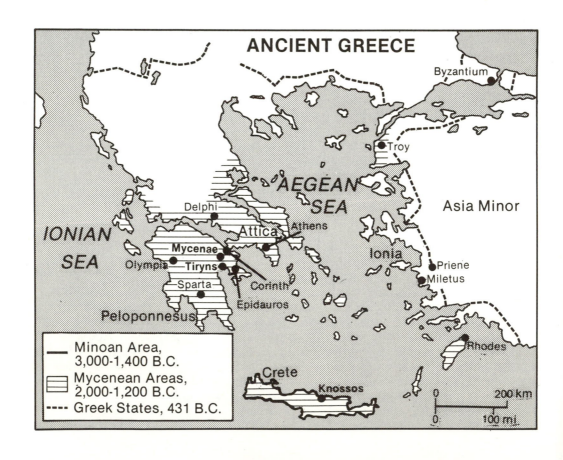

common religion and a rich language that set them apart from those who spoke what they said sounded like nonsense, "bah-bah"—the *barbaroi* or barbarians. The Greeks identified themselves, whatever their particular city-state, as Hellenes and their land, as a whole, Hellas.

Minoan and Mycenaean Greece

The Greeks of what is customarily called the Classic period, roughly 479 B.C. to 338 B.C. (the period focused on here), had descended in stages from Bronze Age cultures which flourished first on the island of Crete, on the islands of the Cyclades in the Aegean Sea, and then on the Peloponnesus and central Greece. The oldest culture was the Minoan, which began as early as 3400 B.C. and reached its peak during 1600 B.C. to 1400 B.C. It was named after the mythical King Minos by the archaeologist Sir Arthur Evans, who believed it had been centered in the immense and sprawling palace and administrative complex at Knossos that Evans began to excavate about 1900 [11.1]. The Knossos palace measured more than 460 feet (140 meters) square, centered about an open court running on a roughly north-south axis from the sacred mountains to the sea. Running through the building was a sophisticated plumbing and drainage system. In places its walls were four and five stories high in a series of setbacks around light courts and stairwells. The principal chambers had walls brilliantly painted with murals depicting religious activities and festive sports, especially contests involving vaulting over charging bulls. It may well be that the complex Knossos palace plan and the bull cult that flourished there formed the basis of the legend of Theseus and the Minotaur, who lived in the fabled labyrinth. The palatial complexes on Crete were remarkable for the complete absence of defensive walls, suggesting that the Minoans had such complete control of the sea they feared no invasion. This focus on the secular life of the palace sets Minoan culture apart from that of Egypt, with its focus on the tomb, or that of Mesopotamia, with its focus on the ziggurat temple.

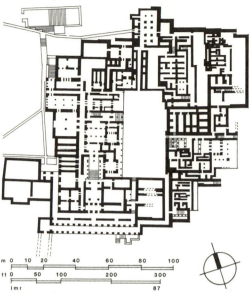

11.1. *Royal Palace, Knossos, Crete, c. 1600 B.C. Plan of the principal living level. This palace was combination residence, administrative center, and storehouse, open at its edges and without protective walls.*

Just prior to 2000 B.C. the outlying Minoan settlements were taken over by a new group which, presumably, moved down from the north. By 1600 B.C. the newcomers had established a distinct culture, called Mycenaean after the city of Mycenae on the Peloponnesus, which appears to have been its center; this Mycenaean culture flourished until 1125 B.C. A more vigorous and aggressive people, the Mycenaeans seem to have been a client state of the older Minoan culture on Crete. Unlike the Cretan cities, however, the Mycenaean settlements were fortified and built on isolated rock plateaus. On the high ground the principal palace was built, behind thick walls of large irregular but carefully fitted stones. The Greeks of the Classic period, looking on these ancient walls of massive rough blocks, imagined they could only have been built by the mythical one-eyed giant Cyclops, and hence this type of masonry came to be called *cyclopean*. All of the major settlements were of this kind, including Mycenae, the seat of King Agamemnon, who led these early Greeks to Troy (Homer's *Iliad* may be an elaborated and imperfectly remembered

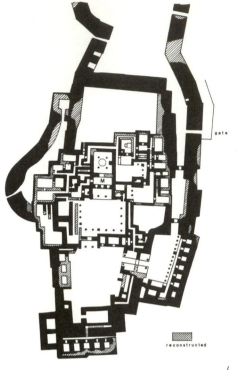

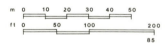

reconstructed

m 0   10   20   30   40   50
ft 0   50   100   200
                                      85

11.2. Akropolis Palace, Tiryns, Greece, c. 1400–1200
B.C. Plan. Mycenaean cities were built atop defensive
strongholds, as at Tiryns. M = Megaron.

11.3. Megaron unit, Akropolis Palace, Tiryns, Greece,
c. 1400–1200 B.C. The form of the central ceremonial
chamber, the megaron, is believed to have provided
the model for the later Greek temple.

m 0   5   10   15
ft 0   10   20   30   40   50
     l m r   87

account of an actual campaign in northern
Asia Minor). At Pylos, in 1939, was found
what has been called the home of King
Nestor, who accompanied Agamemnon in
the Trojan War.

The city of Tiryns (Homer's "Tiryns of the
Great Walls"), just south of Mycenae at the
base of the thumb of the Peloponnesus,
illustrates the basic organization [11.2]. Set
high on a limestone plateau rising from the
plain of Argos, and surrounded by massive
cyclopean walls 20 feet (6 meters) thick, it is
approached by a ramp on the east side.
Attackers would have been forced to
approach along the east wall with their right
side—the side not protected by a shield—
exposed to bowmen on the parapets. Entry
is through a *propylon* gate into a court. In
contrast to the strong outer walls, the inner
structures were built with wooden frames
and of rubble stone infill. Another propylon
gate, on the north side of the court, led to a

smaller palace court ringed with a sheltering
colonnade. This in turn led to the heart of
the palace, what the Greeks called the
megaron [11.3]. It consisted of an entry
porch formed by projecting walls framing
two columns, a vestibule, and the throne
room, nearly square, with its roof carried by
four columns (virtually the same arrangement was found at Mycenae and Pylos). At
the center of the principal room was a raised
circular hearth, suggesting the room was
open at the top.

The traditional view is that about 1150
B.C. the Mycenaean settlements were swept
over by yet another group from the north,
the direct ancestors of the Greeks. The
Greeks called them the Dorians. The Mycenaean culture collapsed, although there
were cultural strongholds that resisted,
especially Athens. Some groups fled the
Peloponnesus and sailed east, setting up
colonies in the islands close to Asia Minor

and on the Anatolian coast itself. Thus remnants of the old Minoan-Mycenaean culture continued to prosper in the easterly region that became Ionia, while the mainland of Greece slipped into a Dark Age. Architecture in stone and the brilliant mural painting of Minoan and Mycenaean palaces disappeared. The Dorians' major cultural contributions were a richly figurative language and a new group of sky-gods, who ruled from the heights of Mount Olympus in north Greece. These gradually replaced the earth deities of the Minoans and Mycenaeans or took over some of their attributes.

Only about 750 B.C. did stone architecture reemerge, and with it the beginnings of Classical Greek civilization. At Sparta there developed a rigorously militaristic society ruled by a landed aristocracy, while at Athens the Dorian culture merged with the surviving Mycenaean, creating a far more cosmopolitan city life, receptive to new ideas. To the clarity and grace of the old Minoan and Mycenaean cultures were added the passion and imagination of the new.

At the same time there began the Greek colonization of the Mediterranean, a response to the poor agricultural conditions at home and the need for raw materials. Almost every major Greek city sent out parties. Euboea established such cities as Neopolis in central Italy (Naples). Megara founded Chersonesus (Sevastopol) at the southern tip of the Crimea in the Black Sea and Selinus in Sicily. Achaea had numerous large settlements in southern Italy, which the Romans came to call Magna Graecia, including Poseidonia (which the Romans translated as Paestum) and Messana (Messina in Italian). Corinth had a number of settlements up the coast of what is now Albania and a major colony at Syracuse, Sicily. Phocaea founded cities along the Spanish and French coasts, including Tarraco (Tarragona), Massilia, near the mouth of the Rhone (Marseilles), Antipolis (Antibes), Herakles Monoecus (Monoco), and Nicaea (Nice). Miletos, the major Ionian city commercially and culturally, founded nine colonies around the Black Sea. Other colonies were planted in Cyrene,

North Africa, and Naucratis in the delta of Lower Egypt. Only where the rival Phoenicians had set up trading bases—in Palestine, Syria, and North Africa—were the Greeks absent.

Although we use the word *colony,* these were not mercantilist sources of raw material, as was the case for eighteenth-century colonies. Greek colonies were wholly independent adjunct communities; the Greeks called them *apoikia,* which means literally "away homes." The result of colonization and the resulting far-flung trade was that Greek ideas and especially the Greek language were spread the length of the Mediterranean and around the Black Sea.

The Greek Character

The mixing together of aspects of the sophisticated Minoan/Mycenaean cultures with the pragmatism of the Dorians produced a unique Greek character, emphasizing inquisitiveness, a love of action, and the desire to perfect human intellectual and physical power. The Greeks wanted to know why the gods did what they did, what the nature of man was, and how the world was formed and how it operated. And, fortunately for us, they perfected a subtle language that enabled them to preserve their speculations. Most of all, the Greeks were supremely confident in their own cultural superiority to the surrounding barbarians.

The Greek quest for truth is best exemplified by the natural philosophy developed by Ionian Greeks during the sixth century B.C. The first of these Ionian scientist-philosophers was Thales of Miletos, a merchant who traveled to Egypt and Mesopotamia, learning geometry and astronomy, which enabled him to predict solar eclipses. He also proposed the idea of a few basic components of which the world was made, an idea that ultimately led to the concept of atoms, the smallest indivisible components of all matter, an idea proposed by Leukippos of Miletos and his pupil Demokritos of Abdera.

The Greeks had an innate love of logic, *logos* (a word that can be variously translated as "reason," "idea," "conception," "word"), a natural order whose opposite was *chaos.* In everything the Greek sought balance and symmetry (*summetria,* "having like measure") as the ideal. Nothing in nature was seen as wholly capricious, for even the gods had reasons for their actions. Hence Heraclitus wrote, "Measure and logos are firm in a changing world." Heraclitus described the cosmos as a balance of such opposites as hot and cold, night and day, health and disease.

Much of this philosophy was based on a priori assumptions rather than observation of how things actually worked, and Plato complained that there was too much variety in natural appearances. Such an approach meant that some philosophers might venture off into pure metaphysical speculation. The Ionian philosopher Pythagoras of Samos, who established a colony of followers at Croton in Italy, took this mystical direction, proposing a natural philosophy based solely on numbers: "all things are number." He and his followers discovered the basis of musical harmony by observing that a taut string one half as long as another produced the same tone an octave higher. From this and other experiments they determined the mathematical basis of musical harmony. They also conceived of triangular and square numbers, and provided a proof of the concept first used by the Egyptians, that the square number on the hypotenuse of a right triangle was the sum of the square numbers of the other two sides.

Small wonder that the Athenian philosopher Protagoras of Abdera, a friend of Perikles, should write in his essay, *Truth,* "Man is the measure of all things, of those which are that they are, and of those which are not that they are not." In the Greek this can also be taken to mean "man is the measurer of all things," meaning that truth is relative to human perception and interpretation. Sokrates was convinced that truth could be found only by constant questioning, refinement, testing. And, as Xenophanes wrote, "The gods did not reveal everything to men at the start; but as time goes on, by searching, they discover more and more."[4]

What the Greeks endeavored to achieve in all things was *arete,* that quality of excellence that results from refinement and testing in all human endeavors—poetry, music, pottery, city government, sculpture, and architecture. *Arete* would be obtained through a contest, *agon* (from which our "agony" is derived). Accordingly, the Greeks regularly sponsored contests, at Argolis, Corinth, Delphi, and, of course, at Olympia, in search of *arete;* the crown of laurel was awarded not only to athletes but also to musicians. Through contest, *agon,* a man learned his capacities and limits, what the priests of Apollo meant when they said, "Know thyself." *Arete,* was an all-encompassing physical, moral, and intellectual excellence, requiring a balance in life achieved through turbulent self-discipline. "Nothing to excess" sums up the Greek view of life, and it was for this reason that Greeks had no time for specialists. A person of *arete* did all things well; he worked his farm outside the city and participated in the town assembly. If he was wealthy, he was expected to pay for the production of public festivals or provide a ship for the city's navy; if not, he accepted his duty to be ready at a moment's notice to march as far as necessary in full armor to defend the honor of his city. To realize a well-ordered life a person endeavored to exercise strength and power in restraint, to value quality before quantity, noble struggle over mere achievement, and personal honor over opulence.

The Greeks ascribed an almost semidivine nature to man. Sophokles has the chorus in *Antigone* sing:

> Wonders are many on earth, and the greatest of these
> Is man. . . .
> The use of language, the wind-swift motion of brain
> He learnt; found out the laws of living together
> In cities, building him shelter against the rain
>   And wintry weather.
> There is nothing beyond his power. . . .[5]

The Olympian gods were thus described in human terms and depicted in perfect human form. The Olympian deities combined male sky-gods introduced by the

Dorians (such as Zeus, hurler of lightning) with female earth deities of the Bronze Age (such as Hera, Zeus' wife). The result is that many temples built to the Olympian gods combine aspects of both masculine and feminine attributes. They are usually Doric in style (that is, built with Doric columns) and are often aligned on an axis that runs to a distant double-peaked mountain sacred to the earth deities of the Bronze Age.[6] The twelve Olympian gods were worshiped by all Greeks, although some had special regional precincts and temples where they received special reverence, such as that of Zeus at Olympia, Poseidon at Sounion at the point of land southeast of Athens, and Apollo at Delphi. Particular gods also were associated with individual cities, so that the Athenians worshiped Athena, the founder of their city, in two temples in her manifestations as Athena Polias, the protectress of the city, and as Athena Parthenos, the warrior maiden.[7] Some Greeks found comfort in mystical cults, but for the most part Greek religion was a straightforward affair of making the proper offerings to the gods. There was no generally accepted notion of an afterlife, as had become common among the Egyptians; perhaps Greek life was too arduous for them to wish it to continue forever. Instead the Greeks sought immortality through the achievement of *arete*, excellence in deeds, so that one's accomplishment would be recorded and remembered forever.

The Greek Polis

The most important political contribution of Greek civilization was the invention of democracy in Athens, spread with particular fervor by Athenians to the cities over which she had influence. As with other Greek words, we have no proper equivalent to *polis* except to render it as "city-state," which says both too much and not enough. The polis was a community of families related by common ancestors; a person did not move into or join a city—one was born a member. Those who traveled and lived in cities other than those where they were born were considered resident aliens; only

in rare instances were they made full citizens with the right and the responsibility of participating in governing the polis. The polis encompassed the farms around it, for Greeks preferred to live in the city in close quarters and walk out to their farms, rather than live in isolated farm villas. As H.D.F. Kitto summed it up, the polis encompassed "the whole communal life of the people, political, cultural, moral, and economic."[8]

To say a polis was a city suggests a size that is too large, for Greeks felt a person ought to be able to cross the entire breadth of the polis on foot in two days. In the *Republic* Plato described the ideal polis as having 5,000 citizens, and Aristotle wrote in *Politics* that a person should be able to recognize all the citizens of his polis by sight. Most poleis were roughly this size, although Athens, Syracuse, and Akragas had populations over 20,000. In 430 B.C., the total population of the region of Attica, including Athens, was roughly 330,000, of which about 15,000 were resident aliens and about 115,000 were slaves in domestic service. Of the remaining 200,000, about 35,000 were male citizens over eighteen, and the remainder were women and children.

In a few places and during times of social disruption, a single individual might impose autocratic rule over the polis, resulting in *tyranny;* in other places a few aristocratic families might exercise rule in an *oligarchy.* In Athens originally there was such an oligarchy of aristocratic *archons,* but through a series of reforms during the sixth and fifth centuries B.C. the governance of the city shifted to *democracy,* the rule of all its male citizens. The entire community of citizens, not just their representatives, met monthly in an open air assembly on a hill called the Pnyx. There everything having to do with the welfare of Athens was argued and voted on, and even the generals and admirals who battled on behalf of the polis were elected to their positions. In this the benign climate of Greece aided significantly, for the Greeks had limited means of covering a volume to hold several thousands. Although smaller committees were chosen by lot to deal with daily matters, overall political leadership was conveyed to whoever was persuasive

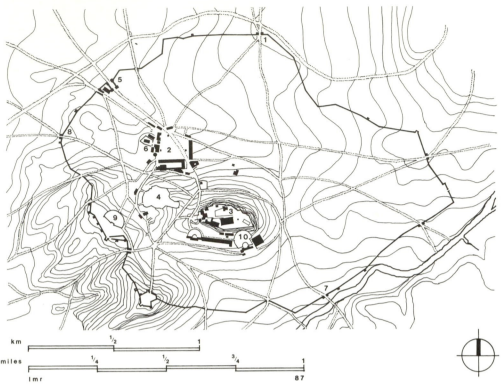

km |_____|_____|
         ½   1
miles |___|___|___|___|
      ¼   ½   ¾   1
l m r |_____|
                        87

11.4. Map of Athens, c. 400 B.C. In Greek cities that developed from Bronze Age settlements, the focal point was the elevated and defensible akropolis ("high city") and the agora ("marketplace") below; streets generally radiated out from these two places, following the topography.

1 = Acharnian Gate   5 = Dipylon Gate   9 = Pynx
2 = Agora   6 = Hephaisteion   10 = Theater of Dionysos
3 = Akropolis   7 = Icaria Gate
4 = Areopagus   8 = Piraeus Gate

11.5. Akropolis, Athens, viewed from the west.

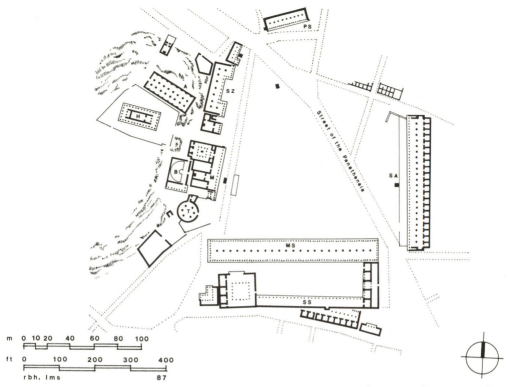

11.6. Agora, Athens, c. 100 B.C. Plan. Running diagonally through the agora was the Dromos, the processional way, extending from the Dipylon Gate (off the plan to the upper left) to the foot of the Akropolis toward the lower right. The Stoa of Attalos is the long building to the east.

A	= Armory	MS	= Middle Stoa	SZ	= Stoa of Zeus
B	= Bouleuterion	PS	= Poikile Stoa	T	= Tholos
H	= Hephaisteion	SA	= Stoa of Attalos		
M	= Metroon	SS	= South Stoa		

and commanded respect. From 461 B.C. to 429 B.C. that leader in Athens was Perikles; he was elected general for fifteen years in a row, and thirty times in all. It was he who led the polis in erecting the major buildings on the Athenian Akropolis.

Greek City Planning

Most poleis grew gradually, focused on the remains of a Bronze Age citadel built on an acropolis, the "high city" or rocky outcropping. This can be seen in Athens, whose Akropolis rises dramatically over the plain of Attica [11.4, 11.5]. Over centuries the household shrines in the Bronze Age Athenian Akropolis palace had become sacred sites dedicated to various Olympian gods,

and later, on these same spots, a succession of temples was built. At the base of the Akropolis, paths leading out to the surrounding farms became streets, and along one of these a roughly triangular open space was set aside as the *agora,* defined by surrounding houses and public buildings. The agora was the communal heart of the Greek city, the open living room where trade was carried on, students were taught, and the business of the polis (politics) was discussed [11.6]. In Athens the agora was defined first by private houses and shops, and in the third century B.C. by *stoas,* long buildings opened by colonnades along one side that provided shelter for artisans selling wares. In the stoas that later enclosed the Athenian agora, Zeno and his followers met to observe and

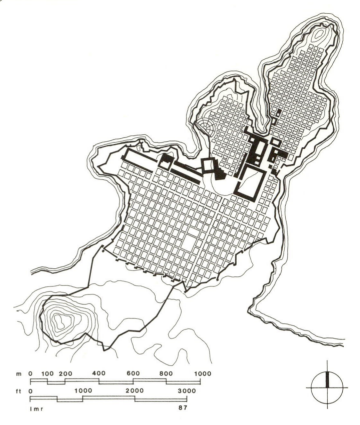

11.7. Hippodamos, plan of
Miletos, Asia Minor, c. 450 B.C.
The regular geometric plan of
Miletos was divided into three
zones, residential to the north
and south, with a commercial
heart at the center around the
agora and near the two harbors.

discuss human nature; they came to be
called Stoics and their philosophy Stoicism.
On the elevated ground immediately west
of the agora stands the Doric temple said to
be dedicated to Hephaistos, god of the
anvil, fire, and the forge, special to the artisans who traded in the agora. Interspersed
about the agora were other, smaller public
buildings and the *bouletarion,* a covered
meeting house for the *boule,* the council of
the polis that met daily. The roofed bouletarion could accommodate up to seven hundred people.

In the Greek colonies cities were laid out
from scratch and a more orderly orthogonal
grid was often employed, as at Poseidonia
(Paestum in Latin). It was not until the Persians razed cities in Ionian Greece during
494 to 479 B.C. that this more objective and
scientific method was applied in the homeland, and it was fitting that it should have
happened first at Miletos, where Greek science had been born a century earlier.

The replanning of Miletos came about as
a result of its destruction by the Persians. By
550 B.C. Ionia had come under the influence
of Croesus, king of Lydia in western Anatolia. Croesus then foolishly attacked the Persian Empire to the east; the Persians
retaliated, conquering Lydia and its allies
and amalgamating the Ionian Greek cities
with the Persian Empire by 540 B.C. The
captive Ionian cities fought back and
pleaded with the Spartans, the Athenians,
and other mainland Greeks to aid them; in
the following struggle many Ionian cities
were destroyed, including Miletos in 494
B.C. To stop the foreign intervention, the
Persian army under Darius crossed into
Greece and advanced toward Attica, but in
490 B.C. they were met at Marathon,
twenty-six miles from Athens, by a small
army of Greeks. Despite being far outnumbered by the Persians, the Greeks defeated
them. In 480 B.C., after Darius' death, a second campaign against Greece was launched

by his son Xerxes. Again greatly outnumbered, the allied Greeks fought bravely but lost; Xerxes' forces then entered Athens and set fire to the Akropolis temples. But then a fleet of two hundred Athenian and allied ships defeated the Persian navy in the Bay of Salamis, within sight of Athens, the first of a series of military reverses for the Persians. By 479 B.C. the Persians had been defeated and pushed back into central Turkey, and the Ionian cities freed from barbarian domination.

With the Persian threat gone, the destroyed Ionian cities were rebuilt, including Miletos. The plan of the new Miletos is usually credited to Hippodamos, a Milesian whom Aristotle describes in *Politics* as the man who "invented the art of planning cities" and who laid out the Athenian port of Peiraeus and the city of Rhodes.[10] The site was a relatively level peninsula jutting into the sea at the mouth of the Meander River, with two deep inlets that formed excellent harbors. Hippodamos adjusted the orthogonal grid to the general direction of the peninsula, rather than orienting it to the points of the compass, and divided the city into three distinct zones [11.7]. To the north was the residential quarter; at the center, running roughly from one harbor to the other, was the agora, divided into two sections by the bouletarion in the middle; to the south was another residential area of larger blocks. The only thing missing was a sacred precinct for the major temples, but this was because the most important Milesian religious site was the great Apollo sanctuary at Didyma, 14 miles (22 kilometers) to the south.

Priene, another city not far to the north of Miletos, was rebuilt in the latter part of the fourth century B.C. [11.8]. Here an orthogonal grid was adapted to a steeply sloping hillside site, with regular blocks of houses measuring approximately 120 by 160 feet (36.5 by 48.8 meters). Six principal streets, generally level, ran east and west; the fifteen minor streets were stepped and ran north and south. Roughly at the center was the rectangular agora, and looking over it, to the north, was the precinct of the temple of Athena and the theater. At the south edge of

the city was the stadium and the palaestra (wrestling school).

Domestic Architecture

Since most civic and commercial business was transacted in the open air in the agora, the private houses of the Greeks generally were small and unelaborated until the fourth century B.C., when Greek culture entered a new phase called Hellenistic. Artisans' houses discovered west of the Athenian acropolis show how, in older cities, the plans were adapted to the irregular street pattern [11.9]. In such artisans' homes there might be a room set aside for the production of pottery or metalwork. Aside from this the house consisted of a small cobblestoned court open to the sky, with a series of rooms opening on to it. Of one story, these houses usually had roofs pitched inward toward the central open court. In Priene, because of the regular blocks, the houses were rectangles [11.10]. Typically these had an *exedra* (e) to the south of a central court, sheltered from the sun and winds, and a megaron type of unit, or *oikos* (o), the major public room.

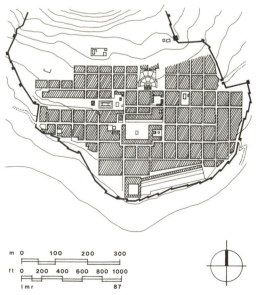

m 0   100   200   300

ft 0   200   400   600   800   1000

l m r   87

11.8. Plan of Priene, Asia Minor, c. 450 B.C. Priene, built atop Mount Micale, shows how a grid plan could be adapted to a sloping hilltop site.

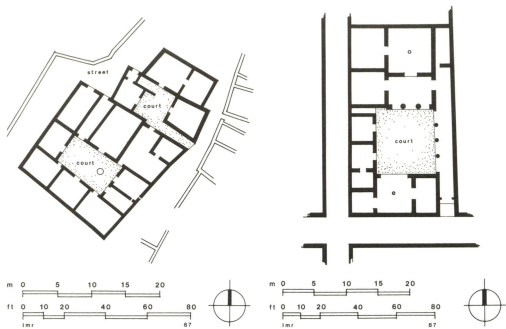

11.9. Artisans' houses near the Agora, Athens, c. 350 B.C. In Athens private houses were fitted into the irregular street pattern.

11.10. House, Priene, Asia Minor, c. 450 B.C. In planned cities such as Priene, private houses had more regular plans. At the south edge of the open central court was the exedra (e), and off the court was the principal public room, the oikos (o).

11.11. Stoa of Attalos, Athens, c. 150 B.C. Built by King Attalos of Pergamum as a gift to the city of Athens, this stoa was meticulously reconstructed in the 1950s. It illustrates well this Hellenistic civic building that began to line and define Greek agoras.

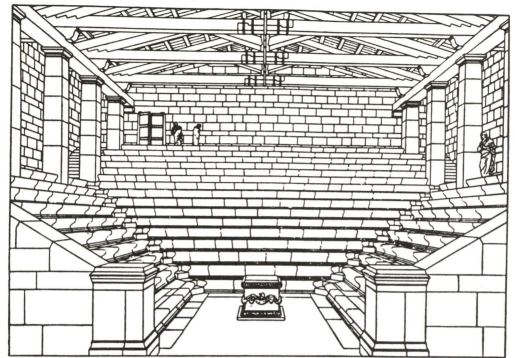

11.12. Bouleuterion, Priene, Asia Minor, c. 200 B.C. Interior view. Such comparatively small covered buildings were built by the Greeks to house their civic councils. This one measured 60 by 66 feet (18.5 by 20 meters) and could seat about 700 people.

Public Buildings

Compared to the number, types, and size of Roman public buildings, Greek public buildings were more limited. Perhaps most important in impact and function were the stoas that lined and defined the agoras. Long rectangular buildings and open on one side to face the agora, these often had an internal row of columns down the middle to support the roof or the upper floor, and small chambers in a row along the back for storekeepers and offices. Following the Classical period, stoas became quite long, as illustrated by the 117-foot (35.7 meters) stoa given to Athens by King Attalos of Pergamum and built c.150 B.C. on the east side of the agora [11.11].

Various covered halls were built to accommodate small groups of people. The bouletarion was one type, designed to house the *boule,* or council, of the polis. The bouletarion of Athens, on the west side of the agora, was larger than most, but the small bouletarion at Priene, built about 200 B.C., survives in better condition. Measuring nearly 60 by 66 feet (18.5 by 20 meters), it had tiers of benches on three sides, providing seating for about seven hundred people, and could probably have housed nearly all the voting citizens of Priene, whose total population must have been about four thousand [11.12]. Around the topmost seats were fourteen supports, reducing the span required of the wooden truss roof to roughly 47½ feet (14.5 meters), a considerable span at that time.

The largest Greek public buildings were open to the air and included theaters and *stadia* for athletic contests. A *stadion*—the Greek word means both a unit of distance of about 656 feet (200 meters) as well as the stadium structure with tiers of seats—might be used only at certain times of the year, but the theater was nearly as important a part of the civic life of the polis as was the agora. Drama productions began as religious rituals for the god Dionysios, and by the time of

11.13. Polykleitos the Younger, Theater, Epidauros, Greece, c. 350 B.C. View. Typically, Greek theaters adjoined religious sites and were built into hillsides. The seats extended around 200 degrees and looked down onto low, temporary skēnē structures.

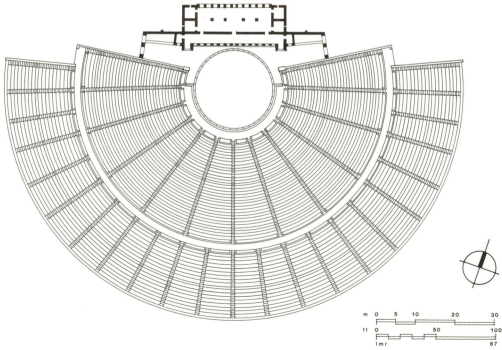

11.14. Theater, Epidauros. Plan.

Perikles had become an important means of defining and elaborating the ideal of civic and moral virtue, or *arete,* as the plays of Aeschylus and Sophokles demonstrate. Even the ribald comedies of Aristophanes played an important part in this. Going to the theater was a celebration of community spirit; the plays contributed importantly to political education and were not merely entertainment, as they became later in the Roman Empire. The fact that the stage structure, or *skēnē,* was relatively low is important, for in becoming part of the drama itself, the audience could raise their eyes to look out over the landscape of their polis, so that, as Vincent Scully writes, "the whole visible universe of men and nature came together in a single, quiet order."[11]

It was fortunate that again the gentle Greek climate made it possible to build theaters in the open, for there was no practicable way to cover a building seating seventeen thousand people, the number accommodated in the theater at Epidauros. In some instances the theater was also used for the assembly of all the citizens of the polis. The theater at Epidauros, built about 350 B.C. on the thumb of the Peloponnesus, after designs by Polykleitos the Younger, retains nearly all its original features [11.13, 11.14]. There were three basic parts: the *theatron* ("seeing place"), the seating for the spectators built into the side of a hill carved out to form a bowl; an *orchestra* ("dancing place"), the circular floor where the actors declaimed and the chorus sang and danced (centered in the orchestra was an altar to Dionysios); and the *skēnē,* a low structure forming a backdrop behind the orchestra. In Greek theaters (as distinct from Roman examples) the seating formed more than a half circle, and the *skēnē* structure was little more than one story high. At Epidauros there are fifty-five semicircular rows of seats, divided by an ambulatory about two-thirds of the way up; the diameter is 387 feet (118 meters).

The Greek Temple

By far the most important Greek building was the temple. Although it served a most vital public function and was a symbol of the polis, it was not a public building in the sense that we use the word, for only priests and selected individuals actually entered it. In contrast to its plain interior, the exterior of the temple was lavished with artistic attention, for public rituals were celebrated at the altar in front of the temple. Because of this and the fact that the temple's enclosed volume was not a public space, the Greek temple has often been described as a monumental sculpture set in the landscape.

The temple was placed in a sacred precinct, or *temenos,* delineated by a low wall or curb, although as these sites were built on over the centuries, stoas and other structures might define the temenos more clearly. There was no effort to align any of these enclosing buildings according to predefined axes; they were adjusted to the topography of the site. Nonetheless, temples were often aligned on axes leading out to mountain peaks in the landscape, sacred since dim prehistory.

Perhaps as early as 1050 B.C. the crude form of the temple emerged, a wooden structure with upright columns completely around the central chamber. Earlier ritual offerings to the gods had been made in sacred groves, the trees decorated with the sacrificial offerings. It is believed that the temple, with its surrounding colonnade, was an attempt to re-create the sacred grove. The columns became those decorated trees, and the many parts of the Doric, Ionic, and later Corinthian orders were named for the actions performed in these rituals [Plate 3]. The architecture seems to have become the concrete form of the ritual, although by the time Vitruvius catalogued this information from his Greek sources in the first century B.C. the original meaning of the Greek architectural terms had already been lost.[12]

The sacred temenos at Olympia [4.35, 11.15] is a good example illustrating temples in their context. The sacred precinct is framed by the bouletarion on the south, a stoa to the east, and a range of small city treasuries nestled against the hill of Kronos to the north. At the north edge of the temenos was a temple to Hera, wife of Zeus, originally built of wood but replaced, part by

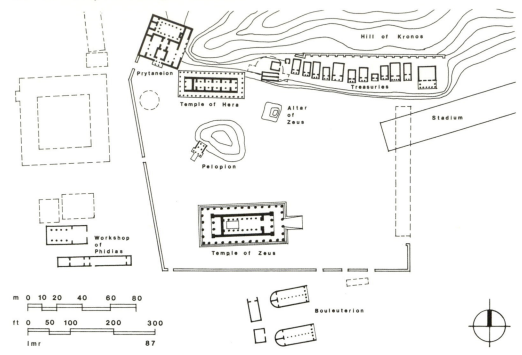

11.15. Temenos, or sacred precinct, Olympia, Greece, fifth century B.C. A temenos encompassed one or more temples, altars, treasury buildings, and other subsidiary buildings. Here the major temples were dedicated to Hera and Zeus. To the east of the temenos at Olympia was the stadion, where the Olympic Games were held.

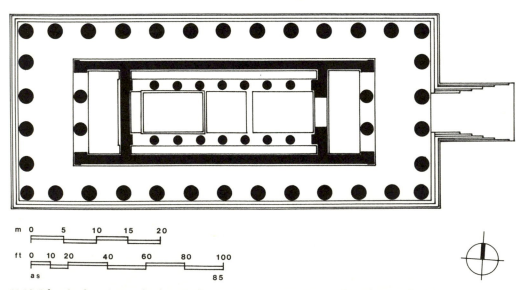

11.16. Libon (architect), Temple of Zeus, Olympia, Greece, c. 468–460 B.C. Plan. The Temple of Zeus incorporates the basic features of the Greek temple during the Classical period, having six Doric columns across the front and thirteen along the sides. Sheltered by the columns is the naos, containing the image of Zeus.

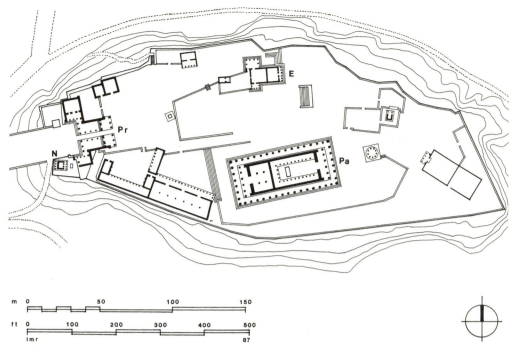

m 0   50   100   150

ft 0   100   200   300   400   500

l m r   87

11.17. Akropolis, Athens. General plan, showing buildings completed in the Periklean building campaign, as of about 400 B.C.

E = Erechtheion   Pa = Temple of Athena Parthenos
N = Temple of Athena Nike   (Parthenon)
                                    Pr = Propylaia

part, with elements of stone as time passed. The principal building was the large temple to Zeus built by the citizens of Elis in 468–60 B.C. and designed by Libon of Elis [11.16]. Measuring 91 by 210 feet (27.7 by 64.1 meters), it was a Doric temple, six massive columns across each end by thirteen columns on the sides (for a discussion of the Greek orders or columns, see Part One). The Greeks built their temples of local stone, and at Olympia it was a coarse limestone covered with a plaster made of marble dust. The temple was peripteral—that is, it had a single row of columns all around, rising from a three-stepped base (the only unusual feature was the ramped approach from the east). Inside was the *naos,* a rectangular chamber with projecting spur walls, *antae,* at each end, with two columns between them. Inside, between rows of Doric columns supporting the roof, was the huge seated image of Zeus, fashioned by the Athenian sculptor

Pheidias, and made of gold and ivory fastened to a wooden armature.

The temple complex embodying most fully the spirit of ancient Greece is found on the Akropolis at Athens. What is seen there today is the remains of a remarkable building program initiated by the Athenian polis under the direction of Perikles several decades after the Akropolis was burned and destroyed by the Persians in 480 B.C.; the buildings were to be the symbol of the victory of Athens and of Greeks generally over barbarism. To prevent the Persians from ever again posing a threat, Perikles had created the Delian League, a confederacy of all the poleis around the Aegean, and a portion of the funds they contributed was used to build the new Akropolis as an emblem of that victory.[13]

The Akropolis was the ideal spot for these new temples. Rising 300 feet (91.5 meters) above the city, it put the gleaming white marble buildings in view of the residents of the polis and also made them visible from the harbor at Piraeus and the Bay of Salamis, where the Persian ships had been sunk [11.4]. It was the focal point of the Panathenaia festival, observed every year on Athena's birthday in late summer but celebrated with special festivities every fourth year. On those occasions pilgrims and celebrants gathered outside the Dipylon gate on the city's northwest side and formed a procession that moved along the street called Dromos, through the agora, and up onto the Akropolis. Gifts for Athena, a specially woven wool robe for the ancient wooden statue of Athena, and sacrificial cattle were taken up the winding approach to the summit of the Akropolis.[14]

On an ancient bastion projecting from the western extremity of the plateau, a small marble temple dedicated to Athena Nike, goddess of victory, was built by Kallikrates about 460–50 B.C.[15] The bastion was subsequently rebuilt and a new temple, the one currently there, was erected during 435–20 B.C. [11.17, 11.18]. The Nike tem-

ple is the first element of the Akropolis seen as one approaches the Akropolis. Its delicate Ionic columns, only four at each end, contrast with the massiveness of the Doric columns of the next element to come into view, the entrance gate to the Akropolis, the *Propylaia.*

The present Propylaia replaced an earlier, smaller gate that had faced more toward the southwest; destroyed in the Persian fire in 480 B.C., it was replaced with a larger, more ceremonial marble entrance in 437–32 B.C., designed by the architect Mnesikles [11.19]. Besides the gate itself, the building included two projecting and flanking chambers for pilgrims. To the left, as one entered, was a gallery for resting, lined with paintings (hence the name *pinakotheke,* or "painting gallery"); the smaller, unfinished gallery to the right may have been planned as a *glyptotheke* ("sculpture gallery"), but despite its unfinished shape, the front was built in such a way that the sense of balance is preserved as one ascends toward the Propylaia. In rebuilding the Propylaia in 437 B.C., Mnesikles turned the building on a new align-

11.18. Temple of Athena Nike, Athens, c. 435–420 B.C. This tiny jewel was built to commemorate the Greek victory over the Persians; it stands over an ancient Bronze Age defensive bastion protecting the gate to the Akropolis. It has Ionic columns only at the front and rear.

11.19. *Mnesikles, Propylaia, Athens, 437–432* B.C. *Having gone past the projecting bastion, the visitor enters the sacred precinct of the Akropolis through the Propylaia gateway.*

11.20. *Propylaia. This restoration view by Gorham Phillips Stevens has some internal Doric columns removed to show better the view into the temenos. To the left can be seen the Erechtheion, left of center the statue of Athena Promachus, and looming on the right the Parthenon.*

11.21. *Erechtheion, Athens, 421–405* B.C. *This complex building housed shrines to a variety of gods, including Athena Polis, protectress of the city. It sits astride a drop in the level of the rock and hence has a split-level plan. It includes the Porch of the Caryatids (Maidens).*

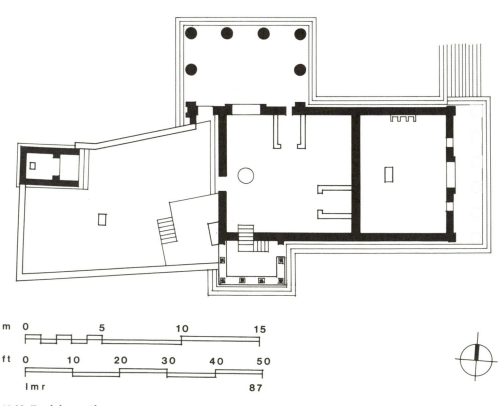

m   0   5   10   15

ft 0   10   20   30   40   50

    I m r   87

11.22. *Erechtheion. Plan.*

ment, placing it nearly parallel to the largest temple on the plateau, the Parthenon, and thus pointing it toward the Bay of Salamis. So, turning back and looking through the gate, the pilgrim saw framed by its columns the site where the Persians had been repulsed.

Beyond the gate and inside the sacred precinct were scores of statues and votive slabs erected as thanks offerings, among which rose a gigantic bronze statue of Athena Promachos ("the Champion") the glint of whose upraised gilded spear tip could be seen at sea [11.20]. Behind this, running parallel to the rear wall of the Propylaia, were the remains of the cyclopean wall of a terrace of the ancient Bronze Age palace, perhaps the palace of the legendary Erechtheus, king of prehistoric Athens.

To the left could be seen the upper part of the complex form of the temple called the Erechtheion, and to the right, over the roofs of lower treasury buildings, rose the great bulk of the Parthenon. Following a ramp along the south side of the cyclopean terrace, the pilgrim reached the west end of the Parthenon and could turn to the north to see the irregular Erechtheion.

The last major building constructed on the Akropolis, the Erechtheion, was also the most unusual [11.21, 11.22]. Built probably from 421 B.C. to 405 B.C. (the architect. is unknown), it housed shrines to a number of gods, local deities, and heroes, and it stood over several sacred spots, including the mark of Poseidon's trident spear and the salt spring he caused to appear, as well as the graves of the legendary Erechtheus and Kekrops; most important, it housed a temple to Athena Polias, protectress of the city and goddess of the hearth.

Originally there had been a traditional Doric temple of Athena Polias, just to the south of the present Erechtheion, which had been burned by the Persians. In building the replacement to the north, the architect faced numerous problems accommodating the many sacred spots and a steep change in grade. As a result the Erechtheion has several levels. To the east, from higher ground, is the six-column Ionic porch leading to the

naos that housed the ancient wooden image of Athena. To the north, at a lower lever, is a larger Ionic porch, four columns wide, leading to the chamber of Erechtheus. In an open court immediately west of the temple there was an olive tree sacred to Athena. That part of the site could not be covered, and so the Erechtheion ends in a blank west wall with engaged Ionic columns. To the south, in the direction of the Parthenon and over the grave of the legendary King Kekrops, is the Porch of the Maidens, or Caryatids, with six supports in the form of maidens with crowns on their heads forming the capitals of the "columns"; it was the most original part of the many novel aspects of this highly unusual building.

If the Parthenon to the south represents *logos,* clarity, and precision, the Erechtheion, with its delicate and highly enriched Ionic details, seems to bring order out of a kind of casual disorder. The Erechtheion is the embodiment of an Ionian flexibility and elegant grace in contrast to the Doric Olympian austerity of the Parthenon. Yet the Erechtheion is not the product of an idyllic and peaceful Golden Age, for the design and construction of the Erechtheion were undertaken during the Peloponnesian War and a concurrent plague that decimated Athens and threatened to destroy the polis. In contrast to the desperation of the times, the Erechtheion is a jewel box of delicate refinement, not the expression of despair.

The building that was first rebuilt on the burnt Akropolis was the largest of them all, dominating the hill and the plain of Attica below; this was the temple to Athena Parthenos, (Maiden), goddess of war and wisdom. An earlier temple on this spot determined the alignment toward Mount Hymettos to the west. A replacement, begun in 490 B.C. and still in the early stages of construction, was destroyed by the Persians. A number of column drums of white marble, quarried from Mount Pentele, survived the fire and were reused for the columns of the new temple. The Parthenon was built 447–38 B.C. from designs by Iktinos (possibly assisted by Kallikrates). In view of this reuse of material, the complete harmonization of proportioned parts in the finished building is especially remarkable, for the architects were using elements originally proportioned for a building of different design.

The Parthenon is unusual in several respects: its large size (it measures 101.5 by 228 feet or 30.9 by 69.5 meters), its eight columns across the ends (when six was more traditional), and its double-chambered naos [11.23]. To the east was the larger chamber, housing a huge standing figure of Athena, helmeted and carrying a spear and a shield; like the gold and ivory figure at Olympia, this too was created by Pheidias, who it is believed supervised all the sculpture carved for the temple. To the west was the nearly square chamber called the Parthenon (the term was later extended to mean the entire building), housing a treasury of offerings to Athena, including the silver throne from which Xerxes watched his ships go down to defeat in the Bay of Salamis. Although the temple was built with the Doric order, massive and austere, and befitting the goddess of war, the roof of the Parthenon chamber was supported by the more delicate Ionic columns.

As at Olympia, all the sculpture on the building related to themes associated with the god and the site. Since this was one of the most Panhellenic of temples, commemorating the victory over the Persians, the sculpture illustrated in various ways the struggle between *logos* and *chaos*, between civilization and barbarism. The ninety-two metopes in the Doric entablature illustrated this in four ways. To the east were images of battle between the Olympian gods and earth giants, to the west were scenes of Greeks fighting Amazons (or Persians), to the north were representations of Greeks against Trojans (another adversary from Asia Minor), and on the south were pairs of battling Lapiths and Centaurs, the same story depicted in the west pediment at Olympia. The pediment figures depicted stories relating more directly to Athens. In the west pediment, facing the Propylaia, was the story of the contest between Athena and Poseidon to determine who should have dominion over Attica. Poseidon attempted to persuade the Athenians by a display of his power in striking the Akropolis with his trident, while Athena caused an olive tree to grow miraculously—the Athenians pre-

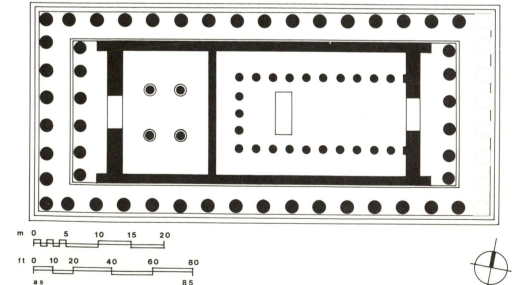

m 0 5 10 15 20

ft 0 10 20 40 60 80

a s   8 5

11.23. Iktinos and Kallikrates, Parthenon, Athens, 447–438 B.C. Plan. This temple has two naos chambers, one for a treasury and one to house the gold and ivory figure of Athena Parthenos, goddess of war. The plan and ratio of columns contain the proportion x : 2x + 1.

11.24. Parthenon. West front viewed from lower court; restoration drawing by Gorham Phillips Stevens.

11.25. Parthenon. View of the west end.

11.26. Parthenon. Detail of corner columns.

ferred Athena's gift [11.24]. In the east pediment, over the door to the principal naos and Pheidias' cult image, was a depiction of the birth of Athena, fully armed, from the brow of her father, Zeus. Most original of all, around the top of the wall outside the naos but inside the encircling Doric peristyle, was a continuous frieze of sculpture, 3½ feet high by 525 feet (1 by 160 meters), showing what appears to be the Panathenaic procession. Prior to this only gods and semidivine heroes were depicted in temple sculpture; now for the first time ordinary mortals appeared. Perhaps these figures represent the original Panathenaia procession, but it is also likely that the Athenians of the Classical period were looking at idealized images of themselves, confidently portrayed celebrating Athena's protection of their city and the way of life it embodied.

What has made the Parthenon special from the time of its creation are the precision of its construction and the subtleties and refinements used in its design [11.25]. Shunning the use of mortar, the builders employed a system of dry masonry called *anathyrosis*. The marble blocks were cut, squared perfectly, and the surfaces ground absolutely flat. For vertical joints the inner surfaces were cut away so that only the edges of adjacent blocks touched in a perfectly tight seam. In this region, prone to earthquakes, the blocks were locked together with iron clamps sealed in molten lead to protect them from oxidation. As an embodiment of logos, the entire design is governed by a proportional system of x to $(2x +1)$ or 4 to 9. Accordingly, if there had to be eight columns across the ends, using the drums already cut, the length would be seventeen columns $(2 \times 8 +1)$. The podium and the naos both have dimensions that have the proportion of 4 to 9 or 1 to 2.25. The same proportional relationship was used for the ratio of the height of the order (including the entablature) to the width of the ends, and in the ratio of the diameter of the columns to the spacing between columns, center to center.

More remarkable still were the subtle visual refinements, what Vitruvius says the Greeks called *alexemata,* or "betterments."

Greek temples were to be designed, he wrote, *quod oculus fallit,* or "with regard to that in which the eye deceives us." He says that if a stylobate platform is built truly flat "it will appear to the eye to be hollowed out," and that corner columns must be thicker since "they are set off against the open air and appear to be more slender than they are." So, he instructs his reader, the stylobate should be raised in the center, with *temperatione adaugeatur,* or "addition . . . made by calculated modulation."[16] In the Parthenon the stylobate is in fact a segment of a huge sphere and rises toward the center; on the long sides it rises nearly 4 inches (10.2 centimeters) in the center, and about 2 inches (5.1 centimeters) on the ends; and every horizontal line parallel to the stylobate is similarly curved. The corner columns are not only nearly 2 inches (5.1 centimeters) thicker than all the others, they are set nearly 2 feet (0.61 meters) closer together.

The Parthenon gives the impression of being a scheme based on absolutely straight lines, a series of perfectly flat horizontals and straight verticals, in perfect equilibrium. Not only are the base and entablature curved, there are no truly straight lines anywhere in the building; it is all a combination of subtle diagonals and curves. The columns have what Vitruvius called *entasis,* a curved taper that starts about two-fifths of the way up the shaft [11.26]; the total reduction in the width of the standard column is eleven-sixteenths of an inch or 1.75 centimeters (this represents a radius of curvature of roughly 1 mile). In the Propylaia the entasis is three-fourths of an inch (1.9 centimeters). Furthermore, none of the columns is perfectly vertical; they all have an inward inclination of 1:150, roughly 2.4 inches or 6 centimeters, and the thicker corner columns incline on the diagonal. If the center lines of the side columns were extended they would meet roughly 1½ miles above the temple stylobate.

Why was such extraordinary care exercised and such energy expended? One compelling reason was *arete,* for the home of the goddess required the most excellent materials and workmanship. In purely practical

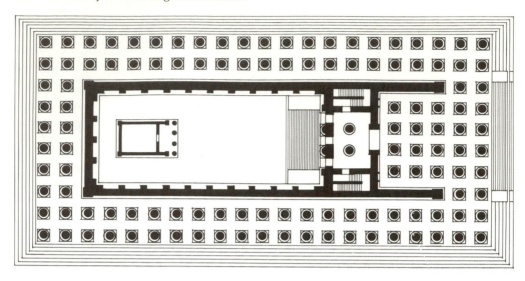

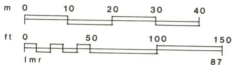

11.27. *Paionios of Ephesos and Daphnis of Miletos, Temple of Apollo at Didyma, outside Miletos, Asia Minor, begun c. 330 B.C. Plan. One of the largest Greek temples ever attempted, this had no roof over the naos but was open to the sky, with a small temple at the end of the open court.*

11.28. *Temple of Apollo at Didyma. Interior of the naos.*

terms the inclined columns would help, however slightly, to resist lateral earthquake movement. (The ruined condition of the Parthenon today, incidentally, is due entirely to human causes. The building was changed from a temple into a Christian church, and then into a mosque, was used as a Turkish gunpowder magazine. In 1687 the Venetians shot an artillery shell through the roof, setting off the gunpowder in an explosion that severely damaged all the buildings on the Akropolis.) As the classicist Jerome J. Pollitt has suggested, perhaps the care taken in the *alexemata* was a way of creating a tension between what the mind expects to see and the information the eye actually sends to the brain—*quod oculus fallit*—so that the two divergent images can never be brought into perfect concordance. The result is a building that seems to quiver with intellectual excitement, and is "vibrant, alive, and continually interesting."[16]

It is significant, too, that no new building was ever built in the center of the reconstructed Akropolis. There, on the remains of the Bronze Age palace, a broad terrace was made between the Erechtheion and the Parthenon. In that most sacred of spots, man is in the middle, the measure and measurer of all things. In one direction was visible the ancient sacred mountain of Hymmetos, and in the other, through the doors of the Propylaia, the Bay of Salamis; myth and human history fused in the experience of the Athenian standing there in the clear light of Attica. As at Olympia, where the figures of Pelops and Hippodameia challenge the athletes in their quest of *arete*, so too atop the Athenian Akropolis the human observer is challenged to contemplate the never-ending struggle between reason and irrationality, civilization and barbarism, *logos* and *chaos*. The Parthenon, in hard marble, serves as proof that the ideal *can* be realized through human action.

Hellenistic Architecture

The cherished independence of the Greek city-states, threatened by Perikles' confederation, was eliminated altogether when the many Greek poleis were amalgamated into a true empire by Philip II of Macedonia and his more famous son, Alexander the Great, during 360–23 B.C. The relative peace this political subjugation brought fostered the flowering of Greek philosophy and science, for it was during this period that Aristotle, Zeno, and Epicurus wrote and taught, that Archimedes and Euclid developed their theorems, and that sculptors such as Praxiteles and Lysippos worked.

Alexander, taught by Aristotle, passionately loved all things Greek and exported Greek art and culture to all the lands he subsequently conquered, including Persia, Egypt, Syria and Palestine, Babylonia, Iran, and the northern regions of India; he also expanded international trade and the exchange of ideas. The visual arts, no longer restrained by the austere Classical Greek ideal, became more elaborate and ornamental, and this more embellished art and architecture is now called Hellenistic. The conservative Roman scholar Pliny even went so far as to say that after the time of Lysippos "art stopped."

Hellenistic architecture underwent some changes. The elegant Ionic and Corinthian orders were made increasingly more elaborate, while the more simply austere Doric of mainland Greece gradually fell from favor, not to be rediscovered until the mid-eighteenth century. The spatial and dimensional elaboration of the Greek temple is well illustrated by the new temple of Apollo at Didyma, outside Miletos, in Asia Minor, begun about 330 B.C. and attributed to the architects Paionios of Ephesos and Daphnis of Miletos [11.27, 11.28]. One of the largest Greek temples ever begun, it rose from a stereobate of seven huge steps, measuring nearly 194 by 387 feet (59 by 118 meters) at the bottom. The naos structure was surrounded by a double row of the tallest and slenderest Ionic columns of any Greek temple, 64 feet 8 inches high (19.7 meters). This double peripteral colonnade was ten columns across the front by twenty-one columns along the sides. The naos, 75 feet (22.8 meters) across, was not roofed but open to the sky; the Ionic pilasters along the inside walls, by themselves, were 6 feet wide and 3 feet deep (1.8 by 0.9 meters). The visitor, no doubt overwhelmed by the sheer size of this vast enclosure, descended into the naos "court," by a flight of stairs 50 feet (15.2 meters) wide. Inside the open naos, amidst a grove of laurel trees, was an Ionic shrine the size of small Ionic temples of the Classical period (about 28 by 48 feet or 8.5 by 14.6 meters). Every part of the typical temple of the Periklean period was enlarged in scale, stretched in length, and more elaborately embellished. The deliberate restraint of the Classical period was giving way to the celebration of worldly wealth, and the balance between civic virtue and public display characterized by Periklean Athens was replaced by a fondness for sumptuous detail.

An Architecture of Excellence

Greek architecture, perhaps best represented in the temple, is the embodiment in stone of the striving for the mean, that ideal balance between extremes. In architectural terms this becomes a balance between the vertical elements of lift (the columns) and the horizontal elements of load (the beams of the entablature), between action and rest. Each component block or column drum, each piece of narrative sculpture, was crafted to perfection, in the best available materials, not as a display of wealth but because it was fitting to honor the gods and one's polis in this way. The goal always was excellence in form, in detail, in workmanship because—as the Greeks believed—that is the only way a human being can achieve the fullest potential. Greek temple architecture represents a unique synthesis of essence and substance, of idealistic form and clearly articulated structure. The Greeks cared little for immortality on a spiritual plane, but rather they sought to ensure their immortality in human memory, through their intellectual and artistic excellence. The Parthenon is proof they succeeded in living forever.

NOTES

1. Quoted in J. G. Frazer, *Pausanias' Description of Greece* (London, 1897), xliii, n. 1.
2. Plato, *Epinomis*, 987d, trans. W.R.M. Lamb (London, 1927), 473.
3. Plato, *Critias*, § 111. Translated in H.D.F. Kitto, *The Greeks*, revised ed. (Baltimore, 1957), 34.
4. C. M. Bakewell, *Source Book in Ancient Philosophy* (New York, 1939), 8–9.
5. Sophokles, *Antigone*, trans. E. F. Watting (Baltimore, Md., 1947), 135.
6. This elemental relationship was first perceived by Vincent Scully; see his *The Earth, the Temple, and the Gods* (New Haven, Conn., 1962); it is a concept still considered extremely controversial by classical scholars.
7. Although the Athenians had several names for Athena, they performed rituals for Athena Polias only in the older, northern temple (later replaced by the Erechtheion) on the Acropolis; the larger, southern temple, the Parthenon, seems to have been built to embody civic ideals. See C. J. Herington, *Athena Parthenos and Athena Polias: A Study in the Religion of Periclean Athens* (Manchester, England, 1955).
8. Kitto, *The Greeks*, p. 75.
9. The modern Olympic Marathon race honors this famous battle and the Greek soldier, Phidippides, who ran the 22.5 miles (36.2 kilometers) from Marathon to Athens with the news of the victory, whereupon he dropped dead.
10. Aristotle, *Politics*, ii. 8, trans. B. Jowett (Oxford, England, 1905), 76.
11. Scully, *The Earth, the Temple, and the Gods*, p. 206.
12. The meaning of the Classical orders, at least in Roman times, and of their numerous component parts, is treated in George Hersey, *The Lost Meaning of Classical Architecture: Speculations on Ornament from Vitruvius to Venturi* (Cambridge, Mass., 1988). For the Corinthian order in particular see Joseph Rykwert, "The Corinthian Order," *Domus* 426 (May 1965), reprinted in Rykwert's anthology *The Necessity of Artifice* (New York, 1982), 33–43. For a modern interpretation of the proportions of the orders, Greek and Roman, see Robert Chitham, *The Classical Orders of Architecture* (New York, 1985).
13. There is, of course, the great irony that the

domination the Persians failed to win Athens easily achieved over the smaller Aegean poleis through the Delian League. Eventually this "empire" proved Athens' undoing, causing the long and disastrous Peloponnesian War, 435–404 B.C.

14. The cattle taken up to the Akropolis altar for slaughter remind us that we are not as close to the Greeks as we sometimes like to imagine. In *A History of Western Architecture* (London, 1986), 38, David Watkin cautions us to remember "the stench, squalor, and noise of such an occasion as the flies settled on the blackening blood in the stifling heat."

15. Although much is now missing from the Akropolis, as at Olympia and all other Greek sites, we have a detailed record of what was on the Akropolis and at other sites in the travel record kept by the Greek traveler Pausanias, who toured Greece in the second century A.D.; see the translation by Peter Levi, *Guide to Greece*, 2 vols. (Harmondsworth and New York, 1971). See also the description of the Panathenaic festival in S. Kostof, *A History of Architecture* (New York, 1985), 149–58.

16. Vitruvius, *On Architecture,* III.4.5. and III.3.11 to 13. Vitruvius lists a treatise by Iktinos and Karpion (misspelling for Kallikrates?) that he says he consulted.

17. J. J. Pollitt, *Art and Experience in Classical Greece* (New York, 1972), 76.

SUGGESTED READING

J. S. Boersma, *Athenian Building Policy from 561/0 to 405/4 B.C.* (Groningen, The Netherlands, 1970).

M. Bieber, *The History of the Greek and Roman Theater* (Princeton, N.J., 1961).

H. Brevé, G. Gruben, and M. Hirmer, *Greek Temples, Theaters, and Shrines* (London, 1963).

V. J. Bruno. ed, *The Parthenon* (New York, 1974).

John M. Camp, *The Athenian Agora: Excavations in the Heart of Classical Athens* (London, 1986).

R. Carpenter, *The Architects of the Parthenon* (Baltimore, Md., 1970).

F. Castagnoli, *Orthogonal Town Planning in Antiquity* (Cambridge, Mass., 1971).

J. J. Coulton, *Ancient Greek Architects at Work* (Ithaca, N. Y., 1977).

———, *The Architectural Development of the Greek Stoa* (Oxford, England, 1976).

W. B. Dinsmoor, *The Architecture of Ancient Greece*, third ed., revised (New York, 1975).

A. Evans, *The Palace of Minos* (New York, 1921), a lively account by the archaeologist who excavated this site.

J. W. Graham, *The Palaces of Crete* (Princeton, N.J. 1962).

R. Higgins, *Minoan and Mycenaean Art* (New York, 1967).

J. M. Hurwit, *The Art and Culture of Early Greece, 1100–480 B.C.* (Ithaca, N.Y., 1985).

H.D.F. Kitto, *The Greeks,* revised ed. (Baltimore, Md., 1957).

A. W. Lawrence, *Greek Architecture,* third ed. (Baltimore, Md., 1983).

P. MacKendrick, *The Greek Stones Speak: The Story of Archaeology in Greek Lands* (New York, 1962).

R. D. Martienssen, *The Idea of Space in Greek Architecture* (Johannesburg, South Africa, 1956).

J. J. Pollitt, *Art and Experience in Classical Greece* (New York, 1972).

D. S. Robertson, *A Handbook of Greek and Roman Architecture*, 2nd ed., rev. (Cambridge, England, 1954).

V. Scully, *The Earth, the Temple, and the Gods,* revised ed. (New Haven, Conn., 1979).

J. Travlos, *Pictorial Dictionary of Ancient Athens* (London, 1971).

J. B. Ward-Perkins, *Cities of Ancient Greece and Italy: Planning in Classical Antiquity* (New York, 1974).

R. E. Wycherley, *How the Greeks Built Cities* (New York, 1962).

———, *The Stones of Athens* (Princeton, N.J., 1978).

12.24. Baths of Caracalla. Interior perspective. Although now shorn of the marble veneers and embellishments, such baths and other public buildings were richly and colorfully ornamented, as this restoration drawing by G. Abel Blonet suggests.

CHAPTER 12

Roman Architecture

Roman architecture shapes spaces.

H. Kähler, *The Art of Rome and Her Empire*, 1965

In contrast to Greek architecture, which can be described as sculptural masses set in balanced contrast to the landscape, Roman architecture, as Heinz Kähler has noted, is an architecture of space, enclosed internal space and outdoor space, on a grand scale. The Egyptians and the Greeks shaped powerfully evocative buildings, but seldom were these buildings meant to contain groups of people; public life was conducted in the out-of-doors, among these sculpted architectural objects, and the buildings' constricted interiors were the domain of a special elite. Only in Hellenistic architecture did public spaces begin to be shaped in a conscious and deliberate way, and this shaping of space was the essence of Roman architecture. No better example exists of the supremacy of space than in the vast interior of the Pantheon in Rome, its concrete dome arching over a clear span of 142½ feet (43.4 meters).

One reason why the Romans attached great importance to public architecture, both enclosed spaces and public spaces, was that from the beginning Roman civilization focused on the city as its basic constituent element. Indeed, the Romans marked the beginning of their history not from a decisive battle or the reign of a particular king, but from the founding of the city of Rome by Romulus and Remus in 753 B.C. Official records were dated from the founding, on the Capitoline Hill in Rome, of the principal temple to Jupiter—Jupiter Optimus Max-imus (Most Supreme Jupiter)—the principal deity of the state religion, dedicated on September 13, 509 B.C., one year after the Republic was instituted. For nearly five centuries the Romans took great pride in the fact that they were free and self-governing, and even during the subsequent empire the emperors who governed most successfully were those who maintained the semblance of the cherished old republic and made themselves appear to be merely the agents of the Senate. Romans were particularly "political animals," in Aristotle's phrase, but in the case of the Romans, their polis came to include the whole of the Mediterranean basin and Europe.

Roman History

Like the Egyptians and the Greeks, the Romans were shaped in large measure by the geography in which they happened to arise and by the impact of the almost incessant warfare which that geography made almost inevitable. Roman history is divided into three phases—the rule of the early kings, the Republic, and the Empire. About 1100 B.C. groups of Balkan settlers moved into the Italian peninsula; among them were the Latins, who settled in the area around the Tiber River in the center of the peninsula. The site the Latins picked was good, on seven hills at a point on the river far enough from the sea to prevent attack but on water still navigable from the sea. Roughly three hundred years later, it is believed, the Etruscans moved into the area north of Rome in what is now Tuscany.[1] Possessing a more advanced culture, they gradually came to dominate the neighboring tribes, including the Latins, over whom they placed a king. In 509 B.C. the inhabitants of the city of Rome rebelled, deposing the king and instituting the Republic, governed by a senate of patricians with executive power vested in two consuls, who served only for a year. Over the next several centuries this system of government was expanded to include an assembly of plebes, or lower classes.

Except for the spine of the Appenine Mountains running the length of the peninsula, there are no truly major barriers to movement in Italy as there are in Greece, nor are there insulating deserts as with Egypt. The citizens of the city of Rome first had to secure their liberty by removing the threat of the Etruscans, and then to the south they secured their borders in stages until they encountered the established Greek colonies. The Greeks then appealed to the mainland mother cities for help. After a series of rigorous battles, the Romans acquired control over the Greek colonies, so that by 265 B.C. Rome was in control of the entire Italian peninsula. The Romans then found themselves in trade rivalry with the Carthaginians of North Africa. Carthage, which was formerly a Phoenician colony, was the center of a bustling Mediterranean commerce and began to view Rome as a possible competitor. This struggle for power resulted in what the Romans called the three Punic Wars (*Punicus* in Latin means "Phoenician"), 265–146 B.C., which led to the eventual destruction of the city of Carthage and the absorption of its colonies into Rome. Meanwhile, the Roman armies and navy encountered challenges from Macedonia and Syria, and defeated them as well. These victories added to Rome's domain much of Alexander's former empire. The consequence of all this was that by the beginning of the first century B.C. Rome was no longer a city but a series of annexed colonies and federated cities stretching from Gibraltar to Syria, with client kingdoms in Asia Minor, Armenia, and Palestine. The Romans began to call the Mediterranean Sea *mare nostrum,* "our sea."

Rome had become in fact an empire, struggling to govern itself as though it was still a republic, with resultant political upheavals. In 46 B.C. Julius Caesar was appointed dictator by the Senate for ten years in the hope of ending periodic civil wars, but two years later he was assassinated by those who sought to reestablish the old republic, but civil war again broke out. In 31 B.C., when Julius Caesar's nephew, Octavian, defeated Mark Antony and Cleopatra and extended Roman rule into Egypt, he was appointed *princeps* ("first citizen") by the Senate and given the *imperium* command, which made him dictator and head of the army; Octavian also took upon himself the title Augustus ("venerable," "majestic"). Even though Augustus was in fact emperor, he retained all the apparatus of republican rule, thereby avoiding a clash with the ardent republicans in the Senate. His reign of forty-one years was marked by peace and the establishment of an imperial bureaucracy that functioned smoothly despite the depredations of the Julio-Claudian emperors who followed him, including the depraved Caligula and the wanton Nero.

Several years after Nero's death, Vespasian was declared emperor by the army, and he began the Flavian dynasty (his family name was Flavius), which ruled successfully A.D. 69–81, ending in fifteen years of terror under Domitian. Upon Domitian's death the Senate appointed Nerva emperor, beginning the era of the Five Good Emperors, which included Trajan, Hadrian, and Marcus Aurelius; their reigns, from A.D. 96 to A.D. 180, marked the longest period of peace and prosperity of the empire and were coincident with the maximum reach of the empire and Roman law under Trajan; these years of efficient administration were the golden years of civil order and peace, Lex Romana and Pax Romana. Much of the best Roman architecture was built during these periods of peace and expansive economic development during the reigns of Augustus, the Flavians, and the Five Good Emperors.

After Marcus Aurelius, the empire began to suffer growing internal rigidity and pressure from invaders outside the imperial boundaries until Diocletian divided the empire into two sections in A.D. 285, administered by two coequal emperors, whereupon he retired to his fortified palace on the Adriatic Coast at Spalatro, Yugoslavia. This system soon fell apart, but the empire was pulled together once more in A.D. 324 by Constantine, who moved the imperial capitol to a new city that he founded at the entrance to the Black Sea on the old Greek city of Byzantium; it was called the New Rome, but soon acquired the name Constantine's City, Constantinople.

The Roman Character

During the early Republican years of struggle, when the constant threat from neighboring tribes required that Roman farmers be ready to take up arms, the Roman character was formed. There developed a sense of ingrained discipline, patriotic responsibility, and serious purpose that is best described by the Latin term *gravitas,* a sense of the importance of matters at hand,

a propensity for austerity, conservatism, and a deep respect for tradition. A good Roman practiced a rigid morality, served the state, had unimpeachable honor, and strived for a physical and spiritual asceticism—traits that Augustus himself exemplified.

As the city of Rome extended its control over the Italian peninsula, there developed a driving compulsion to spread the benefits of Roman law and republican governance to the rest of the world. This imperative had been declared by Jupiter himself, as expressed by Virgil in the *Aeneid:* "To Romans I set no boundary in space or time. I have granted them dominion, and it has no end."[2] It is a great irony that those who thirsted for human blood sports were the very people who created a universal system of law that sustained the rights of citizens the length of the Mediterranean for five centuries. The Romans endeavored to achieve universality and a clearly perceivable order in all of life, and their unique achievement was to visualize this civic order in the urban spaces they shaped, framed by

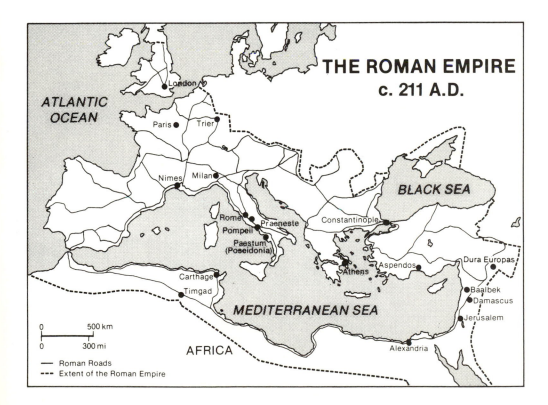

THE ROMAN EMPIRE
c. 211 A.D.

clearly ordered ranks of axially disposed and colonnaded buildings.

The Romans were inherently pragmatic and realistic, unlike the speculative and idealistic Greeks. Although technological advances continued as Rome gained control of the Mediterranean basin, there were no great Roman theoretical scientists. What the Romans produced in abundance was engineers and builders who developed architectural forms on a scale the Greeks could not have conceived, as Strabo boasted in his *Geography*. Roman engineers built a network of roads linking all parts of the empire, from the Portuguese coast to the ends of Turkey and Syria; if a stony mountain outcrop loomed in the way, they simply cut through it. They captured streams and conducted the water more than thirty miles to the cities, tunneling through hills and lifting the aqueducts over valleys on bounding arcades. Rome itself had fourteen aqueducts, over 265 miles (426.5 meters) in total length, carrying 200 million gallons of water into the city daily. In many parts of Europe, the water supply and the sewer systems were far better under the Romans than they are today, and in Segovia, Spain, the city's water is still carried in the Roman aqueduct.

Roman Religion and the Roman Temple

Religion in Rome was centered in the home, the *domus*. It was originally an animistic religion in which gifts were rendered to impersonal spirits that governed every aspect of nature—trees, rocks, water, and the fire of the domestic hearth. In each house were small shrines where offerings were made to these spirits. It was the Etruscans who had introduced a pantheon of Greeklike gods, and who began the construction of temples raised on high platforms with columnar front porticoes. After contact with the Greeks, the Romans invested their civic, or state, gods with much of the character of the Olympian gods, so that Jupiter became nearly the same as Zeus. Jupiter, in particular, became viewed by the Romans as protector of the state. Always fond of clearly specified procedure, the Romans developed detailed rituals in worshiping the gods, rituals carried out by priests who had little contact with the ordinary artisan or merchant. Ordinary Romans still made offerings to the *numina,* the spirits worshiped in their home shrines, but state priests took care of state religion.

12.1. Maison Carrée, Nîmes, France (the Roman Nemausus, Gaul), begun c. 19 B.C. One of the best preserved of all Roman temples, this shows the high base, emphatic front, and engaged columns in the side walls typical of Roman temples.

The Roman temple, *templum,* derived from Etruscan prototypes, was similar to the Greek temple and eventually was embellished with Greek orders and architectural details.[3] The underlying difference in the Roman temple had to do with the way in which the sacred precinct around the temple was consecrated, through actions that set up an axis that dominated the orientation of the temple and the space in front of it, and how the temple was placed in relation to that space. At the dedication of a temple site, the priest, or *augur,* would survey the intended plot and name the boundary lines. He would draw a circle in the earth, dividing it with two perpendicular lines to mark the quadrants of the temple enclosure, laying out an axis in front of him, and a cross axis determining front and back, left and right. Whereas the Greek temple was set down in an open area and approached from all sides, the Roman temple was placed at the end of a clearly defined open space, aligned on the axis of the space. It was set back against the rear of this space, high on a podium—unlike the Greek temple, with its three equal steps all around—and could be approached only from the front up a long flight of stairs. Like the Greek temple, however, the Roman temple had columns, but these were primarily at the front, supporting the gable roof over the entrance to the *cella,* the enclosed chamber. To the sides and rear the wall was dominant, with the columns merged into the wall to form engaged columns integral with the wall of the cella.

Among the best preserved of such Roman temples is that built about 19 B.C. in the provincial town of Nemausus in Gaul (Nîmes, France), called today the Maison Carrée, the "square house," because of its clear rectangular geometry [12.1]. Although built during the reign of Augustus, and therefore an imperial building, it duplicates the form of traditional temples of the earlier Republic. The rectangular enclosed space in front of the Maison Carrée, however, has long since been built over.

The most dramatic example of the rule of the axis in controlling space was for centuries covered up; this is the Sanctuary of Fortuna Primigenia at Praeneste (Palest-

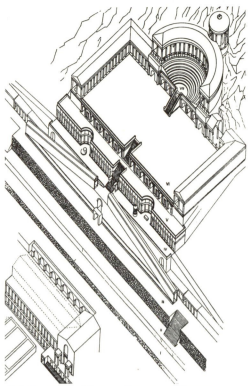

12.2. Sanctuary of Fortuna Primigenia, Praeneste (Palestrina), Italy, c. 80 B.C. This complex of ramps and terraces shows clearly the organization of Roman space around a dominant axis.

rina), Italy [12.2]. Probably built under the direction of Sulla, who conquered Praeneste for Rome in 82 B.C., it accommodated several ancient sacred spots and was part of Sulla's reestablishment of the ancient local cults. Although the site was known through written descriptions such as Cicero's *De divinatione,* it had been built over during the Middle Ages.

As it happened, Palestrina was heavily bombed in World War Two, and when the rubble was cleared away it was discovered that beneath lay the remains of the ancient Sanctuary of Fortuna, enabling scholars to reconstruct its elaborate plan and to study the details of the terraces and colonnades that survived. At the bottom were barrel-vaulted shops leading to three shallow terraces. From there long covered ramps converged on a central axial stair at the fourth level. Here graceful colonnades provided sheltered walks. Above was another terrace and an axial stair leading to the sixth and largest terrace, framed on three sides by stoas. Another stair then led up to a small theaterlike series of concentric steps, culminating in a semicircular colonnade. Behind and rising over this was a circular temple, the focus of the entire composition; from the temple and the semicircular loggia just below it, visitors could look out over the valley to the sea. Inspired perhaps by the terraces of Queen Hatshepsut's mortuary temple west of Thebes, the Romans here transformed an entire hillside, reshaping nature according to their unique vision of the earth yielding to the geometric and axially disposed design of human invention. Built of concrete and tufa masonry, the Sanctuary of Fortuna Primigenia was a hint of the even larger and more complex concrete structures to follow during the Empire.

Roman Urban Planning

As with the Greeks, Roman life was focused on the city, but as the empire grew, the far-

flung cities became part of a federation of participants in self rule rather than subject peoples. The annexed cities were the prime agents in spreading *Romanitas*, the sum of Roman values and culture. By the second century A.D., those who lived outside of cities were considered rustics, and the term used by early urban Christians to describe those not in the cities (that is, those who had not embraced the faith) was *paganus*, "pagan," "a country person."

Early Roman cities and those that grew from Greek settlements, such as the commercial and resort town of Pompeii, south of Neopolis (Naples), had networks of streets forming irregular rectangles [12.3]. As these cities expanded, the blocks might become more regular, but at these ancient sites there was no urgency to align the streets with the points of the compass. At the heart of these old cities, culturally if not always geographically, was the *forum*, the civic open space, lined with stoas and civil buildings. The forum thus served much the same function as the Greek agora.[4] What distinguished the forum, however, was its clear architectural definition and its gener-

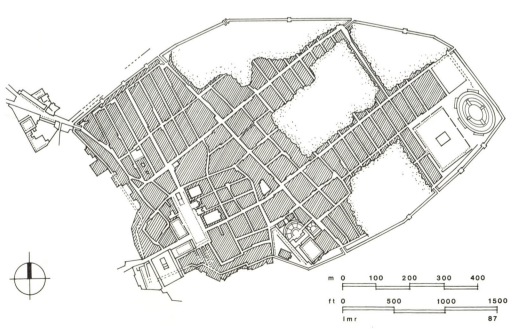

12.3. Pompeii, Italy. Plan of the city. The ancient heart of the city, founded in the sixth century B.C., is to the southeast. Later extensions have a more gridlike system of streets.

ally rectangular shape dominated by a temple of Jupiter at one end on the axis of the forum (the north end at Pompeii). Around the forum, enclosing it and giving it shape, would be found several buildings housing the *curia*, city offices, and a *basilica*, a large roofed building where legal cases were heard, as well as various temples and public buildings. The forum of Pompeii illustrates these elements well [12.4].

From the Hellenistic Greeks the Romans learned the technique of orthogonal planning, and they soon made this the basis of laying out army camps during the second century B.C.[5] Just as in dedicating a temple site, the ground for the camp, *castrum,* was surveyed and the basic governing lines, or *limites,* were established at the center of the camp with an instrument called the *groma.* The principal street running north and south from this point was the *cardo,* the principal east-west street, the *decumanus.* Beyond the walls of the camp this system would be extended on a larger scale (sometimes reoriented in deference to the slope of the land), in blocks called *centuriae,* measuring 2,400 Roman feet to a side.[6] These large squares were equivalent to a hundred small farms, hence their name, centuries.

Military encampments in turn became the basis of countless town plans throughout the empire. In numerous European cities these grid plans survive in various degrees in the medieval streets patterns. In England, especially, the legacy of the Roman camp survives in the names of scores of towns, for "chester" is derived from the Latin *castrum:* Leicester, Chichester, Silchester, Worchester, and Chester are a few examples. One military outpost that has survived in remarkable detail is Thamugadi (Timgad), in the Roman province of Numidia, now eastern Algeria [12.5]. Founded in A.D. 100 as a colony of military veterans guarding a strategic outpost, this was laid out with a rigid orthogonal grid, but as it expanded outside the original walls, the rigid rectilinear order gradually was abandoned. Immediately south of the decumanus is the forum, with the curia to the west and a large basilica on the east side. Just south of the forum was the city's principal theater. Outside the

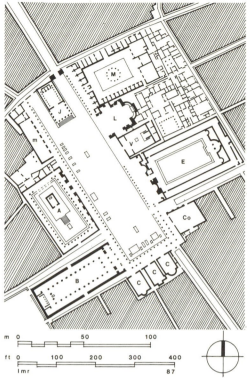

12.4. *Plan of the Forum, Pompeii. The principal public space in Roman cities was enclosed by the curia (city offices) and one or more basilicas (legal chambers), was ringed with colonnades, and was focused on the Temple of Jupiter.*

A	= Temple of Apollo	*J*	= Temple of Jupiter
B	= basilica	*L*	= Lararium
C	= Curia (city offices)	*M*	= Macellum
Co	= Comitium	*m*	= market
E	= Eumachia Building	*V*	= Temple of Vespasian

walls, on the north and south, were the largest of the public baths.

Of all the forums, the most important were those in Rome itself, beginning with the original city square, the Forum Romanum, considered the "head of the world," *caput mundi* [12.6]. Because this had grown bit by bit over several hundred years, it was not rigorously orthogonal, as were those in cities laid out from scratch, but beginning with Julius Caesar additional forums were built north and east of the original forum [12.7]. Julius Caesar's forum, the Forum Iulium, begun c. 54 B.C., provided the model—strictly rectangular, lined with stoas, and focused on a temple of Venus

*12.5. Plan of Thamugadi (Timgad),
Algeria, founded in A.D. 100.
Established as a colony for military
veterans, this city had a military
castrum plan. The main north-south
street is the cardo, and the main
east-west street is the decumanus.*

*12.6. Plan of Rome, third
century A.D. Plan of imperial
Rome, showing major buildings
and the forums.*

A = Amphitheater
B = Basilica of Maxentius
       (Constantine)
BC = Baths of Caracalla
BD = Baths of Diocletian
BT = Baths of Trajan
C = Capitoline Hill
CM = Circus Maximus
CN = Circus of Nero
F = Forum Romanum
IF = Imperial Forums
M = Theater of Marcellus
MH = Mausoleum of Hadrian
P = Pantheon
Pa = Palatine Hill
PC = Praetorian Camp
SD = Stadium of Domitian

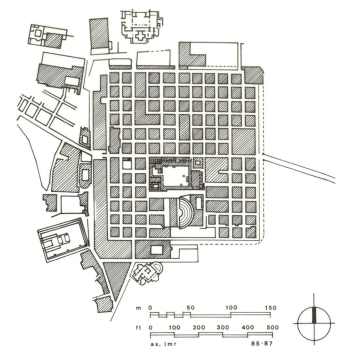

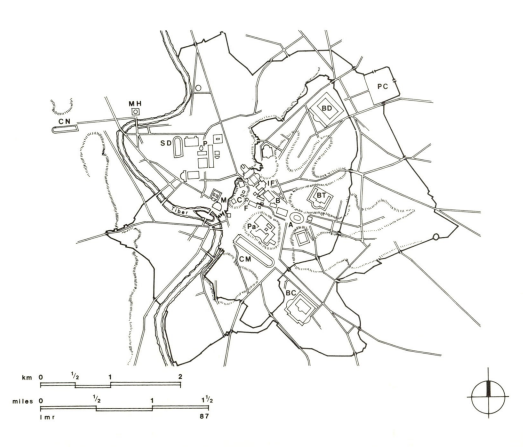

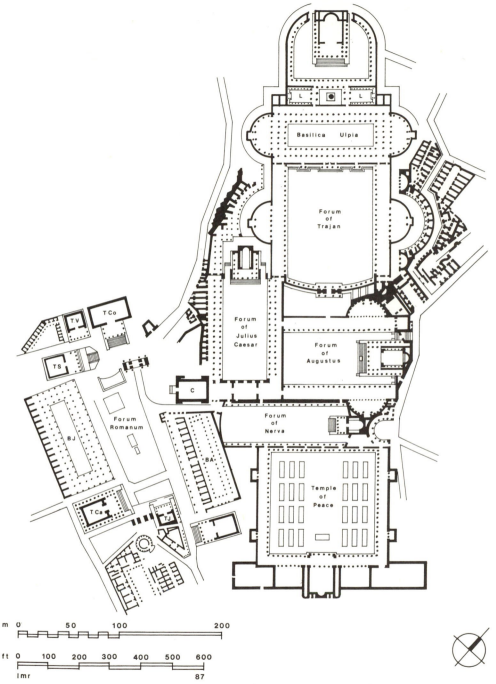

12.7. *The Forum Romanum and the Imperial Forums, Rome, c. 54 B.C. to A.D. 117. The interconnected Imperial Forums were built by successive emperors on interlaced axes next to the ancient Forum Romanun, the center of Roman civic and political life.*

BA	= Basilica Amelia	L	= Libraries	TJ	= Temple of Divus Julius
BJ	= Basilica Julia	TCa	= Temple of Castor	TS	= Temple of Saturn
C	= Curia Julia	TCo	= Temple of Concord	TV	= Temple of Vespasian

Genetrix. Perpendicular to this, Augustus then added his Forum Augustum (dedicated in 2 B.C.), focused on a larger temple of Mars Ultor ("Mars Avenger") which was backed up against a city wall. Additional forums were added by succeeding emperors, each forum commemorating a significant military achievement and dedicated to a god whose attributes were admired by the patron emperor. By means of interlocking and interwoven perpendicular axes, these spaces are linked together to form a complex but coherent system.

The imperial forums culminated in the vast Forum of Trajan, north of the Forum Augustum, designed by Apollodorus of Damascus and built by the emperor in A.D. 98–117 to commemorate his victories in Dacia, north of the Danube. More complex than the earlier forums, this had a broad stoa-lined forecourt measuring 660 by 390 feet (200 by 120 meters), not including the semicircular *exedrae* on each side screened by the stoas. On the hillside overlooking the northern exedra were public markets constructed by Trajan as part of the forum building project. At the far north end of the forum complex was a temple to the deified Trajan, built by his successor Hadrian, in front of which were two libraries, one for Greek and one for Latin manuscripts. Between the libraries stood the great stone column of Trajan, 125 feet (38 meters) high, covered with a spiraling relief depicting the Dacian campaign. The temple to Trajan could not be seen from the open space, for between the temple and the broad court was a large basilica (the Basilica Ulpia), the largest in all Rome.

The Enclosure and Manipulation of Space

The focus on urban life required the development of new building types in Roman architecture, buildings that enclosed space for the use of the public. Although the cellas of Roman temples had several chambers to house the image of the god and a treasury, only priests entered them. Other civic activities, however, such as legal proceedings, required a large covered space where judges

could hear cases, where litigants could wait their turn, and where the public could listen. The basilica was designed to accommodate this need.[7] Normally a long rectangular building placed adjacent to a forum, it had an internal encircling colonnade, with an apse or cylindrical projection at one end (or both ends) where the judges would sit. At the geometric center of the semicircular apse would be an altar acknowledging the spiritual presence of the emperor, for only in his symbolic presence could cases be heard. The Basilica Ulpia (Trajan's family name was Ulpius) illustrates this building type on a grand scale [12.8, 12.9]. Not including the apses, the building was 385 by 182 feet (117.4 by 55.5 meters) wall to wall, with two concentric internal colonnades opening onto a central vertical space, which itself was 260 feet (80 meters) long. The vast center space was covered by a timber truss roof spanning 80 feet (25 meters).

Increasingly during the second century A.D. Roman builders used concrete, *opus caementicum,* for the walls and vaults of these public buildings. Their concrete was a thick mortar (not liquid like modern concrete) laid with bands of brick. Having learned that exposed concrete does not weather well, Roman builders incorporated brick or stone as an outer facing. From about 200 B.C. to 100 B.C. this facing consisted of random masonry blocks, *opus incertum,* but during the next two centuries regular square bricks were used, set on the diagonal, *opus reticulatum.* After about A.D. 100, flat bricks or tiles were used as the facing, *opus testaceum.* Concrete construction reached its height in the public baths of the late empire, and in the three-bay concrete groin vault of the Basilica of Maxentius derived from these baths. Begun by Emperor Maxentius in A.D. 307, this was finished by Constantine in A.D. 325 [2.18, 12.10]. The central circulation space measured 265 by 83 feet (80.8 by 25.3 meters) and was covered by three groin vaults, with a semicircular exedra at the northwest end and three large chambers on each side (whose walls served to buttress the concrete groin vault of the center "nave"). Each of these side chambers, measuring 76 by 56

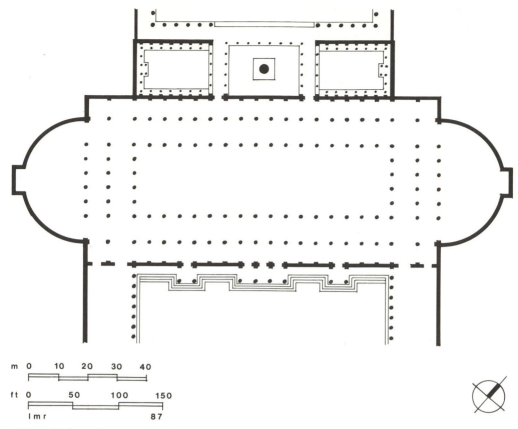

m 0   10   20   30   40

ft 0   50   100   150

l m r   87

12.8. Apollodorus of Damascus, Basilica Ulpia, Forum of Trajan, Rome, A.D. 98–117. Plan. Largest of all the basilicas in Rome, this provided for two legal hearing chambers at each end, with an immense covered volume for public circulation.

12.9. Basilica Ulpia. Interior view.

12.10. Basilica of Maxentius, Rome, A.D. 307–325. View of the surviving three side chambers.

feet (23.2 by 17.1 meters), covered by a barrel vault, could accommodate additional court proceedings; only three of these side chambers survive today.

The building that best symbolizes the Roman enclosure of space and the powerful effect of such defined space is the Pantheon, built by Hadrian between A.D. 118 and A.D. 128 [12.11, 12.12, 2.19]. The Pantheon was a temple to all the gods—from the Greek *pantheos; pan,* "all," plus *theos,* "god"—including the deified emperor Augustus. Since the Romans imagined the earth as a disk covered by a heavenly dome, the new building undertaken by Hadrian was to symbolize that universe of earth and the gods. Who designed it is not known, although Hadrian himself may have played a part in devising the conceptual scheme.[8] Built of concrete of varying density from bottom to top, it is a model of the heavenly dome, the realm of all the gods, measuring

142½ feet (43.4 meters) in diameter. This hemisphere rests on a drum of equal height, so that the distance from the top of the dome to the floor is the same as the width of the dome; hence, one could inscribe a perfect sphere within the enclosed volume. The only source of light (aside from what comes through the sheltered door) is the *oculus,* or eye, at the top, 30 feet across (9.1 meters). Its beam of light slowly creeps across the marble floor and inches up the wall, marking out the cycles of the sun like a gigantic timepiece. As noted in Chapter 2, the concrete of the dome exerts tremendous downward thrust, and this is diverted by eight barrel vaults in the thickness of the drum wall (20 feet; 6.1 meters) to eight piers. Between these piers are eight deep niches (where the statues of the gods were once placed), whose dark interiors are obscured from view by screens of slender Corinthian columns. Thus the enormous weight seems

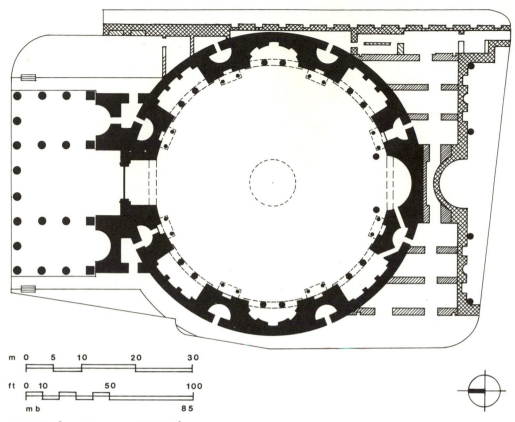

m   0   5   10   20   30

ft   0   10   50   100
     m b   8 5

12.11. Pantheon, Rome, A.D. *118–28. Plan.*

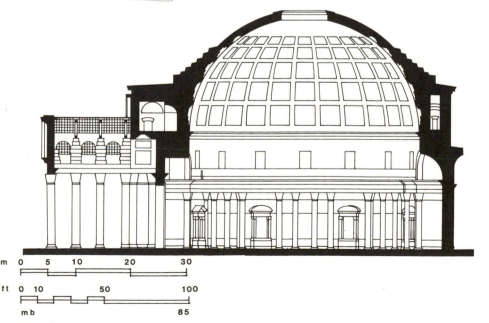

m   0   5   10   20   30

ft   0   10   50   100
     m b   8 5

12.12. Pantheon. Section.

12.13. Forum of the Pantheon. Originally the Pantheon, like other temples, faced an open forum whose enclosing colonnades may have partially obscured the drum of the dome, heightening the sense of surprise one experienced upon entering.

to come down to a wall broken up into shadowy recesses. The reason the building survives in such good condition is that in 609 it was consecrated by Pope Boniface IV as the church of Santa Maria Rotunda.

From the outside, a person approaching originally had little suggestion of the space within the building, for there was a deep, colonnaded rectangular forum in front of the Pantheon that prevented clear views of the cylindrical side walls of the building [12.13]. Facing the forum was the broad octastyle (eight-column) Corinthian portico of monolithic gray Egyptian granite columns with white marble bases and capitals. The portico was backed against a tall square attic block that also prevented full view of the cylinder and dome. The exterior seems always to have been rather plain, but the interior was filled by colored marble.

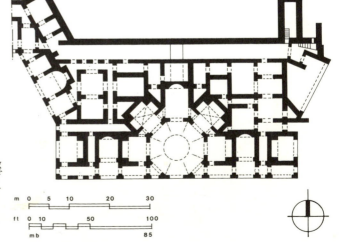

12.14. Severus and Celer, house of Nero, the Domus Aurea (House of Gold), Rome. Partial plan. Overlooking a lush landscape created in the heart of the city, this villa consisted of concrete-vaulted rooms in a wide variety of shapes. Many rooms were illuminated by ingenious oculus windows and reflecting walls.

m   0   5   10   20   30

ft 0 10   50   100

m b   85

The walls and floor were covered with a veneer of marble, granite, and porphyry brought from the corners of the Roman world, evidence of the far-flung trade network made possible by the Pax Romana, the Peace of Rome.

Perhaps no other single building so sums up the Roman achievement as the Pantheon. It exploits concrete to its fullest; it defines simply yet powerfully a clear geometry that assumes universal and cosmic significance, at a scale that never fails to evoke awe. It illustrates highly organized building operations in constructing formwork, in coordinating the flow of building materials, and in the timing of the placement of concrete. It is evidence of the potential of human ingenuity and aspiration. But most important it is evidence that building can transcend utilitarian construction, for the Pantheon becomes "the symbol and the consequence of an immutable union between the gods, nature, man, and the state."[9]

The Pantheon was the culmination of important experiments being made for two centuries. Its distinction was its vast scale, but equally important were the experiments in manipulating space carried out in building the Domus Aurea (Golden House) of Nero in A.D. 64–68. In A.D. 64 a disastrous fire had erupted near the Circus Maximus and had consumed the heart of old Rome. Nero conveniently blamed the fire on a new religious sect, the Christians, and commenced the first of successive waves of persecution. Of Rome's fourteen administrative districts, three had been obliterated in the fire, and ten more were severely damaged. Nero promptly claimed the destroyed districts, appropriating for himself the area around the Esquiline Hill. Here he and his architects, Severus and Celer, set about building a luxurious "country" estate on 350 acres (141.7 hectares) in the center of the city, filling it with fountains and a palace that looked out over an artificial lake. The entrance was built against the Forum

12.15. Domus Aurea. Interior view of the octagon.

12.16. Apartment blocks (insulae), Ostia, Italy, late first and second centuries. This model shows the galleries and balconies that ran around some of the apartment blocks. In places these galleries bridged across the street to allow movement from building to building without having to descend to the congested streets.

Romanum, opening onto a court dominated by a gilded bronze statue of Nero, 120 feet high (36.6 meters), called the Colossus.

The Domus Aurea was a complex of interconnected geometric volumes, its rooms covered by nearly every known type of vault and dome [12.14, 12.15]. In the north wing was a low octagonal room covered by an octagonal vault that became hemispherical toward the top and opened in a large oculus. Around this were taller barrel-vaulted chambers whose open ends looked inward toward the curve of the dome, so that these surrounding vaulted chambers were lit from unseen sources with light bounced from the outer surface of the central dome.

Domestic Architecture

Roman writers, such as Virgil in his *Georgics,* developed a sensitivity to the natural landscape unknown before, an interest reflected in the letters of Cicero and Pliny the Younger that so lovingly describe their country villas. Despite this new appreciation of the landscape, Roman civilization was essentially urban. Cities were the building blocks of the Empire, the centers of trade and commerce. Rome itself was huge, having about a million inhabitants during the reign of Augustus. Complaints were common about the shortage of housing, exorbi-

tant rents, pollution, crime in the streets, and the general high cost of living. Because of congestion, chariots and other vehicles were excluded from the city during daylight, with the result that much commercial traffic was conducted at night.

Most urban citizens lived in apartment houses, large blocks of three or four floors that opened onto landscaped internal courts. These *insulae* ("islands") filled entire blocks. Often hastily and shoddily built as speculative real estate ventures, they sometimes collapsed; in a letter to his friend Atticus, Cicero wrote that two of his shops had fallen down, but that he had a scheme to rebuild that would recover his losses.[10] Augustus decreed that no *insulae* could be built more that 70 feet high (21.3 meters); and after the fire in A.D. 64, Nero decreed numerous additional building regulations, requiring the use of nonflammable materials. The *insulae* in Rome itself have been replaced, but in Rome's port city, Ostia, many have survived, some up to the third floor [12.16]. Built of brick and concrete, they had balconies running around the entire block, many connected by bridges over the narrow streets to neighboring *insulae,* enabling residents to move about the city without descending to the congested streets.

In Pompeii, destroyed in A.D. 79 when

Mount Vesuvius erupted, there is preserved a range of different house types, from small artisans' residences to large patrician residences and expansive country villas.[11] At the northwestern end of Pompeii are a number of blocks in the later more orthogonal extension of the city; these blocks contain a number of houses, ranging from small to very large. One block is nearly filled by the expansive house of Pansa [12.17]. Except for its large garden to the north, it typifies the arrangement of a single-story Roman town house, with its relative closure to the street and inward focus. For the most part, houses had symmetrical floor plans where possible. The entrance connected with a large public room, the *atrium*, open to the sky through an opening in the roof and ringed with cubicles. The roof of the atrium pitched inward, so that rain water dripped into a pool, the *impluvium*, at the center of the room. On the axis beyond the atrium was the principal public room, screened by draperies, the *tablinium*. Beyond this was the open *peristyle*, ringed with a colonnade. Around the peristyle were more cubicles and the *triclinium*, the dining room just large enough to accommodate three broad reclining dining couches. In some houses the peristyle was large enough to be a garden, with another impluvium at the center. Beyond the peristyle, on the axis, was the *oecus*, or reception room. Around the house of Pansa and filling out the block were several small individual residences on the east side, six small shops opening to the street on

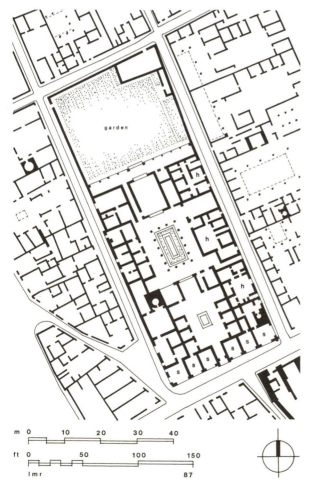

garden

m 0   10   20   30   40

ft 0   50   100   150

l m r   87

12.17. House of Pansa, Pompeii, Italy, second century B.C. Plan. Somewhat larger than other houses in Pompeii, it nonetheless has the same component elements (the major addition here is the large garden to the north). Like other Roman urban houses, it was surrounded by smaller houses and shops open to the street (h = rental houses; s = rental shops).

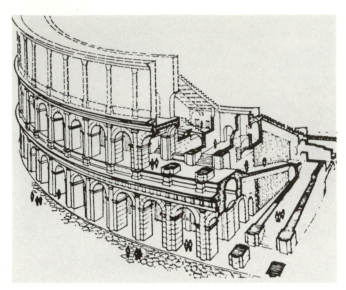

12.18. Theater of Marcellus, Rome, finished 12 B.C. Perspective. This cutaway drawing shows the system of circulation used to admit viewers to the ramped seats. The uppermost floor was removed in the Middle Ages, but the superimposed engaged columns (Ionic over Doric) survive in the lower stories.

the south side, and a bakery and two more shops on the west side. Such surrounding apartments and shops provided income to the owner, whose house was in the center of the block.

The various houses, villas, and public buildings of Pompeii have acquired special importance, for the entire city and the neighboring towns of Herculaneum and Stabiae were buried under up to thirty feet of volcanic ash in the eruption of Mount Vesuvius on August 24, A.D. 79. It happened quickly and yet without a strong blast, so little was damaged physically. Household articles were left where they were dropped, the bread on the bakers' counters was abandoned, the residents who refused to flee suffocated and were buried by the ash where they collapsed. Gradually the streets and houses were filled with the falling ash, covering furniture and wall paintings. When the site was uncovered in the eighteenth century and excavation began in 1748, the first detailed evidence of everyday Roman life came to light.

Public Buildings

Because of their intensive urban life, the Romans developed a range of varied public building types. The largest of these, meant to accommodate public amusements, were

not covered, but others had large volumes covered with concrete vaults of various shapes.

Roman theaters, derived from Greek models, were the scene for revivals of Greek plays as well as the production of newer, Roman works, but they never served the quasi-religious function of the Greek theater. Hence they were not located near temples but instead near the business center of the Roman city; and since they were not built into the sides of sacred acropolises, Roman theaters had their seats ramped up on tilted vaults raised on stone piers. The basic form of the Roman theater was crystallized in the Theater of Marcellus, Rome, projected by Augustus himself, built under the direction of Marcus Agrippa, and dedicated about 12 B.C. [12.18].[12] The seats were inclined on a system of radiating and tilted concrete barrel vaults supported by radiating stone piers, between which threaded the stairs and ramps leading to the sections of seating. The outer curved wall was opened up by superimposed arcades of travertine faced with engaged orders—unfluted Doric at the lower level and Ionic on the second level (the treatment of the third level is not known, for it was rebuilt during the Middle Ages). Unlike Greek theaters, Roman theaters were exactly semicircular, with a half-circle orchestra where Senators were often

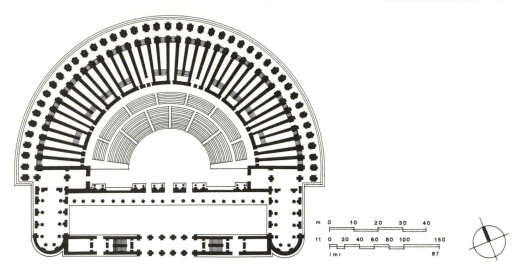

12.19. Theater of Marcellus. Plan.

seated; the Theater of Marcellus measured 365 feet (111 meters) in diameter [12.19]. As was typical of Roman theaters, the seats faced a permanent *scaenae frons,* a wall as high as the rear wall of the semicircular seating. In its three tiers of seats, each one pitched more steeply than the one below, the Theater of Marcellus could accommodate eleven thousand spectators.

Every Roman city had one or more theaters, but the one that has survived best is the theater in Aspendos in the Roman province of Pamphylia, near the coast of south-central Turkey [12.20].[13] Designed about A.D. 155 by Zeno of Theodorus, it was built against a hillside, although the sides of the semicircular seating are carried by vaults and arcades. It is 315 feet (96 meters) in diameter and can accommodate up to seven thousand spectators. The stage and *scaenae frons* still stand, but missing is the sloped, reflecting wooden ceiling that was originally cantilevered 27 feet (8.1 meters) out over the stage. The *scaenae frons* was once richly embellished, with two superimposed colonnades of paired columns carry-

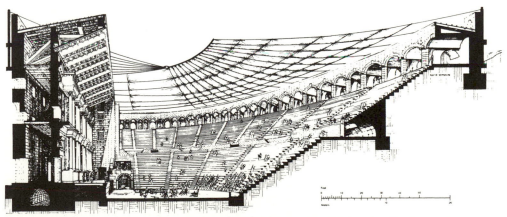

12.20. Zeno of Theodorus, Theater, Aspendos, Pamphylia (Turkey), c. A.D. 155. Interior. The Roman theater focused on a tall, permanent stone scaenae frons, *or backdrop scene, that rose as high as the uppermost seats.*

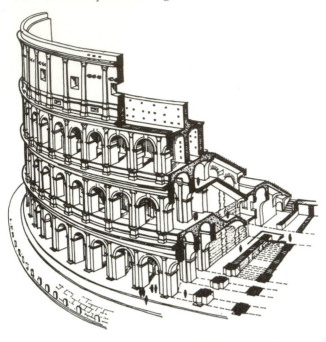

12.21. Flavian Amphitheater (the Colosseum), Rome, begun c. A.D. 80. Perspective. Roman amphitheaters were designed for popular amusements and sports events. This, the largest of them all, could seat up to 55,000 people, admitted through 76 separate gates.

12.22. Flavian Amphitheater. Interior of arena. Originally the floor was covered with heavy wooden planks covered with sand for gladiatorial contests. Below were the animal cages. For special occasions the floor was removed and the arena flooded for mock naval battles.

ing alternated segmental and triangular pediments. To shield theater-goers, a *velarium,* supported by fifty-eight masts planted in sockets at the rear of the seating, could be pulled over the audience.

The principal Roman innovation in theater design was to combine two theaters to form the oval *amphitheater* devoted to gladiatorial contests and other large-scale amusements. The oldest surviving example is that at Pompeii, built about 80 B.C. It measures 500 by 350 feet (150 by 105 meters) and could hold twenty-thousand spectators. The word amphitheater, however, has become nearly synonymous with the huge Flavian amphitheater in Rome, popularly called the Colosseum [12.21, 12.22]. This was begun by Emperor Vespasian in A.D. 80, after the end of Nero's unpopular reign, when the grounds of his Domus Aurea were appropriated for new public buildings; Vespasian's amphitheater in fact was built in the basin where Nero's artificial lake had been and stood next to Nero's colossal statue—hence the name. (Nero's Domus Aurea was later covered by the Baths of Trajan). The unknown architect of the Flavian amphitheater was a master of logistics and construction deployment, for the building was under construction in several areas at once by different work crews. On a foundation ring of concrete, piers of tufa and travertine were placed to carry the concrete vaults forming the shell for the tiers of seating. Overall, the amphitheater measured 615 by 510 feet (188 by 156 meters), with a clear arena floor of 280 by 175 feet (86 by 54 meters). The floor was laid with wood planks over a series of subterranean chambers and passageways through which lions and other animals could be admitted to the arena floor; the floor could be removed and the entire lower level flooded for water sports. The seats rose in tiers to 159 feet (48.5 meters), with a curved outer wall of four superimposed arcades. As in the Theater of Marcellus, the stone arcades incorporated engaged columns— unfluted Doric on the ground floor, and Ionic, Corinthian, and finally Corinthian pilasters on the uppermost, fourth story. At the fourth level, too, were sockets holding masts for the velarium that could be stretched over the audience. The individual wedge sections of seats were divided into seventy-six separate blocks, each with its own entrance and exit stairs and ramps incorporated in the vaulted passages under the seats, a system nearly identical to that used in many modern sports arenas. Between forty-five thousand and fifty-five thousand people could be seated in the Flavian amphitheater at one time.

Even larger were the stadiums, or circuses, used for chariot races. The biggest of them all in Rome was the Circus Maximus, in the valley between the Palatine and Aventine hills and begun in 329 B.C. [12.6]. Shaped rather like a modern football stadium, but much longer, the Circus Maximus was about 1,820 feet (555 meters) from the stables at one end to the curve at the other. It was approximately 380 feet (115.8 meters) wide. The Circus Maximus has disappeared, but the smaller Circus of Domitian survives as a ghost image in the open space of the Piazza Navona, for the enclosing walls of the circus's seating were reused in medieval buildings that were themselves replaced with new buildings in the Renaissance [17.19].

The unique Roman structural achievement was covering large spaces for public use, as in the creation of the basilica as a legal court. Another special Roman creation was the public bath, examples of which were built in profusion throughout the empire during the second century A.D. In Rome itself, according to a catalogue of buildings drawn up in A.D. 354, there were 952 baths of varying size.[14] Roman baths, *thermae,* were used for much more than simply washing. They combined aspects of a modern health club with that of a public library and school, for the biggest baths (such as the Baths of Caracalla in Rome [12.23]) contained shops, restaurants, exercise yards (*palaestrae*), libraries, and lecture halls and reading rooms (*gymnasia*), all arranged around spacious gardens filled with sculpture (in fact, many of the surviving Roman copies of Greek sculpture were found in the gardens of these baths). In the Baths of Caracalla, the largest in Rome, more than

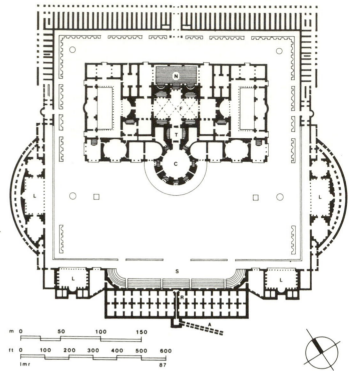

12.23. Baths of Caracalla, Rome, A.D. 212–216. Plan of the bath complex, showing surrounding gardens and reading rooms.

A = Marcian Aqueduct
C = Calidarium (hot baths)
F = Frigidarium (cold baths)
L = Libraries
T = Tepidarium (warm baths)
N = Natatio (swimming pool)
R = Water reservoir
S = Stadium

1,600 bathers of one gender could be accommodated at one time in its sprawling 33 acres. The entire complex was 1,152 feet wide (351 meters; excluding the curved exedrae) and 1,240 feet (378 meters) in depth, including the reservoirs at the south end fed by the Marcian aqueduct. Along the north side were shops and in the exedrae on the sides were libraries and lecture halls; flanking the reservoirs were additional libraries. The remaining space within the walls was shaded by groves of trees. In the northerly half of the enclosure was the principal bath building, 750 by 380 feet (228 by 116 meters). On the central axis, on the south side, was the domed hot room, the *calidarium*, 115 feet (35 meters) in diameter, with hot pools in niches in the wall of the drum. Immediately north of this was the warm room, the *tepidarium*, with two pools at the sides of this hall. The tepidarium led to the large three-bay cold room, the *frigidarium*, 183 feet by 79 feet (55.7 by 24 meters). At the heart of the building, the frigidarium had three groin vaults rising 108 feet (32.9

meters) above the roof, with light pouring through the eight semicircular lunette windows [12.24]. To the north of the frigidarium was the swimming pool, the *natatio*, open to the sky but apparently illuminated by bronze mirrors attached to metal fixtures overhead. The entire complex, including gardens and enclosing facilities, was built on a platform 20 feet high (6 meters) that provided for vaulted storage rooms and the furnaces that heated the tepidarium and calidarium by means of flues in the floors and walls through which hot air circulated.

Every Roman city of any significance had a theater and a bath. Timgad had fourteen baths in all, with two large establishments on the north and south edges of the city [12.5] built in the third and mid-second centuries A.D., respectively. In the northern outpost of Augusta Treverorum (Trier, Germany) on the Moselle River, the spacious heated baths built in the fourth century must have been especially welcome. Trier had a number of other large public buildings; the basilica still stands nearly intact. In

Britain the Romans took advantage of mineral hot springs that bubbled up next to the Avon River, building there *thermae* and a city they called Aquae Sulis, a city that exists today as Bath, England.

Although the great circuses and baths were built at public expense, there was much private philanthropy as well. One example is the Celsus library at Ephesus, on the western coast of Turkey, built in A.D. 135 by the son and grandson of Caius Julius Celsus Polemaeanus in his honor. It was a two story rectangular block, 55 by 36 feet (16.8 by 10.9 meters), lined on three sides by recesses that held cupboards for the books (rolled into scrolls). Centered on the back wall was a semicircular niche that may well have had a statue of Celsus.

Roman theaters, circuses, and baths were built and operated with imperial funds and were available at no charge to the public. The purpose of these expensive enterprises was to keep the unruly populace occupied, for tens of thousands in the city of Rome were unemployed. The construction of such buildings itself provided work for those in the building trades, and the continual games and the pleasures of the baths served to divert the populace. Grain was dispersed as well; free "bread and circuses" in the cities soon became imperial policy. There was, of course, a price to be paid for such state largess, in the form of increasingly burdensome taxes throughout the empire. By the time of Diocletian's reign, A.D. 284–305, restrictions bound sons to the trade of their fathers and farmers to the land, and thus the basis of medieval serfdom was created.

Roman "Baroque" Architecture

During the later Roman Empire, architectural forms became larger, more extensively

12.24. Baths of Caracalla. Interior perspective. Although now shorn of the marble veneers and embellishments, such baths and other public buildings were richly and colorfully ornamented, as this restoration drawing suggests.

embellished, and formally complex. This move toward elaboration and complexity was especially pronounced in the provinces, removed from the influence of the austere models in Rome. In such areas as Syria the official Roman state religion was amalgamated with local cults, resulting in temple buildings and complexes that differed significantly from those in the capital city. Several striking examples are found in the city of Baalbek, Syria, a Roman colony established about 16 B.C. The principal temple there was dedicated to Baal, the great god of storm who had become equated with Jupiter; next to it was a temple to Tammuz (synonymous with the Roman god Bacchus). Begun soon after the establishment of the colony, the vast temple complex was under construction for nearly two hundred fifty years. The large Temple of Jupiter was raised on an immense podium 40 feet (12.2 meters) high; it faced a square forum court 380 feet square (115.8 meters), which in turn opened onto a hexagonal forecourt 192 feet (58.5 meters) across. The adjoining Temple of Bacchus had richly ornamented interior cella walls, the spaces between its engaged Corinthian columns filled with heavily ornamented architectural detail.

Such spatially complex architecture nowadays is said to be baroque, using the modern term developed to describe the richly modeled architecture of the seventeenth century in Italy. One such late Imperial Roman building is the temple of Venus in Baalbek, built in the third century A.D., a combination of a round temple fronted by a rectangular portico carrying a pediment. The entablature of the enclosing Corinthian colonnade is pushed back in deep concave curves, as is the podium of the temple, so that the building reads more like a molded sculptural mass rather than a structural arrangement of stone posts and beams.

Just as Hellenistic architecture moved away from the formal clarity of Periklean architecture, so too did late Roman provincial architecture move away from the austerity of the architecture of the Augustan age in Rome. Instead the emphasis was on experimentation and on pushing stone to its plastic limits.

An Architecture of Universality

While the Pax Romana endured, during the peaceful and prosperous reigns of Augustus, the Flavians, and the so-called Five Good Emperors in the second century A.D., the Romans perfected an architecture unlike that ever seen before and spread it the length of the Mediterranean world. A Greco-Roman architecture, it combined the elegance of detail and refinement of form of Greece with the pragmatic functionalism, civic scale, and sense of power of Rome. It was a universal architecture, embodying the essence of Romanitas wherever it was built, whether in Rome, Palmyra in Syria, Alexandria in Egypt, Timgad in Africa, Trier in Germany, Olisipo (Lisbon) in Portugal, or Londinium (London) in Britain. Unlike Egyptian architecture, which focused on the next world, Roman architecture focused on this; Roman buildings, like the more elemental Greek buildings that influenced them, addressed not the mysteries of the hereafter but the problems of the present. They were visually and intellectually comprehensible, composed of parts that had recognizable proportional relationships and clear connections. Having found a new and pliable material in concrete, Roman architects discovered ways of shaping and playing with space, of molding light and shadow, that has repeatedly inspired architects ever since.

After the second century A.D., the Pax Romana gradually disintegrated before the pressure of barbarian tribes at the borders of the empire. Diocletian attempted to facilitate administration by dividing the empire in smaller sections in A.D. 285, but his short-lived success was gained through political ruthlessness. After his death the disintegration continued and central authority virtually collapsed until Constantine restored a measure of order. But when Constantine then relocated the imperial capital to the east, the light of Classical learning dimmed and was nearly snuffed out in Western Europe. The glory that had been pagan Imperial Rome was transported to Constantine's new Christian Rome being built at Byzantium.

NOTES

1. This may be the basis of the legend, transcribed by Virgil in the *Aeneid,* that Rome was founded by Aeneas, fleeing from the ruins of Troy after its capture by the Greeks.
2. Virgil, *Aeneid,* I. 278, trans. W. F. Jackson Knight (Harmondsworth, England, 1956), 36.
3. The proper design of the temple is described in Vitruvius, *On Architecture,* III and IV.
4. Vitruvius suggests that the ideal proportions of a rectangular forum are two to three; for the planning of a forum see Vitruvius, *On Architecture,* V.i.
5. Vitruvius discusses the considerations in city planning in *On Architecture,* I.iv–vii.
6. William L. MacDonald notes that the Roman foot was somewhat shorter than the modern foot, about 11.625 inches (29.5 centimeters). Hence 2,400 Roman feet was roughly equal to 2,325 modern feet (708.7 meters); see MacDonald, *Pantheon* (Cambridge, Mass., 1976), 62.
7. Rules for the design of basilicas are given in Vitruvius, *On Architecture,* V.i.iv–x.
8. On the pediment of this building, the second Pantheon, Hadrian retained the inscription that had appeared on the original: *M . AGRIPPA . L . F . COS . TERTIUM . FECIT* (Marcus Agrippa the son of Lucius, three times Consul, built this).
9. David Watkin, *A History of Western Architecture* (London and New York, 1986), 60.
10. Cicero, *Ad Atticum,* XIV.9, (letter to Atticus, April 17, 44 B.C.), trans. E. O. Winstedt (London, 1918), 231.
11. Vitruvius discusses the proper design of houses in *On Architecture,* II.i and VI.i–viii.
12. Vitruvius discusses theater design in *On Architecture,* V.iii–viii.
13. For the theater at Aspendus, see George C. Izenour, *Theater Design* (New York, 1977), 182–83, 263–64.
14. Cited in Axel Boethius and J. B. Ward-Perkins, *Etruscan and Roman Architecture* (Baltimore, 1970), 271. Vitruvius discusses the design of baths in *On Architecture,* V.x.

SUGGESTED READING

R. H. Barrow, *The Romans* (Baltimore, Md., 1949).

Axel Boethius, *Etruscan and Early Roman Architecture,* second ed., revised (New York, 1978).

Axel Boëthius and J. B. Ward Perkins, *Etruscan and Roman Architecture* (Baltimore, Md., 1970).

Frank E. Brown, *Roman Architecture* (New York, 1961).

Heinz Kähler, *The Art of Rome and Her Empire* (New York, 1963).

T. Kraus and L. von Matt, *Pompeii and Herculaneum,* trans. E. Wolf (New York, 1973).

William L. MacDonald, *The Architecture of the Roman Empire, I: An Introductory Story* (New Haven, Conn., 1965).

————, *The Architecture of Rome, II: An Urban Appraisal* (New Haven, Conn., 1986).

————, *The Pantheon: Design, Meaning, and Progeny* (Cambridge, Mass., 1976).

A. G. Mackay, *Houses, Villas, and Palaces in the Roman World* (London, 1975).

Paul MacKendrick, *The Mute Stones Speak: The Story of Archaeology in Italy* (New York, 1960).

L. S. Mazzolani, *The Idea of the City in Roman Thought,* trans. S. O'Donnell (Bloomington, Ind., 1970).

R. Meiggs, *Roman Ostia* (Oxford, England, 1973).

E. Nash, *Pictorial Dictionary of Ancient Rome,* 2 vols. (London, 1961–62).

D. S. Robertson, *A Handbook of Greek and Roman Architecture,* second. ed. (Cambridge, England, 1954).

F. Sear, *Roman Architecture* (London, 1982).

M. Vitruvius, *On Architecture,* 2 vols., trans. F. Granger, (Cambridge, Mass., 1931). See also the translation by Morris Hicky Morgan, *The Ten Books of Architecture* (Cambridge, Mass., 1914).

J. B. Ward-Perkins, *Cities of Ancient Greece and Italy: Planning in Classical Antiquity* (New York, 1974).

————, *Roman Imperial Architecture* (New York, 1977).

Mortimer Wheeler, *Roman Art and Architecture* (New York, 1964).

2.21. Hagia Sophia (Church of Divine Wisdom), Istanbul (Constantinople), Turkey, 532–537. Interior view.

CHAPTER 13

Early Christian and Byzantine Architecture

The dome of Hagia Sophia was not there to mark an object of veneration, as domes did in martyria. . . . the thought of crowning Hagia Sophia with a dome related to the sanctity of the whole building as an earthly analogue to heaven. The visible universe was concretized in the Byzantine mind as a cube surmounted by a dome.

Spiro Kostof, *A History of Architecture,* 1985

Roman life focused on temporal comforts and pleasures, as the Roman bath illustrates well. The bath was designed to serve the needs of the body in its pools and exercise gardens, to feed the mind in its libraries, and to reward the eyes in its vast molded spaces lined in multicolored marble brought from the far corners of the Roman Empire. This emphasis of Roman life on the here and now, however, was gradually replaced with a new concern for the hereafter through the influence of a new religion that reshaped the way Romans began to think about the world and themselves. Even as the Roman Empire began to come apart politically, it was being reshaped from within, so that no longer was the sole emphasis on secular concerns but on religious concerns. As a result new building needs arose necessitating new building types. Courts, administration buildings, and houses continued to be built as required, but architectural innovation shifted to solving the problem of how to house communal groups of worshipers. This new church building, however, was not elaborated in form or detail, as the baths had been. Those external qualities of architecture that had appealed to a cultivated visual sensibility

gradually were replaced by an architecture of simpler elements, fostering a sense of mysticism. The new architecture, with its shimmering interiors lined with mosaic and encrusted with gold, served to direct the mind away from its concerns with the here and now to life in the hereafter.

The Transformation of the Roman Empire

We sometimes speak of "the fall of the Roman Empire," as though on a particular day there was a sudden collapse. In fact it was more a gradual transformation, occurring over more than a century, marking the change from the pagan empire to a Christian empire. Constantine's relocation in A.D. 330 of the entire imperial bureaucracy of the old Rome on the Tiber to the New Rome at the mouth of the Black Sea was symbolic of a number of sweeping changes in the Roman world. It was no longer Roman, as that term had been used before. The empire fashioned by Augustus and enlarged by Trajan had come apart, for the social cooperation and mutual trust that had enabled the empire to function was disappearing by the third century A.D. Although numerically there were now more Roman citizens, they were no longer free but tied by law to the land or to their occupations. Along the length of the northern borders, Germanic tribes were pressing for admission into the empire, and they in turn were being pressed from behind by other tribes being driven west from deep in central Asia by the Huns. One by one, Germanic tribes were allowed across the borders, and although they provided excellent soldiers for the Roman army, the character of Rome and of its legions meanwhile was gradually changed.

The other change, and the one that had the most far-reaching effect, was the impact of the new religion that had sprung up in a backwater of the empire, in the rebellious and troublesome province of Palestine. At first a sect among the Jews, the new faith was quickly embraced by adherents in Asia Minor, Egypt, Greece, and the city of Rome itself. It went from twelve disciples in Galilee to a tenth of the population in the Roman Empire, dramatically transforming the empire from within. This change in the hearts of the believers was so all-embracing that, when they went to carve the date of building on the walls of their new houses of worship, they used not the year of reign of the current emperor but the year of the lord to whom they owed a more personal spiritual allegiance. They scratched "A.D." for *anno domini*, the year of the lord, reckoned from the date of birth of the son of a Palestinian Jewish carpenter. The force that was reshaping the new Roman Empire was Christianity.

Diocletian found himself head of an empire splitting apart in A.D. 284, torn by a half century of civil war, too big and complex for one person to rule. He divided the empire, setting up two coequal emperors, each titled Augustus and assisted by a subordinate caesar designated as successor. Diocletian ruled the Eastern, Greek-speaking half of the empire, consisting of Greece, Asia Minor, and Egypt; his coemperor, Maximian, ruled the Latin-speaking half, made up of Italy, Gaul, Africa, and Spain. The city of Rome ceased to be the western center of imperial rule, as the imperial seat was alternately at Trier, Germany, or in Milan; in the East it was at Nicomedia, in northwest Turkey.

In 305 Diocletian abdicated and retired to the fortress-palace he had built for himself at Spalato (Split), on the Yugoslavian coast, forcing Maximian to step down as well. The two remaining caesars soon faced other aspirants to the imperial throne and civil war erupted once again. In the West the contest was between Constantine in Trier and Maxentius in Rome. When Constantine marched on Rome in 312, Maxentius inexplicably left the safety of its walls and confronted Constantine's army where the via Flaminia crosses the Tiber on the Mulvian Bridge. Constantine's biographer, Eusebius, recorded that, in a dream on the eve of battle, Constantine had a vision in which he saw a cross in the sky with the inscription *in hoc signo vince*, "in this sign conquer." He thereupon had the letters *chi* and *rho,* the first letters of the name *christos,* emblazoned on his soldiers' standards, and marched out to defeat Maxentius, becoming emperor in the West. From that date Constantine embraced the Christian faith, becoming its champion and defender, and in 313 he issued the Edict of Milan, in which Christianity was given full equality with other religions in the empire. He continued his struggle with the Eastern caesars and by 324 was sole ruler of a once-more united Roman Empire.

The religion that Constantine now proclaimed at first had been given little notice in Rome, for there were so many mystery religions then being practiced in the empire. To understand the appeal of Christianity for first-century Romans it is necessary to understand the life and teaching of Jesus of Nazareth.[1] The son of a carpenter, born in Bethlehem in Judea in southern Palestine, Jesus studied Jewish scripture and at about the age of thirty began a career as an itinerant rabbi, or teacher. He preached brotherly love, charity, humility, and adherence to the spirit of Jewish law, but he enraged Jewish religious authorities by forgiving sins in the name of God, whom he called his father. He strongly criticized hypocritical religious practices that outwardly adhered to the letter of Jewish law but promoted insensitivity to human needs. Religious authorities were also infuriated that Jesus' followers believed him to be the *christos,* Greek for "the anointed," the promised Messiah, the son of God, who would deliver Israel from Roman rule. Instead of political revolt, Jesus preached personal spiritual renewal. Eventually Jewish religious authorities forced the Roman governor, Pontius Pilate, to have Jesus crucified, a degrading form of execution. But on the third day after his death, Jesus' disciples believed, he rose from the dead and later ascended to heaven.

Initially the followers of Jesus were Jews in Palestine. As Hellenized Jews from the eastern Mediterranean came to Jerusalem for religious festivals, converts were made, since the teachings of Jesus fitted well with late Classical Greek philosophy, particularly in his emphasis on a renewal of spirit and nurturing of the soul rather than an endless search for physical gratification. Soon groups of these converted Hellenized Jews were found in Alexandria, Egypt, and in most of the major cities of Asia Minor. The most important factor in spreading Christian teaching was the work and travels of Paul of Tarsus, a native of the city in Cilicia in southwestern Turkey. A well-educated Jew, he was also a Roman citizen and thus able to travel freely to the early Christian communities in Asia Minor and Greece. The letters he wrote in Greek to these early churches quickly became sacred scripture for the Christians. When Paul was arrested and about to be scourged he reminded the centurion that it was unlawful to whip an uncharged Roman citizen; subsequently, when Paul was brought before the Roman governor, Felix, he claimed his right as a citizen to have his case heard by Caesar. Accordingly, he was sent to Rome, where he joined Peter, one of the original apostles. Both were later executed when Nero began persecution of the Christians after the fire in A.D. 64.

At first the teachings of Jesus appealed to slaves and artisans, to those for whom the present life held little appeal and for whom a heavenly paradise was most attractive, but gradually patricians embraced the faith as well. By A.D. 200 there were numerous Christian communities throughout Palestine, Syria, over half of Asia Minor, Greece, in central Italy and Rome, scattered groups in Gaul, and North Africa. By 400, parts of Spain were Christian, as was nearly all of Gaul, Italy, and Egypt. In another two centuries Ireland was staunchly Christian, as was a large part of England, all of Spain, North Africa, Yugoslavia and the Balkans, and all of Turkey and Armenia, stretching to the Caspian Sea.

As the early Christian churches proliferated despite periodic suppression by Roman authorities, a form of church organization developed, with volunteer *episkopoi,* overseers or bishops, supervising the congregations in a single city. There might also be *presbyters,* councils of elders. Eventually the bishop of Rome was accorded primacy among the bishops in the Latin West, since it was believed Peter had been the first bishop of Rome and had received his authority directly from Jesus. As Christ had said, "You are Peter [*petros* in Greek], and upon this rock [*petra* in Greek] I shall found my church."[2] The metropolitan bishop of Constantinople, who described himself as the Universal Patriarch, was accorded first rank among the Eastern, Greek-speaking Christians. This division between the heads of the church in the two Romes, coupled with the difference in language, would in time also split the church.

Early Christian Architecture

During the early periods of persecution, Christians tried not to direct attention to themselves. They gathered privately in the homes of fellow Christians, collecting donations to help those in their group who needed aid and sharing a communal meal of bread and wine to commemorate the supper Christ had shared with his disciples on the eve of his death. During this communion the faithful believed that the spirit of the risen Christ was in their midst.

At first there was no need for specialized architecture, for the small Christian groups adapted their worship to the available spaces in private homes. The church, *ecclesia* (which in Greek means "the assembly"), was not a building but the people themselves. Those who desired to become Christians could watch the first part of worship, but then had to withdraw to another room or to the peristyle of larger houses while the confirmed celebrated the *agape,* "love

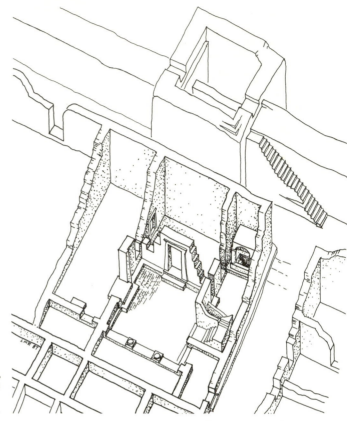

13.1. Christian church, Dura-Europus, Syrian-Iraqi border, c. A.D. 230–232. A small Roman house, this was converted for the use of the Christian community in A.D. 231–232 in this Roman outpost city.

feast," and the *eucharist,* "thanksgiving"; only those who had been ritually baptized could participate in the Mass of the Faithful. When the occasion demanded, as when Paul visited Ephesus, a hall might be rented.[3]

In the city of Dura-Europus, established by Alexander's army on the Euphrates River (now on the Syrian-Iraqi border), was discovered the oldest known Christian church [13.1]. A house, built about 230 adjacent to the town wall, was converted for the use of the congregation about 231–32; both it and a nearby Jewish synagogue were then preserved when the buildings were filled with earth to strengthen the wall during an attack by the Persians in 257. In modifying the house for church use, two rooms were merged by removing a wall, and another chamber was made into a baptistery with the construction of a small pool covered by a canopy on four columns.

As Christianity spread beyond the Jews and was taken up the length of the Mediterranean, variations in religious interpretation inevitably sprang up and the problem of heresy emerged. By 385 Christian leaders, only recently themselves the subject of imperial persecutions, began to order the death of Christian heretics. Such was the growing power of church authorities that in 390 Ambrose, Bishop of Milan, was able to excommunicate Emperor Theodosius and force him to rescind an imperial decree. Four years later Theodosius banned pagan religions altogether, making Christianity the sole religion of the empire.

Constantine's Churches

Faced with the deteriorating political situation in the West, and desiring to be closer to the threatened Danube frontier, Constantine shifted the capital of the empire eastward. He selected the old Greek city of Byzantium, on a peninsula jutting into the Bosporus, the narrow neck of water that connects the Black Sea with the Sea of Marmara and the Aegean Sea—at the juncture of Asia and Europe. There he built a new Christian capital city, free of the entrenched pagan traditions of old Rome, and filled it with new administrative buildings and churches. In 330 the entire mechanism of government was moved to the New Rome, which came to be called Constantine's City, Constantinople.

Constantine took an active role in church administration, personally determining church doctrine and policy. He saw himself as the earthly vicar of Christ the Eternal King, as is evident in the letter addressed to his bishops in which he admonished them to inform him promptly of divisions within the church, for "by them God may be moved not only against the human race, but also against me myself to whose care by His heavenly will He has entrusted the guidance of the affairs of earth."[4] He soon learned how extensive those differences of interpretation were, for in 325, just a year after he reunited the empire and made Christianity the favored imperial religion, he was obliged to call the ecumenical, or universal, Council at Nicaea to settle the question of the Arian heresy, the result of which was the Nicene Creed, which all orthodox Christians were obliged to embrace.

Once Christianity became the official religion of the empire, there arose the pressing problem of devising a building type appropriate both functionally and symbolically for public worship. Unlike older religions, in which individuals made private offerings, Christianity was a congregational religion, with a liturgy (from the Greek *leitourgia*, "public service") in which the faithful gathered together as a body to offer gifts and share a common meal. The Christians required buildings that would accommodate large numbers of converts, enclosed spaces that would facilitate hearing the spoken work and chanted psalms. Clearly, the ancient temple form could not be used, for it was doubly unsuitable; first, because it did not have broad internal spaces suitable for

housing a group of people, and second, because it so thoroughly symbolized pagan gods and Roman emperor worship.

Constantine and church officials looked to secular public buildings, and the type they selected was the basilica [12.8, 12.9]. The basilica had originally been devised for public gatherings, and its symbolic connotation, having to do with the equitable administration of earthly justice, was positive. It was a simple matter to replace the small altar devoted to the emperor with one at which the Eucharist, or ritual communal meal, could be celebrated. Since the basilica was axial in spatial organization, that axis served to focus attention on the altar.

The other building type favored by the early Christians had a centralized plan, whether round, octagonal, or square, and was derived from royal tombs; the octagonal tomb Diocletian built for himself in his palace compound at Spalato is an example. The centralized plan was also derived from the pagan *heroa,* a building commemorating the deeds of a divinity or the deceased member of a prominent family. Early Christians began to employ this form for *martyria,* structures marking the place of suffering or death of a martyr, and also for mausoleums of prominent Christians. A passage from Revelation provided the basis for this practice, for John wrote, "And when he had opened the fifth seal, I saw under the altar the souls of them that were slain for the word of God, and for the testimony which they held."[5] Centralized buildings also came to be used for baptisteries, where symbolically believers died to the old life and rose renewed from the water; an octagon was the form used for the Baptistery of the Lateran Basilica in Rome, the first in the city, built c. 315.

Constantine put the imperial treasury at the disposal of church officials in building numerous churches, particularly at the sites held most sacred by the Christians. In building major churches in Rome and Palestine, he and his bishops gave direction to the later development of church architecture in the two ends of the empire during the next thousand years. In Italy basilical axial churches were favored, while in the East

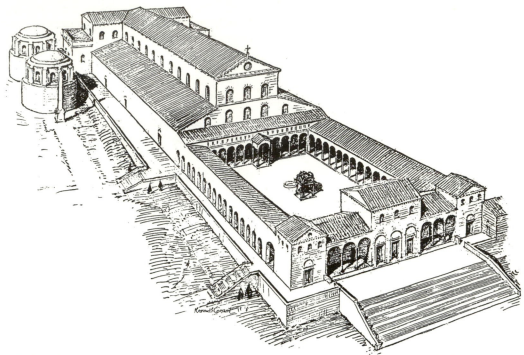

13.2. Basilica of Saint Peter (Old Saint Peter's), Rome, A.D. 319–329. Aerial perspective. One of the largest basilicas in Rome, this was built by Constantine over the spot where Saint Peter was believed to have been buried after his martyrdom.

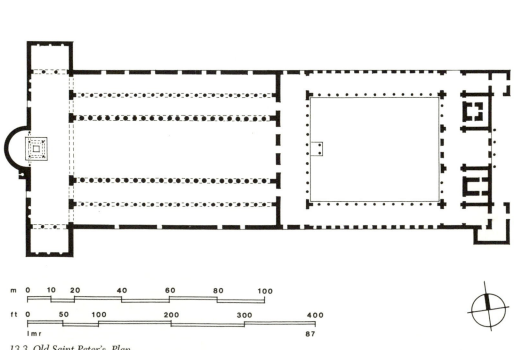

13.3. Old Saint Peter's. Plan.

centralized plans were favored. Almost immediately after officially recognizing Christianity, in 313, Constantine donated the imperial palace of the Lateran in Rome for the residence of the bishop of Rome. Soon thereafter construction began, next to the palace, on the cathedral of Rome dedicated to Saint John, San Giovanni in Laterano. It should be noted that the term *basilica* refers first to a public gathering place and only second to a particular form of public building. *Cathedral,* however, means specifically a church containing the official chair of the bishop, the *cathedra,* from which official pronouncements are made *ex cathedra;* hence a basilica may be a cathedral but is not always so. The Lateran cathedral, as the principal parish church of Rome, was large, measuring about 245 feet (75 meters) in length and 180 feet (55 meters) in width. It could hold several thousand worshipers. Unfortunately it was extensively rebuilt in the seventeenth and nineteenth centuries, and little of the Constantinian building remains.

The other major Constantinian church in Rome was the basilica of Saint Peter, built outside the walls of the city on the Vatican Hill, in an area that had formerly been a cemetery, next to the remains of the Circus of Nero. It was in this circus, according to tradition, that Peter had been crucified and then hastily buried nearby. The place of his interment was soon venerated, and it was over this martyrium that the Constantinian church was built, begun about 319–22 and finished about 329 (the atrium probably not until 390). It was an immense basilica, rivaling the Basilica Ulpia in size [13.2, 13.3]. The principal vessel, the nave of the basilica, was 301 feet (92 meters) long; along the sides ran two aisles, making the total width 216 feet (65.9 meters).[6] The nave rose in a clerestory pierced with many tall windows to a ceiling height of 104½ feet (31.8 meters) high; thus the ceiling was exactly half as high as the building was wide to the inner surfaces of the walls. Attached to the nave at the west end was a cross arm, or transept, 297 feet (90.7 meters) long and 69 feet (21 meters) wide, giving the plan of the basilica the form of a T. (The resemblance of such a basilican form to that of a cross was deeply symbolic for these early Christians.) From the center of the transept extended a semicircular apse capped by a half-dome; the apse was centered directly over the tomb of Peter and thus served as a martyrium. Unlike the Lateran basilica, Saint Peter's was a pilgrimage church, and although not used for services every day, it needed to be extremely large to accommodate crowds on special festival days.

Saint Peter's and other early churches were clearly derived from the great imperial basilicas, but additional modifications were necessitated by the special needs of Christian worship. In particular, at the end of the nave was added an entrance vestibule, or narthex, and beyond that a large atrium ringed with colonnades, where the unbaptized withdrew during the Mass of the Faithful. At Saint Peter's, entrance to the atrium was through an imposing propylon or gate. Including the narthex and atrium, the total length of Saint Peter's was 669 feet (203.9 meters) from transept to propylon.

Subsequent churches in Italy and other parts of the West tended to follow the pattern provided by the Constantinian basilicas. An example is Santa Sabina on the Aventine Hill, Rome, built 422–32 [13.4]. Another well-preserved example is San Apollinare, in Classe, the harbor town of Ravenna, built c. 532–49, and paid for in large part by the financier Julianus Argentarius (the freestanding *campanile,* or bell tower, is of a later date) [13.5, 13.6, 13.7]. Although the floor of the apse was raised to allow for a crypt below, and some of the marble veneer of the interior has been removed, the Corinthian arcade of veined Hymettos marble from Greece and the sparkling mosaics in the half-dome of the apse illustrate the reach of Byzantine influence when the church was built and when Ravenna was the capital of the emperor's Western governor, or *exarch.*

In the Eastern part of Constantine's empire, new churches took a different form, incorporating in a more dramatic way centralized martyria in the buildings erected on the spots associated with the life and death of Christ. Constantine's mother, Helena, a

13.4. Santa Sabina, Rome,
A.D. *422–432. Plan. This is a*
good example of the small,
basilica-plan Christian
churches built throughout
the city once Christianity
became established as the
state religion.

13.5. San Apollinare in
Classe, outside Ravenna,
Italy, c. 532–549. Aerial
view. The freestanding bell
tower (campanile) is of a
later date.

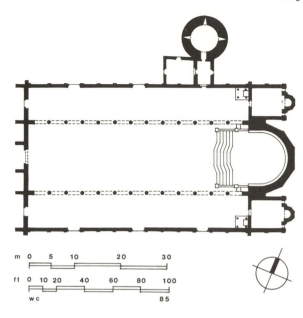

m 0   5   10   20   30

ft 0 10 20   40   60   80   100

w c   85

13.6. *San Apollinare in Classe. Plan.*

13.7. *San Apollinare in Classe. Interior, looking toward the altar.*

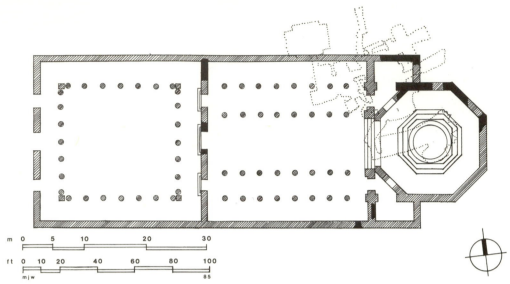

13.8. Church of the Nativity, Bethlehem, Israel, c. A.D. 326–333. Plan. Although it was completely rebuilt in the sixth century, sufficient traces of the original church survive to enable reconstruction of the approximate Constantinian plan, with an octagon over the cave where Christ was believed to have been born.

Christian long before her son's conversion, had made a pilgrimage to Palestine to retrace Christ's steps, discovering what were believed to be the stable cave in Bethlehem where he had been born and the hill of Golgotha in Jerusalem where he had been crucified.

As early as 326, Constantine resolved to build a church over the Bethlehem grotto, and although that building was replaced by

another in the sixth century, enough remains to suggest the general outline of Constantine's church, finished in 333 [13.8]. Like the early churches in the West, it had an atrium (roughly 148 by 92 feet, or 45 by 28 meters) for the reception of the nonbaptized, and a basilica with side aisles (in all, 95 by 93 feet, or 29 by 28.3 meters) for the assembly of the faithful, but instead of having a transept and an apse it terminated in a

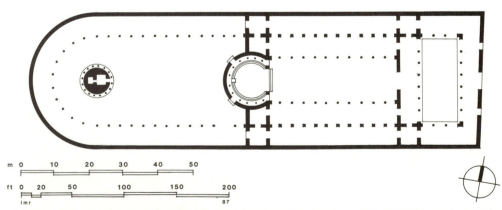

13.9. Zenobius (architect), Church of the Holy Sepulcher, Jerusalem, Israel, A.D. 325–336. This complex building covered the sites where Christ was believed to have died and been buried. The circular apse of the basilica was centered over where remains of the cross were believed to have been found, and the round structure surrounded the tomb.

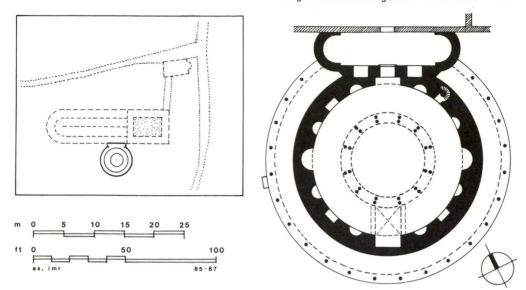

13.10. *Mausoleum of Constantina (Santa Costanza), Rome, c.* A.D. *350. Plan (the inset shows the location of the mausoleum adjoining the Church of Sant' Agnese). The large square niche opposite the entrance originally held the sarcophagus of Constantina.*

large domed octagon, with an opening in the floor through which pilgrims could look down into the cave.

Even more imperial attention was given to the church complex covering the sites of Christ's death, burial, and resurrection in Jerusalem. In an official imperial decree of 325, Constantine ordered that there be built in Jerusalem "a basilica more beautiful than any on earth."[7] The architect appears to have been Zenobius, working from general plans possibly sent from Constantinople; construction began about 326, leading to dedication in 336 [13.9]. The basilica had a compact atrium court, nave, and two side aisles, but ended in a unique "apse" consisting of an almost completely circular structure lined by twelve columns, symbolic of the twelve apostles, supporting a dome. The focal point of this centralized feature was directly over where the remains of the cross had been unearthed by Helena. Immediately east of the wall of the basilica was a rock cube—the cut-down remains of the hill of Golgotha—in a large, atriumlike court ending in a hemicycle. At the center of the circular end was a round structure, also of twelve columns carrying a dome, inside of which was a cone-shaped rock containing

the tomb. During 350–80 this martyrium over the tomb was replaced by the much larger Anastasis Dome, a rotunda 55 feet (16.8 meters) in diameter and three stories high, with an arcaded passageway or ambulatory, around the periphery.

Centralized structures were used for Christian mausoleums in the West as well. One example in Rome, the mausoleum of Constantine's daughter Constantina, survives in excellent condition and suggests the character of Constantinian building in general [13.10, 13.11, 13.12]. It had become the practice for the faithful to build their tombs as close as possible to spots associated with the early martyrs; the mausoleum of Constantine himself was attached to the basilica of Saints Marcellinus and Peter in Rome. Constantina's tomb was built about 350 against the side aisle of the church of Sant' Agnese (Saint Agnes), outside the walls of Rome, a typical basilican church after the pattern of the Lateran and Saint Peter's. The church of Sant' Agnese is now gone, so that the tomb, later dedicated as the church of Santa Costanza, now stands isolated. At the center is a tall cylinder, 40 feet (12.2 meters) in diameter, pierced at the top by twelve large windows and capped by a

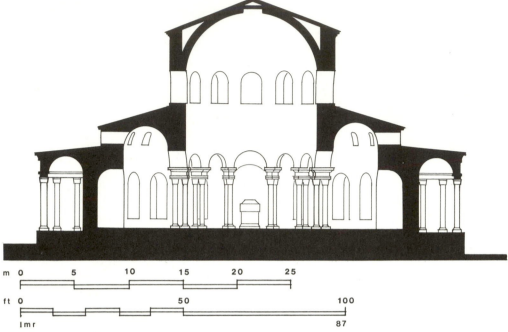

m 0   5   10   15   20   25

ft 0   50   100

l m r   87

13.11. Mausoleum of Constantina (Santa Costanza). Section.

13.12. Mausoleum of Constantina (Santa Costanza). Interior.

dome. This cylinder is raised on twelve pairs of reused columns from a pagan building. Around this is an ambulatory covered by a circular, or annular, barrel vault decorated with mosaics. The thick outer wall is hollowed out by niches, larger ones on the cross axes and a deep, square niche opposite the entrance to contain the sarcophagus of Constantina. Around the exterior is a circular colonnaded porch and a vestibule that once connected the mausoleum to the side wall of Sant' Agnese. The exterior, then and now, was exceedingly plain whereas the interior was ablaze with mosaics and colored marble, characteristic of Constantinian buildings. External appearances of these early Christian buildings were of little consequence; the interior, like the soul, was the focus of concern.

Post-Constantinian Developments

By the time San Apollinare in Classe was built at Ravenna, the West had been overrun several times by Germanic peoples from the north, causing political and economic upheavals. The first to arrive, in 376, were the Visigoths, who came from what is now Hungary, and after them wave after wave of invaders pushed into Italy and across the Western empire. Having long lived next to the imperial borders, however, most of these groups were already converted to Christianity. So, although the invaders brought no immediate drastic change in religion, the political, social, and economic effects of these successive invasions were indeed devastating. The city of Rome was besieged but never actually entered until the Visigoths, under Alaric, sacked Rome in 410; Virgil's "Eternal Rome" was no more. The Visigoths eventually moved out of Italy and on into what is now southern France and Spain. They were followed by the Vandals who moved down from Poland through Italy, destroying nearly everything in their path; they pillaged Rome in 455 and then pushed into Spain and across the Strait of Gibraltar into North Africa. After that the

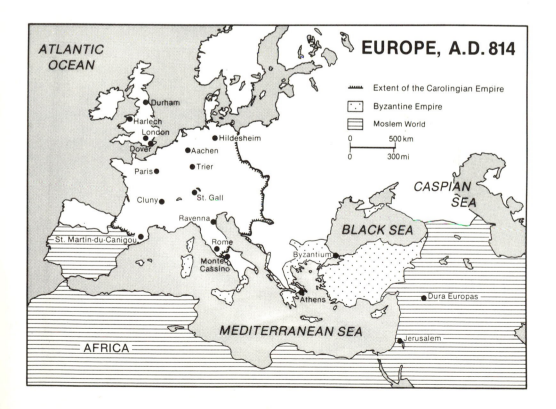

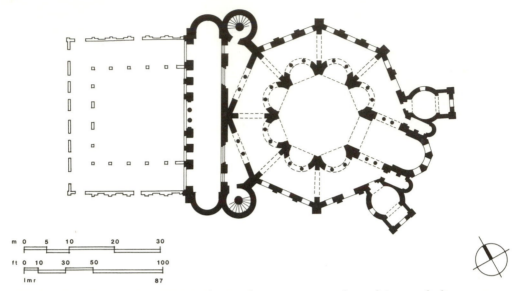

13.13. *San Vitale, Ravenna, Italy, 532–548. Plan. For this western provincial capital, Justinian built a variant on the octagon-dome scheme.*

Ostrogoths, from southern Russia, moved into Italy, where they remained. In 476 the last Western Roman emperor was deposed by Odoacer who set himself up as King of the Romans, a claim recognized by the Eastern emperor. Finally, in 493, Theodoric established the kingdom of the Ostrogoths in Italy. Roman Gaul (what is now France), in the meantime, had become the new home of the Franks, who moved in from the east and occupied northern Gaul, with the Burgundians in the south. Britain was overrun by the Angles and Saxons from Denmark. Only in the East, closer to the supervision of the emperor in Constantinople, did the borders remain relatively firm. In the West, where there was no longer a central imperial administration, the glories of the Roman Empire became only a memory. Yet, except for the Vandals, the invaders were far more affected by the people they ruled than the other way around. They adopted Roman law, Roman civil administrative institutions, and the Christian religion. They attempted to speak a crude form of Latin, thereby gradually transforming their own languages into early medieval Italian, French, Spanish, and Romanian.

Classical literature did survive the invasions, in a fashion, first being used as texts in Christian schools and universities, and then nurtured and protected by monastic copyists in a new institution that arose in the East. In Egypt, toward the end of the third century A.D., a Christian named Anthony retreated into the desert as a way of conquering evil spirits, beginning the monastic movement. Groups of monks began to organize themselves into ordered communities in southern Egypt. During the mid-fourth century, Basil the Great established monasteries in the East, and an early form of monasticism was introduced in France by Martin of Tours. Finally, in the early sixth century, the basis of Western monastic communal life was provided by Benedict of Nursia in his *Rule for Monasteries*. In 529, Benedict established the mother of Western monasteries atop the hill at Monte Cassino in central Italy. In the monasteries that soon dotted the European landscape, ancient manuscripts were stored, copied, and thus saved from the turmoil around them, to be rediscovered, recopied, and studied five hundred years later when a new light of human reason began to challenge the orthodoxy of the Middle Ages.

Byzantine Architecture

Justinian's Churches

Once Constantine moved the capital of the Roman Empire to Constantinople, the centers of political and church administration there tended to merge, resulting in what has been termed Caesaropapism, in which imperial civil authority and control over the church became intertwined. In the West, political and church affairs were increasingly left to take care of themselves in the face of barbarian intrusion.

The Roman Empire, in its new form in the East, endured and achieved its pinnacle of cultural and political importance during the reign of Justinian (483–565), who came to the throne in 527. Justinian came from peasant stock in Illyrium (Yugoslavia) and even late in life was said to speak poor Greek. His uncle, Justin, however, had become emperor in 518 following a military career, and it was he who brought Justinian to Constantinople and educated him. Justinian was given the title Caesar by his uncle, then was made coemperor, and upon

13.14. San Vitale. Interior.

13.15. Anthemios of Tralles and Isidoros of Miletos, Hagia Sophia (Church of Divine Wisdom), Istanbul (Constantinople), Turkey, 532–537. View. The minaret towers were added later, when this church was converted into a mosque by the Turks who conquered Constantinople.

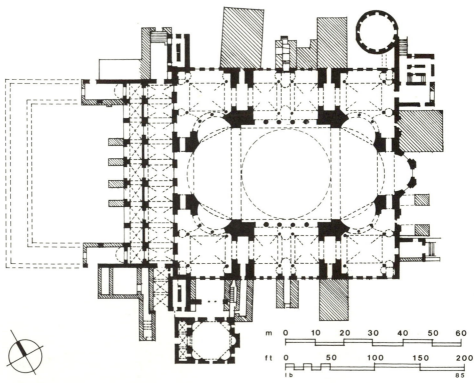

13.16. Hagia Sophia. Plan. This combines the central focus of domed Roman buildings with the directional focus of the Roman basilica.

Justin's death he became sole emperor. Justinian waged successful military campaigns against the Persians and also regained control of Italy and the coasts of North Africa and Spain, establishing an exarch, or viceroy, at Ravenna in Italy (Italy was lost to the Lombards after Justinian's death). It was during this period of Byzantine expansion that the major churches in Italy were built, such as San Vitale and San Apollinare at Ravenna.

Justinian's two most lasting achievements were the codification of Roman law and church building—the latter, in Constantinople at least, partly the result of the former. In 528 Justinian had set up a commission of legal scholars to draw up a new code of imperial enactments (published in 529), and then he turned to a codification of the entire body of Roman law, an endeavor that produced in 533 the *Codex Justinianus*, which eventually became the basis of nearly all legal systems in Europe except in Britain. This legal codification was accompanied by attempts to root out corruption and abuses in the government, measures that were unpopular with some factions of the populace. In 532 groups of citizens, disgruntled with the reforms and high taxes, rioted. Shouting *nika* (meaning "conquer" or "win"), the mobs attacked and burned city offices, public buildings, part of the imperial palace, and the church of Hagia Sophia (Holy Wisdom) adjacent to it. There was a virtual collapse of civil authority, and a rival emperor was elevated by the people. Bol-

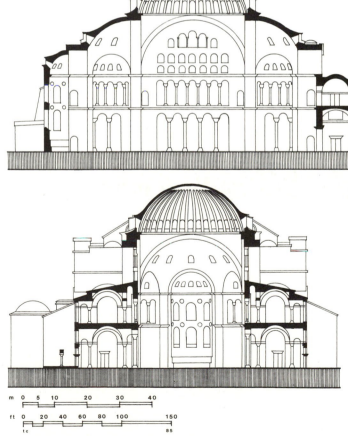

13.17. *Hagia Sophia. Longitudinal section. Along the main axis the outward thrust of the central dome is transmitted downward by a series of half domes and barrel vaults, forming a stable triangular profile.*

13.18. *Hagia Sophia. Cross section. In comparison with the longitudinal section, this shows relatively little lateral support for the dome, requiring the addition of bulky buttresses at the corners.*

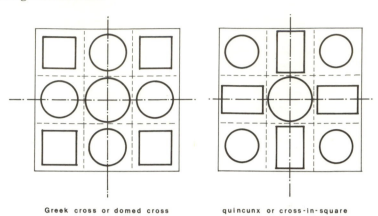

13.19. Diagram of Byzantine church types, showing arrangement of domes.

Greek cross or domed cross   quincunx or cross-in-square

stered by his wife, Theodora, Justinian stood firm, mustered what imperial troops were available, and crushed the rioters. When struggle was over, thirty thousand people lay dead in the streets.

Justinian then faced the task of restoring order and concord, as well as of rebuilding large parts of the city. He resolved immediately to rebuild Hagia Sophia as a monument to his rule and as a celebration of his victory. It was to be a centralized building on a vast scale. He had already built the church of Saints Sergios and Bakchos, 527–32, on a constricted site near his former residence in Constantinople. It is a double-shell structure, with piers forming an octagon inside an irregular square; over the octagon rises a dome with a diameter of roughly 58 feet (17.6 meters). A similar scheme was then used for the church of San Vitale in Ravenna, the base of Justinian's Italian exarch. Built in 532–48 [13.13, 13.14], San Vitale also has a double shell of two octagons, with an adjacent atrium now

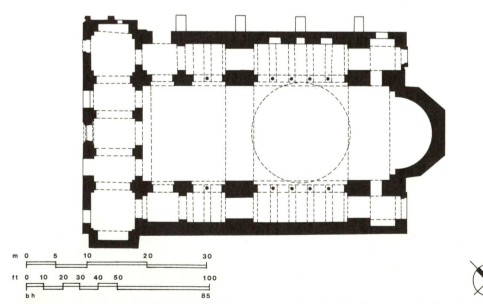

m 0   5   10   20   30

ft 0   10   20 30 40   50   100

b h   85

13.20. Hagia Eirene (Church of the Holy Peace), Constantinople (Istanbul), Turkey, begun 532. Plan. This shows perhaps more clearly than the larger Hagia Sophia how a dome could be placed over a square or slightly rectangular plan.

destroyed. In San Vitale the openings of the inner octagon push out in arcaded exedrae; over the octagonal clerestory in the center is a dome, 54.7 feet (16.7 meters) in diameter.

For the new Hagia Sophia, however, Justinian had in mind something far larger. Instead of employing the usual master-builder for the new Hagia Sophia, Justinian engaged two philosophers known for their studies in theoretical geometry. It is a testimonial to the lingering tradition of Classical Greek science that Anthemios should come from Tralles and Isidoros from Miletos. Experts in theoretical physics and statics, only they could design the kind of ethereal, dematerialized building that Justinian wanted. The new church filled a rectangle measuring 225 by 240 Byzantine feet (230 by 250 feet, 71 by 77 meters). This, too, was to be a double-shell building, for at the center was a square marked by four massive piers, 100 Byzantine feet (102 feet, 31.1 meters) to a side, capped by a dome on pendentives [13.15, 13.16]. The plan was centralized but axial as well, for along the principal axis the inner square was extended in deep semicircular apses rising to half-dome vaults below the main dome, and these apses were further extended by barrel-vaulted extensions on the axis and arcaded exedrae on the diagonals [13.17]. But on the lesser cross axis the walls were flat and pierced with many windows [13.18]. In fact, all the surfaces of the vast church were pierced, with windows in the exterior walls and screens of arcades on all sides of the interior volume. Even the base of the dome was pierced, with forty windows between the radiating ribs, so that Justinian's historian, Procopius, wrote that the dome "seems not to rest upon solid masonry, but to cover the space with its golden dome suspended from Heaven."[8] The remaining solid surfaces, such as the huge pendentives of the dome, measuring 60 feet across (18.3 meters), were covered with mosaics with a gold-leaf background, and the lower interior was sheathed with white, green, blue, black, and other marble from throughout the Byzantine Empire; dark-green marble columns in the aisles came from the temple of Artemis at Eph-

esos and the dark-red porphyry columns in each of the four exedrae had been removed from the temple of Zeus at Baalbek [2.21].

Hagia Sophia was a stupendous achievement—perilously balanced masses and shells of brickwork laced with stone reinforcement, lifted into the air. The central dome, although not as broad as that of the Pantheon in Rome, rises from a ring already 120 feet (36.6 meters) in the air, to a total height of 180 feet (54.9 meters). It was a physical representation of the union of empire and church; for to the Byzantine mind the cube surmounted by a dome was a model of the universe, the earth covered with the dome of heaven. Unlike the static and rationally perceivable forms and spaces of Classical architecture, here all seems in motion, surfaces curving and intersecting, bathed in a mystical light. The interior is awash with light from the hundreds of windows, reflecting from marbled walls and mosaics. The importance of Anthemios' and Isidoros' achievement was clearly understood by Procopius, for he described how the interior

> abounds exceedingly in sunlight and in the reflection of the sun's rays from the marble. Indeed, one might say that its interior is not illuminated from without by the sun, but that the radiance comes into being within it, such an abundance of light bathes this shrine.... All these details, fitted together with incredible skill in midair and floating off from each other and resting only on the parts next to them, produce a single and most extraordinary harmony in the work, and yet do not permit the spectator to linger much over the study of any one of them, but each detail attracts the eye and draws it on irresistibly to itself. So the vision constantly shifts suddenly, for the beholder is utterly unable to select which particular detail he should admire more than all the other.[9]

On December 27, 537, when Hagia Sophia was finished, it was reported that Justinian entered the new church with the Patriarch of Constantinople, rushed alone to the center, and exclaimed: "Glory be to God, Who has deemed me worthy of this task. O, Solomon, I have surpassed thee."[10] In Hagia Sophia, Justinian gave definitive form to Byzantine architecture, fusing Roman constructive practice with Greek science in the

13.21. Hagia Eirene. Interior.

service of theological speculation, with an oriental luxuriousness celebrating the mystery of Divine Wisdom.

Even as the dome was rising, it appeared that the structure below was insufficient to resist the outward thrust, and so towers were added over the buttress piers in the northeast and southwest aisles to increase the downward component of the dome's thrust [13.15]. Following earthquakes in 553 and 557, the original low saucer dome collapsed and was rebuilt by Isidoros' son with a steeper hemispherical profile. The original weakness was the result, in part, of the speed of construction, for the slow-setting lime mortar allowed the arches, pendentives, and buttressing half-domes to deform and spread out as they rose. In 989 a portion of the 557 dome fell, and in 1346 the remaining portion of the 557 dome fell. In the successive repairs and rebuilding,

additional massive buttresses were added to the exterior of the church, principally on the northeast and southwest sides, where the original design had left the dome inadequately counterbalanced.

Once the Byzantine pendentive had been developed, allowing round domes to be placed over square volumes, Byzantine architects evolved numerous plan variations in which large squares were divided into nine component squares, with domes at the center and the corners (the quincunx plan), or at the center and on the cross axes [13.19]. Hagia Eirene (Saint Irene, or Holy Peace), another church rebuilt in Constantinople after the Nika riot in 532 by Justinian [13.20, 13.21], illustrates one type from which later Byzantine and Russian Orthodox churches derived over the next thousand years. Although Byzantine churches customarily had centralized plans, Hagia Eirene is axial, but

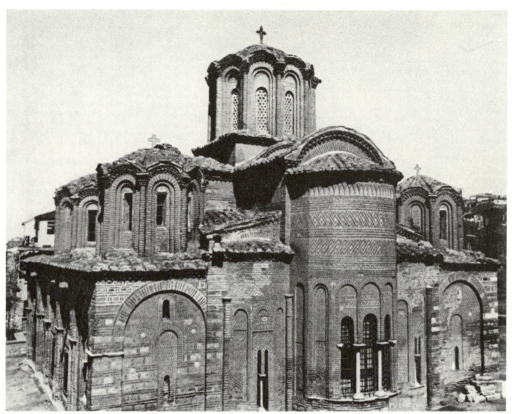

13.22. Church of the Holy Apostles, Salonika, Greece, 1312–15. View from the east.

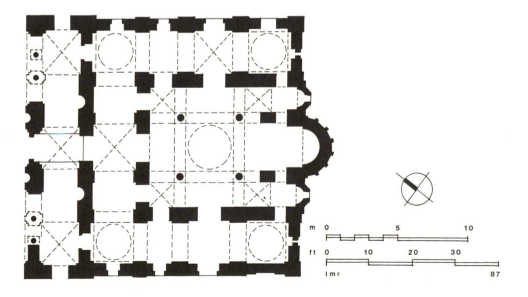

13.23. Church of the Holy Apostles. Plan.

13.24. Church of San Marco (Saint Mark's), Venice, Italy, 1063–95. Interior.

the basic component elements of dome-toped square bays connected by short barrel vaults are present.

Later Byzantine Churches

The later development of Orthodox churches in northern Greece can be seen in the Church of the Holy Apostles, Salonica, 1312–15 [13.22, 13.23]. A basically square plan contains another square divided into a Greek cross, with a tall dome rising over the center. In each corner of the outer square are smaller domes. This theme was pushed further in the church at Gračanica, Serbia, begun in 1321 by Miljutin, king of Serbia. The volumes forming the slightly elongated quincunx plan rise in stages, so that the

brick exterior has an almost pyramidal silhouette.

Eastern Orthodox Christianity was carried northward into Russia, and with it the modular domed church. Just as the Russian church gradually assumed its own unique identity, liturgy, and self-governance, so too the Byzantine church form it received was modified and made something uniquely Russian. Kiev, in the Ukraine in southern Russia, was then the cultural center and capital of Kiev-Rus; in 988 its ruler, Prince Vladimir, embraced Byzantine orthodoxy. Through Kiev, Russia adopted the spiritual, artistic, and cultural heritage of Byzantine civilization. The character of Russian churches was determined by examples such as Saint Sophia in Kiev, begun about 1037,

13.25. Church of San Marco. Aerial view. This shows clearly the five domes, somewhat obscured by the Late Gothic embellishment added to the facade of the church.

13.26. Church of San Marco. Plan. Built perhaps by Byzantine architects, the church was based on Justinian's Church of the Holy Apostles, Constantinople (now destroyed).

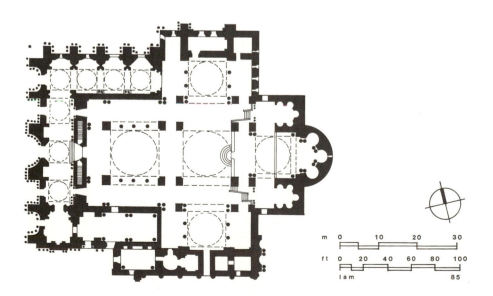

which stressed the vertical character in narrow, soaring domed chambers; the exterior, however, has been greatly modified over the centuries.

The Byzantine tradition even had a limited impact in the West, especially in Venice, which carried on extensive trade with Constantinople and the eastern Mediterranean. It is possible that Byzantine architects and workmen were employed in building the new church of San Marco, Venice, begun in 830 and rebuilt in 1063–95 [13.24, 13.25], using as their model Justinian's Church of the Apostles in Constantinople, 536–50, now destroyed. Saint Mark's in Venice, the chapel of the doges, or dukes, of Venice (rather than the bishop's seat), was built to house the remains of Mark removed from Alexandria when it became Islamic territory. Saint Mark's is a good example of the Greek cross five-dome church, in which four square arms project from a central slightly larger square, each square covered by a dome (the vestibule to the west was added later). Here the walls are covered entirely in gold-backed mosaic, with figures of the apostles, saints, and angels. San Marco, however, had little influence in the West, for it was a transplanted form. In eleventh-century Europe a very different tradition in church architecture, evolved from the Western Constantinian basilica, was just then beginning to reach its peak.

The Byzantine Empire survived for nine hundred years after Justinian's reign, gradually shrinking in influence; its outlying territories were lost piecemeal to the advance of an especially fervent new religion that originated in Arabia. About 610, in the city of Mecca, the prophet Muhammad preached the new faith of Islam; by 632 Islam had swept the Arabian peninsula. In another thirty years soldiers of Islam had conquered Persia, Syria, Palestine, Egypt, and North Africa as far as Algeria. The Christians in these territories, bitterly divided by relatively minor religious differences, offered little resistance; in any case, they were able to practice their religions after conquest so long as they paid the required taxes. By 750 Islamic territory included all of North Africa and Spain in the West, and Pakistan and the Hindu Kush to the east. In 673 Constantinople itself had come under siege by Islamic armies but successfully withstood it; this was but the first of many such sieges, until the city finally fell to the Seljuk Turks in 1453 and became Istanbul. Yet Justinian's extended architectural influence continued to shape Islamic buildings, in the domed mosques of Suleyman and the Sultan Ahmed in Istanbul, and the white marble dome of the tomb of the Taj Mahal, all built from 1550 to 1650.

An Architecture of Heaven

As the Roman Empire was transformed into a Christian empire, churches and other religious buildings emerged as the preeminent architecture. Other public buildings and residences faded into relative obscurity. Churches were internalized, their exteriors deliberately restrained in spatial modeling, detail, and color. The artistic focus shifted to the building's interior, on creating a mystic image of heaven that was the very opposite of the architecture of the work-a-day world outside. Byzantine art and architecture were devoted to reinforcing religious experience, in which the familiar physical world of human sensation is transformed into a suggestion of the transcendental world. Images of conventional reality, captured in the glittering mosaics, evoke a spiritual presence in an otherworldly atmosphere of resplendent grandeur. In an atmosphere of shimmering light from countless windows, reflected from high mosaic-lined domes, and the flickering of innumerable lamps and candles, filtered through the haze of pungent incense, the early Christian and Byzantine liturgy celebrated the fusion of secular and religious rule and the endeavor to create a heaven on earth.

NOTES

1. For the rise and spread of Christianity, see Roland Bainton's excellent survey *Christendom: A Short History of Christianity and Its Impact on Western Civilization*, 2 vols., revised ed. (New York, 1966).
2. Matthew 16:18.
3. The Acts of the Apostles 19:9. In Acts 2:46, Luke writes that the first Christians broke bread together "in private houses"; *The New English Bible: The New Testament*, second ed. (New York, 1971).
4. Constantine to his bishops, quoted in R. H. Barrow, *The Romans* (Baltimore, Md., 1949), 185–86.
5. Revelation 6:9.
6. The dimensions of old Saint Peter's basilica are taken from Turpin C. Bannister, "The Constantinian Basilica of St. Peter at Rome," *Journal, Society of Architecture Historians* 27 (March 1968); 3–32; included in this issue is Kenneth J. Conant, "The After-life of Vitruvius in the Middle Ages," 33–38.
7. The decree and an early description of the Church of the Holy Sepulcher in Jerusalem are given in Eusebius, *Life of Constantine*, III.26; for this and the other Constantinian churches see Richard Krautheimer, *Early Christian and Byzantine Architecture*, third ed. (New York, 1979), passim.
8. Procopius of Caesarea, *Buildings*, trans. H. B. Dewing and G. Downey (Cambridge, Mass., 1940), I.i.45–47.
9. Procopius, *Buildings* I.i.29, 47–49.
10. This often-repeated phrase, suggesting Justinian's self-importance, seems to be legendary, and was first written down in the eleventh century; see John W. Baker, *Justinian and the Later Roman Empire* (Madison, Wis., 1966), 183, n. 12.

SUGGESTED READING

Roland H. Bainton, *Christendom: A Short History of Christianity*, 2 vols. (New York, 1974).

J. Beckwith, *The Art of Constantinople* (New York, 1961).

William C. Brumfield, *Gold in Azure: One Thousand Years of Russian Architecture* (Boston, 1983).

J. Davies, *The Origin and Development of Early Christian Church Art* (London, 1952).

O. Demus, *The Church of San Marco in Venice* (Cambridge, Mass., 1960).

George Heard Hamilton, *The Art and Architecture of Russia*, second ed. (Baltimore, Md., 1975).

Heinz Kähler, *Hagia Sophia*, trans. E. Childs (New York, 1967).

Spiro Kostof, *The Orthodox Baptistery of Ravenna* (New Haven, Conn., 1965).

Richard Krautheimer, *Early Christian and Byzantine Architecture*. third ed., revised (New York, 1981).

———, *Rome, Profile of a City, 312–1308* (Princeton, N.J., 1980).

William L. MacDonald, *Early Christian and Byzantine Architecture* (New York, 1962).

Cyril Mango, *Byzantine Architecture* (New York, 1977).

T. F. Mathews, *Early Churches of Constantinople, Architecture and Liturgy* (University Park, Pa., 1971).

David Talbot Rice, *Art of the Byzantine Era* (New York, 1963).

S. Runciman, *Byzantine Style and Civilization* (Harmondsworth, England, 1975).

E. B. Smith, *The Dome: A Study in the History of Ideas* (Princeton, N.J., 1950).

E. H. Swift, *Hagia Sophia* (New York, 1940).

Robert L. Van Nice, *Saint Sophia in Istanbul: An Architectural Survey* (Washington, D.C., 1965).

14.2. Odo of Metz, Palace Chapel of Charlemagne, Aachen, Germany, 792–805. The interior, little touched since Charlemagne's time, shows the clear debt to the Church of San Vitale in Ravenna.

CHAPTER 14

Early Medieval Architecture

The most conspicuous property of Carolingian and
Romanesque buildings is their combination of massive
enclosure and manifest verticality. . . . So the
Romanesque church is simultaneously stronghold and
gate to heaven, and the two main building types of the
period, the church and castle, are profoundly related.

Christian Norberg-Schulz, *Meaning in Western
Architecture,* 1975

Once the Roman Empire ceased to function
administratively, there was no central government to commission buildings. Public
building nearly stopped during the fifth
century A.D. and did not resume in any significant way until about 800, with the
appearance of Charlemagne. This Carolingian architecture, although consciously built
to resemble Roman models, was rather
crude compared to the Roman ruins scattered about the old empire. What a true
Corinthian capital was supposed to look like
had been largely forgotten. In the unsettled
centuries that followed the end of the
Roman Empire, internal divisions and
external invasions repeatedly disrupted civil
life; civil and religious building forms therefore became both heavy and massive defensive refuges from the uncertainties of
everyday life and impressive gateways to a
promised better afterlife.

The Western church survived the disintegration of the Roman Empire by embracing
the hierarchical structure of the Roman
bureaucracy. The bishop of Rome assumed
the imperial title *pontifex maximus,* or chief
priest, shortened to pontiff or pope, gradually asserting his primacy not only over the
other bishops but over kings as well. Charlemagne later was to take crucial advantage of

the pope's blessing in creating a new empire
in Western Europe. But central international political authority disappeared, and
the complex Roman network of public institutions and utilities broke down. Roads fell
into disrepair and aqueducts were broken,
spilling water over the low country around
Rome which went back to swamp.

The Middle Ages—as Renaissance scholars would later characterize the long centuries between enlightened ancient civilization and their own period—is now generally
divided into three periods: the Early Middle
Ages (450 to 900), the High Middle Ages
(900 to 1200), and the Late Middle Ages
(1200–1450). The first includes the end of
the Roman Empire and the following true
Dark Age that did occur between 500 and
800 but which ended with the rise of
Charlemagne and the Frankish Empire in
the ninth century. The next period, the
High Middle Ages, is characterized by the
development of a more stable feudal system, the gradual resumption of travel and
trade across Europe that coincided with the
first of eight Crusades against the Muslims
in the East, and the revival of building on a
large scale, especially of churches. Despite
these positive developments, the High Middle Ages witnessed continued onslaughts by
invaders from the north and east. From
Hungary came the Magyars on horseback,
while from Denmark and Sweden came the
Norsemen in their longboats, raiding coastal
and riverbank settlements. The concluding
Late Middle Ages, the subject of the next
chapter, witnessed the rise of cities and the
development of a light and graceful Gothic

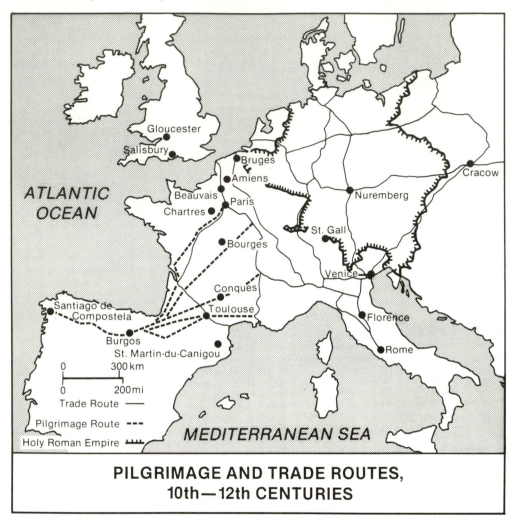

PILGRIMAGE AND TRADE ROUTES, 10th—12th CENTURIES

architecture in church, educational, and private buildings, but it also suffered the devastation of the Black Death (bubonic plague) and the political turmoil of the Hundred Years' War.

The Carolingian Renaissance

When the history of the West began to be written in the fifteenth century, Renaissance scholars wrote of the dark ages that intervened between the glory of Greece and Rome and their own enlightened age. But in actuality, the ten centuries following Constantine's death were not quite the cultural wasteland that Renaissance writers sug-

gested. During those long years there had been recurrent attempts to recapture something of the accomplishment of the Romans, so that there was a series of rebirths of Classical learning accompanied by efforts to reunite parts of what had once been the Roman Empire.[1] The first of these was the remarkable Carolingian renaissance in the ninth century, initiated by Charlemagne with the reestablishment of centers of learning in his Frankish kingdom that included what is now France and part of Germany and extended down into central Italy.

As the Roman Empire crumbled, Europe was divided into individual kingdoms by whichever group was strong enough to take and hold territory. The Visigoths and then the Ostrogoths descended into Italy and ruled for a time until replaced by the Lombards. Central Italy was also controlled for a time by the Byzantine emperor through his exarch at Ravenna. But meanwhile the Germanic Franks were pushing westward into northern Gaul, and the Burgundians moved into central Gaul. The Franks gradually emerged as the most powerful of the groups in Gaul under their Christian king, Clovis. In 732 the Franks, under the leader Charles Martel, successfully repelled an Arab invasion at Poitiers, limiting Arabic expansion in Europe to Spain. Charlemagne (768–814) then consolidated the Frankish areas and extended the borders, absorbing northeastern Spain, central Germany, and the northern Italian kingdom of Lombardy, extending down to the monastery of Benedict at Monte Cassino. In the annexed territories entire populations were forcibly converted to Christianity, new churches established, and monasteries founded. Finally, in recognition of his military protection of the pope, Charlemagne was crowned emperor by Leo III in 800 at a Christmas eve ceremony in Saint Peter's basilica, Rome.

Charlemagne truly hoped to recapture something of the intellectual achievement of Rome before it vanished altogether. Although he himself read and wrote Latin imperfectly, he initiated intensive programs to revive Classical arts and letters, setting up schools and putting teams of scholars and scribes to work copying old manuscripts. In copying these works, the scholars and scribes developed a clear, rounded form of calligraphy that was later revived by fifteenth-century Renaissance printers and made the basis of our modern lower-case letters added to the Latin upper-case capital characters.

Charlemagne and his court traveled from one royal residence to another in the area of northern France, Belgium, and northwest Germany, and hence there was no single imperial capital, but the principal city of residence was Aachen (Aix-la-Chapelle), west of Cologne and the Rhine. This quickly became the cultural center of Europe. In Aachen the revival of Roman architecture

resulted in the construction of an octagonal palace chapel modeled closely on the imperial Byzantine church of San Vitale in Ravenna. Designed by Odo of Metz, it was built of cut stone in 792–805, and its central vertical space was covered with a stone vault, a building tradition that by then had almost been lost [14.1, 14.2].

Medieval Domestic Architecture and Castles

During the period of Charlemagne's Frankish Empire, the basis was laid for the feudal system and rural manorial life that came to characterize the rest of the Middle Ages.

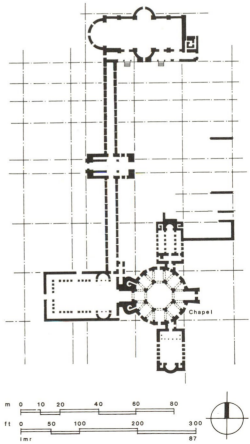

14.1. Palace of Charlemagne, Aachen, Germany, c. 790–810. Plan. Although new buildings replaced this during the Gothic period, fragments of the Audience Hall and connecting hall survive, and the interior of the palace chapel remains nearly intact.

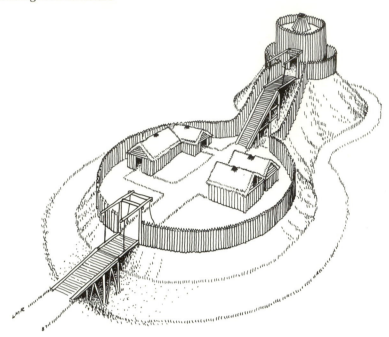

14.3. View of a bailey and motte castle.

The allegiance to a distant central government and a single ruler that had prevailed during the Roman Empire was replaced by a pyramidal system of direct personal contracts, in which a vassal pledged service to a lord, and farmers pledged their farm production to their vassal ruler, and so on down to the lowest peasant. Cities shrank in upon themselves as productivity shifted to the manors and fortified villas in the countryside; those manor houses, in turn, became the focus of small rural villages. The minting of coins for an urban money economy ceased, replaced by an agrarian barter economy.

Along with the wood-framed manor house, the other major form of domestic construction was the castle. At first this took

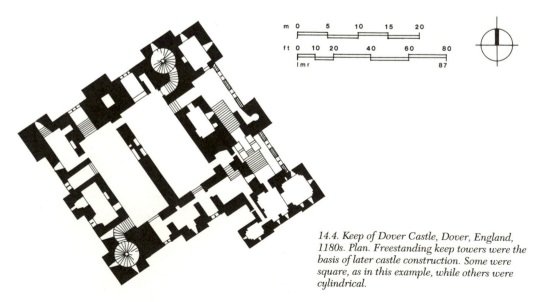

14.4. Keep of Dover Castle, Dover, England, 1180s. Plan. Freestanding keep towers were the basis of later castle construction. Some were square, as in this example, while others were cylindrical.

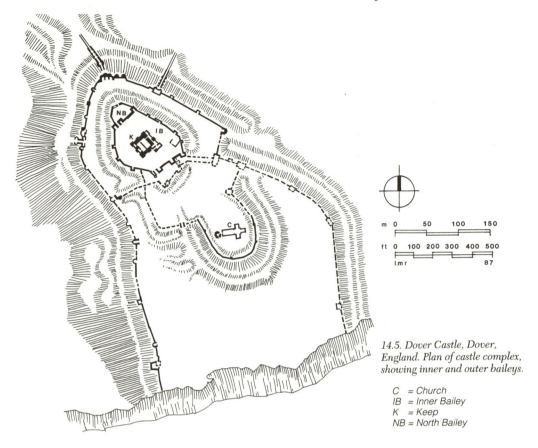

14.5. *Dover Castle, Dover, England. Plan of castle complex, showing inner and outer baileys.*

C   = Church
IB = Inner Bailey
K   = Keep
NB = North Bailey

the form of a motte and then a motte and bailey castle, beginning about 750 during the time of Charlemagne [14.3]. Atop a motte ("mound" in Old French)—either a natural hillock or heaped-up earth—a wooden tower structure was built, serving as both place of refuge and residence of the local lord. Attached to the base of the motte, in time, would be a bailey, or walled enclosure, containing storage buildings, workshops, and assorted houses, all of wood, and protected by a wooden palisade. The bailey and palisade might be further protected by a surrounding ditch, either dry or water-filled. Although the remains of many of these mounds survive, the wooden structures long ago disappeared.

With a view to increasing security, the wooden towers of such castles were rebuilt as stone *keeps* beginning about 1000, sometimes directly on the ground and not on a mound. These keeps were square, or nearly

so, although there were numerous cylindrical keeps, with four or more floors of storage cellars and living quarters stacked atop each other. The walls were up to fifteen feet thick at the base. The keeps were entered by means of a wooden ramp or stair up to the second level (perhaps this accounts for the European practice of calling this the first floor, distinguishing it from the lower, ground floor). The White Tower, built c. 1047–97, at the center of the Tower of London, is one well-known and well-preserved example. The keep of Dover Castle, built by Henry II in the 1180s, is a later similar example [14.4].

As improving economic conditions permitted more elaborate construction, the baileys adjacent to the keeps were also ringed with stone walls, and eventually the keep was pulled entirely inside the fortified perimeter, becoming the *donjon*, resulting in the walled, or mural, castle typical of the

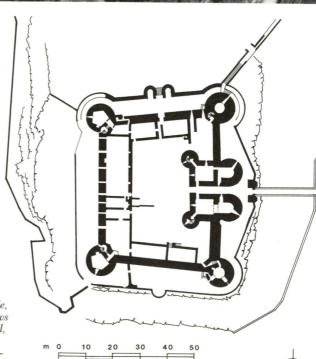

14.6. James of Saint George, Harlech Castle, Merionethshire, Wales, 1283–90. This shows the typical configuration of medieval mural, or walled, castles, with towers (spaced at bow-shot intervals along the walls), double-tower gate, and a central keep, or donjon.

14.7. Harlech Castle. Plan.

twelfth century. The outer walls were punctuated by projecting towers spaced at regular intervals determined by the range of
bowshot, so that through raking fire from
the towers attackers could be kept from
scaling the walls. Henry II's keep at Dover
Castle is surrounded by two such fortified
concentric walls, resulting in an inner bailey
and an outer bailey [14.5]. Similarly, the
White Tower, at that time outside London,
was wrapped with a stone bailey wall in
1270–1300 and then by a second one immediately afterward. Around the outer bailey
wall would be a dry or wet moat if the castle
did sit on a natural prominence or next to a
body of water. Immediately next to the principal gate into the inner bailey would be a
smaller enclosure, the barbican, which
forced attackers to expose their unshielded
right sides to archers on the battlements
atop the bailey wall.

Many later innovations in European castle design were inspired in part by what the
Crusaders saw of the fortifications around
Constantinople (their stopover on the way
to the Holy Land) and also from what they
learned of fortifications built by the Muslims. The First Crusade, of 1095–99, was
the most militarily successful, resulting in
the conquest of some the limited territory in
Palestine and Syria. This was followed in
1147–49 by the Second Crusade, when the
eastern territories won previously were fortified. The European masons building castles in the Holy Land adopted Muslim
improvements that, soon after, they incorporated in the castles they built upon
returning to their homelands. The now
ruined Château Gaillard, built in 1196–98
by Richard I on a chalk cliff overlooking the
Seine River in Normandy, is one example; it
had three irregularly shaped baileys, separated by moats, wrapped around the hill. Its
fame arises from the fact that it was so
strong that it resisted a siege lasting a year,
1203–1204, until its walls were tunneled
under. Another castle of this type, so clear
and functional in form that it has become
the symbol of them all, is Harlech Castle,
built in 1283–90, on the west coast of Wales,
on a promontory overlooking the Irish Sea
[14.6, 14.7]. One of the many castles built by
Edward I in his conquest of Wales, it was
designed by James of Saint George, who
also had charge of the king's other Welsh
castles, with at least four major works in
progress at all times between 1277 and
1300, and up to 1,500 workmen toiling at
each site. With a trapezoidal plan adjusted
to the rock outcrop on which it sits, Harlech
Castle has enormous drum towers at the
corners and a twin-towered gatehouse.
Inside there was a granary against the south
wall, a kitchen in the southwest corner, with
the main hall north of it, and a chapel built
against the north wall.

Within another century, however, such
castle building came to an end, as gunpowder made these exposed artillery targets
obsolete. Yet the basic castle shape—a rectangular solid or a hollow, marked by corner
towers and a prominent central gate
tower—was to remain a model of ideal residential form, especially in France, well into
the Renaissance and Baroque periods.

Medieval Monasteries

Aside from military construction and residential facilities associated with it, all other
building activity during the High Middle
Ages involved religious structures. Monastic
communities flourished, requiring the
development of new building complexes.
Although some monastic communities
appeared spontaneously, most adopted the
Rule written by Benedict of Nursia and patterned themselves on the monastery he had
founded atop Monte Cassino in central Italy
in 529. These monasteries provided the stabilizing influence throughout the West that
had formerly been exercised by the Roman
government bureaucracy. To the monasteries came men and women who sought to
serve God; pledging celibacy, poverty, and
obedience, the monks and nuns spent their
days reciting the prescribed sequence of
prayers, studying and copying manuscripts,
guided by their abbot or abbess in a life of
prayer and manual labor. Gradually, the
monasteries became the repositories of
sacred and pagan texts. They became places
of refuge from uncertainty in the outer
world, and the recipients of gifts of land and

14.8. Monastery of Saint-Martin-du-Canigou in the French Pyrenees, 1001–26. Aerial view. Secluded in the rugged mountains of southwestern France, this monastery illustrates well the isolation from worldly distractions that early medieval monks sought.

buildings from local lords seeking absolution from sin or the assurance of heaven. As a result, monasteries came to function as the political, cultural, and agricultural centers of their surrounding regions.

Saint-Martin-du-Canigou

The Monastery of Saint-Martin-du-Canigou illustrates well the quality of isolation that monks sought [14.8, 14.9, 14.10]. Built at the top of a steeply sloped rocky knob in the lower slopes of the French Pyrenees above Prades, it is reached only after an arduous forty-five minute climb on foot. A small monastery, its irregular plan is adjusted to the site. It was built from 1001 to 1026, under the direction of a monk, Sclua, who became its first abbot. It was paid for by Guilfred, Count of Cerdagne, who eventually left his family and lived in seclusion in the monastery for the last years of his life. It has two church sanctuaries, one atop the other, with the upper church covered by three narrow parallel barrel vaults over both aisles and the nave; the center, or, nave vault is not quite 10 by 40 feet (3 by 12 meters). Lighting is dim, for the only windows are at the ends of the barrel vault, illustrating clearly the low levels of illumina-

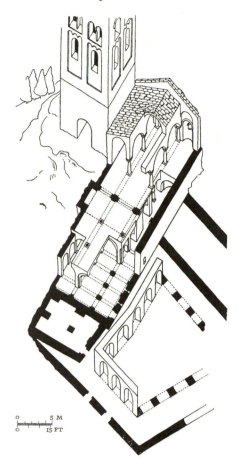

14.9. Saint-Martin-du-Canigou. *Cutaway perspective, showing the organization of the monastery church.*

14.10. Saint-Martin-du-Canigou. *Interior of upper church. Although perhaps conducive to meditation, the darkness of the interior shows the problem in creating openings in barrel vaults.*

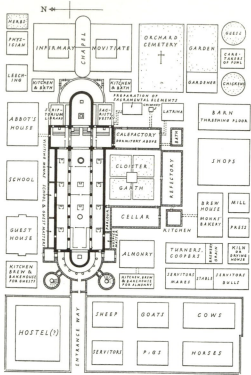

14.11. *Plan at Saint Gall, Switzerland, c. 814. Layout of the various buildings. Diagram by Kenneth Conant.*

tion that customarily resulted from using barrel vaults.

The Saint Gall Monastery Plan

Lacking an established far-flung administrative corps such as the Romans had enjoyed, Charlemagne relied on a network of Benedictine monasteries to run his Frankish Empire and to provide a stabilizing influence across his domains. This accounts for the importance of a meeting of monastic officials about 814, just prior to his death. Summing up the discussions at the conference, Abbot Haito of the monastery at Reichenau (on the German-Swiss border) prepared a diagrammatic plan of a model monastery that he sent to his friend, Abbot Gozbertus of the monastery at Saint Gallen, or Saint Gall, Switzerland (then part of the Carolingian province of Alemanni), for Gozbertus had been unable to attend.[2] The drawing is a most remarkable document, for

it is the oldest such plan to survive from the Middle Ages. On several sheets of parchment, stitched together to form a rectangle roughly 44 by 30 inches (112 × 77 centimeters), was drawn a comprehensive plan of the ideal monastery scheme [6.5, 14.11].

The principal building was a large church, filled with altars for the use of seventy-seven monks and oriented west to east, facing toward the Holy Land and the rising sun. On the sunny southerly side were to be (clockwise) a dormitory for the monks so arranged that they could easily pass into the church for the first prayers of the day at 4:00 A.M.; next to that the refectory for meals; and to the west a cellar for food and beverages, with offices above. These three buildings, together with the church, enclosed a cloister court, ringed with a colonnaded portico for easy circulation whatever the weather. Clockwise around this central cluster were the numerous service buildings for the religious and for visitors, since monasteries served as "hotels" during the Middle Ages for the few travelers there were. Opposite the west end of the church was the principal public entrance. Along the north perimeter were dining and sleeping buildings for guests, a school, and the abbot's private residence. Along the east side were the physician's residence and a large infirmary for both monks and novices, bisected at its center by two chapels back to back. Next to this was the cemetery, which also served as an orchard, and gardens that supplied the kitchen with vegetables and the infirmary with herbs and medicinal plants. Along the south edge were the kitchen facilities, including a threshing barn, a granary, a bake house, a brew house, shops, and a cooperage. To the west of this farming operations were housed, including stables for sheep, pigs, goats, horses, and cattle, along with housing for farm workers.

The Monastery at Cluny

How this ideal scheme was realized in an actual monastery is illustrated well by the example of Cluny. The monastery at Cluny, in southern Burgundy near the Saône River, was founded in 910 by William the Pious,

Duke of Aquitaine. A Benedictine community, Cluny early focused its energies on restoring liturgical purity and effecting church reform, advocating papal authority over all priests and bishops, denouncing the practice of clergy keeping concubines, and attacking simony, or the sale of church offices. Soon it became the center of a strong reform movement, and eventually more than 1,500 daughter monasteries were founded throughout Europe devoted to extending monastic and church reform. Within a century the measures advocated by the Cluniac reformers were embraced and promulgated by the papacy. For these reasons, the mother abbey at Cluny came to be seen as the most important in the West, and its influence was international. It also grew

rapidly and prospered handsomely through gifts of land.

In 915–27 the first church at Cluny was built, but by 955 this was replaced by a larger building. At that time there were seventy permanent monks, but by 1080, only forty years after completion of the second church, there were two hundred professed monks and another new building was required. Thus, in 1088–1130 the last and largest complex, Cluny III, was built under the direction of Abbot Hugh and designed by Gunzo, a cleric who was also a mathematician and a musician [14.12, 14.13]. Much of the initial cost of this last building campaign was paid by the king and queen of Castile and León in Spain as a thanks offering for the Christian recapture of Toledo in

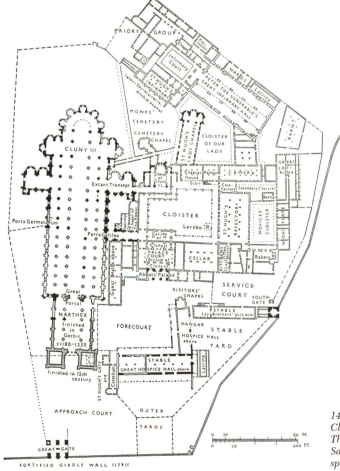

14.12. *Gunzo (architect), Monastery of Cluny III, Cluny, France, 1088–1130. The plan shows how the concept of the Saint Gall plan could be adapted to a specific setting.*

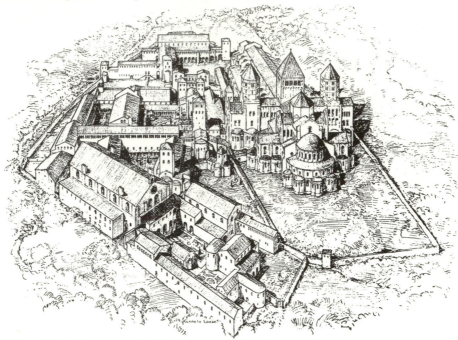

14.13. *Cluny III. Aerial perspective by Kenneth Conant. Although much larger than the Saint Gall scheme, the placement and relationship of the numerous buildings at Cluny are the same as shown in that diagram.*

1086 from the Muslims.[3] Regrettably, in the antireligious frenzy following the French Revolution, the great monastic community at Cluny and its vast church were almost utterly demolished, but the prolonged researches of Kenneth Conant have yielded a picture of Cluny as clear as if the monastery still operated.

Here, too, the church was oriented west to east; in front of it were the principal gate and an approach court. The church itself had large western towers, and a narthex of five bays (nearly as long as many entire churches). Beyond this, through the great portal, was the long nave with two side aisles, ending with a curved *chevet* with five radiating chapels. Altogether the huge church was almost 614 feet long (187.1 meters) from its west towers to the radiating chapels, comparable in scale to the enormous Constantinian basilicas in Rome. South of the west towers was a stable, with a hospice above for visitors, and south of the narthex was a forecourt ringed with other facilities for visitors and lay brothers. South of the main body of the nave was the cloister

enclosed by storage cellars and the abbot's residence to the west, the monks' refectory and kitchen to the south, and by chapels and chapter house to the east. Running at an angle to the east of the cloister and church was a large infirmary complex. Hence, with the exception of specialized chapels and other buildings specific to this monastery, the general layout corresponds in the disposition of its main parts to the Carolingian diagram preserved at Saint Gall.

Romanesque Churches

As political conditions became somewhat more settled across Europe after 1000, building activity flourished, particularly the construction of churches. Yet the memory of invasions in more uncertain times was fresh enough to encourage buildings in which structural masses dominated over void and in which windows were kept small. The memory of Rome lingered as well, especially in southern France, where many Roman ruins served as models, so that the sturdy piers and round arches of the newly

14.14. *Monastery Church of Saint Michael, Hildesheim, Germany, 993–1022. View. Because this was built outside and north of the walls of the city, the church has massive stone walls to withstand attack. Yet the towers point heavenward, so that the church is both a stronghold and a gate to heaven.*

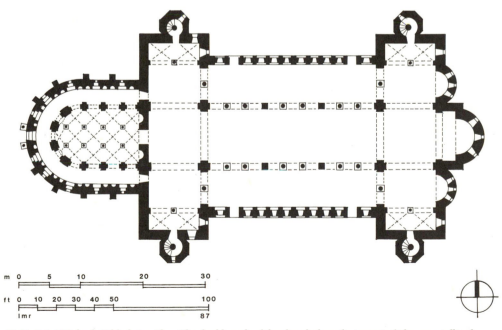

14.15. *Saint Michael, Hildesheim. Plan. The double ends of the church show the impact of ideas crystallized in the Saint Gall plan.*

emerging architecture attempted to recall the substantial presence and clear circular geometries of Roman construction. This is one reason why the massive round-arched architecture of the period 1000 to 1150 is called Romanesque.

Saint Michael's, Hildesheim

The massiveness of Romanesque architecture is well illustrated in the monastic church of Saint Michael, built as an offering by Bernward, bishop of Hildesheim, in north-central Germany [14.14, 14.15]. Built in 993–1022 just north of Hildesheim, it was unprotected by the town walls, accounting perhaps for its relatively small windows at ground level; its walls are more than five feet thick. It was what Martin Luther might have described later as *eine feste Burg*, or "a mighty fortress," for the attacks of the Magyars and Vikings had only just begun to end. That massiveness and sense of security reflects the uncertainty of temporal life, paralleled in the passage from the Gallican liturgy, for in France the moonlight raids of the Vikings, silently slipping upriver in their longboats, were an ever-recurring danger: "Let not our own malice within us, but the sense of thy longsuffering be ever before us, that it may unceasingly keep us from evil delights and graciously guard us from the disasters of this night."[4]

Saint Michael's, severely damaged during World War Two but carefully restored, is a modified basilican plan, whose basic pattern is very similar to that suggested in the Saint Gall plan. Not only does it have an eastern transept with small apses flanking the larger traditional one in the center, but there is a western transept as well, connecting to a large chapel-like apse, where the main altar may have been placed (in German medieval churches this came to be called a *westwork*). Underneath this westwork is a vaulted crypt where Bishop Bernward was buried. The eastern apses and the double transepts provided for as many as twenty-five altars where various relics could be displayed and where the monks could say Mass during the course of each day. For the same reason the monastic church at Cluny had two transepts

and a wealth of apses, also originally housing multiple altars.

Pilgrimage Churches

Although many religious buildings were paid for by the tithes exacted from peasants and freemen, the two centuries after 1000 were also marked by genuine piety and religious fervor, and an upsurge in contributions for religious building, especially after the reforms advocated by the Cluniac clergy began to have effect. People of the High Middle Ages, whether farmwife, cleric, knight, princess, or bishop, lived far more in anticipation of the next life than Europeans or Americans generally have since that time. An eternal life of damnation or bliss in heaven was very real for them, and the sculpture that began to embellish the portals of monastic churches served to crystalize their aspirations. An integral part of the architecture, such sculpture served a practical instructive function for a population that was largely illiterate, including many parish priests who could read only enough to get through daily Masses.

The rise in religious fervor in the tenth through twelfth centuries was paralleled by the cult of relics, in which the bones of saints and martyrs were believed to effect miraculous cures. Whether in fact these ancient bones, encased in bejeweled and gilded reliquaries, truly had miraculous power or whether the intense faith of the believers worked the miracles, the effect was the same. As travel became more feasible, with settled conditions, the faithful began the practice of visiting those churches and sites with relics reported to work cures. Those churches and monasteries that found themselves lacking suitably powerful relics went to great lengths to get them—even so far as stealing them from other churches or monasteries. Typically, the French churches of the tenth through twelfth centuries were dedicated to local saints, Gauls who had been executed in the periodic Roman persecutions, becoming early martyrs for the faith.

The pilgrimage journey was itself nearly as important as visiting the churches, for the

*14.16. Church of Sainte-Foy,
Conques, France, 1040–1130.*

pilgrims developed a spirit of comradeship that made the long and arduous trek more pleasant. Although the fourteenth-century pilgrimage described by Geoffrey Chaucer is of a later time and in a different land, his *Canterbury Tales* reveal much of the life and of the people who undertook them:

When April with his showers sweet with fruit
The drought of March has pierced unto the
   root
And bathed each vein with liquor that has
   power
To generate therein and sire the flower . . . ,
Then do folk long to go on pilgrimage,

And palmers to go seeking out strange
   strands,
To distant shrines well known in sundry
   lands.
And specially from every shire's end
Of England they to Canterbury wend,
The holy blessed martyr there to seek
Who helped them when they lay so ill and
   weak.[5]

During the eleventh and twelfth centuries in France, churches and monasteries set up a network of way stations like a giant fan that directed the faithful toward the Pyrenees, where the pilgrimage roads merged into one

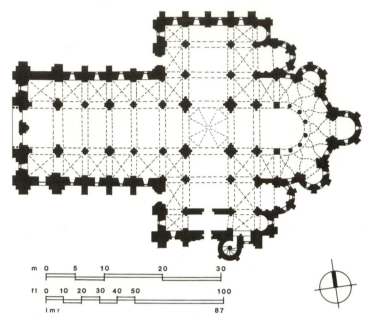

14.17. Sainte-Foy. The plan
shows the solution to circulation
through the church, with a
continuous ambulatory passage
around the choir.

m	0	5	10		20		30
ft	0	10 20 30 40 50					100
l m r							87

that led west through Spain to the ultimate goal, the great church of Saint James, Santiago de Compostela. The routes started in the north at Chartres, at the abbey of Saint-Denis near Paris, at Vézelay with its valuable relics of Mary Magdalene, at Le Puy, and to the south at Arles and Saint-Gilles. Two monastic churches along the pilgrimage route illustrate the type that came to characterize the Romanesque pilgrimage church: the smaller church of Sainte-Foy at Conques, and the larger church of Saint-Sernin at Toulouse.

Sainte-Foy, Conques

Rising over the pilgrimage road from Le Puy to Moissac and Spain, on the slopes of the low mountains of the Massif Central at Conques, is the church of Sainte-Foy, originally part of a monastery that is now gone, although the church survives in good condition. Miraculously the church was untouched during the French Revolution, including its many rare reliquary treasures, the most important of which is the gold statuette that houses the remains of Sainte Foy, a twelve-year-old Christian girl who was martyred in 303. Although she died

elsewhere, in the ninth century a monk plotted carefully to steal the remains and bring them to Conques where they have remained.

To house the gold reliquary and other treasures, the church was built in 1040–1130 [14.16, 14.17, 14.18]. Its plan incorporates a new arrangement developed at Tours, where the growing attraction of relics had presented problems in conducting normal monastic church services. The crowds of pilgrims kept crossing paths with the processing monks. The solution devised at Tours, and used at Conques, was to give the church two spatial shells—one a series of connected outer passages for the visitors, leading to chapels holding the relics, and the other the inner basilica for the monks and clergy. Because monastic churches had to accommodate a number of monks near the altar, what had once been a simple semicircular apse became a deeper space called a choir. Around this, and behind a screen of columns that supported the curved upper wall, was a walkway, or *ambulatory,* from which radiated three apsidial chapels containing the relics. This entire easterly combination of parts—choir, ambulatory, and radiating chapels—came to be called the *chevet* in France. The transept was now shifted nearer the center of the church, and it too had side aisles connecting to the ambulatory around the choir and to the traditional side aisles of the nave. Thus, pilgrims could move from the narthex inside the west doors to the side aisles and pass completely around the church, while the clergy occupied the choir and celebrated Mass.

Sainte-Foy at Conques also incorporated stone vaulting over all internal spaces, whereas previous churches such as Saint Michael's at Hildesheim had flat ceilings fastened to wooden roof trusses. At Sainte-Foy the nave has a barrel vault 68 feet (20.7 meters) from the floor. The vault is about two feet thick, stiffened by transverse arches. The nave vault's considerable outward thrust is absorbed by the arches and vaults in the gallery over the side aisles, which then transmit the forces to the thick buttresses in the outer wall. There are, therefore, no clerestory windows directly into the nave, but instead windows along the side aisles and in the gallery over the aisles, with the result that the overall illumination level in the church is low.

14.18. *Sainte-Foy. Interior.*

14.19. Church of Saint-Sernin,
Toulouse, France, 1077–1125.
Aerial view of the east end
(chevet), showing the ring of
ambulatory chapels.

Saint-Sernin, Toulouse

The church of Saint-Sernin in Toulouse, built 1077–96, with the nave vaulted about 1125, was dedicated to Sernin (Saturnin), the first bishop of Toulouse, martyred in the fourth century [14.19, 14.20, 14.21, 14.22]. Although much longer than Sainte-Foy (359 as opposed to 173 feet, or 109.4 versus 52.7 meters) and broader in the transept, Saint-Sernin has a nave only slightly higher than that of Sainte-Foy and with nearly the same proportions of width to height, 1:2.5. Furthermore, Saint-Sernin is more complicated spatially, since it has two side aisles along the nave. But as at Conques, the inner side aisle has a gallery over it sheltering the arches that resist the outer pressure of the immense barrel vault over the nave, and similarly the light here is low. The major source of light in the nave is from the large rose window, constructed later over the western entrance.

Saint-Philibert, Tournous

The problem of getting more light into the church was one that pushed Romanesque architects to find new solutions. It was perhaps not purely a physical concern, for they felt drawn to light as a spiritual metaphor, in a way prefiguring Abbot Suger's concept of sunlight filtered through stained glass as a symbol of divine light (discussed in the next chapter). However, the technical means

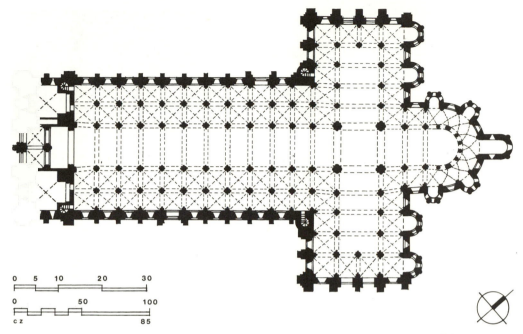

14.20. *Saint-Sernin. Plan. When the tower was built over the crossing, the crossing piers were greatly enlarged; they are shown here as they were prior to this addition.*

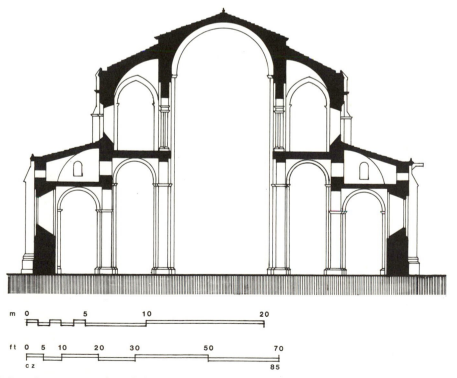

14.21. *Saint-Sernin. Section through the nave.*

14.22. Saint-Sernin. In this interior, too, the difficulty of admitting light in a barrel-vaulted nave is clear. Much of the light comes through the later Gothic rose window at the west end.

available to masons during the period 1000 to 1150 were limited, resulting in some interesting solutions. One of the more innovative is found in the nave vaulting of the church of Saint-Philibert at Tournous, just north of Cluny in Burgundy, France. Originally built to house relics of Saint Valérien, the church received the additional relics of Saint Philibert when monks driven from their northern island monastery by the Norsemen brought their precious relics to Tournous. The monastery at Tournous suffered attacks by the Magyars in 937, followed by destruction by fire in 1007. The monastery church at Tournous was then rebuilt, with special emphasis on vaulting the nave and chevet spaces with stone to reduce the danger of fire. The solution worked out in the nave was unique [14.23]. Tall, undecorated, cylindrical piers carry semicircular arches opening into the side aisles; these side aisles are themselves covered by traditional groin vaults. Resting on the massive cylindrical piers are stout engaged columns from which spring diaphragm arches that span across the nave. These diaphragm arches in turn support transverse barrel vaults (there is a wooden roof above). The barrel vaults running across the nave cancel out each other's lateral thrusts, leaving only minimal lateral forces at the outer wall. Even though the clerestory windows were not opened up to take full advantage of the wall space available, the level of light in the nave of Saint-Philibert is relatively high.

Romanesque Churches in Italy

The Romanesque style was used in Italy as well. Masonry nave vaulting, however, was not always used there, even for such large groups as the impressive cathedral complex at Pisa, whose cathedral was built 1063–1272 following a decisive battle in which the Pisan and Genovese navies defeated the Saracens of Sicily. The cathedral complex, Pisa's thanks offering, has an exterior encrusted with row upon row of decorative white marble arcades In front of the cathedral the round baptistery was built, in 1153–1265, and the famous freestanding bell tower in 1174–1271, which immediately started to lean in the soft soil. Despite bending the axis of the tower shaft to counter the lean (giving the tower a curve),

14.23. *Saint-Philibert, Tournous, France, c. 1008–c. 1120. Interior. To bring in light, the masons devised a unique scheme of transverse barrel vaults carried by arches crossing the nave.*

14.24. San Miniato al Monte, Florence, Italy, 1062–c. 1200. At San Miniato the continuing influence of Roman architecture is seen in the clear geometric patterns in the marble veneer.

the tipping continued until stopped recently through construction of a new foundation. Reaching 179 feet (54.5 meters), it is slightly more than thirteen feet out of plumb.

An adherence in central Italy to the Classical tradition in design is well demonstrated in the small Benedictine abbey church of San Miniato al Monte, just outside Florence, Italy [14.24]. This hillside church, overlooking Florence, the chief commercial rival of Pisa, was built in 1062–c.1200. It is an aisled basilica without transept. The wooden truss roof over the nave and "choir" rests on marble-veneered walls carried by

arcades of near-correct Classical Corinthian columns. Even more significant, the facade is encrusted with a system of rectangular panels and a Corinthian arcade made up of numerous inlaid colored marbles. This facade is not so very far distant from the geometries of Roman architecture, so that San Miniato makes it understandable why the Renaissance would begin in Florence.

Durham Cathedral

One of the last Romanesque churches to rely solely on the sheer mass of its walls to support its vaulting is the cathedral at Durham, England, built by Bishop William de Carlief in 1093–1133 [14.25, 14.26]. Rising on the bluff over the curve of the Weir River at this northern outpost of Norman England, the cathedral shared this natural defensive site with a castle. The nave arcade alternates between huge square piers with engaged colonettes and massive cylindrical piers carved in various chevron and geometric patterns. Over the side aisles is a gallery, and over the gallery clerestory windows, made possible by the daring and innovative use of rib vaults over the nave. Yet the lateral forces exerted by the massive vaults are gathered in the thick wall of the nave and conducted down through the stout piers and columns of the nave. Although there are perpendicular arches in the gallery that appear in section drawings to be roofed-over flying buttresses, they were not connected structurally to the piers receiving the weight of the vaults [14.26]; they seem to have been built only to carry the sloping roof over the gallery. Accordingly, the round-headed clerestory windows are smaller than the space available, for the wall was still required to convey the weight of the vault to the piers below. But much more innovative was the use of segmented, or pointed, arches in the vaults, so that the tops of the vault centers are roughly the same

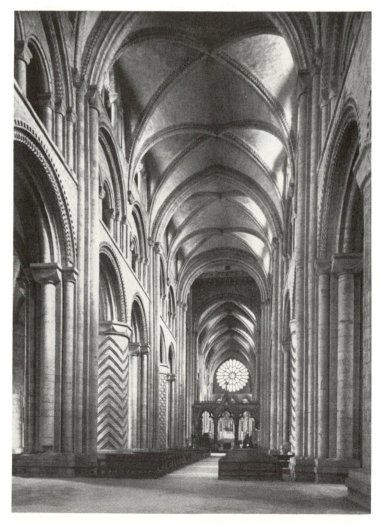

14.25. *Durham Cathedral, Durham, England, 1093–1133. The nave vaults of Durham were among the first in England to have diagonal ribs and the first in which the ribs have pointed profiles.*

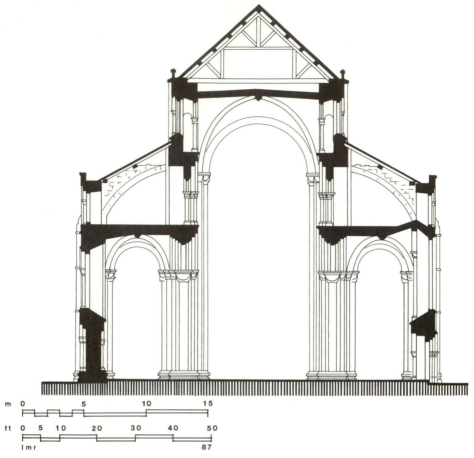

14.26. Durham Cathedral. Cross section. Although there seem to be arches buttressing the nave piers, these arches carry only the roofs over the side galleries.

height as the outer edges. Nonetheless, even though one finds here all the basic elements necessary for Gothic rib vaulting—ribs, pointed arches, and lateral "external" bracing (flying buttresses)—the emphasis is still on mass resisting weight, and all of the working parts of the structure are shown to the eye in the nave.

An Architecture of Refuge

To Western Europeans in the fifth century, it may have seemed that the world had come to an end. Roman civilization had vanished and there was a kind of starting over, resulting in an architecture that was able to withstand periodic contests for power as well as the onslaughts from the north and east. The round-arched architecture of the Early

Middle Ages that gradually became Romanesque never quite rid itself of that massiveness bred of defense. The great vaulted naves of Saint-Sernin and the similar Santiago de Compostela further demonstrated the limitations of Romanesque construction. Reliant on the sheer power of mass to abut and restrain the tremendous outward thrust of thick nave barrel vaults, Romanesque architecture could not open up to the light, not even with the innovations employed at Durham. In the new phase into which medieval architecture now passed, the presence of light, the symbol of God's divine Grace, became the preeminent symbol; the church had to become transparent, and when it did so it was no longer Romanesque but Gothic.

NOTES

1. This idea is explored in Erwin Panofsky, *Renaissance and Renascences in Western Art,* second ed. (New York, 1972).
2. This interpretation of the origin and purpose of the plan of Saint Gall is based on recent research by Warren Sanderson, Paul Mayvaert, Norbert Stachura, and others; see Warren Sanderson, "The Plan of St. Gall Reconsidered," *Speculum* 60 (July 1985); 615–32. In their major publication *The Plan of St. Gall,* 3 vols. (Berkeley, 1979), Walter Horn and Ernest Born interpret the inscription on the plan to mean that Abbot Haito sent the plan to Abbot Gozbertus as a result of the synods held at Aachen in 816–17 to effect Benedictine reform, and that it was a duplication of some other plan prepared at the Aachen meetings, intended as a model for emulation throughout the Carolingian Empire. Recent study of the inscription and of the physical evidence of the original parchment has led to differing conclusions. I am indebted to my colleague Richard Sundt for pointing out this shift in interpretation to me.
3. The Christian reconquest of Islamic Spain was to have an enormous influence on the development of European culture, for in the great centers of Islamic learning in Spain were found vast libraries of Greek manuscripts, many of them works of theoretical science translated into Arabic and previously unknown in Europe; in translating these back into Greek and Latin, some of the Arabic technical terms, such as *azimuth,* had to be left in Arabic because no substitute could be found.
4. From the Gallican liturgy quoted in Gregory Dix, *The Shape of the Liturgy* (London, 1952), 581.
5. Geoffrey Chaucer, *The Canterbury Tales,* prologue, translation by J. U. Nicolson (New York, 1934). The martyr mentioned is Saint Thomas Becket, archbishop of Canterbury, killed in 1170 and canonized in 1172. Chaucer describes a pilgrimage that he joined in the spring of 1387; in the party were thirty people, including a knight, a miller, a monk, a nun, a clerk, a merchant, a physician, and a farmer—a cross section of medieval society. The tales he relates are based on those told by the travelers while on the road for their mutual amusement and edification.

SUGGESTED READING

William Anderson, *Castles of Europe from Charlemagne to the Renaissance* (London, 1970).

John Beckwith, *Early Medieval Art* (New York, 1964).

W. Braunfels, *Monasteries of Western Europe,* trans. A. Laing (Princeton, N.J., 1973).

R. Allen Brown, *The Architecture of Castles: A Visual Guide* (New York, 1984).

D. Bullough, *The Age of Charlemagne* (New York and London, 1966).

A. W. Clapham, *Romanesque Architecture in Western Europe* (Oxford, England, 1936).

Kenneth J. Conant, *Carolingian and Romanesque Architecture* second ed., revised (New York, 1978).

G. G. Coulton, *The Medieval Village* (Cambridge, England, 1925).

Joan Evans, *Monastic Life at Cluny, 910–1157* (London, 1931).

Henri Focillon, *The Art of the West,* vol. I, *Romanesque Art* (London, 1963).

G. Henderson, *Early Medieval* (Harmondsworth, England, 1972).

W. Horn and E. Born, *The Plan of St. Gall,* 3 vols. (Berkeley, Calif., 1979).

Hans Erich Kubach, *Romanesque Architecture* (New York, 1972).

Talbot D. Rice, ed., *Dawn of European Civilization* (New York, 1965).

J. C. Russell, *Medieval Cities and Their Regions* (Bloomington, Ind., 1972).

Howard Saalman, *Medieval Architecture* (New York, 1962).

E. B. Smith, *The Architectural Symbolism of Imperial Rome and the Middle Ages* (Princeton, N.J., 1956).

R. W. Southern, *The Making of the Middle Ages* (New Haven, Conn., 1953).

Whitney Stoddard, *Monastery and Cathedral in France* (Middletown, Ct., 1966; republished as *Art and Architecture in Medieval France,* New York, 1972).

Marilyn Stokstad, *Medieval Art* (New York, 1986).

15.1. *Abbey Church of Saint-Denis, Saint-Denis, France, 1135–40. West facade. In his first addition to the Carolingian church, Abbot Suger provided the basis for subsequent Gothic church facades, particularly in the large round rose window.*

CHAPTER 15

Gothic Architecture

The cathedral was the house of God, this term understood not as a pale commonplace but as a fearful reality. The Middle Ages lived in the presence of the supernatural, which impressed itself upon every aspect of human life. The sanctuary was the threshold to heaven.

Otto von Simson, *The Gothic Cathedral,* 1956.

It is possible to say that Gothic architecture was invented in 1141 for Suger, abbot of the monastery of Saint-Denis, a town just north of Paris [15.1]. What Suger and his architects and builders did was to bring together a number of improvements in late Romanesque church architecture, including pointed arches and rib vaulting. Somehow they sensed these elements of design might work together synergetically, each expanding the potential of the other, to create a lighter and more visually transparent architecture. For what Suger wanted was to replace walls of stone with walls of stained glass, which filtered and transformed sunlight so that it symbolized divine illumination.

Gothic architecture was also the physical expression of a new, assertive positive outlook on life here and now, as contrasted to the emphatic focus of the Romanesque period on a life in the hereafter that was certain to be better than life now. The audacity of thirteenth-century bishops, burghers, and masons in starting churches so large and complex that they required several generations to be completed is an indication of the confidence of the period. By 1200 the apprehensive outlook of previous centuries had begun to be replaced with a more positive outlook. That is not to say that life expectancy suddenly was appreciably longer

or that warfare had decreased, but rather that people looked to temporal life with greater anticipation. The curious contradiction was that this embrace of earthly life should have resulted in an architecture that so emphatically aspired to heaven. It is significant, too, that the new joy in human existence paralleled a growing adoration of the Virgin Mary as an exemplar of earthly womanhood, and indeed a new respect for women in general.

The unifying agent across Europe continued to be the church, reinvigorated by the reforms instituted by Cluniac monks. The focus of human action remained religious life, so that the buildings that most advanced architectural design and technology were those built by the church, whether cathedrals, monasteries, schools, hospitals, or the new universities that began to emerge in this period.

Political and Social Changes— The Reemergence of the City

The most important political change in Europe was the growing awareness of nation states united by a common culture and language. In England and France strong central monarchies emerged that gained power as the nobles lost some of their sovereignty. In France this consolidation of royal authority began around Paris and the province of the Île-de-France, extending to the north into Flanders (what is now Belgium), with its rich trade in wool and textiles, and south into central France and Burgundy. Louis VI, with the political advice of his friend Abbot Suger, greatly advanced this process of consolidation during 1140 to 1180. The west of France, however, still consisted of areas governed by the Duke of Normandy, who also claimed the throne of England. After the Norman conquest of England in 1066, therefore, these were English territories. The ensuing bitter and bloody struggle of English and French monarchs for dominion in western France—the Hundred Years' War, lasting from 1337 to 1453—was one development that marked the end of the Middle Ages.

Europe was transformed socially during the late Middle Ages by two forces that reinforced each other—the reemergence of cities and the growth of trade. In some places old Roman towns on major trade routes were reinhabited, elsewhere new towns appeared. The principal agent in invigorating urban growth was the Crusades. As ineffective as the Crusades were in establishing a permanent Western settlement in the eastern Mediterranean, they were enormously successful in generating a spirit of adventurousness in the Western mind. As a result of the travel initiated by the Crusades and the necessity of establishing supply lines, Europeans moved out into the Mediterranean, creating the basis of a trade network. Spices and cotton cloth were brought back from the Arab territories of the Eastern Mediterranean, funneled through Venice and Genoa, and transported into northern Europe. Amber, furs, and other goods traveled southward from Germany and Russia into Italy for shipment to the East. Farm lands, exhausted by a thousand years of agriculture, were converted to pasture for sheep, and the weaving of woolen cloth became an important industry in England, Flanders, and Italy. Florence, Italy, became a center for the cloth trade in the south, while Bruges became the comparable northern center in Flanders. Pisa became a center for finance, especially for the papacy. Paris and Marseilles in France, London, Bristol, and York in England, Bruges and Ghent in Flanders, and Frankfurt and Nuremberg among the German cities—all became important centers of trans-shipment of trade goods.

These cities were small by twentieth-century standards, with populations of ten thousand to seventy thousand people; only such cities as London, Paris, Florence, and Venice had populations that reached one hundred thousand. Ninety-five percent of the total population of Europe was still rural, but the five percent who congregated in cities soon dominated the life and culture of Europe. The old agrarian feudal culture was gradually replaced by an urban mercantile culture. A new word entered the European vocabulary: *burgher,* or *bourgeois,* meaning a person who lived in a city, and usually someone who operated a business. The rising *bourgeoisie,* this new class of merchants and bankers, soon rivaled the nobles and clergy in influence. Joining the merchants in controlling the emerging cities were craft guilds, organizations that trained apprentices, set standards of conduct and workmanship, and aided members' widows and children. The cities were places of increased personal freedom, and serfs who longed for this had only to remain within the walls of a city for a year and a day to be freed from the bonds to their lord.

The rising bourgeoisie had fluid wealth, for money was again being coined, and they used this money to make profitable loans to kings and princes to finance their military campaigns (despite the church's prohibition of charging interest for the use of money). With the development of a money economy instead of a barter economy came changes in business, such as accounting, double-entry bookkeeping (first used in such Italian commercial centers as Florence), letters of credit, and insurance companies.

The consequence of these various developments, and the resulting reemergence of cities as a major economic force during the thirteenth and fourteenth centuries, is that Gothic architecture is largely an urban architecture. As the following pages will show, the great monuments documenting the rise of Gothic architecture are not isolated monasteries but urban cathedrals, building projects initiated by influential urban bishops and paid for by wealthy urban businessmen and craft guilds.

These Gothic cathedrals differed not only

from their Romanesque predecessors in structural form but also in their dedication, and this bears on important related social and religious changes. Almost uniformly the urban cathedrals (particularly in France) were dedicated to the Virgin Mother of Christ, to Our Lady, *Notre-Dame,* and not to local saints (although they did contain subsidiary chapels dedicated to local saints). This change in dedication was due to the veneration being given to Mary, the Mother of Christ, by the early twelfth century, and this paralleled an important shift in attitude toward women in general in the later Middle Ages. From the time of Saint Augustine in the fifth century, women had been viewed as temptresses and as the source of evil (had not Eve tempted Adam and caused the expulsion from the Garden of Eden?). As the courts of the medieval lords ceased to be centers of military power, they fostered the development of a refined court etiquette and an interest in the arts and literature that elevated the position of women. The result was the code of chivalry and the concept of unconsummated romantic love. The Virgin was seen as incorporating the perfect virtues of the noble lady; she was the Queen of Heaven who interceded on behalf of humankind like a mother for her children, just as the lady of the manor might intercede with her lord on behalf of their subjects. Accordingly, one after another the soaring new churches built in Europe were dedicated to the Virgin Mary.

Religious Changes—Scholasticism

Christianity, benefiting from the invigorating effects of the Cluniac reforms, enjoyed a time of renewed fervor. Yet the growing interest in the secular world also had an impact on religion. There arose a thirst for knowledge and a rational statement of religious faith that resulted in the establishment of universities in many major cities. The University of Bologna, founded in 1158, was the first, and gradually became known as a center for the study of religious and civil law. The University of Paris, founded in 1200, specialized in the study of theology. It should be remembered, too,

that all universities were then branches of the church and that their faculty members were clerics.

The method used to ascertain truth by the scholars of the thirteenth century was *scholasticism,* the application of the process of Classical Aristotelian reason to explain and reconcile differences between scripture and church doctrine. It was inevitable that such investigations would lead to doubt, but as Abelard, one of the principal philosophers in Paris, observed, doubt would lead to inquiry and inquiry to truth. In the universities were collected the works of Aristotle and other classical authors, many of them obtained as Arabic translations from Islamic scholars, and these were studied and debated.[1] This endeavor to fully reconcile faith and reason reached its zenith in the work of Thomas Aquinas (c. 1225–1274), who set himself the task of reconciling Aristotelian logic with the writings of the early church fathers. His *Summa theologica* systematically covered the entire literature of the church, beginning with the earliest writings, and attempted to create one coherent logical doctrine. It is a hierarchical construction of greater principles dominating subsidiary ideas.

The Gothic Cathedral

The Gothic cathedral was another by-product of the Crusades, for when the first Crusaders saw Constantinople on their way to the Holy Land, they marveled at the size and wealth of the city and the vast scale and splendor of Hagia Sophia. There was nothing to compare with either that city or that church in France. It is no mere coincidence that cathedral building started shortly after the First Crusade ended and the Crusaders returned home.

The urban cathedral was also the physical expression of Saint Thomas Aquinas's *Summa theologica;* it was a hierarchical organization of related parts representing a balance of structural forces that corresponded to the reconciliation of Classical logic and Christian faith. The Gothic cathedrals were covered virtually from top to bottom with sculptural representation of biblical stories. The most dramatic innovation was the virtual elimination of the walls of the church; in their place appeared membranes of colored glass depicting stories from scripture. Thus, in stone and colored glass, the entire building became a bible for the illiterate, and what was especially important, the visual imagery was known and accessible to all—lord, merchant, servant, and serf alike.

The Abbey Church at Saint-Denis

The opening up of the wall for stained glass windows was first achieved in the new abbey church at Saint-Denis, begun by Abbot Suger about 1135. Suger (1081–1151), the son of peasants, demonstrated such unusual intelligence as a boy that he was admitted to the abbey school at Saint-Denis. There he became a close friend of his fellow student, Louis Capet, who was to become King Louis VII. Suger rose through the ranks of the monks, became the assistant of Abbot Adam, and after Adam's death was elected abbot of Saint-Denis in 1122. The Benedictine abbey of St.-Denis, about 6 miles (9.6 kilometers) north of Paris, had existed before the time of Charlemagne; it was dedicated to Denis, martyred in the third century, one of the first missionaries to the Gauls and believed to have been the first bishop of Paris. In subsequent centuries myths proliferated concerning Saint Denis. Since the seventh century, Frankish and French kings had been buried in the abbey church rebuilt by Charlemagne, and after 1120 the insignia of the French monarchs were kept at the abbey. As a result Saint Denis came to be seen as the patron saint of France. While Louis VII was leading the Second Crusade, 1147–49, Suger was appointed his regent, so that to Suger the fate of the abbey, of its church, and of France became intricately linked.

Upon becoming abbot, Suger embarked on a program of returning the monks to a life of piety and of repairing the greatly dilapidated monastic buildings, especially the abbey church, which had become far too small for the urban population that crowded into it on feast days. In 1135–40 Suger constructed a broad and soaring new west facade of the church, with two towers over a three-bay narthex [15.1]. Three innovations distinguished the new facade. First, there was a clear geometrical compositional scheme, which Suger wrote was devised "by means of geometrical and arithmetical instruments" and which governed the placement of the masses of the tower and the position of the grouped window openings.[2] Second, between the towers, and admitting light to the extension of the old church nave, was a great round window, the first of the rose windows that so distinguished later Gothic churches. And third, the three entrance doors of the new west front were recessed behind ranks of successive jamb columns and concentric archivolts, all covered with carefully organized sculpture relating to the biblical kings and queens and, by extension, those of France. Regrettably, much of this sculpture was deliberately defaced in subsequent centuries.

The most important change, however, was the new choir built by Suger in 1141–44. In the library at Saint-Denis, then one of the largest in France, were ancient documents said to have been written by Dionysius the Areopagite, erroneously believed to be Saint Denis himself. These mystical writings merged Christian doctrine with what Erwin Panofsky has described as the "fundamental oneness and luminous aliveness of the world." Throughout the writings of Dionysius, God is described as "the superessential Light" or "the Father of Lights," and Christ is described as the "first Radiance." Such passages suggested that this pure, heavenly radiance could be simulated through an analogy to earthly light. To Suger, humans need not be ashamed of their sensory perception and sense-controlled imagination; instead of rejecting physical sensory reality they could hope to transcend it by absorbing it. He wrote:

Thus, when—out of my delight in the beauty of the house of God—the loveliness of the many-colored gems [on the new altar reliquaries] has called me away from external cares, and worthy meditation has induced me to reflect, transferring that which is material to that which is immaterial, on the diversity of

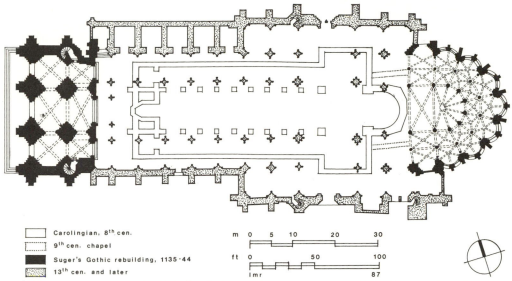

m   0   5   10   20   30

ft 0   50   100

1mr   87

15.2. Saint-Denis, 1141–44. Plan of the church, showing the new west towers and choir by Suger; the old Carolingian church is shown in dotted outline, and the later Gothic nave is shown in solid outline. (Note: The ninth-century east end is not shown in its entirety, so as to clarify the reflected rib plan of Suger's new choir.)

15.3. Saint-Denis. Interior of the choir ambulatory. By combining rib vaults and pointed arches with careful resolution of structural forces, Suger's architects were able to achieve unprecedented lightness of structure and to open the walls to large panes of stained glass.

the sacred virtues: then it seems to me that I see myself dwelling, as it were, in some strange region of the universe which neither exists entirely in the slime of the earth nor entirely in the purity of Heaven; and that, by the Grace of God, I can be transported from this inferior to that higher world in an anagogical manner.[3]

The new choir of Saint-Denis was to be suffused by a divine radiance, earthly light filtered through the sacred images of stained glass. As Suger wrote, "Bright is the noble edifice which is pervaded by the new light."[4] Around the foundations of the old Carolingian choir, and more than doubling its capacity, was a double ambulatory [15.2, 15.3]. From the outer ambulatory extended seven chapels, each with two large windows that reduced the walls to narrow bands adjoining buttresses. Suger described them as "a circular string of chapels by virtue of which the whole [church] would shine with the wonderful and uninterrupted light of the most luminous windows, pervading the interior beauty."[5] The inner ambulatory and the outer ambulatory chapels were covered by vaults articulated by ribs of pointed arches. To put the central keystone of the pointed arch ribs at roughly the geometric center of the vault, the ribs were broken in plan. The resolution of the structural forces was such that the vaults were supported on the slenderest of twelve columns (which Suger wrote were symbolic of the apostles), giving the interior a lightness that made the vaults appear to be rising and tied down by the columns rather than being massive and bearing down upon the columns, as had been characteristic of Romanesque vaults. What had been, by comparison, the somber dirge of Romanesque architecture, suddenly became the hymn of praise of Gothic lightness. (The medieval French, it should be noted, used the term *style ogivale,* or "pointed-arch style," to identify this new construction technique; *Gothic* is a later, derogatory term invented by later Renaissance historians to suggest barbarism.)

Notre-Dame of Amiens

Within a half century, in a score of cities radiating out from Saint-Denis and Paris, and inspired by the lightness and structural articulation of Suger's church, Gothic cathedrals sprang up. Before 1450, in France alone, over eighty cathedrals were built, plus five hundred monastic churches and hundreds of smaller parish churches. As Jean Gimpel has suggested, once it became apparent that the military reconquest of the Holy Land was impossible, the conquest of architectural space was undertaken, leading to a new "cathedral crusade."[6] Medieval masons did not immediately open up walls to glass, despite Suger's eloquent writing; but gradually, as they experimented in pushing masonry technology to its limits, the cathedrals became larger and lighter. After Saint-Denis came the cathedrals at Noyon, begun in 1151; Laon in 1160; and Paris in 1163 [15.4]. Up to this time the ribbed vaults over the central naves were no higher than 80 feet (24.3 meters). Below them, however, opened up expansive clerestory windows, a radical departure from the heaviness and darkness of Romanesque barrel vaults. At Notre-Dame in Paris, in extending the 108-foot (32.9 meters) nave westward from the chevet, the decision was made to increase the size of the gallery windows, which meant that the nave vaults had to be braced in an unconventional way. Previously, oblique tilted arches, resisting the outward thrust of the nave vaults, had been hidden under the side aisle roofs, but now they would need to be placed above the aisle roof, outside and exposed, sloping from the upper nave wall to vertical extensions of the buttresses of the side aisle walls [15.5]. Thus flying buttresses were created. This innovation then led to the Early Gothic churches of Chartres in 1194, Rouen in 1202, and Reims in 1211. By the time the last of these was begun, cathedral architecture had reached the stage called High Gothic, fully developed in all its constituent and integrated parts—pointed arches and broken rib vaulting, skeletonized structure, and flying buttress.

The cathedral of Notre-Dame at Amiens, the next to follow of these great churches, exploits all of these and was built in a relatively brief period, beginning in 1220 and finished in 1269, so it incorporates fewer

15.4. *Church of Notre-Dame de Paris, 1163–1250. In the choir and nave of Notre-Dame in Paris the innovations of Suger's architects at Saint-Denis were used to transform the upper clerestory windows into huge panels of stained glass.*

15.5. *Notre-Dame de Paris. Cross section of the nave, showing the flying buttresses used to transmit the lateral forces of the roof and vaults down to the outer buttresses.*

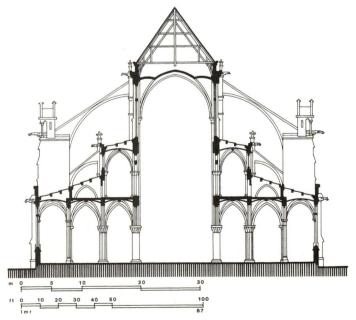

15.6. *Robert de Luzarches, Thomas de Cormont, and Regnault de Cormont, Notre-Dame de Amiens, Amiens, France, 1220–69. View of the west front. Built in a relatively short period, this cathedral exemplifies the High Gothic in France.*

modifications to the original scheme than many cathedrals. For that reason it is often said to be the classic example of the fully developed French Gothic cathedral [15.6]. Notre-Dame at Amiens, like so many other Gothic cathedrals, such as that at Chartres, replaced an older church destroyed by fire. The decision to rebuild was made immediately after the fire at Amiens in 1218, but construction was not ready to get under way until 1220. The bishops directing the work were Evrard de Fouilly and his successor,

Geoffrey d'Eu. Three architects supervised construction, although the basic design seems to have been decided by the first, Robert de Luzarches, who began construction at the western towers, narthex, and nave. The transept and choir were carried forward by Thomas de Cormont and the church brought to completion in 1269 (except for the tops of the west towers) by his son, Regnault de Cormont. The towers were then finished at the end of the fourteenth century.

More than any previous medieval building type, the Gothic cathedral was quickly standardized in its plan and basic components. There were, of course, distinctive regional variations in Gothic cathedrals, such as the lowness and horizontality of English churches, or the more highly colored ornamentation of Italian examples. Yet the basic organization was relatively uniform. The plan was derived from Romanesque pilgrimage churches, with nave, side aisles, transept arms and crossing, and the chevet with ambulatory and radiating chapels enclosing a round-ended choir [15.7]. The radiating chevet chapels were dedicated to various saints, often local martyrs, with the central chapel dedicated to the Virgin, Notre-Dame.

The principal change in plan was the greater size of the choir, for often the choir had nearly as many bay units as the nave, so that the transept was roughly at the middle of the body of the church. This arrangement reflected directly the way the cathedrals were paid for and how they were used, for typically only the choir (sometimes excluding the surrounding ambulatory and chapels) legally belonged to the clergy of the diocese. The nave, transept, and aisles, in contrast, legally belonged to the city, were paid for by the various craft guilds, and often were used for secular gatherings. The other major change from the Romanesque plan was the creation of elaborated entrances not only at the west end of the nave but at the end of each transept arm.

Externally, aside from the exposed and increasingly thin flying buttresses, the major changes in the Gothic cathedral included towers. In France this took the form of a pair of towers at the west entrance, whereas in England there was more typically a great tower perched over the crossing.

Internally, the cathedral consisted of side aisles (sometimes two on each side of the nave) covered with rib vaults [15.8, 15.9]. These opened through an arcade of tall pointed arches to the nave. Above the arcade was a dark narrow passage in the thickness of the nave wall, the triforium gallery, whose height corresponded to that of the sloping wooden shed roof protecting the side aisle vaults. Above the triforium passage, the wall opened up in broad stained glass clerestory windows subdivided by delicate stone tracery. A cluster of elongated colonnettes continued up from the capital of the arcade pier, each colonnette

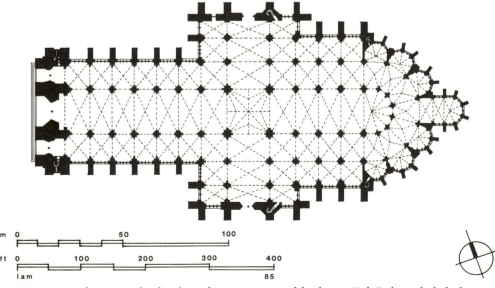

15.7. Notre-Dame de Amiens. The plan shows the increasing size of the choir in High Gothic cathedrals, forcing the transept arms toward the middle of the building.

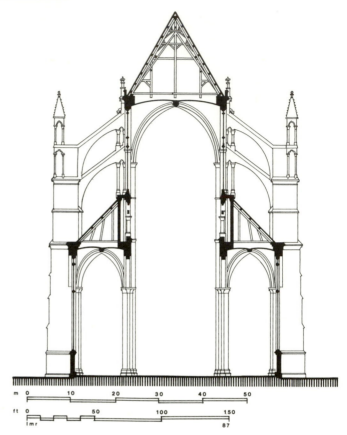

15.8. Notre-Dame de Amiens. Cross section through the nave. Pairs of flying buttresses were used to transmit the forces of roof and nave vaults to the external buttress piers. (The roof trusses shown here have been adapted from Viollet-le-Duc's drawing of those at Reims; the original wooden trusses at Amiens were replaced long ago.)

corresponding to one of the ribs of the longitudinal, transverse, or diagonal arches in the rib vault over the nave.

The network of thin colonnettes in the clerestory piers, as well as the stone tracery, emphasized the vertical reach of the Gothic cathedral. This strong sense of verticality was also emphasized by an optical illusion. Actually a cross section of Amiens would nearly fit inside a cross section of the Pantheon in Rome, which measures 142½ feet (43.4 meters) in height and diameter, for the vaults of Amiens rise 138 feet (42.1 meters) from the nave floor, and the width is nearly 150 feet (45.7 meters) to the aisle walls. Yet Amiens and the other Gothic cathedrals appear much higher than they actually are, since all the elements of the design reach upward. Contributing to the optical illusion of great height are the proportions of the nave. At Amiens the nave width is roughly 45 feet (13.7 meters), so the

ratio of width to height is 1:3.1, whereas the ratio at both Sainte-Foy at Conques and Saint-Sernin in Toulouse is lower, 1:2.5. Further strengthening the sensation of height is the infusion of light in the Gothic cathedral, for the upper walls dissolve in light. There are, in fact, no true upper walls but rather a series of slender piers carrying an umbrella of stone vaults; between the piers are panels of stained glass, through which passes an ethereal light, casting soft-edged colored patterns on the limestone piers and arcades below [Plate 4].

Above the stone nave vaults of a Gothic cathedral was yet another substantial structure, a steep wooden trussed roof. At Amiens the peak of the roof is 200 feet (60.9 meters) above ground. These steep roofs, effective in shedding rain and snow, also caught the wind, so that typically two sets of flying buttresses were required: the lower flyers to transmit the outward thrusts of the

15.9. *Notre-Dame de Amiens. Interior.*

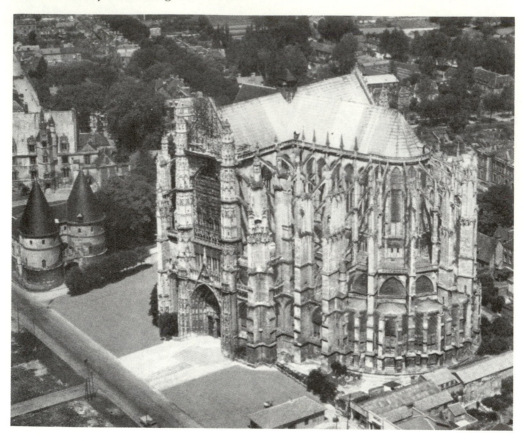

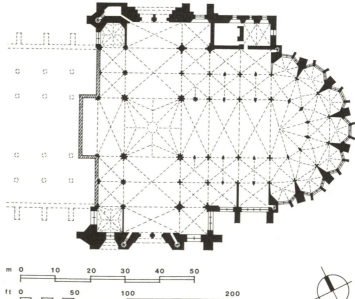

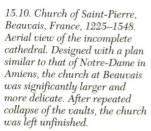

15.10. Church of Saint-Pierre, Beauvais, France, 1225–1548. Aerial view of the incomplete cathedral. Designed with a plan similar to that of Notre-Dame in Amiens, the church at Beauvais was significantly larger and more delicate. After repeated collapse of the vaults, the church was left unfinished.

15.11. Saint-Pierre, Beauvais. Plan. The solid portion shows what was finished; the outlined section shows where the bays of the nave would have continued.

15.12. *Saint-Pierre,*
Beauvais. View of the choir.

nave vaults to the externalized buttresses, and the upper ones to carry the wind loads of the tall roofs to the buttresses.

Saint-Pierre, Beauvais

Like twentieth-century architects, medieval master masons sought to dematerialize structure, but their objective was to make the church an analogue of the ethereal heavenly city. Yet there were limits beyond which their empirical knowledge, gained by trial and error, could not pass. These were reached in the huge church of Saint-Pierre at Beauvais, another prosperous trading center in wool and textiles, about 44 miles (71 kilometers) north of Paris. The earlier, tenth-century cathedral was partially burned in 1180 and then completely destroyed by fire in 1225. Immediately a new church was proposed by Bishop Milon de Nanteuil. Three successive (and as yet

unidentified) masters constructed the choir, ambulatory, and chapels, and covered the chevet in stone vaults between 1225 and 1272 [15.10, 15.11, 15.12]. The original vaults were quadrapartite, divided into four segments by two diagonal ribs; in this and other respects the plan was nearly the same in its parts as that of the chevet of Amiens (as yet incomplete, since Amiens was built from the west eastward). But at Beauvais the scale was grander, for the choir vaults were 51 feet wide (15.5 meters) and soared to 157½ feet (48 meters); the ratio of width to height was therefore exactly the same as that at Amiens, but the actual size was 14 percent larger. The arches of the ambulatory arcade by themselves were 69.67 feet high (21.2 meters), one foot higher than the nave barrel vault at Conques. Even more light flooded Beauvais, for the triforium passage was glazed as well, eliminating the last suggestion of solid wall.

15.13. Salisbury Cathedral, Salisbury, England, 1220–66. Viewed from the air, Salisbury has more open space around it than did urban French cathedrals.

Apparently because of design errors in making the external buttresses too small to resist the forces created by wind loads, the buttresses gradually bent and cracked; on November 29, 1284, the choir vaults at Beauvais collapsed.[7] Repairs were undertaken in 1322–37 by another unknown master mason. Believing that an inadequate system of support in the ambulatory piers had caused the collapse, he inserted additional piers between the original piers of the choir and rebuilt the vaults in sexpartite form, with diagonal ribs and an additional cross rib. The extra piers stabilized the structure and the vaults have stood firm since. The inserted piers, however, doubled the number of verticals, further emphasizing the unsurpassed height of the vaults. A

decade after the choir was finished, construction of the crossing and nave was halted first by the Black Death and then the Hundred Years' War. Not until 1500 were the transept arms and crossing built by Martin Cambiges and finished by Jean Vast in 1548. It was then proposed to build a great tower over the crossing, and in 1564–69, after prolonged study and discussion, Jean Vast built a stone spire reaching up 490 feet (150 meters). Unbraced by any adjoining nave structure on the west side, the delicate transept piers under the tower bulged outward, and finally, on April 30, 1573, the tower collapsed. After the rubble was cleared away, it was decided not to complete the church. The transept vaults were rebuilt and the west side enclosed, but

Saint-Pierre at Beauvais has remained truncated ever since. As the French historian Desjardin observed: "This was not the time to build cathedrals anymore. The schools for masters, sculptors, glaziers, and painters, which had been inspired by their creation, were dying all over the place."[8]

Salisbury Cathedral

In French cathedrals the vertical line dominated everywhere, and although the interior elevation was divided into three distinct zones (arcade, triforium, and clerestory), increasingly the lines between those zones were crossed by thin *colonnettes* that ran from floor to vault top and back down to the floor, symbolic representations of the way the forces of gravity were conveyed to the ground. In England a very different model evolved in cathedral design, in which the horizontal line was stressed by lateral exten-

sion of the cathedral, by keeping the vertical dimensions much lower than they were on the Continent, and by stressing the horizontal moldings and string-courses of masonry that marked the edges of the three horizontal divisions of the interior elevation. English churches also incorporated two basic plan differences, compared to Continental counterparts. First, since they were often inspired by Cistercian monastic models, they had two transepts; and second, they had flat east ends, as advocated by the Cistercian monks, so that instead of a curved chevet there is a flat stained glass window-wall.

Salisbury Cathedral, built in 1220–66, illustrates all these typically English attributes [15.13, 15.14, 3.10]; the strikingly vertical tower was an addition of the early fourteenth century, not altogether in sympathy with the original horizontality. Salisbury Cathedral is an interesting contrast to

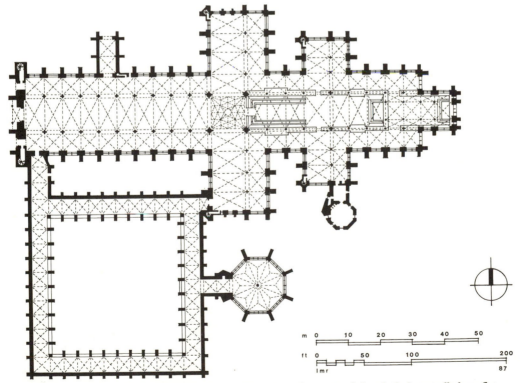

15.14. *Salisbury Cathedral. Plan. Because of strong Cistercian influence, English cathedrals typically have flat east ends with a large window instead of a rounded chapel.*

Amiens, especially since both were started the same year, 1220, and both are nearly exactly the same length—450 feet (137.2 meters). Salisbury Cathedral was built on new ground, outside the old city of Sarum, and hence had far more open space around it than was typical of Continental Gothic urban churches; eventually a new city, a trading center for wool and cloth, grew up around the new cathedral. Although nearly as long as Amiens, Salisbury Cathedral is only 78 feet (23.8 meters) wide. Its nave is 37 feet wide (11.3 meters), with vaults 81 feet high (24.7 meters), so the ratio of width to height is just 1:2.2, much less than in Amiens or Beauvais.

The Sainte-Chapelle, Paris

In France the drive to make the building frame a true skeleton, to eliminate all sense of the wall as a structural mass, was achieved in the lofty choir of Beauvais, but it is especially clear in the small private chapel of the king, the Sainte-Chapelle, attached to the royal palace on the Île-de-la-Cité in Paris. This project was undertaken by Louis IX and his architect, Thomas de Cormont, in 1240–47, to house the relics Louis had collected, including pieces of Christ's Crown of Thorns, and pieces of the True Cross, as well as the iron lance, the sponge, and a nail used in Christ's crucifixion. The chapel, measuring 32 feet in width and 99.5 feet in length (9.75 by 30.33 meters), was attached to the royal palace, with a relatively low

ground-floor chapel for palace retainers and lesser nobility and a tall upper chapel on the main floor (the second floor), connecting to the royal apartments. The structure of this upper chapel was reduced to nothing more than a series of buttresses spaced 15 feet apart [15.15, Plate 4]. The walls were entirely of stained glass, and the stone vaults were painted deep blue with gold fleur-de-lis stars, the royal emblem seemingly in the vault of heaven. Damaged in the French Revolution but restored to lustrous brilliance in the nineteenth century by Eugène Viollet-le-Duc, the chapel is luxurious in the extreme. Perhaps we should perceive this less as a church in the usual sense of the word and more as an architecturally scaled reliquary, filled with precious religious objects.

Wooden-Roofed Churches

The cut stone vaulting used so effectively in cathedrals and royal chapels was beyond the means of rural parishes, so these smaller village churches were covered with wooden roofs. In medieval England, especially, timber roof construction achieved an excellence of structure and a delicacy of sculptural enrichment that remained unsurpassed. In addition to covering parish churches, various forms of roof trusses were used over meeting halls and to enclose large tithe barns used to protect offerings of grain. The same technology was used to construct the heavy timber roofs over the

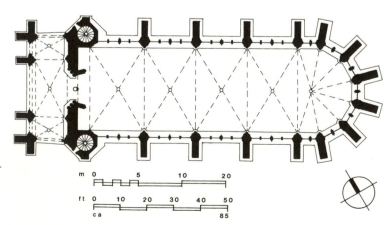

15.15. Sainte-Chapelle. Plan. In the upper chapel, the building is reduced to isolated piers and walls made up entirely of glass.

15.16. Henry Yevele and Hugh Herland, Westminster Hall, Palace of Westminster, London, 1394. Interior. Spanning 68 feet (20.7 meters), this is one of the largest surviving medieval wooden roof trusses.

masonry vaults of the cathedrals. For spans wider than 20 feet or 6 meters, hammerbeam trusses were developed with the principal uprights supported by projecting brackets or hammerbeams [2.24]. Numerous Late Gothic examples of hammerbeam truss roofs survive in England, such as in Saint Botolph's at Trunch in Norfolk, or the double hammerbeam roof of Saint Wendreda's, March, in Cambridgeshire. The culmination of this technique was reached in the massive hammerbeam roof over the hall of Westminster Palace, a royal palace then outside the city of London [15.16]. The

hall itself, built by Henry Yevele in 1394–1400, was covered by a hammerbeam roof spanning 68 feet (20.7 meters) designed by the king's master carpenter, Hugh Herland.

Late Gothic Architecture

As happened with Greek and then Roman architecture, basic forms were first worked out, and then, in succeeding centuries, they were made increasingly complicated and more heavily ornamented, as exemplified in the so-called Roman Baroque architecture of the late Roman Empire. The same kind

15.17. Saint-Maclou, Rouen, France, 1434–1514. The elaborate open tracery of the facade marks this as Flamboyant Gothic.

of movement away from structural directness in favor of ornamental extravagance occurred in the Late Gothic period as well. In France this appeared in decorative forms, particularly in the stone tracery of stained glass windows that had the wavy fluidity of flames; such curvilinear forms were said by the French to be *flambant*, "flaming," or flamboyant, a word still used to convey a sense of extravagant excess. Perhaps the best example of an entire church in this late Gothic style is Saint-Maclou in Rouen, near the mouth of the Seine River in Normandy [15.17]. When the Hundred Years' War ended and the English finally were driven out of Normandy, a period of active building commenced there. One of the buildings undertaken was Saint-Maclou, 1434–1514. A parish church, it is 180 feet (55.9 meters) long, with nave vaults that rise

75 feet (22.8 meters). Its most flamboyant portion is the five-sided porch, built last, in 1500–1514; the hoods over the doors are stretched vertically and transformed into an open interlace of curving flamelike tendrils.

In England the final form of the Gothic was called Perpendicular, because of the emphasis on the vertical in closely spaced repeated lines. An early use of Perpendicular Gothic was in the rebuilding of the cathedral at Gloucester, a Norman building that had formerly been the abbey church of Saint Peter. The repository of the remains of the murdered King Edward II, the church at Gloucester prospered greatly as a point of pilgrimage, permitting extensive reconstruction. The Perpendicular style is illustrated most clearly in the rebuilt choir there, 1331–51, designed perhaps by William Ramsey or Thomas of Canterbury

[15.18]. The round-headed arches of the Romanesque lower arcade were overlaid with delicate tracery, and broad clerestory windows were opened up above. The entire east wall was filled with an enormous window, its tracery illustrating the character of Perpendicular Gothic. The new vaulting of the choir also illustrates what happened to rib vaulting in England; in these *lierne vaults* the ribs were multiplied to the point at which, as here, they become a decorative filigree over the surface.

Also introduced, in the cloister walk at Gloucester in 1351–1412, was the unique form of English fan vaulting in which a dense cluster of thin ribs radiates out from each column like an inverted curved cone. This type of vault reached its fullest expression in such buildings as King's College Chapel, Cambridge University, built by Reginald Ely, with vaults by John Wastell, 1508–15 [15.19]. Commissioned by King Henry VI, this was larger than other college chapels and patterned more after the choirs

15.18. New choir, Gloucester Cathedral, Gloucester, England, 1337–51. Interior. In England, Late Gothic architecture became emphatically vertical, as demonstrated in the numerous vertical mullions of the window in the new choir of Gloucester Cathedral.

15.19. Reginald Ely and John Wastell, King's College Chapel, Cambridge University, Cambridge, England, 1446–1515. Interior. Unique to England was the fan vault, as found in King's College Chapel, suggesting a grove of trees.

of cathedrals, that at Gloucester being the particular model. When construction was completed under Henry VII, the technique of fan vaulting was used here at its grandest scale; the walls are completely dissolved in glass, and the vaults, windows, and detailing are a complete harmony. King's College Chapel is said to be the most majestic of all Perpendicular interiors.[9]

In Germany and the Holy Roman Empire, vaulting also became more elaborated, with proliferating ribs in "net vaulting," which seemed to break the surface into a series of facets. In time the German masons made the ribs completely independent of the vault surface, creating the *flying rib*, a network of lacelike ligaments in the air below the faceted vault surface; one example is the church of Saint Leonard, Frankfurt, 1507. There also arose a preference for simpler spaces, freed of the spatial complexities of transepts and crossings, low side aisles, and high naves. German masons devised the *hall church*, in which there is only one volume of uniform height, divided into nave/choir and aisles by rows of columns. This hall church type, with net vaults, is well illustrated in the choir portion of the church of Saint Lorenz, Nuremberg, Germany, built 1439–77 by Konrad Heinzelman and Konrad Roriczer.

Domestic and Public Architecture

With the rise of cities again, and the accumulation of private wealth, a new urban residential architecture emerged. Adjacent to the cathedrals appeared the houses of the bishop and archbishop, and residences of the clergy associated with operation of the cathedral, often enclosing in an irregular way (as in front of the cathedral at Noyon) a plaza that was the site of fairs and religious plays. Early cities sprang up around monasteries, and the rich and active monastery at Cluny had many houses built around it in the twelfth century. Although the facades of some of these survive, the interiors have been rebuilt. Nonetheless, Viollet-le-Duc was able to reconstruct a typical house plan [15.20], with a large shop room on the ground floor opening to the street by means of a broad, arched window-wall. Behind this commercial space was a court and behind that the kitchen. On the upper level were the living quarters, with a combined living-dining room and a bedroom in front overlooking the street, an open court to the rear, and a rear bedroom over the kitchen. The third floor had sleeping quarters for apprentices and storage for merchandise and supplies.

Just as cities became a new driving force in late medieval culture, so too did merchants increase the scope of their business, becoming bankers and money brokers. Merchant bankers became the new patrons of architecture, and the late buildings of the Middle Ages were buildings they commissioned—their residences, guild halls, and

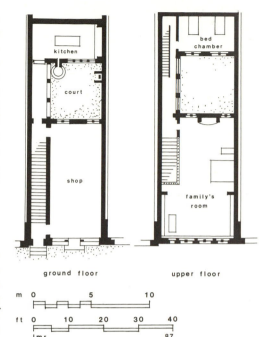

ground floor   upper floor

15.20. *Merchant's house, Cluny, France, twelfth century. Plan (as reconstructed by Viollet-le-Duc).*

town halls. The large house of Jacques Coeur in Bourges illustrates this new urban type well [15.21, 15.22]. Jacques Coeur (1395–1456), the son of a furrier, was born in Bourges, a cloth-producing city in the virtual center of France. He became a merchant, gradually becoming one of the most important businessmen in France due to his international trading contacts. His operations included trading exchanges for cloth, silk, jewels, armor, spices, salt, wheat, and wool, with warehouses across France, Belgium, Scotland, and Italy, supplied by his own fleet of merchant ships. He became steward of the royal funds and banker for the court during the reign of Charles VIII, lending money to the king for the conquest of Normandy, which made Jacques Coeur in essence the French minister of finance.[10]

Altogether Jacques Coeur acquired forty manors throughout France, but in 1443–51 he built a magnificent house for his family in Bourges, purchasing a portion of the old defensive walls of the city, and adding wings wrapping around a commodious court that

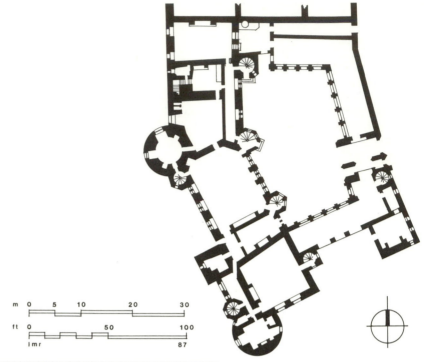

m 0   5   10   20   30

ft 0   50   100

1 m r   87

15.21. House of Jacques Coeur, Bourges, France, 1443–51. Plan. In the construction of this grand house, new sections were added to the old city walls, incorporating the old round towers.

15.22. House of Jacques Coeur. View of the courtyard. Although the building has the complex geometries of something that has been added to over centuries, this was built in one campaign.

15.23. *Cloth Hall, Bruges, Belgium, c. 1240 to late fifteenth century. By the end of the Middle Ages, secular architecture was beginning to assume great importance, borrowing forms and decorative details from earlier religious architecture. Guild halls, such as this one, became symbols of civic pride.*

opened to the street. Although built in one continual operation, the parts of the house present an irregularity of plan and profile, a flexibility and freedom of delicate ornament, that suggests numerous additions over time. It had public rooms and galleries on the ground floor, with large kitchens and an equally large general dining room. The family's private chambers were on the second floor and included a richly embellished private chapel.

Important expressions of municipal prestige and power were the large town halls and cloth-trading halls built in the commercial centers of northern France and Belgium at the end of the Middle Ages. Although designed in plan to accommodate their new commercial and municipal functions, stylistically these buildings borrowed extensively from the vocabulary developed for church buildings, using pointed arches and elaborate tracery. The town hall in Bruges, Belgium, survives nearly intact, a fortunate accident of the historical development of that cloth-trading center [15.23]. Ten miles (16.1 kilometers) from the sea and just thirty miles (48.3 kilometers) north of the present French border, Bruges (Brugge in Flemish) emerged during the twelfth and thirteenth centuries as the single most important port city in the Flemish textile trade and the fur trade with England and Scandinavia. The money funneled through the city made its burghers wealthy, and this affluence and municipal pride were expressed in the construction of a town hall, 1376–1420, and of the cloth hall, with its rather top-heavy tower finished in 1482 which dominates the plaza in the old part of the city. The reason medieval Bruges survives almost intact is that the Zwijn River, the city's access to the sea, silted up in the fifteenth century, and commercial activity then shifted to Antwerp. Later, when a canal was opened to the sea, Bruges grew only slowly. It never became a vital commercial hub in modern times, as Antwerp did, and thus never became a target for bombardment during the wars of the twentieth century that leveled Antwerp and destroyed so much European architecture.

An Architecture of Aspiration

Despite the rise of cities as economic and political centers in the Gothic period, and the resultant flourishing of secular life in the growing cities, the basic concern of earthly life remained gaining assurance of heaven. Accordingly, the building of great urban cathedrals, arising both from swaggering civic pride and sincere religious piety, provided the arena of the most probing architectural experimentation. The Gothic architecture of town halls and private residences was therefore derived from the forms developed for the cathedral, and the result was an urban form of organic integration, rising in vertical lines that reached ever heavenward.

The Middle Ages ended in a series of concurrent disasters. Certainly, to the pessimistic and fainthearted of the fourteenth century, the end of the world must have seemed imminent. For over two centuries people had been gathering into the cities, and the rate of population growth increased so that the population of Europe nearly

doubled from 1000 to 1300. But then depleted fields failed to produce, and famine struck in 1315–17, followed soon after by plague. In 1348, in the port cities of central Italy, there appeared a disease that swept through the population, disfiguring its victims with black pustulant sores that preceded a lingering death. A form of bubonic plague, it was called the Black Death. Because medieval physicians were unable to discover that the disease was spread by fleas on rats, their preventive measures had no effect. As the plague spread the length and breadth of the Continent in the next two years, upward of two-fifths of Europe's population perished—at least twenty-five million people died.

Meanwhile the church hierarchy became splintered. The popes left Rome and took up residence in Avignon, in southern France, from 1309 to 1377, in what became known as the Babylonian Captivity. Various political factions within the church supported different claimants to the papal crown, and during 1378 to 1417 there were no fewer than three competing popes.

From the East appeared yet another threat, the Islamic Seljuk Turks, who conquered all of what is now Turkey and pressed hard against the fragment of the Byzantine Empire, now shrunk within the walls of Constantinople. In 1453, after long resistance, Constantinople finally fell to the Turks, and Greek scholars began their exodus to Italy.

Yet, curiously, despite this apparent outward disintegration, there began to emerge a fervent optimism in human potential, and a profound respect for the intellectual and artistic achievements of Classical Greece and Rome. Encouraged in part by the arrival of Greeks from the beleaguered East, Italian scholars, painters, sculptors, and architects set out to equal and surpass the endeavors of thirteenth-century theologians to reconcile Christian belief with the intellectual rigor of Classical thought, but they proposed to do it in symbolic artistic forms, to make a new art that was both Christian and Classical. As the Middle Ages faded, a new spirit was born, a rebirth of an old humanism, a renaissance.

NOTES

1. For an interesting description of the conflicts within the medieval monastic community concerning the study of Classical literature, see the mystery novel by Umberto Eco, *The Name of the Rose,* trans., William Weaver (New York, 1983).
2. Suger, *De consecratione . . . ,* trans. and ed. by Erwin Panofsky, in *Abbot Suger on the Abbey Church of St.-Denis and Its Art Treasures,* second ed. (Princeton, N.J., 1979), 101.
3. Panofsky, *Abbot Suger,* 19, and quoting from Suger, *De administratione . . . ,* 63–65.
4. Ibid., 51.
5. Ibid., 101.
6. Jean Gimpel, *The Cathedral Builders,* trans. Teresa Waugh (New York, 1983).
7. A technical explanation of the failure is given in Robert Mark, *Experiments in Gothic Structure* (Cambridge, Mass., 1982), 58–77; see also Stephen Murray, "The Choir of the Church of St. Pierre, Cathedral of Beauvais: A Study of Gothic Architectural Planning and Construction Chronology in its Historical Context." *Art Bulletin* 62 (December 1980); 533–51.
8. Desjardin, quoted in Mario Salvadori, *Why Buildings Stand Up* (New York, 1980), 222–24.
9. Peter Kidson, Peter Murray, and Paul Thompson, *A History of English Architecture* (Harmondsworth, England, 1965), 135.
10. See A. B. Kerr, *Jacques Coeur: Merchant Prince of the Middle Ages* (New York, 1927).

SUGGESTED READING

Marc Bloch, *Feudal Society* (Chicago, 1968).

Jean Bony, *French Gothic Architecture of the Twelfth and Thirteenth Centuries* (Berkeley, Calif., 1983).

Robert Branner, *Chartres Cathedral* (New York, 1969).

———, *Gothic Architecture* (New York, 1961).

John Fitchen, *The Construction of Gothic Cathedrals: A Study of Medieval Vault Erection* (New York, 1961).

Henri Focillon, *The Art of the West in the Middle Ages,* vol. II, *Gothic Art* (New York, 1963).

Paul Frankl, *Gothic Architecture* (Harmondsworth, England, 1962).

J. Gies and F. Gies, *Life in a Medieval City* (New York, 1981).

Jean Gimpel, *The Cathedral Builders,* trans. Michael Russell (New York, 1983).

Louis Grodecki, *Gothic Architecture,* trans. I. M. Paris (New York, 1977).

John Harvey, *The Gothic World, 1100–1600* (London, 1950).

———, *The Master Builders: Architecture in the Middle Ages* (London, 1971).

Denys Hay, *Europe in the Fourteenth and Fifteenth Centuries* (New York, 1966).

George Henderson, *Gothic* (Harmondsworth, England, 1967).

Johan Huizinga, *The Waning of the Middle Ages* (London, 1924; New York, 1954).

Hans Jantzen, *High Gothic: The Classic Cathedrals of Chartres, Reims, Amiens,* trans. James Palmes (Princeton, N.J., 1983).

Walter Leedy, *Fan Vaulting* (London, 1980).

Robert Mark, *Experiments in Gothic Structure* (Cambridge, Mass., 1982); highly interesting accounts of engineering analyses of selected Gothic churches.

Erwin Panofsky, *Abbot Suger on the Abbey Church of St.-Denis and Its Art Treasures,* second ed. (Princeton, N.J., 1979).

———, *Gothic Architecture and Scholasticism* (New York, 1957).

Henri Pirenne, *Medieval Cities: Their Origins and the Revival of Trade,* trans. Frank D. Halsey (Princeton, N.J., 1952).

Fritz Rörig, *The Medieval Town* (Berkeley, Calif., 1971).

Howard Saalman, *Medieval Cities* (New York, 1968).

Otto von Simson, *The Gothic Cathedral: Origins of Gothic Architecture and the Medieval Concept of Order,* second ed. (New York, 1962).

Whitney S. Stoddard, *Monastery and Cathedral in France* (Middletown, Ct., 1966; republished as *Art and Architecture in Medieval France* (New York, 1972).

Marilyn Stokstad, *Medieval Art* (New York, 1986).

G. F. Webb, *Architecture in Britain: The Middle Ages* (Harmondsworth, England, 1965).

16.1. *Filippo Brunelleschi, dome of Florence Cathedral, Florence, Italy, 1418–36. The dome of the cathedral of Florence rises over the city as a bold gesture of civic ambition. It was the largest such dome attempted since antiquity.*

CHAPTER 16

Renaissance and Mannerist Architecture

Renaissance artists firmly adhered to the Pythagorean concept "All is Number". . . . Architecture was regarded by them as a mathematical science which worked with spatial units: parts of that universal space for the scientific interpretation of which they had discovered the key in the laws of perspective. Thus they were made to believe that they could re-create the universally valid ratios and expose them pure and absolute, as close to abstract geometry as possible. And they were convinced that universal harmony could not reveal itself entirely unless it were realized in space through architecture conceived in the service of religion.

Rudolf Wittkower, *Architectural Principles in the Age of Humanism,* 1949

Gothic architecture was an assembly of parts worked out for each building individually. It was an architecture adaptable to any situation, but it was not an architecture determined by universal norms. To the Italians of the fifteenth century, Gothic architecture, with its roots in northern European sources, evoked an uncivilized brutish period that they began to call the dark age that separated the glories of ancient Greece and Rome from their own time. Emboldened by their flourishing urban (and urbane) culture, they set out to match the intellectual and artistic achievements of the ancients.

The Italians, and the Florentines especially, began to view history in a new way. They perceived human history not as a divinely ordained continuum but as successive periods, some characterized by great human accomplishment. More important, they sensed that they were at the start of a new age of vast possibilities, an age that could equal the achievement of the ancients. They had a new confidence in their intellectual capacity and desired a new architecture, one no longer based in the traditions of the church but expressing the mathematical clarity and rationality they perceived in the divine order of the universe. Such a new architecture needed no longer to point heavenward but, like Roman architecture, would stress the earth-bound horizontal. This new architecture, visually clear and rationally organized, first appeared in Filippo Brunelleschi's Ospedale degli Innocenti, (Foundling Hospital) in Florence [16.6]. Light and graceful, this building was based on Roman sources and governed in the arrangement of its parts by an evident proportional system. Here was an architecture rooted in the human intellect, serving not to impress religious dogma but built to provide for the very human needs of orphaned children.

Coupled with this new sense of human potential and history was the perception of the artist as a humanist scholar—not simply an artisan or a craftsman but a philosopher in paint and stone. Thus, it became extremely important to record the aspirations and achievements of contemporary artists, a task the painter Giorgio Vasari took upon himself. Writing in 1550 about the fourteenth-century painter Giotto, Vasari said Giotto's work marked a *rinascinta,* a "rebirth," of Classical solidity of form and human expression.[1] This Italian term, translated into French, became *renaissance.*

Italy in the Fifteenth Century

When the Renaissance began about 1400, there was no single Italy but rather a series of duchies, republics, and kingdoms along the Italian peninsula. These city-states were in constant competition with each other, periodically leading to armed conflict. Such internal division encouraged the strong monarchies of neighboring France and Spain to intervene frequently, and in fact the southern half of Italy and Sicily became a client kingdom of Spain. Running across central Italy toward Venice were the Papal States, provinces ruled by the Pope as a purely secular kingdom. North of the Papal States were various sovereign states dominated by the duchy of Milan, which was ruled by the Sforza family; the duchy of Ferrara, ruled by the d'Este family; and the republics of Venice and Florence. Both Venice and Florence prospered through commerce, Venice through maritime trade to the east, and Florence through the wool trade to northern Europe.

Florence had been a relatively quiet and minor town during the Early Middle Ages. Founded on the Arno River as Florentia in the first century B.C., a colony for Roman soldiers, by the third century it was a provincial capital. During the successive rule of the Goths, the Byzantines, and the Lombards, monasteries in Florence kept alive the older culture. Beginning as part of the southern edge of Charlemagne's empire, Florence gradually won greater autonomy in the Holy Roman Empire. Early in the twelfth century the Commune of Florence became a free city and by the end of the twelfth century had gained control of the surrounding region of Tuscany. During the thirteenth and fourteen centuries Florence suffered politically, with warring factions respectively supporting and resisting papal power. These internal conflicts sometimes escalated into conflict with nearby cities. Nonetheless, Florentine businessmen gradually came to dominate others in Italy, and the florin they began minting in the thirteenth century soon became the currency of Europe.

The Renaissance Patron

Another change that marked the emergence of the Renaissance concerned the patronage of art and architecture. Increasingly individuals, cardinals, and popes, but especially merchants and bankers commissioned buildings both for themselves and for their cities. In northern Europe, once the Reformation was under way, the church as a corporate body gradually ceased to be an important patron of architecture.

In Italy the first major patrons of the new architecture were the merchants who governed Florence, especially the Medicis. Following the Black Death and continuing up to 1434, Florence had experienced chaotic rule until the ascent of Giovanni di Bicci de' Medici (1360–1429) and his son Cosimo (1389–1464), merchants who prospered in the Florentine textile industry. Cosimo and his grandson Lorenzo, although without benefit of official title, ruled Florence through skillful diplomacy, frequent magnanimity, and personal flourish. Beginning with Giovanni, the Medicis made it the duty of a wealthy citizen to provide public and religious buildings for the citizens. Giovanni de' Medici began the rebuilding of the church and monastery of San Lorenzo and he was especially involved in the building of the Foundling Hospital (discussed below). His son, Cosimo, built major additions at three churches in Florence, constructed a monastery at Fiesole outside the city, paid for the renovation of Santo Spirito in Jerusalem, and sponsored additions to two monasteries in Assisi and San Marino. In addition, he refurbished several family villas outside Florence, one of which he put at the disposal of Marsilio Fincio where, free of disruption, Fincio could pursue his translation of Plato into Latin.

Cosimo's grandsons Lorenzo, Giovanni (Pope Leo X), and Giulio (Pope Clement VII) continued this creative work. Of them all, perhaps Lorenzo, called the Magnificent (1449–1492), was the most dazzling political and artistic figure—businessman, banker, connoisseur of art and literature. He was a friend and a colleague of such writers and philosophers as Pico della Mirandola and Marsilio Fincio, the theorist and architect Alberti, the sculptor Donatello, the painters Ghirlandaio and Botticelli, and the young sculptor Michelangelo. Lorenzo and his contemporary, Duke Federico di Montefeltro of Urbino, provided the models for the ideal Renaissance prince. They were adept at political diplomacy (and the art of war when necessary), were skilled linguists and writers, were collectors of ancient manuscripts and works of art, and were highly discriminating patrons of painting, sculpture, and architecture. They were the very embodiment of the Renaissance Man. Federico di Montefeltro built a well-proportioned and elegantly simple ducal palace at Urbino, where he installed one of the most important private libraries in Italy; there he and members of his court discussed at length what made for the well-conducted life, conversations later transcribed by Baldassare Castiglione as *The Book of the Courtier* (written 1508–18). This in turn became the textbook for the education of a humanist gentleman for the next three centuries.

Humanism

The renewed interest in antiquity that marked the Renaissance began with the rereading of the works of the ancient authors, especially Latin authors such as Cicero and Virgil, and such Greek works by Plato and Aristotle as were available in Latin. But what set this younger generation of scholars apart from the earlier Scholastics was that they were less interested in how the ancients corroborated scripture and church dogma and more in what the ancients themselves had to say. The mid-fourteenth century Florentine poet Petrarch stressed the study of the ancient authors and reliance on one's own observations, as evident in his famous climb of Mount Ventoux in southern France in 1336, a journey taken solely for the pleasure of surveying the beauty of the countryside. Saint Augustine had warned against drawing too much pleasure from the senses, but Petrarch contradicted this, carrying up the mountain a copy of Virgil, on which he reflected upon the way. Adjoining Duke Federico's study at Urbino was an open loggia, or porch, from which he could scan the surrounding countryside. This new awareness and appreciation of the natural landscape was one of the important contributions of the Renaissance.

Moreover, the new generation of scholars wanted to read the original words of the ancients, not medieval glosses or commentaries, and thus was set in motion the search for ancient documents in Latin and Greek in monastic libraries. Indeed, for the humanists Greek and Roman history became more real than that of their own recent past, which Leonardo Bruni called a "dark middle age." Such study also meant humanists had to develop linguistic skills to correct the errors in medieval copies of ancient manuscripts. This objective inquiry was reinforced by the appearance of numerous Eastern Greek scholars, especially in Florence in the early fifteenth century, as they fled beleaguered Constantinople. In the mid-fifteenth century, with Cosimo de' Medici's help, the Florentine Marsilio Fincio focused his energies on translating into Latin all the works of Plato. In 1462 Cosimo de' Medici established what came to be called the Florentine Academy, supervised by Fincio and Pico della Mirandola, where Platonic Greek philosophy was discussed by scholars, students, and such amateurs as Cosimo.

There emerged from such intensive reading of Classical literature a new program of instruction, rooted in *humanitas,* or "humanism," a term first used by the Florentine scholar Leonardo Bruni. Humanism was a philosophical view that emphasized the importance of human values and achievement as distinct from religious dogma. Humanism stressed objective inquiry guided by human reason, leading eventually to a statistical approach to comprehending and configuring reality. The humanists viewed history as the record of human aspiration and fallible judgments rather than an inevitable unfolding of God's will. They did not reject Christianity but

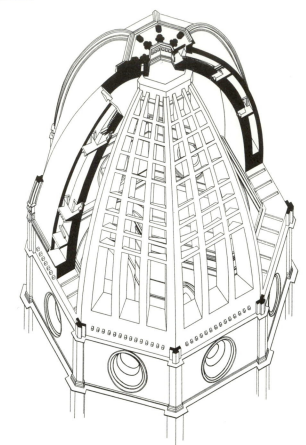

16.2. Dome of Florence Cathedral.
Axonometric cut-away view, showing
the method of construction, employing
ribs and double shells.

rather sought to reconcile the Classical view of human potential with Christian belief. Humans were still viewed as God's creation, possessing free will to pursue their own destiny, but humanists also celebrated the dignity of the individual human being and the wonder of human achievement.

Perhaps the best summary of the humanist view of human potential was given by Giovanni Pico della Mirandola, in his "Oration on the Dignity of Man," written in 1486 almost as an echo of Virgil's repudiation of limits for the Romans. God had assigned Adam no fixed place in creation, writes Pico, and

> neither a fixed abode nor a form that is thine alone nor any function peculiar to thyself have We given thee [Pico has God say to Adam], to the end that according to thy longing and according to thy judgement thou mayest have and possess what abode, what form, and what functions thou thyself shalt desire. . . . Thus, constrained by no limits, in accordance with

thine own free will, in whose hand We have placed thee, shalt ordain for thyself the limits of thy nature. We have set thee at the world's center that thou mayest from thence more easily observe whatever is in the world.[2]

Everything was possible for humankind, believed Pico, for to man "it is granted to have whatever he chooses, to be whatever he wills." There was also rekindled that desire for excellence in human achievement that the Greeks had called *arete,* for as Pico also observed, humans are "not content with the mediocre, [but] we shall pant after the highest and (since we may if we wish) toil with all our strength to obtain it."[3]

This desire to stretch human limits was boldly exemplified in the dome Filippo Brunelleschi completed over the crossing of the cathedral in Florence, Santa Maria della Fiore. The large cruciform Gothic church was begun about 1300 after designs by Arnolfo di Cambio. Its east end, consisting of octagonal chapels around an octagonal crossing, was greatly enlarged by Francesco Talenti half a century later, creating a crossing 138½ feet (42.2 meters) across that now had to be vaulted. Moreover, church officials decreed that no centering resting on the floor could be used, so that so far as traditional medieval building practices were concerned the dome was impossible to build. And yet, as Brunelleschi knew from his detailed examination of the ancient buildings in Rome, the Pantheon was proof that such a span had been vaulted once and he resolved it could be done again. Brunelleschi began studying how it could be done in 1404. By 1418 he had devised a way, and construction began in 1420 [16.1]. Technically the dome of the Florence cathedral is not a Classical design; it is more properly termed a medieval eight-sided cloister vault. It has a steep pointed profile and its construction method owes much to Gothic technique, for it is built of eight major brick ribs at the corners, with two lesser ribs in between; on these ribs two concentric brick shells of the dome are supported [16.2]. It is not so much the formal or ornamental properties but the sheer size of the dome that marks it as a Renaissance creation, its construction is Roman in scale. Big things were being done again in Italy.[4]

Vitruvius and Ideal Form

The Bible for the new generation of humanist patrons and architects was the *Ten Books on Architecture* by the Roman architect Vitruvius, much discussed during the fifteenth century and published in one edition after another beginning in 1486, with the first illustrated edition by Fra Giocondo in 1511. The ideally proportioned forms described by Vitruvius were derived from the ideal geometric forms discussed by Plato in *Philebus*—forms generated by straight lines and circles, as well as the solids formed by them in three dimensions. Plato was convinced such forms not only had inherent beauty but were "eternally and absolutely beautiful."[5] Vitruvius drew from such ideas in his third book, devoted to the design of temples, for basic to temple design were symmetry and

proportion. Ideal systems of proportion, he observed, can be found in the perfect proportions of the human body. For example, the foot is one sixth the height to the top of the head; and the face—from chin to nostrils, nostrils to eyebrows, and eyebrows to hair line—is divided into thirds. He also described how the ideal Platonic Phileban shapes, the square and the circle, are incorporated in the proportions of the human body [16.3]:

> For if a man be placed flat on his back, with his hands and feet extended, and a pair of compasses centered at his navel, the fingers and toes of his two hands and feet will touch the circumference of a circle described therefrom. And just as the human body yields a circular outline, so too a square figure may be found from it. For if we measure the distance from the soles of the feet to the top of the head, and then apply the measure to the outstretched arms, the breadth will be found to be the same as the height, as in the case of plane surfaces which are perfectly square.[6]

Renaissance architects sought clearly expressed numerical relationships in their designs, recalling the mysticism of Pythagoras and his followers. Galileo Galilei wrote that it was not possible to understand the "book" of creation "if we do not first learn the language and grasp the symbols in which it is written. This book is written in the mathematical language, and the symbols are triangles, circles, and other geometrical figures, without whose help it is impossible to comprehend a single word of it."[7]

The circle was an especially attractive form for Renaissance designers, symbolizing the perfection of the deity. Not only did the circle and the square thus provide the ideal forms for church plans, but planners even adapted circular schemes in plans for new towns. Antonio Avellino, called Filarete, worked in Milan during the 1460s on a manuscript discussing the new rational and classically inspired architecture, and in it he laid out a model new town, called Sforzinda, after his patron, consisting of an octagonal star-shaped city with streets radiating from a central market square [16.4]. Because of the political difficulties then besetting Italy, no new towns were built, although a number of urban piazzas were opened up. In 1593 such an ideal city was built when the Republic of Venice began construction of Palmanuova, a fortress city northeast of Venice to protect the exposed plain of Fruili from attack by the Turks [16.5]. Believed to have been designed by Vincenzo Scamozzi, it is a nine-pointed star, with bastions for artillery. Its nine principal radial streets and circumferential connectors, besides conforming to the ideal pattern, served the practical purpose of enabling supplies and munitions to be moved equally well from centralized storehouses to wherever they were needed.

Renaissance architects sought to shape space using modular units based on whole-number proportional relationships. The circle and the square became the basic design modules of their architecture, with the boundaries of these modules being delineated by Classical columns, arches, and entablatures derived from Roman sources. Beauty was seen to rest in the careful arrangement of proportionally related parts. The humanist scholar and theorist Leon Battista Alberti (1404–1472) offered this summary in his book *De re aedificatoria* (On Building), written about 1450: "Beauty is that reasoned harmony of all the parts within a body, so that nothing can be added, taken away, or altered, but for the worse."[8] Echoing Pythagoras, Alberti was convinced that "the very same numbers that cause sounds to have that *concinnitas,* pleasing to the ears, can also fill the eyes and mind with wondrous delight."[9]

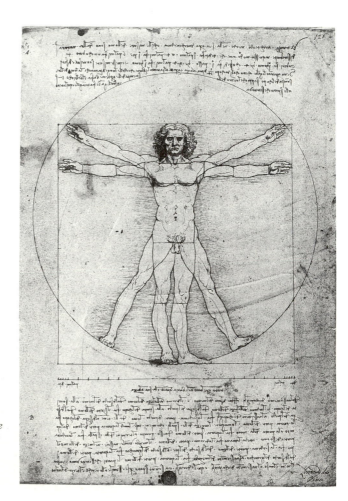

16.3. Leonardo da Vinci, drawing of the ideal Vitruvian man, c. 1485–90. For Leonardo, as for Vitruvius, the form of the human body contained within it the essence of ideal form (the perfect geometry of the circle and the square) as well as ideal proportional relationships. Leonardo reveals these in the dividing lines marked on the body.

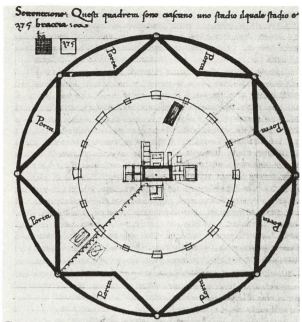

Settentrione: Questi quadretti sono ciascuno uno stadio ilquale stadio e 375 braccia : oo

I nella testa doriente Io fo lachiesa maggiore & inquella doccidente fo ilpalazzo reale lequali grandezze alpresente non tocho pche quando l

16.4. Antonio Averlino (called Filarete), plan of the ideal city of Sforzinda, from his treatise on architecture written c. 1461–62. Filarete (a name adapted from Greek, meaning "Lover of Virtue") was the first Renaissance designer to use the ideal form of the circle as the basis for a city plan.

16.5. Vincenzo Scamozzi(?), Palmanuova, Italy, begun 1593. Palmanuova was a new town, built according to the ideal circular model.

Brunelleschi and Rationally Ordered Space

The first building to demonstrate this mathematical proportioning was Brunelleschi's Foundling Hospital in Florence, designed in 1419 for his patron Giovanni de' Medici and the silk guild [16.6, 3.13]. Across the front of the building and facing the piazza, Brunelleschi created an arcade with monolithic Corinthian columns carrying the lightest of curved architraves and a stretched entablature. The columns are so proportioned that they are spaced exactly as far as they are tall, defining squares in elevation; the columns are also as far from the rear wall as they are high, thus delineating cubes in space. The delicate semicircular arches carried by the columns are half as high again, so that in terms of the length of the radius of the arch, the bays have a whole-number proportional ratio of 2:2:3.

Like nearly all other Renaissance architects, Filippo Brunelleschi (1377–1446) was trained as an artist, a master goldsmith in the silk guild, but, more unusual, he was also a scholar who read Latin. Vasari reports in his *Lives of the Artists* that Brunelleschi turned to the study of architecture after losing the competition for new bronze doors for the Florentine baptistery because he felt architecture was "more useful to mankind than either sculpture or painting."[10] While he was perfecting his constructional scheme for the cathedral dome as well as designing the Foundling Hospital, Brunelleschi also tackled the problem of developing a rational mathematical scheme for accurately depicting on a painted two-dimensional surface the arrangement of objects on real three-dimensional space—that is, the rediscovery of mathematical perspective such as Roman painters had used. Alberti was working on this problem at the same time in Rome.

Once Brunelleschi had formulated the basis of mathematical perspective, he then turned his attention to duplicating this objective order in his architecture. In 1418 he was engaged by Giovanni de' Medici to rebuild the church of San Lorenzo in Florence, beginning with a new square sacristy capped by a dome on pendentives, and then turning to reconstruction of the main vessel of the monastic church [16.7, 16.8]. His objective was to create a volume organized into cubes of space: large cubes forming the

16.6. Filippo Brunelleschi, Foundling Hospital, Florence, Italy, 1419–24. Brunelleschi used the ideal of pure circles, squares, and cubes to determine the proportions of the arcade across the front of this orphans' asylum.

choir and transept arms, with four cubes forming the naves; and with smaller cubical units, defined by dark stone Corinthian columns and pilasters, forming the side aisles.

Because he had to adapt the plan of San Lorenzo to fit among existing structures, Brunelleschi was unable to make this mathematical scheme fully coherent throughout, but in his church of Santo Spirito, begun in 1436, Brunelleschi created what he considered his most successful design, due in large part to construction in an open area unhampered by existing walls [16.9, 16.10]. The plan of the church is generated by the central cubical bay of the crossing, surmounted by a dome on pendentives. From this duplicate cubes extend to form the choir and transept arms. Each of these, in turn, is flanked by two smaller cube units forming the side aisles; each is one-fourth the volume of the larger units. From the central crossing extend four large cubical bays for the nave. Along the side aisles around the church Brunelleschi wanted to have semicircular apses (these were later filled in). Since their radius would have been one-half the width and height of the side aisle bays, what the viewer would have seen from the end of the nave would have been a series of units increasing in a proportional progression of 1:2:3:4:5, from the diameter of the side aisle apses to the height of the central nave—in other words, a fully three-dimensional representation of a building as a constructed perspective, each architectural element assigned a precise position in a rationally ordered scheme. Instead of the medieval transcendent mystical experience here was a celebration of human reason in the service of the church.

Ideal Form and the Centrally Planned Church

To theorists such as Alberti, the circle and the centralized plan generated from it were highly evocative religious symbols of the perfection of divinity. A dome, placed over the center, became the outward manifestation of this centrally focused plan. An early example of the square plan surmounted by a dome was Brunelleschi's Pazzi Chapel, 1429–46, built for the Pazzi family in the cloister court of the church of Santa Croce, Florence, but here again Brunelleschi had to modify an otherwise ideal plan to fit the chapel among the existing buildings. In 1460 Alberti devised a square plan with short arms for the church of San Sebastiano in Mantua, but construction was changed after his death and little remains today of Albert's own design.

Perhaps the clearest expression of the use of the circle and the square as generative modules is the small church of Santa Maria della Carceri by Giuliano da Sangallo (1445–1516). Built in 1485–91 in the town of Prato, eleven miles (17.7 kilometers) northwest of Florence, it is based on a square plan projected vertically into a cube [16.11, 16.12, 16.13]. Above the cube, pendentives form a circular plan from which rises a short drum and a ribbed dome, lit by twelve bull's-eye windows at the base and a lantern at its top. From the cube base half-cubes project, forming the arms of a Greek cross plan. Internally, the edges of the volume are marked by dark stone Corinthian pilasters, entablature, and architraves, sharply contrasting with the unadorned white stucco walls. Externally, each component of the interior is revealed by the stone trim attached to the brick structural wall. The outer entablature corresponds to that inside; the upper attic level corresponds to the barrel vaults over the arms; the pediments (and the central block they run into) correspond to the short drum inside carrying the dome. Consequently, the church is a rational exercise in the extrapolation of parts from the central cube module, extended by halves and semicircles in every direction; every part of the exterior announces what is to be found inside. There are no intellectual surprises but rather perfect conformity throughout to proportional harmony.

Alberti's Latin Cross Churches

In many instances the Renaissance architect did not have an open site on which to build but rather had to adapt his centralizing Classical preferences to an existing late Gothic

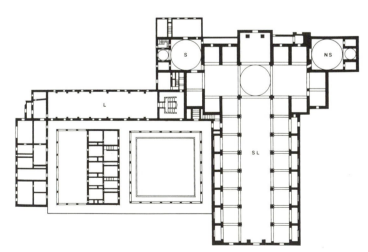

16.7. Filippo Brunelleschi,
Church of San Lorenzo,
Florence, Italy, 1418–46. View
of the nave. In rebuilding this
monastic church for the Medici
family, Brunelleschi attempted
to use mathematically pure
proportions throughout.

16.8. San Lorenzo. Plan.

L   = Library (Michelangelo)
NS = New Sacristy
      (Michelangelo)
S   = Sacristy (Brunelleschi)
SL = Church of San Lorenzo
      (Brunelleschi)

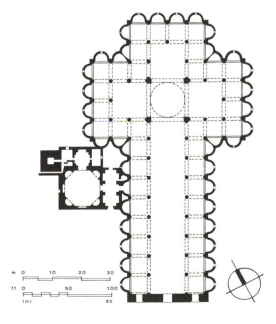

16.9. Filippo Brunelleschi, Church of Santo Spirito, Florence, Italy, 1436–82. View of the nave. Given an open site, Brunelleschi was able to realize his goal of a building completely determined by mathematical proportions.

16.10. Santo Spirito. Plan.

16.11. Giuliano da Sangallo,
Santa Maria delle Carceri,
Prato, Italy, 1485–91. Sangallo
used the proportional ideal to
construct a centralized church
generated by a square and cube
at its center.

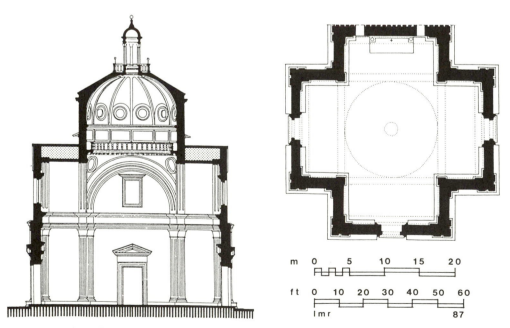

16.12. Santa Maria delle Carceri. The plan and section, viewed together with the exterior, demonstrate the exact
correspondence of part to part, inside and out, an idea central to the Renaissance concept of ideal form.

16.13. Santa Maria delle Carceri. Interior.

basilican plan. Alberti had confronted this problem in 1450–61 in putting a new exterior shell around the church of San Francesco in Rimini, a coastal city on the Adriatic ruled by Sigismondo Malatesta [16.14]. Alongside the old church walls Alberti created a deeply arcaded new wall, recalling the massiveness of the Colosseum in Rome; in the arched voids was room for ceremonial sarcophagi for members of the Malatesta court. At the end of the church Alberti devised an entry derived from Roman triumphal arches, with arches to the left and right repeating the rhythm of the arches on the side walls (these were to have been deep niches as well, containing the sarcophagi of the duke and his mistress, but out of structural necessity they had to be filled in). Between them a central arch encloses a door framed by a Classical architrave and capped by a pediment. The details throughout reveal Alberti's detailed study of Roman ruins.

Above the entry Alberti was confronted with the problem of making a graceful transition from the tall center nave to the lower side aisles with their shed roofs. Unfortunately this upper section was never finished following Alberti's design, but in a letter of November 18, 1454, to his supervising architect, Matteo de' Pasti, Alberti gives us an idea not only of what he had in mind but also the importance of proportional relationships throughout the entire scheme: "Remember and bear well in mind," Alberti instructs Matteo, "that in the model, on the right and left sides along the edge of the roof, there is a thing like this," and here he inserted a little sketch [16.15], "and I told you I am putting it there to conceal that part of the roof that will be put on inside the church. . . . You can see where the sizes and proportions of the pilasters come from; if you alter anything you will spoil all that harmony."[11] Later, in 1458–71, Alberti improved on this connection between side

16.14. Leon Battista Alberti, Church of San Francesco (the Tempio Malatestiano), Rimini, Italy, 1450–61. This new shell, wrapped around an existing medieval church, is based on Roman triumphal arches.

aisles and nave in the facade he designed for the existing church of Santa Maria Novella in Florence [16.16]. This time he used long curved volutes to make a graceful transition from the square of the upper part of the nave block to the two squares of the lower part of the facade.

Because the design was developed through correspondence with his supervising architect, the church of San Francesco at Rimini was not fully resolved in all its parts. Much more thoroughly studied was Alberti's last building, the church of Sant' Andrea in Mantua, designed in 1470 but built closely following his intentions by Luca Fancelli and finished in 1493 after Alberti's death in 1472 [16.17, 16.18, 16.19]. Once again Alberti had to deal with existing con-

ditions, fitting his new facade against the existing bell tower that could not be removed; hence the facade is a slightly reduced version of the main part of the church. But the major problem that Alberti confronted, and one that contradicted his strong predisposition for symbolic centralized plans, was that such plans simply do not accommodate the processional liturgical service of the church; for such a liturgy, the longitudinal basilican plan had long before proved itself superior. Repeatedly Renaissance architects would propose idealized centralized plans, either circular or square, only to have church officials insist on a Latin cross plan; this struggle between the ideal and the practical is documented in the dramatic pendulum swings in the designs for

16.15. Alberti, detail from letter to Matteo de' Pasti, November 18, 1454. Inserted in the text of Alberti's letter is a sketch of this detail, showing Matteo de' Pasti how to make the transition from the lower side aisles to the taller center nave.

the new Saint Peter's basilica in Rome. Thus, in Sant' Andrea, Alberti had to do what Brunelleschi had done previously in Florence: devise a scheme that was both centralized around the crossing and yet provided the focus toward the altar of a basilican plan. His solution, inspired by Brunelleschi perhaps, had the massive solidity of Roman baths instead of the lightness of San Spirito. The crossing cube extends in three barrel-vaulted wings, forming transepts and choir. On the fourth side the barrel vault is extended in three bays to form the nave. Like the heavy vaults of the Basilica of Maxentius, Alberti's coffered nave vault, 60 feet (18.3 meters) across, is supported by massive lateral piers connected by smaller barrel vaults. These buttressing side vaults cover deep chapels between the piers.

This internal organization, consisting of a nave barrel vault supported by vaulted side chapels, Alberti clearly announced in the reduced entrance facade. The facade, with its recessed entry, is also another variation on the Roman triumphal arch, with a lower Corinthian order supporting the central arch and a colossal Corinthian pilaster order carrying the broad Classical pediment. As a further demonstration of proportional design, the entire facade, from edge to edge, and from pavement to the pediment crown, neatly fits inside a square.

Bramante and the New Saint Peter's, Rome

Like Alberti, Donato Bramante (1444–1514) preferred centralized plans for religious buildings. Bramante was trained as a

16.16. Alberti, facade of Santa Maria Novella, Florence, Italy, 1458–71. In this facade design for an existing medieval church, Alberti pursued further his ideas of uniting the parts of the design by means of proportional systems.

16.17. Alberti, Sant' Andrea,
Mantua, Italy, 1470–93. Facade.
Slightly reduced in size to fit next
to the existing tower, the facade
mirrors every part of the interior
of the church and is so
proportioned that it fits into a
perfect square.

16.18. Sant' Andrea, Mantua.
Plan. Although Alberti preferred
centralized plans based on squares
and circles, here he bowed to the
wishes of the clergy and developed
a traditional Latin cross plan,
carefully proportioned and using
repeated modules. The hatched
area is the existing tower.

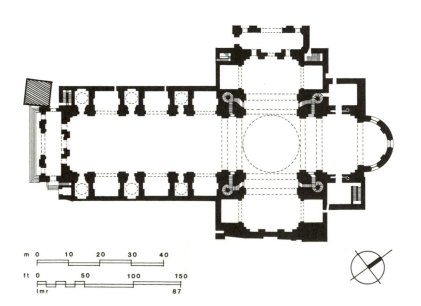

painter in Urbino but switched to designing buildings when he moved to Milan. In 1499, when the French occupied Milan, he moved to Rome, where he received the commission for a small martyrium to mark the spot where, according to one traditional account, Saint Peter had been crucified. His patrons were Ferdinand and Isabella of Spain, more widely known to posterity for their patronage of Columbus's voyages to the New World. In writing about the ideal centralized church, Alberti had used the Latin word *templum,* "temple"; Bramante took Alberti literally, deriving his martyrium for Saint Peter from such round peripteral Roman temples at that at Tivoli. The result was the Tempietto (Little Temple) in the cloister of San Pietro in Montorio, Rome, 1500–1502 [16.20]. Bramante carefully proportioned the Tempietto so that its overall height to the base of the dome is equal to its width, and the ratio of width to height in the encircling Doric colonnade is repeated in the width to height of the drum of the dome. The Doric columns were reused

Roman artifacts, but the frieze was designed by Bramante after that of the Temple of Vespasian, with the instruments of pagan ritual in the Roman model transmuted into instruments of the Mass and papal symbols. Hence, in form, proportion, and ornamental detail, the diminutive building recalls Roman architecture at its purest, re-created and reshaped in the service of the church.

With the election of Giuliano della Rovere as Pope Julius II in 1503, an aggressive and vigorous humanism was introduced to the papal court. Besides consolidating his temporal power in the Papal States, Julius II had great ambitions for Rome as the queen city of the church, ending its medieval slumber and giving it something of the glory it had displayed in antiquity. Throughout the city stood the mammoth ruins of pagan Rome, rising proud if rather dilapidated over the medieval city that had shriveled in upon itself. The venerable Constantinian basilicas built nearly twelve centuries before had been in constant use and had withstood the onslaughts of successive invaders. Chief

16.19. Sant' Andrea, Mantua. The nave is covered by a massive brick barrel vault with deep coffers, recalling Roman baths.

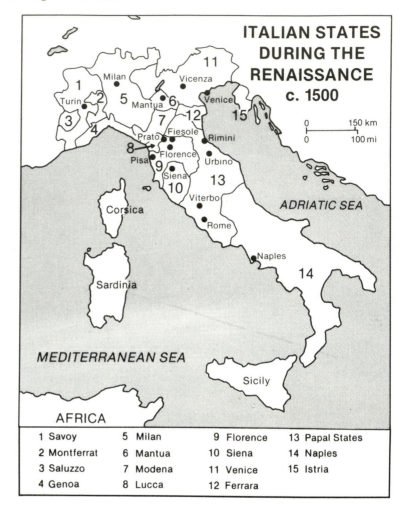

ITALIAN STATES DURING THE RENAISSANCE c. 1500

1 Savoy	5 Milan	9 Florence	13 Papal States
2 Montferrat	6 Mantua	10 Siena	14 Naples
3 Saluzzo	7 Modena	11 Venice	15 Istria
4 Genoa	8 Lucca	12 Ferrara	

of these, and next to the papal palace on the Vatican Hill west of the Tiber and thus outside the actual city of Rome, was the great pilgrimage basilica of Saint Peter's.

Gathered in Rome at this time were humanist artists of the highest caliber—the sculptor Michelangelo, the young painter Raphael Santi, and Bramante, his uncle. Julius II resolved to put them to work rebuilding the papal possessions according to the new vision of human power, a testament to the glory of God as well as to the power of the papacy. He sent Michelangelo up the scaffold in the Vatican chapel built by his uncle Pope Sixtus IV (the Sistine Chapel) to paint the ceiling frescoes. Raphael was assigned to paint frescoes in

the papal apartments, depicting the victory of humanist theology. And in 1504 Bramante was appointed to design and build a new Saint Peter's, bigger than Constantine's church, embodying the ideals of the new architecture and proclaiming the power of an invigorated Christianity while surpassing the achievement of pagan antiquity.

Bramante devised a plan for a vast martyrium, providing for a gigantic dome over the crypt of Saint Peter's burial and the apse of Constantine's basilica [16.21, 16.22]. The dome was to be 136 feet (41.5 meters) in diameter, nearly equal in size to that of the ancient Pantheon but raised far higher. Instead of resting on a massive ring wall, this dome was to be lifted aloft on four moulded

16.20. Donato Bramante, Tempietto of San Pietro in Montorio, Rome, 1500–2. Originally planned to be surrounded by a circular arcade, this little temple uses pagan Roman forms and motifs to proclaim the importance of Saint Peter as founder of the Christian church in Rome.

corner piers and pendentives, its outward thrust transmitted to the barrel vaults radiating out from the pendentives between the piers. Around the four central piers would run an ambulatory connecting with four vast chapels on the axes of the arches. In the corners of the vast square plan were to be auxiliary chapels. Bramante's scheme, inspired by a drawing in one of Leonardo da Vinci's sketchbooks that Bramante may well have seen in Milan, combined the clear logical form of the Greek cross with Roman barrel vaults and hemispherical domes. Circles and squares, cubes and hemispheres were nested together and wrapped around each other in a huge pyramidal pile. Altogether the church would have been roughly 528

feet (161 meters) square, and Bramante may have intended to create an even larger, paved square piazza around the church. Clearly this was a project to rival in scale those of the Romans. Construction began on the piers of the great dome in 1505, when Bramante was sixty-one years of age; when he died, in 1514, only the piers, the barrel vaults connecting the piers, and the lower portions of the radiating walls had been completed [16.23].

Such a project was enormously expensive, and to finance it Julius had authorized the sale of papal indulgences. These indulgences had been first granted in 1343 by Pope Clement VI, who declared that because of the great piety of the religious during the

16.21. *Bramante, San Pietro in Vaticano (the new Saint Peter's), Rome, 1504–14. The medal, struck by Cristoforo Caradosso when the foundations of Bramante's church were laid, records the original design. Bramante proposed a huge martyrium with an elevated dome nearly as big as that of the Roman Pantheon.*

16.22. *Bramante, Saint Peter's, Rome. Plan. The simple scheme of Saint Peter's has a central square surmounted by a dome, surrounded by an ambulatory passage, apses at the ends of the crossed axes, and towers at the four corners.*

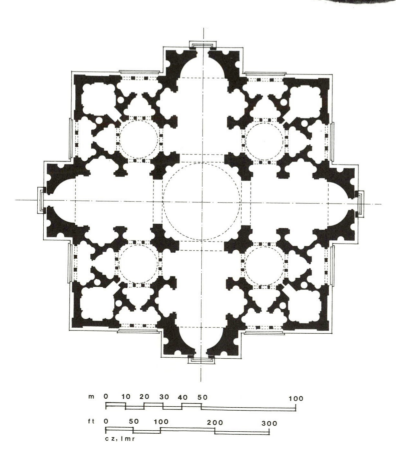

m   0   10 20 30 40 50   100

ft   0   50   100   200   300

c z, l m r

early years of the church, a heavenly "treasury of merit" had accumulated. Those who feared eternal damnation could obtain some of this merit through a papal indulgence by doing good works; later this was changed to giving alms. In time this practice deteriorated to the outright sale of indulgences. In Germany, where the indulgences were vigorously hawked by Johannes Tetzel, an agent specially hired for the purpose, such flagrant abuses prompted a Franciscan monk to question the sale and post ninety-five theses for debate on the door of the castle church of Wittenberg on October 31, 1517. The monk was Martin Luther and that act immediately polarized German princes, many of whom wished to be freed of papal control. Wishing only to argue for reform within the church, Luther succeeded instead in setting off the Reformation, splintering Christianity into argumentative factions.

The popes who followed Julius II (who died in 1513 and thus was spared seeing how his architectural project split the church) had to deal with this problem, the most serious the church had faced since the split with the Eastern Orthodox (Greek) Church. There were external threats as well, particularly the invasion of Italy by German troops of the Holy Roman Emperor, who sacked Rome in 1527. Consequently, after 1517 there was little construction on the new basilica; the new portions stood only partly constructed, and the old Constantinian fragments remained only partly demolished.

Under succeeding popes and their selected architects, Bramante's centralized plan was changed on paper, first into a more traditional longitudinal basilica and then returned to some variant of a centralized plan, and this ambivalence continued for decades. Not until the election of Alessandro Farnese as Pope Paul III in 1547 was

16.23. *Maerten van Heemskerck, drawing of Saint Peter's under construction, c. 1532–35. The Dutch artist van Heemskerck visited Rome when building on Saint Peter's was temporarily halted; he recorded these views of the arches silhouetted against the sky.*

work seriously resumed, when new plans were prepared by the aged Michelangelo. Perhaps Michelangelo's training as a sculptor, as someone familiar with the weight of stone, enabled him to see the flaws in Bramante's original design; it had far too much volume and height and far too little mass to support the huge elevated dome. Michelangelo pulled in the walls, thickening them and creating a tighter and more solid perimeter to the plan [16.24]. He also made another important change, for although he retained the sense of a centralized plan with four arms of equal length, he proposed making one of them the entry by ending it in a huge colonnaded temple front, thereby creating a sense of ambiguity—was the design centralized or not? Under his direction the western walls were built, organized with immense Corinthian pilasters whose scale defies comprehension [4.16]. Michelangelo's dome was finished in 1585–90, after his death, by Giacomo della Porta and the engineer Domenico Fontana, but the church was still not finished, for the east end stood incomplete and the approach toward the building had not yet been made clear; these tasks would be undertaken by later architects in the Baroque period.

Residential Architecture—Merchant Prince Palaces

The Palazzo de' Medici

In prosperous mercantile Florence a new standard of urban residential design, sponsored by the rising merchant princes, replaced the cramped houses of the fourteenth century with large residences of Classical grace. In 1444 Cosimo de' Medici proposed to build a large residence for his family, with space on the ground floor to accommodate his business offices. It was to be located on the via Larga, then at the edge of town. At first Cosimo had Brunelleschi prepare a model of the new house, but the design was so novel and imposing that Cosimo rejected it, fearing it would excite his townsmen to envy. As Vasari reports, Brunelleschi was so furious he smashed the model "to smithereens."[12] Cosimo then engaged a more conservative architect, Michelozzo di Bartolommeo (1396–1472). The palazzo that Michelozzo designed combined the sobriety of traditional medieval Florentine residences with a sense of gravity and proportion, and attention to Classical Roman detail [16.25, 16.26]. The rusticated joints of the masonry was a gesture to local

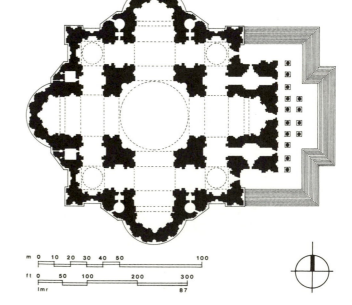

16.24. Michelangelo Buonarroti, Saint Peter's, Rome, 1547–90. Plan. In comparison to Bramante's plan, Michelangelo's is denser and provides more support for the dome; it also deviates from Bramante's strict centrality by providing for an entrance portico on the east side.

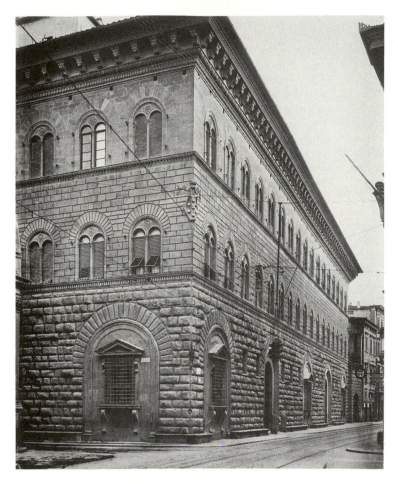

16.25. Michelozzo di Bartolommeo, Palazzo Medici, Florence, Italy, 1444–60. Although the heaviness of the palazzo and the window details were derived from earlier Florentine city houses, the careful proportioning of parts and the massive classical cornice show Michelozzo's study of antiquity.

16.26. Palazzo Medici. Plan.

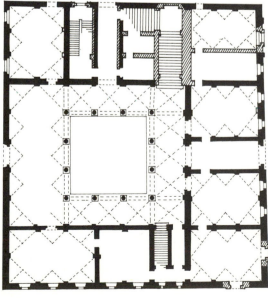

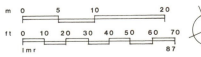

tradition, but the graduation from rough quarry-faced masonry on the ground level, to channeled joints in the middle floor, to a perfectly smooth surface in the upper floor was new. Also modern was the massive cornice, adapted from ancient Roman models; it was decidedly Classical and proportioned to the overall height of the building, as though associated with an invisible order of pilasters or engaged columns. Inside, the rooms were arranged around a central court, which opened up at the bottom through an encircling arcade of delicate Corinthian columns. Appearing quiet and empty in modern photographs, the court then was alive with the comings and goings of clients and family members, artists and writers Cosimo supported, and it was ornamented with ancient statuary and such contemporary sculptures as Donatello's heroic *David*.

The Palazzo Rucellai

A more radical departure in facade design was made by the theorist Alberti in his remodeling of the Palazzo Rucellai, begun about 1452 [16.27]. Giovanni Rucellai, whose fortune derived from making *oricello,* the red dye for which Florence was famous and from which the family name derived, purchased the houses adjoining his birthplace at the corner of the via della Vigna and the via del Palchetto. Alberti was asked to design a new facade, unifying the combined properties. Wishing to give a sense of modular order to the traditional rusticated Florentine wall, Alberti superimposed three orders of pilasters, as the Romans had done in the orders applied to the Theater of Marcellus in Rome and the Colosseum, with Tuscan Doric on the bottom, a variant of Ionic in the middle, and a

16.27. Leon Battista Alberti, Palazzo Rucellai, Florence, Italy, begun c. 1452. Alberti based his facade (a remodeling of existing houses) on Roman sources, using superimposed pilasters to create a varied rhythm and to visually support the crowning cornice.

16.28. *Antonio da Sangallo the Younger (and Michelangelo), Palazzo Farnese, Rome, 1515–59. This palazzo, a regal and imposing residence befitting the status of newly elected Pope Paul III, brings to subtle perfection the ideas and forms used by Alberti in the Palazzo Rucellai.*

loosely interpreted Corinthian at the top. The entablatures of the orders serve as bases for the surmounting pilasters and windows, and the uppermost pilasters carry a large cornice proportioned roughly to the height of the building. The pedestal base at the street is rusticated to suggest Roman *opus reticulatum* concrete. Thus Alberti combined selected traditional elements with the new interest in Roman architecture and a logical reuse of Classical orders to create a proportioned module across the facade.

The Palazzo Farnese

The sense of balance, repose, and order was maintained and developed in subsequent urban palazzi, as illustrated in the immense Palazzo Farnese begun in 1515 by the architect Antonio da Sangallo the Younger (1485–1546) for Cardinal Alessandro Far-

nese before he became Pope Paul III [16.28]. By the early sixteenth century, Rome had become a center of power again, and princes of the church vied to display their importance through imposing architectural projects. The Palazzo Farnese was one such example, surpassing anything done in Rome. Cardinal Farnese held enormous power in the Vatican, having a retinue of three hundred persons. Following his election to the papacy as Paul III in 1534, he had Sangallo enlarge the palazzo, then still under construction. Eventually the third floor of the facade and much of the rear of the palazzo was completed during 1547–59 by Michelangelo, who modified the third-floor design.

The Villas of Palladio

By the time Michelangelo had finished the third floor of the Palazzo Farnese in 1559,

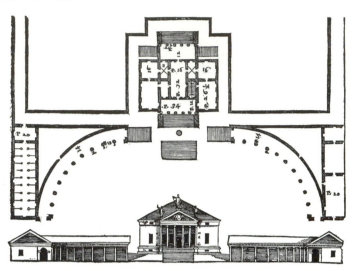

16.29. Andrea Palladio, Villa
Badoer, Fratta Polesine, Italy,
begun 1556. Basing his theories on
studies of music, Palladio designed
his farm villas using proportional
number systems, shown clearly in
the dimensions he noted on the
plans published in his Four Books
of Architecture.

Renaissance architecture as the clear and intellectual expression of form through simple mathematical proportions was being replaced with a more subtle and complicated idiom called Mannerism (discussed below). Nonetheless, one architect working in the mid-sixteenth century in the region of the Veneto, the area north and west of Venice, continued to exploit the simple cubic volumes and elemental forms of the early Renaissance. He was Andrea Palladio (1508–1580), one of the few architects of this period to be trained as a builder; it was later in his life that he was given a humanist education in the classics, with the support of his patron, Giangiorgio Trissino. During his career he built public buildings and urban palazzi in his adopted city, Vicenza, two important churches in Venice, and finally the Teatro Olimpico in Vicenza. But in numbers alone, the buildings Palladio designed the most were farm villas, producing more than forty around Venice and Vicenza.

Early in the sixteenth century, desiring to make their finances more secure, Venetian nobles used funds made in commerce to buy up and reclaim low-lying marshy lands that had been unproductive for centuries. Palladio was commissioned to design numerous working farms for these lands, and he devised a variety of plans, simple in layout, proportionally composed, and yet

functionally practical. The Villa Badoer at Fratta Polesine, 37 miles (60 kilometers) southwest of Venice, begun in 1556, exemplifies in plan the practical use of curved Classical colonnades to connect the stables and storage sheds with the main house and the exploitation of whole number proportional systems in the sizes of the rooms [16.29]. In nearly all of these villas, Palladio incorporated a temple front, because he believed that Romans had adapted that form from their early houses and, desiring to emulate the ancients, he "restored" the colonnaded portico to the private house.

His best known and most imitated villa was not strictly a working farm but more a suburban retreat for Paolo Almerico, a retired papal court official, just outside the city of Vicenza. Palladio in fact used the word suburbana to describe its location in the book he published of his own work, I Quatro libri dell' architettura (Venice, 1570), the Four Books of Architecture. This was the Villa Capra, called the Villa Rotonda because it focused not on a single entrance facade but on a cylindrical rotunda at the center capped by a dome visibly poking through the roof [16.30, 6.11]. The use of a dome in a private residence was a novel departure on the part of Palladio, for up to this time such a form, symbolizing the heavens and divinity, had been reserved for churches. The house was, as Palladio wrote, not strictly a villa but a *belvedere,* an elevated pavilion designed to offer views over the surrounding countryside. From the central rotunda passages extend to the temple porticoes on each of the four sides of the square house, so that even from the center of the house one can view the pastoral landscape. In its symmetry, and the proud way it is lifted up on the hill surveying the landscape below, the Villa Capra summarizes the confident spirit of the Renaissance and its ideal of a rational, intelligible order superimposed on nature. At the center of it all—quite literally in this case, at the focus of the domed rotunda—stands man, the "measure and measurer of all things." Palladio almost literally translated into architectural forms Pico's "Oration," for the human being is indeed set "at the world's center that thou mayest from thence more easily observe whatever is in the world."

Mannerism— The Renaissance in Transition

Classical order in Florentine architecture appeared in 1418 in the work of Brunelleschi. By the time Bramante had completed the Tempietto in 1502, Renaissance architecture had achieved a clarity of form and precision in the adaptive reuse of Classical architectural forms that is called the High Renaissance. The goal of this architecture was purity, a state of absolute balance and rational order. Yet once this state of perfection was achieved in such designs as Bramante's Tempietto and the new Saint Peter's—once the rules had been set down—they were quickly flouted in favor of variations on the rules, deviations from the established norm. In their restless quest of innovation, Renaissance architects were not content to stop their manipulation of form once the rules had been defined. The result was that High Renaissance architecture lasted less than half a century before it was replaced, about 1530, by a subtle tension and a willful playfulness in design known as Mannerism. It is also possible that the artists' deliberate rejection of High Renaissance pure form was a cynical reaction to the sack of Rome in 1527. The sense of universal order and rationality so carefully nurtured during the fifteenth century was suddenly swept away, and artists found an escape in exercising their fancy and rejecting formal discipline.

One artist whose work dramatically il-

16.30. Palladio, Villa Capra (Villa Rotonda), outside Vicenza, Italy, begun c. 1550. Taking advantage of the elevated setting, Palladio gave this villa four identical facades opening out to the countryside, all governed by a system of proportional relationships.

lustrates this change is Michelangelo Buonarroti (1475–1564). Michelangelo's later architecture is built up of ambiguous and complex forms. His revised design for Saint Peter's, for example, was both centralized and yet also had an emphasized portico entrance. His replanning of the Capitoline Hill in Rome, the Campidoglio, conceived as early as 1536 and built during the mid-sixteenth century, gave a measure of order to the irregular geometry of the existing buildings. In the new facades and buildings he added, Michelangelo shaped a trapezoidal space, in the center of which is not an ideal and unequivocal circle but an oval drawn in the paving [16.31]. His Medici Chapel, added to San Lorenzo in Florence, 1520–26, has blank windows whose crown-

ing pediments (carried by brackets, not pilasters) are squeezed into their allotted space between paired pilasters [16.32]. His staircase, providing entrance into his library at San Lorenzo, 1558–71 [16.33, 16.34, 16.35], has pairs of muscular Tuscan Doric columns recessed into niches in the wall. Instead of bearing down on substantial pedestal bases, the heavy pairs of columns appear to be carried by light, curved scrolls attached to the wall. In the center of the room the staircase has three parallel flights (which one to choose?), which fan out toward the bottom, creating a perspective illusion of depth greater than there truly is. The staircase is thus made a major element of the experience of this space, in direct contradiction to Alberti's explicit instruc-

16.31. Michelangelo, Capitoline Hill (Campidoglio), Rome, designed 1536. Intended to give new civic importance to the heart of ancient and medieval Rome, Michelangelo's Campidoglio incorporated new facades in front of existing buildings to enclose a trapezoidal space reinforcing a processional axis.

16.32. *Michelangelo, Medici Chapel in San Lorenzo, Florence, Italy, 1520–26. Designed to complement the sacristy added to San Lorenzo by Brunelleschi, this was to hold the tombs of the Medici family members. In addition to the sculpture of the tombs, the walls were filled with invented architectural ornament.*

16.33. Michelangelo, staircase, Library of San Lorenzo, Florence, Italy, 1558–71. The tiny room accommodating the staircase up to Michelangelo's library is crammed with dark, massive architectural elements contrasted to the white walls.

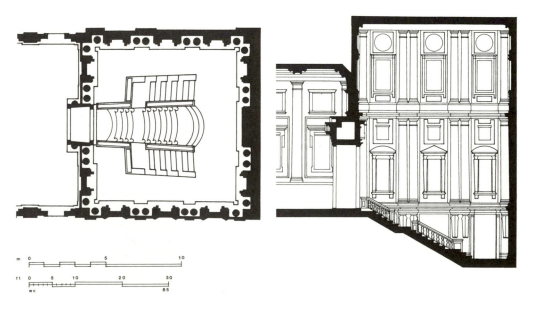

16.34. Staircase, Library of San Lorenzo. Plan.   *16.35. Staircase, Library of San Lorenzo. Section.*

tions in his *De re aedificatoria:* "The fewer staircases in a building and the less room they take up, the less of an inconvenience they will be."[13] In every one of Michelangelo's architectural designs what appear at first to be standard Classical architectural elements are in fact used in defiance of the conventions of Classical design, for Michelangelo was manipulating them as elements in gigantic sculpture. Vasari, who knew Michelangelo well, recounted that in the work at San Lorenzo "he did the ornamentation in a composite order, in a style more varied and more original than any other master, ancient or modern, has ever been able to achieve. . . . He departed a great deal from the kind of architecture regulated by proportion, order, and rule which other artists did according to common usage and following Vitruvius and the works of antiquity but from which Michelangelo wanted to break away."[14]

In Mannerist planning the circle was replaced by the oval as a governing modular device, beginning with Michelangelo's Piazza del Campidoglio. The ambiguity of the oval typifies the Mannerist method of design. It is at the same time centered and yet suggests two foci; it is round and yet has one major and one minor axis. Giacomo Barozzi da Vignola used the oval in two small Roman churches, first in Sant' Andrea in the via Flaminia, 1550–54, only 28 feet (8.5 meters) across the short dimension, and then in the slightly larger Sant' Anna dei Palafrenieri, begun about 1565 [16.36].

The Palazzo del Te

The playfulness of Mannerist architecture is perhaps most evident in the Palazzo del Te, 1525–32, built just outside Mantua for Duke Federigo Gonzaga by Giulio Romano (c. 1492–1546). It was to house the duke's well-known stud farm and to provide a pleasant suburban retreat. Having a relatively open site, Giulio Romano spread the building out, placing the living quarters in one principal level in a large square around a spacious central court (Giulio Romano was obliged, however, to incorporate portions of a building that already stood on the

site). The exterior masonry of the one story building is deeply rusticated and has heavy pilasters, which correspond to no upper load at all; since the pilasters are disposed in different rhythms on each wall they create odd combinations when they meet at the corners. Toward the garden, the existing building was faced with new, arcaded bays that give the initial impression of being identical in their constituent elements but which, on closer inspection, turn out to differ in each bay [4.18; see the discussion of this building in Chapter 4].

But the most dramatic flouting of the Classical orders is in the court [16.37]. There the rustication is even more pronounced, and the pilasters have been transformed into more emphatic, engaged Tuscan Doric columns. In the wide bays are windows (some of them blind) capped by what appear to be triangular pediments, yet the bottom cornice of the pediment is missing, and instead of being supported by pilasters, the parts of the pediment are carried by brackets. Inside the would-be pediment, the keystone of the flat arch of the window swells to fill completely the available space. Above the entrances to the court are larger pediments, also carried by brack-

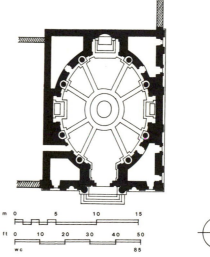

16.36. *Giacomo Barozzi da Vignola, Church of Santa Anna dei Palafrenieri, Rome, begun c. 1565. Plan. Vignola was among the first architects to turn away from the circle as a generating form for buildings, using instead the more ambiguous oval.*

16.37. *Palazzo del Te. In the inner court, architectural elements are exaggerated, some are missing altogether, and what should be a straight architrave beam has keystones slipping out of place.*

16.38. *Giulio Romano, house of the architect, Mantua, Italy, 1544. In this design, too, what appears at first to be in accordance with the rules of design is full of omissions, changes, and invention.*

ets, their bottom cornices replaced by huge keystones pushing up from the arch below. Resting on the engaged columns, where there should be straight entablatures, are what appear to be flat arches, and as a kind of architectural joke the keystones seem to be slipping out of place. In fact, inside the palazzo, Giulio Romano painted highly illusionistic frescoes that show the building falling down around the observer.

Giulio Romano enjoyed the full support of the duke, who paid him handsomely, making possible the construction of Romano's own house in Mantua in 1544. The facade is similarly filled with unorthodox architectural gamesmanship [16.38]. The masonry is again rusticated, the surfaces of the stones having the appearance of having been worm-eaten, what is called *vermiculated.* The windows of the basement were designed to disappear below the street without a base line. What should be a sill course, or molding, just above the ground-floor windows is displaced by the large voussoirs of the flat arches, so the molding reads instead as a dotted line across the facade. Another molding, or belt course, with a most unusual profile, marks the line between floors and serves as the base line for the upper windows, but in the center it is heaved up over the central door by the entrance arch to suggest an incomplete pediment. Within the arcade of the upper floor are inset windows framed with architraves of novel design, missing the bottom cornice of their crowning pediments. And the entablature that brings the entire composition to an end is resting on nothing more than the oversized keystones of the arches below. There is hardly one element in the Classical vocabulary that Giulio Romano has not willfully changed in detail or violated in some way, and yet the effect is subtle; only a person who knew the rules of Classical design would grasp the irony and whimsy of Giulio Romano's facade.

Late Renaissance Gardens

The other area in which Mannerist designers excelled, preparing the way for artists in the Baroque period, was garden design.

Landscape architecture had been revived early in the fifteenth century as another manifestation of Classical civilization. The new gardens were inspired by the villas described by Scipio, Cicero, and Horace, and especially by the two villas that Pliny the Younger described at length in his *Letters*. Early Renaissance gardens, as in the villas of the Medici, were usually orthogonal grids of planted beds (parterres), delineated by gravel walks and disposed in one or more flat terraces. The increasing subtlety and variety of Mannerist architecture finds its landscape parallel in the Villa Lante at Bagnaia, a small village five miles east of Viterbo about thirty-seven miles (60 kilometers) north of Rome. Towards the end of the fifteenth century the woods on the hill above the village were enclosed by Cardinal Raphael Riario, bishop of Viterbo, as a summer retreat. The present villa was developed by Cardinal Gambara, then bishop of Viterbo, beginning in 1566; it was finished by Cardinal Montalto by 1590. After 1875 it was in the charge of the Lante family. Who precisely was the designer is not known, but Vignola is one possible candidate.

The plan of the Villa Lante exploits the sloping topography [16.39, 16.40]. At the lowest point, next to the village, is a large square terrace with twelve planted beds around its perimeter and a fountain at the center. West of this the land rises sharply, and the visitor ascends ramped and angled stairs between twin casinos that frame the central controlling axis. Behind these casinos are further terraces, reached by stairs built into the retaining walls. Each terrace is progressively more enclosed, planted with larger trees and having a denser canopy. The uppermost terraces also are more restricted in size, with a water chain (a long narrow cascade) spilling down the axis. At the top of the hill is a small pavilion covering a grotto, from which the water issues; all the lower cascades and fountains are fed by the water that pours forth here. Around this uppermost pavilion the trees and shrubs are wilder in form, so that the garden terraces proceed from the most cultivated at the lower lever to the most primitive at the top. All of this graduation and shift in detail is

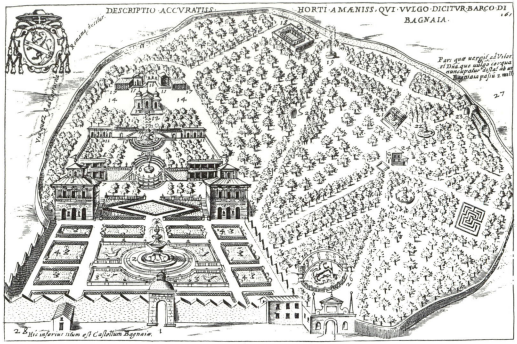

16.39. *Villa Lante (attributed to Vignola), Bagnaia, near Viterbo, Italy, begun 1566. Aerial perspective.*

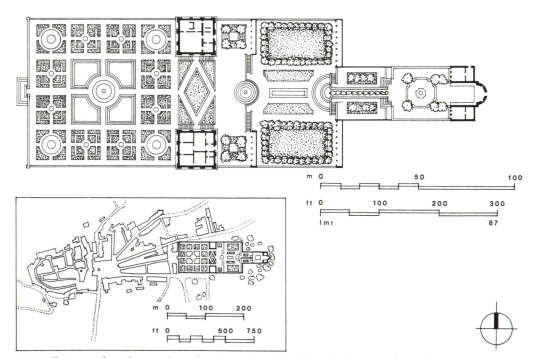

16.40. *Villa Lante. Plan. The inset shows the relationship of the villa to the adjoining village of Bagnaia.*

contained in an area no more than 756 feet (230.3 meters) long and 250 feet (76 meters) wide at the widest, easily comprehensible and toured in a single afternoon (although well worth much longer stays).

More complex and larger in scale is the Villa d'Este, designed for Cardinal Ippolito d'Este at the ancient resort of Tivoli in the hills sixteen miles (25 kilometers) east of Rome. The general design of the site, nearly 700 feet (213 meters) square, was devised about 1550 by Pirrio Ligorio; the hydraulic engineer who diverted water from the Aniene River for the waterworks was Orazio Olivieri, and the famous waterworks themselves were designed by Tommaso da Siena [16.41]. Here, too, the land was rugged, rising sharply on the southeast and northeast sides, and the garden design exploited the changes in elevation for dramatic fountains. Running on an axis extending northwest from the rather plain villa building, the gardens are laid out in terraces descending to a

large parterre on the northwest side. This is divided into the more traditional square planted beds, but on approaching from the southeast the visitor passes one cross axis after another. At the southerly edge of the large terrace is a major cross axis, called the Terrace of the Hundred Fountains, for its retaining walls are lined with hundreds of jets in cascading rows [16.42]. At each end of the walk are focal points marked by large fountains.

Perhaps even Petrarch, who ventured up Mount Ventoux solely for the pleasure of the view, would have been surprised at the sensual pleasures such gardens thrust upon their visitors, for every sense was touched, by the color of clipped plant materials, the sound of wind and water, the feel of moss and stone, the scent of shrub and blossom, and the taste of the water. Such captivating examples of the Italians' mastery of natural elements were much admired by ambassadors of the French king to the papal court,

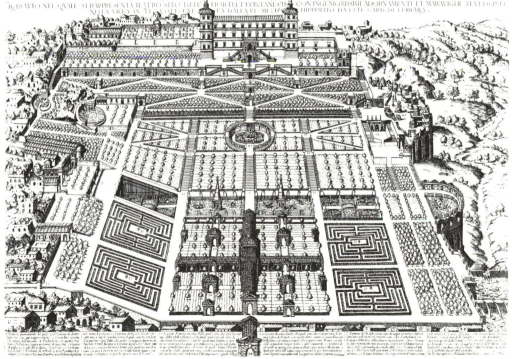

16.41. Pirrio Ligorio, Orazio Olivieri, and Tommaso da Siena, Villa d'Este, Tivoli, Italy, begun c. 1550. This garden takes advantage of the rugged landscape for the creation of terraces and innumerable fountains; such Mannerist designs provided a total sensory experience.

16.42. Terrace of the Hundred Fountains, Villa d'Este.

and would soon inspire garden architecture in France.

The Renaissance Exported

The use of Classical details and of Renaissance architectural ideals had begun to move beyond Italy by the end of the fifteenth century. One of the most important agents in this diffusion was the printing press, as architectural treatises aimed at both patron and practicing architect began to appear in growing numbers.[15] The crucial *Ten Books on Architecture* by the Roman architect Vitruvius appeared in Latin versions in 1486, in an illustrated edition in 1511, was translated into the vernacular Italian in 1521, and then was translated into other European languages. Alberti's *De re aedificatoria* was published in 1485, followed by translations into Italian, French, and Spanish during the following century. Sebastiano Serlio began to produce practical and popular books on Renaissance design in 1537; eventually this series grew to seven volumes, of which the last was published in 1575, after his death. Giacomo Barozzi da Vignola's *Rules of the Five Orders* appeared in Italian in 1562 [6.10]. Palladio's *Four Books on Architecture* was published in 1570: an English translation in 1715 set off a Palladian revival in England and its American colonies [6.11].

But direct contact also spread the new architecture. Due to numerous military expeditions into Italy, the French monarch Francis I was acquainted with contemporary developments there. In fact, a number of Italian artists and architects decided that political conditions were so unsettled at home that they accepted invitations to work in France. The best known of these artists is Leonardo da Vinci, who was supported by Francis I in his last years, but among the architects who moved to France was Serlio, who was commissioned to work on the royal château at Fontainebleau and who published several of his volumes in France.

When the Renaissance first appeared outside Italy, it was always fused with national building forms that grew out of the building traditions of the Middle Ages. But in each country this took on a particular and recognizable character. In Germany and the Netherlands, small-scale Classical details were applied to the vertically oriented urban houses, with their distinctive stepped gables fronting on the street. In Spain, particularly in the southerly provinces just recently won back from the Islamic Moors, small-scale Classical ornamentation was clustered in dense profusion around central doors and windows, continuing in different form the Moorish tendency toward intricate ornamental patterns. In England, fortified country houses were opened up to walls of glass and overlaid with loosely interpreted engaged columns and entablatures. A good example is Wollaton Hall, Nottinghamshire, 1580–88. It was designed by the master mason Robert Smythson for Sir Francis Willoughby, sheriff of Nottinghamshire, in anticipation of official visits by Queen Elizabeth. Its medieval antecedents are evident, but the exterior is covered with Classical details that stress the horizontal layers.

In France, too, generic medieval forms were encrusted with Classical details, as can be seen in the royal château at Chambord, on a branch of the Loire River about ninety-seven miles (160 kilometers) southeast of Paris. It was begun for Francis I in 1519 and was built c. 1520–50. As with Wollaton Hall, the plan of Chambord clearly reflects medieval military forms, with a lower enclosure and a tall keep tower. Every section is capped by its own steep roof form, especially the round towers, with their pointed cones. The overall design was by the relo-

cated Italian architect Domenico da Cortona, while the construction was supervised by the French master mason Pierre Nepveu. Significant for the future was the extension of the axis of the château out into the vast hunting park of more than 13,000 acres (5,261 hectares).

Gradually, as the Renaissance matured in northern Europe, building forms tended to become more austere and more carefully studied in the proportion and placement of Classical details. The national forms, however, never entirely disappeared. The mature Renaissance in England is well represented by the Banqueting House, 1619–22, designed by Inigo Jones as an addition to the royal palace at Whitehall, then just outside London [16.43]. Retaining the nearly flat roof hidden behind a balustrade, it shows Jones' close study of the work of Palladio. In addition to the carefully proportioned engaged orders (Tuscan Doric below and Ionic above), the building is so proportioned that the single internal room, used for state banquets, formal receptions, and court masques, had the form of a perfect double cube. The comparable French example would be the Château de Maisons, built outside Paris in 1642–46 for René de

16.43. Inigo Jones, *Banqueting House, Palace at Whitehall, London, 1619–22.*

16.44. François Mansart, Château de Maisons, Maisons, near Paris, 1642–46. Although the forms have been clarified and the classical details thoroughly mastered, the separation of pavilions and wall segments remains, and the pavilions are capped by tall roofs that soon came to bear the architect's name (spelled "mansard" in English).

Longueil by François Mansart [16.44]. The separate masses of the building are still evident (although the round corner towers have now become flattened corner pavilions), and each has its own steep roof contributing to a picturesque skyline. As in Jones's Banqueting House, the Classical details are used sparingly to accentuate the precise portioning of the parts of the building, inside and out.

An Architecture of Humanist Ideals

The humanist scholar architects of the Renaissance, most of them trained as painters or sculptors, sought to create a new architecture cleansed of the mystical hierarchy of what they liked to call the crude work of the Goths. The new architecture was to be rationally comprehensible, formed of planes and spaces organized according to clear numerical proportions, its edges and intervals delineated by the crisp elements of the ancient architectural orders. It was to be a celebration of human intellectual powers, but it was also an architecture that invited pleasurable human response, and once that door to sensory delight was open there was no holding it shut. Indeed, political and religious developments during the sixteenth century soon demanded that Italian painters, sculptors, and architects create a new fusion of the arts, with the explicit purpose of exciting the emotions and reinvigorating religious mysticism. The Classical elements of column, entablature, pediment, and arch remained, but the intellectual formal clarity was replaced with a new sensualism. This change was only hinted at in Mannerist whimsy; shortly it would be transformed into full-blown Baroque theatricality.

NOTES

1. Giorgio Vasari, a student of Michelangelo, wrote *Vite de' più eccellenti architetti, pittori e scultori italiani* during 1546 to 1550. See the edited version, trans. George Bull, *Lives of the Artists* (Baltimore, 1965). The concept of the Renaissance is discussed in Erwin Panofsky, *Renaissance and Renascences in Western Art* (Stockholm, 1960).

2. Giovanni Pico della Mirandola, "Oration on the Dignity of Man," trans. Elizabeth L. Forbes, in Ernst Cassirer et al., eds., *The Renaissance Philosophy of Man* (Chicago,

1948), 224–25. The quotations in Pico's text reveal his knowledge of Greek and Latin sources. Also included in this anthology are selections by Francesco Petrarch (such as his account of the ascent of Mount Ventoux), Marsilio Fincio, and others.

3. Pico, "Oration," 225, 227.
4. The intriguing story of Brunelleschi's solution to the Florence dome dilemma is told in detail in E. Battisti, *Filippo Brunelleschi* (New York, 1981); and in F. D. Prager and G. Scaglia, *Brunelleschi: Studies of His Technology and Inventions* (Cambridge, Mass.,1970).
5. Plato, *Philebus,* trans. B. Jowett (Oxford, 1953), 610–11.
6. Vitruvius, *Ten Books on Architecture,* trans. Morris H. Morgan (Cambridge, Mass., 1914), 73.
7. Galileo, quoted in E. A. Burtt, *The Metaphysical Foundations of Modern Physical Science* (Garden City, N.Y., 1954), 75.
8. Leon Battista Alberti, *De re aedificatoria: On the Art of Building in Ten Books,* trans. J. Rykwert et al. (Cambridge,Mass.,1988),VI.ii.
9. Alberti, *De re aedificatoria,* IX.v.
10. Vasari, *Lives of the Artists,* trans. G. Bull 139. Vasari drew much of his information from the contemporary biography of Brunelleschi by Antonio Manetti, written about 1448–49 shortly after the architect's death. Manetti described Brunelleschi as the innovator of "true architecture." See the translation in Elizabeth Gilmore Holt, *A Documentary History of Art,* vol. 1 (Garden City, N.Y., 1957), 167–79.
11. Alberti to Matteo de' Pasti, quoted in Peter Murray, *The Architecture of the Italian Renaissance* (New York, 1963), 50.
12. Vasari, *Lives of the Artists,* 164.
13. Alberti, *De re aedificatoria,* I.xiii.
14. Vasari, *Lives of the Artists,* 366.
15. See the catalogue of such architectural books in Dora Wiebenson, ed., *Architectural Theory and Practice from Alberti to Ledoux* (Chicago, 1982).

SUGGESTED READING

James Ackerman, *The Architecture of Michelangelo,* second ed. (London, 1986).
———, *Palladio* (Baltimore, Md., 1966).
Leon Battista Alberti, *De re aldificatoria: On the Art of Building in Ten Books,* trans. J. Rykwert, N. Leach, R. Tavernor (Cambridge, Mass., 1988).
Giulio C. Aragon, *The Renaissance City* (New York, 1969).
E. Battisti, *Filippo Brunelleschi* (New York,1981).

Leonardo Benevolo, *The Architecture of the Renaissance* 2 vols., trans. J. Landry (Boulder, Colo., 1978).
Anthony Blunt, *Art and Architecture in France, 1500 to 1700,* fourth ed. (New York, 1980).
———, *Artistic Theory in Italy, 1450–1600* (Oxford, England, 1940).
Bruce Cole, *Italian Art, 1250–1550: The Relation of Renaissance Art to Life and Society* (New York, 1987).
Giovanni Fanelli, *Brunelleschi* (Florence, Italy, 1980).
Joan Gadol, *Leon Battista Alberti, Universal Man of the Renaissance* (Chicago, 1969).
Richard Goldthwaite, *The Building of Renaissance Florence: An Economic and Social History* (Baltimore, Md., 1980).
Ludwig H. Heydenreich and Wolfgang Lotz, *Architecture in Italy, 1400 to 1600,* trans. Mary Hottinger, (Baltimore, Md., 1974).
Christopher Hibbert, *The Rise and Fall of the House of Medici* (London, 1974).
Norman Johnston, *Cities in the Round* (Seattle, 1983).
Bates Lowry, *Renaissance Architecture* (New York, 1962).
G. Masson, *Italian Villas and Palaces* (London, 1959).
Peter Murray, *The Architecture of the Italian Renaissance* (London, 1963).
———, *Renaissance Architecture* (New York, 1977).
Norman Newton, *Design on the Land: The Development of Landscape Architecture* (Cambridge, Mass., 1971); contains excellent discussions of Renaissance villas and gardens.
Paolo Portoghesi, *Rome of the Renaissance,* trans. P Sanders, (London, 1972).
John Shearman, *Mannerism* (Harmondsworth, England, 1967).
J. C. Shepherd and G. A. Jellicoe, *Italian Gardens of the Renaissance* (London, 1925; new ed., Princeton, N.J., 1986).
John Summerson, *Architecture in Britain, 1530 to 1830,* sixth ed. (New York, 1977).
M. Wackernagel, *The World of the Florentine Renaissance Artist,* trans. A. Luchs, (Princeton, N.J., 1981).
David Watkin, *A History of Western Architecture* (London and New York, 1986); has good summaries of the spread of Renaissance architecture throughout Europe.
Dora Wiebenson, ed., *Architectural Theory and Practice from Alberti to Ledoux* (Chicago, 1982).
Rudolf Wittkower, *Architectural Principles in the Age of Humanism* revised ed. (London, 1962).

17.44. Vierzehnheiligen. View of the nave. In such southern German pilgrimage churches as this, much of the credit for the dazzling interiors must go to the stucco carvers, gilders, and painters; at Vierzehnheiligen these artists included Johann Michael Feichtmayr, Johann Georg Übelhör, and Giuseppe Appiani.

CHAPTER 17

Baroque and Rococo Architecture

The Renaissance building exists to be admired in its splendid isolated perfection. The Baroque building can only be grasped through one's experiencing it in its variety of effects. . . . Baroque unity is achieved—at the expense of the clearly defined elements—through the subordination of the individual elements to invigorate the whole. Baroque space is independent and alive—it flows and leads to dramatic culminations.

Henry A. Millon, *Baroque and Rococo Architecture*, 1961

Renaissance architects of the fifteenth and sixteenth centuries endeavored to create new rational forms based on what they understood of the Classical architecture of ancient Rome. They even invented a term to describe their decisive break with the Gothic past, saying their work marked a renaissance, or rebirth. The architects of the seventeenth century, however, who continued to develop this Classical architecture, made of it something quite different from what had been intended by Alberti and Brunelleschi. These later architects seem not to have recognized the dramatic nature of this change themselves and they coined no universally accepted term to contrast their work with that of the fifteenth century.[1] In continuing to seek new forms, in exercising their newly won artistic prerogative to invent, they created an architecture that was everything the Renaissance was not.

The nature of Baroque architecture is clearly illustrated in one of the last buildings to adhere to these principles, the church of Vierzehnheiligen (Pilgrimage Church of the Fourteen Saints) in Franconia, Germany, built by Johann Balthasar Neumann in

1742–72 [17.44]. Whereas Renaissance architecture gave the visual impression of being simple, Baroque architecture was deliberately complex. Instead of clarity there was ambiguity; instead of the uniformity of elements and overall effect, there was studied variety; instead of regularity, contrast. Where there had been planar forms, with an emphasis on the surface, now the emphasis was on plasticity and spatial depth. The Early Renaissance buildings had most often been human in scale; seventeenth-century architecture became superhuman in scale. Renaissance architecture had stressed easily perceived forms, but the new architecture projected a sense of mystery, so that where the interest had once been in intellectual comprehension and cerebral satisfaction, now it shifted to creating an emotional impact.

As Gothic architecture was named in derision by Renaissance writers, so too the term *baroque* was used to denigrate the architecture of the seventeenth and early eighteenth centuries, by French critics of the mid-eighteenth century. To them, the curving, heavily embellished architecture of seventeenth-century Rome, with its corkscrew columns and bent entablatures, was as much a deviation from architectural propriety as a twisted pearl deviated from the spherical norm, and they applied to that architecture the derogatory Portuguese term used for misshapen pearls: *barocco,* "baroque." Gradually, however, the term *baroque* came to be used by late-nineteenth-century art historians such as Heinrich Wölfflin in a more positive sense, to describe any art that has become elabo-

357

rated, embellished, and complex by developing from simpler forms.

An Architecture for the Senses

The reasons for the shift toward visual complexity about 1600 are several. First, as in any period of artistic creativity in which the goal is to achieve a state of absolute balanced order, once that goal is reached a reaction sets in. The Classical perfection and restraint of Athenian architecture of the fifth century B.C. was transformed into the more complex, Hellenistic architecture of the fourth and third centuries B.C., and the austere architecture of the Roman Republic became the heavily ornamented architecture of the Roman Empire. So, too, Late Gothic architecture became more and more elaborated, with proliferating vault ribs that eventually became free of the vault surface altogether. In each of these periods the latter stages of development are what can be described as baroque.

Second, in Italy, France, and southern Europe, there was a particular religious aspect to this dramatic change in architectural character. This cultural and religious stimulus was the Counter Reformation, the delayed but emphatic reaction to the church reforms advocated by Luther. For numerous political and ecclesiastical reasons, Popes Leo X and Clement VII postponed reacting to Luther; those first years free of challenge were critical in allowing the German states and the Baltic region to reject the domination of Rome and refute basic tenets of Roman church dogma. Soon other splinter groups moved beyond Luther's modest position, advocating even more drastic restructuring of the church and changes in worship. These more radical factions were led by Ulrich Zwingli in Zurich and John Calvin in Geneva, Switzerland; the Calvinists, as they came to be called, soon controlled half of Switzerland, several duchies in Germany, the Netherlands, and Scotland. For a time the continued existence of the Roman church seemed in question.

Not until 1545 did Pope Paul III (Alessandro Farnese) convene the first of several church councils that met at Trent to respond to the Protestant revolt. The final decrees of the Council of Trent were deliberately and decidedly not conciliatory toward the Protestants, and thus the breach was made irreparable. Some of the flagrant abuses of the church identified by Luther were corrected, but whereas Luther had advised priests to marry, the Council absolutely reaffirmed priestly celibacy. Whereas Luther and Calvin rejected the authority of the church as the sole interpreter of scripture, the Council adamantly insisted on it. These and other points had to do with dogma, but other points had a direct bearing on church design and visual imagery. Luther (and Calvin even more so) rejected the veneration of saints, but the Council now vigorously endorsed the practice. Whereas the Calvinists preached the elimination of all sensory stimulation in worship, the Council insisted that music, painting, sculpture, and architecture, properly handled, were among the most powerful instruments enhancing religious devotion. (For his part, Luther made congregational singing an important part of Lutheran worship.) Accordingly the Council strongly encouraged the use of architecture, painting, and sculpted images to create a mystical atmosphere for worship.

Roman Baroque Churches

The most active campaign within the Roman church to bring back the faithful was led by Ignatius Loyola, a Spaniard who had established a new militant religious order in 1540, the Society of Jesus. Ignatius was only one of many zealous champions of the Roman church who were quickly canonized after their deaths. Other religious orders also arose in response to the Protestant threat, including the Theatines (1524) and the Capuchins (1535), but it was the Jesuits especially who led the fight against the heretics. In 1568 the Jesuits began construction of a central administrative convent and mother church, the church of the Gesù, Rome, from designs by Vignola [17.1]. It was a large church clearly adapted from Alberti's Sant' Andrea in Mantua but

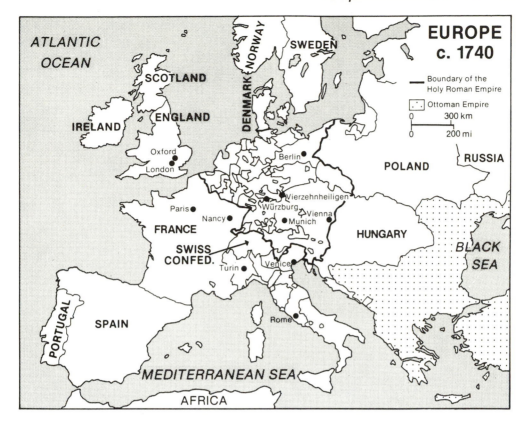

designed following the explicit instructions of the patron, Cardinal Alessandro Farnese, to facilitate preaching. It had short transept arms covered with barrel vaults and a third short arm forming the choir, terminating in a semicircular apse. The broad nave, covered by a barrel vault, was flanked by square side chapels. This aspect of the church was Late Renaissance in its clarity of form; only in the facade, designed by Giacomo della Porta in 1573 [17.2], was there a hint of the complexity that would develop into Baroque complexity. The facade, too, is derived from Alberti, from his facade for Santa Maria Novella in Florence [16.16], but it is far more plastically molded, with paired engaged columns and nested pediments, one inside the other. This church image the Jesuits carried with them, and its variations appear across Europe, as in Saint Michael's in Louvain, Flanders (Belgium), and throughout the New World.

In strictly architectural terms, the Baroque emphasis on sculptural plasticity can be seen clearly in the facade of the Church of Saints Vincent and Anastasius (Santi Vincenzo ed Anastasio), Rome [17.3]. Built by the architect Martino Lunghi the Younger, in 1646–50 for Cardinal Jules Mazarin of France, it is another variant on the pattern established by the Gesù seventy years before. Now, however, the pilasters have become fully disengaged, freestanding columns, and in the center section they stand in triplicate, carrying three nested pediments. The pediments, moreover, are cut away at the top, opening voids that are filled with garlands and carved figures. There is, in fact, no part of the surface that is not enlivened with projecting architectural members or figural sculpture. This compulsion to enrich, embellish, and overlay reached its zenith in Spain, where the Classical architectural vocabulary of the Renaissance was combined with a love for pattern and surface ornament, the legacy of

17.1. *Giacomo Barozzi da Vignola, Church of the Gesù, Rome, 1568–77. Plan. In order to emphasize preaching in this new mother church of the newly founded Jesuit order, Vignola used a Latin cross plan, directing the attention of the worshipers on the altar. The plan was closely patterned after Alberti's Sant' Andrea in Mantua.*

17.2. *Giacomo della Porta, facade of the Gesù, 1573–77. Giacomo della Porta, too, was inspired by Alberti, and used large curved volutes to make the transition from the high nave to the lower side chapels.*

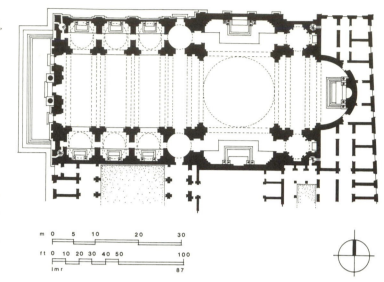

the Islamic Moors. This can be seen in the interior of the sacristy of the Cartuja in Granada, begun in 1730 by Francisco Hurtado and decorated in 1742–47 by an unidentified stucco carver [17.4]. Here, on a system of arches resting on pilasters, is layer upon layer of ornament, so that the basic structural system is obscured and everything becomes an intricate pattern of light and shadow in which the eye is drawn endlessly from part to part.

An Architecture of Emotional Impact

It was the sculptor and architect Gian Lorenzo Bernini (1598–1680) who summa-

rized most clearly the impact of the Council of Trent and who provided the prototype for the emotion-inducing function of the arts. In 1645 Bernini began work on a chapel for Cardinal Federico Cornaro of Venice, to be built in the left transept of the church of Santa Maria della Vittoria (one of the many churches in Rome built on the model of the Gesù, this was designed by Carlo Maderno and built in 1608–20, with the facade finished later). In the upper part of the transept-chapel, Bernini designed an illusionistic fresco around the window, showing billowing clouds and angels, some of the clouds carved in high relief in stucco and covering up parts of the architectural moldings [17.5]. The surfaces of wall and vault

17.3. Martino Lunghi the Younger, Church of Saints Vincent and Anastasius, Rome, 1646–50. In Italy the Baroque church facade reached its point of fullest development in this example; no part of the surface is free of embellishment.

17.4. Francisco Hurtado,
Sacristy of La Cartuja,
Granada, Spain, 1730–47.
Interior. Baroque
enrichment was most
elaborate in Spain and its
dominions, and perhaps
nowhere as elaborate as in
the carved stucco work of
this interior.

curve together and are covered with molded clouds so that the intersection of wall and vault disappears and the physical boundaries of the space become blurred.

Below is a miniature theater. The marble-paneled side walls contain "box seats," in which Bernini depicted members of the Cornaro family reading and discussing the miraculous event being enacted on the "stage" in the end wall of the chapel. At the center of the composition, paneled in yellow, gray, and green marble, is an aedicule that curves forward as though pushed forward by some force behind it, breaking the pediment. On the "stage" is the figure of Saint Teresa of Ávila, one of the new Counter Reformation saints, who described

in her autobiographical meditations a visitation by an angel carrying a golden spear, with which he penetrated her heart, causing her exquisite spiritual ecstasy. Bernini re-creates that moment in his *Ecstasy of Saint Teresa*, conveying it in carnal physical terms so that the observer could easily grasp a spiritual experience through its physical equivalent. The miraculous event is illuminated from a hidden source, a window behind the pediment of the stage, whose flood of light is symbolized by the gilded rays that stream down behind the figures. The autonomy of architecture is here eliminated, becoming now an armature for sculpture and painting meant to impress upon the viewer a mystical experience. Architec-

17.5. *Gianlorenzo Bernini, Cornaro Chapel, Santa Maria della Vittoria, Rome, 1647–52. In the arm of the transept of this church, Bernini created a miniature theater, with the members of the Cornaro family in boxes overlooking the divine mystery of the* Ecstasy of Saint Teresa *onstage; above them the heavens open up.*

ture as an independent rational structural frame is transformed into a fusion of the arts as propaganda. Architecture has become but one constituent part in what is best expressed by the German term *Gesamtkunstwerk*, "a total work of art."

In Baroque architecture and art the line between three-dimensional reality and mystical illusion was increasingly blurred. In 1672–85 the ceiling decoration of the Gesù was completed by Giovanni Battista Gaulli. On the barrel vaults of the Gesù thickly modeled architectural moldings of stucco were placed, framing illusionistic frescoes showing clouds and angels rising to heaven, but in places the billowing clouds spill out of the frames, making it difficult for the viewer

to distinguish between the real paneled vault surface and the perspective illusion. Even more dramatic was the nave vault fresco of the church dedicated to Saint Ignatius (San Ignazio), Rome, designed by Padre Orazio Grassi in 1626–50 [17.6]. The vaults were painted by Padre Andrea Pozzo in 1691–94, showing the *Glory of Saint Ignatius*, in an illusion of architectural elements extending into the open sky, with clouds and angelic figures accompanying the figure of Saint Ignatius. When this is viewed from the floor of the church, it is nearly impossible to tell that one is actually looking up at a curved barrel vault, for the reality of the curved planar surface has been completely eradicated by the illusion of the

17.6. *Padre Andrea Pozzo,*
nave vault fresco, Church of
San Ignazio, Rome, 1691–94.
Pozzo completely disguised
the intersection lines of the
groin vaults, and the viewer
can scarcely guess that this is
a curved barrel vault;
instead the viewer looks up
into the heavens, witnessing
the "Glory of Saint Ignatius."

perspective. Reason has been overpowered by mystical experience.

This kind of mystical presence appealed greatly to the southern Germans, who remained loyal to the Church of Rome and rejected Luther's reforms. In the richly embellished pilgrimage and monastic churches built in Bavaria in southern Germany in the early eighteenth century, such rhapsodic illusionism was pushed even further. Among the most skilled practitioners were the brothers Cosmas Damian and Egid Quirin Asam, both trained in Italy, Cosmas as a fresco painter and stuccoist, and Egid as a sculptor. Hence they combined to a high degree all the skills necessary to produce the most powerful

emotional effects. One of their most striking creations was the sculptural complex at the end of the choir of the Augustinian Priory Church of the Assumption at Rohr, Germany, a tiny village near Regensburg, built in 1717–22 [17.7]. A series of screens of columns carrying pieces of broken pediments serves to shield the eye from the sources of light to the sides. Beyond these "wings" or "tormentors" (to use theatrical terminology once again), on the "stage" is the figure of the Virgin Mary ascending to heaven, rising from an open sepulcher surrounded by figures dramatically registering various stages of amazement. The figure of the Virgin actually hovers in the air, assisted by two angels, in apparent defiance of grav-

17.7. *Cosmas Damien Asam and Egid Quirin Asam, altar of the Priory Church of the Assumption, Rohr, Germany, 1717–22. The Asam brothers pushed the illusionism of Bernini to the logical extreme, depicting the Virgin Mary hovering in space, lit by hidden windows to the sides.*

ity, for she is supported from behind by hidden projecting bars of iron. Here the emotional impact of Bernini was pushed as far as technology then allowed. If Bernini's *Saint Teresa* is a *portrayal* of a miraculous event, at the Rohr church such a miracle actually seems to be taking place before our very eyes.

The Central Plan Modified

Bernini's Churches

The broad longitudinal plan of the Gesù quickly became the model for seventeenth-century Roman Catholic churches, but the centralized plan did not disappear alto-

gether. For smaller chapels and votive churches the oval was often the generating form. This direction had already been suggested by Vignola in his Sant' Anna dei Palafrenieri, Rome, 1570 [16.36], which served as the point of departure for Bernini's church of Sant' Andrea al Quirinale, Rome, 1658–70, a church sponsored by Cardinal Camillo Pamphili to serve the Jesuit novices living on the Quirinal Hill. The fact that this is a rounded church is clearly evident from the curve of the upper walls visible as one nears the church [17.8, 17.9]. The half-oval walls, curving out to enclose the entry, greet the approaching worshiper and give a hint of what one may expect to find inside. This concave curve is

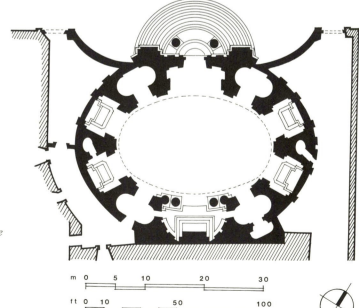

17.8. Gianlorenzo Bernini,
Church of Sant' Andrea al
Quirinale, Rome, 1658–70.
Bernini anticipated the oval of the
plan in the curving arms of the
walls shaping the entry.

17.9. Sant' Andrea al Quirinale.
Plan. Bernini turned the oval so
that the principal line of
movement is along the short axis.

17.10. *Gianlorenzo Bernini, Piazza of Saint Peter's, Rome, 1656–67. Aerial view. The arms of the vast piazza, adjusted to miss existing Vatican Palace buildings, were intended by Bernini to symbolize the embracing arms of the church.*

countered in the convex curve of the portico, capped with a broken curved pediment. Around the portico and framing it is a heavily overscaled temple front. Inside, one discovers that the line of movement is along the short axis of an oval plan, not along the more usually dominant longer axis. In fact, there is no true perpendicular axis, for there are four chapels on each side, meaning that a customary perpendicular cross axis would run into the ends of spur walls and not into chapel recesses. The principal altar on the short axis is contained in a niche behind a portico made with paired red-veined marble Corinthian columns; behind the altar is a painting of the martyrdom of Andrew illuminated by a hidden source of light. The Corinthian columns carry a pediment scooped out at its center to accommodate an ascending figure of Saint Andrew. Over all rises an oval dome, punctuated by carved figures of angelic putti who flit among the architectural elements.

Bernini also used an oval to solve his largest building project, the great piazza in front of Saint Peter's basilica in Rome, which finally brought this ambitious church to completion in 1667, a century and a half after it had been started by Bramante [17.10, 17.11]. Before Bernini was given this task, the basilica itself finally had been enclosed by Carlo Maderno and given a facade, but not until the last change was made in the plan. After the incessant vacillation between central and longitudinal plans, the final decision was to extend a nave from Michelangelo's east arm. Maderno added the bays of the nave in 1605 and finished the broad facade in 1612.

Still, the space in front of Saint Peter's was ill-defined. A broad space was needed to accommodate the crowds who gathered at Easter to receive the papal benediction, *urbi et orbi*. Bernini's problem was that the existing buildings of the Vatican palace intruded from the north, making it impossible to create one large, simple, geometric enclosure. His solution was to divide the

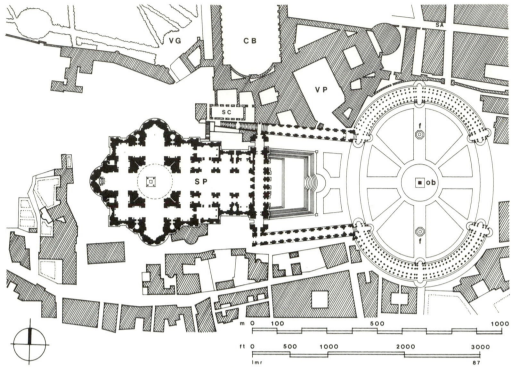

17.11. *Piazza of Saint Peter's. Plan. Bernini carefully planned the open space to incorporate existing fountains and the Egyptian obelisk re-erected by Domenico Fontana.*

CB = Cortile del Belvedere   SA = Sant' Anna dei Palafrenieri   VG = Vatican Gardens
f   = fountains   SC = Sistine Chapel   VP = Vatican Palace
ob = obelisk   SP = Basilica of Saint Peter

piazza into two parts, the portion immediately next to the facade being a trapezoid and the more distant portion an oval enclosed by curved Tuscan Doric colonnades focused on two fountains in a vast piazza. Between them was an Egyptian obelisk, erected here at the instructions of Pope Sixtus V as part of his replanning of Rome in 1585–90. Bernini viewed the encircling colonnades as the motherly arms of the church, which, he said, "embrace Catholics to reinforce their belief, heretics to re-unite them with the Church, and unbelievers to enlighten them with the true faith."[2]

Borromini's Churches

Bernini's chief rival in Rome was Francesco Borromini (1599–1667). The two were unlike in almost every way. Bernini, trained

as a sculptor, had the support and patronage of some of the most powerful figures in the Roman Church, including Maffeo Barberini who reigned as Pope Urban VIII and Fabio Chigi who became Pope Alexander VII. Bernini's prodigious creations in architecture, sculpture, painting, and theater design, coupled with his air of confident buoyancy and social ease, brought him international acclaim. Borromini, a reclusive and brooding man, trained as an architect, but gained limited recognition and received his commissions from smaller organizations. Yet he manipulated space and the traditional Classical orders even more sculpturally than did Bernini. Borromini rose to prominence with the small church and monastery he designed for the Spanish Trinitarian Order, San Carlo alle Quattro Fontane in 1634 (built 1634–67), often called simply San Carlino because of

17.12. Francesco Borromini, Church of San Carlo alle Quattro Fontane, Rome, 1634–67. Interior. The heavily sculpted elements of this miniature church are positioned according to a proportional system generated by equilateral triangles.

17.13. San Carlo alle Quattro Fontane. The plan combines elements of the oval with joined equilateral triangles. The dashed lines revealing the triangular basis of the design are shown by Borromini in his own drawings.

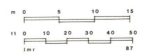

17.14. San Carlo alle Quattro
Fontane. Exterior, facade.

its diminutive size [17.12, 17.13]. Its name derives from the fact that it sits at the intersection of two new streets cut through Rome by Sixtus V, at the corners of which four new public fountains were built.

Borromini's radical departure in the design of San Carlino was to base the entire composition, both in plan and in section, not on the traditional module of the column diameter—as had been the rule since the time of the Greeks—but rather on the module of a symbolic equilateral triangle. This approach may have been inspired by Borromini's contemporary, Galileo, who described the universe as being based on geometrical, triangular relationships. Borromini's surviving drawings show this modular derivation quite clearly, for the delicate lines of the overlapped triangles are clearly visible among the heavier outlines of the walls.[3] He began with two large equilateral triangles joined on a common base and then enclosed them in an oval; this determined the basic ground plan. In enclosing the ground floor, however, he used spaced pairs of columns carrying an undulating cornice that has the fluidity of extruded clay rather than the linearity of traditional stone lintels. Above this is a transitional level, with four pendentives that rise to form the oval base ring for a deeply coffered oval dome. The dome, in turn, is opened at the top by a lantern, at the very top of which is the figure of the dove of the Holy Spirit circumscribed by an equilateral triangle—the key to the entire composition.

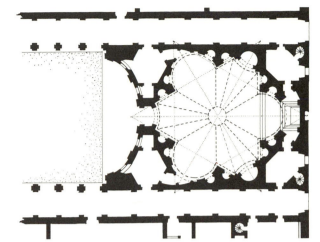

17.15. Francesco Borromini, Collegiate Church of Sant' Ivo della Sapienza, Rome, 1642–60. This plan, too, was generated by equilateral triangles, to form a Star of David.

In 1665–67 Borromini began construction of the facade, designed earlier [17.14]. In this, too, he used a system of generating triangles related in plan to the triangles he had employed in the interior, resulting in a facade that undulates like rolling waves, one of the first such undulating Baroque facades. The curved entablatures and the surfaces packed with architectural and sculptural ornament prepare the visitor for the unorthodox interior. Despite its striking departures from the canons of Classical design, the church was immediately sought out by visitors to Rome, and the Procurator General of the Order wrote that members from numerous countries asked for plans of the church because of its "artistic merit, caprice, excellence, and singularity." The Procurator General was clearly aware of the special character of the building, a character that would become common in Baroque architecture, for he wrote that it "is arranged in such manner that one part supplements the other and that the spectator is

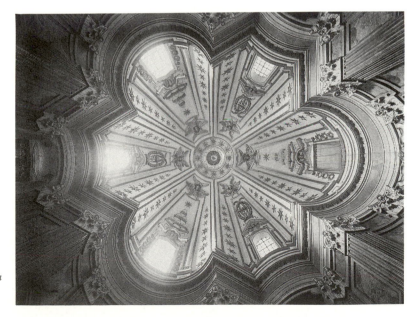

17.16. Sant' Ivo della Sapienza. Interior, dome.

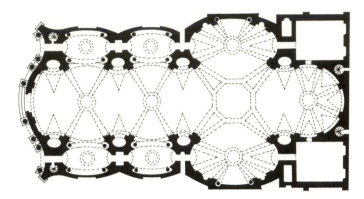

17.17. Guarino Guarini, Santa
Maria della Divina Providenza,
Lisbon, Portugal, 1652–63
(destroyed 1755). Plan. Guarini
used a series of overlapping ovals
as the generating elements in this
church.

stimulated to let his eye wander about ceaselessly."[4]

Borromini again used a centralized plan in the chapel of Sant' Ivo della Sapienza, which he added to the University of Rome in 1642–60 [17.15, 17.16]. This was built at the end of the long courtyard designed by Giacomo della Porta in 1585–90. This church, too, was based on a system of equilateral triangles, but in this instance they were laid atop one another, forming a six-pointed star around a hexagon. Such a form had almost never been used before, since it makes no provision for crossed axes, as does a square or an octagonal plan. Three of the lobes of San' Ivo, corresponding to the points of one triangle, end in semicircular apses, whereas the other three, corresponding to the second triangle, are pointed but have convex walls pushing in at the points. The inherent conflict in this system (since opposing faces of the interior are different in form) is reconciled by a massive molded cornice, resting on the substantial Corinthian pilasters that articulate the planes of the walls; this cornice undulates around the space and holds it together. A unique and deeply molded dome rises directly from this cornice, following the convolutions of the star-shaped plan below.

Guarini's Churches

This molding of space, as though by tremendous forces that bend and curve walls, was further extended in the city of Turin in northern Italy, by Guarino Guarini (1624–

1683). Guarini entered the Theatine Order at age fifteen and was sent to Rome, where he studied theology, philosophy, mathematics, and architecture. The architecture of Borromini, then under construction, was a powerful influence on him, and, to a lesser extent, that of Bernini. He traveled across Europe on behalf of the Theatines, building churches for the order in Portugal and France. In 1652–63, the church of Santa Maria della Divina Providenza in Lisbon, Portugal, was built to his design [17.17]. Although the church was later destroyed in the earthquake of 1755 that damaged much of Lisbon, its design was recorded in engraved plates in Guarini's posthumous book *Architettura civile,* published in Turin in 1737. The curve of the facade recalled the facade of San Carlino, then just ten years old, but the interior was a reshaping of the traditional Latin cross plan exemplified in the Gesù; each of the component spaces was based on an oval—ovals overlapping ovals, in fact—and the ribs of the vaults, instead of crossing transversely from one pier to another, crossed the bays of the nave diagonally.

Guarini was then hired by Carlo Emanuele of Savoy, who was engaged in rebuilding and enlarging Turin as the capital city of the emerging Duchy of Savoy. The House of Savoy possessed one of Christendom's most famous relics, the Holy Shroud, believed to have received the imprint of the body of Christ when he was buried. Carlo Emanuele desired to build a special chapel at the end of the cathedral of Turin to house the precious shroud, and he gave the task to Guarini. Built in 1667–90, the Cappella della Santissima Sindone (Chapel of the Holy Shroud) consists of a round base from which rise *three* pendentives, converging to a smaller circular ring [17.18]. On this rests a hexagonal arcade that forms the base of a dome. This dome, however, was unlike any every built before, for it consists of six segmental arches resting on the arcade, and six smaller segmental arches resting on the crowns of the first six, and six smaller arches resting on the crowns of the second layer, and so on, diminishing by stages to the top of the dome. Within each of these superimposed arches is a window, so that the dome is filled with light filtering in through the stacked window openings. It is an architecture that Galileo might well have understood, perhaps, for although complex in form, it has a mathematical clarity and a directness of structural function.

Baroque Scale

Another of the attributes that sets Baroque architecture apart is the great jump in scale, from the circumspect arcades of Brunelleschi and the superimposed orders of Alberti to vast complexes that surpass the limits of human visual perception. A Renaissance building, as exemplified by Sangallo's diminutive church of Santa Maria della Carceri [16.11], can be taken in at a glance, and the relationship of its component parts is almost immediately recognized. Baroque buildings, in contrast, are so large and complex that they cannot possibly be comprehended in a single view [17.18].

This change in complexity and scale was one of the first manifestations of the Baroque spirit, declared in the proposal of Pope Sixtus V to replan the city of Rome [17.19]. Although Sixtus V occupied the papal throne only five years, 1585–90, his vision has determined the shape of Rome ever since. This sweeping reorganization of the city was another response of the Counter Reformation; it was, in part, an effort to encourage pilgrims to visit Rome to see the major sites associated with the earliest years of Christendom. When the Christian churches, especially the large major basilicas, were first built in Rome in the

17.18. *Guarino Guarini, Cappella della Santissima Sindone (Chapel of the Holy Shroud), Turin, Italy, 1667–90. This dome, sheltering the famous Shroud of Turin, is built up of superimposed diminishing arches, admitting a diffuse light into the chapel.*

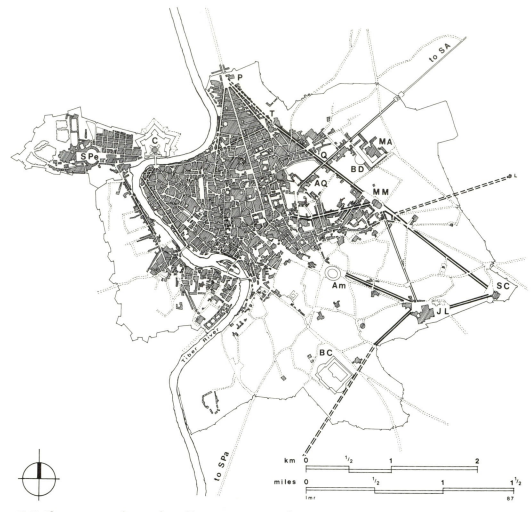

17.19. The new streets of Rome planned by Sixtus V in 1585. Plan.

AM	= Flavian Amphitheater	L	= San Lorenzo fuori le Mura	SC	= Santa Croce
AQ	= Sant' Andrea al Quirinale	MA	= Santa Maria degli Angeli	SPe	= San Pietro in Vaticano
BC	= Baths of Caracalla	MM	= Santa Maria Maggiore		(Basilica of Saint Peter)
BD	= Baths of Diocletian	P	= Piazza del Popolo	SPa	= San Paolo fuori le Mura
C	= Castel Sant' Angelo	Q	= San Carlo alle Quattro Fontane	T	= Santa Trinità dei Monti
JL	= San Giovanni in Laterano	SA	= Sant' Agnese		

fourth and fifth centuries, they rose near the edges of the city, in those areas where there was available property. Several, such as Sant' Agnese and Saint Peter's, were built over cemeteries. As a result, the great basilicas of San Lorenzo, Santa Croce, San Giovanni in Laterano, and of course San Pietro (Saint Peter) were scattered at the edges of what had been the ancient Roman metropolis; these peripheral areas had been largely

abandoned during the Middle Ages. The principal entry to the city was at the north, through the Porta del Popolo, into the irregular Piazza del Popolo. To get to these dispersed ancient basilicas from the Porta del Popolo was difficult and meant traversing large parts of the ruin-strewn expanses of the ancient city. Sixtus V resolved to bring order out of this chaos.

Although the pope conceived the grand

scheme, its implementation was left to his engineer and architect, Domenico Fontana. He and Sixtus V cut a new street, the strada Felice (Felix, or Felice, was the pope's given name), from the Piazza del Popolo straight through the center of the ruins of the old city, toward the huge basilica of Santa Maria Maggiore at the center of the old city, continuing on to Santa Croce to the south [17.20]. Where the strada Felice crossed the existing strada Pia, the intersection of the four fountains was created (San Carlino would be built there later). The alignment of the existing via Gregoriana, radiating off the Piazza Santa Maria Maggiore and running toward the cathedral of San Giovanni in Laterano, was corrected by Sixtus V to improve its circulatory function. Another major street was cut to the east, from the strada Felice to San Lorenzo. And a new street was cut from the Piazza Santa Maria Maggiore, the hub of Sixtus V's design, to the vicinity of the Capitoline Hill (Michelangelo's Campidoglio) and the hub of medieval Rome. Other streets were planned by Sixtus V as well, intended to further knit together the dispersed basilicas, but these were not immediately built. In addition to the street layout, Sixtus V built an aqueduct, the first influx of fresh water

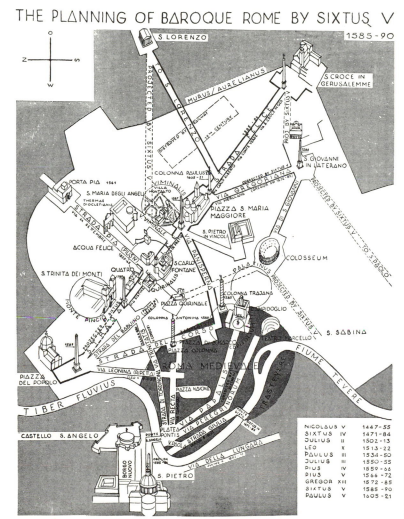

THE PLANNING OF BAROQUE ROME BY SIXTUS V   1585-90

17.20. *Diagram of the replanning of Rome by Sixtus V. North is toward the lower left.*

since Roman times, and this, the Aqua Felice, also bore his name. Its waters were discharged in a public fountain on the strada Pia.

The nodes of Sixtus V's plan were the great basilicas, and in front of each a piazza was carved out. To mark these spots, and to make them visible along the new, straight streets, Sixtus V had Fontana reerect Egyptian obelisks that lay about in the ruins of the ancient city. Not since Roman times had such huge monoliths been moved and erected, and Fontana had to invent the necessary machinery and organize the synchronized teams of men and horses to do the work. So, in front of each basilica, as beacons and place markers to the pilgrim, rose again the reconsecrated obelisks. One of these was the obelisk in front of Saint Peter's, raised in 1586, around which Bernini later shaped his piazza.

For French ambassadors in the seventeenth century, and for nineteenth-century urban planners such as Baron Haussmann of Paris, the restructuring of Rome by Sixtus V and Fontana showed what unfaltering will and centralized power could accomplish in reshaping the landscape. Ironically, as Sixtus V reorganized Rome, the secular power of the papacy was beginning to diminish, and few of his successors were able to summon the resources to initiate such vast projects. The kings of the European nation states, however, were increasing their power at just this time—particularly the French monarchs—and very shortly they were able to undertake even more expansive projects.

The Spread of the Baroque Outside Italy

French Baroque—Versailles

The idea of extending the axis of the château at Chambord out into the landscape was

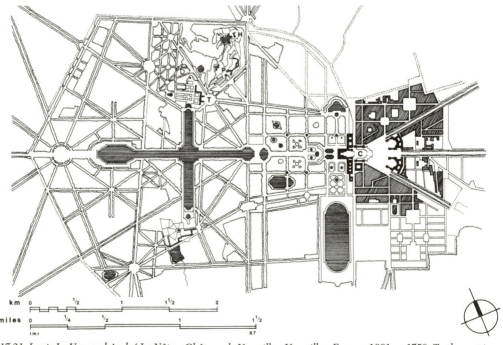

17.21. Louis Le Vau and André Le Nôtre, Château de Versailles, Versailles, France, 1661–c. 1750. To the east is the village and to the west the gardens; both are laid out around a single axis that runs through the center of the king's chambers at the core of the château.

C = Château de Versailles   P = Petit Trianon
T = Grand Trianon   H = Hameau

pushed to its limit in the royal château at Versailles. Like Blois and Chambord, Versailles was originally a royal hunting lodge not far from Paris, but from 1661 to 1710 it was enlarged by Louis XIV on a scale rivaling that of the Rome of Sixtus V. The grounds were extended farther by later monarchs, until the French Revolution in 1789.

Versailles, about 14 miles (22 kilometers) southeast of the heart of Paris, had been a favored hunting retreat of Louis XIII, a love he passed on to his son, Louis XIV. The father had built a relatively modest hunting lodge in 1624, enlarged it in 1631–36, and had several geometric parterres laid out around the house, defining an axis centered on the lodge and stretching westward into the landscape. When Louis XIV reached maturity in 1661 and assumed personal control of the government operations, he began extensive enlargement of Versailles, using the team of architect, landscape architect, and painter/decorator that his minister of finance, Nicholas Fouquet, had assembled to build and landscape his own private country house outside Paris at Vaux-le-Vicomte in 1657–61. Fouquet had made the unforgivable tactical error of building a country estate finer than anything owned by the king, and a month after Fouquet played host to the nobles at a grand celebration at Vaux-le-Vicomte—replete with a ballet by Molière, music by Lully, décor by Le Brun, and fireworks—he was arrested on charges of embezzlement. Vaux-le-Vicomte was confiscated by the king, and its designers and builders put to work rebuilding Versailles to make it even larger and grander.

The architect Louis Le Vau (1612–1670) was instructed by the king to wrap a new and larger building around his father's château. The painter/decorator Charles Le Brun was charged with designing all the interiors, including the allegorical paintings celebrating the king, his rule, and his military victories through allusions to Apollo, the sun god. And the landscape architect André Le Nôtre (1613–1700) was to begin the first of several extensions of the gardens in terraces to the north, south, and especially west of the château. All of the parter-res (the hedge-framed planted beds) and the radiating *allées* were laid out in relationship to the grand axis of the château, running through the king's own rooms at the center [17.21]. Le Nôtre's gardens combined the intricacy of texture, detail, and color of the best Italian gardens with the sense of vast scale of Sixtus V's plan for Rome. Since there were no dramatic changes of level in the landscape, as in Italy, Le Nôtre maintained visual interest by using water in basins, long pools (the Grand Canal was over a mile long), and hundreds of fountains. The fountains were supplied by a system of pipes and aqueducts fed by a huge pumping apparatus called simply the Machine at Marly, which raised water from the Seine River.

During 1678–88 there was a second major phase of construction at Versailles, when the architect Jules Hardouin-Mansart added the Galérie des Glaces (Hall of Mirrors) along the west front [17.22]. Then wings tripling the bulk of the château were added to the north and south [17.23]. These wings housed much of the nobility now required to reside at Versailles, for Louis XIV had moved the entire mechanism of government to his rural retreat, abandoning Paris. The population at Versailles continually expanded; when Louis XIV died, in 1715, the nobility numbered 20,000 persons (of which 5,000 lived in the château itself), military staff and servants numbered 14,000, and the townspeople, who provided services for the court, numbered another 30,000, making a total population in the château and town of Versailles of roughly 64,000 people. The expanded château building alone measured 1,250 feet (381 meters) in length, and the entire landscape of Versailles, including both the park and the town, measured more than 2.7 miles by 2 miles (4.2 by 2.9 kilometers). Here was an expansion of scale that Roman Baroque architects could only have begun to imagine. In contrast to the compact Villa Lante at Bagnaia, here was a building complex and a landscape that could hardly be understood even over a lifetime of observation, a manmade landscape that stretched along the great east-west axis extending from the

17.22. Jules Hardouin-Mansart, Galerie des Glaces (Hall of Mirrors), Versailles, 1678–88. This grand room replaced a terrace overlooking the gardens; windows face the gardens westward, and banks of mirrors on the opposite walls reflect the light throughout the room.

17.23. Louis Le Vau and Jules Hardouin-Mansart, aerial view of the Château de Versailles, 1661–88, and later. With the wings added by Hardouin-Mansart, the château stretched nearly 1,250 feet (381 meters) in length.

heart of the château as far as the eye could see.

English Baroque

Baroque architecture can be described as a celebration of absolutism, whether the absolute majesty of religious mysticism or the absolute rule, by divine right, of pope and king. In England, however, no such absolutism determined politics, for the power of the crown had been reduced by the rise of the conservative Whig aristocracy, which governed through Parliament. Hence, English monarchs never built for themselves a Versailles and thereby spared themselves that sense of privileged isolation that led in part to the bloodbath of the French Revolution. Not that the English people were spared the expense of such building enterprise, however, for an equivalent to Versailles was built, but presented as the gift of the nation to a private citizen. The building was Blenheim Palace, built 1705–25 at the request of Queen Anne, paid for by Parliament, and built by way of thanks to John Churchill. The reason for this generosity was that Churchill, general of the English army and head of forces allied with England, had defeated the armies of Louis XIV at the small German village of Blenheim in 1704, establishing a new balance of power on the Continent. In gratitude Churchill was created Duke of Marlborough and granted the royal manor of Woodstock outside Oxford, where the great house was to be built. Since the house was being paid for with public funds, its designer, the talented amateur Sir John Vanbrugh (1664–1726), continually enlarged the plans, so that it became more a monument to the deed than the doer; eventually the exorbitant cost put John and Sarah Churchill into royal and public disfavor.

Vanbrugh, working with the architect Nicholas Hawksmoor, laid out the house in three huge parts—a kitchen court, a stable court, and the main block of the house—enclosing a vast entrance court [17.24, 17.25]. The components of this ensemble,

17.24. Sir John Vanbrugh with Nicholas Hawksmoor, Blenheim Palace, Oxfordshire, England, 1705–25. Aerial view. This English version of Versailles was built by the nation as a gift to John Churchill, general of the king's army. The grounds visible here are the result of later relandscaping by landscape architect Lancelot "Capability" Brown in the 1760s in the new style of the English garden.

17.25. Entrance court, Blenheim Palace. The design builds in scale toward the center, overpowering the
approaching visitor. This is more museum than a private residence, more a monument to the deed than the doer.

each highly molded with extensive ornamentation, build toward the center, leading
to the curved quadrants and the central
pedimented portico that rises over the axial
entrance. The scale, of both ornament and
building elements, is huge. It is, in fact, less
a private residence than a national monument, and the ornament everywhere bears
this out. In the pediments are images of

17.26. Blenheim Palace. Detail of the ornament used
atop the chimneys, showing a duke's crown on a
cannonball crushing the French fleur-de-lis.

heaped-up battle trophies, and peppered all
over the picturesque roof line on the massive clustered chimneys are clear symbols of
the house's meaning. The finials are in fact
stylized representations of a ducal coronet
atop a cannonball crushing a fleur-de-lis—
the duke victorious over the French king
[17.26]. Such theatricality was basic to
Baroque architecture, and it is significant
that the bombast of Blenheim Palace was
created by Vanbrugh, who was by profession a dramatist.

The complexity associated with Baroque
architecture is also found in the churches
designed by Sir Christopher Wren (1632–
1723) to replace those destroyed in a catastrophic fire that swept through medieval
London in the late summer of 1666, burning
itself out after ten days. Wren was by education a mathematician, an astronomer, and a
scientist, but his avocation in architecture
and construction had led him to be
appointed Surveyor-General of the King's
Works in 1669, which meant he was in
effect chief architect to the crown. He had
already designed a number of buildings and
had completed a trip to France (where he
met Bernini briefly) when the fire gave him
his unparalleled opportunity. First he

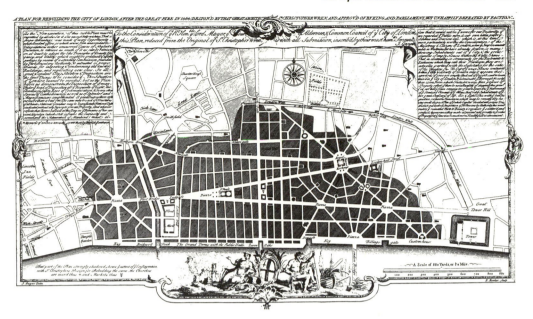

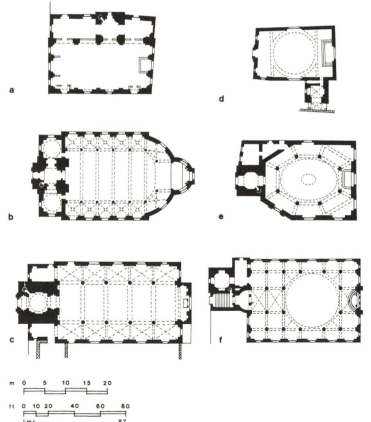

17.27. Sir Christopher Wren, new plan for the City of London, 1666. In working out a new plan for the city after the disastrous fire of 1666, Wren used broad, straight thoroughfares focused on several nodes, as in the scheme of Sixtus V for the new Rome.

17.28. Sir Christopher Wren, assorted plans for London churches, 1670–85. No two of the scores of churches that Wren designed had the same plan; some were essentially longitudinal in form and others were centrally planned.

a = All Hallows the Great (demolished)
b = Saint Clement Danes
c = Saint Bride, Fleet Street
d = Saint Mildred, Bread Street
e = Saint Antholin, Watling Street (demolished)
f = Saint Stephen, Walbrook

17.29. *Sir Christopher Wren, Church of Saint Mary-le-Bow, London, 1670–80. In re-creating the image of tall Gothic spires in the new City churches, Wren used stacked classical elements.*

devised a plan for rebuilding the heart of London, with broad major thoroughfares radiating from public squares and focusing on the Royal Exchange and the great cathedral of Saint Paul's [17.27]. In the rush to rebuild the city, however, nothing came of this, but Wren's plan shows his familiarity with French and Italian ideals.

As surveyor-general, it was Wren's responsibility to provide designs for the scores of small London parish churches consumed in the flames. Of the eighty-seven Gothic churches that vanished, fifty-one were rebuilt, since several parishes were consolidated. Almost no new churches had been built in England since medieval times, so that the problem Wren faced was how modern English Protestant churches ought to be designed. The building sites were often constricted between adjoining properties and hardly any had true rectangular lots. Wren's ingenuity demonstrated itself in the unending variety of plans he devised for these churches, some centralized in plan, others rectangular [17.28]. All were devised, as Wren wrote, to facilitate the worshipers' hearing the words of the speaker. Prior to the fire, London's medieval skyline had been a forest of slender Gothic spires rising over the old churches, and Wren also resolved to restore that image—in Classical terms. The new towers he designed consisted of diminishing stages of Classical squares and octagons, belvederes and cupolas, rising to slender spires [17.29].

Wren's greatest achievement was the rebuilding of Saint Paul's Cathedral, whose Gothic bulk formerly rose over old London. When it was determined that the old stone walls were too badly damaged by the fire to permit reconstruction, the site was cleared, giving Wren his opportunity to design an ideal centralized cathedral. This first scheme, prepared in 1670, was an enormous Greek cross (the arms connected by curved quadrants rather than meeting in more traditional right angles), the whole capped by a great dome resembling that of Saint Peter's, Rome, but simpler in ornamentation [17.30]. Wren then modified the design by adding a domed vestibule at the west, resulting in an axial building. The clergy

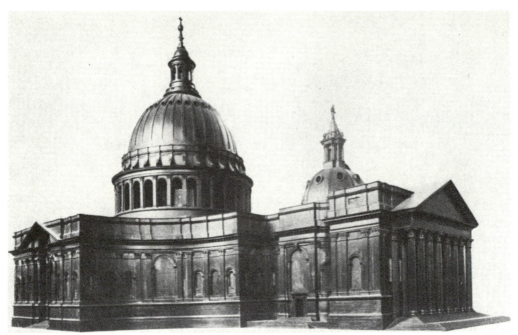

17.30. *Sir Christopher Wren, Great Model design for Saint Paul's Cathedral, London, 1673. In his early schemes for Saint Paul's, Wren employed the ideal forms of the Renaissance.*

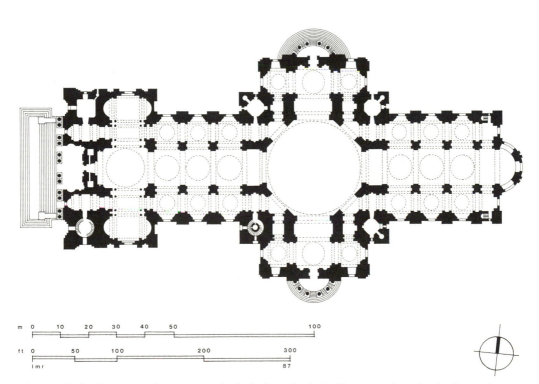

17.31. *Final plan for Saint Paul's, c. 1675. In the final scheme for the building, Wren bowed to the clergy's desire for a more traditional Latin cross, but he still retained his great dome for the crossing.*

17.32. Saint Paul's. Exterior.

were still not satisfied, insisting that Wren devise a more traditional basilican plan, with choir, transept wings, and nave. This he did, devising the final plan that was the basis of construction started in 1675 [17.31]. The upper portions of the cathedral underwent continued study by Wren, particularly the dome, finished in 1709 [17.32, 17.33]. The end result is a building of studied proportions full of curious paradoxes. The choir and nave have a traditional high-nave, low-side-aisle profile; as with the individual bays of the nave they are covered by Classical shallow saucer domes on pendentives. The outward thrusts of these vaults are transferred to the outer side walls by parabolic flying buttresses hidden behind the upper walls, which are simply a screen (their "windows" are blank). Instead of four massive piers under the dome in the manner of Bramante, Wren used eight smaller pendentives over eight slender piers to support the broad dome. The principal inner structural wall of the drum actually slopes inward, for

Wren's mathematical and geometrical studies indicated that this was the direction the forces would take coming down from the upper dome [17.34]. Moreover, the dome has three shells: the inner visible shell, a brick cone to support the crowning stone lantern, and the outer shell of timber and lead sheeting proportioned to the overall size of the cathedral. Saint Paul's is a complex and brilliant fusion of traditional plan and Renaissance/Baroque formal elements, its structure mathematically studied for utmost efficiency.

The Baroque Staircase

Baroque architects derived special satisfaction from the molding of sequences of interior spaces, alternately light and then dark, some confining, some expansive. This development was especially vigorous north of Italy, in the German-speaking areas of Bavaria and Austria, where it was focused on the architectural development of the staircase. The German and Austrian architects of the early eighteenth century deliberately violated Alberti's instructions, placing the staircase in a room of its own, exploiting its spatial potential. It was not unusual for the staircase to be the single *most* developed part of a German or an Austrian Baroque building.

The two best examples of stair design are by the German architect Johann Balthasar Neumann (1687–1753). For the sprawling palace for Prince-Bishop Johann Philipp Franz Schönborn in Würzburg, in central Germany, Neumann was brought in to complete the staircase in 1737–42, inside a building started from plans by two other architects. The palace itself was in the form of a wide U, with a center pavilion opened up by three huge doors so that, in accordance with the prince-bishop's wishes, his

17.33. Saint Paul's. Exterior of the dome.

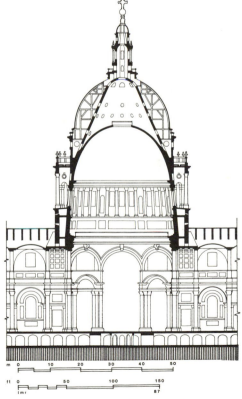

17.34. Saint Paul's. Section through the dome.

17.35. Johann Balthasar Neumann, Prince-Bishop's Palace, Würzburg, Germany, stair, 1737–42. In Baroque buildings the most important space was the ceremonial stair hall.

carriage could escape the rain and pass into the building, where he could alight at the foot of the staircase. The staircase was housed in the largest single room on the ground floor. In technical terms the stair has what is called an imperial plan, meaning that it has a central flight that ends in a landing at the rear wall and that it then divides into two flights (running parallel to the lower flight), which ascend the remaining distance [17.35]. The entire staircase is enclosed in a room almost twice as long and wide as the stair itself; this permits an enclosing balcony at the upper level, so that one ascends into a larger, lighter space. The coved ceiling vault was later embellished by the Venetian fresco painter Tiepolo, 1752–53, with figures representing the four continents and, in front of the illusionistic attic level, a portrait of Neumann himself.

Neumann's other major staircase was also designed for a Schönborn, Damian Hugo, the brother of Johann. Damian Hugo Schönborn had been elected to the prince-bishopric of Speyer, in eastern Germany on the Rhine River. In 1728–52 he began

building a palace at Bruchsal, south of Speyer, with a rectangular central block focused on a cylinder set in a light well at its core; flanking buildings formed a U-shaped entry court. Damian Hugo drew up much of the conceptual design himself, engaging various architects as consultants. It was he, apparently, who devised the scheme for the central cylinder housing curved stairs rising to a round landing at the upper floor, but his architects despaired of building it [17.36]. In 1728 Damian Hugo obtained the services of Neumann, who finished the stair. The ascent begins in a dark grotto vestibule on the ground floor; from there two staircases diverge, rising in curves along the sides of the cylinder. Past intermediate landings halfway up, the stairs rise to the upper domed cylindrical chamber, flooded by light from three tall arched windows on each side [17.37]. The lightness of the chamber is heightened by the lacy Rococo gilded ornament and the illusionist vault painting, both done in 1752. Here again one ascends from contained darkness by stages to expansive lightness.

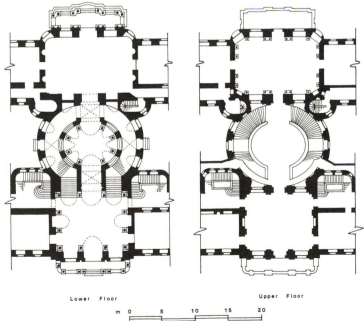

Lower Floor

Upper Floor

m 0   5   10   15   20

ft 0   10   20   30   40   50   60

l m r   87

17.36. *Johann Balthasar Neumann, Prince-Bishop's Palace, Bruchsal, Germany, 1728–52. Plan of the stair hall. The steps curve upward toward a central circular landing.*

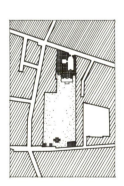

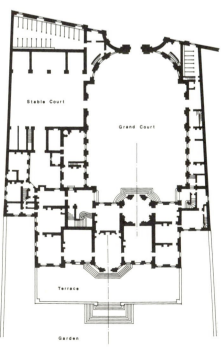

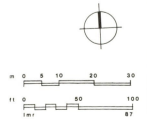

17.37. Stair hall, Prince-Bishop's Palace, Bruchsal. The upper chamber was completed with delicate Rococo ornament in 1752.

17.38. Jean Courtonne, Hôtel de Matignon, Paris, 1722–24. Plan. After the death of Louis XIV in 1715, the nobility returned to Paris, where they built new residences with one or two stories on large irregular parcels in the open outer fringes of Paris. The axial formal plans were adjusted to the irregularities of the sites.

Rococo Architecture—
The End of the Baroque

A particularly attractive element of the Bruchsal stair is its Rococo ornament. This light and irregular curvilinear ornament, so different from the heavy sculptural Classical orders and moldings of the seventeenth century, was part of an architectural reaction that began in Paris in the 1720s and swept through Europe in the mid-eighteenth century. As with other stylistic labels, this was coined as a derogatory term by the later Neo-Classicists, in the 1790s. They derived the word *rococo* from the French *rocaille,* used to describe the shell-encrusted grottos fashionable in gardens at the beginning of the eighteenth century.

During the lifetime of Louis XIV, when all members of court were required to live at Versailles, they found themselves either in cramped, ill-maintained quarters in the château itself, or in whatever accommodations they could find in the town. Le Brun's pervasive heavy Baroque Classical interiors came to be viewed as oppressive. As soon as Louis XIV died there was a mass exodus from Versailles (and a collapse of the local real estate market). The nobles moved to Paris, where they erected spacious private houses, *hôtels,* in what were then the outskirts of the city. These *hôtels* were built on

17.39. Germain Bouffrand, Salon de Princesse, Hôtel de Soubise, Paris, 1732–45. In the salons of the Parisian hotels, a new, light and airy style of interior decoration— Rococo—was developed, as exemplified in this room.

large, irregular parcels that permitted an entrance court off the street, leading to the entry pavilion of the house and to the stables, and a spacious private garden to the rear. A good example of the new freedom in domestic design is the Hôtel de Matignon, Paris, by Jean Courtonne, 1722–24 [17.38]. The plan shows another break from the insistent axial symmetries of Versailles, for the entrance court facade is much narrower than the garden facade, yet both are bilaterally symmetrical. This means that the axis of the entry is shifted to the side in a complex interlocking of rooms to become the axis of the garden facade.

The *hôtels* were built low to the ground, with the principal rooms on the ground floor, opening to garden terraces by means of what came to be called French doors.

Those parts of the wall not filled with windows or doors were often glazed with mirrors, and the effect of the tall doors and the many mirrors was to create a blaze of light, deemphasizing the sense of structure. The rooms inside these *hôtels*—painted white or in pale pastel tints and paneled with delicate gilded frames formed of lacy tendrils and wisps of ornament—must have seemed like a breath of fresh air after the somber interiors of Versailles, with their heavy pilasters and entablatures. Instead of the static orders of antiquity, this new Rococo ornament derived from natural forms—shells, flowers, seaweed—particularly if it had a double S-curve. The character of the Parisian style is epitomized in the interior of the Salon de Princesse of the Hôtel de Soubise, remodeled by Germain Bouffrand

17.40. *François Cuvilliés, Amalienburg Pavilion, on the grounds of the Nymphenburg Palace outside Munich, Germany, 1734–39. The fullest expressions of Rococo were made by French artists working in Germany, as in this hunting pavilion. The central round salon is completely lined with glass, either in French doors or mirrors.*

in 1732–45 [17.39]. Whereas Baroque architecture and its illusionistic visions had begun in Rome to express religious mysteries, Rococo architecture was developed in Paris as a purely secular style; it was also perhaps the first architectural idiom to arise primarily as a style of residential interior decoration.

The Amalienburg

Within a decade, Rococo had become the fashionable style of interior decorating across Europe, and in fact the most fully developed examples are those by French designers working in Germany. Even more resplendent than the interiors of the Salon de Princesse are those of the small hunting lodge, the Amalienburg, built in the grounds of the Nymphenburg, the royal Bavarian retreat outside Munich inspired by Versailles. The Amalienburg was built for Amalia, wife of the elector of Bavaria, in 1734–39 by François Cuvilliés (1695–1768), who was born in France and trained in Paris but employed in the royal household in Bavaria from the age of thirteen. The relatively plain white exterior of the diminutive Amalienburg gives one little preparation for the delicate encrustation of silver filigree, set against an azure blue background, that covers nearly every surface of the central Mirror Salon not glazed or covered by mirrors [17.40]. In the adjoining rooms the walls are pale yellow with silver leaf on the delicate paneling. The delicate profusion of carved and gilded stucco work by Johann Baptist Zimmermann made painted panels unnecessary. No other Rococo interior ever surpassed this.

Vierzehnheiligen

In Germany the intensity of ornamentation in eighteenth-century buildings was in large part compensation for the long period of deprivation caused by the Thirty Years' War, 1618–48, which devastated the economies of all the German bishoprics and principalities (although those in the Catholic south less than in the Protestant north). Fought by Swedish, French, Span-ish, and Austrian imperial armies on German soil, this bitter clash of Catholics and Protestants, together with the famine that followed, reduced the population across Germany by 15 percent and in some areas of the north and along the Rhine by as much as 66 percent. The various shattered economies did not fully recover until about 1715, precisely when the great palaces and pilgrimage churches in southern Germany began to be built.

The many eighteenth-century pilgrimage churches built in Bavaria and Franconia, in southern Germany, were also emblems of a rise in religious fervor. In 1445, on a hill in Franconia roughly 45 miles (72 kilometers) north of Nuremberg and overlooking the Main River, a shepherd had a vision of the Christ Child surrounded by fourteen childlike angels, who later came to be called the Fourteen Saints in Time of Need. The pilgrimage church of Vierzehnheiligen (Fourteen Saints) was soon built there, and in 1742 work began on replacing that building following plans supplied by Johann Balthasar Neumann. The supervising builder, G. H. Krohne, blithely deviated from Neumann's design, however, modifying the plan so that the principal altar of the Fourteen Saints would be in the center of the nave instead of in the choir. In 1744 Neumann was engaged to take over construction himself, to rectify as best he could the errors that Krohne had introduced. Since the position of the altar with respect to the outer foundations was now fixed, Neumann decided to make the spatial divisions of the church more fluid, reshaping the interior plan as a series of interlocked and overlapping ovals, the largest one containing the misplaced main altar [17.41, 17.42, 17.43]. Hence the internal curved arcades, capped by ellipsoidal plaster domes, have no direct relationship to the exterior of the church. In particular, the domes of the choir and the large nave oval meet in curved rib arches *over* the crossing where one would expect to find a dome. The main pilgrimage altar was placed at the center of the large oval in the nave (over the spot where the vision occurred), within the separate internal shell of the church; this arrangement allowed pil-

17.41. *Johann Balthasar Neumann, Vierzehnheiligen (Pilgrimage Church of the Fourteen Saints), Franconia, Germany, 1742–72. Exterior. From the outside, this pilgrimage church would appear to have a traditional Latin cross nave-with-side-aisles plan.*

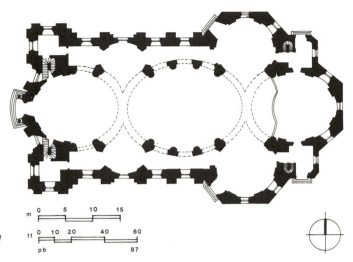

17.42. Vierzehnheiligen. Plan. Neumann's plan uses overlapped ovals throughout, creating a fluidity of movement from part to part.

grims to circulate around the church and not disturb the celebration of the Mass at the altar in the choir.

The interior embellishment, carried out in 1744–72, is also a superb example of the work of the Late Rococo stuccoists Johann Michael Feichtmayr and Johann Georg Übelhör and the painter Giuseppe Appiani [17.44, Plate 5]. Its white piers and vaults are covered with gilded tendrils framing the vault paintings. Here, as in most Rococo German and Austrian churches, the colorful and beautifully veined marble columns are not stone but actually painted plaster called *scagliola*. There was no desire to express structural reality, for even the vaults overhead are plaster on wooden lath suspended from the wooden roof trusses. On the con-

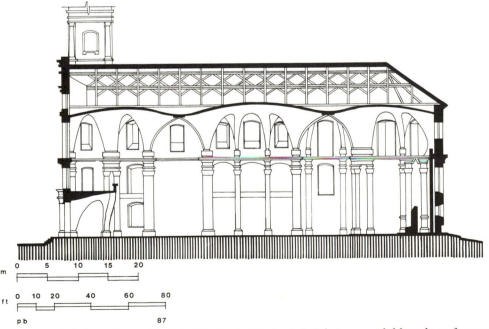

17.43. Vierzehnheiligen. Section. The curved vaults are in fact a shell of plaster suspended from the roof trusses.

17.44. Vierzehnheiligen. View of the nave. In such southern German pilgrimage churches as this, much of the credit for the dazzling interiors must go to the stucco carvers, gilders, and painters; at Vierzehnheiligen these artists included Johann Michael Feichtmayr, Johann Georg Übelhör, and Giuseppe Appiani.

trary, this is an environmental shell, defining interconnected spaces and manipulating light, bouncing it from the inner side of the encircling piers, suffusing the interior with a soft radiance. The interior is a world of delicate and joyful artifice, making the strongest possible contrast with the grim world outside. To pilgrims entering the church it must have seemed like the shepherd's vision—a foretaste of paradise.

An Architecture of Artifice

In their striving for the fullest possible effects of molded space, manipulated light, brilliant color, and sensuous detail, Baroque architects and their later Rococo counterparts created an architecture that, increasingly, was concerned predominantly with the shaping of space and almost not at all

with expression of the fundamental structure of architecture. Architecture became, quite literally, an exquisite and colorful veneer that was applied over something else; it was visual effect with very little structural truth. By the time Vierzehnheiligen was being completed in the 1760s, however, a radical change was under way in France, an abrupt turn toward a fully rational architecture in which, conversely, structural truth now controlled visual effect. The pendulum was swinging sharply back to the rationalism of Renaissance purists. Yet there was no immediate return to a Renaissance style, for an objective knowledge of history as a scientific discipline had emerged in the meantime. Architects now sought to create a rational modern architecture reformulated from the ground up in the light of a new understanding of ancient architecture.

NOTES

1. The nearest equivalent is the *maniera,* used by Vasari to describe affectation and deliberate stylization. This is the origin of the modern term *Mannerism.* See John Shearman, *Mannerism* (Harmondsworth, England, 1967), 15–22.
2. Bernini, quoted in Anthony Blunt, ed., *Baroque and Rococo: Architecture and Decoration* (New York, 1978), 35.
3. The generating modules are clear in Borromini's own drawings reproduced in Paolo Portoghesi, *The Rome of Borromini: Architecture as Language* (New York, 1968).
4. Quoted in Wittkower, *Art and Architecture in Italy, 1600 to 1750,* third ed., revised (New York, 1980) 203.

SELECTED READINGS

William Howard Adams, *The French Garden* (New York, 1979).

Germain Bazin, *Baroque and Rococo* (New York, 1964).

Leonardo Benevolo, *The Architecture of the Renaissance,* 2 vols., trans. J. Landry.(Boulder, Colo., 1978).

Anthony Blunt, *Art and Architecture in France, 1500 to 1700,* fourth ed. (New York, 1980).

———, ed., *Baroque and Rococo: Architecture and Decoration* (New York, 1978).

Kerry Downes, *English Baroque Architecture* (London, 1966).

Sigfried Giedion, *Space, Time, and Architecture,* fifth ed. (Cambridge, Mass., 1967); contains a good survey of the planning of Rome by Sixtus V.

Karsten Harries, *The Bavarian Rococo Church* (New Haven, Conn., 1983).

Francis Haskell, *Patrons and Painters: A Study in the Relations Between Italian Art and Society in the Age of the Baroque* (London, 1963).

Julius S. Held and Donald Posner, *17th and 18th Century Art: Baroque Painting, Sculpture, Architecture* (New York, 1972).

Eberhard Hempel, *Baroque Art and Architecture in Central Europe* (Baltimore, Md., 1965).

Howard Hibbard, *Bernini* (Baltimore, Md., 1965).

Henry-Russell Hitchcock, *German Rococo: The Zimmermann Brothers* (London, 1968).

———, *Rococo Architecture in Southern Germany* (London, 1968).

Wend Graf Kalnein and Michael Levy, *Art and Architecture of the Eighteenth Century in France* (Baltimore, Md., 1972).

Richard Krautheimer, *The Rome of Alexander VII, 1655–1667* (Princeton, N.J., 1985).

George Kubler and Martin Soria, *Art and Architecture in Spain and Portugal and Their American Dominions* (Baltimore, Md., 1959).

John Rupert Martin, *Baroque* (New York, 1977).

Henry A. Millon, *Baroque and Rococo Architecture* (New York, 1961).

Christian Norberg-Schulz, *Baroque Architecture* (New York, 1974).

———, *Late Baroque and Rococo Architecture* (New York, 1974).

Christian Otto, *Space into Light: The Churches of Balthasar Neumann* (New York, 1979).

Paolo Portoghesi, *Borromini* (London, 1968).

———, *Roma Barocca: The History of an Architectonic Culture* (Cambridge, Mass., 1970).

John Summerson, *Architecture in Britain, 1530 to 1830,* sixth ed. (New York, 1977).

V. L. Tapié, *The Age of Grandeur: Baroque and Classicism in Europe* (London, 1960).

John Varriano, *Italian Baroque and Rococo Architecture* (New York, 1986).

Rudolf Wittkower, *Art and Architecture in Italy, 1600 to 1750,* third ed., revised (New York, 1980).

———, *Studies in the Italian Baroque* (London, 1975).

18.10. *Étienne-Louis Boullée, Project for a metropolitan church, c. 1781–85 (detail). Although not intended to be built, such vast and geometrically severe projects as this ushered in the new scale of the industrial age.*

CHAPTER 18

Architecture in the Age of Enlightenment, 1720–1800

Modern architecture is a product of Western Civilization. It began to take shape during the later eighteenth century, with the democratic and industrial revolutions that formed the modern age. Like all architecture, it has attempted to create a special environment for human life and to image the thoughts and actions of human beings as they have wished to believe themselves to be. In these two fundamental attempts the modern man has faced psychic difficulties unparalleled in the West since the time of the breakup of Rome. The old, Christian, preindustrial, predemocratic way of life has progressively broken away around him so that he has come to stand in a place no human beings have ever quite occupied.

Vincent Scully, *Modern Architecture,* 1961

From the time of the Egyptians up to about 1750, Western architecture in any given time or region was relatively uniform—one expression for each relatively homogeneous culture. This homogeneity had just begun to change during the Renaissance as the new humanist architecture spread outside Italy and mixed for a time with regional and national architectural traditions. During the eighteenth century, however, there began to appear a multiplicity of architectural options.

This multiplicity is evident in the contrast between two important churches both under construction in mid-century, one an expression of illusion and the other a celebration of fact. Vierzehnheiligen, begun in 1742, was still being decorated as the 1770s began, its stucco carving and scagliola painting the product of the most accomplished skills of Baroque and Rococo illusion. Meanwhile a very different view concerning architecture was being embodied in the church of Sainte-Geneviève, Paris, begun in

1755 and midway to completion when the stuccowork of Vierzehnheiligen was being finished. Although Classical elements were employed in Sainte-Geneviève, they are no longer decorative and painted to look like marble; the columns serve a vital structural function, and the vaults are solid stone, not suspended plaster shells. Vierzehnheiligen is a chimera; Sainte Geneviève is "real."

An early indication of the growing yearning for a return to clear forms and proportional relationships was the revival of Palladian architecture in England, brought on by the appearance of the first English translation of Palladio's *Four Books of Architecture* in 1715. An active promoter of Palladian ideals was Richard Boyle, Third Earl of Burlington (1694–1753), and his architect, William Kent (1685–1748). Burlington designed Chiswick Villa in 1725 as a wing to his family residence, Chiswick House, clearly inspired by Palladio's Villa Capra but incorporating other elements as well [18.1]. Kent and Robert Adam designed a number of other country houses early in the eighteenth century, exploiting the proportioned geometries of Palladio's designs. To Burlington this simplified "un-Baroque" architecture embodied the ideals of balance of the ruling Whig oligarchy.

By the middle of the eighteenth century in France, the artifice of Rococo art and architecture came to be viewed as symptomatic of the artificiality and corruption of what was called the *ancien régime,* the reigns of kings Louis XV and Louis XVI. As social critics such as Denis Diderot (1713–1784) viewed such lascivious images as the cavorting plump pink nudes by

18.1. *Richard Boyle, Third Earl of Burlington, Chiswick House, Chiswick, outside London, 1725. The English in the early eighteenth century developed a new appreciation for the proportional clarity of Palladio's architecture, resulting in several country houses such as this based on the Villa Capra.*

François Boucher at the annual painting exhibitions, they felt the need for a new art and architecture, which served not to pander but to instruct and uplift. Diderot intended to write a book on the subject of art criticism (it would have been one of the very first), and his notes for this book reveal deep misgivings concerning how the arts represented the social values of his period. One finds among these notes such comments as these:

> Every work of sculpture or painting must be the expression of a great principle, a lesson for the spectator.

> I am no Capuchin [monk—i.e., prude], but I confess that I should gladly sacrifice the pleasure of seeing attractive nudities, if I could hasten the moment when painting and sculpture, having become more decent and moral, will compete with the other arts in inspiring virtue and purifying manners. It seems to me that I have seen enough tits and behinds. These seductive things interfere with the soul's emotions by troubling the senses.[1]

He could easily have made the same observations regarding Rococo deceit in hiding a building's structure and the overt sensual display in Rococo interiors.

Diderot was a champion of the *philosophes,* the moral and social philosophers in

France who advocated radical change in society; he edited and published the *Encyclopédie,* a richly illustrated summation of knowledge that also advanced new social ideas.[2] The philosophes, progressive-minded members of the growing middle class as well as philosophers, scattered across Europe, believed it was imperative to strip away the corrupting influence of the culture of the ancien régime to arrive at the natural condition of humankind and to create through deliberate and rational design a new social order, and with it a new, purer, more functionally and structurally expressive architecture. The philosophes had an implicit faith in human reason which pursued to its logical ends, they believed, would result in enlightenment. They rejected the idea of supernatural religion and the notion of a divine plan directed toward some preordained human end. Instead they believed in the power and potential of enlightened human reason.

The philosophes believed that knowledge comes only from a close study of the natural world. Since human understanding would therefore always be incomplete, humans could be certain of no absolute truth. Such a view fostered tolerance, something that religious dogma—whether Catholic, Protestant, Jewish, Islamic—has tended to make impossible. The philosophes emulated the critical objectivity of Ionian Greek scientists, adding to it disciplined observation and the modern idea of proof through experimentation. The only knowledge one could be certain of was what one could demonstrate by scientific observation and measurement, and out of this emerged modern notions of science and the mathematical model of the universe. Sir Isaac Newton's explanation of celestial movements, published in 1687, made the universe seem like a giant clock, perfectly made and operating without fault since the time of creation according to rational mathematical principles. Inspired by Newton's model, scientists endeavored to explain other natural phenomena in an effort to make the whole observable world an expression of rational processes.

Reinventing a Rational Architecture

The philosophes attributed to primitive nature an almost sacred importance, searching for qualities of the primitive, the pure, and the uncorrupted in art and architecture. With the statement of the nineteenth-century American writer Henry David Thoreau that "in wilderness is the preservation of the world" they might have agreed.[3] In architectural terms this meant that the purest architecture, that most suited to fundamental human needs and to basic human society, was what had appeared at the dawn of civilization. But with the philosophes' insistence on direct observation, it was now apparent that very little was truly known about ancient architecture. It was possible to read Vitruvius, but as to what the Roman houses of his time really looked like no one was positive. From what Vitruvius wrote, however, it was clear that in antiquity it was the column that was the basis of architectural structure, not the wall. This was where Alberti had made a fundamental error, basing his system of Renaissance architecture on the wall, embellished with engaged columns or pilasters, whereas it was from the orders themselves that the entire system

of proportion derived according to Vitruvius. Yet when eighteenth-century critics looked about them at contemporary architecture, what they saw was walls that swelled in and out, plaster masquerading as stone, and ornament so thick it obscured the structure. That ornament had to be stripped away; architecture had to get back to essentials.

This radical view was first expressed by Jean-Louis de Cordemoy in 1706 and then further elaborated in a little book, the *Essai sur l'architecture* (Paris, 1753), by Marc-Antoine Laugier (1713–1769), which gave instant form to the feelings of many architects of the period. The frontispiece of the book [18.2], its only illustration, shows the muse of architecture pointing out to a human infant (the first of his race) the mythical "primitive hut," a pure structure of columns and beams in which in fact the columns are the trunks of living trees. That, according to Laugier, was the beginning of architecture (and he was not so very far from describing the hut of *Homo erectus* at Terra Amata, Nice). Architecture, Laugier asserted, in contrast to Rococo embellishment was the art of pure structure, the essential elements of which are column, architrave, and pediment, serving their original structural functions and not applied as ornament. Yet he also appreciated the structural directness of Gothic vault construction (he was, after all, a patriotic Frenchman). In many ways his little book was the first manifesto on modern architecture, for it sparked lively discussion and a search for a pure architecture, freed of deceptive ornamental overlay. An even more extreme position was taken by the Italian theorist Carlo Lodoli (1690–1761), who insisted that architecture be determined solely by its internal function or use.

The first civilized people had been closer to the natural state, so it was believed, and hence their architecture had been purer, but the precise appearance of ancient domestic architecture was still a mystery. At least, that is, until 1748, when workmen digging a canal near Naples came upon the remains of Pompeii. The destruction of Pompeii in A.D. 79 was well known, for it

18.2. Frontispiece of Marc-Antoine Laugier, Essai sur l'architecture (Paris, 1753), showing the Muse of Architecture demonstrating what true architecture is.

was described at length by Pliny the Younger, who watched it from the safety of a ship at sea. But it is indicative of the theoretical bias of Renaissance architects that they had never bothered to find Pompeii and uncover it. In 1721 the Viennese architect Johann Fischer von Erlach had published a remarkable book, *Entwürf einer historischen Architektur* (A Study of Historical Architecture), presenting the great buildings of antiquity in large engraved plates. Although the plates revealed a new interest in the successive phases of architectural history, the images were largely artistic invention. What was needed instead was

hard evidence concerning ancient architecture, and that literally began to come to light in the mid-eighteenth century. Through the excavations of Pompeii and its surrounding towns, actual Roman homes, furniture, garden ornaments, jewelry, and other objects of everyday use were revealed, put on display, and eventually published.

To this new physical evidence was added a critical philosophical structure in the writing of the German art historian Johann Joachim Winckelmann (1717–1768). Winckelmann visited the diggings at Herculaneum and Pompeii to observe operations; what he saw prompted him to write a series of open letters that resulted in the expulsion of amateur treasure hunters and placing the excavations in competent hands. For this he is credited as the father of archaeology. His study of Greek sculpture (carried out unknowingly using Roman copies of Greek statuary) resulted in two epochal works, *Reflections on the Painting and Sculpture of the Greeks* (1755) and the more sweeping *History of the Art of the Ancients* (1764). The first defined the Greek aesthetic, and in it appears Winckelmann's famous characterization of Greek art: filled with "noble simplicity and calm grandeur." His history, though imperfect, was the first to outline the organic growth of art, passing from a period of youth to maturity of expression and then to a period of decline; he also attributed such natural, social, and cultural factors as climate, politics, and craftsmanship to the development of art. While Winckelmann helped to establish the strong affinity of Germans for Greek art, even more important was the stress he placed on the ennobling moral impact of the study of Classical art, suggesting that making such works of art available to the public would improve the moral consciousness of the nation, an idea German monarchs readily accepted and that

led to the creation of public art museums in the early part of the following century (discussed in the next chapter).

As the archaeological evidence began to accumulate, and with Winckelmann's writing for instruction, a perception of the successive phases of history began to be formulated. Although the concept of the distinct phases of Greek, Hellenistic, and Roman civilization was not yet fully developed, there were those like Winckelmann who argued in favor of Greek architecture's being superior because older and purer than Roman. But ancient Greek architecture was even more imperfectly understood than Roman, and soon expeditions of architects and natural scientists set out for remote sites around the Mediterranean to record in an objective way the appearance, dimensions, and proportions of Greek buildings. The first expedition to Greece itself was led by James Stuart and Nicholas Revett of England. During 1751–55 they traveled across Greece, visiting Corinth, Delos, and Delphi, but the focus of their attention was Athens. In 1761 appeared the first of their four engraved volumes, *The Antiquities of Athens,* presenting the buildings of the Akropolis in crisp engravings

18.3. James Stuart and Nicholas Revett, restoration drawing of the Parthenon, Athens, c. 1785. Published in the second volume of their Antiquities of Athens, *showing the result of intensive archaeological study in Athens, this was the first truly accurate representation of the Parthenon and introduced the austere beauty of Greek architecture to Europe.*

18.4. Robert Adam, library, Kenwood House, London, 1767–68. Such interiors as this resulted from Adams's study of Roman architecture, such as the Palace of Diocletion at Spalato, Yugoslavia, which he visited and published.

[18.3].[4] In 1750–51 Madame du Pompadour, mistress of Louis XV, sponsored a team that visited Greek Paestum in Italy; one member of this party was the young architect Jacques–Germain Soufflot (1713–1780). The published result of this expedition was *Ruines de Paestum* (Paris, 1764). Roman sites also began to receive attention. An English expedition to Yugoslavia resulted in Robert Adam's *Ruins of the Palace of the Emperor Diocletian at Spalato . . .* (London, 1764), and Adam's fellow Briton, Robert Wood, traveled extensively, producing *Ruins of Palmyra* (London, 1753) as well as *Ruins of Baalbec* (London, 1757). In England such investigations helped support a revival of Roman forms and spatial config-

urations in interior design, of which Robert Adam (1728–1792) was the leader. His column-screened library in Kenwood House, London, 1767–68 [18.4], is based on similar Roman rooms. Even the delicate decoration is inspired by Pompeiian prototypes, but with the flat painted Roman designs translated into low-relief carved plaster, and the atmosphere of the whole room elevated by lighter, pastel colors.

Sainte-Geneviève, Paris

How the study of antiquity might point toward a new architecture was demonstrated in the design of the church of Sainte-Geneviève, Paris, designed in 1755 by

Soufflot just four years after his visit to Paestum. There he had seen Greek columns boldly silhouetted against the sky, powerfully evocative images of load and support. And where the roof of the temple of Poseidon had been supported there were superimposed columns, one atop the other. For the plan of his church, Soufflot used a Greek cross, much admired at this time [18.5], but it was like a temple turned inside out. Its external walls were opened up with numerous windows, and its internal structure was a colonnade (Corinthian in this case—Soufflot was not yet prepared to use the more massive and austere Greek Doric). The columns in turn support the domical vaults over the arms of the church, each dome carried by pendentives that come down in points precisely over the columns [18.6]. The vaults are exactly what they purport to be—structural shells of solid cut

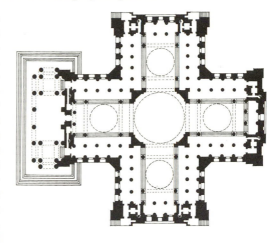

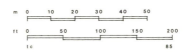

18.5. *Jacques-Germain Soufflot, Church of Sainte-Geneviève (Panthéon), Paris, 1755–90. The Greek cross plan, with four arms of equal length, was one popular with academically trained French architects, but the use of freestanding structural colonnades internally was new.*

18.6. *Sainte-Geneviève (Panthéon). Interior. The vaults are true structural shells of cut stone, not plaster illusions; they rest on points over the structural Corinthian columns.*

stone, and not a false work of plaster suspended from some hidden armature. It was this structural realism, combining the best of the post and lintel with the arch and vault systems, that caused Laugier to praise Sainte-Geneviève as "the premier model of perfect architecture."[5] Over the crossing was to be a dome on four piers, but construction of the dome was delayed, and the finished dome is not entirely Soufflot's design. Across the front runs a Classical temple portico of Corinthian columns [18.7]. The entire building was designed by Soufflot with the new mathematics of architectural statics, allowing him to calculate pressure and thrust; there was no stone that was superfluous. Furthermore, in the portico he incorporated a complex system of iron bar reinforcements in the flat arches of what appears to be the entablature (it was not possible to find stone to span the distance between columns). In its clarity of form and structural expression, Sainte-Geneviève seemed to its generation to announce a new era in architecture.

"Speaking Architecture"

Some French architects endeavored to push Soufflot's ideas to their inevitable conclusion, creating an architecture of pure elemental form expressing function. What these architects proposed was an architectural "revolution," although politically they were actually quite conservative; indeed, Claude-Nicolas Ledoux (1736–1806) nearly went to the guillotine for building royal tax-collecting stations in a ring around Paris. Yet those stations had a boldness of form and a simplicity of detail that was radically new. Few survive, as they were ripped apart when the French Revolution erupted. One tollhouse that did survive is the Barrière de la Villette, 1784–89, composed of a square base and a cylindrical upper section [18.8]. Windows, doors, and arched openings are

18.7. Sainte-Geneviève (Panthéon). The facade incorporates a Roman temple portico.

18.8. *Claude-Nicolas Ledoux, Barrière de la Villette, Paris, 1784–89. Ledoux's consciously modern architecture was reduced to the simplest possible geometries.*

18.9. *Étienne-Louis Boullée, Project for a cenotaph for Isaac Newton, c. 1784.*

18.11. Claude-Nicolas Ledoux, house for a river surveyor, project, c. 1785–90. The new architecture envisioned by Ledoux and Boullée was to speak directly of its function—in this case, providing residence for a hydraulic engineer in charge of moderating the flow of a river.

18.12. Claude-Nicolas Ledoux, Royal Saltworks, Chaux (Saline de Chaux), Arc-et-Senans, near Besançon, France, begun c. 1775. Begun as a royal saltworks, this was redesigned by Ledoux as an ideal industrial town, with the saltworks and housing in the center oval, other civic buildings around that, and all surrounded by an agricultural green belt.

completely free of embellished frames, and the entry portico is supported by square Doric piers.

Ledoux's contemporary, Étienne-Louis Boullée (1728–1799), built several *hôtels,* but his principal impact came through his teaching at the royal academy of architecture. Like Ledoux, he proposed in his theoretical designs a boldly scaled and austere architecture whose symbolic forms would evoke a sense of function. Such architecture was intended to communicate its purpose directly to the observer, to be *l'architecture parlent,* or, literally, "speaking architecture." Boullée's most expressive buildings were funerary monuments of enormous scale, and his best known is a cenotaph for Isaac Newton designed about 1784 [18.9]. Deriving its basic form from the round tumulus mausoleums of the Romans, the Newton cenotaph was to have a vast cylindrical base supporting a pure hemispherical dome. Inside, and reached by means of a tunnel passing through the base of the building, was an enormous spherical chamber, with a massive sarcophagus at its base. The upper masonry shell was to be penetrated by tiny apertures that admitted pinpricks of daylight; these points of light, viewed against the black interior of the dome, re-created the vault of the heavens, whose planetary motions Newton had explained. Equally large in scale was Boullée's project for a huge metropolitan church, designed about 1782–83 [18.10, page 396]. Considering the state of building technology of the late eighteenth century, these vast projects were clearly unbuildable, but even if never intended for construction, the Newton cenotaph and church exemplified a new scale and a new simplicity of form, and were beacons for a new age.

In his drawings and projects Ledoux was freer than in his tollhouses to create an architecture of pure volumes declaring functional use. The best known of these idealistic designs is his house for a river surveyor, done about 1785–90 [18.11]. The house is a hollow cylinder lying on a cradling base; through the hollow of the cylinder the river flows, as dramatic an expression of control of the water as Ledoux was able to make.

The boldness of this new architecture is contrasted to the old mills and their water wheels shown in the foreground.

Another of Ledoux's royal commissions was a saltworks, begun in 1775 between the small villages of Arc and Senans in western France, not far from the Swiss border. This too had caused him political trouble at the time of the French Revolution, but while in prison he redesigned the town, creating an ideal industrial community. After the Revolution he published engravings of his ideal town, now called the Saline de Chaux (Saltworks at Chaux), along with other designs, in a volume entitled *L'Architecture considérée sous le rapport de l'art, des moeurs et de la legislation* (Architecture Considered in Relation to Art, Habits [or Morals], and Legislation) (Paris, 1804). The buildings were arranged to enclose an oval, a form Ledoux wrote he used because it was "as pure as that of the sun in its course." At the center of the oval plan [18.12] the first buildings actually had been constructed: the house of the administrator, flanked by the reduction buildings where the brine pumped up from the salt mines was boiled down to obtain the salt. The stark geometry of the administrator's house was emphasized by overscaled details, particularly the columns of the portico, built up of alternated cylindrical and square blocks of stone. The only ornaments in the otherwise stark walls of the reduction buildings are openings from which protrude carvings of a thick fluid, the sculpted representation of the brine. The carvings thus expressed the function—*l'architecture parlent.* Around the workshops in the oval ring and framing a communal park were to be the residential apartments for the workers, with gardens in rear yards. Beyond the ring were to be public facilities, markets, and more gardens and open land forming a green belt.

Designing the City

Ledoux's project for Chaux is an example of the increasing attention that some architects were giving to the form of the city, and his is especially noteworthy as an example of an ideal industrial community. In England the

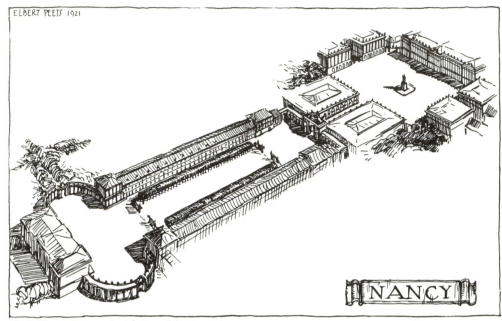

ELBERT PEETS 1921

NANCY

18.13. Nancy, France. Aerial view of the new urban squares.

most coherent demonstration of urban design was Bath, a spa that increasingly began to attract London society during the summer months. John Wood (1704–1754) undertook to remake the town, designing clusters of town houses shaping urban spaces, beginning with Queen Square in 1729–36 and adding the Circus in 1754, a circle of thirty-three residences facing inward toward a common park. His son, John (1728–1781), continued this work, adding the Assembly Rooms, 1769–71, and the majestic Royal Crescent, 1767–75, a group of thirty houses in a broad half-ellipse.

Versailles continued to set the example for royal estates and parks, and in the eighteenth century several more were laid out, including the park at Aranjuez of 1746–78 south of Madrid for Philip V of Spain, and Karlsruhe in southern Germany, begun by J. F. von Betzendorf in 1715 as a hunting lodge for Karl Wilhelm, Margrave of Brandenburg. Eventually thirty-two avenues would radiate out from the palace, some toward the village and others into the forest. Urban squares were designed in Paris, Bordeaux, and Copenhagen, all of them royal

projects, but perhaps the most intriguing case of urban design is Nancy, the capital of Lorraine in western France. The duchy of Lorraine was given by Louis XV to Stanislas Leczinski, father of his bride and former king of Poland. A king without a country, Stanislas set out to make Nancy his own capital city, befitting his station. With the financial aid of Louis XV, he engaged the architect Emmanuel Héré de Corny (1705–1763) to design a series of linked urban squares, with his residence at one end and a major urban space at the other, connected by a tree-lined boulevard framed with rows of identical houses [18.13]. The new town center was built during 1741–53. At the end of the boulevard (the Place de la Carrière) is a Roman triumphal arch, foreshadowing the Neoclassicism that would become a major movement in another quarter century, while the large Place Royale (now the Place Stanislas) was embellished with wrought iron gates and lamps that epitomize Rococo delicacy. It was fitting, perhaps, that one of the last such royally sponsored urban rebuilding projects should have been so well done.

The English Garden

The arrangement of Ledoux's city of Chaux on the landscape was still formal, in the French tradition of Le Nôtre, but it is significant that so much open space was protected around it in Ledoux's green belt. Ledoux was reflecting the new sensitivity to nature that arose in the Age of Reason. Whereas in the seventeenth century nature was seen as something to be tamed and controlled, having no inherent form or beauty in its own right, early in the eighteenth century that perception radically changed. The English gentry began to develop an entirely new approach to planning the grounds around their country houses. Instead of imposing an arbitrary geometric pattern of parterres, they endeavored to augment the natural contours of the land, damming streams to create irregular lakes, and planting groups of trees so as to frame asymmetrical vistas across the landscape. One of the best-preserved examples is the garden at

Stourhead, England, designed and planted during 1741 to 1781 by its owner, Sir Henry Hoare [18.14, 18.15]. What these Englishmen were trying to do was to re-create in real materials, in soil, water, and carefully arranged plants, the pastoral Classical landscapes described by the Roman author Virgil. Not content with viewing the painted versions of these landscapes in the seventeenth-century canvases of Nicolas Poussin or Claude Lorrain, they sculpted the earth itself to re-create those yearned-for landscapes. The result was the creation of the English garden and the new aesthetic of the Picturesque that prized irregularity, roughness, asymmetry, and the surprise of unexpected vistas as one moved through the landscape.

Carefully put down in these constructed "natural" landscapes were representations of historic or exotic buildings intended to induce reflection, so that seated on a bench at Stourhead and facing the mock Pantheon across the lake, one might have read Virgil's

m　0　　100　　200　　300　　400

ft　0　　　　500　　　1000　　　1500

I m r　　　　　　　　　　　　87

18.14. Sir Henry Hoare, Garden, Stourhead, England, 1741–81. Plan. The picturesque English garden, looking deceptively "natural," is totally a product of human design, imitating the paintings of Claude Lorrain and the nature writing of ancient authors.

18.15. View of the Pantheon, Stourhead. Scattered at strategic points in the English garden were buildings evoking places far away or times far distant, meant to be objects of contemplation.

pastoral *Georgics* or perhaps even have reflected on the implications of Edward Gibbon's newly published history of the decline and fall of the Roman Empire. Other buildings might provoke different associations with different periods; for example, an allusion to Greece was made at Hagley Park in Worcestershire, where in 1758 James Stuart built a garden pavilion with a facade adapted from the Parthenon, which he had just returned from measuring in Athens [18.16].

Or the intent might be to induce reflections on local history by showing medieval architecture, an idea that had first emerged a half-century earlier. In 1705, when Sir John Vanbrugh inspected the royal estate where he was to build Blenheim Palace, he discovered on the grounds the ruins of the medieval Woodstock Manor, which Sarah Churchill insisted be removed. For several years Vanbrugh argued against this, writing in a letter of 1709 that such ruins "move lively and pleasing reflections . . . on the persons who have inhabited them [and] on the remarkable things which have been transacted in them." If the ruins were

planted, he wrote, "with trees (principally fine yews and hollys), promiscuously set to grow up in a wild thicket, so that all the buildings left . . . might appear in two risings amongst them, it would make one of the most agreeable objects that the best of landscape painters can invent."[6] As Vanbrugh clearly suggested, it was the associations the mind made with the old buildings and their stylistic qualities that were important. If real ruins did not exist, fake medieval buildings could be built and knocked down to create instant ruins. In 1747 at Hagley, a mock ruin of a Gothic building had been built in the park by Sanderson Miller [18.17].

In France a sensitivity to nature was awakened by the philosopher Jean-Jacques Rousseau. In his *Discourses* (1750–54) he made an eloquent plea for the natural man, writing that human beings were essentially free, virtuous, and happy but were corrupted by society and urban ills. A friend of Rousseau, the Marquis de Girardin, resolved to create at Ermenonville, outside Paris, the kind of landscape in which the natural man could rediscover himself.

18.16. *James Stuart, "Doric Portico," Hagley Park, Worcestershire, England, 1758. Stuart based this garden pavilion on the Parthenon, which he had just returned from measuring in Athens.*

18.17. *Sanderson Miller, sham Gothic ruin, Hagley Park, Worcestershire, England, 1747. If no real medieval ruins existed in the grounds of English gardens, fake ruins such as this were sometimes built.*

18.18. *Richard Miqué, Antoine Richard, and Hubert Robert, Hameau (Hamlet), Versailles, France, 1778–82. In this mock rural village, tucked into a corner of the forest of Versailles relandscaped as an English garden, Marie Antoinette liked to play at being a peasant.*

Assisted by J.-M. Morel and the painter Hubert Robert, the Marquis had the park constructed in 1754 to 1778, with a variety of open or wooded landscapes with picturesque buildings, all permeated with the pastoral and arcadian atmosphere of Rousseau's book *Julie ou la Nouvelle Hèloïse.* Even at Versailles, in a far corner of the grounds away from Le Nôtre's insistent geometries, around an irregular lily pond Marie Antoinette had a mock *hameau,* or farm hamlet, built in 1778–82, where she tried desperately to recapture the simple life [18.18, 17.21].

The picturesque garden, in its embrace of nature and all its untidiness and irregularity, was one of the first expressions of another view of the world that eventually would challenge Enlightenment rationality; this was Romanticism. Named after the literary "romances" of mystery and suspense that writers modeled after medieval stories, Romanticism was a reaction against the nar-

row and restrictive mathematical models of the philosophes, which the Romantics felt belittled feeling and imagination. Early Gothic novels, such as Ann Radcliffe's *Mysteries of Udolpho* and Horace Walpole's *Castle of Otranto,* were set in dark, mysterious, ancient houses in which the single governing principle of their rambling design seems to have been irregularity and asymmetry. As in the gardens, it was roughness and irregularity that was prized. Another literary foundation for the emerging Romanticism was provided by Edmund Burke's essay *A Philosophical Inquiry into the Origin of Our Ideas of the Sublime and Beautiful,* 1756. Contradicting the philosophes at every turn, Burke discussed the heightening of the senses caused by darkness, danger, and great forces of nature, such as roaring waterfalls, storms, and volcanic eruptions. So, in addition to the refined symmetry and proportion of the Enlightenment, and the irregular roughness of the Picturesque, there was the awe-inspiring danger of the Sublime.

The Romanticists' vivid imagination and something of their sense of awe were expressed in the engravings of Giovanni Battista Piranesi (1720–1778). An Italian architect who built very little, he nonetheless had an enormous impact on architects in the last half of the eighteenth century through the various series of engravings he produced. In his *Veduta* (Views of Rome), he presented fanciful visions of Roman ruins and recent buildings, suggesting a scale that absolutely dwarfed ant-sized humans. Piranesi's creativity reached its zenith in his *Carceri* (Prisons), which presented visions of limitless spaces, delineated by broken architectural fragments of overpowering scale [18.19]. Like Boullée, Piranesi proposed an architecture whose scope far outreached the technology of the time but that soon became the prototype for

the building needs of the nineteenth century.

Eclecticism— The Architecture of Choice

The idea inherent in the pavilions in the English Garden was that architecture derived its value in direct proportion to its literary associations—that is, to the degree the historical references were in accord with the building's function. Thomas Jefferson (1743–1826) seized on this idea as a way of inculcating in his American countrymen not only a taste for good architecture but also as a way of visually reinforcing the function of republican government. The republican form of government created in the new American federal government following the American Revolution, and then in each of the individual states, were the first true republican governments since early Roman

18.19. *Giovanni Battista Piranesi, plate from the* Carceri *(Prisons), c. 1745–61. In these visions of boundless spaces, of ramparts connected by bridges stretching away in vistas beyond comprehension, Piranesi gave form to a uniquely modern view of architecture on a vast scale.*

18.20. Thomas Jefferson, Virginia State Capitol, Richmond, Virginia, 1785–89. Jefferson deliberately selected a Roman temple, the Maison Carrée, in Nîmes, France, as his model, since he believed it to be an example of superior Roman Republican architecture and therefore symbolic of republican self-government.

times. What sort of building did a modern republican form of government require? What sort of image should it project? Those were the questions that Jefferson faced when he was asked by his fellow Virginians to provide them a design for the new Virginia State Capitol. What he wanted was a building image that would provide the appropriate associations in the minds of his colleagues.

As a result of designing his own home, Monticello, beginning in 1770, Jefferson became known for his abilities in architectural design. At the time that Jefferson received the request for the Virginia capitol design in 1785, he was serving as the first ambassador of the United States to the court of France. He had moved beyond his early admiration for the proportioned Renaissance architecture of Palladio (he taught himself Italian so he could read the original), and now was an ardent admirer of Roman Classical architecture. Working in association with the Parisian architect Charles-Louis Clérisseau, who had recently published measured drawings of the Maison Carrée in Nîmes, Jefferson took the Maison Carrée as his model [18.20, 12.1]. He prepared sets of drawings, using the new graph paper then being used by French engineers, putting the various state governmental functions into rooms fitted into the shell of a Roman temple, and had a plaster model made in Paris for shipment to Richmond, Virginia. Jefferson did make some changes from his model. In place of the Corinthian columns of the Maison Carrée, Jefferson called for the somewhat simpler Ionic. The side walls of Jefferson's building were punctuated by two stories of windows, lighting the various chambers inside. He wrote to his colleagues in Virginia that because the prototype in Nîmes was "noble beyond expression" he was dismayed to hear that major changes were being considered in his plans. He implored his friends to follow his designs, for "how is a taste in this beautiful art to be formed in our countrymen unless we avail ourselves of every occasion, when public buildings are to be erected, of presenting to them models for their study and imitation?"[7] Persuaded by his arguments, the Virginia committee had the building erected with only minor deviations from Jefferson's drawings and model. On the bluff over the James River rose a white Roman temple.

Jefferson's Virginia capitol was the first

functionally habitable building, on either side of the Atlantic, whose form was based on a specific historical model. Since that form was meant to exemplify the architecture of people governing themselves in a republic, it was an example of *associational eclecticism.*[8] But Jefferson's adaptation of a specific building also gave authoritative sanction to the idea that a new building could successfully duplicate an ancient model; this would soon lead to an outright Greek Revival. By the beginning of the nineteenth century, architects were turning increasingly to specific source models, in a wide variety of historical styles, resulting in revivals of Greek and Roman classicism, medieval and Gothic architecture, as well as Egyptian and even more exotic re-creations. Publishers obligingly provided architects with increasing numbers of folios with engravings of historical ancient buildings. The measured drawings by Stuart and Revett were just the beginning of such architectural publications.

With Jefferson began eclecticism as a basis of architectural design. Fundamental to this approach was the associational connection between the form or ornamental detail of a contemporary building with another architecture, distant either in time or location. This initial *associational eclecticism* lasted from about 1740 to 1785. The fact that garden pavilions were meant to be seen from a distance meant that they did not need costly building materials painstakingly detailed, nor did the historical references need to be especially precise (and in any case, archaeological knowledge in 1750 as to the specifics of Greek or Gothic architecture was just emerging). So, for instance, although the columns of Stuart's Greek Doric pavilion at Hagley are true Greek Doric, heavily proportioned and devoid of a base, the corner columns are not thicker nor do any of the columns have true entasis.

This initial associational phase of eclecticism gradually changed to a *synthetic eclecticism,* lasting from about 1755 through 1815. This approach advocated using various historical styles from a range of historical periods combined in a single structure. Souflot's Sainte Geneviève in Paris is a good example of this. The Corinthian columns are used as structural supports in the sense that the Greeks used them (although they are inside the building); the entrance portico is Roman in detail and scale; the plan form is contemporary, but the saucer domes on pendentives in the arms of the church are Byzantine; the cut stone construction of the domes and the resolution of structural forces is Gothic in spirit (and the crossing dome, as finally built, is a derivative of Wren's dome for Saint Paul's, London). Yet these various references are combined to create an organic whole, not a collection of ill-related parts.

The Baltimore Cathedral in the United States, designed by Benjamin Henry Latrobe (1764–1820) in 1804, is a similar synthesis of various elements. It too has a plan inspired largely by Byzantine examples, covered with cut stone vaults [6.15], with an entry portico supported by some of the most beautifully carved Ionic columns of the period. When Latrobe was first asked to develop a design for the diocese, he drew up two completely different and independent proposals. One was a version of a Gothic church (not very accurate in detail), for Latrobe recognized that the Gothic style had been developed by the medieval church and he thought it might have symbolic meaning for the clergy. His alternative design was the Classical domed scheme that was built. The fact that Latrobe was able to provide his client with two alternative designs, however, points up the fact that he was professionally trained.

Synthetic eclecticism was employed by the early Romantics just as it was by the early Neoclassicists, as is evident in Strawberry Hill, the country house Horace Walpole designed as his own Castle of Otranto and the setting for his life as a literary romance [18.21]. Walpole began Strawberry Hill, outside London at Twickenham, in 1748, and construction continued for almost forty years, as section after section was added, supervised by various architects. It is a mixture of every conceivable expression from the Middle Ages, ranging from twelfth-century battlements to sixteenth-century Tudor moldings; it even was given a library in a new "Gothick" style greatly influenced by the contemporary craze for intricate Chinese design.[9]

Revolution and Architecture

Today virtually every aspect of modern Western civilization is influenced by sweeping cultural changes begun in the eighteenth century. That period is often called a time of revolution, even if few of the changes occurred as fast as the word *revolution* suggests. Yet the cultural changes begun then have had effects as profound as the political upheavals that began when the American colonies threw off British domination and declared themselves the United States (1775–83), followed by the bloody fratricidal French Revolution (1789–94).

Most essential, perhaps, was the new perception of humans and their relationship to the universe that grew out of the rise of modern science. The beginnings of this new perception were laid in the Renaissance, in Nicolaus Copernicus's theory of a sun-centered solar system, proved when Galileo turned his telescope on the heavens in 1609. Galileo also proposed a mathematical model of the universe, writing that everything in nature was governed by numbers. How the heavenly bodies remained in perpetual motion without flying apart or crashing together was finally explained in Isaac Newton's *Philosophiae naturalis principia mathematica,* 1687. Thus emerged the concept of a wholly rational universe, a gigantic clocklike mechanism, created by a distant rational deity. And as Francis Bacon had

proposed much earlier, the operating principles of such an understandable universe could and should be deciphered by the human mind and used to improve human life.

If this new attitude meant that humans began to take more control of their own destiny, it also had the unfortunate effect of further weakening the connection between religious practice and social conscience, between religion and civil life. The impact of religious authorities on civil life diminished still further. Western civilization became a secular society, and the days when the noblest ambition of an architect was to build the house of God rapidly came to an end.

Once the idea that the noblest objective of human inquiry was to change and improve the physical world took hold in the late seventeenth century, the rate of social and economic change increased dramatically. Agriculture was affected early with the introduction of the iron plowshare, able to cut hard, previously untillable land. In Holland the practice began of rotating crops. This and other changes in farming practice resulted in greater farm yields, producing more food for humans and fodder for improved breeds of farm animals. New sources of food also appeared in plants brought from the New World.

The increase in food production, coupled with the lowering of the death rate through improved hygiene, and improvements in medical care toward the end of the century, all meant that the population of Europe

18.21. Horace Walpole, Strawberry Hill, Twickenham, near London, begun 1748. For his own home, the author Horace Walpole assembled a collection of miscellaneous medieval details to create an evocative and romantic setting.

suddenly began to grow at an exponential rate. In 1700 the population of Europe was about 110 million, but by the end of the century it had almost doubled, to 190 million, and by 1850 it was 260 million. As the productivity of farm workers increased, there was a migration of rural workers to the rapidly expanding cities in search of employment and food. London grew by over 50 percent from 1700 to 1800, reaching a million inhabitants. Other European cities experienced similar rates of growth. This shift in population meant that European culture increasingly was a middle-class urban culture, and the principal architectural problems the next generation would face would be learning how to house, transport, entertain, and accommodate the governing institutions of ever-larger urban populations.

As the urban populations swelled, they were employed in proliferating shops and factories. This change in production of goods also radically restructured the European economy, for it meant replacing traditionally rigid economic practices with new procedures that fostered ever-expanding production of goods for general consumers. This increase in production began in Great Britain in the textile industry. The first step in the transformation of the textile industry was the mechanical twisting of thread in 1765 and then Richard Awkright's invention of the water-powered loom in 1769. With these inventions, soon powered by the steam engine perfected by Watt and Boulton in 1769–76, the production of cloth in Britain increased by 800 percent by the end of the eighteenth century.

The most important change in industry, perhaps, was using machines in place of skilled labor to make other machines, first done in 1799 by Marc Brunel, who designed machines in England to make pulley blocks for ships' rigging. Brunel's crude apparatus was surpassed in 1798–1801, when the American Eli Whitney used division of labor, together with standardized machine jigs, to enable workers to produce identical musket components; finished firearms could then be assembled from the standardized parts by anyone. With the application of simple machines to perform repetitive tasks, mass production of consumer goods began. The result was a dramatic increase in production and a lowering of production costs, meaning that goods formerly available only to the aristocracy became available to the growing middle class and even to the workers themselves.

The increased manufacture of consumer goods was dependent on the production of less expensive component materials, and of these the most important was iron. Iron was not a new material, but the smelting of iron ore had been hampered from the beginning by the use of charcoal for fuel. At the very time that the need for iron began to rise, the English forests were fast disappearing into the charcoal furnaces. Abraham Darby devised a system of heating mineral coal to drive off its sulfur content, creating coke; this material could then be used to fire iron furnaces. Darby began to use this process in his works at Coalbrookdale, England, in 1709. Not only did coke allow for larger furnaces and hotter temperatures, it also produced a better grade of molten iron, which could be cast into thin-walled pots and other everyday items in great demand. Darby's son and grandson continued to develop the iron industry and worked with Boulton and Watt to perfect precision boring of the pistons of steam engines. As the technique of iron smelting was improved by the Darbys, the cost per ton gradually dropped, so that cast iron and its tension-resisting derivative, wrought iron, became the basic materials for industrial growth.

One of the landmarks in the emergence of iron as a new building material was the construction of a cast iron bridge over the Severn River near Coalbrookdale in 1777–79, based on an idea of John Wilkinson after designs by Thomas F. Pritchard and manufactured by Abraham Darby III [18.22]. Traditional in its arch form, it was made of five half arches on each side (ten pieces in all), with a total clear span of 100 feet (30.5 meters). Each half-arch was cast as a single piece, a formidable job of iron casting. Soon other bridges of cast iron voussoirlike sections were proposed, as were suspension bridges using wrought iron chains. Cast iron was also being exploited for thin structural columns needed in textile factories during the 1780s, and in 1786 the architect Victor Louis designed a light iron truss for the roof of his Théâtre-Français in Paris. By the end of the eighteenth century, iron was a major building material, although its full potential was just beginning to be understood.

Each of these developments affected and intensified the social impact of the others. The end result was the rise of utilitarianism by political theorists, such as the Englishman Jeremy Bentham. In his *Fragment on Government* (1776), and his *Introduction to the Principles of Morals and Legislation* (1789), Bentham proposed that the most rationally ordered society would promote the greatest good for the greatest number. This accorded well with the economic ideas of Adam Smith, presented in his *Inquiry into the Nature and Causes of the Wealth of Nations* (1776). Smith advocated the elimination of trade restrictions, allowing production and trade to be governed solely by the law of supply and demand—capitalism at its purest. In this way the self-interest of every producer would promote the general welfare, resulting in the greatest good for the greatest number. Producers of raw materials, manufacturers, merchants, and consumers would all benefit.

The architectural corollary to these late eighteenth-century processes of industrialization and economic growth was this: the building tasks that soon were the most pressing were those that provided the greatest use for the greatest number, the greatest public service to the community. The most

important commissions very shortly were no longer churches or great palaces but legislative halls, courts, museums, galleries; the new patrons of architecture were industrialists and governmental bodies. As the eighteenth century came to a close, the basis of the bourgeois middle-class culture of the nineteenth century, clothed and supplied by means of mass-produced goods, was being created.

An Architecture of Rationality

Guided by the philosophes, European architects by the mid-eighteenth century began to reject the visual excesses of Rococo architecture in favor of a structural discipline shorn of extraneous ornament; the generative basis of architecture was transformed. Increasingly architects were faced with devising solutions and using new building materials for the new buildings needed by the exploding urban populations. The church, splintered into ever more numerous factions, was no longer a dominant unifying cultural, moral, or political force, nor was it any longer the most important patron of architectural innovation. It says much of the times that during the French Revolution Soufflot's Sainte-Geneviève ceased to be a church and was secularized as the Panthéon, a monument to the great figures of French history and culture. A bourgeois middle class was evolving, and with it a new secular culture and an architecture inspired by egalitarian ideals and industrial enterprise. The old religious and aristocratic architectural models would no longer suffice.

18.22. *John Wilkinson, Thomas F. Pritchard, and Abraham Darby III, Coalbrookdale Bridge, Coalbrookdale, England, 1777–79. One of the first demonstrations of the dramatic potential of cast iron as a structural material, this bridge was cast in 50-foot half sections.*

NOTES

1. Denis Diderot, "Random Thoughts on Painting," in Lorenz Eitner, *Neoclassicism and Romanticism: 1750–1850* (Englewood Cliffs, N.J., 1970), 64–66.
2. The full title was *Encyclopédie, ou dictionnaire raisonné des sciences, des arts et des métiers.* The first volume appeared in 1751 and the seventeenth in 1780. It was richly illustrated with engravings showing contemporary achievements in the sciences, construction, and industry. As many as sixteen thousand copies were published, exerting a great influence on the dissemination of progressive ideas.
3. Henry David Thoreau, "Walking," 1851, in *The Works of Thoreau,* Henry S. Canby, ed. (Boston, 1937).
4. For all the care taken in measuring the Parthenon, Stuart and Revett failed, however, to notice the entasis of the columns and the curvature of the stereobate.
5. Laugier, quoted in W. G. Kalnein and M. Levy, *Art and Architecture of the Eighteenth Century in France* (Baltimore, Md., 1972), 319.
6. See Vanbrugh's letter in Geoffrey Webb, *The Works of Sir John Vanbrugh,* vol. 4, *The Letters* (London, 1928), 28–30
7. Thomas Jefferson to James Madison, September 20, 1785, reprinted in Leland M. Roth, *America Builds: Source Documents in American Architecture and Planning* (New York, 1983), 28.
8. Although the Maison Carrée was built during the reign of Augustus Caesar, and is thus technically an imperial building, it does follow the type of the earlier Republican temple, of which several small examples survive in Rome, but these were not known to Jefferson.
9. The eighteenth-century spelling *Gothick* is used to distinguish this early adaptation of this historical style.

SUGGESTED READING

Carl Becker, *The Heavenly City of the Eighteenth Century Philosophers* (New Haven, Conn., 1932); controversial but informative.

Leonardo Benevolo, *History of Modern Architecture,* 2 vols., trans. H. J. Landry (Cambridge, Mass., 1971); especially 1: 3–37.

A. Branham, *The Architecture of the French Enlightenment* (Berkeley, 1980).

Peter Collins, *Changing Ideals in Modern Architecture* (London, 1965).

Peter Gay, *Age of Enlightenment* (New York, 1966).

———, *The Enlightenment: An Interpretation,* 2 vols. (London, 1966–69).

N. Hampson, *The Enlightenment* (Harmondsworth, Eng., 1968).

W. Herrmann, *Laugier and Eighteenth-Century French Theory* (London, 1962).

Henry-Russell Hitchcock, *Architecture; Nineteenth and Twentieth Centuries,* fourth ed. (Baltimore, Md., 1977).

Hugh Honour, *Neo-classicism* (Baltimore, Md., 1968).

Christopher Hussey, *The Picturesque* (London, 1927).

Edward Hyams, *The English Garden* (London, 1962).

W. G. Kalnein and M. Levy, *Art and Architecture of the Eighteenth Century in France* (Baltimore, Md., 1972).

Emil Kaufmann, *Architecture in the Age of Reason* (Cambridge, Mass., 1955, and New York, 1968).

Dominique de Ménil, *Visionary Architects: Boullée, Ledoux, Lequeu* (Houston, 1968).

Robin Middleton and David Watkin, *Neo-Classical and 19th Century Architecture* (New York, 1977).

Norman T. Newton, *Design on the Land: The Development of Landscape Architecture* (Cambridge, Mass., 1971).

Joseph Rykwert, *The First Moderns: The Architects of the Eighteenth Century* (Cambridge, Mass., 1980).

———, *On Adam's House in Paradise* (New York, 1972).

John Summerson, *The Architecture of the Eighteenth Century* (London, 1986).

Dora Wiebenson, *The Picturesque Garden in France* (Princeton, N.J., 1978).

———, *Sources of Greek Revival Architecture* (London, 1969).

Rudolf Wittkower, *Palladio and English Palladianism* (London, 1974).

19.16. Paris Opéra. In the staircase, Garnier provided a place for Parisians to promenade—to see and be seen.

CHAPTER 19

Architecture
in the Nineteenth Century

It is very important for architects, engineers, both civil and military, painters of both historical and landscape scenes, sculptors, draftsmen, theatrical decorators, in a word, for all those who build or depict buildings and monuments, to study and know all the most interesting things that have been done in architecture in every country throughout the ages.

Jean-Nicolas-Louis Durand, *Recueil et parallèle des édifices en tout genre, anciens at modernes,* 1801

Must the nineteenth century, then, come to a close without ever possessing an architecture of its own? Is this epoch, so fertile in discoveries, so abounding in vital force, to transmit to posterity nothing better in art than imitations, hybrid works without character and impossible to classify?

Eugène-Emanuel Viollet-le-Duc, *Entretiens sur l'architecture,* 1863–72

Architects at the beginning of the nineteenth century were confronted with multiple problems, all urgently demanding answers. They had to devise plans for buildings that had never existed before—covered public markets, railroad stations, public and charitable institutions, hospitals, insane asylums, housing for the workers being drawn to rapidly expanding industrial cities, to mention only a few of the new building types. Moreover, these buildings had to be larger than any had been since Roman times. Architects were also presented with new building materials, cast and wrought iron as well as glass, in quantities never available before thanks to improvements in mass production.

These logistical and technical problems were perplexing enough in themselves, but architects also found themselves in an awkward position. Architects in the early nineteenth century now knew the history of architecture, and they could never again

have the innocence of not knowing history. Once the evolutionary stages of the history of civilization had been sketched out, the historical development of architecture and its successive styles had begun to be codified. Intoxicated with this new knowledge, architects wanted to make buildings like those they were learning about. Furthermore, the growing nationalistic fervor, particularly in those countries overrun by Napoleon and now seeking to establish their unique national identities, impelled architects to use historical references to establish recognizable national architectural styles.

Architects inherited Romantic literary associationalism from the eighteenth century, causing them to ask what the appropriate images of these new building types should be. For buildings such as churches and residences it was possible to look to native vernacular models for appropriate expression, as Augustus Pugin and William Morris were to do in England in the design of churches and houses. But for other new building types, the temptation to draw analogies and to think of contemporary buildings in terms of similar ancient examples was very persuasive.

Moreover, all too readily available were proliferating portfolios of engravings of measured drawings, first of Classical buildings, then of Gothic churches, and even of exotic non-European architecture, such as the views of Egypt that excited so much interest after Napoleon's campaign there in 1797–98. During the Renaissance, architects had had to visit Rome and other ancient sites to make sketches of Classical ruins and to abstract their own principles of composition and proportion. Although nineteenth-century architects were able to travel even more easily, now they could also purchase engravings and photographs, and they became deluged with information as to the accuracy of details.

The major emphasis of eclecticism now became archaeological accuracy, making sure the entasis of a column was exactly like that of its prototype, the curve of a capital was correct, the number of cusps on a Gothic finial was accurate, the arrangement of tracery of a Perpendicular Gothic window was authentic, or the inclination of the wall of an Egyptian pylon was right. Eclecticism thus entered a third phase, growing out of general associationalism and synthetic accretions—**Revivalism,** lasting from about 1800 to 1850, in which two criteria determined the success of a design: how appropriate the historical allusion in conveying the image of the internal function was, and how archaeologically correct the form of the building and its details were. Jefferson's Virginia capitol would have been only a qualified success in this respect, for its side walls had been punctured by un-Roman windows.

Neoclassicism

The image of Classical order came to be strongly associated with public buildings and the role of public buildings in elevating public virtue. One early example was Leo von Klenze's sculpture gallery built in Munich, 1816–30, for Ludwig of Bavaria [19.1]. Bavaria had just achieved the status of an independent kingdom, having allied itself with Napoleon, and Ludwig, an ardent patron of architecture and a firm believer in the public function of architecture, quickly set about rebuilding Munich as a royal capital and a symbol to the German people. Leo von Klenze (1784–1864) faced the dual problem of developing a new building type and of giving it a recognizable and appropriate image. This was to be the first public sculpture museum, making available to the public the remarkable early Classical Greek pediment sculpture from the temple of Aphaia on the island of Aegina excavated in 1811. The newly recovered sculpture had just been purchased by the Bavarian king and its missing fragments restored by the Danish Neoclassical sculptor Bertel Thorvaldsen. During the preceding decades

19.1. Leo von Klenze, Glyptothek (Sculpture Gallery), Munich, Germany, 1816–30. Designed as part of the campaign to embellish Munich as capital of Bavaria, this public museum was designed by von Klenze especially to house the Greek sculpture recently discovered at the Temple of Aphaia on the island of Aegina, Greece.

19.2. Karl Friedrich Schinkel, Altes Museum, Berlin, 1822–30. This, too, was a major public art museum; its novel plan was carefully designed by Schinkel to provide ease of circulation and good light, and to promote the educational function of the building.

European monarchs and princes had been opening their residences to the public so their collections of ancient sculpture could be viewed and studied by their subjects. As Diderot and Winckelmann suggested, if Classical art could be viewed by the general public it would have an uplifting and moralizing impact. Starting with von Klenze's building, other buildings began to be built solely for this purpose, the museum becoming an extension of the art being housed in it, enhancing its educational function.

Because of this view, and because of what von Klenze's building was designed to contain, it was given the Greek name Glyptothek, "sculpture gallery." And because this museum was to present Greek sculpture, von Klenze made his Glyptothek Classical in its details. The plan, however, was not Greek, but composed of identical square cubicles, each capped by a dome; it was based directly on a plan for a public gallery published by Jean-Nicolas-Louis Durand (1760–1834) in his *Précis de leçons données à l'École Royale Polytechnique* (Paris, 1802–5). Durand had been von Klenze's teacher in Paris. The exterior of the Glyptothek has no windows, but rather blind aedicules containing sculpture (another announcement of what one will find inside),

and at the center of the building is a Greco-Roman Ionic temple block serving as the entrance portico, its details inspired by Greek sources.

Since 1798 much the same concern for making the royal collections available to the public had been on the mind of Friedrich Wilhelm II, King of Prussia, and his curator of art, Alois Hirt. Their resolve was further strengthened by the ideas of Alexander von Humboldt on the role cultural institutions played in public education. As early as 1800 the architect Karl Friedrich Schinkel (1781–1841) prepared schemes for a museum to hold the royal collections of painting and sculpture, but it was not until Napoleon had been defeated in 1815 and the art he had removed to Paris had been returned to Berlin that final plans for the Altes (Old) Museum were undertaken (the name was adopted after a new museum was built in 1841–55).

The Altes Museum, designed by Schinkel in 1822 and built 1824–30, is a large rectangular block on an island in the Spree River in central Berlin [19.2, 19.3, 19.4]. Its broad front closes off the end of the old royal pleasure garden and faces the Baroque royal palace. Perhaps because it was to define and enclose a major public space, Schinkel gave

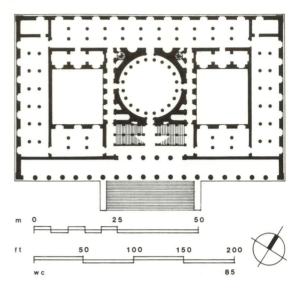

19.3. Altes Museum. Plan of the main floor.

his museum the form of a Greek stoa; its long Ionic colonnade continues the average cornice height of surrounding Baroque buildings. The art works to be displayed inside included sculpture and painting, so the building was divided into two zones, with a central Pantheon-like rotunda to house the sculpture, and surrounding galleries for the paintings. Lighting the paintings was of paramount concern to Schinkel, so he devised a system of galleries arranged around light courts. The court and the outer walls are opened up with tall windows, and perpendicular to these are spur walls or panels on which the paintings could be hung, thus eliminating glare on the varnished surfaces of the paintings.

In the Altes Museum Schinkel devised a logical plan and a circulation pattern based on a thorough study of the building's function of displaying works of art as an educational task, creating around it a crisply and accurately detailed Greek envelope. It was designed as the ancient Greek architects

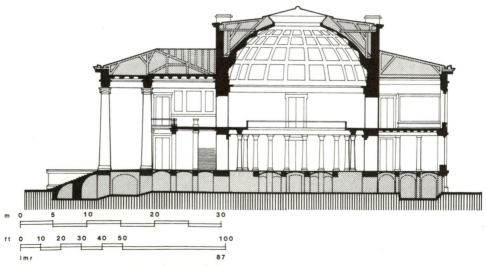

19.4. Altes Museum. Cross section. The central, domed rotunda was designed to house the sculpture collection.

themselves might have done if they had been required to design such a large public museum. In buildings such as this, Neoclassicism became firmly linked with public service and educational aspirations; this museum and Schinkel's other buildings also helped to establish Berlin as the preeminent German cultural and architectural center.

Both von Klenze's and Schinkel's galleries used Greek details selectively, in buildings whose plans were evolved almost solely with a view to function. They can be called Revivalist because of the fidelity to Greek and Roman source material in their details. In other instances architects duplicated whole Greek temples, in form as well as in detail. Von Klenze did this in his memorial temple Walhalla, 1821–42, a Germanic pantheon commissioned by Ludwig of Bavaria to commemorate the great figures in German literature and history, built atop an immense ziggurat podium on a bluff over-

looking the Danube near Regensburg, Germany. Although the building was given the name of the Norse paradise, it is a replica of a Doric Greek temple.

American architects faced a similar need to make buildings express a national character. Following the example provided by Jefferson in his Virginia State Capitol, they built a number of state capitols in the early years of the nineteenth century. Like Jefferson they wanted to give these governmental buildings the image of democracy, and so they attempted to fit all the requirements of state government into building shells patterned after Greek temples. One particularly well-detailed example is the Kentucky capitol at Frankfort, Kentucky, 1827–30, by Gideon Shryock, built of white marble. But perhaps the most elaborate of all the American examples is Thomas Ustick Walter's Greek temple for Girard College in Philadelphia, 1833–47. Built entirely of cut stone,

19.5. Thomas Ustick Walter, Girard College, Philadelphia, 1833–47. The accurate Grecian details of this building reinforced and ennobled its functional purpose, for this housed a college for young men from the working classes in Philadelphia.

it has beautifully and most accurately detailed Greek Corinthian columns completely surrounding the temple block [19.5]. The problem that all Revivalists faced, however, especially those trying to fit modern public functions inside a Classical temple, was that it was not possible to make changes in the established model to allow for modern needs without losing the image. The American sculptor Horatio Greenough recognized this problem, and in 1843 said his countrymen were going about architecture backward, trying to bend the Greek temple to contemporary needs. If, he wrote, Americans would only design buildings the way they built their ships, with lean economy of form dictated by function, they would soon create buildings "superior to the Parthenon."[1]

The Gothic Revival

Neoclassicism was only one manifestation of how the interest in history influenced design, for medieval, Egyptian, Asian Indian, and other exotic styles were also being re-created with increasingly correct details.

The major alternative to Neoclassicism in public architecture was the Gothic style. Religious and educational activities were housed in Gothic adaptations since the earliest colleges and universities had been developed by the church in the Middle Ages. The use of Gothic forms also corresponded to the more romantic side of eclecticism; for just as the trabeated Neoclassical orders suggested enlightened logic and ennobling probity, so craggy and dark Gothic architecture corresponded to the Romanticists' desire for mystery and irregularity of form.

The Houses of Parliament, London

In northern Europe, especially, Gothic architecture was viewed as inherently national in expression, the French and Germans seeing it as embodying their particular national character, but the English had a particular affinity for Gothic architecture. This became evident in 1834 following a catastrophic fire that consumed the medieval palace of Westminster, where Parliament had been assembling since the

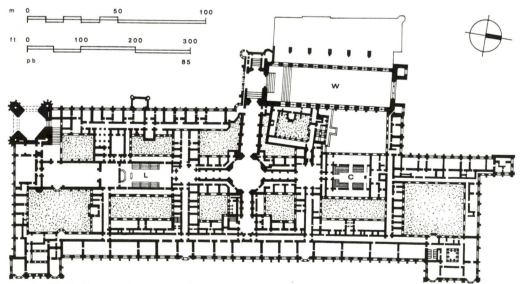

19.6. Sir Charles Barry and Augustus Welby Northmore Pugin, New Palace of Westminster (Houses of Parliament), London, 1836–70. Although the new Houses of Parliament were designed in the Perpendicular Gothic style to better incorporate portions of medieval Westminster Hall (W), the plan was strictly symmetrical about the center, reflecting the two governing bodies—the House of Lords (L) and the House of Commons (C). The stippled areas are internal courts.

19.7. Houses of Parliament. River facade.

thirteenth century. In 1052 an abbey had been established there by Edward the Confessor, and next to it a royal palace was built and enlarged over the centuries. One major addition was Westminster Hall, in 1397, the great public room with its hammerbeam wooden trusses [15.16]. Another was the mid-twelfth-century palace chapel of Saint Stephen. Because subsequent monarchs preferred other residences, the palace at Westminster was made available to Parliament, and in Saint Stephen's chapel the upper and lower houses of Parliament alternately sat for debate. It was not an arrangement specifically designed for this parliamentary function, but over the years Parliament adjusted its mode of operation to the spaces provided.

In 1834 royal tax records that had accumulated over eight centuries were burned to make room in the government vaults. The incineration went on nonstop in the palace furnaces for days, and finally one night the heat ignited the wooden structure near the furnaces; by the time the blaze was discovered it was too late to contain the fire. The ancient houses of Parliament were almost totally consumed, in a great conflagration stirringly depicted in the bold color sketches

of the landscape painter Joseph Mallord William Turner.

After the fire it was quickly decided that the houses of Parliament should be rebuilt on the same spot. It was also decided that the general style of the new buildings should be medieval, so as to better accommodate the surviving portions of the original buildings, especially Westminster Hall. A competition held to procure the best design was won by the team of Charles Barry (1795–1860) working with the young designer Augustus Welby Northmore Pugin (1812–1852). Pugin and his father had been among the leading advocates of Gothic architecture and had already published several books presenting measured details of thirteenth- and fourteenth-century churches. The symmetrically Classical and rationally clear plan of the new Houses of Parliament was devised by Barry, with two wings balanced about a central circulation corridor and rotunda [19.6]. At the center of each wing was the principal chamber, for the Lords and the Commons, each surrounded by associated committee rooms, offices, and libraries arranged around light courts; on the Lords' side were additional robing rooms and special preparation chambers for the monarch

19.8. *Interior, House of Lords, Houses of Parliament, A.W.N. Pugin, designer.*

when opening parliamentary sessions. All of this was clothed in the most accurate late English Perpendicular Gothic detail. This style made possible the repetition of many identical small bay units (thereby permitting repetitive cutting of ornamental detail) and also provided for large banks of glass [19.7]. To provide for better ventilation—one of the great faults of the original buildings—large plenum chambers were created over the meeting halls into which the warm, stale air rose and was passed to large iron ventilators on the roof. Iron was used for the framing of the roof trusses so as to eliminate combustible material that might contribute to future fires.

Thus the new Houses of Parliament combined a rational plan, carefully devised to enhance functional use, with a new structural material exploited to improve mechan-

ical services and fire safety, and with historical references in the detailing that enhanced the functional meaning of the building in three ways. First, the Gothic details of the new work allowed it to join with the surviving medieval portions in such a way that the line between the two is nearly undiscernible [15.16]. Second, Perpendicular Gothic was viewed by the mid-nineteenth-century Englishman as being an inherently English architecture. And third, because of the long association of Parliament with the medieval palace of Westminster, the Gothic style was viewed as being connected with the parliamentary form of government. In fact, when designing the new chambers for the Lords and Commons [19.8], Barry and Pugin were careful to retain the medieval chapel seating arrangement. Hence, it could be argued that the

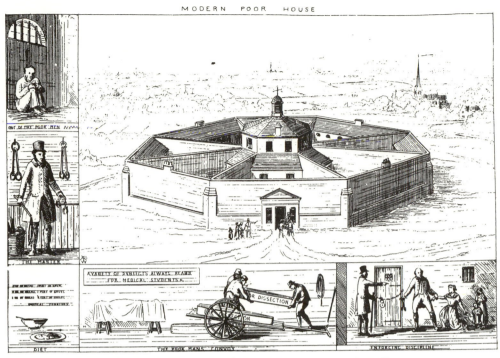

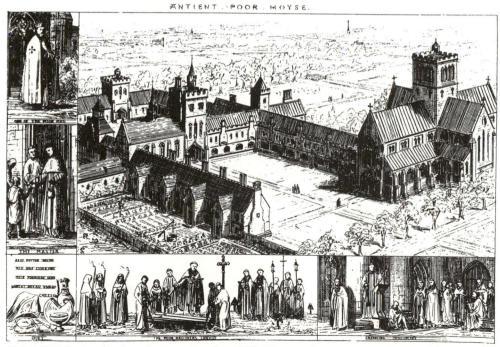

19.9. A.W.N. Pugin, plate from Contrasts *(London, 1836). This pair of views contrasts the care of the poor in the fifteenth century in a Christian almshouse with that in a nineteenth-century poorhouse. Pugin suggested that the character of architecture reflected the quality of social concern and interaction.*

19.10. A.W.N. Pugin, *Church of Saint Giles, Cheadle, Staffordshire, England, 1840–46. For his revitalized church architecture, Pugin drew from English parish churches of the fourteenth and fifteenth centuries.*

Gothic style was perhaps the only one that could have been used in building the Houses of Parliament.

Saint Giles, Cheadle

The revival of the Gothic style coincided with and gave support to the resurgence of mysticism in religion that grew out of Romanticism. The Gothic Revival phase of eclecticism that emerged in the 1840s in England coincided with a liturgical reform movement within the English Anglican Church. Impassioned students at Oxford and Cambridge began a movement to return to the pre-Reformation English liturgy, and this required a return to the church architecture of that period. The acknowledged arbiter of taste in this revival of archaeologically correct Gothic church architecture was Pugin. In 1836 he had published a highly propagandistic and persuasive book called *Contrasts,* in which he presented side-by-side drawings of fifteenth-century buildings with their nineteenth century counterparts, which unvaryingly lacked a humane spirit and convincing architectural form [19.9]. Clearly, according to Pugin, Gothic architecture had been far better.

For Anglican churches, the Gothic Revival worked very well, for the reinvigorated architecture fitted perfectly with the building's renewed function. One of the best examples of Pugin's adaptation of fourteenth- and fifteenth-century parish church models is his church of Saint Giles in Cheadle, Staffordshire, 1840–46 [19.10, 19.11]. The compact plan of the church, with a separately articulated chancel, side porch, and tower, recalls such prototypes as Saint Andrew's, Heckington, Lincolnshire, 1345–80. In building Saint Giles's, Pugin had the patronage of the Earl of Shrewsbury, who provided funds for the building so that Pugin was able to realize the intensive interior ornamentation he desired. Following Pugin's example, in England and in the United States Gothic architecture was used extensively for churches and collegiate buildings, although few were as richly embellished as Saint Giles.

Creative Eclecticism

There were limits to the literal reuse of established architectural forms, as the many ill-formed variations on the Greek temple made clear. For four decades such replication was feasible, but by 1850 it was no longer possible to fit the ever-expanding needs of the nineteenth century into fifth-century B.C. building envelopes. The alternative was a new mode of design, with historical details in buildings planned strictly in accord with functional requirements. At first the historical references were employed in highly personal, creative, and often idiosyncratic ways, but later with greater restraint and archaeological accuracy in proportion and detail.

Second Empire Baroque

For public buildings the Classical alternative was developed by the architects Louis Visconti and Hector-Martin Lefuel in the extensive additions to the Louvre in Paris, 1852–57 [19.12]. What they created was a lavishly embellished variation on the French

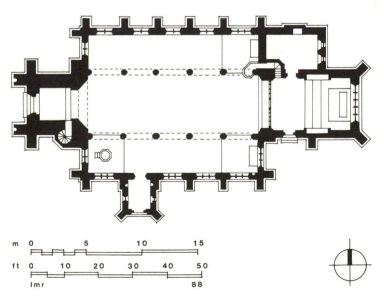

m 0   5   10   15

ft 0   10   20   30   40   50

1 m r   88

19.11. Saint Giles, Cheadle. Plan. Just as in medieval churches, the chancel area containing the altar is a separate smaller space.

19.12. Louis Visconti and Hector-Martin Lefuel, the new Louvre, Paris, 1852–57. The richly embellished French Baroque style was developed by Visconti and Lefuel to integrate the new addition with the original portions of the Louvre, built in the sixteenth and seventeenth centuries.

19.13. Charles Garnier, Paris Opéra, 1861–75. Garnier designed the exterior to accomplish several public functions, including expressing each of the three major sections of the building, providing a fitting terminus to the new Avenue de l'Opéra, and celebrating the act of going to the opera.

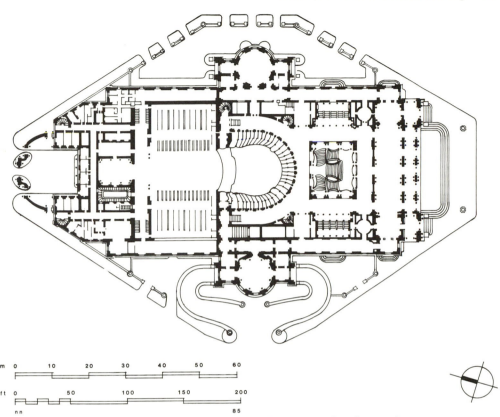

m 0   10   20   30   40   50   60

ft 0   50   100   150   200

n n   85

19.14. Paris Opéra. The divisions of the plan show that Garnier gave special emphasis to the public circulation areas of the opera house, and somewhat less to sight lines of the stage.

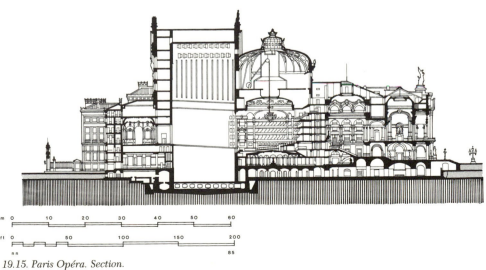

m 0   10   20   30   40   50   60

ft 0   50   100   150   200

n n   85

19.15. Paris Opéra. Section.

19.16. Paris Opéra. In the staircase, Garnier provided a place for Parisians to promenade—to see and be seen.

19.17. Sir George Gilbert Scott, Midland Grand Hotel, London, 1868–74. Built of multicolored stone and other materials, this vigorously modeled building celebrated the power and status of the railroad.

Baroque in what came to be called Second Empire Baroque, since their patron was Louis-Napoléon, who declared himself emperor of the Second Empire, fashioned after that of his more famous uncle, Napoléon Bonaparte.

The embellished character of Second Empire Baroque was further elaborated in the sumptuous new opera for Paris built in 1861–75 by Charles Garnier (1825–1898) [19.13, 19.14, 19.15]. During the mid-twentieth century this building was considered by knowledgeable architects and critics to be the low point of rationality in design, but in fact Garnier had made a careful study of how the opera functioned in Paris. As a result he developed a carefully plotted circulation pattern for each of the four types of operagoers he identified: those arriving by carriage, those on foot, those who already had tickets, and those who bought them at the box office. But above all, he perceived that late-nineteenth-century Parisians went to the opera principally for social reasons, rather than to hear the music—they went "to see and be seen." Accordingly, Garnier used a traditional horseshoe auditorium with layered galleries around the auditorium so operagoers could better see each other. But most important, by far the greatest proportion of space in the building is devoted to circulation spaces and lobbies, focused on the elaborate staircase, which provides the perfect stage on which the operagoers can parade and exchange greetings [19.16]. In many ways, on reaching the auditorium after having passed through the staircase and the successive lobbies, an operagoer may have experienced something of an anticlimax.[2]

High Victorian Gothic

The Gothic alternative in this more creative phase of nineteenth-century eclecticism has come to be called High Victorian Gothic, because of its elaborate character, its development in England during Victoria's reign, and its use of Gothic forms. It likewise appeared about 1850, and is well illustrated by the Midland Grand Hotel designed by Sir George Gilbert Scott (1811–1878) as the

head house for the Saint Pancras Railroad Station, London, 1868–74 [19.17, 19.18]. Now converted to offices, it is a long J-shaped building fitted to its irregular site, originally not only providing facilities for ticket offices, waiting rooms, and baggage handling for the station but also serving as a terminus hotel for travelers, with lounges, dining rooms, and private rooms on the upper floors. Its skyline is among the most picturesque in London, with a variety of clock towers, dormers, chimneys, ventilators, and miscellaneous projections. The colorful character of the profile is enriched by the multiple colors of the building materials, including red brick, stone, slate, and marble of various hues in the polished columns.

This external representation of internal function through varied building masses, and the expressive use of various building materials in their natural colors, derived from the writings of the architectural critic John Ruskin (1819–1900). Although not an architect, he exerted a profound influence on architectural development, primarily through two books. In *The Seven Lamps of*

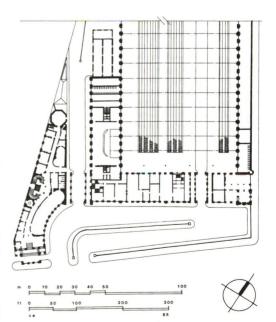

19.18. *Saint Pancras Station and Midland Grand Hotel. Plan. Behind the hotel rises the great train shed covering all the tracks.*

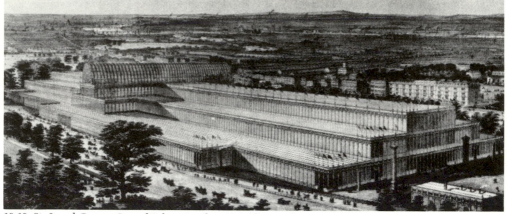

19.19. Sir Joseph Paxton, Crystal Palace, London, 1851 (destroyed 1936). View.

Architecture (London, 1849), he argued in favor seven criteria: the use of functionally expressive ornament, truth in expression of building materials and structure, expressive massing, beauty derived from observation of nature, bold and irregular forms, durable construction, and adherence to traditional Christian architectural forms (that is, Gothic architecture). In his other influential work, *The Stones of Venice* (London, 1851, 1853), he extolled the architecture of Venice, suggesting that it provided the perfect point of departure for developing a modern Gothic architecture suited to a capitalist, mercantile culture. It was also a highly colored architecture. In the Midland Grand Hotel, Scott showed how Ruskin's arguments could be applied to real situations.

The Architecture of the New Industrialism

The Impact of Industry

In the nineteenth century there arose building needs that had never existed before, leaving architects perplexed just how to design the required structures. This is well illustrated by the dilemma faced by Prince Albert and his supporters. The prince had conceived of a comprehensive international exhibition of industrial products, the first world's fair. Various executive and architectural committees were set up and the exhibition scheduled for 1851. The most notable

English architects of the day submitted designs for the exhibition building, none of which were found satisfactory and all of which would have required too much time to build. The solution was provided not by an architect but by Joseph Paxton (1801–1865), a horticulturalist and a builder of greenhouses. He proposed a large building, essentially a grandly oversized greenhouse, to be assembled of identical modular cast iron columns and beams, with a wall membrane almost entirely of standardized panes of glass. His initial sketch was drawn on June 11, 1850; in eight days he prepared the necessary drawings for approval; in July a contract for construction was accepted; and within nine months all parts had been manufactured and shipped to Hyde Park, London, ready for assembly. On May 1, 1851, the building was opened with great fanfare by Queen Victoria [19.19]. It was almost immediately dubbed the Crystal Palace by the London magazine *Punch*.

Paxton made full use of all that the English had learned of metal building technology in the construction of train stations and greenhouses in the preceding two decades, but his innovations produced a giant leap in building scale, in the prefabrication of standardized building parts in factories across England, and in methodical organization of the building process. The Crystal Palace covered an enormous area, 1,848 by 408 feet (563.3 by 124.4 meters), with cast iron columns set 48 feet (14.6

meters) apart. As in no building before, Paxton had created a building in which the volume enclosed far surpassed the mass of the building. Compared to all prior buildings, it was like a bubble, and so Paxton introduced cross bracing in wrought iron diagonal rods in the upper parts of the structure to resist lateral wind pressures [19.20]. But he also created a transparent building without visual limits. Its cast iron members were painted predominantly blue, so they tended to merge with the sky. Even better, it was a demountable building, and when the exhibition was over the parts were disassembled and removed to Sydenham, where an enlarged Crystal Palace was reerected and served as a cultural center for London until destruction by fire in 1936.

The greatest limitation of historical styles was in meeting the growing demand for such large public buildings as train stations. Boulton and Watt's steam engine was put on wheels in 1804 to move mining cars, and in 1825 the first passenger railway began oper-

ation between Darlington and Stockton, England. During the following decade other passenger rail systems were set up in England, with small depot buildings erected to the sides of the tracks, sometimes with the roofs extended toward the tracks to provide cover for passengers. Within thirty years the technology of rail transport was fully developed and several different types of rail stations had been defined. Perhaps never before in human history had a building need arisen, been solved, and pushed to its limits so quickly as in the invention of the railroad station.[3] (In a few years the same rapidity in invention and perfection would occur in the development of the high-rise office building in the United States.)

Since Roman times, buildings covering large spans had been built with wooden trusses, but the railroad buildings posed a particular challenge. What was required was buildings for locomotive roundhouses and passenger depots that could cover the tracks and yet not be susceptible to fire caused by

19.20. Crystal Palace. Interior. Forming an X in nearly all of the upper bays are rods of wrought iron that provided the diagonal wind bracing.

19.21. W. H. Barlow and R. M. Ordish, engineers, Saint Pancras Station train shed, London, 1863–65. Covering all the tracks of the station, the clear span of this metal and glass roof is 234 feet (71.3 meters).

embers blown from the smokestacks. The rapidly developing technology in building in iron provided the answer, allowing extremely light trusses to be made of wrought iron bars and rods. The railroad station reached a culmination in the vast arching metal shed built at the Saint Pancras station in London, 1863–65, by the Midland Railway Company, designed by the engineers W. H. Barlow and R. M. Ordish [19.21]. Barlow, who was the engineer of the Midland Railway Company, had earlier helped Paxton in the design of the Crystal Palace. Like the Crystal Palace, this is a great bubble, of vast Piranesian dimensions but little building mass—a structure in which, compared to the massive masonry of Roman and even Gothic construction, the greatest possible work is done by the least amount of material. The arch of the shed spans 234 feet (71.3 meters) and rises 100 feet (30.5 meters) with a slightly pointed profile; its length is 689 feet (210 meters). In actuality the shed was built first and the

head-house hotel built afterward, but it would be a mistake to assume that Barlow or other nineteenth century observers saw in this juxtaposition of dissimilar elements any profound discordance. Only mid-twentieth-century observers felt that the shed was superior to the hotel, because it openly exploited metal structure. To nineteenth-century users each part of the building was well designed to serve its appointed function—the shed to protect passengers and baggage handlers from the weather, and the head-house hotel to advertise the railroad and provide the most commodious and luxuriant accommodations for travelers. Because the symbolic connotation, the meaning, of each section was quite different, the forms and structures correspondingly differed.

Few train sheds exceeded Saint Pancras in size, and the only structures that did were temporary buildings for exhibitions, the lineal descendants of Paxton's Crystal Palace. The best known was the cavernous Palais

19.22. *Charles-Louis-Ferdinand Dutert with Contanmin, Pierron, and Charton, Palais des Machines, Paris, 1886–89. Designed to house all the major machinery exhibits of the Paris World's Fair of 1889, on the centennial of the French Revolution, this vast shed had a span of 377.3 feet (115 meters).*

des Machines, built to house the large industrial exhibits at the World's Fair in Paris, 1889, celebrating the centennial of the French Revolution [19.22].[4] Designed by the architect Ferdinand Dutert in 1886, in collaboration with the engineers Contanmin, Pierron, and Charton, it was an enormous pointed barrel vault 1,407½ feet (429 meters) long, with a clear span of 377¼ feet (115 meters), rising to a height of 142½ feet (43.5 meters). The roof was supported by twenty transverse trusses. As never before, the forces of nature pulled on this building, for its huge wrought iron and steel structure expanded and contracted over the course of the day as the sun passed from one side to the other, during the changes in temperature from midday to the cold of night, and during the changes in temperature from summer to the dead of winter. Accordingly, the trusses were hinged at their bases and at the crown, so that they might bend and flex at those points and not tear themselves apart. There seemed to be a denial of weight

as well, for there were no massive stone or concrete buttresses to resist the lateral thrust at the bottom of the arch. Instead the trussed arches came to rest on the pins of gigantic hinges, the lateral forces taken up by tensile rods running under the floor. Like the Crystal Palace, the Palais des Machines was translucent, with glazed roof and end walls, and this apparent openness (particularly in photographs taken before the exhibits were installed) accentuated the already vast scale. Such buildings as this and the great mid-nineteenth century train sheds, all of them nearly pure structure, were the logical extension of the insistence on rationalism in design begun by Laugier and Lodoli in the eighteenth century.

Reactions to the Machine

The Palais des Machines and the Crystal Palace that had inspired it were made possible by the growth of industry in producing iron and steel, as well as by the application

19.23. William Morris with Philip Webb, Red House, Bexley Heath, near London, 1859–60. In his own house, Morris returned to English vernacular architectural traditions, exposing the materials and revealing the method of construction.

of mathematical statics to determine the forces at work in such large structures. They were manifestations of the impact of the machine on architecture. The Crystal Palace had been created, in fact, to house exhibited products of mechanized industry, the kinds of mass-produced goods that made nineteenth-century middle class culture possible—pianos, rugs, chairs, pitchers, goblets, scissors, and thousands of other objects. To the English artist and designer William Morris (1834–1896) it was also an exhibition of the worst possible design, in which bad variations on Classical and medieval forms were adapted to mechanized reproduction. The results were pitchers with handles so contorted as to be impossible to hold and chairs no person could relax in. How could the taste of the middle class be improved, Morris pondered, if such was the caliber of goods offered for sale?

Taking a theme first proposed by Pugin and then Ruskin, that Gothic architecture was good because it was hand made by workmen who took joy in their work, Morris set about to reform standards in design. He began by designing, with the architect

Philip Webb, a house for himself, simple in design and based on medieval vernacular prototypes yet free of any attempt at deliberate copying [19.23]. His house, at Bexley Heath in Kent, built in 1859–60 of exposed common red brick without a coat of fashionable stucco, came to be called Red House. Inside, the rooms were finished in simple moldings of stained wood, with some built-in pieces of wooden furniture, and free-standing pieces inspired by medieval models but designed to facilitate use and handmade with emphasis on the constructive process. If wallpaper or rugs were required, they were designed with comparatively simple, flat curvilinear foliate patterns, instead of the illusionistic flowers and landscapes that were then fashionable. Morris then began to gather about him artisans who made furniture, tableware, and other objects used in domestic interiors. Although their designs were deliberately kept uncomplicated, the objects they produced could never be made cheaply enough to appeal to a broad audience. In the end the Arts and Crafts Movement that Morris initiated in the 1860s, and that continued up through 1920, was able to attract the interest of a few devoted affluent followers. Morris's greatest impact on design, however, was to be made by later disciples such as Charles Francis Annesley Voysey in England and Frank Lloyd Wright in the United States.

Industry and Urban Growth

The relocation of large segments of the population that had begun in the eighteenth century, first in England and then across Europe, accelerated as the nineteenth century began. Old cities such as London grew from just under a million inhabitants in 1800 to nearly 4.3 million by 1900. Paris expanded from over a half million in 1800 to 2.5 million in 1900. Industrial cities in Great Britain—such as Manchester, Birmingham, Liverpool, and Glasgow—which all had populations of about 70,000 to 80,000 at the beginning of the century, grew to almost three-quarters of a million each by the end of the century. In the United States the rate of urban growth was even greater, for New York, which had 63,000 people in 1800, was second only to London in 1900, with 2.8 million. Even more dramatic was the explosive growth of Chicago, which had fewer than thirty permanent residents in 1833, when it was formally established; by 1900 Chicago had over a million inhabitants and was the sixth-largest city in the world.[5]

The results, most especially in those cities spawned by the proliferating factories, tended to be grim indeed. Charles Dickens, whose sense of public moral responsibility was especially keen, sketched a revealing caricature of the mid-nineteenth-century no-nonsense industrial city, Coketown, in his novel *Hard Times* (1845). Coketown, he wrote, was a creation of economic determinism.

> It was a town of machinery and tall chimneys, out of which interminable serpents of smoke trailed themselves forever and ever, and never got uncoiled. It had a black canal in it, and a river that ran purple with ill-smelling dye, and vast piles of building full of windows where there was a rattling and a trembling all day long, and where the piston of the steam-engine worked monotonously up and down like the head of an elephant in a state of melancholy madness. . . . You saw nothing in

Coketown but what was severely workful . . . everything was fact between the lying-in hospital and the cemetery, and what you couldn't state in figures, or show to be purchaseable in the cheapest market and saleable in the dearest, was not, and never should be, world without end, Amen.

In the United States, where laissez faire capitalism controlled business as well as politics, no direction was given to urban growth, but in Europe, where governmental and bureaucratic control was more customary, steps were taken to shape urban growth in a few places, as illustrated in the replanning of Paris from 1852 to 1870. The growth of Paris was due only in part to the influx of rural immigrants, for the city also grew through the annexation of outlying suburbs. The water and sewer systems of the city were a patchwork of seventeenth- and eighteenth-century additions. Cholera was an annual epidemic, since drinking water was drawn from the Seine *downriver* from where major sewers emptied into the river. The twisted and narrow streets of the medieval part of the city were repeatedly blocked by barricades during uprisings that convulsed the capital city almost every twenty years.

When Louis-Napoléon declared himself emperor in 1852, he embarked on a rebuilding of the city of Paris following the designs of his chief engineer of the Department of the Seine, Baron Georges-Eugène Haussmann (1809–1891) [19.24]. To connect the railway stations scattered around the periphery of the city, Haussmann cut new streets through the heart of the city, and had entire sections of the medieval core demolished. It was also believed that the broad new tree-lined boulevards would make civil insurrection impossible (a hope that was dashed in the uprising of 1870). New aqueducts were built, extending thirty miles to the tributaries of the Seine, and the fabled sewers of Paris were laid under the new street system to carry the effluent of the city several miles downstream from the city. Several small parks were built throughout the city, and two enormous park preserves were created from royal hunting grounds at the west and east edges of the city; these Haussmann called "the lungs of the city."

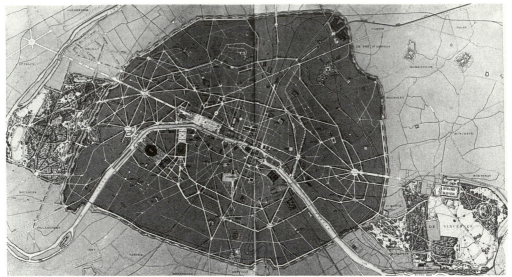

19.24. Baron Georges-Eugène Haussmann. Plan for Paris, 1852. With the support of Emperor Louis-Napoléon, Haussmann undertook the rebuilding of the city, cutting major new streets, laying new water and sewer systems, and adding new parks.

Not even Sixtus V had dreamed of a rebuilding scheme so vast as this.

Although there was criticism concerning the historical medieval architecture wantonly destroyed, Napoléon III's and Haussmann's determination to restructure the city was a challenge to planners in other cities, who likewise attempted to reshape jumbled medieval cities, transforming them into modern metropolises. Certain that the Turks would never again be a threat to Vienna, in 1857 the Austrian Emperor Franz Joseph decreed that the city's fortifications be removed and a boulevard, lined with public buildings and parks, built in its place, uniting the medieval core of the city with the suburbs that had grown up outside the walls. The result was the Ringstrasse, designed by Ludwig Förster and carried to completion, with major public buildings by various architects, up to the time of World War I, in 1914.

A new problem that architects and planners faced was creating new industrial towns on open land, including all necessary civil amenities and housing for the workers. One of the first of the planned industrial communities was the textile factory town of Saltaire, outside Bradford, England, begun in 1852 by Titus Salt. In 1879 the Cadbury family began construction of Bournville, outside Birmingham, as the site of the Cadbury chocolate factory, with rows of housing and communal facilities set on winding landscaped roads. Even more picturesque was Port Sunlight, built by the Lever family beginning in 1888, in which the houses were specially designed and arranged on winding landscaped streets so as to suggest the quaint atmosphere of a preindustrial English village [19.25]. In the United States several similar industrial towns were planned and built, of which perhaps the most elaborate architecturally (if not the most progressive socially) was Pullman, 12 miles (19.3 kilometers) south of Chicago, designed by the landscape architect Nathan F. Barrett and the architect Solon S. Beman and built largely from 1879 to 1895 to house workers making the luxurious Pullman sleeper railroad cars [19.26].[6]

Rational Eclecticism— The École des Beaux-Arts

The multiplicity of building tasks and the sheer scale of building activity during the nineteenth century meant that the appren-

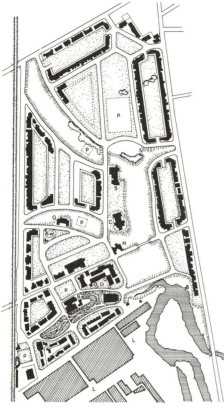

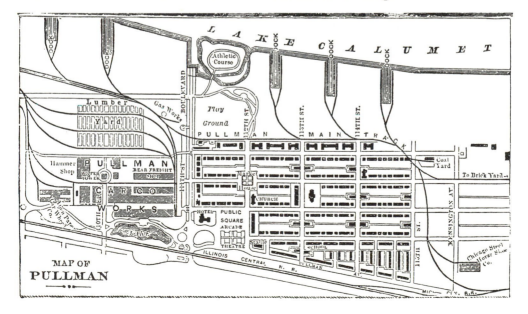

19.25. *Port Sunlight, England. General plan. This model industrial community, begun in 1888, was built for employees of the Lever Company.*

C = church
G = gymnasium
H = inn
L = Lever Company factories
p = playing fields
S = schools
sw = swimming pool

19.26. *Nathan F. Barrett and Solon S. Beman. Pullman (now in Chicago), Illinois, 1879–95. Barrett designed the street and park system, and Beman designed the public buildings and houses of this ideal American industrial village.*

tice method of training architects and engineers in the offices of practitioners was no longer adequate. The French had already confronted this problem in the building programs of Louis XIV and had established the Royal Academy of Architecture in 1671 to train architects for state building projects. The Royal Academy, transformed during the French Revolution, became the École des Beaux-Arts (School of Fine Arts); it soon became the largest and most influential school of architecture during the nineteenth century. One important but less influential school was the Prussian Bauakademie in Berlin, under the direction of Karl Friedrich Schinkel. By the end of the nineteenth century there were also schools of architecture at numerous American universities patterned after these two.

With architectural students at the École des Beaux-Arts were also students of painting and sculpture (in the tradition of the Renaissance), whereas those who wished to study the various branches of mechanics and engineering were taught in the completely separate École Polytechnique, un-

fortunately encouraging a split between architects and structural engineers. While it is true that students at the École des Beaux-Arts were taught structural design and construction techniques, design instruction at the École des Beaux-Arts focused strongly on plan organization, with a view to the simplest possible circulation into and through the building, and on expression of the character of the function housed.

The architect who has come to best represent École des Beaux-Arts precepts of functional planning and character expression is Henri Labrouste (1801–1875).[7] He entered the École in 1819 at the age of eighteen, progressed through the successive levels of instruction, and won various design competitions, which culminated in his winning first prize in the Prix de Rome competition in 1824. This allowed him to live in Rome for the next five years, where he prepared the required series of restoration drawings of Roman buildings. For his last project, however, Labrouste chose to study the ancient Greek temples at Paestum. In the course of working on these drawings, Labrouste came

19.27. Henri Labrouste, Bibliothèque Sainte-Geneviève, Paris, 1838–50. With this public reference library, Labrouste took care to define urban space and to let the external form and details of the building speak of its internal function in the glazed arcade and inscribed authors' names.

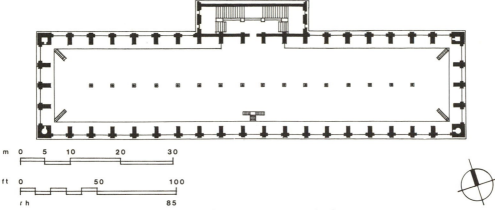

19.28. Bibliothèque Sainte-Geneviève. Plan at the upper reading-room level.

to a new understanding of the relationship between form and expressive structural function in Greek architecture, which determined the development of his own design. He scandalized his teachers in Paris when he sent back detailed drawings showing the temples in use rather than as remote Classical ideals, suggesting that buildings arise as expressions of unique functional and social environments and not as universal prototypes. So upset were École officials they prevented Labrouste from getting any government commissions for ten years.

Finally, in 1838, Labrouste was given the commission to design a large new reference library on the Place du Panthéon, the Bibliothèque Sainte-Geneviève (1838–50), north of Soufflot's church, now converted to

19.29. Bibliothèque Sainte-Geneviève. View of the reading room.

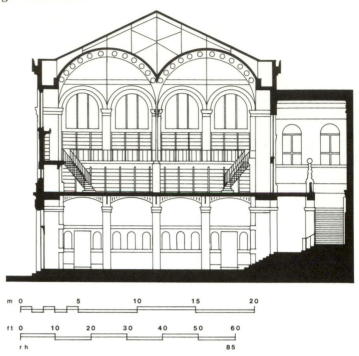

m 0   5   10   15   20

ft 0   10   20   30   40   50   60

r h   85

19.30. Bibliothèque Sainte-
Geneviève. Section.

a museum. One of the civic functions of the building was to define this edge of the Place around the Panthéon. Internally, the building had to provide a large reading room, for books were not to be taken from the library [19.27, 19.28]. Accordingly Labrouste placed the reading room on the upper level. Even though the building was to be the first library in Paris illuminated with gas, and hence the first library to have regular hours irrespective of the amount of daylight, the need for daylight was still great. Labrouste opened up the upper level by creating an arcade running completely around the building so that sunlight could stream through its broad glazed openings [19.29]. The lower portion of the arcade corresponded to the two levels of book shelves around the perimeter of the reading room, so Labrouste inserted there stone panels bearing the inscribed names of authors, symbolic of the books housed just on the other side of the stone panels. Covering the reading room are two parallel barrel vaults carried by delicate open web transverse arches of cast iron [19.30]. These are fastened to the stone piers of the perimeter

walls, but down the center of the room they are carried by the slenderest of cast iron columns. What Labrouste achieved in the library was the combination of clarity of functional arrangement and directness of circulation with a structure that exploited new building materials and expressed in a straightforward way just what the building was used for. Moreover, he had done all this without applying extraneous Classical ornament. Understandably, among students and progressive architects, the Bibliothèque Sainte-Geneviève quickly became a model of what a modern library ought to be.

The basic principles of architectural design followed at the École des Beaux-Arts were codified by Julien Guadet (1834–1908) in 1901. He summarized the instruction given there during the last half of the nineteenth century, when so many young Americans attended the École. Guadet wrote that the first requirement in design is to understand the function of the building and accommodate it, but that secondly the building site and the prevailing climate will necessarily modify the way function is accommodated. Third, a good design must be easily buildable and does not require complicated and costly structural gymnastics. Fourth, truth in architectural expression must be maintained. Fifth, a building must look strong as well as be structurally sound. Sixth, a good design has easy and inevitable patterns of circulation for the movement of people, for admitting light, and for carrying off rainwater. And seventh, he wrote: "Composition proceeds by necessary sacrifices. Composition must be good first, but it must be beautiful as well. You must therefore compose a building with a view towards its usefulness and its beauty. You will seek character, which contributes to beauty by creating variety."[8]

This triple goal (derived from Vitruvius) of clear structural expression and functional composition in beautiful designs was sought by American architects who had studied at the École des Beaux-Arts. When American students returned from Paris, they were asked by businessmen to design large commercial blocks of offices or warehouses, a building type that had seldom engaged the attention of architects before. For these Paris-trained American architects, the idea of wrapping a functionally designed commercial building in an appliqué of unrelated Second Empire Baroque or High Victorian Gothic details was unsatisfactory. The external character of the building had to result from the inside function projected to the outside. Henry Hobson Richardson (1838–1886), the second American to study at the École, during 1860–65, tackled this problem. He created for himself a personalized and simplified Romanesque style that used

19.31. Henry Hobson Richardson, Allegheny County Courthouse, Pittsburgh, Pennsylvania, 1885–87. Richardson attempted to suggest permanency in American buildings by the massiveness and roughness of his Romanesque masonry, devising plans dictated by internal functional requirements.

19.32. Henry Hobson Richardson, Marshall Field Wholesale Store, Chicago, 1885–87 (demolished 1930). For this utilitarian building, Richardson simplified his masonry even more, unifying this sprawling commercial block by means of repeated tall arcades.

masses of masonry in strongly expressive ways to accentuate points of entry into a building, bands of windows, and solid structural supports. His last two buildings, designed in 1885 as nephritis was gradually killing him, summarized his views concerning the expression of character in large urban buildings. His Allegheny County Courthouse in Pittsburgh, Pennsylvania, is divided into two parts [19.31]. The courthouse section focuses on a massive tower that serves as a civic symbol; its external walls are modeled with projecting towers that correspond to the alternation of court rooms and private judges' chambers inside. To the rear, however, is the county jail, enclosed in a wall of gigantic granite blocks and unadorned with any of the delicate Romanesque details that grace the public areas of the courthouse.

Richardson's Marshall Field Wholesale Store, Chicago, 1885–87, was also austere [19.32]. Field had asked for a huge building, occupying an entire city block, on the west side of Chicago's warehouse district. It was to contain showrooms for the wholesale branch of Field's department store (he operated a catalogue-sales division like that conducted today by Sears, Roebuck and Company, who adapted their techniques from Field). Field's was the largest single business building in the city, and Richardson expressed this by a unity of massing and a singularity of effect by superimposing masonry arcades in the exterior wall. Since it was to be a strictly utilitarian building, it was stripped of almost all historical ornament, employing only the roughness of the stones themselves to provide visual texture. The Marshall Field Wholesale Store had a most dramatic impact on Chicago architects, showing them how to express the scale of the increasingly large commercial blocks without falling into the pitfall of overusing ornament.

Richardson's Marshall Field Wholesale Store was structurally quite traditional, with heavy outer masonry walls that carried their

19.33. *William Le Baron Jenney, Home Insurance Building, Chicago, 1883–86 (demolished 1931). When a bricklayers' strike interrupted progress in construction, Jenney substituted a metal skeleton to allow work to continue; later the outer masonry veneer was attached to the standing skeleton. This was the first constructed metal frame skyscraper.*

own weight and that of adjacent floor loads, and an interior structural skeleton of heavy wooden timbers. Almost at the moment Richardson began designing the Field store, however, there appeared in Chicago a radically new technique for supporting office blocks. In 1883 the architect William Le Baron Jenney (1832–1907) had begun construction of the Home Insurance Building in Chicago, with outer walls of solid brick piers, when a bricklayers' strike brought work to a halt [19.33]. Wishing to finish the building, Jenney decided to use a metal skeletal frame, not only on the inside but in the exterior walls as well. When the bricklayers came back to work, the metal skeleton was wrapped with protective masonry cladding attached to the metal skeleton instead of supporting its own weight. Within five years Chicago architects had almost completely changed over to using metal frames, first of cast and wrought iron and then steel, for this techniques solved two troublesome problems—it reduced the total

weight of the office blocks by a half or more (and consequently reduced settlement in the soft subsoil of Chicago), and it eliminated the thick supporting walls at the ground floor and in the basement.

As business buildings got higher and higher, the movement of people within these buildings was mechanized by the introduction of the passenger elevator. This stimulated architects and the clients to build ever higher office blocks, going from five to ten, to sixteen, and finally to twenty stories. And yet, while the various technological advances making possible this height were being perfected, few architects were considering how this new verticality might affect design. What Chicago architects and structural engineers had done in the space of five years was to invent a wholly new building type, and yet architects were still thinking of the vertical office towers as composed of two- and three-story units stacked atop one another.

It was the architect Louis H. Sullivan

19.34. McKim, Mead and White, Boston Public Library, 1887–95. Like Labrouste, McKim, Mead and White defined an urban space while at the same time expressing the fact that this was a library open to the public.

(1856–1924), a student at the École during 1874–75, who first analyzed this new problem in his essay of 1896, "The Tall Office Building Artistically Considered." In this he insisted that "form follows function," and he correctly perceived that the office block had four principal functional zones. The Guaranty Building in Buffalo, New York, which he and his partner, Dankmar Adler, had designed the year before, embodied all the points Sullivan expressed in his essay [1.2]. First, there is a basement area filled largely with mechanical equipment and utilities, but this had little bearing on the external expression, as it was not visible. Above this is the ground-floor zone, a mixture of street-oriented shops at the perimeter, public entrances, elevator lobbies, and a mezzanine level of offices reached by stairs from the internal lobbies. Above this is the second major visible zone, the stacked identical office cells grouped along corridors that radiate from the central elevator spine. Atop all of this is the third, terminating zone, with some offices, elevator machinery, and other utilities. Sullivan proposed that the new office blocks were decidedly vertical buildings and ought, therefore, to emphasize and celebrate that character. Moreover, since

they were a cage of thin steel columns and beams, the external protective skin should not appear to be heavy supporting masonry. In the Guaranty Building, Sullivan used protective blocks of terra cotta embellished with his own unique foliate ornamental patterns stressing the different character of the three visible zones and indicating that this skin was clearly not the structural support. Above all, Sullivan gave expression to his image of the modern commercial skyscraper: "It must be every inch a proud and soaring thing, rising in sheer exultation that from bottom to top it is a unit without a single dissenting line."[9]

What Sullivan did in applying École principles to the design of the new commercial high rise office building, the architects McKim, Mead & White accomplished in the design of urban public buildings (McKim had been a student at the École during 1967–70). One of their earliest successes was the Boston Public Library, 1887–95 [19.34]. Forming a defining wall along the southwest side of Copley Square, a major open space in a newly developed portion of Boston, the library was inspired by Labrouste's Bibliothèque in Paris. Although its internal plan arrangement was

19.35. McKim, Mead and White, Pennsylvania Station, New York, 1902–10 (demolished 1963–65). Aerial view. Like G. G. Scott in London, McKim, Mead and White wanted to celebrate the power of the railroad, creating an imposing gateway for the city.

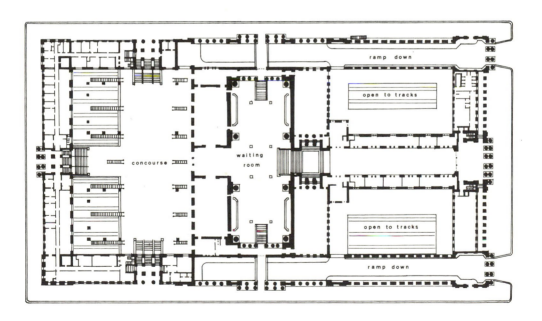

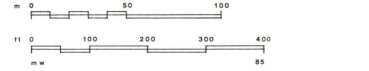

19.36. Pennsylvania Station. The main working floor was below street level and was reached by stairs and ramps for vehicles; from the Concourse area additional stairs led down to the train tracks, about 45 feet below the street.

not as forthright as Labrouste's—for the Boston library officials kept changing their minds as to what they wanted, even as the walls were being built—it was richly embellished inside and out with painting and sculpture as a way of inviting the populace into the building, for this was the first large urban lending library. The entrance doors were tripled, for example, and the stair to the upper reading room was much larger than Labrouste's.

The most commanding example of McKim, Mead & White's attempt to merge functional clarity with expressive form was their Pennsylvania Station in New York, designed in conjunction with engineers for the Pennsylvania Railroad during 1902–5, built 1905–10, and demolished in 1963 [19.35, 19.36]. Wishing to draw off some of the transcontinental business of the rival New York Central Railroad, the Pennsylvania Railroad built this new station over tunnels that brought the trains under the Hudson River from New Jersey, under Manhattan Island, and under the East River to Long Island. The station had a double function, providing for crowds of commuters who poured into the city from Long Island in the morning and funneled back through the station in the afternoon on their return home, and also providing for the different needs of long-distance travelers, with their more extensive baggage. The paths of these two groups of users were carefully studied so that they would not cross; commuters could exit the station going in any direction or connect directly with subterranean mass transit subways.

At the heart of the building, which filled two entire blocks in the heart of Manhattan, was the soaring General Waiting Room [8.1], modeled after the huge public spaces of the Roman baths, specifically the Baths of Caracalla [12.24]. Beyond the Waiting Room was the Concourse, in which stairs descended to the nineteen parallel track platforms below the station; the Concourse was covered by a glazed system of groin vaults, recalling the form of the Roman groin vaults of the Waiting Room but constructed of exposed steel columns, steel arches, and glass. The Waiting Room was designed as a great gate to the city, a monumental termination of a long journey, whereas the Concourse was a calculated transition from the monumental architecture of the Waiting Room to the mechanical utilitarianism of the trains themselves. Hence, the Waiting Room and Concourse were an envelope molded to recall historical forms but built of twentieth-century materials.[10]

An Architecture of Pragmatic Utility and Symbolic Expression

Critics and architects in the nineteenth century were consumed with an interest in style. As they studied Greek, Roman, and Gothic architecture, they came to understand by the end of the nineteenth century that these expressions had begun first as vernacular construction, then had been clarified and stylized, becoming cultural expressions rich in meaning. As Ruskin had written in the Preface to *St. Mark's Rest* (1877), great nations write their autobiographies in the "books" of their literature, their political histories, and their art; "of the three," he insisted, "the only quite trustworthy one is the last."[11] What then, as Viollet-le-Duc asked, was the nineteenth-century architectural expression that summarized its culture; what style was it creating that embodied the spirit of adventurousness of the age? This was the question that Louis Sullivan struggled with. Although Sullivan attempted to develop an American approach to design broad enough to be applied to any building task, his most notable successes were commercial and office buildings rather than churches and residences, of which he designed relatively few. Sullivan rejected the literal reuse of styles and historical architecture, while at the same time observing the lesson of history that the best design always grew out of a cultural response to function.

Other architects responded in their own ways in developing a method of building unique to their own place and time. Some put the emphasis on exploiting local vernacular traditions, as Morris had suggested in Red House. Perhaps the most unusual of such architects was Antoni Gaudí (1852–1926), of Barcelona, Spain, who developed

19.37. Antoni Gaudí, Casa Milá (La Pedrera, *The Quarry*), *Barcelona, Spain, 1905–10. View. Gaudí sought to create an architecture that was modern yet inspired by Moorish traditions, as well as uniquely identified with Barcelona.*

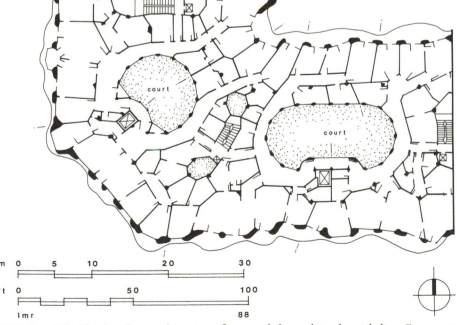

19.38. Casa Milá. The plan of a typical apartment floor reveals few traditional straight lines. Four apartments (their party walls are indicated by the dotted lines extending from the periphery) are arranged around internal light courts.

an architecture of brilliant color (inspired by Moorish ceramic tiles) and molded forms based on curved structural walls and thin masonry vaults. Catalonia, the province of which Barcelona is the chief city, has continually chafed under the rule of Madrid, and at the end of the nineteenth century the province witnessed a resurgence of separatist sentiment. Gaudí created an architecture rooted in Catalonia's Moorish and medieval past, ablaze with colored tile, exploiting the thin, curved tile vault construction for which Catalonia had long been famous. His architecture was also closely studied from nature, as well as being carefully analyzed mathematically, so that supporting columns were inclined and vaults were twisted and ramped to follow the lines of structural action. As a result he was able to eliminate all external flying buttresses in the immense church of the Sagrada Familia, on which he began work in 1884 and which remained incomplete at his death. His fusion of organic naturalism and the structural logic of curved vaults is demonstrated in the large apartment block, the Casa Milá, he designed for Doña Rosario Milá on the Paseo de Gracia, Barcelona, 1905–10 [19.37, 19.38]. Its plan of irregular walls, looking like a microscopic enlargement of the cross section of a plant stem, provides for four apartments per floor, grouped around interior light courts. On the exterior the massive walls of cut stone give the appearance of a weathered cliff (closely resembling the sea cliffs outside Barcelona), with balcony balustrades of wrought iron fashioned in the likeness of tangles of kelp seaweed. The attic roof, whose undulations, ventilators, and mechanical houses create a surreal roof garden, is supported by diaphragm tile arches and thin parabolic vaults [19.39]. It is a unique vision of a functional, structurally utilitarian, organic architecture that could have been created only in Barcelona.

In Brussels, Belgium, the architect Victor Horta (1861–1947) deliberately rejected

19.39. *Casa Milá. The roof of the attic level is formed of curved tile vaults supported by thin parabolic diaphragm arches.*

19.40. *Victor Horta, Tassel House, Brussels, Belgium, 1893. Stair hall. Horta's modernity came from the use of metal for both structural and decorative elements and the artistic assimilation of lighting fixtures, all woven together in a continuous curvilinear pattern.*

historical styles and invented a new architectural idiom for his progressive, wealthy industrialist clients, using ornamental motifs in metal and glass derived from plant forms. As with Rococo architecture, whose delicacy and irregularity in detail it resembled, this "new art"—or as the Parisian collectors called it, *Art Nouveau*—was employed largely for interiors. It appeared fully developed in the interiors of the Tassel house, Brussels, that Horta designed in 1893 [19.40]. The Tassel house staircase, with its integration of pattern and line in floor mosaic, foliate column with budlike capital, wall painting, tendrillike gas lighting fixture, and curvilinear stair balustrade, was the prototype for the other houses Horta designed in Brussels and was matched by similar work by Hector Guimard in Paris at the turn of the century. This was a self-consciously modern expression, owing little in a strictly formal sense to earlier historical periods. Art Nouveau embraced the modern age, with its electric lighting and new materials—iron, steel, and ceramic panels—but as with the Arts and Crafts Movement, the result was an architecture created only with intensive and costly handcraftsmanship. By 1910 the cost of such handmade buildings would bring Art Nouveau to an end. As Frank Lloyd Wright correctly perceived in his address of 1901, "The Art and Craft of the Machine," the architecture of the future would be built of machine-formed elements; the modern architect would of necessity need to embrace the machine in every aspect of design.[12] Fashioning a decorative curvilinear idiom of metal, independent of any historical style, was not enough. Although the architects and engineers of the nineteenth century had solved the extraordinary planning and structural problems of their time, they had yet to evolve a characteristic cultural expression of their own time.

NOTES

1. Horatio Greenough's critique "American Architecture" first appeared in *The United States Magazine, and Democratic Review* 13 (August, 1843): 206–210, and is reprinted in L. M. Roth, ed., *America Builds* (New York, 1983), 77–84.

2. Exactly the opposite approach was taken by the composer Richard Wagner in 1870, when he began sketching plans for an opera house at Bayreuth, Germany. For him the primary purpose was for the audience to hear the music-drama and see clearly the action on the stage. Accordingly, little space was given over to the circulation, and all seats are placed on a single steeply pitched fan for maximum visibility. This contrast in the interpretation of functional needs and resulting building design is discussed in a chapter devoted to the Paris Opéra and the Festival Hall in Bayreuth in Michael Forsyth, *Buildings for Music* (Cambridge, Mass., 1985), 163–196. See Chapter 5.

3. The development and evolution of this new building type is treated in Carroll L. V. Meeks, *The Railroad Station* (New Haven, Conn., 1955).

4. For a dated but still highly useful and informative account of the development of metal train sheds and international exhibition buildings, see Sigfried Giedion, *Space, Time, and Architecture*, fifth ed. (Cambridge, Mass., 1967), 165–290.

5. For statistics of urban growth in the nineteenth century, see Adna Ferrin Weber, *The Growth of Cities in the Nineteenth Century* (New York, 1899; reprinted Ithaca, N.Y., 1963).

6. Concerning Pullman, see the illustrated and annotated contemporary assessment by Richard T. Ely, "Pullman: A Social Study," *Harper's Magazine* 70 (February 1885): 452–66, reprinted in part in L. M. Roth, ed., *America Builds* (New York, 1983), 202–16. Although architecturally elaborate, Pullman was not truly representative of planned industrial communities built in the United States; see Gwendolyn Wright, *Building the Dream: A Social History of Housing in America* (New York, 1981), 58–72, 177–192.

7. Only in recent years has Henri Labrouste been viewed as a typical product of the École; in his own time he was considered something of a radical: See Neil Levine, "The Romantic Idea of Architectural Legibility: Henri Labrouste and the Néo-Grec," in Arthur Drexler, ed., *The Architecture of the*

École des Beaux-Arts (New York, 1977).

8. Julien Guadet, *Eléments et théories de l'architecture,* 4 vols. (Paris, 1901–4), vol. 1, ch. 3; translated by L. M. Roth and Jean-François Blassel, in L. M. Roth, *America Builds* (New York, 1983), 334.

9. Louis Sullivan, "The Tall Office Building Artistically Considered," originally published in *Lippincott's Magazine* 57 (March 1896): 403–9; reprinted in L. M. Roth, ed., *America Builds: Source Documents of American Architecture and Planning* (New York, 1983), 340–46.

10. The published statements of the architects regarding their intent in the design of Pennsylvania Station are quoted in Leland M. Roth, *McKim, Mead & White, Architects* (New York, 1983).

11. John Ruskin, preface of *St. Mark's Rest* (London, 1877).

12. Frank Lloyd Wright, "The Art and Craft of the Machine," a lecture Wright delivered in several versions, beginning in 1901, is reprinted in part in Frederick Gutheim, ed., *Frank Lloyd Wright on Architecture: Selected Writings, 1894–1940* (New York, 1941), 23–24, and in its entirety in Wright's *Modern Architecture* (Princeton, N.J., 1930), 7–23, and in Leland M. Roth, ed., *America Builds* (New York, 1983), 364–76.

SUGGESTED READING

Leonardo Benevolo, *History of Modern Architecture,* 2 vols., trans. H. J. Landry (Cambridge, Mass., 1971).

———, *The Origins of Modern Town Planning,* trans H. J. Landry (Cambridge, Mass., 1967).

Richard G. Carrott, *The Egyptian Revival: Its Sources, Monuments, and Meaning, 1808–1858* (Berkeley, Calif., 1978).

Françoise Choay, *The Modern City: Planning in the Nineteenth Century* (New York, 1969).

Peter Collins, *Changing Ideals in Modern Architecture* (London, 1965).

Carl W. Condit, *American Building,* second ed. (Chicago, 1982).

———, *The Chicago School of Architecture* (Chicago, 1964).

Roger Dixon and Stefan Muthesius, *Victorian Architecture* (New York, 1978).

Arthur Drexler, ed., *The Architecture of the École des Beaux-Arts* (New York, 1977); includes an essay on Labrouste's Bibliothèque Sainte-Geneviève by Neil Levine.

Georg Germann, *Gothic Revival in Europe and Britain,* trans. G. Onn (London, 1972).

Sigfried Giedion, *Space, Time, and Architecture,* fifth ed. (Cambridge, Mass., 1967).

Alan Gowans, *Images of American Living: Four Centuries of Architecture and Furniture as Cultural Expression* (New York, 1976).

David Handlin, *American Architecture* (London, 1985).

George Hersey, *High Victorian Gothic* (Baltimore, Md., 1972).

Henry-Russell Hitchcock, *Architecture: Nineteenth and Twentieth Centuries,* fourth ed. (New York, 1977).

———, *Early Victorian Architecture in Britain,* 2 vols. (New Haven, Conn., 1954).

F. Loyer, *Architecture of the Industrial Age* (New York, 1983).

Carroll L. V. Meeks, *The Railroad Station* (New Haven, Conn., 1955).

Nikolaus Pevsner, *Some Architectural Writers of the Nineteenth Century* (Oxford, England, 1972).

David H. Pinkney, *Napoleon III and the Rebuilding of Paris* (Princeton, N.J., 1958).

M. H. Port, ed., *The Houses of Parliament* (New Haven, Conn., 1976).

Hermann G. Pundt, *Schinkel's Berlin* (Cambridge, Mass., 1972).

Leland M. Roth, *A Concise History of American Architecture* (New York, 1978).

———, *McKim, Mead & White, Architects* (New York, 1983).

Howard Saalman, *Haussmann: Paris Transformed* (New York, 1971).

Vincent Scully, *American Architecture and Urbanism* (New York, 1969).

———, *Modern Architecture,* revised ed. (New York, 1974).

R. Schmutzler, *Art Nouveau* (New York, 1962).

Phoebe Stanton, *The Gothic Revival and American Church Architecture* (Baltimore, Md., 1968).

20.14. Ludwig Mies van der Rohe, Lake Shore Drive Apartments, Chicago, 1948–51. In the United States following the Second World War, Mies had access to the kind of industrial production that enabled him, at last, to realize his long-standing dream of a glass tower. This view shows the impact the buildings made in their original setting.

CHAPTER 20

Early-Twentieth-Century Architecture: The Perfection of Utility

Architecture is the will of the epoch translated into space. Until this simple truth is clearly recognized, the new architecture will be uncertain and tentative. Until then it must remain a chaos of undirected forces. The question as to the nature of architecture is of decisive importance. It must be understood that all architecture is bound up with its own time, that it can only be manifested in living tasks and in the medium of its epoch. In no age has it been otherwise.

Ludwig Mies van der Rohe, "Baukunst und Zeitwille," 1924

We have had enough and to spare of the arbitrary reproduction of historic styles. In the progress of our advance from the vagaries of mere architectural caprice to the dictates of structural logic, we have learned to seek concrete expression of the life of our epoch in clear and crisply simplified forms.

Walter Gropius, *The New Architecture and the Bauhaus*, 1935

Since the dawn of human consciousness, architecture has provided utilitarian shelter while at the same time serving as the physical expression of how humans have seen themselves in relation to the cosmos—to the universe, to their gods, and to each other. It has given form to their whole social and religious natures. This was the basis of Paleolithic construction, of the temples at Malta, of Sumerian ziggurats, of Egyptian funerary building, of Greek sacred precincts, and of everything that followed until the rise of the secular philosophies of empiricism, utilitarianism, and positivism in the eighteenth and nineteenth centuries. Then architecture lost its vital cosmological significance and became a symbolic vehicle for conveying historic traditions and a practical vessel for accommodating functional activity.

Meanwhile, during the nineteenth century, philosophers and art historians such as Hegel and Jakob Burckhardt developed the interrelated views that history evolves as the result of an inner spiritual necessity, and that each period in history is shaped by its unique zeitgeist, the spirit of the age. The art historian Heinrich Wölfflin then extended this idea to the interpretation of architecture, writing in 1888 that "architecture expresses the attitude to life of an epoch."[1] Thus it was up to architects at the end of the nineteenth century to express the character of their time, but what that character was proved difficult to define. Further complicating the issue was the fact that a new millennium was beginning; clearly the architecture of the twentieth century ought to declare its uniqueness, to celebrate electric illumination, radio communications, the automobile, and the airplane. The dawning century was to be one of the machine, of speed, and of mobility, and the architecture of the new epoch would surely proclaim this mechanization.

The forces of change in the nineteenth century had dramatically changed Western society from monarchy to democracy, from religious devotion to secular concerns, and from an aristocratic taste in the arts to one dominated by industrial entrepreneurs and the middle class. To achieve a sense of order in this apparent chaos architects turned to one of several design alternatives: eclecticism, vernacular traditionalism, personal invention, or functional/structural determinism.

Some architects took the position that the new mechanical conveniences simply made

459

easier traditional modes of life, and they used the machine to continue Late Romantic eclecticism. These more conservative-minded architects, many of them university educated, École trained, and well traveled, developed a creative academic eclecticism, correct in the manipulation of historicist detail, carefully planned to accommodate movement, full of readily grasped symbolic images of public function. The firm of McKim, Mead & White, in its Pennsylvania Station, New York (see the last chapter), epitomized this approach and its influence lasted well into the twentieth century. Few Europeans or Americans would have diffi-

culty today understanding that the building illustrated in Figure 20.1 is a state capitol, in this instance the Washington State Capitol in Olympia, Washington, 1911–28, by W. R. Wilder and H. K. White, once assistants in the McKim, Mead & White office.

Another alternative some architects followed was to abstract and clarify vernacular architecture to accommodate modern functional needs, using the forms, textures, and details of medieval domestic models. This alternative worked especially well for residential architecture. One such architect was Edwin Lutyens (1869–1944), and his country house, The Deanery, at Sonning, Berk-

20.1. W. R. Wilder and H. K. White, Washington State Capitol, Olympia, Washington, 1911–28. Wilder and White based their domed capitol design on the model for many state capitols, the Capitol in Washington, D.C., begun in 1792.

20.2. Charles Francis Annesley Voysey, The Orchard, Chorleywood, near London, 1899–1900. Voysey used this sharp-edged white-stuccoed vernacular expression for his residential designs up to 1915.

shire, 1900–1901, is a good example of the extension of William Morris's theories in later Arts and Crafts architecture. Built of red brick, with a red tile roof, it is set against an old brick wall, facing an orchard and a series of garden terraces designed by the landscape architect Gertrude Jekyll (1843–1932). Although derived ultimately from medieval sources that determined such things as the two-story living hall at the center of the garden facade, The Deanery nonetheless has a carefully studied functional plan and deliberate artful geometries in the arrangement of windows, masses, and planes.

By 1906 Lutyens had turned by stages to a heavy Neoclassicism reminiscent of the English Baroque architecture of Hawksmoor and Vanbrugh, but the vernacular tradition remained the very essence of the domestic architecture of Charles Francis Annesley Voysey (1857–1941) from the time he designed his first house in 1885 through 1914, when his practice began to decline.

His houses employed tight plans, often fitted into clear rectangles, with long unbroken wall surfaces punctuated by repeated sharp roof gables. The basic type is well illustrated in Voysey's own house, The Orchard at Chorleywood, a suburb of London, 1899–1900 [20.2]. The walls were built of solid rubble stone, carefully dressed only at the windows and doors, with the broad surfaces covered with rough stucco painted white. The result was a traditional design rendered with abstract clarity. A similar approach was taken by the Scottish architect Charles Rennie Mackintosh (1868–1928), best known in his native land for his Glasgow School of Art, 1896–1909.

The formal clarity of Voysey's houses, based on functional use and highlighted by sharp, clean wall surfaces, began to interest German architects and theorists in the 1920s. Later, when he was praised by Nikolaus Pevsner for being the grandfather of the emerging International Modernism, Voysey vigorously objected, saying he never had any

20.3. *Frank Lloyd Wright, Ward Willits House, Highland Park, Illinois, 1900–1902. Wright's houses, superficially similar to those of Voysey and Mackintosh, were partly inspired by Japanese architecture but were shaped by Wright's unique conception of expanding, interwoven spaces.*

intention of spawning a new architecture but rather of improving the old. Yet Voysey did have an influence on the Continent, for during the early years of the new century the ideals of English Arts and Crafts architecture, particularly the insistence on excellence in design and craftsmanship, were carried to Germany and Austria by writers such as Hermann Muthesius. Muthesius then helped establish the Deutscher Werkbund in Germany to promote these ideals.

Other architects, possessed of unshakable self-confidence and guided by a unique vision, simply invented their own idiom. Of these individualist architects the American Frank Lloyd Wright (1869–1959) was one of the very few who developed a philosophy of design capable of being unfolded through-

20.4. *Frank Lloyd Wright, Frederick C. Robie House, Chicago, 1908–9. Wright exaggerated the horizontal lines to integrate his houses with their prairie settings, creating a strong connection with the earth.*

out his long life. In part this was because his architecture was rooted in the philosophy of William Morris. Hence, Wright is often described as the leader of the American contingent of the Arts and Crafts Movement, and it was because of this connection that he came to the attention of English Arts and Crafts leaders. His earliest work, such as his own residence in Oak Park, Illinois, 1889, was greatly indebted to the American Shingle Style that had been developed on the Eastern seaboard during the 1880s. Wright, who had been the principal assistant in Adler & Sullivan's Chicago office during 1888–93, shared with Sullivan the belief that American architecture ought to evolve its own forms, derived from unique American circumstances.

As Wright built suburban residences in the flat prairie land around Chicago, he began to stretch them out into the landscape and to emphasize the horizontal lines in the design. The first fully developed expression of what he called the Prairie House was the Ward Willits residence [20.3]. In designing this house Wright had the advantage of working on a large lot, so that the house could expand outward from the chimney mass at the center in four wings accommodating separate functional sections. Inspired by Japanese architecture, the exterior of the wood-frame house is reduced to a stark pattern of dark-stained wooden members contrasting to the white stucco of the walls.

In 1906 Wright began work on what has generally been regarded as the finest of the Prairie Houses, the Frederick C. Robie house on the South Side of Chicago, 1908–9 [20.4, 20.5]. Wright pulled the house up out of the damp clay of the prairie, so that the main living level is on the upper level, with three bedrooms in the cupola on the third level. At every point the horizontal line is stretched and emphasized, internally as well as externally. The main living level is one long space, divided into living room and dining room by a freestanding fireplace. To achieve the long internal spans, and to support the long cantilever where the roof to the west covers the porch, Wright had to use steel beams inside the roof. Wright also integrated the lighting and heating into the ceiling and floor, and designed nearly all the furniture, using machine-cut oak components given only a dark stain [20.6].[2]

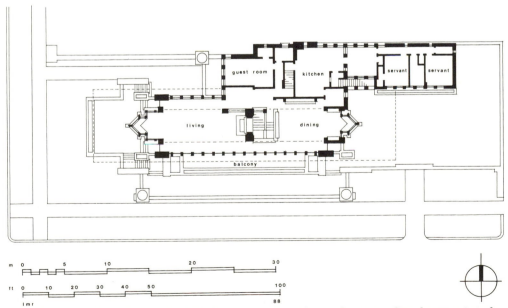

20.5. *Robie House. Plan of the living level, lifted to the second story for visual protection from the street. A single living space is defined, divided into two parts by the freestanding fireplace.*

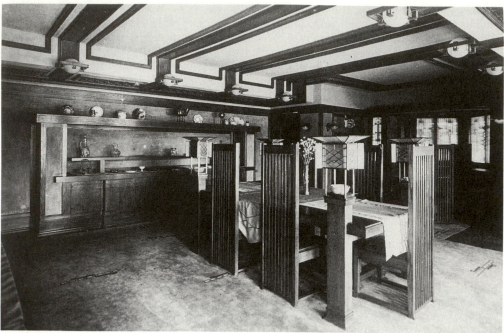

20.6. *Robie House. View of the dining room, showing the interior fixtures and furniture specially designed by Wright.*

The fourth approach was to let functional requirements and structural solutions determine the final design. To an extent Sullivan had done this, using ornament to delineate the three zones of internal function in his skyscrapers. But Sullivan was no strict structural determinist, for to emphasize the verticality of his skyscrapers he used *twice* the number of required vertical piers. This had the practical advantage of reducing the size of windowpanes, but it also made the building look much higher than it actually was [1.2].

For designers seeking a purely utilitarian architecture, the form could be (or appear to be) absolutely determined by internal function and necessary structure. American buildings that particularly fascinated European observers were the stark, tall, cylindrical, concrete grain elevators and the bare utilitarian concrete-frame American factories with structural bays filled with panels of brick and steel sash windows. These seemed to be building forms determined in every part by internal functional necessity. Such architects as Charles-Édouard Jeanneret

(Le Corbusier) saw in photographs of such utilitarian structures a hint of what twentieth century architecture might become.

Architecture: "The will of the age conceived in spatial terms"

How the machine might inspire a new architecture was demonstrated first in Berlin, in a Germany just beginning at the turn of the century to develop its potential as a political and industrial power. The creation of a new architecture to express the aspirations of industrialism in the rising German empire was strongly encouraged by German industrial leaders. Its originator was Peter Behrens.

Peter Behrens (1868–1940)

Behrens, trained in Karlsruhe and Munich as an artist and designer, quickly became a central figure in the progressive art movement in Munich, a center for the German equivalent of Art Nouveau, *Jugendstil*, (Youthful Style). He trained himself as an architect-designer, viewing the architect as a leader of the cultural elite who would provide the correct form for the new social order. Meanwhile he taught and practiced design in a wide variety of fields, becoming especially well known for his graphic and typographical design. Whereas his early architectural leanings had been toward an austere Greek Classicism, he gradually turned to abstract geometrical forms, dominated by the purity of the circle and the square and their derivatives.

In 1907 Behrens was appointed industrial designer for the Allgemeine Elektricitäts Gesellschaft (German General Electric Company), first designing some of their lamps, then all of their electrical appliances, their trade catalogues and other publications, and finally the various buildings in which AEG products were assembled. Behrens was also one of the founders of the Deutscher Werkbund, an organization of architects, artists, designers, craftsmen, political economists, and industrialists who sought educational and industrial reform in

various ways: through a reconciliation of fine and applied arts, the elevation of the position of the artist in an industrial society, the improvement of architecture and interior design, and especially the expansion of German influence and economic strength in the world.[3] Behrens saw that his position as designer for the AEG allowed him an unusual opportunity to advance these causes.

In the following year, 1908, Behrens and the company engineer, Karl Bernhard, designed the first major assembly building for the AEG, the Turbine Factory, where large turbines were being manufactured for ships. Since Germany was rapidly expanding its maritime trade and its navy, the demand for these turbines was high and new facilities urgently needed. Behrens viewed this as an excellent opportunity to create a factory building determined, like the machinery built inside it, by primary mechanical functions, raising the factory to the higher realm of architecture [20.7]. First the technical requirements were provided for, with two

20.7. *Peter Behrens, AEG Turbine Factory, Berlin, 1908. Behrens hoped in such factory buildings to create an elevated architecture, to raise the design of the factory to a higher aesthetic plane as a type for all architecture.*

20.8. Walter Gropius and Adolf Meyer, Fagus Factory administrative wing, Alfeld-an-der-Leine, Germany, 1911–12. Gropius pursued the lead provided by his teacher Behrens in using an industrial expression for the administrative office wing of the factory.

gantry cranes riding on rails in the upper walls of a long rectangular block. These cranes had to be able to lift loads of fifty tons to a height of 49 feet (15 meters). The basic frame of the building was 123 feet (39.3 meters) across by 402 feet (123 meters) in length. Twenty-two girder frames supported the rails for the gantries as well as the glazed roof. The box-section columns of these frames had to be thicker at the top; the outer surface was kept perfectly vertical and the inner face sloping inward. Rising between the columns along the inclined inner edge were walls of windows, so that the steel columns openly revealed to the street. At the end of the building the faceted profile of the inner roof girders determined the line of the gable. Below this hangs a curtain-wall of windows. Enclosing the corner is an inclined concrete membrane (its inclination matches that of the side window-walls) stripped with bands of steel. Ironically this corner, originally intended by Behrens to suggest the thinness and non-supportive function of the corner, has often been misinterpreted as representing containment and support. What Behrens set out to create was "a compelling symbol for electricity," and his work for the AEG, beginning with this building, was soon lauded for its clarity of form determined by function.[4] Subsequent buildings for the

AEG included the Small Motors Factory, 1909–13, and the High-Tension Material Factory (1908).

Walter Gropius (1883–1969)

Behrens's conception of the architect as the shaper of form and taste, exemplified in his buildings for the AEG, attracted a number of young architects to his Berlin office. One was Walter Gropius, the son of a family of teachers, civil servants, and architects prominent through the nineteenth century (his grand-uncle, Martin Gropius, had been the architect of the Neues Gewandhaus in Leipzig). Walter Gropius was trained in Berlin to become an architect, in the noble tradition of Schinkel. During 1907–8 he was Behrens's chief assistant, but by 1909 he had set up his own practice, with Adolf Meyer. His first major commission was the Fagus Factory, where shoe lasts were made, given to him by the owner Carl Benscheidt, who shared Gropius's progressive social ideals. In the administrative wing of the factory [20.8], Gropius created an austere block inspired by Behrens's turbine factory. Here too the structural supports taper inward as they rise to a flat roof, with the glass curtain walls seemingly hung from the roof. The building appears to be reduced to planes of windows (with the panes at the floor lines replaced by opaque metal panels), but here significantly the corners are not solid masses but the merging of transparent planes. In the yellow brick walls, the grid of the windows is repeated in recessed courses of dark brick recalling the banding of Behrens's corners in the turbine factory. As in Behrens's turbine factory, here is the image of a mechanized architecture.

Gropius's career was then interrupted by World War One, and after the conflict, like so many other artists, he joined revolutionary groups seeking to replace the old social order with one more socially progressive and responsive to modern needs in industrial design and housing. In 1919 he was invited to take over the direction of the School of Arts and Crafts at Weimar, originally established by the Grand Duke of Sachsen-Weimar. Gropius merged with this the Weimar Academy of Fine Arts, forming an institute of design he called the Bauhaus. He reorganized the curriculum to stress basic principles of design. His objectives were proclaimed in numerous manifestoes and publications; in the Bauhaus manifesto of 1919 he wrote:

> The ultimate aim of all visual arts is the complete building. . . . Together let us desire, conceive, and create the new structure of the future, which will embrace architecture and sculpture and painting in one unity and which will one day rise toward heaven from the hands of a million workers like the crystal symbol of a new faith.[5]

In these early years the character of the Bauhaus was greatly influenced by Johannes Itten (1888–1967), who taught the basic *Vorkurs,* the introductory course in design. After Lázlo Moholy-Nagy took his place in 1923, and with the arrival of the Dutch architect Theo van Doesburg, the focus on crafts diminished in favor of an emphasis on industrial production and the development of normative industrial standards.

Gropius's concept of the Bauhaus changed as the school gained new teachers, and when the Bauhaus relocated in 1926 to new buildings in Dessau (designed by Gropius and Meyer), Gropius summarized the emphasis of the modified curriculum:

> Modern man, who no longer dresses in historical garments but wears modern clothes, also needs a modern house appropriate to him and his time, equipped with all the modern devices of daily use.
>
> The nature of an object is determined by what it does. Before a container, a chair, or a house can function properly its nature must first be studied, for it must perfectly serve its purpose; in other words, it must fulfil its function practically, must be cheap, durable, and "beautiful."[6]

It is significant that Gropius should have set apart the word *beautiful,* for by what standards was something to be considered beautiful in this new functionally ordered world? The architect Bruno Taut, a contemporary of Gropius then working in Berlin, held similar views and believed that adaptation to function and beauty were intertwined, for as he wrote in his *Modern Architecture,* "The aim of architecture is the creation of the

20.9. Walter Gropius and Adolf Meyer, Bauhaus, Dessau, Germany, 1925–26. Aerial view. The school of design organized by Gropius provided the model for the proposed new, efficient, and objective architecture.

20.10. Workshop wing, Bauhaus. In the workshop wing particularly, Gropius succeeded in suggesting a weightless, transparent architecture; the wall, entirely of glass, is hung away from the supporting structure.

perfect, and therefore also beautiful, efficiency."[7] In his essay of 1926, Gropius summarized the Bauhaus approach:

> The creation of standard types for all practical commodities of everyday use is a social necessity.
>
> On the whole, the necessities of life are the same for the majority of people. The home and its furnishing are mass consumer goods, and their design is more a matter of reason than a matter of passion. . . . The Bauhaus workshops are essentially laboratories in which prototypes of products suitable for mass production and typical of our time are carefully developed and constantly improved.[8]

In another description of the program, Gropius wrote, "The Bauhaus believes the machine to be our modern medium of design and seeks to come to terms with it." An architecture generated by this principle, he was certain, would be clear and organic, "whose inner logic will be radiant and naked, unencumbered by lying facades and trickeries." If the modern designer was to understand the role of the machine in design and production, Gropius believed his or her education "must include a thorough, practical manual training in workshops, actively engaged in production, coupled with sound theoretical instruction in the laws of design."[9]

These ideas regarding design were perfectly realized in the architecture of the new Bauhaus at Dessau designed by Gropius and Meyer [20.9]. The school building had a pin-wheel plan straddling a street. Faculty offices formed a bridge over the street, linking the classrooms, dining hall, and student housing to the workshop wing, in many ways the most symbolic portion of the entire building. Everywhere the surfaces of the school were of smooth stucco or glass, but in the workshop wing the wall was entirely of glass, fully transparent (no visually disruptive opaque panels) and suspended away from the reinforced concrete floor slab [20.10]. It was intended as the model of what all architecture should become.

Although Behrens (and Gropius) had hoped to raise the factory to the level of architecture, the economy of a war-ravaged Germany redirected Behrens's dream. Forced by the Treaty of Versailles to pay enormous reparations to the victorious allies after World War One, Germany suffered disastrous inflation, with the result that in many buildings the desired excellence of construction and durability of materials had to be sacrificed. Instead of Behrens's hope of raising the factory to the higher plane of architecture, architecture was reduced to the perfunctory quality of the factory.

Ludwig Mies van der Rohe (1886–1969)

Gropius's two concerns—the development of an industrialized architecture, and social responsiveness to housing needs—were shared by his colleagues in Behrens's office, Ludwig Mies and Charles-Édouard Jeanneret. Mies, who later added his mother's surname, van der Rohe, chose to concentrate on perfection of the industrial image in consummately crafted buildings, whereas Jeanneret (who adopted the pen name Le Corbusier) gave special concern to housing.

Ludwig Mies van der Rohe was born in Aachen to a family of stonemasons, and from them inherited a strong sense of craft in building construction. In 1905 he moved to Berlin and entered the office of the designer Bruno Paul. Three years later Mies moved to the office of Peter Behrens, where, after the departure of Gropius, he became Behrens's chief assistant. It was from Behrens that Mies derived the concept of the artist as agent of the taste of the age, and of architecture as being an expression of technical power. He also learned from Behrens a keen appreciation of detail and precision in both design and construction, for in 1907 Behrens began an intensive study of the work of Schinkel, in which he involved his whole office staff. During 1913–14, Mies produced several austere and almost Neoclassical residences, but then his career, too, was interrupted by the war. In 1919 Mies joined the Novembergruppe, and together with three other young idealists published a magazine, *G*, devoted to creating a New Architecture. Mies's postwar designs were dramatically evocative, as evident in several projects he exhibited in 1919. Among them were two designs for soaring skyscrapers, free-form in

20.11. Ludwig Mies van der Rohe, Weissenhof Siedlung (White Housing Estate), Stuttgart, Germany, 1927. Planned by Mies and incorporating designs by sixteen major progressive European architects (including Gropius and Le Corbusier), this was to be a model workers' housing complex.

20.12. Ludwig Mies van der Rohe, German Pavilion, Barcelona, Spain, 1929. This open-air pavilion was designed as an expression of the precision of German industry for an international exhibition held in Barcelona during the summer of 1929; demolished at the end of the year, it was reconstructed on the same spot in 1984–86.

plan and completely sheathed in glass, as well as a project for a horizontal concrete office block. In *G* appeared statements of Mies's design principles, including such epigrams as "architecture is the will of the age conceived in spatial terms" and "create form out of the nature of the task with the means of our time."[10] Mies's view of the connection between architecture and industry was similar to that of Gropius: "I see in industrialization," wrote Mies, "the central problem of building in our time. If we succeed in carrying out this industrialization, the social, economic, technical, and also artistic problems will be readily solved."[11]

Given the condition of the German economy in the postwar Weimar republic, construction of Mies's idealized glass towers was not feasible. Yet Mies was able to build country houses for a few wealthy intellectuals who shared his views. He also rose to professional prominence organizing and directing the Werkbund housing exhibition at Stuttgart, Germany, in 1927—the Weisenhof Siedlung (White House Estate) [20.11]. Conceived as a demonstration of the best in housing design, the exhibition involved major avant-garde architects from across Europe, each designing a cluster of apartment units built on a hill outside Stuttgart and sold after the exhibition. As a result of this success, Mies was put in charge of the German exhibits at a small international trade fair held in Barcelona in the summer of 1929. Mies's particular responsibility was to design a pavilion for official ceremonies, and on this pavilion Mies lavished his attention [20.12, 20.13]. At the same time he was designing a residence for the Tugendhats at Brno, Czechoslovakia, 1928–30, and the two buildings are much the same in their free organization of space. Both the main living level of the Tugendhat house and the single level of the German Pavilion consist essentially of a single space delineated into subsidiary spaces by planes arranged in space. In both the best materials were selected—golden and green onyx, travertine, marble, macassar wood veneers, raw silk for the draperies in the Tugendhat house, smoked glass, and chrome-plated steel—assembled with infinite care. The

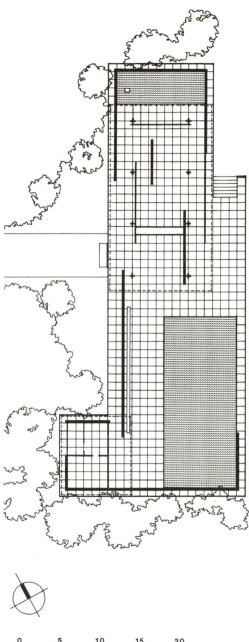

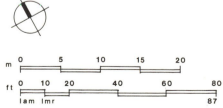

20.13. German Pavilion, Barcelona. Plan.

20.14. Ludwig Mies van der Rohe, Lake Shore Drive Apartments, Chicago, 1948–51. In the United States following the Second World War, Mies had access to the kind of industrial production that enabled him, at last, to realize his long-standing dream of a glass tower. This view shows the impact the buildings made in their original setting.

curious irony in the German Pavilion, designed as it was to demonstrate the highest ideals of German industry, was that it was painstakingly handmade. Indeed, all of Mies's later architecture—as industrialized as it appears, and despite the importance of mass production and prefabrication of parts to its realization—required patient hand assembly to achieve its apparent mechanical simplicity.

In 1937 Mies van der Rohe left Germany, where he had been prevented from working for several years by the National Socialists. He accepted the position of head of the Architecture Department at the Illinois Institute of Technology, Chicago, and began a career of international impact. That impact was first felt through the design and construction of the Lake Shore Drive Apartment towers at 860–880 Lake Shore Drive, Chicago, 1948–51 [20.14, 20.15]. At last, with the industrial production of the United States available to him, Mies was able to realize the dream of the glass tower con-

ceived in his cloud-covered north German homeland. The apartment blocks were reduced to their simplest terms, functionally and structurally, with a small glass-enclosed lobby at the ground floor, freestanding structural columns (actually steel-sheathed concrete-enclosed structural steel columns), and a flat top. The major structural bays, three on the short side and five on the long side, were then subdivided by pre-fabricated aluminum window mullions whose alternation of widths sets up a counter rhythm to the regular rhythm of the structure (this is discussed in Chapter 3).

These glass towers, together with others being designed at the very same time for New York City by Skidmore, Owings & Merrill and for Portland, Oregon, by Pietro Belluschi, provided the prototype for the glass towers that soon became the mark of modernization and urban renewal in cities across the United States and then around the world. Mies himself perfected the type in his office tower for the Seagram Corporation on Park Avenue in New York, 1954–58 [7.10], in which the glass curtain-wall window was hung in front of the structural columns, hiding them completely except where they stand clear at the base. Mies had done just what Gropius said was necessary, discovering and perfecting a type that could be used to the widest degree, and by the time of his death Mies could see adaptations of his glass tower, both good and bad, around the globe.

Le Corbusier (1887–1966)

Le Corbusier (Charles-Édouard Jeanneret-Gris) was born in La Chaux-du-Fonds, Switzerland. He was initially trained in the local Arts and Crafts school to take up the family trade of watch engraver and enameler; his teacher was Charles L'Eplattenier,

who inculcated ideals of the social responsibility of the artist and the role of architecture as symbolic expression. After 1908 Jeanneret moved to Paris, where he began working for the architect Auguste Perret, the early master of reinforced concrete, learning from Perret the potential of that material.

In 1910 Jeanneret began traveling, going to Berlin, where for six months he worked in the office of Peter Behrens. Then he toured the Balkans, Turkey, and Greece, returning through Italy. A northern European, he was captivated by the sharpness of forms in the crisp Mediterranean sunlight (unlike Mies, who always remained partial to the cloud-covered skies of his native Aachen); he lingered for days on the Akropolis in Athens, sketching the Parthenon. Despite the war, in 1917 Jeanneret settled permanently in

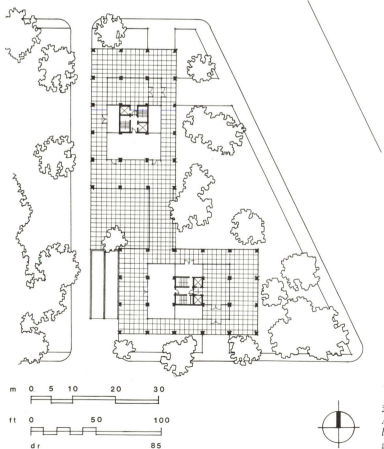

m   0   5   10   20   30

ft   0   50   100

d r   85

20.15. *Lake Shore Drive Apartments. Plan at ground level, showing the open, glass-enclosed lobby areas.*

Cliché Albert Morancé.　　　　　　　　　　　　　PARTHÉNON, de 447 à 434 av. J.-C.

faire mieux que l'adversaire *dans toutes les parties*, dans la ligne
d'ensemble et dans tous les détails. C'est alors l'étude poussée des
parties. Progrès.

　　Le standart est une nécessité d'ordre apporté dans le travail
humain.

　　Le standart s'établit sur des bases certaines, non pas arbi-

DELAGE, Grand-Sport 1921.

20.16. *Le Corbusier, page 125 from* Vers une architecture, *Paris, 1923 (translated as* Towards a New
Architecture, *London, 1927). Through such comparisons, Le Corbusier suggested that modern automobiles were
like Greek temples, in their adaptation to function, economy of form, and precision of assembly; modern
architecture, he argued, should aspire to the same qualities.*

Paris, painting, writing, and joining with Amédée Ozenfant in promoting a new spirit in art and architecture. They published the journal *L'Esprit nouveau* (New Spirit), in which Jeanneret expounded a theory of a new socially responsive architecture built around structural necessity. In these articles he adopted the pen name Le Corbusier, a loose derivative of the French for raven, *le corbeau,* which he used professionally for the rest of his life.

Out of these essays came Le Corbusier's personal manifesto, *Vers une architecture* (Paris, 1923), translated as *Towards a New Architecture* (London, 1927). Although he acknowledged that "architecture goes beyond utilitarian needs," Le Corbusier extolled the mechanical perfection of the airplane, steamship, and automobile as supreme expressions of the beauty of form determined by absolute response to function. He placed photographs of these modern machines side by side with views of the Parthenon, arguing that twentieth-century machines possessed the same elegance of form [20.16]. The problem, he wrote, was that the functional requirements of modern

architecture had not yet been clearly stated. Once that was done, as with designing an automobile, the appropriate form would automatically and immediately spring forth. After all, he pointed out, "the house is a machine for living in." And lest his readers underestimate the urgency of completely reshaping modern architecture, Le Corbusier issued this ultimatum: "it is a question of building which is at the root of social unrest today: architecture or revolution."

Meanwhile Le Corbusier busied himself designing prototypes for the new architecture. In 1920–22 he produced what he called the Citrohan house, a concrete-framed single family unit with one bedroom on a balcony overlooking a two-story living room [20.17]. The name was a pun on Citroën, the popular French automobile, since it was Le Corbusier's hope that such houses, using standardized factory architecture components, would be as easy and cheap to build as low-priced automobiles and, similarly, available to everyone. Simultaneously he drew up a scheme for a City for Three Million. At its center was to be an aerodrome set in the center of a cluster of regu-

20.17. *Le Corbusier, model of the Citrohan House, 1920–22. This was Le Corbusier's proposal for mass-produced housing. The name was wordplay on the Citroën automobile, since Le Corbusier wanted the same production techniques to be used to lower the cost of housing.*

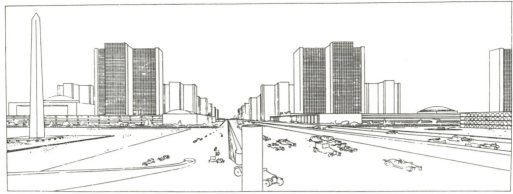

20.18. *Le Corbusier, drawing for the City for Three Million, project, 1922. Le Corbusier proposed that the city of the future consist of regularly spaced office towers and low-rise apartment blocks connected by multilane automobile expressways.*

larly spaced office towers, with biplanes buzzing about the buildings [20.18]. Around this core ranged five-story apartment blocks set in large grassy parks dotted with playing fields and athletic facilities. The entire city was criss-crossed by multilane automobile freeways, and in one of his drawings Le Corbusier provided a basic blueprint of the city of the future, with high-rise towers flanking such a broad thoroughfare.

In the City for Three Million, Le Corbusier made a clear functional distinction between the lofty high-rise towers to house business and governmental offices and the lower linear buildings for housing. For a particular functional use, however, all buildings were identical. After World War Two, when American planners began to use Le Corbusier's ideas as the basis for actual building, they often misappropriated the high-rise tower for housing since it allowed greater population density per acre. One example of the many public housing developments built in the United States following

20.19. *Le Corbusier, Villa Savoye, Poissy, near Paris, 1928–31. View. Le Corbusier perfected his vision of a dematerialized architecture, lifted free of the earth, in this house. It is also architecture that arises from transportation by private automobile, for it sits atop a three-car garage.*

this model was the Pruitt-Igoe complex built by the city of Saint Louis, Missouri, in 1952–55, after designs by the architect Minoru Yamasaki (see Chapter 6).

The clear separation of business and residential districts in the City for Three Million, each with its distinct architectural forms, exemplified what also became one of the major planning tools of the modernists—zoning, or the absolute separation of functional activities. Although there are sound reasons for keeping noxious industrial processes away from residential areas, there was no compelling reason for separating all workplaces from all residences, and yet this quickly became standard legal practice in the West, particularly in the United States. The result was that half of all gasoline consumed in private automobiles in the United States in 1970 was used getting from bedroom to workplace in the morning and shuttling back again in the afternoon.

Although Le Corbusier produced several city plans on paper in the 1920s, he was able to build only fifty model housing units at Pessac, outside Bordeaux, in 1924–26, and then the two apartment buildings in the Weisenhof housing exhibition, Stuttgart, in 1927. What he actually built in the 1920s were private suburban villas for members of the artistic avant-garde in Paris. These culminated in the Villa Savoye at Poissy, outside Paris, 1928–31. The house is a square, lifted up on what Le Corbusier called *pilotis*, stilts, set in a broad field with a view of the Seine [20.19, 20.20]. An elaborate retreat, it incorporated all of the five points that Le Corbusier had stipulated in an article published in 1926.[12]

First, the building has a structural frame, with slender *pilotis* that lift the building free of the earth. This eliminates problems of dampness as well as providing usable space under the house. At the Villa Savoye the minimum turning radius of an automobile determined the curvature of the glass wall of the ground floor, for there, under the shelter provided by the raised living level, is a covered driveway, a three-car garage, a reception area, and other auxiliary spaces. Visitors may mount to the living level by means of a helical curved stair or a long

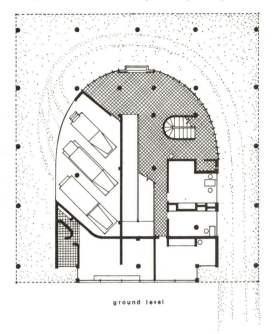

ground level

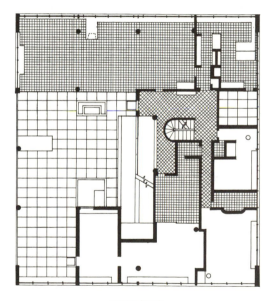

upper level

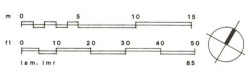

20.20. *Villa Savoye. Plans of the ground floor and main living level. The curve of the glass wall around the entry vestibule in the lower level was determined by the turning radius of automobiles. Above the living level was a roof garden.*

20.21. *Villa Savoye. View of the outdoor living room, showing the ramp to the upper roof garden.*

sloping ramp that doubles back through the center of the house.

By using the concrete frame Le Corbusier could achieve the second of his five points, the free plan, for no wall is structurally determined. On the third level of the Villa Savoye, for example, walls are curved to shape special spaces.

By projecting the floors beyond the column supports, the third point was realized, for the facade wall was also freed of any supporting function and could be opened or closed as function and artistic decisions determined.

The fourth point was exemplified in "free fenestration," the horizontal ribbon window that Le Corbusier was convinced provided better illumination of the interior.

The fifth point was provision of a roof garden, showing the influence of Le Corbusier's study of Mediterranean vernacular

architecture. In the Villa Savoye the main living level is divided into the usual enclosed living, dining, kitchen, and bedroom spaces, but there is also a large outdoor living space [20.21]. Some of the long horizontal window strips are the glazed windows of the enclosed living quarters, while others are openings onto the outdoor living room through which the spreading countryside is viewed as though it were a broad panorama painting. From the outdoor living room the ramp rises through one more switchback to an upper roof garden.

Le Corbusier continued to press for housing reform and eventually, in 1928, convinced officials of the Salvation Army in Paris to build a hostel for single men, the Cité de Refuge. Built in 1929–33, it was a long glass-enclosed austere slab block [7.8]. Le Corbusier called it an *usine du bien*, a "factory of goodwill." Along the south wall he experimented with a double glazing as a way of generating heat in the winter, and he stipulated a mechanical ventilation system to cool the building in the summer, for all the glass panes were to be fixed—this was one of the first hermetically sealed buildings. Unfortunately the double glazing was omitted as was the mechanical system, so the building became a hothouse in the summer, and after 1947 Pierre Jeanneret was called in to replace the windows with operable sashes set in a concrete screen wall that provided deep sunshades to keep sunlight off the glass.

Le Corbusier made a similar mistake in not protecting the southern glass wall of the dormitory for Swiss students at the City University in Paris (the Pavillon Suisse), 1930–32, but within a year he had begun to use deep concrete walls with vertical and horizontal louvers to prevent sunlight from reaching glazed wall surfaces; he called these *brise soleils,* "sun breakers." Even as late as 1948, however, Mies van der Rohe was still specifying all-glass buildings (with single panes) that mandated elaborate and expensive mechanical systems for cooling such hothouses in the summer and heating such radiators in the winter (see Chapter 7). The driving cause of International Modernism in its early years had been social utilitarianism, to provide the most supportive and heathful environment for the greatest number of people. Now it seemed that the new architecture was inflicting itself on its inhabitants. Something had gone amiss in the pure logic and social concern that had originally called modern architecture into being.

An Architecture of Perfect Function: Success or Failure?

The invention of what was called the International Style or International Modernism did not usher in the millennium, as its early proponents had prophesied.[13] A growing discontent with what was viewed increasingly as the straitjacket of the modern style

20.22. *Dynamiting the Pruitt-Igoe Housing Complex, Saint Louis, Missouri. At 3:32 P.M., July 15, 1972, the first charges of dynamite were detonated, demolishing what had once been considered a model public housing complex. All the high ideals of International Modern architecture seemed to come crashing down with it.*

occasioned a frank admission, even by some who had once been champions of the cause, that modern architecture was a failure. The moment, some said, when modern architecture died was 3:32 P.M., July 15, 1972, when dynamite charges were set off to level the Pruitt-Igoe housing complex at Saint Louis [20.22].[14] The housing complex had been thoroughly vandalized by its residents, for, due to socially biased judgmental errors in design, it had become a seedbed for crime. Eventually people flatly refused to move into it. What had been a demonstration of the highest ideals of modern architecture in the service of social engineering had to be destroyed less than a quarter century after its construction.[15]

Still, the pioneers of modern architecture achieved notable successes. In pursuit of a modern style, Behrens, Gropius, Mies, and Le Corbusier had grappled with the industrial processes of making building components; they exploited materials and forms evocative of the machine age. To an extent they reestablished the connection between architecture and engineering, and laid the basis for a rationalized architecture expansive enough in scale to meet the challenges of the twentieth century. They developed an architectural image of extended smooth planes and sharp cubic volumes, relieved of the tyranny of bilateral symmetry, an unfortunate legacy of the École des Beaux-Arts. But to their discredit, they insisted on using the flat roof everywhere, even in climates where it could never be properly sealed against seepage from melting snow.

International Modernism failed in significant ways, some of which did not become clearly apparent until a half century had passed.[16] It was not the inevitable result of new materials, but simply another style; not a radical new conception of architecture, but an iconoclastic image of the modern age which as often as not was unbuildable. And it was rooted in ideas that had nothing to do with architecture. From capitalist industrial production it had adopted the notion that lean and maximum efficiency was *always* best. The luxurious extravagance of ornament had been equated with "crime" in 1908 by Adolf Loos, and its brutal and total elimination became an article of faith of the new creed. As centuries of weathering have demonstrated, however, historical ornament provides very practical and visually satisfying ways of shedding water, accommodating expansion joints, or otherwise making provision for buildings to age gracefully. Within two decades, in contrast, buildings like the Villa Savoye began to self-destruct, revealing that International Modernism is a very fragile architecture.

From Protestant evangelicalism came the notion of truth and honesty in architecture, so that all materials and methods of construction had to be expressed for exactly what they are; plumbing was proudly displayed and bare light bulbs dangled in the centers of cubical white rooms. From this root, too, came the evangelical zeal of bringing the word to the unenlightened, so that International Modernism—and the Western cultural values that shaped it—were exported to all parts of the globe; whether or not this new architecture was appropriate to local climatic conditions or social institutions was never considered. Gropius exposed his upper-middle-class European chauvinism when he wrote that "on the whole, the necessities of life are the same for the majority of people."[17] While this may have been essentially true in the 1920s for the German workers he intended to house, that philosophy was applied by adherents of International Modernism in such places as Pakistan, Yemen, Kenya, and Iran, where glass-sheathed skyscrapers rose in the deserts. Le Corbusier's proud boast of devising "one building, for all nations and climates" was attempted by the next generation of modernists.[18] In fact, emerging third-world countries were eager to accept the gifts of "foreign" architecture as evidence of arriving in the international political arena.

The early modernists also believed fervently in a kind of inverted Social Darwinism. They were convinced that if the environment were changed, if the crowded slums and congested streets that were a legacy from the Middle Ages were swept away and replaced by gleaming housing blocks arranged in neat rational rows, crime and poverty would be eradicated. As Le

Corbusier had said, unless such radiant cities were built, the inevitable alternative was revolution.

For all its seductive simplicity and beauty, International Modernism was based on a number of fundamental fallacies. The most pervasive was that function in architecture was simple and therefore as easily analyzed as in a linear industrial manufacturing process. Ambiguity, surprise, and delight in architecture were disregarded as irrelevant, and circulation as a primary social function of architecture was also undervalued.

The modernist insistence on the direct relationship between function and beauty faltered too, when, after mid-century, old buildings increasingly were converted to new uses, often accommodating their new uses better than the ones they had been designed for. As Stanley Abercrombie has pointed out in *Architecture as Art*, function and beauty had very little connection. The three surviving side bays of the Basilica of Maxentius in Rome, he observes, each accommodate different uses, and one, in fact, is closed because of suspected structural instability. Which bay, then, is the more beautiful? Or, as he also notes, Brunelleschi's Foundling Hospital in Florence was not actually occupied and put to its designed use until twenty years after its completion.[19] At what time did it become beautiful: when built or when put into use?

Because of the implicit faith in technology, architects in the mid-twentieth century stopped bothering to think about the relationship of a building to its climatic or environmental setting. If a building was too hot or too cold, it was a simple matter of fortifying the cooling or heating equipment. If a new building material was required, the building-materials industry would eagerly supply the need; but, as good capitalists, these suppliers were more interested in expanding their markets than in providing safe, stable, durable materials. Whether a sealant, plastic, or adhesive would last even

as long as the mortgage on the building was anyone's guess.

International Modernism was based on an implicit faith in deified reason, in the ability of the human mind to perceive, analyze, and solve any problem, a faith that has been deeply shaken in the third quarter of the twentieth century. Where science had once been proclaimed the source of ultimate truth, it turned out also to be the source of the ultimate threat, for science had made easy the possibility of nuclear suicide. And even if that global holocaust can be indefinitely postponed, the ever-accumulating toxins of nuclear and industrial waste that technology produces so abundantly, technicians and politicians find impossible to dispose of. Hence the poisons produced during the span of the single generation of humans alive today will threaten life for an eon, stretching into a future as long as all the thousands of centuries that have passed since *Homo erectus* built that first hut at Terra Amata. Just how dangerous peaceful nuclear energy can be was amply demonstrated in April 1986, when the Russian nuclear electrical power plant at Chernobyl exploded, devastating parts of Ukraine for the remainder of this century. And in January of 1986 the confidence of a generation raised to think technology always works, that tomorrow would always be better, withered in the flames that engulfed the American space shuttle *Challenger*. Were our buildings, bridges, and dams being built and maintained any better than our most carefully supervised scientific apparatus? Could we be certain?

In the end, sadly and ironically, the proponents of modernism who had sought crystalline architectural purity and social conscience simply became arrogant purveyors of merely another style. And yet, there had always been alternatives to the seductive imperative of the machine, alternatives that had arisen at the very time that Gropius formulated his version of utopia.

NOTES

1. Heinrich Wölfflin, *Renaissance and Baroque,* 1888, trans. K. Simon (Ithaca, N.Y., 1966) 78.
2. The original interiors of the Robie house are shown in rare photographs in Donald Hoffman, *Frank Lloyd Wright's Robie House: The Illustrated Story of an Architectural Masterpiece* (New York, 1984). For Wright's architecture see Peter Blake, *Frank Lloyd Wright: Architecture and Space* (Baltimore, Md., 1964); Vincent Scully, *Frank Lloyd Wright* (New York, 1962); and Leland M. Roth, *A Concise History of American Architecture* (New York, 1978).
3. See Joan Campbell, *The German Werkbund: The Politics of Reform in the Applied Arts* (Princeton, N.J., 1978).
4. This contemporary assessment is by R. Breuer, *Werkkunst* 3 (1908); 145–49.
5. Walter Gropius, "Program of the Stätliches Bauhaus in Weimar," 1919, trans. Michael Bullock, in Ulrich Conrads, *Programs and Manifestoes on 20th-Century Architecture* (Cambridge, Mass., 1970), 49.
6. Walter Gropius, "Dessau Bauhaus—Principles of Bauhaus Production," March, 1926, in Conrads, *Programs and Manifestoes,* 95–96. Another translation appears in Frank Whitford, *Bauhaus* (London, 1984), 205–6.
7. Bruno Taut, *Modern Architecture* (London, 1929), 9.
8. Walter Gropius, "Principles of Bauhaus Production," 1926, trans. Michael Bullock, in Conrads, *Programs and Manifestoes,* 95–96.
9. Herbert Bayer, Ise and Walter Gropius, *Bauhaus, 1919–1928* (New York, 1938), 24–30, 127.
10. Ludwig Mies van der Rohe, "Working Theses," 1923, trans. Michael Bullock, in Conrads, *Programs and Manifestoes,* 74.
11. Mies van der Rohe, "Industrialized Building," 1924, trans. Michael Bullock, in Conrads, *Programs and Manifestoes,* 81.
12. Le Corbusier and Pierre Jeanneret, "Five Points Towards a New Architecture," originally published in Alfred Roth, *Zwei Wohnhäuser von Le Corbusier und Pierre Jeanneret* (Stuttgart, 1927), and in Conrads, *Programs and Manifestoes,* pp. 99–101.
13. The name International Style was coined by the architectural historian Henry-Russell Hitchcock and the architect Philip Johnson for an exhibition entitled *The International Style: Architecture Since 1922,* held at the new Museum of Modern Art, New York, in 1932. Their catalogue, illustrated with 140 plans and photographs of the most recent work of European and American architects, defined the elements of the new architecture, with its clear emphases on space enclosed by thin planes, regularity as distinct from bilateral symmetry, and a dependence on material, technical precision, and proportions in replacing applied ornament. Their epochal catalogue is still in print: H.-R. Hitchcock and P. Johnson, *The International Style* (New York, 1966).
14. See Peter Blake, *Form Follows Fiasco: Why Modern Architecture Hasn't Worked* (Boston, 1977).
15. For an analysis of the design problems of the Pruitt-Igoe housing complex, see Oscar Newman, *Defensible Space: Crime Prevention Through Urban Design* (New York, 1972).
16. For criticisms of modernism see Brent C. Brolin, *The Failure of Modern Architecture* (New York, 1976), and Peter Blake, *Form Follows Fiasco.*
17. Walter Gropius, "Principles of Bauhaus Production," in Conrads, *Programs and Manifestoes,* 96.
18. Le Corbusier, *Précisions sur un état présent de l'architecture et de l'urbanisme* (Paris, 1930), 64.
19. Stanley Abercrombie, *Architecture as Art: An Aesthetic Analysis* (New York, 1984), 99.

SUGGESTED READING

Reyner Banham, *The Architecture of the Well-Tempered Environment,* second ed. (Chicago, 1984).
———, *Theory and Design in the First Machine Age,* second ed. (Cambridge, Mass., 1980).
Tim and Charlotte Benton, with Dennis Sharp, *Architecture and Design, 1890–1930: An International Anthology of Original Articles* (New York, 1975).
Peter Blake, *Le Corbusier: Architecture and Form* (Baltimore, Md., 1964).
———, *Form Follows Fiasco: Why Modern Architecture Hasn't Worked* (Boston, 1977).
———, *Frank Lloyd Wright: Architecture and Space* (Baltimore, Md., 1964).
———, *Mies van der Rohe: Architecture and Structure* (Baltimore, Md., 1964).
Brent C. Brolin, *The Failure of Modern Architecture* (New York, 1976).

Joan Campbell, *The German Werkbund: The Politics of Reform in the Applied Arts* (Princeton, N.J., 1978).

Ulrich Conrads, *Programs and Manifestoes on 20th-Century Architecture*, trans. Michael Bullock (Cambridge, Mass., 1970).

Le Corbusier, *Towards a New Architecture*, trans. Frederick Etchells (London, 1927).

William J. R. Curtis, *Le Corbusier: Ideas and Forms* (New York, 1986).

———, *Modern Architecture Since 1900*, second ed. (Englewood Cliffs, N.J., 1987); one of the best general surveys.

Norma Evenson, *Le Corbusier: The Machine and the Grand Design* (New York, 1969).

James Marston Fitch, *Walter Gropius* (New York, 1960).

Kenneth Frampton, *Modern Architecture: A Critical History* (New York, 1980).

Marcel Franciscono, *Walter Gropius and the Creation of the Bauhaus in Weimar* (Urbana, Ill., 1971).

Walter Gropius, *The New Architecture and the Bauhaus* (London, 1935).

———, *The Scope of Total Architecture* (New York, 1962).

Henry-Russell Hitchcock and Philip Johnson, *The International Style; Architecture Since 1922* (New York, 1932); reissued as *The International Style* (New York, 1966).

Charles Jencks, *Modern Movements in Architecture* (Garden City, N.Y., 1973).

Barbara Miller Lane, *Architecture and Politics in Germany, 1918–1945* (Cambridge, Mass., 1968).

C. Lodder, *Russian Constructivism* (New Haven, Conn., 1983).

Nikolaus Pevsner, *Pioneers of Modern Design: From William Morris to Walter Gropius* (Baltimore, Md., 1974).

Franz Schulze, *Mies van der Rohe: A Critical Biography* (Chicago, 1985).

Nancy J. Troy, *The De Stijl Environment* (Cambridge, Mass., 1983).

Stanislaus von Moos, *Le Corbusier: Elements of a Synthesis* (Cambridge, Mass., 1979).

Frank Whitford, *Bauhaus* (London, 1984).

Alan Windsor, *Peter Behrens, Architect and Designer* (London, 1981).

H. Wingler, *The Bauhaus: Weimar, Dessau, Berlin, and Chicago* (Cambridge, Mass., 1969).

21.40. Mario Botta, house, Viganello, Switzerland, 1981–82. Botta has managed to find a way of using bold geometric forms, built of ordinary materials, that accommodate function and create powerful images at the same time.

CHAPTER 21

Late-Twentieth-Century Architecture: A Question of Meaning

... architecture is not a science. It is still the same great synthetic process of combining thousands of definite human functions, and remains architecture. Its purpose is still to bring the material world into harmony with human life. To make architecture more human means better architecture, and it means a functionalism much larger than the merely technical one.

Alvar Aalto, "The Humanizing of Architecture," 1940

I believe that today there is a need for images, for emotion in architecture; a need for architecture to speak once again to people, to become "presence" once again, to become material, to reacquire a meaning that can sometimes be erotic; a need to reestablish a partnership with people, after decades in which architecture was so antiseptic, distant, after the International Style ruined all possibility of communication.

Mario Botta, interview with Stuart Wrede, in *Mario Botta*, 1986

The pioneers of modern architecture tried to create a wholly new idiom generated solely by functional use and the structural means necessary to accommodate use. Their new architecture was to make no statement other than to reveal itself. And yet in making an architecture of nonstatement these theorists were, in fact, making a statement. They had caught themselves up in an endless means-and-end cycle. Unwilling to acknowledge that architecture was something in and of itself, they insisted it was only a means to the end of utility. And as the philosopher Hannah Arendt observed in 1958, "Utility established as meaning generates meaninglessness."[1] There were, however, other architects in the 1920s who believed conversely that architecture is far more than a utilitarian appliance—that it is,

in fact, primarily a vehicle for conveying communal values expressible in no other way.

German Expressionism (1918–30)

During the years just before and after World War One, some progressive architects in Germany and Italy attempted to create a totally new and dynamic symbolic architecture, inventing bold sculptural forms expressive of the modern fascination with movement. One building that may serve to illustrate the intent of the German Expressionists is the Einstein Tower, built in Potsdam, Germany, outside Berlin. It was the work of the architect Erich Mendelsohn (1887–1953), designed in 1917–19 and built in 1919–21 [21.1]. Mendelsohn had been educated for a career in architecture in Munich, then the center for the Expressionist painters led by Wassily Kandinsky. From them Mendelsohn learned to think of the function of architecture as the symbolic expression of inner human emotions realized in physical form. He had just set up a practice in Berlin when World War One interrupted his career. In the trenches he began to write out his theory of architecture and to make small sketches, some of them no bigger than postage stamps. The small size enabled him to concentrate on a few bold energetic lines conveying a sense of mass and motion. Some of the visionary projects were for garden pavilions and great public halls, some were done in response to hearing pieces of music, but many were hypothetical sketches for industrial build-

21.1. Erich Mendelsohn, Einstein Tower, Potsdam, near Berlin, 1917–21. Designed especially to house equipment to test Einstein's theory of relativity, this also was to suggest an image of modern Promethean power.

21.2. Erich Mendelsohn, sketch for an optical instrument factory, project, 1917. This sketch, one of many done in the trenches during World War I, was the inspiration for the Einstein Tower commission.

ings—railway stations, automobile plants, foundries, and a design for a factory of optical instruments [21.2].

It was this last sketch that was to lead to Mendelsohn's first major commission, built immediately after the war. He had become a friend of Erwin Freundlich, a research associate of Albert Einstein, and immersed himself in studying their scientific investigations. Once the war was over, Mendelsohn was invited to redraw his thumbnail sketches for exhibition in Berlin, and thereby he was brought to the attention of a group of supporters who undertook to build an observatory and a laboratory where Einstein's theories about the relationship between energy and matter could be proved. The hypothetical observatory project of 1917–19 was converted into detailed drawings for a boldly molded building, to be built of reinforced concrete, the material that for Mendelsohn symbolized the potential of the new century. However, when it came time to build the tower in Potsdam, the postwar German economy was collapsing and the necessary concrete could not be found. So the structure was built of concrete foundations, with a tower of brick covered in concrete stucco. Such a substitution of material would have been unthinkable to Gropius or Mies without changing the form, but for Mendelsohn the form was paramount and the substitution posed no significant problem. In the rotating dome atop the tower was a system of lenses and mirrors that reflected starlight to another mirror at the base of the tower, which in turn reflected it to various instruments in the laboratory base of the structure. Instead of encasing this in a light framework of industrial steel (which would not have given the necessary thermal insulation nor provided the mass necessary to prevent vibrations disturbing the delicate instruments), Mendelsohn sculpted a heavy mass that was not so much a direct expression of the mechanics of the scientific/technological age as it was a symbol of Promethean power. How prophetic Mendelsohn's gesture was, for in 1917 only a few scientists imagined how Einstein had put the fire of the gods into the hands of mankind.

Neoexpressionism (1955–70)

The difficulties in building the sculpted masses of the Einstein Tower prompted Mendelsohn to adopt more regular but nonetheless sweeping geometries for his department stores and movie theaters built in the 1920s. Mendelsohn was forced to leave Germany in 1933; his work in the United States thereafter lost something of the expressive power of his earlier work. Under the Nazis other German architects gave up altogether their experiments in expressive form. Only Frank Lloyd Wright in the United States, unconcerned with public opinion, continued his explorations of strongly evocative architectural forms. Since the 1920s Wright had been fascinated with the spiral helix as a means of both wrapping and defining space and also as a means of vertical movement, using it in a number of unbuilt projects. In 1943 Wright was approached by Solomon R. Guggenheim to design a museum to house Guggenheim's unparalleled collection of modern art, and in this Wright saw his opportunity to build a helical ramp. By 1945 Wright had worked out the basis of a solution, but another eleven years passed as the details were designed and as New York building officials were persuaded it was safe to build; construction took place in 1956–59.

What Wright proposed was a gigantic helical ramp in reinforced concrete, expanding outward as it rose, enclosing a vast space to be covered by a glass skylight, a modern-day Pantheon whose space was contained not by enormous masses but by a dynamic curve [21.3, 21.4, 21.5, 21.6].[2] Perhaps not since Schinkel had a museum building itself been as important a statement as the art it contained. Indeed, to some observers Wright's building promised to overpower the paintings. Certainly, Wright was declaring in this, the last building he supervised personally, that the form of a building could be as important, perhaps even *more* important, than utilitarian accommodation of function.

Virtually all of the buildings Mies van der Rohe designed after coming to the United States were prototypes, models for all sub-

21.3. Frank Lloyd Wright, Solomon R. Guggenheim Museum, New York, 1943–59. Wright's museum, one of his last works, makes few concessions to its setting, but instead grew out of Wright's concept of a long, curved processional path.

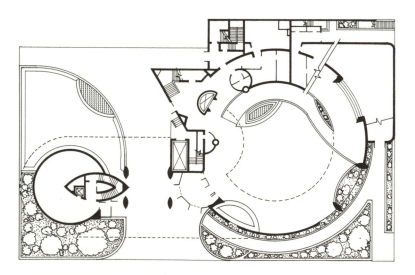

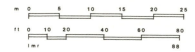

21.4. Guggenheim Museum. The plan is based on circular modules.

21.5. *Guggenheim Museum. Interior.*

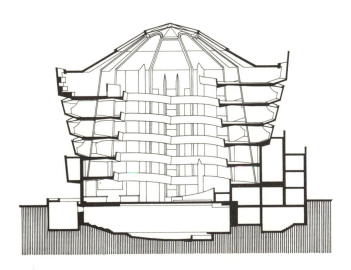

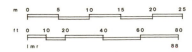

21.6. *Guggenheim Museum.*
The section shows clearly
how the spiral ramp swells
outward as it rises.

sequent buildings of that type. This was
abundantly clear in the Lake Shore Drive
apartments, 1948–51. The site available for
building was a trapezoid looking eastward to
the drive and Lake Michigan. Mies might
have devised a molded building, presenting
the largest possible number of windows to
the lake, the preferred view, but instead,
desiring maximum uniformity, he created
two identical towers, each with the Classically proportioned bay structure of three by
five. By turning one perpendicular to the
other, he arrived at an L-shaped arrangement that would fit in the trapezoid [20.14,
20.15]. All the facades of the two towers are
identical; there is no recognition that some
face the lake, while others face south and
west, where their glass-walled apartments
become hothouses in summer afternoons.
Not only could these buildings be turned to
any orientation (as in fact they are), but they
could also house a wide variety of functions,
such as luxury apartments, speculative
rental offices, and corporate headquarters
(as in fact this building type was used in the
next several years).

The alternative was to design in response
to the site and specific functional requirements, as the Finnish architect Alvar Aalto
(1898–1976) did in his dormitory for the
Massachusetts Institute of Technology in
1946–48 [21.7]. During World War Two,
Aalto had taught at MIT and had consequently gotten to know well the physical
environment of the university and its placement on the banks of the Charles River,
overlooking Boston. When he was asked to
design the dormitory, Aalto was given a site
on the drive along the Charles River
between two existing buildings. He resolved
to orient the rooms toward the river, so that
residents could see the city and watch the
activity in the water. To fit the required
number of student rooms into the available
space, he bent the form of the building,
which resulted in the visually commanding
S or W curve. Along the back side of the
building, away from the river, are lounge
rooms, lavatories, baths, and the stairs. The
entire building is of brick—rough, misshapen, irregular in color, in contrast to the
mathematically uniform brick that Mies was

21.7. *Alvar Aalto, Baker House, Massachusetts Institute of Technology, Cambridge, 1946–48. Aerial view. Aalto*
bent his dormitory building to fit into the available space; in doing so he provided oblique views across the
Charles River and created a powerfully evocative form.

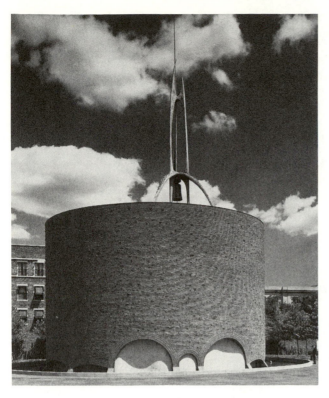

21.8. Eero Saarinen, Chapel, Massachusetts Institute of Technology, Cambridge, 1953–55. Saarinen's chapel uses a simple cylinder form, unique to this campus, built of the red brick typical of the Boston and Cambridge area.

using at the very same time for his buildings on the Illinois Institute of Technology campus. The south wall of Baker House, facing the river, is punctured by individual windows at each room, so that by the simple selection of this traditional material Aalto provided himself with easy solutions to potential scale, thermal, and textural problems. The Lake Shore Drive Apartments can be anywhere; Baker House can only be here, looking out across the Charles River.

Other examples of differing responses to the same problem are the chapels built at the Massachusetts Institute of Technology and the Illinois Institute of Technology almost simultaneously. At IIT, the chapel and all the other institute buildings were designed by Mies van der Rohe from 1938 through 1969. The chapel is a steel-framed cubical block, built 1949–52, with in-fill walls of uniform buff glazed brick [1.4]. At one end is a glass wall providing the entrance. The interior is decidedly unmystical, evenly illuminated by diffused light bounced off the glazed brick walls. As originally conceived, there would have been only a panel at the end behind the altar and no raised dais. It would have been the perfect all-purpose space, immediately adaptable for a handball court or a physics lab. (As built, it had enclosed spaces behind the altar for office and sacristy as well as a dais denoting a chancel area.)

The contrast between this and the chapel built at MIT, by Eero Saarinen, is revealing. Saarinen was an architect who spared no effort searching for *the* unique form for each one of his commissions. At MIT he was given the dual task of designing a large auditorium for general university functions and a small chapel suitable for meditation. These were to be near each other in a common quadrangle. Both structures, built in 1953–55, had forms generated by circular or spherical forms, the auditorium a triangular segment one-eighth of a sphere, and the chapel a brick cylinder [21.8]. The chapel was built of the rough, irregular brick simi-

21.9. Chapel, Massachusetts
Institute of Technology. Interior.
The main source of light is a
circular oculus at the top.

lar to that Aalto had used in Baker House, but its outer cylindrical wall was supported by arches resting on stone blocks in a surrounding pool of water at the base. The principal source of light is through a single oculus in the roof, whose beam of light is caught, so to speak, on the twinkling metal blades of a sculpture by Harry Bertoia [21.9]. There is no figure of heavenly rapture, à la Bernini, yet the effect of focused light is much the same in Bernini's Cornaro chapel.

Mies van der Rohe never deviated from the path of selective refinement in form and building materials he set for himself in the 1930s, but Le Corbusier radically changed his architecture during the 1930s, and the most dramatic result of this appeared in the first buildings he designed after World War Two. These changes involved molding of space, but more importantly they revolved around a change in materials, away from the smooth stucco and seamless surfaces of the 1920s to rough materials and deliberately crude workmanship, giving the surfaces of Le Corbusier's postwar buildings a rich texture. The concrete he had used previously in thin structural frames hidden from view was now revealed on the surface in bold masses and, as was noted in Chapter 4, imprinted with patterns left by the rough lumber used for formwork, as in the Unité d'Habitation in Marseilles, 1946–52. The Unité, although taller, cruder in execution, and composed of apartments with an L-shaped cross section, in many ways continued the themes begun in the apartment blocks Le Corbusier had been designing since the 1920s.

The most vivid break with his past, and

one for which most observers were unprepared, was Le Corbusier's chapel at Ronchamp, France, built just after the war. Notre-Dame-du-Haut at Ronchamp had been a site of pilgrimage since the twelfth century. There, on a hill at the base of the Vosges Mountains, a few miles from Belfort and the Swiss border, a statue of the Virgin Mary had long been the object of special veneration. Ronchamp had never become a major commercial pilgrimage city, and hence had retained a particular rural character, but it was nonetheless a strategic spot and a succession of chapels housing the statue had been built, destroyed, and rebuilt over the centuries. The nineteenth-century neo-Gothic chapel had been completely destroyed during World War Two. In 1950,

at the strong recommendation of several leaders of a reform movement in the French Catholic church, Le Corbusier was selected to rebuild the chapel; he was given a completely free hand. Le Corbusier spent several days on the site in the ruins of the old chapel, sketching the profile of the surrounding forested hills. He absorbed the setting and gradually the new chapel formed itself in his mind, creating what he called "a visual echo of the landscape."[3]

Although the plan of the chapel was based on a mathematically proportioned Modulor grid incised in the concrete floor, the chapel seemed to be completely at odds with the rational precision of Le Corbusier's prewar work. The thick outer walls curve in, and the heavy roof swells and sinks in the middle;

21.10. *Le Corbusier, Notre-Dame-du-Haut, Ronchamp, France, 1950–55. Viewed from the southeast, the church seems like a huge piece of sculpture, molded according to some individual whim of the architect.*

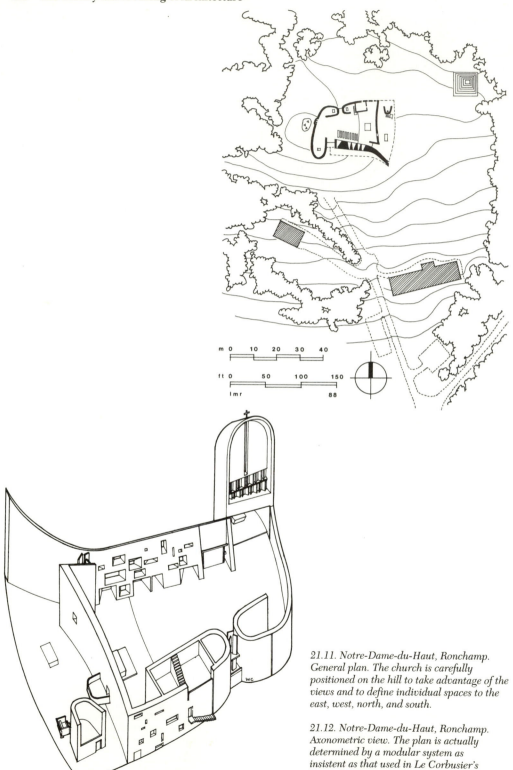

21.11. Notre-Dame-du-Haut, Ronchamp.
General plan. The church is carefully
positioned on the hill to take advantage of the
views and to define individual spaces to the
east, west, north, and south.

21.12. Notre-Dame-du-Haut, Ronchamp.
Axonometric view. The plan is actually
determined by a modular system as
insistent as that used in Le Corbusier's
Unité d'Habitation in Marseilles.

21.13. Notre-Dame-du-Haut, Ronchamp. Interior. The roof, apparently massive when viewed from the exterior, appears much different when viewed from the interior, for it hovers above the walls, carried by widely spaced, slender piers.

the curves that seem to open out to the landscape when seen outside give a sense of compression and containment when experienced from within [21.10, 21.11, 21.12]. To the east, the concave indentation of the wall and the overhanging curve of the roof frame an outdoor chancel that faces a hillside sanctuary where large crowds can gather for worship at special times of pilgrimage. The brilliant whiteness of the rough stucco exterior is in the sharpest contrast to the interior, lit only by small apertures in the south wall filled with colored glass, and by the reflected light scooped up in the towers and splashed down on the altars below (the manipulation of light at Ronchamp is discussed in Chapter 4).

To critics and historians of the rationalist camp, such as Nikolaus Pevsner and James Stirling, this apparent about-face by Le Corbusier was greatly disturbing.[4] Yet the free-form walls were not so different from the poetic shapes of the roof terrace of the Villa Savoye. What Le Corbusier intended to cre-

ate here was a sculptural response to the site, an expression of what Stanislaus von Moos has called the "atavistic mysticism of nature."[5] It was a sacred building in a way far more profound than representing a particular religious institution; it spoke instead of the mystical union of man and the cosmos. When the building was finished in 1955, Le Corbusier said to the Archbishop of Besançon at the dedication ceremonies: "When I built this chapel, I wanted to create a place of silence, of prayer, of peace and inner joy. The feeling of the sacred inspired our efforts."[6] To some it was surprising that a person who was not a practicing Catholic could design what they saw as the most religious building of modern times. Le Corbusier refuted sectarian narrowness. For him the building was a symbol of the sacral element of life and not of a specific creed, for, as he said to the archbishop, "Some things are sacred and others are not, regardless of whether or not they are religious."

If Le Corbusier's earlier buildings sug-

21.14. *Eero Saarinen, Trans World Airlines Terminal, John F. Kennedy Airport, New York, 1956–62. Saarinen consciously set out to shape a building that would suggest the magic of flight.*

gested the utilitarian efficiency of ocean lin-ers in their abstract economy of form, the swelling roof of Ronchamp suggested many things—a nun's cowl, a monk's hood, a ship's prow, praying hands. Le Corbusier himself said his inspiration was a clam shell he had picked up on the beaches of Long Island in 1946.[7] That Ronchamp repre-sented something larger than itself was compounded by the fact that the building was not what it seemed. In places the walls were concrete, elsewhere they were rubble, but all were covered with a uniform, rough stucco so as to suggest a single material. Moreover, once inside and adjusted to the cavelike light, the visitor can see that what seems from the outside to be a massive heavy roof is actually light and is raised aloft by slender columns, hovering 10 inches (25 centimeters) above the thick walls [21.13]. Clearly the structure is a delicate frame and not the massive-looking walls. And the south wall, pierced by the tiny windows on the outside, is actually hollow but made deliberately thick and opened in broad embouchures inside so that the tiny colored windows can be see from around the sanctu-

ary. Le Corbusier was putting into concrete and stucco what the Polish-American archi-tect Matthew Nowicki was then saying in print—that the primary function of a build-ing is to mold space, to create form. As Nowicki put it, "In the overwhelming majority of modern design, form follows *form* and not *function*."[8]

Thus the injunction of the International Style against symbolic expression was swept away and a new generation of expressionists blossomed. Among the most inquisitive in search of communicative form was the American architect Eero Saarinen (1910–1961). When presented with the commis-sion to design the "flagship" terminal build-ing for Trans World Airlines at Kennedy (then Idlewild) Airport in New York, 1956–62 [21.14], Saarinen decided to make a building that would suggest the miracle of flight. He and his assistants, working with large-scale design models, shaped a cluster of shells cantilevered out from central "feet," and before the glass was installed, enclosing the volume below the shells, the cantilevered shells had very much the pro-file of a gull's outstretched wings.

21.15. *Hans Scharoun, Berlin Philharmonie, Berlin, 1957–65. Exterior. The unusual plan and profile of this building were shaped by the desire to put music at the center of the audience.*

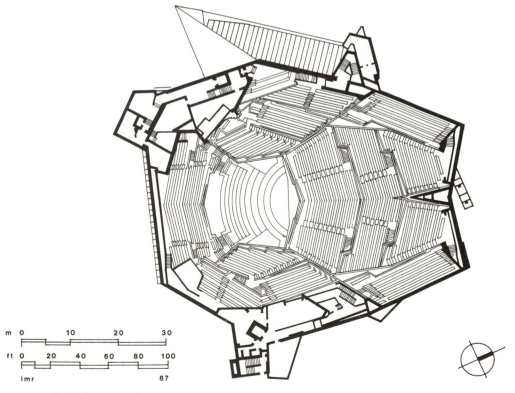

m 0   10   20   30

ft 0   20   40   60   80   100

1mr   87

21.16. *Berlin Philharmonie. Plan.*

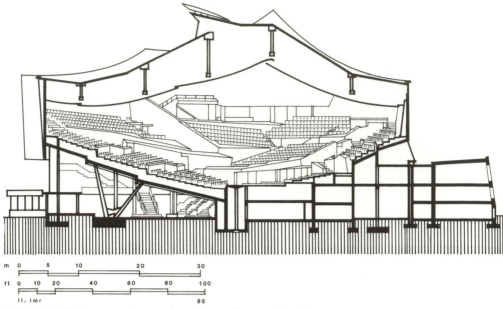

m 0   5   10   20   30

ft 0   10   20   40   60   80   100

II, Imr   85

21.17. Berlin Philharmonie. Section. The exterior is determined in all its parts by internal functional requirements.

21.18. Berlin Philharmonie. Interior. According to the architect, "Music as the focal point, this was the keynote from the very beginning."

Perhaps the best of these formally evocative and yet functional buildings is the Philharmonie in Berlin, 1957–65, by Hans Scharoun (1893–1972). The symphony hall is one of the last works of an Expressionist of the older generation [21.15, 21.16, 21.17, 21.18]. In this instance, however, the form is shaped by the music, with the audience surrounding the musicians, seated on elevated sections lifted over lobbies on the ground floor below. The many angled surfaces and the convex curves of the ceiling (mirrored by the angles and curves of the exterior) disperse the sound well. Scharoun made clear his objectives: "Music as the focal point. This was the keynote from the very beginning. . . . The orchestra and conductor stand spatially and optically in the very middle of things; and if not in the mathematical center, then certainly they are completely enveloped by the audience. Here you will find no segregation of "producers" and "consumers," but rather a community of listeners grouped around an orchestra."[9]

The inherent danger in such monumental symbolism was that the image could eventually completely dominate the building, just as, at the other extreme, in International Modernism, structural systems or reputed function had become dominant. This point was reached in the captivating design of 1957 for the Sydney Opera House, built in 1965–73 at the end of Bennelong Point, jutting into the middle of the harbor of Sydney, Australia [21.19]. The design was based on the sketch submitted by the Danish architect Jørn Utzon (born 1918) in a celebrated international competition in 1957, even though it was not at all clear how to build the nested shells Utzon had conceived. The image was simply too compelling not to build. The rising shells suggested sails in the harbor, and the undulating ceilings of the auditoria recalled not only the surrounding water but also suggested sound waves. Yet how Utzon proposed to build the shells, and how many of the details of the building were to be resolved, was far from clear. Utzon

21.19. *Jørn Utzon, Sydney Opera House, Sydney, Australia, 1957–73. Despite enormous cost overruns, the Sydney Opera House was carried to completion as a symbol of the cultural aspirations of Sydney and of Australia.*

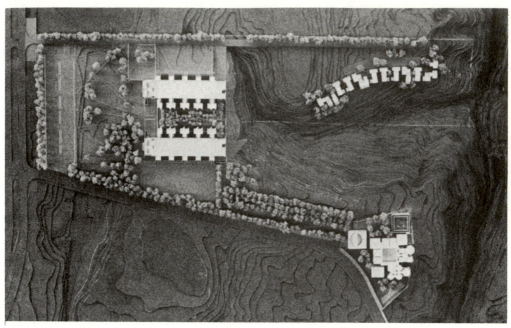

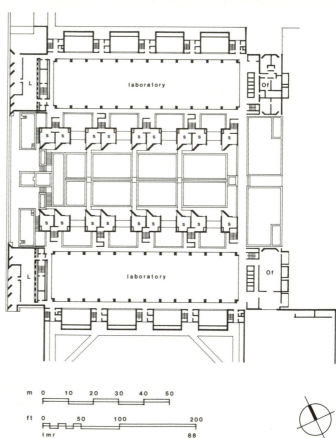

21.20. Louis I. Kahn, Jonas Salk
Institute for Biological Studies, La
Jolla, California, 1959–65. View of
study model, showing all three
portions of the complex—housing,
laboratory, and community
center.

21.21. Salk Institute. Plan.
Although the drawing suggests
that the laboratory spaces and the
studies are on one level, the
studies are actually one-half
flight up.

L = Libraries
Of = Offices
S = Private Studies

21.22. *Venturi and Rauch with Cope and Lippincott, Guild House, Philadelphia, 1960–65.*

worked on the design through 1965, when he resigned. The profile of the design was changed by the subsequent architects and engineers to make the shells pairs of triangles cut from the same sphere; the shells were fabricated of wedge-shaped precast concrete segments. The details of the structural design were worked out by the engineer Ove Arup, and changes were made in the interiors of the auditoriums. The original estimated cost of $9 million spiraled to $131 million and eventually reached $400 million. Finally, in 1973, the Sydney Opera House opened to acclaim even though its two auditoria did not always work especially well and were small. Without doubt, however, the Opera has become the preeminent worldwide symbol of the spirit of Sydney and Australia.

"Both/And" Architecture

By 1960–65 numerous architects, especially in the United States, were asking why architecture had to move to such extremes. Was it not possible to create an architecture that accommodated function to an optimum

degree and yet expressed that function in clearly recognizable ways? Two approaches were proposed by architects in Philadelphia, the older Louis Kahn and the younger Robert Venturi. Kahn (1902–1974), trained in the École tradition at the University of Pennsylvania, viewed the purpose of architecture as elevating human institutions and human activity to an almost metaphysical plane. This is well illustrated in his Jonas Salk Institute for Biological Studies at La Jolla, California, 1959–65 [21.20, 21.21, 1.8]. Kahn was fortunate in having as his client scientist Jonas Salk, who shared Kahn's conviction that the element of majestic mystery was to be integral to the design of the laboratory. Kahn's original scheme for a complex of buildings on a cliff overlooking the Pacific Ocean called for three distinct groups around the edges of a ravine—a residential quarter, a research laboratory, and a community center—forming a balance of living, working, and communal activities. Of the three parts only the laboratory was built. The laboratory is U-shaped, enclosing a court. The actual working labs are layered between open floors

21.23. Renzo Piano and Richard Rogers, Centre Georges Pompidou, Paris, 1971–77. This museum has been turned inside out, with the structure and utilities externalized so that the interior can be opened up to large spaces.

21.24. Peter Eisenman, House 10, 1976–82.

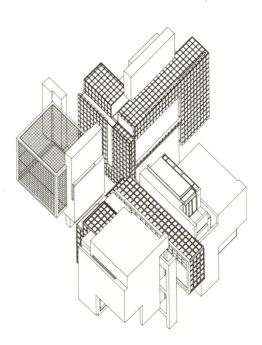

containing plumbing, wiring, and every conceivable utility. On the inner court sides of these laboratory blocks are the researchers' individual studies, small domestically scaled dens paneled in teak whose intimate character contrasts dramatically with the scientific objectivity of the laboratory spaces. The structural masses throughout are of reinforced concrete, carefully detailed to reveal the method of construction. There is imbued in the building the sense of a monastic community gathered together in search of truth, given a clarity of form that grows out of the work being performed. Kahn's Salk Institute is a monument to the celebration of human reason, but with the clear admonition, embodied in the studies clustered at the center, that part of scientific inquiry is contemplating the extended impact one is making in nature.

21.25. *Richard Meier, High Art Museum, Atlanta, Georgia, 1980–83. The crisp, white volumes of this building were achieved with enameled metal panels.*

Kahn's Philadelphia colleague, Robert Venturi (born 1925) clearly expressed his view, in several articles and books, that good architecture consists of multiple overlaid messages. His first major statement of this philosophy and the most influential was *Complexity and Contradiction in Architecture* (New York, 1966). How this multiplicity of meanings could be created he demonstrated in an apartment house for elderly Quakers, Guild House, Philadelphia, 1960–65 [21.22]. The plan was complex, contained in a block that stepped back from the entrance at the sidewalk; the individual apartments, therefore, had irregular floor plans similar to those in apartment blocks of the 1920s. The red brick exterior was based on the surrounding ordinary brick buildings of this dense urban setting. Yet Venturi suggested the organization of a Classical build-

ing in the white tile base and the band of white glazed brick that sets off an attic story. The broad segmental window of the upper lounge recalled Classical pediments, and there was even ornament provided in the gold-plated television antenna at the very center; it was, in fact, a symbolic antenna, since the real antenna was at the back of the building, in those pre-cable TV days pointing toward the broadcasting station. Venturi found a way to combine abstract references to traditional ornament and Classical form, and yet accommodate function in a building that endeavored to become part of its immediate environment.

Late Modernism

Architects after 1965 seemed to divide into two main groups, one extending and amplifying the expressive qualities of Modernism (these could be called Late Modernists) while the other group consciously sought to reinvest modern architecture with levels of meaning accessible to its users (the so-called Post-Modernists). The exaggeration and reductivism of Late Modernism reached a high point in the vast new museum in Paris, the Centre Georges Pompidou, 1971–77, designed by Renzo Piano and Richard Rogers [21.23]. It is an immense rectangular box of glass, with all of its hardware pulled to the exterior so that the interior can be a series of huge Miesian universal spaces. The exterior, therefore, is a maze of color-coded air ducts, electrical conduits, and plexiglass-enclosed escalators. It is architecture-as-machine elevated to the highest level.

Some Late Modern American architects practiced a kind of historicism, reviving and continuing the character of the Early Modernism of the 1920s as represented in the early work of Le Corbusier. Peter Eisenman (born 1932) pursued this path, developing a purely formal architecture totally devoid, he insisted, of any reference to outside systems

of references; his was a completely self-referential abstract architecture (even if coincidentally it did look like early Le Corbusier) [21.24]. To emphasize this nonreferential quality, Eisenman has identified the houses he designed by number rather than by the client's name.

The debt to early Le Corbusier is even clearer in the work of Richard Meier (born 1934), who has stressed purity of form and surface while exploiting the expressive power of the irregular form introduced into an otherwise insistent structural grid. These attributes, as well as his borrowings, are clear in his High Art Museum, Atlanta, 1980–83 [21.25]. The building has five cubic masses arranged in an L that forms the sides of an atrium that sweeps around in a quarter circle. This glass-enclosed atrium, with its cramped ramp providing vertical circulation, comes from Wright's Guggenheim but without the amplitude of space. The sleek white wall surfaces (of porcelain-enameled squares attached to an underlying steel frame) and the pipe railings are derived from Le Corbusier. Yet in its formal and constructive purity, this building typifies

21.26. Philip Johnson, "Roofless Church," for the Blaffer Trust, New Harmony, Indiana, 1960. The molded form recalls the rose, an important symbol for this utopian community, while the shingles refer to a traditional American material.

21.27. *Philip Johnson, Pennzoil Place, Houston, 1972–76. Johnson was among the first to move away from the boxy glass office tower and to invent unique forms as a way of creating identifiable office buildings.*

one of the problems of reductivist Late Modernism; it turns its back on the adjoining museum, built in the 1960s. There is no link between the two. The High Museum makes no effort to become integrated into its urban context.

Post-Modernism

Post-Modern architecture can be said to have begun with such work as Robert Venturi's Guild House. He and later Post-Modernists have not so much rejected Modernism as they have attempted to revise it to make it referential—addressing context and tradition, giving architecture a civic meaning beyond the esoteric formal concerns that may appeal only to a handful of similarly inclined architects. Venturi's Guild House suggested the possibilities of referring to the long-standing Classical traditions of Western architecture, particularly in older cities like Philadelphia. A British

example is the Hillingdon Civic Center, London, 1974–77, by the architect Andrew Derbyshire of Robert Matthew, Johnson-Marshall and Partners. Derbyshire drew upon English urban vernacular brick architecture of the nineteenth century but deliberately broke down the scale of his large building, introducing multiple pitched roofs. Derbyshire designed the entire mass of brick, giving particular attention to careful detailing. His purpose, he said, was "to design a building that spoke a language of form intelligible to its users," a goal in which he was successful.[10]

Shaping an architecture that communicates to the user became the goal of even avowed Modernists, most notably Philip Johnson (born 1906). Once the disciple of Mies (he once quipped of being called "Mies van der Johnson"), Johnson was Mies's associated architect in the design of the Seagram Building in New York. Johnson began his conversion to symbol-making in

21.28. *Philip Johnson, AT&T Building, New York, 1978–83. In this corporate headquarters building, Johnson used bold ornament and pattern, recalling similar New York skyscrapers of the 1920s.*

the curved shingled roof of his "Roofless Church," for the Blaffer Trust at New Harmony, Indiana, in 1960 [21.26]. The undulating form of the molded roof recalled the rose that had been the symbol of the utopian community founded in New Harmony at the beginning of the nineteenth century, while at the same time Johnson made a gesture to the Shingle Style domestic architecture popular on the American eastern seaboard in the 1880s and 90s.

In corporate and speculative high-rise office towers of the 1970s, Johnson evolved new skyscraper forms with canted and stepped tops, best illustrated perhaps by his

Pennzoil Place, Houston, Texas, 1972–76 [21.27]. In this instance Johnson was using standard elements of Modernist glass-wall corporate architecture, but in new evocative forms. More historicist references appeared in his granite-clad AT&T building, New York, 1978–83 [21.28], whose Classical loggia base and so-called Chippendale top made clear allusions to such New York skyscrapers of the 1920s as Warren & Wetmore's New York Central Building (Helmsley Building) of 1929.

European architects also began to turn away from the empty nonreferential qualities of Late Modernism. The public presentation of their new direction was the exhibition held in Venice in 1980, the Biennale, whose theme for that year was "The Presence of the Past." Within the large hall used for the exhibition, twenty architects contributed facades along the "Strada Nouvissima" exploring this theme; among them were such American architects as Charles Moore, Robert Venturi, and Robert A. M. Stern; the Spaniard Ricardo Bofil; and the Viennese Hans Hollein. The striking thing about the designs was how many were Classically derived, ranging from the curiously idiosyncratic to virtual Neoclassicism. Clearly, both European and American architects were ready for ornament once again.

Some architects have, in fact, moved in the direction of outright historical revival, such as the American architects Allan Greenberg and (in some of his work) Robert A. M. Stern. Stern, a student of architecture at Yale, where he came under the influence of the architectural historian Vincent Scully, is at his most convincing in his summer and weekend residences, making allusions to America's Shingle Style architecture of the nineteenth century. One example is his shingled house at Farm Neck, Massachusetts, 1980–83, based on the Low house by McKim, Mead & White, 1885–86 [21.29]. The most intriguing (and also difficult to classify) is the literal re-creation of the Roman Villa dei Papiri (destroyed by Mount Vesuvius) built in 1970–75 to house the J. Paul Getty Museum on the hills at Malibu, California [21.30]. The architects were Langdon and Wilson of Los Angeles,

21.29. *Robert A. M. Stern, house, Farm Neck, Martha's Vineyard, Massachusetts, 1980–83. In some of his residences, Stern has aimed at outright historical revival, creating summer houses that equal those of McKim, Mead and White of a century earlier.*

21.30. *Langdon and Wilson, with Dr. Norman Neuerberg, J. Paul Getty Museum, Malibu, California, 1970–75. To house the Getty Museum (at Getty's direction), the architects meticulously re-created a Roman villa buried outside Pompeii in* A.D. *79.*

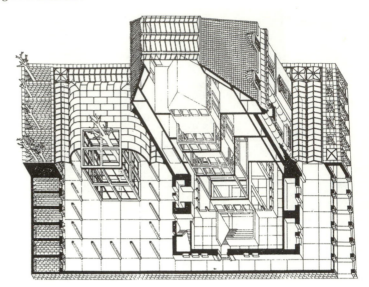

21.31. Oswald Mathias Ungers, Deutsches Architekturmuseum (German Architecture Museum), Frankfurt, Germany, 1979–84. For this museum of contemporary German architecture, Ungers combined old and new elements.

21.32. Ricardo Bofil, Palace of Abraxas Apartment Complex, Marne-la-Vallée, near Paris, 1978–82. This and Bofil's other apartment complexes outside Paris establish clear identities, avoiding the monotonous sterility of much twentieth-century housing developments.

21.33. Charles Moore, designer, Piazza d'Italia, New Orleans, 1975–80. In such designs as this, late-twentieth-century architects have attempted to create places where, once again, people can play.

with archaeological advice by Dr. Norman Neuerberg.

The task of gracefully placing contemporary work into our inherited architectural environment has proved to be a particular challenge. One intriguing example of how this might be done is in the German Architecture Museum (Deutsches Architekturmuseum, or DAM), Frankfurt, 1979–84 [21.31]. The site for the museum was a large Neoclassical villa of 1901, with a garden that ran down to the Main River. The architect Oswald Mathias Ungers (born 1926) wrapped the existing house in a new base that ran out to the street and side lot lines; this base was then used to house circulation around and into the house. The old structure was gutted and new offices and gallery space constructed around its periphery, opening up a large atrium in the center of the old building. Through this rises an abstracted "house within a house" ending in an archetypal gable roof just under the skylight that covers the old building. Thus old and new are fused in a new entity, commenting on Germany's architectural legacy while providing space for the presentation of Germany's most recent architecture in drawings and models.

Perhaps the great challenge, and one that has confounded architects since the dawn of the industrial age, is the creation of large-scale housing that is both economical and yet creates recognizable environments that residents can grow to identify with and to care about. Whether the last of these objec-

21.34. Michael Graves, Portland Building, Portland, Oregon, 1978–82. In this office block, Graves tried to make a visual connection to the turn-of-the-century City Hall next door and to evoke early-twentieth-century gracious public architecture.

tives has been met is too early yet to tell, but certainly the Barcelona architect Ricardo Bofil (born 1939) has succeeded in creating identifiable housing groups that project a monumental image. In four huge housing complexes outside Paris, built over a period from 1971 to 1985, he has added over 1,900 apartment units. The complex called the Palace of Abraxas at Marne-la-Vallée, near Paris, 1978–82, is one example [21.32]. This and the other complexes are uniquely identifiable, vast and Baroque in scale, but Neo-classical in detail and broken down into varied component sections. Despite the apparent historicism, what makes these housing complexes possible is prefabrication of massive precast concrete parts.

Post-Modern eclecticism has also proved a fertile field for whimsy in architecture, as illustrated in the work of Charles Moore and Hans Hollein of Austria. One of Moore's most controversial and yet intriguing designs is the Piazza d'Italia in New Orleans, Louisiana, 1975–80, conceived specifically as a gathering place for New Orleans' small Sicilian community, especially on the feast day of Saint Joseph [21.33]. The piazza, fitted in among existing buildings, focuses on a map of the boot of Italy (with Sicily at the very center) that rises in steps toward a Palladian door centered in a semicircular Corinthian colonnade. Highly colored and ringed with neon tubing, the "Classical" elements are impishly rendered in chrome steel, and jets of water sprout from unexpected places, such as the abstracted leaves of the Corinthian capitals.

Similar to this is Hans Hollein's Austrian Travel Agency headquarters in Vienna, 1978–79. Since this is a place where travelers come to dream of escape to other places and climates, the lobby is filled with allusions to faraway places—tropical palm columns with the metal fronds, a Mogul Indian pavilion, a fragment of a pyramid, a Classical column whose broken shaft is transmuted to a gleaming chrome cylinder. Other fragments refer to automobiles, ships, and planes, and all of this is covered by a curved milk-glass vault recalling the similar glass-vaulted banking room of Otto Wagner's Postal Savings Bank, 1904–6, which stands a few blocks away.

Such flights of fancy and tongue-in-cheek allusions work best in buildings of festive function. Much more difficult is eclectic allusion in buildings of more solemn public service. This dilemma was evident in the first major American Post-Modern public building, Michael Graves's Portland Building for the City of Portland, Oregon, 1978–82 [21.34]. Graves was responding to the restrained Neoclassical Portland City Hall, 1893, in his enormous abstracted column forms, swags, garlands, and three-story keystone. Yet for all the architect's written assertions and visual intimations that this was a return to the gracious public architecture of the turn of the century, the gesture rings hollow, for the ornament is painted plaster, not marble, the entrances are constricted and not inviting, and the interior public spaces are cramped and not generous. Despite Graves's claim that this building is unique to its site, the four facades are sufficiently equal that the building could be

turned any direction. Post-Modernism is bold and, as here, often audacious, but the results are often mannered and more than a little grotesque. Caprice, charm, and willful gesture ought to be welcomed in architecture, but in much Post-Modernism the result all too often has been a modern idiom that has been changed but not improved.

Yet not far from Graves's experiment is a building that proves it is possible to combine functional clarity and formal expressiveness with artistic elegance in ways that satisfy the mind as nourish the spirit. It is no longer among the newest of buildings, nor does it, like Graves's Portland Building, loudly proclaim its importance. And yet, like all of Alvar Aalto's creations, it is a building that works in every detail and at every moment to enhance human use. Aalto's library for the Abbey at Mount Angel, Oregon, 1967–71, is shaped around functional requirements, with a fan-shaped book-stack area that lends itself to easy supervision from one vantage point [21.35, 21.36, 21.37]. To one side are tightly clustered offices, and on the other a small auditorium. Because the library is on the crest of a plateau, the building is only one story high where it faces the neighboring monastic buildings, but it is three levels deep as it descends the hill, providing for sufficient stack area without overpowering adjoining buildings of the monastic quadrangle. Following the curve of the book-stack fan is a long skylight bouncing light down to the stacks below [21.38]. Every detail was studied by Aalto—the steel columns sheathed in wood and warm to the touch, the door handles angled to match the grip of the outstretched hand, and the lighting fixtures louvered to soften the illumination.

If Aalto's architecture appears just a bit too abstract to some users, his concern for clarity of form and direct statement of materials is being carried forward in the late twentieth century by the Swiss architect Mario Botta (born 1943). To these qualities Botta has added a primal imagery that makes his building look very old as well as very new, as in a house in Viganello, Switzerland, 1981–82 [21.40]. The precision of form and the careful handling of brick

21.35. Alvar Aalto, Mount Angel Abbey Library, Mount Angel, Oregon, 1967–71. Aalto's work repeatedly demonstrates that responding to function and human psychology can produce architecture of both noble purpose and pleasing form.

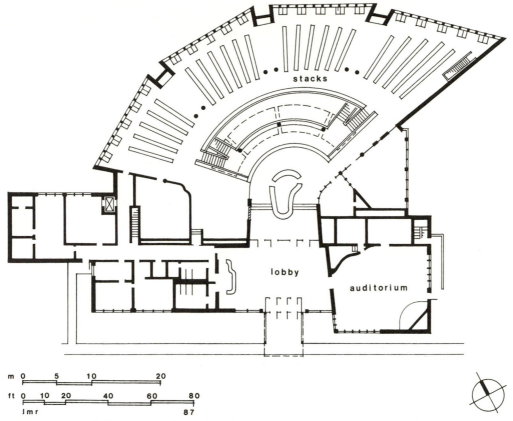

m 0   5   10   20

ft 0   10   20   40   60   80

l m r   87

21.36. *Mount Angel Abbey Library. Plan. Aalto's plans, too, show that varying functions can be successfully accommodated in differing forms, knitted together.*

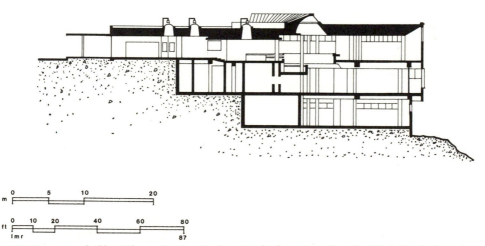

0   5   10   20
m

0   10   20   40   60   80
ft

l m r   87

21.37. *Mount Angel Abbey Library. Section. By dropping the floors down the side of the hill, Aalto kept the main-entry story low and simple in deference to adjoining campus buildings.*

21.38. *Mount Angel Abbey Library.*
Interior of the book-stack and
reading area.

and concrete block clearly reveal Botta's debts to his two mentors, Le Corbusier and especially Louis I. Kahn (he worked briefly for both men). But Botta has moved away from the nonreferential abstraction of their work, seeking forms that echo images dwelling deep in the human subconscious, endeavoring to make an "architecture to speak once again to people."[11]

An Architecture of Substance

Function is far more than utility, as Aalto understood perhaps better than any of his colleagues, and as Botta reasserts. In an article written in 1940, Aalto sharply contrasted "architecture whose main concern is the formalistic style a building shall wear" with "architecture that we know as functionalist." Function he realized is an elusive commodity, for "since architecture covers the entire field of human life, *real* functional architecture must be functional mainly from the human point of view." Despite the rigorous purity of the empiricists of the 1920s, or the heroic neofunctionalism of a half-century later, Aalto reminds us that architecture is not a precise science; it is not simply defining mechanical function and putting the most economical structure around it. Nor, if he could be present to remind today's Post-Modernists, is it an exercise in slick, superficial, or esoteric allusionism. As Aalto understood well, architecture "is still the same great synthetic process of combining thousands of definite human functions, and remains *architecture*. Its purpose is still to bring the material world into harmony with human life."[12]

Aalto's words have a special significance now, a generation after he spoke them, for a very contrary perception of architecture has arisen that asserts that architecture has no fixed symbolic relationship to its time or place, nor any particular reference to human form or activity. Labeled "De-Construction," in reference to a contemporary movement in literary criticism, its architectural inspiration comes in part from the industrial designs of Russian Constructivism of the twenties. Architecture, according to this radical view, exists as an isolated abstract phenomenon, and its "function" is to promote a sense of dislocation and disorientation.[13]

Architecture arose in the dimly understood eons of prehistory as a way of reconciling the vagaries of human existence with what humans perceived as the truth of the cosmos; architecture gave its builders an enduring way of giving meaning to life and to the religious and political structure of the community. This remained the essential function of architecture for thousands of years, from the earliest time of the Egyptians up through the eighteenth century. An architecture of substance arises not simply from exploiting new structural techniques or materials; it is not created through the refinement of form or the playful manipulation of fashionable details. It does not result automatically even from the most penetrating analysis of utilitarian function. It springs from the inner conviction of an individual and a culture, in response to the necessities of human material need and expressing a perception of human values measured against the total complexity of the universe. It springs, in other words, from impulses that might be described—for want of more precise words—as ethical and cosmological.

From this, then, comes the dilemma faced by architects today in the industrialized West, for the culture that shapes life in the West is frequently controlled by the monetary values of the marketplace, and such values by themselves have never had much to do with creating art or architecture of substance or significance. An architecture generated by the values of the marketplace

21.39. Balkrishna Doshi, Gandhi Labor Institute, Ahmedabad, India, 1980–84. Doshi has brought together influences from his teachers Le Corbusier and Kahn, in forms shaped by the ancient cultures of the subcontinent.

21.40. Mario Botta, house, Viganello, Switzerland, 1981–82. Botta has managed to find a way of using bold geometric forms, built of ordinary materials, that accommodate function and create powerful images at the same time.

has merit only so long as it serves, and as soon as it no longer serves the marketplace it is replaced by something deemed more profitable.

In contrast, cultures in the so-called less developed Third World countries have recently experienced a resurgence of vigorous architecture whose forms are shaped by traditional cultural and religious patterns, in reaction, perhaps, to the symbolic emptiness of imported Western architectural forms. Examples are found in the work of two Indian architects, Charles Correa and Balkrishna Doshi [21.39], who have successfully merged the lessons of form and material found in the architecture of Le Corbusier and Louis Kahn with the architectural traditions of their country.[14] The work of the Swiss architect Mario Botta also

fits into this category, for his forms evoke ancestral and ancient memories rather than specific "isms" of the recent past.

Architecture is the art we cannot escape; it is over, under, and around us virtually every second of our lives. As Aalto insisted in his work and writing, an architecture of substance is more than simply a benevolent protective umbrella; at its best, it interacts with us on our behalf, allowing us to become more human. It is far more than shelter, more than a commodity for speculation, more than an expedient package, more than a capricious gambol. It is the built record of how we have ordered our cultural priorities, of who and what we are, and what we believe in. It is our testament in stone. What, then, is the testament we are building today?

NOTES

1. Hannah Arendt, *The Human Condition* (Chicago, 1958), 154.
2. The most penetrating analysis of the design and function of the Guggenheim Museum is found in William Jordy, *American Buildings and Their Architects, IV: The Impact of European Modernism in the Mid-Twentieth Century* (Garden City, N.Y., 1972), 279–360.
3. Le Corbusier, *Ronchamp* (Zurich, 1957), 89;

translated as *The Chapel at Ronchamp* (London, 1960).
4. See Nikolaus Pevsner, *An Outline of European Architecture*, seventh ed. (Baltimore, Md., 1963), 429; and James Stirling, "Le Corbusier's Chapel and the Crisis of Rationalism," *Architectural Review* (March 1956), 155–61.
5. Stanislaus von Moos, *Le Corbusier: Elements*

of a Synthesis (Cambridge, Mass., 1979), 254.

6. Le Corbusier, *Ronchamp*, 7.

7. Le Corbusier, *Text et dessins pour Ronchamp* (Paris, 1965).

8. Matthew Nowicki, "Origins and Trends in Modern Architecture," *Magazine of Art* 44 (November 1951), reprinted in Roth, *America Builds,* 564.

9. Hans Scharoun, quoted in Michael Forsyth, *Buildings for Music* (Cambridge, Mass., 1985), 303.

10. Andrew Derbyshire, "Building the Welfare State," in Barbara Goldstein, ed., *Architecture: Opportunities, Achievements* (London, 1977), 29. His success is noted in Linda Groat and David Canter, "Does Post-Modernism Communicate?" *Progressive Architecture* 60 (December 1979).

11. "Interview with Mario Botta," in Stuart Wrede, *Mario Botta,* exhibition catalogue, Museum of Modern Art (New York, 1986).

12. Alvar Aalto, "The Humanizing of Architecture," *Technology Review,* trans. Stuart Wrede, in *Sketches: Alvar Aalto* (Cambridge, Mass., 1978), 76–77.

13. See Philip Johnson and Mark Wigley, *Deconstructivist Architecture* (New York, 1988).

14. See the discussion in Chapter 27 and the Addendum in William J. R. Curtis, *Modern Architecture Since 1900,* second ed. (Englewood Cliffs, N.J., 1987) 356–66, 389–403.

SUGGESTED READING

Reyner Banham, *The New Brutalism: Ethic or Aesthetic* (London, 1966).

Brent Brolin, *Flight of Fancy: The Banishment and Return of Ornament* (New York, 1985).

William J. R. Curtis, *Le Corbusier: Ideas and Forms* (New York, 1986).

———, *Modern Architecture Since 1900,* second ed. (Englewood Cliffs, N.J., 1987).

Arthur Drexler, *Transformations in Modern Architecture* (New York, 1979).

Kenneth Frampton, *Modern Architecture: A Critical History* (New York, 1980).

John Jacobus, *Twentieth Century Architecture: The Middle Years, 1940–65* (New York, 1966).

Charles Jencks, *Architecture Today,* revised ed. (New York, 1982).

———, *The Language of Post-Modern Architecture,* fourth ed. (New York, 1984).

———, *Modern Movements in Architecture,*

revised ed. (New York, 1987).

———, *What Is Post-Modernism?,* second ed. (New York, 1988).

Philip Johnson and Mark Wigley, *Deconstructivist Architecture* (New York, 1988).

William H. Jordy, *American Building and Their Architects,* vol 4: *The Impact of European Modernism in the Mid-Twentieth Century* (Garden City, N.Y., 1972).

Heinrich Klotz, ed., *Postmodern Visions: Drawings, Paintings, and Models by Contemporary Architects* (Munich, 1984; New York, 1985).

Udo Kultermann, *Architecture in the Seventies* (New York, 1980).

Richard A. Miller, ed., *Four Great Makers of Modern Architecture: Gropius, Le Corbusier, Mies van der Rohe, Wright* (New York, 1963).

Stanislaus von Moos, *Le Corbusier: Elements of a Synthesis* (Cambridge, Mass., 1979).

Wolfgang Pehnt, *Expressionist Architecture,* trans. J. A. Underwood and E. Kustner (New York, 1973).

Paolo Portoghesi, *After Modern Architecture* (New York, 1980).

Leland M. Roth, *America Builds: Source Documents in American Architecture and Planning* (New York, 1983).

———, *A Concise History of American Architecture* (New York, 1978).

Roger Scruton, *The Aesthetics of Architecture* (Princeton, N.J., 1979).

Vincent Scully, *American Architecture and Urbanism* (New York, 1969).

———, *Louis I. Kahn* (New York, 1962).

———, *The Shingle Style* (New Haven, Conn., 1955).

———, *The Shingle Style Today, or, The Historian's Revenge* (New York, 1972).

Dennis Sharp, *Modern Architecture and Expressionism* (New York, 1966).

Robert A. M. Stern, *Modern Classicism* (New York, 1988).

Robert Venturi, *Complexity and Contradiction in Architecture* (New York, 1966).

K. Wheeler et al., eds., *Michael Graves: Building and Projects, 1966–1981* (New York, 1982).

Arnold Whittick, *Erich Mendelsohn,* second ed. (London, 1956).

Stuart Wrede, *Mario Botta* (New York, 1986).

———, *Sketches: Alvar Aalto* (Cambridge, Mass., 1978); contains translations of Aalto's speeches and published articles.

Richard Saul Wurman, ed., *What Will Be Has Always Been: The Words of Louis I. Kahn* (New York, 1986).

Bruno Zevi, *Erich Mendelsohn* (London, 1985).

Glossary

abacus (from Greek *abax*, "counting board") The square slab that forms the topmost element of a Classical capital. See *order*.

abbey (from Old French *abaie*, which comes from Latin, *abbas*, "abbot") A monastery or convent, a place of residence, work, worship, and study for monks or nuns.

acanthus (from Greek *akanthos*, thorn plant) A plant, native to the Mediterranean region, whose thick, serrated leaves provided the model for the leaflike forms of the Corinthian capital. See *order*.

acropolis (from Greek *akropolis*, from *akro*, "top," plus *polis*, "city") Generic sense: the elevated plateau or citadel containing the principal municipal and religious buildings of a city. Specific sense: the ancient citadel of Athens, the site of the Erechtheion, the Parthenon, and other temples.

aedicule (from Latin) A framing motif, around a *blind* window or door, or around an actual opening, consisting of columns or *pilasters* supporting an *entablature* and *pediment*.

aggregate (from Latin *aggregare*, "to add together") The crushed stone, sand, and other solid material used to make *concrete*.

agora (Greek) An open area used as a marketplace; in Greek cities of the Hellenistic period often lined by *stoa* buildings.

aisle (from Old French and from Latin *ala*). A passage or open corridor running parallel to the principal space or *nave* of a church or *basilica* and separated from it by an *arcade*.

ambulatory (from Latin *ambulare*, "to walk") A curved or polygonal *aisle* forming a passageway around the *choir* or *chevet* of a church.

amphitheater (from Greek *amphi*, "around," plus *theatron*, "watching place") Originating in Roman architecture, a round or oval arena for sports events, surrounded by tiers of seats.

annular vault (from Latin *anulus*, "ring") A tunnel or barrel vault (see *vault*) that curves around in a closed ring.

anta (from Latin *antae*, "pilasters") The pier or *pilaster* formed by the projection of the side walls of a building, often found at the ends of the *naos* chamber of Greek temples.

apse (from Latin *apsis*, "arch" or "vault") A semicircular projection from an enclosed space, typically covered by a hemispherical vault, often found on the short side of a Roman *basilica* or at the end of an Early Christian church.

aqueduct (from Latin *aqua*, "water," plus *ductus*, past participle of "to lead") A channel used to carry water, often raised up on a long *arcade*.

arcade (from Italian *arcata*, from Latin *arcus*, "arch") A series of arches, often raised on piers or columns; a covered passage with such arches on one or both sides; a covered passage with such arches on each side opening into shops or offices (used figuratively even when no true arch forms are present).

arch (from Latin *arcus*, "arch") A structure, formed of wedge-shaped blocks laid to form a semicircle or a parabola or some other curve, that spans an opening. A *flat arch* is formed by a segment of a semicircle and can have very little curvature.

architecture parlent (French) Literally, "speaking architecture." First used in eighteenth-century France to describe an architecture that clearly expressed its functional purpose.

architrave   (from Old French and Old Italian *arch* plus *trabs*, "chief beam") Specifically, the lowest element in the *entablatures* of the Ionic and Corinthian columnar orders (see *order*), with two or three stepped back faces; by extension the frame around windows, doors, and arches in classical architecture.

arcuated   A structural form composed of numerous arches, in contrast to *trabeated*.

arris   (from Old French *areste*, "ridge") The edge formed when two surfaces meet at an angle, as in the *flutes* of a classical column.

ashlar   A dressed or squared stone, and a masonry wall or structure built of such hewn stone. Ashlar masonry may be coursed (with continuous joints) or random (with discontinuous joints).

atelier   (from Old French *astelier*, "carpenter shop," from Old French *astele*, "splinter," from Latin *astula*, "board") A studio or workshop, particularly an artist's or architect's studio in which younger students are trained.

atrium   (from Latin *atrium*) In Roman houses, the central court, open to the sky, that provided access to the principal rooms; by extension any central circulation space, open to the sky or covered by a skylight.

attic   A story above the main cornice level in classical architecture.

axis   An imaginary line about which parts of a building or individual buildings in a group are disposed, usually with careful attention to bilateral symmetry.

axonometric projection   A method of mechanical drawing to represent a building in three dimensions in which vertical lines are drawn vertically and horizontal lines are drawn at unequal angles to the true horizontal, usually 30 degrees and 60 degrees.

bailey   (Middle English from Old French, *baille*) The outer wall of a castle, and by extension the open court enclosed by this wall.

balloon frame   (from *balloon*, since the frame was said to go up as fast as a balloon) A building frame, historically developed in the mid–United States about 1830, made of slender wooden members, or studs, spaced about 16 inches (.5 meters) apart. In a true balloon frame, the wooden studs rise through two floors. In a *platform frame*, the studs rise only one floor and support a platform that forms the base for the next floor.

baluster   (from French and Italian derivatives of Greek *balaustion*, the flower of the pomegranate, because of the shape of the post) An upright vase-shaped post used to support a rail.

balustrade   A series of balusters supporting a rail.

baptistery   In Christian architecture, a chamber or often a separate building used for the sacramental ceremony of baptism.

barrel vault   A masonry *vault* resting on two parallel walls and having the form of a half cylinder; sometimes called *tunnel vault;* also, by extension, a nonstructural wooden ceiling of the same form.

base   (from Latin and Greek *basis*) The lowest element of a column, pier, or wall.

basilica   (from Latin and Greek *basilike*, "royal portico") In Roman architecture, a large meeting hall, most often used to hold law courts. Adapted for Early Christian churches, often with the addition of *aisles* on the long sides and terminating in an *apse*.

batter   The upward and inward slope of a masonry wall, generally resulting in diminishing thickness.

battlement   (from Old French *battillement*) A parapet built atop a wall with openings (*crenels*) for defense.

bay   In a building, a regular and repeated structural or spatial unit or module marked by repeated beams or ribs.

blind arch   An arch within a wall framing a recessed flat panel rather than an opening; used to enliven an otherwise plain expanse of masonry or to decrease the dead weight of a wall.

boss   (from Old French *boce*) In architecture, a round ornamented keystone at the intersection of *ribs* in a rib vault.

bouletarion   (from Greek *boule*, the council of ancient Athens) The council chamber of ancient Greek cities.

boulevard   (from Old French *boloart*, a rampart converted to a promenade) A major thoroughfare in a town, usually laid out where old fortifications were removed, often lined with rows of trees.

bracket   A projecting brace used under cornices, eaves, balconies, or windows to provide structural support or visual support.

buttress   (from Middle English and Old French *bouteret*, from *bouter*, "to strike against") A pier built into or against a wall to help it resist lateral forces (see *flying buttress*).

caisson foundation   (from French *caisse*, "box") A technique for constructing deep foundations in loose, saturated soils, developed in the United States, 1865–90. An open-bottom airtight chamber is lowered into the soil and the earth is excavated from beneath it by workmen called "sand hogs." As the chamber descends, the air pressure inside the chamber is increased to match the water pressure outside; meanwhile the hole left above is lined or filled with stones or *concrete.* When dense soils or solid rock is reached, the chamber is filled with concrete.

cantilever (from Middle English and Norman French *cant,* "side," plus *levier,* "to raise") A beam or a part of a building supported by such beams that is supported at one end only, with the other end hovering in the air.

capital The topmost part of a column (see *order*), above the shaft, which carries the *entablature.*

cardo The principal north-south street in an ancient Roman town or military camp (see *decumanus*).

cartouche (French, from Italian *cartoccio,* "card") A decorative tablet or panel, with carved edges resembling curled paper.

caryatid (from Latin and Greek *Karuatides,* the maidens of Karui, a village in ancient Greece) A building column sculpted in the form of a female figure.

castellated Having battlements (parapet walls with notched openings) and turrets like those of a medieval castle.

castrum (Latin) An ancient Roman military camp, with streets laid out in a rectalinear grid (see *cardo* and *decumanus*).

catacomb (from late Latin *catacumbae*) An underground passage or chamber used as a cemetery.

cathedral (from Latin *cathedra,* "chair") A church that contains the bishop's throne, from which official pronouncements are made. Usually, but not always, the largest church in the diocese.

causeway (from Middle English *caucewei,* "raised road") A roadway on a raised embankment.

cella (Latin) The Latin term for the *naos,* the inner chamber of a classical temple.

cement (from Latin *caementa,* "broken stones") Term used to identify the bonding agent in concrete; nowadays made from pulverized baked limestone.

cenotaph (from Greek *kenos,* "empty," plus *taphos,* "tomb") An empty tomb built as a monument to a person buried elsewhere.

centering Term used to describe the temporary support used to carry a vault or an arch until the keystone is put in place.

central plan A building plan focused on a central point and usually laid out on two axes crossed at right angles; square and octagonal plans are examples.

centuriation The system of land division practiced in ancient Rome, with units large enough to contain one hundred traditional farms.

chamfer (from French *chanfrein,* "a bevel") To remove the edge or corner; also, the flat surface left after the corner is cut away.

chancel (from Old French) In a Latin cross-plan church, the eastern end, including the choir, side aisles, ambulatory, and chapels. (In France this is called the *chevet*).

chapel (from medieval Latin *capella,* a diminutive of the Latin *cappa,* "cloak"; derived from the name of a small chamber at the church Saint-Martin, Tours, France, which contained the cloak of Saint Martin) A small chamber containing an altar and used for private worship; a similar room within a larger church or religious building. A *Lady Chapel* is one dedicated to the Virgin Mary.

chevet The French term for the *chancel,* or east end of a church, including side aisles, choir, ambulatory, and chapels.

choir (from Middle English *quer* and Old French *cuer,* from Latin *chorus*) An organized group of singers, such as medieval monks; hence that part of the church in which the monks gathered for services, usually the area between the crossing and the altar at the east end of the *chancel* or *chevet.*

church (from Middle English *chirche* and from Greek *kuriakos,* "of the lord") The principal building used for Christian public worship.

circus (Latin, "circle") In ancient Roman architecture, a long, open arena used for chariot races and other contests. In the eighteenth century, this term was used to describe curved ranges of connected town houses.

classic Of the highest order, or representing the best of its type; often capitalized, referring to the art or architecture of ancient Greece or Rome.

Classical Referring to the art or architecture of ancient Greece or Rome; architecture employing the forms and proportions derived from ancient Greek and Roman architecture.

Classicism The principles of design and proportion, as well as the repertoire of forms and details, found in ancient Greek and Roman architecture, as well as later Renaissance and Baroque architecture. See also *Neoclassicism.*

clerestory (from Middle English *clere,* "lighted," plus "story") Originally the upper section of the nave of a Gothic cathedral, with its banks of large windows; hence, any elevated series of windows for light and ventilation.

cloister (from Latin *claustrum,* "enclosed

place") In a medieval monastery, the courtyard and its surrounding covered walkways enclosed by the church, dormitory wing, refectory, and storage buildings.

cloister vault   A form of *dome,* with curved surfaces that rise from a square or polygonal plan; the intersections of the curved surfaces form *groins* or have *ribs* (example: the dome of Santa Maria del Fiore, Florence, by Filippo Brunelleschi).

coffer   (from Middle English *coffre,* "box," and Latin *cophinus,* "basket") A recessed boxlike panel in a ceiling or vault; usually square but sometimes octagonal or lozenge-shaped.

colonnade   (from Italian *colonnato,* from Latin *columna,* "column") A row of evenly spaced columns, usually carrying a continuous entablature.

colonnette   (French, diminutive of *colonne,* "column") A small, slender, or greatly elongated column, more often used for visual effect than for structural support.

column   (from Latin *columna,* "column") A narrow round support post, often having a *base* and a *capital.* See *order.*

composite order   See *order.*

compression   A force within a structure that tends to push, crush, or squeeze. Many materials, whether crystalline or fibrous, are strong in compression.

concrete   (from Latin *concretus,* past participle of *concrescere,* "to grow together" or "to harden") An artificial stone made by mixing water, *aggregate* made of crushed stone and sand, and a cementing or bonding material. Like crystalline stone, concrete is relatively weak in *tension;* the addition of iron or steel bars to resist the tensile forces creates *reinforced concrete.*

console   (from Latin *consolator,* "one who consoles"; hence, figuratively, a support) See *bracket.*

corbel   (from Middle English *corp* and Latin *corvus,* "raven") A block of masonry projecting from the plane of the wall used to support an upper element such as a cornice, battlements, or an upper wall.

Corinthian order   See *order.*

cornice   (from Greek *koronos,* "curved," referring to the curved profile) Specifically, the uppermost and projecting section of the entablature; hence, the uppermost projecting molding or combination of brackets and moldings used to crown a building or to define the meeting of wall and ceiling. See *order.*

corps de logis   In French classical architecture,

the dominant center motif or element, in contrast to the flanking wings.

crennelation   (from Latin *crena,* "notch") A series of openings or large notches in a parapet. See *battlement.*

crocket   (from Old French *crochet,* "hook") In Gothic architecture, a carved, foliate, hooklike projection used along the edges of roofs, spires, towers, and other upper elements.

cromlech   (from Welsh *crwm,* "arched," plus *llech,* "stone") A prehistoric structure consisting of *monoliths* encircling a mound; the term is sometimes used in place of *dolmen.*

crossing   In a Latin cross-plan church, the area where the four sections (nave, transepts, and chancel) come together; the area where the two axes of nave-chancel and of the two transepts cross.

cross-in-square plan   A Byzantine centralized church plan of nine bays in which the central bay and the middle bay on each side are domed. See *quincunx plan.*

crypt   (from Latin and Greek *kruptos,* "hidden") A chamber or story beneath the main floor of a church, often below ground, usually containing graves.

cupola   (from late Latin *cupula,* diminutive form for "tub") A rounded towerlike device rising from the roof of a classical building (usually Renaissance or Baroque), typically terminating in a miniature dome.

curtain wall   In modern architecture since 1885, a non–load-bearing wall attached to an internal structural skeleton; since 1920, the outer skin or curtain has often been composed of panels of glass, steel, aluminum, or composites.

cyclopean   (from Greek *Cyclops,* the one-eyed giant in Homer's *Odyssey*) A type of dry masonry characterized by huge irregular stones laid in random patterns.

dentil   (from Latin *dens,* "tooth") A small rectangular block used in a series below the cornice in the Corinthian order; any such block used to form a molding below a cornice. See *order.*

dependency   An outbuilding or other subordinate structure that serves as an adjunct to a central, dominant building.

diaphragm arch   An arch that spans a space crosswise to support a ceiling or other superstructure; often an arch that spans across the nave of a church (example: Saint-Philbert of Tournous).

dolmen   (from Celtic and Breton *tol,* "table," plus *men,* "stone") A prehistoric European structure consisting of two or three upright stones carrying a stone slab as a roof.

dome   A convex roof with a smooth curved surface rising either from a circular or a polygonal base (if the latter, then it is more accurately a *cloister vault*). The simplest true dome is a *hemispherical* dome; an *onion* dome may have a shape that is somewhat more than a half sphere and may be pointed at the top (example: the Taj Mahal); a *saucer* dome is a low dome that is less than a half sphere; a *melon* or *umbrella* dome is divided into radiating sections or gores by ribs (example: Santa Maria delle Carceri, Prato).

donjon   (variation of dungeon, from Middle English and from Latin *dominus*, "master") The fortified tower at the center of medieval castles, either square or round in plan; the dwelling of the lord.

Doric order   See *order*.

dormer   (from Old French *dormeor*, "bedroom window") A vertical window and its housing, which projects outward from a sloping roof.

drum   (because it resembles the musical instrument) A circular or polygonal wall that carries a dome; also one of the individual cylindrical blocks of stone used to build columns.

dry masonry   Blocks of stone, either regular or irregular in shape, laid in a wall without *mortar*.

duomo   The Italian term for a cathedral.

echinus   (from Latin and Greek *ekhinos*, "sea urchin") In the capital of the Doric order, the circular flaring block that carries the *abacus*.

eclecticism   (from Greek *ek*, "out," plus *legein*, "to choose," "to select") The combination of selected elements from different sources to form one whole; in architecture, the use of historic styles from previous time periods to make associational links between appearance and functional use.

egg and dart   A form of molding, or decorative band, in Classical architecture made up of forms that resemble alternated eggs and darts.

elevation   (from Latin *elevare*, "to raise up") A drawing of the walls of one side of a building (either interior or exterior) with all lines of true dimension and shown vertical and horizontal; also used in reference to the vertical plane of a building, as in "the west elevation."

engaged column   A column that is attached to and appears to emerge from the wall; in plan it forms a half to three-quarters of a fully rounded column. It is usually purely decorative and may serve as a buttresslike thickening of the wall.

entablature   (French, from Italian *intavolatura*, "to put on a table," "to support") The horizontal beamlike member supported by Classical columns. See *order*. Although the details and proportions of the entablatures of the Doric, Ionic, and Corinthian orders vary, each has three component parts: the lower *architrave*, the middle *frieze*, and the crowning *cornice*.

entasis   The subtly curved diminution of the thickness of the Classical column. See *order*.

epistyle   (from Greek *epi*, "upon," plus *stulos*, "column") The Greek term for *architrave*. See also *order*.

esplanade   (from Italian and Latin *explanare*, "to flatten out") A flat open space, often laid out as a walkway.

estipite   Spanish, for a *pilaster* whose surface is covered by elaborate secondary decorations, sometimes to such an extent that the basic pilaster is difficult to see (example: Cartuja, Granada, Spain).

exedra   (from Greek *ex*, "out" plus *hedra*, "seat") A seat with a high back, curved in a semicircle; also a semicircular roofed recess in a building with seats or a curved bench.

facade   (from Italian and Latin *facies*, "face") The face of a building, especially the principal face or front.

fenestration   (from Latin *fenestra*, "window") A general term used to denote the pattern or arrangement of windows.

fillet   (from Middle English and Old French, diminutive of Latin *filum*, "thread") A narrow flat molding, usually between two larger elements, as between the indented *flutes* of a Classical column.

finial   (Middle English, variant of Latin *finis*, "end") A decorative ornament that ends a gable, pinnacle, or spire, usually foliate in form.

fireproof construction   A system of construction employing masonry bearing walls and arches. When iron and steel frames were introduced in the nineteenth century, the metal was protected from fire by tile cladding or concrete/plaster.

flute   One of the several shallow vertical grooves cut into the shaft of Classical columns or pilasters. See *order*.

flying buttress   An inclined or ramped arch extending from the wall of a building to an outer, freestanding buttress pier, thus transmitting outward thrusts from the main building to externalized supports.

folly   In eighteenth-century English gardens and landscape design, a garden ornament building such as a tower or fake ruin constructed to highlight a view.

forum   (Latin) An open space in a Roman town used as a marketplace and public gathering place; hence, a place for civic discussion.

foundation   See *caisson* foundation, *raft* foundation, and *spread* footing.

frame   A structural support composed of separate linear members (columns and beams) joined together to form a cage, as contrasted to solid masonry construction. Traditionally, a wooden frame was composed of large hewn hardwood members, connected with complex interlocking joints. See *mortise and tenon*. Also called braced frame.

fresco   (from Italian for "fresh") A form of wall painting in which pigments are mixed into the wet, fresh plaster immediately after it is applied to the wall.

frieze   (from Old French *frise*, from Latin *Phrygia*, the name of an ancient country in Asia Minor) In Classical architecture, the flat horizontal panel in the *entablature* of the Ionic order, between the lower *architrave* and the crowning *cornice*, ornamented with low relief sculpture. Hence, by extension, the center panel or section of all entablatures, even of the much different Doric order, which has grooved stylized beam ends (*triglyphs*) with the spaces between filled with panels of low relief sculpture (*metopes*). See *order*. By further extension, any projecting horizontal decorative band or panel.

gable   The triangularly shaped area enclosed by the two sloped surfaces of a *gable roof* and the wall below; a generic term distinct from *pediment*, which refers to a portion of a Classical facade.

gable roof   A simple roof composed of two angled flat surfaces meeting to form a straight ridge.

gallery   (from Middle English *galerie*, from medieval Latin *galeria*) In medieval architecture, especially Gothic churches, a passage above the side aisle and below the clerestory window that provided access to the roof over the side aisles; in general, a long passage, often with windows on one side, sometimes used for the display of paintings.

gambrel roof   (from Old North French *gamberel*, from late Latin *gamba*, "leg," referring to the bent or crooked stick used by butchers to suspend carcasses) A roof, similar to a *gable roof*, but with two slopes on each side, a steeper pitch to the lower, outer portion of the roof, and a lower pitch to the upper, center portion of the roof. In England this term is used to denote a *mansard* roof.

gargoyle   (from Middle English *gargoyl* and Old French *gargoule*) A rain spout carved in the form of a fantastical creature or demon;

any such projecting ornamental feature in the form of a grotesque.

glacis   (from Old French *glacier*, "to slide") In medieval military architecture, a long, gentle, open slope outside a fortified wall.

golden section   A proportional ratio devised by the ancient Greeks that expresses the ideal relationship of unequal parts. Capable of being demonstrated by Euclidian geometry, it can also be stated thus: a is to b as b is to $a + b$; or $a/b = b/(a + b)$. If this is rewritten as a quadratic equation and the value 1 assigned to a, and then solved for b, the value of b is 1.618034. Hence, the ratio of the golden section is 1 : 1.618.

Greek cross   A type of centralized plan with two axes at right angles and with identical elements on each of the axes around the central element (example: San Marco, Venice, Italy).

groin   (from Middle English *grinde*) The junction of the intersection of two curved vaults.

groin vault   A vault formed when two barrel vaults intersect at right angles; sometimes called a cross vault (example: Baths of Caracalla).

hall church   A late Gothic type of church in which the side aisles are as high as, or nearly as high as, the central nave.

hammerbeam   A short beam projecting from a wall, supported from below by a hammer brace and used in turn as the support for the collar brace in a hammerbeam *truss*.

henge   A circle of upright stones or wooden posts.

heroum   (plural, *heroa*) (Latin) In ancient Greek and Roman architecture, a building or sacred enclosure dedicated to a hero, usually over a grave; such buildings typically had *central plans*.

hexastyle   (from Greek *hex*, "six," plus *stulos*, "column") Having six columns; used to describe Classical temples according to the number of columns across the short side.

historicism   The reference to historic periods in the past; the use of architectural forms derived from the past. In contrast to eclecticism, which may result in the combination of elements of many historic periods in one building, historicism may be said to confine the references in a single building to a single time period.

hôtel   (French) A French town house of the eighteenth century, usually of one or two floors, spread out horizontally in a large suburban estate. The main living level was at ground level (see the contrast with *piano nobile*), with large casement windows or French doors that provided easy access to the garden terraces.

hypocaust   (from Latin *hypocaustum*, from

Greek *hupo,* "underneath," plus *kaiein,* "to burn") In Roman architecture, a type of hollow floor, honeycombed with passages, through which hot air and smoke from fires were channeled as a means of heating the interior; used extensively in Roman baths.

hypostyle (from Greek *hupo,* "underneath," plus *stulos,* "column") Used to describe a hall or chamber whose roof is supported by many columns.

impost (from Old French *imposte,* from medieval Latin *impostum,* past participle of *imponere,* "to place upon") The block or line upon which the foot of an arch rests.

in antis (from Latin and Greek, meaning "within the walls") Used to describe the placement of two or four columns in the porch of a Classical building between the projecting *antae* or *spur walls* of the *naos* behind the columns.

insula (Latin, "island") Latin term for an ancient Roman multilevel apartment building that filled an entire city block.

intercolumniation (from Latin *inter,* "between," plus *columna,* "column") Term used to describe the distance between columns in a colonnade; expressed in terms of fractions of the diameter of the individual columns.

Ionic See *order.*

isometric projection (from Greek *isometros,* "of equal measure") A method of mechanical drawing to represent a building in three dimensions in which vertical lines are drawn vertical and horizontal lines are drawn at equal angles to the true horizontal, usually 30 degrees or 45 degrees.

jamb (from Middle English *jambe,* from late Latin *gamba,* "hoof") The vertical posts forming the sides of a door or window.

keep Also called *donjon,* the central fortified tower inside medieval castles.

keystone The uppermost central *voussoir* of an arch that locks all the others together, often bearing carved embellishment.

Lady Chapel See *chapel.*

lancet (Middle English *launcea,* from Latin *lancea,* a lance or spear) Used to describe tall, extremely narrow, spearlike windows, particularly in early English Gothic architecture.

lantern In architecture, a small glass-enclosed square or round structure built atop a larger structure to admit light.

Latin cross Term used to describe the plan type of many Western medieval churches shaped like a cross, with a long *nave,* north and south *transepts,* and *chancel* or *chevet.*

lierne (French) A subordinate, often purely decorative, *rib* that connects a principal rib to a tierceron.

lintel (Middle English from Old French and Latin *limes,* "boundary" or "threshold") A beam used to carry a load over an opening or to span between two columns.

loggia (Italian, from French *loge,* "small house," "hut") A covered but open gallery, often in the upper part of a building; also, a covered passageway, often with an open trellis roof, connecting two buildings.

lunette (from Old French and Latin *luna,* "moon") A semicircular or crescent-shaped area, often opened with a semicircular window.

machicolation (from Old French *macher,* "to crush," plus *col,* "neck") In medieval castles, a projecting gallery at the top of the castle wall, supported by *corbeled* arches, with openings in the floor through which stones or boiling oil could be dropped on attackers.

mansard roof (from François Mansart, French Baroque architect, 1598–1666, who employed this roof form extensively) A roof with two slopes on each of its four sides, a steep and nearly vertical slope on the outside and a gentle, nearly flat slope on the top; the steeper outer roof slope may be flat, convex, or concave in profile.

martyrium (from Latin and Greek *martus,* "witness") A site that witnessed events in the life of Christ or of an apostle, or where the relics of a Christian martyr were deposited; also often used to identify the building (usually centrally planned) constructed over such a spot.

mass In architecture, term used to describe the sense of bulk, density, and weight of architectural forms.

mastaba or *mastabah* (from Arabic *mastabah,* "bench") Term used to identify ancient Egyptian tombs with flat tops and *battered* sides, built over subterranean burial chambers.

megalith (from Greek *megas,* "big," plus *lithos,* "stone") A stone of great size, moved in prehistoric times by teams of builders. *Megalithic* is used to describe prehistoric structures.

megaron (from Greek *megas,* "great") The principal reception room of a Mycenaean residence or palace; rectangular in plan, with a central hearth, and entered through a porch with two columns *in antis.*

melon dome See *dome.*

menhir (from Celtic and Breton *men,* "stone," plus *hir,* "long") A prehistoric monument, a *megalith,* consisting of a large single upright stone; sometimes set in long parallel rows.

metope (Greek *meta,* "between," plus *ope,* "opening") In the Classical Doric *order,* a square stone panel placed between the beam ends covered by *triglyph* panels; the metope panel was embellished with narrative figural sculpture.

moat (from Middle English and Old French *mote,* "mound") A wide, deep ditch, either dry or filled with water, used for defense purposes. See also *motte.*

modillion (from French and Italian *modiglione,* from Latin *mutulus,* from an Etruscan root meaning "to stand out") A small curved and ornamented *bracket* used to support the upper part of the *cornice* in the Corinthian *order;* any such small curved ornamented bracket used in series.

module (from Latin *modulus,* diminutive of *modus,* "measure") A unit of measurement governing the proportions of a building. In Classical architecture, the module was either the diameter or half the diameter of the column at the base of the shaft. In modern architecture, the module is any unit of measurement devised by the architect, usually to facilitate prefabrication.

monolithic (from Greek *monos,* "single," plus *lithos,* "stone") Made from a single stone.

mortar (from Middle English *morter,* from Latin *mortarium*) A mixture of lime with sand and water used as a bed for setting stones in masonry walls. In medieval buildings, the lime mortar required oxygen to set properly; modern mortar is made with Portland cement instead of lime and cures without the presence of external oxygen.

mortise and tenon One of the basic wood joining methods; one member is cut with a rectangular or square hole (*mortise*) to receive the other member, cut with a rectangular or square tongue (*tenon*).

mosaic (from Greek *mouseios,* "of the Muses") A wall or floor covering made of small cubes (*tesserae*) of colored stone or glass, often laid out to form a figural image.

motte (from Middle English and Old French *mote,* "mound") A steep mound of earth surrounded by a ditch and surmounted by a timber stockade.

mullion (from Middle English *moniel,* from Latin *medianus,* "median") Originally the large vertical stone divider in medieval windows; later the vertical supports in glazed windows; often now any support strip, vertical or horizontal, in a glazed window.

naos (Greek) The enclosed inner chamber of an ancient Greek temple.

narthex (from Greek *narthex,* "box") A vestibule or entry lobby in an Early Christian church.

nave (from medieval Latin *navis,* "ship") In a Roman basilica, the taller central space lit by clerestory windows; in a Christian church, the taller space in the western arm, lit by clerestory windows.

Neoclassicism Beginning in the late eighteenth century, the intentional reproduction of Classical Greek or Roman buildings in their entirety or in selected details such as orders from specific ancient buildings.

niche (from Old French *nichier,* "to nest") A recess or hollow in a wall, often meant to contain a statue.

nymphaeum (from Greek *numphe,* a female spirit of woodland and water) A Classical building or room, decorated with plants and fountains, often located in a garden and intended as a place for relaxation.

obelisk (from Old French *obelisque,* from Greek *obeliskos,* "spit or pointed pillar") A tall, narrow square shaft, tapering and ending in a pyramidal point.

octastyle (from Greek *okta,* "eight," plus *stulos,* "column") Having eight columns; used to describe Classical temples according to the number of columns across the short side.

oculus (Latin, "eye") A round window in a wall or at the apex of a dome.

ogee (alteration of Old French *augive*) A double or reverse S-shaped curve.

ogive (from Old French *augive*) A diagonal *rib* in a Gothic vault; a pointed arch.

opus incertum Roman concrete faced with irregularly shaped stones.

opus quadratum Roman masonry of squared stones.

opus reticulatum Roman concrete faced with small pyramidal stones with their points embedded in the wall and laid on the diagonal, forming a netlike pattern.

opus sectile In Roman architecture, a wall or floor covering of stone laid out in a geometric pattern.

order (from Old French *ordre,* from Latin *ordo,* "line" or "row," possibly from Greek *arariskein,* "to fit together") Any of the several types of Classical columns, including pedestal bases and *entablatures.* The Greeks developed three orders, the Doric, Ionic, and Corinthian, of which the Romans adopted the latter two and added Tuscan Doric and the Composite, merging the features of Ionic and Corinthian. See Figure 2.9.

    1. The Greek Doric, developed in the west-

ern Dorian region of Greece, is the heaviest and most massive of the orders. It rises from the stylobate without any base; it is from four to six times as tall as its diameter; it has twenty broad flutes; the capital consists simply of a banded necking swelling out into a smooth echinus, which carries a flat square abacus; the Doric entablature is also the heaviest, being about one-fourth the height column. The Greek Doric order was not used after c. 100 B.C. until its "rediscovery" in the mid-eighteenth century.

2. The Ionic order was developed along the west coast of what is now Turkey, once Ionian Greece. It is generally about nine times as high as its diameter; it has a base, twenty-four flutes, and a much more elaborate capital, consisting of a decorative band and a circular egg-and-dart molding on which rests the distinctive volute; the volute in turn supports a thin, flat abacus. The Ionic entablature is about one-fifth the height of the column.

3. The Corinthian order, the most attenuated and richly embellished, was the least used by the Greeks. It is about ten times as high as its diameter, rising from a base, with twenty-four flutes and a tall capital consisting of a band from which spread upward three or four layers of curling acanthus leaves ending in tight volutes in the four corners and supporting a concave abacus. The Corinthian entablature is about one-fifth the height of the column.

4. The Roman Doric order is much slimmer than the Greek prototype, being nearly as slender as the Ionic order; moreover, it has a short base. Derived from this is the thicker Roman Tuscan Doric order, which has a base and an unfluted shaft and is about seven times as high as its diameter; its capital is similar to that of the Greek original but more strongly articulated.

5. The Composite order was formed by the Romans by combining the Ionic and Corinthian orders, and placing volutes atop acanthus leaves; this is the most sculpturally elaborate of all the orders.

oriel (from Middle English and medieval Latin *oriolum*, "porch") A projecting bay window, supported from below by a corbel or bracket.

palace (from Old French *palais*, from Latin *palatium*, the Palatine Hill, the site of the residence of the Roman emperors) The official residence of a royal person or high dignitary; hence, any splendid or elaborate residence.

palazzo (Italian) An urban residence, often including family business quarters as well as facilities for the extended family and retainers.

palisade (French *palissade*, from Latin *palus*, "stake") A fence of stakes forming a defense barrier.

Palladian motif (from Andrea Palladio, 1508–1580, who employed this device frequently) A window or door with three openings, the center opening having a semicircular arch springing from the entablature of narrow flanking bays. Since it was illustrated in a treatise of 1537 by Sebastiano Serlio, this motif has also been called a Serliana.

parti (French, from *prendre parti*, "to make a decision") A basic compositional scheme for a building plan or group of buildings. Emphasis on a clear, rational parti was a cornerstone of the instruction of the Ecole des Beaux-Arts, Paris, during the nineteenth century.

pavilion (from Old English *pavilon*, from Latin *papilio*, "butterfly," perhaps because of the resemblance of ornamental tents to butterfly wings) Originally a tent, especially an elaborately ornamented shelter; later, any portion of a building projected forward and otherwise set apart, or even a separate structure. Much favored in French Renaissance and especially Baroque architecture, and later in Second Empire Baroque architecture, 1850–90.

pediment (from a variation of obsolete English, *perement*, perhaps from pyramid) Originally the triangular gable above the entablature of Greek and Roman temples, enclosed by the horizontal *cornice* of the *entablature* and raking cornices following the edges of the roof; later, any such cornice-framed embellishment over a door or window, either triangular, segmental, broken, or consisting of curved broken cornices ending in volutes.

pendentive (from French *pendentif*, from Latin *pendens*, "hanging") A curved triangular element that effects the change from the circular base of a dome down to a square plan below; first employed extensively in Byzantine architecture (example: Hagia Sophia, Istanbul, Turkey).

peripteral (from Greek *peri*, "around," plus *pteron*, "wing") Used to designate temples with a single row of columns all around.

peristyle (from Greek *peri*, "around," plus *stulos*, "column") A *colonnade* surrounding a building, or a court completely enclosed by an encircling colonnade.

perpendicular Gothic Term used to identify the phase of late Gothic architecture in England, c. 1330 to c. 1580, characterized by multiple and emphasized vertical elements.

piano nobile (from Italian, figuratively "the noble level") In a European building, the main living level with reception and state rooms, usually the first floor above ground level.

piazza (Italian) A public square in an Italian town.

picturesque A term defined in the eighteenth century to describe landscapes or other designs characterized by ruggedness, irregularity, asymmetry, and a variety of textures and forms.

pier (Middle English *per,* from Latin *pera*) A solid support, often rectangular or square in plan and thick relative to its height.

pilaster (Old French *pilastre,* from Latin *pila,* "pillar") In Classical architecture, a flat protrusion from a wall, with ornamental elements corresponding to one of the Classical *orders* and having the same proportions.

piles, piling (from Middle English and Latin *pilum,* "spear") A heavy wooden timber or shaft of metal or concrete driven into the earth as a support for a foundation. Groups of piles may be driven in a close pattern to support a *spread* or *raft* foundation.

pillar (from Middle English and Latin *pila,* "pillar") A freestanding support or column.

pilotis (French, "stilt") An extremely thin vertical support; used by Le Corbusier to lift his buildings free of the ground.

place (French) An open public space in a French town.

plaza (Spanish, from Latin *platea,* "broad street") A broad street or an open public space in a Spanish town.

plinth (from Greek *plinthos,* "tile") Specifically, in Classical architecture the square slab forming the bottom element of a column base; by extension, any platformlike base for a building.

polis (Greek) An ancient Greek city-state.

polychromy (from Greek *polus,* "many," plus *khroma,* "color") In architecture, the use of many building materials of contrasting colors.

porch (from Middle English *porche,* from Latin *porta,* "gate") A covered or roofed entrance to a building, often employing columns to support the roof. See *portico.*

portal (from Latin *porta,* "gate") An entrance to a building or enclosure, particularly one that is imposing.

porte cochère (from French, "coach door") A covered area, attached to a house, providing shelter for those alighting from carriages.

portico (from Latin *porticus* and *porta,* "gate") A covered entrance, often using Classical columns to support a *pediment* or other roof.

Portland cement A binding cement made of burned pulverized selected limestone and clay, so called because the finished concrete closely resembled the high-quality limestone from Portland, England.

post and lintel Term used to describe a generic structural type in which upright columns support horizontal beams; the structure may be stone, wood, or iron and steel.

propylaia (from Greek *pro,* "before," plus *pule,* "gate") An entrance gateway; refers to entrance gateways to Greek temple enclosures.

propylon See *propylaia.* An entrance gateway, but especially the large freestanding monumental entrances to Egyptian temples.

pylon (from Greek *pule,* "gate") The large, imposing entrance to an Egyptian temple.

quarry-faced masonry Masonry built of stone blocks whose outer faces are left rough and irregular, much as they come from the quarry.

quincunx (from Latin *quinque,* "five," plus *uncia,* "twelfth," or "five-twelfths") A Byzantine centralized church plan of nine bays in which the central bay and the corner bays are domed. See *cross-in-square plan.*

quoin (from Old French *coing,* "wedge") Originally the structural use of large masonry blocks to reinforce the corner of a brick or other masonry wall; but often used as a decorative embellishment in non–load-bearing materials.

radiating chapel One of a group of *chapels* in a Gothic church arranged around the curved ambulatory of the *chancel* or *chevet* and seeming to radiate out from the *choir.*

raft foundation A foundation type developed in Chicago in the 1870s in which beams of either wood or steel are laid crosswise over *piles* and encased in concrete to form a pad for the base of a structural pier or column.

refectory (from Latin *reficere,* "to refresh") In a monastery, a room where meals are served.

reinforced concrete See *concrete.*

revetment (from Old French *revestir,* "to reclothe") A wall facing or veneer consisting of panels of stone, marble, metal, or other material.

rib A slender arch used in the construction of Gothic rib *vaults.* The principal ribs are the transverse ribs that run across the nave from pier to pier, the diagonal ribs that cross over the nave and intersect at the center *boss,* and the ridge ribs that extend lengthwise and crosswise from the boss along the length of the nave and from side wall to side wall. The secondary ribs and more decorative ribs, used in later English and German Gothic architecture, are tierceron ribs, which extend from the wall piers to the longitudinal ridge rib; and lierne ribs, which extend from the center boss to the side walls, or from diagonal ribs to other lierne ribs. See photograph 2.23, page 33.

rib vault   The medieval variation on the tunnel vault in which the vault surface was divided into membranes or webs separated by arch ribs. The ribs of a bay were built first, forming a skeleton, and the webs then filled in.

rond-point   (French for "round point") In French Baroque landscape design and town planning, a circular plaza on which streets converge.

rustication   (from Latin *rusticus*, "of the country, rude, coarse") The treatment of stone masonry with the joints between the blocks deeply cut back; the surfaces of the blocks may be smoothly dressed, textured, or extremely rough (*quarry-faced*).

sacristy   A room in a church housing sacred vessels and vestments; also called vestry.

sanctuary   (from Latin *sanctus*, "holy") A sacred place, such as a church, temple, or mosque, but especially the most holy part of that place; in a Christian church, the altar and the area immediately around the altar.

sash   (from French *châssis*, "frame") The frame in which glass windowpanes are set.

scenae frons   (from Latin and Greek *skene*, "scene," plus *frons*, "facade") In a Roman theater, the richly embellished wall rising behind the stage area.

section   (from Latin *sectio*, "act of cutting") In architecture, a drawing showing a slice through a building, either lengthwise (longitudinal section) or crosswise (cross section), with all horizontal and vertical lines shown at their full length as in an *elevation* drawing. In detailed section drawings the interior is drawn in elevation.

serdab   In ancient Egyptian architecture, a closed chamber meant to contain a statue.

Serliana   See *Palladian motif*.

setback   A recessed upper section of a building; used in New York and Chicago skyscrapers of the 1920s as a way of admitting more light and air to the streets below.

shaft   (from Old English *scheaft*) The main part of a column, between the base and the capital. See *order*. The main part of a pier.

skeleton frame   See *skyscraper construction*.

skyscraper construction   The method of construction developed in Chicago in which all building loads are transmitted to a ferrous metal skeleton, so that any external masonry is simply a protective cladding. See *curtain wall*.

space frame   A form of *truss*, made of relatively short wooden or metal pieces, that extends in three dimensions and can be supported at virtually any of the points where the members are joined.

spandrel   (from Middle English *spaundrell*, from Latin *expandere*, "to spread out") In *arcuated* structures, the wall area between the adjacent arches and an imaginary line drawn across their tops; in *curtain wall* structures, the panel between structural columns.

spire   (from Old English *spir*) In architecture, an elongated, tapering structure that comes to a point.

spread foundation   For a column or pier load, a foundation built like a pyramid to spread the weight over a large area. In soft soils, a spread foundation may be built over a cluster of *piles*. Spread foundations can be extended in a line for wall loads.

spring line   The imaginary line from which an arch springs or starts to curve.

spur wall   A short wall extending out from a main wall.

square   In architectural planning, an open public space in a town, usually surrounded by buildings.

stele   (Greek, "pillar") An upright stone slab, usually bearing an engraved inscription and figural relief carving, placed to mark a grave or as a votive offering.

stoa   (Greek, "porch") In Classical Greek architecture, a long roofed *portico* open along one long side, most often facing out onto the *agora*.

stucco   (Italian) An exterior plaster finish similar to *mortar* and mixed of lime cement (now Portland cement) and sand.

temenos   (Greek) The sacred enclosure around a temple site.

temple front   In Neoclassical architecture, a decorative facade treatment consisting of columns carrying a *pediment* and resembling a Classical temple.

tension   (from Old French and Latin *tendere*, "to stretch") In architecture, a force that tends to stretch and pull apart.

terra cotta   (Italian *terra*, "earth," plus *cotta*, "baked") A thick clay material, mixed with crushed baked clay, molded and fired; used as a floor, wall, and roof covering.

thrust   (Middle English) In architecture, an outward, oblique, or downward force generated by gravity, wind pressure, or both working together.

torsion   (from Latin *torsus*, "twisted") A force that tends to twist; often a problem in large modern skyscrapers due to wind pressure.

trabeated   (from Latin *trabs*, "beam") Used to describe a structure consisting of posts and beams, or having a frame, in contrast to *arcuated*.

tracery (from Old French *trait*, "strap") Ornamental design of interlaced lines or straps, particularly the thin stone interlaces of Gothic windows.

transept (from Latin *trans*, "through," plus *saeptum*, "partition") Either of the two lateral arms in a *Latin cross* plan church.

triforium (origin unknown) In a Gothic church, a narrow arcaded passage between the arcade of the side aisles and the clerestory windows; corresponds to the shed roof over the side aisles.

triglyph (Greek *treis*, "three," plus *gluphe*, "carving") In the frieze area of the Classical Doric *order*, the stone panel cut with three grooves originally used to protect the open-grain end of wooden beams.

truss (from Middle English *trusse*, from Old French *trousser*, "to secure tightly") In architecture, a rigid frame, constructed of timbers or metal pieces forming triangular units; this rigid structure cannot be deflected without deforming one of its component members.

turret, tourelle (from Old French *tourete*, diminutive for "tower") A small tower, sometimes corbeled out from the corner of a building.

tympanum (Latin, from Greek *tumpanon*, "drum") The triangular space enclosed between the entablature and the moldings of a Classical *pediment;* the panel enclosed between a lintel and an arch rising above it.

vault (Middle English *vaute*, from Latin *volvere*, "to roll") A curved or arched masonry (or concrete) roof such as a *tunnel* or *barrel* vault

that has the shape of a half cylinder; a *groin* vault formed by the intersection of two tunnel vaults at right angles; an *annular* vault that results when a tunnel vault is curved into a circle, or a *rib* vault (see *rib*).

veranda, verandah (from Hindi *varanda*, which is partly from Portuguese *varanda*, akin to Spanish *baranda*, "railing") An extensive open gallery or porch.

vestibule (Latin *vestibulum*) A lobby or entrance hall.

viaduct (Latin *via*, "road," plus *ductus*, past participle of verb "to lead") A raised series of arches carrying a roadway.

villa (Italian from Latin) A country house, with associated outbuildings. A *villa rustica* was a working farm, whereas a *villa urbana* was primarily intended for recreational purposes.

volume (from Latin *volvere*, "to roll") In architecture, the amount of space contained within a three-dimensional enclosure.

volute (from Latin *voluta*, "that which is rolled") A spiral ornament or whorl, best represented in the Classical *Ionic capital.*

voussoir (from Old French *vossoir*, ultimately from Latin *volvere*, "to roll") Any of the wedge-shaped blocks that make up an arch or a vault.

westwork The elaborated western end of Carolingian and German Romanesque churches, which consisted of western transept arms and towers, a low entrance hall, and an upper room open to the nave (example: Saint Michael's, Hildesheim, Germany).

ziggurat (from Assyrian *zigguratu*, "summit," "mountaintop") A temple-tower of multiple stepped-back stages built by the Babylonians and Assyrians.

Index

DUE